CW00542152

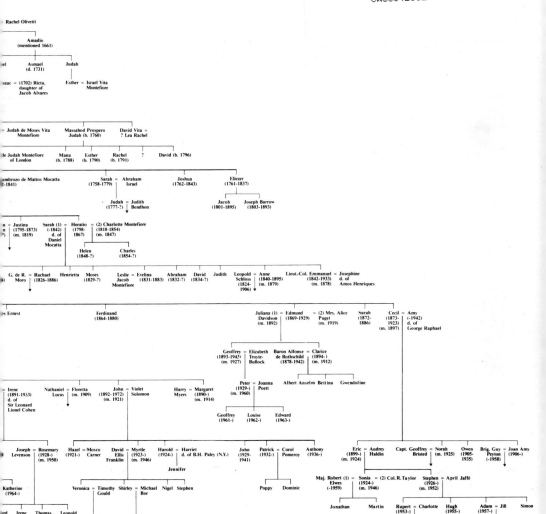

8" Eyre & Spottiswoode 1971; and partially brought up to date by S.W. Massil 1984

The Century of
Moses Montefiore

THE LITTMAN LIBRARY OF
JEWISH CIVILIZATION

FOUNDER
L. T. S. Littman

EDITORS
David Goldstein
Louis Jacobs
Vivian D. Lipman

For the love of God
and in memory of
JOSEPH AARON LITTMAN

'Get wisdom, get understanding:
Forsake her not and she shall preserve thee'

THE JEWISH HISTORICAL SOCIETY OF ENGLAND
University College London
Gower Street, W.C.1

The Century of
Moses Montefiore

Edited by

Sonia and V. D. Lipman

Published for
THE LITTMAN LIBRARY OF JEWISH CIVILIZATION
IN ASSOCIATION WITH THE JEWISH HISTORICAL SOCIETY OF ENGLAND
by
OXFORD UNIVERSITY PRESS
1985

Oxford University Press, Walton Street, Oxford OX2 6DP

London New York Toronto
Delhi Bombay Calcutta Madras Karachi
Kuala Lumpur Singapore Hong Kong Tokyo
Nairobi Dar es Salaam Cape Town
Melbourne Auckland

and associated companies in
Beirut Berlin Ibadan Mexico City Nicosia

Oxford is a trade mark of Oxford University Press

Published in the United States
by Oxford University Press, New York

British Library Cataloguing in Publication Data
The Century of Moses Montefiore. —
(The Littman library of Jewish civilization)
1. Montefiore, Sir Moses
2. Jews — Great Britain — Biography
3. Philanthropists — Great Britain — Biography
I. Lipman, Vivian D.   II. Lipman, Sonia L.
III. Series
942.07'3'0924   DS135.E6M7
ISBN 0-19-710041-4

Library of Congress Cataloging in Publication Data
Main entry under title:
The Century of Moses Montefiore.
(The Littman library of Jewish civilization)
Includes Index.
1. Montefiore, Moses, Sir, 1784—1855.   2. Jews —
Great Britain — Biography.   3. Jews — Syria — Damascus —
Persecutions.   4. Jews — Morocco.   5. Jewish pilgrims and
pilgrimages — Palestine.   I. Lipman, Sonia L., 1926—   .
II. Lipman, V. D. (Vivian David), 1921—   .
III. Series.
DS135.E6M719   1985   909'.0492404 [B]   84-27225
ISBN 0-19-710041-4

Printed in Great Britain by
The Alden Press, Oxford

Preface

The century of Sir Moses Montefiore's life spans the period from the age of enlightenment to the late Victorian era. When he was born the American Revolution had just ended and the French Revolution had not begun; he died two years before Queen Victoria's Golden Jubilee. He grew up in the world of the stagecoach and the sailing ship; he lived through that of railways, steamships and the electric telegraph. His life began in the aristocratic and elegant England of the eighteenth century; it ended in the respectable, bourgeois, and increasingly democratic society of Victorian Britain.

There were correspondingly dramatic changes in the Jewish world of which he formed part. When he was born, Jews nowhere in Europe enjoyed civic rights and their conditions in parts of Central and Eastern Europe could justifiably be described as medieval. During his years of youth and maturity, Jews — beginning with the French Revolution — gained civic rights in Western and Central Europe. It was widely believed by many, including Montefiore, that this progress would be maintained and would in time extend to Eastern Europe. There was a movement to reform Judaism as a religion, which Montefiore vehemently opposed, and also to acculturate Jewish life socially to that of their neighbours, which Montefiore approved. But the last decades of his life saw the resurgence of anti-semitism in modern form in Central Europe and the pogroms in Russia, developments which troubled him not only for the present suffering they caused but because they called into question much of his view of the Jewish future.

In addition to Montefiore's civic, business and social life, the missions he undertook on behalf of oppressed Jews in many countries and his seven visits to the Holy Land (which in part were in the nature of pilgrimages) brought him into contact with an immense variety of milieux — ranging from English county society through western courts, Russian autocracy and the Vatican, to the oriental regimes of Turkey, Egypt and Morocco. Montefiore's life touched modern Jewish history at perhaps more points than that of any other single figure, because he was concerned with so many Jewish communities, in widely varying environments and stages of cultural development. Yet there was an underlying continuity about his life and attitudes, as well as about the objectives which he pursued with the aid of his wife, Judith, and a small group of trusted and long-serving associates.

When preparing to commemorate the bicentenary of Montefiore's birth in 1984 and the centenary of his death in 1985, the Jewish Historical Society of England decided that the celebrations should include the publication of an appropriate book. No major biography of Montefiore has appeared for half a century; and Montefiore had already in his life-time become such a legend that myth often obscures reality. It was felt that such a major figure merited a re-assessment, taking account of original material which had become accessible, or specialized research which had been undertaken, in recent years. But because he lived so long and did so many different things, the sources and other relevant literature required knowledge of many different languages and areas of scholarship. It seemed unlikely that at this stage any one author could compass the whole field with an authoritative biography. It was decided therefore to invite a number of authors each to contribute a study on a subject, connected with Montefiore, of which he or she had expert knowledge. The object was to provide new information not only about Montefiore's life but on the background to the problems with which he had to deal. The authors have corrected previously accepted statements about Montefiore, brought to light new facts from archival sources, and given a new evaluation of many of his activities. In doing so they have sometimes expressed different views on certain issues. The editors have tried, however, to exclude passages in which authors have duplicated material covered in other studies in the volume, although in studies devoted to different facets of the life of the same man, it is impracticable to avoid any overlapping at all.

This volume has been planned as one of a number of publications due to appear before or during the Montefiore celebrations; it was therefore decided to avoid duplication with material in them. In particular, the Jewish Historical Society has been associated with the publication of the 1983 facsimile reprint of the *Diaries of Sir Moses and Lady Montefiore,* with an introduction by Professor Raphael Loewe; and of the papers given at a symposium at Yarnton Manor, Oxford and published in 1982 as *Sir Moses Montefiore: A Symposium,* edited by V. D. Lipman. There is therefore in this volume no introduction to the sources for the study of Montefiore, no general survey of Sir Moses and Palestine, and no narrative of the Damascus Affair because papers on these subjects were included in the Yarnton volume.

The editors thank Mr Cordy, Miss Bayley and Miss Ashby and other members of the Oxford University Press for constant help and guidance.

V D LIPMAN

Contents

Contents

Transliterations have been left as written by each contributor.

Chronology of Montefiore's Life

1784	Born in Leghorn during a visit by his parents
1803	Member of London Stock Exchange
1804	Death of his father, Joseph Elias Montefiore
1809	Captain in the Surrey Local Militia until its disbandment in 1814
1812	Marries Judith, daughter of Levi Barent Cohen and sister-in-law of Nathan Mayer Rothschild. Becomes a freemason, though no evidence that he was actively involved, and resigns in 1819
1814	First visit to Paris
1816	Travels in France and Italy
1817–18	First visit to his birthplace Leghorn
1824	Death of his younger brother Abraham. Retirement at the age of forty. Continues as a company director.
1827	First visit to the Holy Land
1831	Buys East Cliff Lodge, Ramsgate.
1835	Elected President of the Board of Deputies of British Jews. Holds presidency (except for brief periods when travelling) until 1874.
1837–8	Sheriff of London and Middlesex. Knighted. In 1838 appointed to City Lieutenancy
1838	Second visit to the Holy Land
1840	The Damascus Affair. Obtains firman from the Sultan in Constantinople. Achieves international fame and becomes a roving ambassador to ameliorate sufferings of persecuted Jewish communities
1845	High Sheriff of Kent
1846	First visit to Russia
1849	Third visit to the Holy Land
1850–1	Member of Committee organizing Great Exhibition and Chairman of its Fine Arts section

1855	Fourth visit to the Holy Land
1857	Fifth visit to the Holy Land
1859	The Mortara affair. Journeys to Rome but fails to rescue Edgar Mortara who had been baptised by his nurse.
1862	Death of Judith Montefiore
1863	Visit to Constantinople where firman renewed by the new Sultan
1863–4	The Moroccan mission
1864	Endowment of Judith Lady Montefiore College at Ramsgate
1866	Sixth visit to the Holy Land. Death of Dr Hodgkin at Jaffa
1867	Mission to Romania
1872	Visits Tsar Alexander II of Russia.
1875	Last visit to the Holy Land
1884	International celebrations of his hundredth birthday
1885	Death of Montefiore on 28 July

List of Illustrations

Notes on Contributors

*C. ABRAMSKY MA: Former Goldsmid Professor of Hebrew and Jewish Studies at University College London; Senior Fellow St Antony's College, Oxford

*R. D. BARNETT CBE, Litt.D., FBA: Former Keeper, Department of Western Asiatic Antiquities, British Museum

P. L. COTTRELL BSc. (Econ.), PhD.: Senior Lecturer in Economic and Social History and Dean of the Faculty of Social Sciences, University of Leicester, is a financial historian interested in the development of the Modern European Capital Market 1815–1939

*I. FINESTEIN QC, MA: Circuit Judge; Honorary Research Fellow, University College London

URSULA R. Q. HENRIQUES MA: Former Professor in the Department of History, University College, Cardiff; has written extensively on British nineteenth century history

AMALIE M. KASS BA, M.Ed.: Research Associate, Francis A. Countway Library of Medicine, Harvard University, is engaged, with her husband, Professor Edward H. Kass, in writing a major biography of Dr Thomas Hodgkin

MARILYN LEHRER MA: Chairman, Jewish Book Council. Her associate, Peter Salinger, is Hebrew Librarian at the School of Oriental and African Studies, London

DAVID LITTMAN MA: Historian of the Jews of North Africa and the Levant

*RAPHAEL LOEWE MC, MA: Former Goldsmid Professor of Hebrew and Director of the Institute of Jewish Studies, University College London

TUDOR PARFITT D.Phil.: Lecturer in Hebrew, School of Oriental and African Studies, London

HELEN A. ROSENAU D.Phil. (Hamburg), PhD. (London): Former Reader in the History of Art, University of Manchester. Dr Rosenau died on 27 October 1984

A. SCHISCHA: Scholar and bibliophile, London

THE EDITORS:

SONIA L. LIPMAN BA: Writer on Anglo-Jewish history

*V. D. LIPMAN CVO, D.Phil., FSA: Former Director of Ancient Monuments and Historic Buildings for England; Honorary Research Fellow, University College London

*Has served as President of the Jewish Historical Society of England

PART I

The Man and His Circle

1

The Making of a Victorian Gentleman

SONIA L. LIPMAN

The lasting reputation of Moses Montefiore was shaped during the second half-century of his life when his activities caught the imagination both of those for whose benefit they were undertaken and of British public opinion. Not only was he news, but he had become so established as the grand old man of Anglo-Jewry that *The Times* celebrated his ninety-ninth and hundredth birthdays[1] with flattering 'leaders', as well as publishing biographical articles in October 1883. Accordingly, he remains entrenched as a figure larger than life and of perfect character, of whom the future Chief Rabbi Hermann Adler said in 1883, '... his firmness and constancy had been further shown .... He had never touched forbidden food, no matter where he might have been ...'.[2] In fact, modern research has shown that he and his wife did not observe the dietary laws in the early years of their marriage, at least when they were travelling.[3]

Because he lived so long none of his early contemporaries survived to confirm or contradict the sparse accounts of his youth which have survived, and because he had no direct descendants, the stories and family jokes recounted by parents to children from generation to generation in ordinary households were not handed down. Moreover, his reputed reminiscences, though they fill some of the lacunae and explain certain discrepancies, yet contain inaccuracies, and perhaps for this reason have been totally neglected.[4]

It is now certain that some at least of the traditional account of Moses Montefiore's early life cannot be correct, although it is not always possible to substitute irrefutable fact for what must be discarded. Nor is it possible to judge whether there was deliberate deception in order to safeguard the image, or whether the old man's memory was defective.

The sources for our knowledge of Moses Montefiore's family and youth are Louis Loewe's introduction to, and his extracts from, the *Diaries of Sir Moses and Lady Montefiore* (published in 1890) and the *Centennial Biography* written by Lucien Wolf (published in 1884). Wolf was obviously conscious of the limitations of this book. In the early 1890s he intended to spend a summer holiday examining the diaries and papers of Sir Moses which had been deposited in the library of the Judith Lady Montefiore College at Ramsgate.[5] To his chagrin, the plan was thwarted when Sir Moses' heir, Sir Joseph Sebag Montefiore, had the diaries and papers burned, supposedly on the instructions of Sir Moses himself, though whether because they contained sensitive material — and this is possible in intimate journals kept over a long period — or for some other reason is unknown. Thus it is only possible — where primary sources do not exist — to use the traditional accounts and where they are found to be incorrect, point out the errors or reinterpret the conclusions reached by the authors.

The story of the English Montefiores begins with the arrival in London of Moses Vita Montefiore of Leghorn.[6] Born in 1712, he married the seventeen-year-old, reputedly beautiful, Esther Racah, in 1752. He had evidently in the early 1740s made some contacts in England, where members of his mother's family, the Medinas, had achieved great wealth; and his name was included in a list of *yehidim* (ordinary members) of the Spanish and Portuguese Synagogue assessed in Adar 5504 (1744).[7] But he was cautious and it was only in the early 1750s that he made his final move to London. He first appears in Kent's *London Directory* of 1754 as 'Moses Montefiore Merchant, Fenchurch Street'. A year later in the *London Directory* he is listed as 'Moses Montefiore, Philpot Lane, Fenchurch Street'. This implies that he set up his permanent home in London between 1752 and 1753. In 1755 he was allowed by the East India Company to export a quantity of coral on condition that there was enough shipping space,[8] a transaction which associates him with the diamond trade — and with the business activities of his brother-in-law, Moses Racah of Leghorn, who is also said to have been a coral merchant.[9] However, he is usually regarded as an importer of Italian commodities. By 1760 he was sufficiently well established to be among the 800 merchants who presented loyal addresses to George III on his accession and kissed the King's hand.[10] Later he was able to acquire an estate in Mutton Lane, Hackney.

His fourth son, Joseph Elias, was born in London in 1759. He was obviously trained for business and spent time in Leghorn, possibly acting as his father's agent, for when his brother Samuel and his sister Jayley arrived in the city in 1782 to celebrate the marriages arranged for them, Joseph Elias was there to meet them, and he made the return journey with them in February 1783.[11] His Italian was fluent. In 1839, when Moses Montefiore was in Carrara, he was shown some of his father's letters 'in Italian, and beautifully written', but the recipient would not part with them in spite of Montefiore's offer to acquire them.[12]

Joseph Elias' own marriage was a stroke of good fortune. The wealthy Abraham de Mattos Mocatta was also the father of a very large family, including a number of daughters for whom husbands had to be provided. Evidently the son of Moses Vita Montefiore was an acceptable son-in-law and in 1783 Joseph Elias and Rachel Mocatta were married. A further connection between the two families occurred when the widowed Samuel married Grace Mocatta, Rachel's sister, in 1785, though he later proved an unfaithful husband, fathering several illegitimate children — of whom he was very fond — by non-Jewish women.[13] The marriage of Joseph and Rachel seems, however, to have been not only fruitful but happy. Rachel, from what is known about her in later years, seems to have been genuinely loved and trusted by her children and grandchildren, and, even more commendably, regarded with affection by her daughters-in-law and sons-in-law, whom she treated equally with her own children.

The traditional view is that Joseph and Rachel lived at 3 Kennington Terrace from their marriage in 1783. This is impossible. It is true that with the opening of Westminster Bridge in 1750 and Blackfriars Bridge in 1769, development south of the river was accelerated, aided by the breaking up of landed estates for housing. With easy access to the City, middle class families were able to move to the new residential areas in Southwark and Vauxhall. However, Kennington Terrace was not built until the 1790s, as one of the groups of terraces which were interspersed along Kennington Lane.[14] In 1795 Moses Mocatta, Rachel's brother, married Abigail Lindo and settled at No. 2, where one of his neighbours was David Ricardo at No. 5.[15] Mocatta moved to a better — or at least larger — house in the same area before 1800, while the Montefiores moved into their house at 3 Kennington Terrace when it became vacant in that year. Obviously they would have known the houses and the district from their visits to the Mocattas. Rachel lived in the house until her own death in 1841, thirty-six years after that of her husband.

Since the records show no other address for Joseph Elias south of the river, it must be assumed that he lived until 1800 in the City.[16] Before 1787 he is not found in any directory and it is possible that he was his father's tenant in Philpot Lane, since Moses Vita had his other home in Hackney. However, in 1787 he was at 25 Abchurch Lane, and from 1788 until 1790 at 24 Jewry Street. He would seem to have taken over the Philpot Lane property after his father died in 1789, although it was not bequeathed to him in Moses Vita's will, and later he gave it up. In the mid-1790s he was in business, first with one of the Mocattas at 19 Great Alie Street, and then on his own account. Great Alie Street was, however, a residential area for the well-to-do and Abraham Goldsmid, one of the leading

Part of a map of London in 1795 by J. Fairburn engraved by E. Mogg, showing Kennington Lane and

Kennington Lane Abchurch Lane Philpot Lane Jewry Street Gt. Alie Street

y (by courtesy of the British Library)

financiers of the day, lived at number 18. It is unlikely therefore that 19 Great Alie Street was merely a business address and we may assume that Joseph and his family lived there, since the premises were valued at £50 and his Land Tax assessment was £4. 11s. 8d. By 1798 the Montefiores had gone, Abraham Goldsmid taking over part of the property, for which he was assessed £1. 5s. 0d. for 'premises late Montefiore'. Joseph then worked from the New York Coffee House, and, in the early 1800s, at Old City Chambers. His residential address between 1798 and 1800 is unknown.

In 1784, the young Montefiores went on a business trip to Leghorn taking with them the sixteen year old Moses Mocatta, and it was in that city on 24 October that their eldest son, Moses Haim, was born.[17] However exciting the event was to the parents, to Moses Mocatta and to great-uncle Moses Racah and his wife, it is unlikely that this child was any more special to the grandparents on both sides than the other children being born to their sons and daughters. Moses Vita already had a grandson bearing his name and it is noteworthy that in the wills of both grandfathers Joseph and Rachel's children do not appear. Moses Vita, who died in 1789, left £5 to each of his sons, his landed estate in rigid order of primogeniture, and everything else to his wife.[18] Since this was before the levy of estate duty his fortune is not known, but his widow left under £10,000 in 1812. She may of course have reduced her inheritance by living on capital and making gifts. In her will[19] she assigned one-fourteenth of the proceeds of the sale of her estate (after legacies) to be divided between Joseph Elias' children. Since her residence and other effects raised £309. 19s. 2d., her grandchildren can hardly have benefited greatly.

Abraham Mocatta died in 1800. He was a much richer man and a widower, whose fortune, £150,000, would by today's standards place him in the millionaire class. In his will,[20] after arranging that his grave should be watched day and night for a year (i.e. before the tombstone was set) to thwart body snatchers, a very real danger at the time, he remitted the debts and returned the mortgages, securities and rents of his sons-in-law to them; and he left £8,000 to each of his daughters in 3 per cent stock. Dividends and interest were to be paid only to the daughters for their own use and not to their husbands. The women were also left their shares in annuities and in a tontine.

Little is known of Moses Montefiore's childhood and education. He is supposed to have had Hebrew lessons from his uncle Moses Mocatta,[21] but while the latter was a scholar and author, Montefiore seems never to have acquired much learning, although as an adult he enjoyed listening to the Torah being expounded, especially by Louis Loewe in later years; and he was meticulous about saying his prayers.

There is doubt, too, about his secular education. Since the family did not live in Kennington until he was sixteen, it is most unlikely that he went to school there, as has been assumed by his biographers.[22] Indeed, they tend to dismiss his schooling as being elementary and unimportant, since there was no point in him having an academic education when as a Jew he could not go to university. This is strange, for while he would have been excluded from certain schools connected with the established church or the livery companies, there were various dissenters' establishments and private academies which were non-denominational, and some were of very high academic standard. They, unlike the traditional grammar and public schools, provided an up-to-date curriculum, often concentrating on modern languages and commercial subjects, and they were patronised by the growing merchant and industrial middle class.[23] Isaac Lyon Goldsmid, for instance, is said to have been educated in Finsbury Square. If he went to the Mercantile School kept by Patrick Kelly, he would have received a first class education, studying mathematics, navigation and commercial subjects. Robert Hamilton kept a well-known academy in Leman Street, while William Milns' City Commercial School in George Yard, Lombard Street, aimed to combine a 'literary with commercial, mathematical and philosophical education'.[24]

It is suggested that Moses Montefiore may have gone to a 'small private school in Hackney much patronised by the better class of Jew in those days'.[25] Hackney was a favoured area for schools and it is impossible to identify the establishment described. A novel written by Samuel Cooper in 1890 purports to tell the story of his education in a school based on the English public school, where Montefiore's nobility of character triumphs over the anti-semitic bullying of his schoolmates, the cheating of his enemy and the prejudices of his instructors.[26] Since for the purposes of the story Isaac Lyon Goldsmid, his senior by six years, appears as his contemporary, the work's authenticity is not to be commended.

If his educational background is unknown, his early career is also obscure. Traditionally, he is said to have been apprenticed to the firm of Johnson McCulloch, wholesale grocers and tea merchants, whose principal was a neighbour, Robert Johnson.[27] But he cannot have been formally apprenticed, since there is no record of such an apprenticeship in the official records, although there are dozens of Jewish indentures.[28] More likely he filled in the time before he could join the Stock Exchange by working as a clerk in the firm from the age of sixteen, perhaps in its, or in another, counting house. He is supposed to have recounted how he had to work very hard for exceedingly long hours, walking home afterwards to Kennington between ten o'clock and midnight and there 'astonishing his good mother by his onslaughts upon cold boiled beef — his favourite dish as long as he lived — after fifteen hours work and a six mile walk.'[29] Exaggeration or fact? At any rate it complies with the Victorian recipe for success: if not quite 'rags to riches' at least character and hard work.

Moses Montefiore is first found in business in 1803, aged eighteen plus, when for the annual fee of ten guineas, and recommended by his uncle Moses Mocatta among others, he became a member of the Stock Exchange.[30] The story of his being one of the Jew brokers, the position having been bought for him by his uncles is false, since he bought the right himself in 1815, when he was an affluent stock-broker;[31] and to be a stockbroker by the nineteenth century a Jew did not have to be a Jew broker at all.

It is significant that none of Joseph Elias' three sons went into their father's business, suggesting that it was not a flourishing concern. Indeed, biographical accounts of Sir Moses in the last years of his life or in the obituary notices, state unequivocally that his parents were 'persons of moderate means' or that his father was a 'not very wealthy merchant' or 'only moderately successful in commerce'.[32] If this information was supplied by Sir Moses himself in his later years, or if he gave the impression, it is an interesting comment on his opinion of his father's standing: at his death in 1804 Joseph Elias left between £9,000 and £10,000,[33] a respectable sum which would not condemn his family to penury but would limit, for instance, the amount that could be given the daughters as dowries. Fortunately, the girls do not seem to have suffered and made good marriages, although they may have been helped by their wealthier relatives.

However, Abraham, dying only twenty years after his father, left his daughters by the former Henrietta Rothschild £25,000 each, and his daughter by his first marriage £15,000, having already given her a dowry on her marriage to Benjamin Mocatta.[34]

In fact, Joseph Elias would seem to have been a victim of the international situation and of changes in fashion. If indeed his livelihood largely depended on the import of Leghorn straw hats, the trade which saw the import of 15,972 dozen in 1782 and 6160 dozen in 1792, had declined to 1602 dozen in 1800.[35] The French Revolutionary wars had undoubtedly played their part, but imports of skins and silks both raw and thrown were still large in 1800. While Joseph Montefiore's major business would seem to have collapsed therefore for reasons outside his control, it appears that he had not been sufficiently flexible or enterprising to diversify, so as to deal in lucrative alternative commodities.

In 1802 tragedy struck the Montefiores. *The Times* of Friday 5 March reported: 'On Sunday died Miss Montefiore, daughter of Mr Joseph Montefiore of Kennington. Her death was occasioned by her dress having accidentally caught fire. This melancholy event must be severely felt by all who knew her; at the bloom of sixteen she possessed every charm of person and mind, united to the most amiable disposition. May her unhappy fate inspire the breast of every Female Reader with that degree of precaution and care that may for ever prevent a repetition of a similar calamity.' And the *Gentleman's Magazine* for March, in reporting the tragedy, mentions that 'within these few months not less than six ladies have literally been burnt to death'.

Esther was the second of Joseph and Rachel's eight children. According to Moses Montefiore, his father 'was at one time of a most cheerful disposition, but after he had the misfortune to lose one of his daughters at a fire which occurred in his house, he was never seen to smile.'[36] He died in January 1804 at the age of forty-five, leaving £10 to each of his sons and the residue of his estate to his wife.

It may have been this bereavement, which now made him the head of the family, rather than excess of religious zeal or a desire for praise, which prompted Moses to apply for membership of the Spanish and Portuguese Synagogue in 1804 instead of waiting until the normal age of twenty-one. His father, while a loyal member of the Sephardi community — and assiduous in attendance at synagogue during the year of mourning for his own father, 1789—90, — had never, so far as is known, been invited to serve as one of its officers. In this he did not follow in the footsteps of his own father or his father-in-law, both of whom held office on occasion and declined it at other times, presumably paying the requisite fines when they did so. In fact, in 1776, Moses Haim held the important office of one of the *fintadores* (assessors of the congregational tax).[37] In 1790, Joseph Elias was assessed at £1 a year. At this date, 75 per cent of members paid under £4, of whom 43 per cent paid under £1, 14 per cent £1—£2 (his category) and 17½ per cent £2—£4. The highest contribution was £18. 15s. 0d., paid by a few Sephardi magnates.

Moses Montefiore, in his turn, remained all his life a loyal and active member of the synagogue, serving first as one of the *lavadores* (washers of the dead) and later holding all the synagogal offices in turn. In 1823 he presented thirteen houses in Cock Court, Jewry Street, to the synagogue for use as almshouses for the congregational poor.

In spite of this, he was not in his younger days a strict adherent of the religious practices he later adopted so enthusiastically. After his marriage, it is obvious that although he did not break the Sabbath by riding, he did, when away from home, eat non-kasher food. As late as 1823, when the Montefiores were in Italy, Judith wrote to her sister, Hannah Rothschild: 'We are well pleased with the cookery when a slice of bacon does not cover the roasted poulay [sic], in that case Mr Mezzara continues to finish the dish.'[38] They drew the line at prohibited animals, such as pig, and presumably, at shellfish, but did not have scruples over eating meat or poultry which had not been ritually slaughtered. However, his change of heart in the late 1820s was completely sincere and from that time he observed the dietary laws, even employing his own *shochet* (ritual slaughterer) to travel with him, though continuing to eat fish in non-Jewish houses and restaurants.[39]

In 1803, the very real threat of an invasion by Napoleon, after the breakdown of the peace of Amiens, resulted in the setting up all over Britain of corps of Volunteers to combat the danger. These corps were organized by committees and financed by local collections and individual subscriptions;[40] in the City of London and Whitechapel, wealthy Jews were prominent as members of the committees. Many young Jews joined up as enthusiastically as non-Jews, both as officers and in the ranks. Isaac Lyon Goldsmid, for instance, became a captain in the Loyal Whitechapel Volunteers, while Abraham Goldsmid Jr. was a captain in the Portsoken Ward Corps and Solomon Levien, a connection of the Goldsmids, became an officer in the Southwark Volunteers. Their commissions were not difficult to obtain, since officers in the Volunteer Corps were either appointed by the committees or elected — and official confirmation was automatically forthcoming.[41]

There is no record of Moses Montefiore having served as an officer at this time and he does not appear until 1809 as a captain in the Surrey Local Militia. This is surprising. By 1809 the danger was over. The Battle of Trafalgar had removed the threat of an invasion of Britain and Napoleon had turned his attention to the continental monarchies. As a result, the enthusiasm for military vigilance waned. In the Volunteers both officers and men were, in many cases, undisciplined and ineffective, with absenteeism and frequent resignations leading to the depletion of companies. Accordingly, when the Regular Army was due to go to the Peninsula with Wellington in 1808 and the Militia was destined for service in Ireland, the Government introduced legislation to set up a local militia for home defence. The men, like ordinary militia troops, were drafted by ballot, but, unlike them, those ballotted were not allowed to send substitutes or buy themselves out. The officers came either from the Volunteers or from retired regulars or militia. In addition, new officers had to be recruited.[42]

The Surrey Local Militia was to consist of 5,958 men, of whom 3,228 were already enrolled and 2,736 had to be recruited. Lord Cranley (a deputy Lord Lieutenant for Surrey) suggested three regiments, with Thomas Alcock as lieutenant colonel of the Third Regiment. Each regiment would have ten companies, and each company would be headed by a captain. The arrangements were approved by Lord Liverpool, the minister for war.[43] Montefiore's commission, among others, was confirmed by Liverpool on 5 July 1809, in response to Lt. Col. Alcock's recommendation of June 29 to Lord Cranley.[44] Solomon Levien had received his captaincy earlier that year. That Montefiore should have become a captain immediately without ever having served as an ensign or lieutenant would seem to argue that there was a dearth of applicants for commissions especially of mediocre companies, or that he was powerfully recommended, perhaps by Solomon Levien. On the other hand, why he should have wanted to serve at this time is a bit of a mystery. There was no stigma on civilians and the literature of the time shows many gentlemen following their normal pursuits. Perhaps the idea of drills, the camaraderie of the mess, or the stirring of social ambitions played a part. In his old age, Montefiore seems to have recounted a story of having joined up in 1803—4 in the Lambeth Volunteers as a private and having risen to the rank of sergeant. He told how there was some difficulty in swearing him in because he was a Jew, but that when the officer who was consulted saw this tall well-built young man, he ordered that he be sworn in first and the lawyers consulted afterwards.[45]

Two things are wrong with this story. The muster rolls of the Loyal Lambeth Volunteers (the only unit with Lambeth Volunteers in its title) do not contain his name,[46] while the oath was innocuous, since it read:

'I do sincerely promise and swear that I will be faithful and bear true Allegiance to His Majesty King George the Third, and that I will faithfully serve His Majesty in Great Britain for the Defence of the same, against all His Enemies and Opposers whatsoever. So help me God.'[47]

He obviously enjoyed his years as an officer, attending drills regularly, learning to play the bugle and taking part in the annual muster on Epsom Common. His Order Book survives in the National Army Museum, but disappointingly gives no personal information. His service ended in 1814 when the Local Militia was disbanded, to his regret.

His military activities did not interfere with his personal life. In

June 1812 he married Judith Cohen, a daughter (by his second marriage) of Levi Barent Cohen, who had settled in London in the 1770s from Amersfoort in Holland.[48] Levi Barent Cohen is celebrated as the ancestor of the 'Cousinhood'[49] which provided Anglo-Jewry with its most prominent personalities for over a century. A successful merchant and stockbroker, he was a leading member of the Ashkenazi Great Synagogue, and his standing is attested by his son Selig who wrote in 1808: 'Thank God he died with a very good name, rich and old, which is everything one can leave behind . . . We have lost a good father and friend.[50] Most important for Montefiore's future, Levi Barent Cohen's daughter Hannah was the wife of Nathan Mayer Rothschild. Reportedly, that marriage had not met with great enthusiasm from Hannah's father, but Nathan Mayer had had his way, and there is no doubt that he had shown equal shrewdness in his choice of a wife as in his business operations. Hannah had beauty, poise and charm and was able to mix with ease in society. Her husband doted on her, respected her judgment and was lost in her absence.[51] His regard for her was expressed in his will in 1836: 'My dear wife Hannah . . . is to cooperate with my sons on all important occasions and to have a vote upon all consultations. It is my express desire that they shall not embark in any transactions of importance without having previously demanded her motherly advice, and that all my children sons and daughters are to treat her with true love, kind affection and every possible respect, which she deserves in the highest degree . . . .'[52]

Hannah therefore was a woman of calibre and it was from the same background that Montefiore chose his wife. Judith was to prove equally valued by her husband during the fifty years of their marriage. In 1844, he wrote: 'On this happy day, the 10th of June, 32 years have passed since the Almighty God of Israel in His great goodness, blessed me with my dear Judith, and for ever will I be most grateful for this blessing, the great cause of my happiness through life. A better and kinder wife never existed, one whose whole study has been to render her husband good and happy.'[53] And many years later Lucien Wolf recorded his reply to someone who expressed gratification at meeting so great a man: 'I am no great man . . . the little good I have accomplished or rather that I intended to accomplish, I am indebted for it to my never-to-be-forgotten wife, whose enthusiasm for everything that is noble and whose religiousness sustained me in my career.'[54]

Judith was undoubtedly well educated, cultured, possessed of financial flair and secure in the affections of her family. The last is implicit in what Selig wrote to Hannah at their father's death: 'You can have no idea what attention Mamma and Judy paid our late father in his illness.'[55]

In considering this marriage it is essential that not too much is read into the Sephardi-Ashkenazi aspect.[56] Other such alliances had been accepted without dissension in recent years; and though both families were respectable and comparatively wealthy, they were not yet leaders or spokesmen of the Jews of England. While Judith naturally joined her husband's congregation, both were always conscious of, and sympathetic to, each other's heritage. Many years later, when the couple built their own synagogue in Ramsgate, they adopted the Ashkenazi custom of making *kiddush* at the end of the service on Friday evenings.[57] They supported both Ashkenazi and Sephardi charities in England and in the Holy Land, and Moses Montefiore made a point of consulting the Ashkenazi rabbinate as well as his own in communal affairs. After Judith's death, he presented two annual scholarships, one for £100 to a pupil of Jews College School, a boy, the other, slightly less munificent, for a female pupil of the Jews' Free School. Where merit was equal, preference was to be given to the child of a 'mixed marriage' such as he and his wife had enjoyed.[58]

There is no evidence that Moses Montefiore and Nathan Mayer Rothschild had business dealings before the marriage and their first recorded transaction seems only to have been in 1813. But the two men were *en rapport* from the beginning. They became neighbours in New Court on Montefiore's marriage and remained so until the Montefiores moved, first to Green Street in 1825 and then to Grosvenor Gate, Park Lane — his London home for the rest of his life — soon to be followed by the Rothschilds to 107 Piccadilly.

The family connection became even closer in 1815, when Abraham Montefiore, Moses' brother and partner, married as his second wife Henrietta Rothschild, the only unmarried sister of Nathan Mayer. Although this marriage lasted only nine years, until Abraham's early death in 1824, it produced four children.[59] Moses and Judith, on the other hand, were childless, but had a close relationship with their Montefiore, Cohen and Rothschild nephews and nieces, among whom there was considerable intermarriage, as there was between the resultant families in later generations.

They were also drawn unreservedly into the orbit of the Continental Rothschilds, over the years visiting them in Paris, Naples, Vienna and Frankfurt.[60] In 1814, Moses wrote to Nathan Mayer from Paris that 'Mr Salomon Rothschild entertained us with the friendship of a brother and the hospitality of a Prince'[61] and Salomon expressed his opinion of Montefiore to Nathan Mayer in a letter of 1817: 'Moses . . . is a fundamentally honest, fine man.'[62]

All accounts tell of Nathan Mayer's lack of interest in his appearance and clothes, his devotion to his home and family, his impatience of the polite society with which he had increasingly to mix: 'After dinner I have nothing to do. I do not read books. I do not play cards, I do not go to the theatre. My only pleasure is business . . .'[63] Moses Montefiore, impressive in appearance (he was six feet, three inches tall), well dressed and gentlemanly in speech, was a definite asset, both as envoy and companion, to the benefit of both. Moses was also becoming known to people who were to be useful to him in later life. Both men were participating in non-Jewish charities and meeting their wealthy and influential promoters, as the Goldsmids and Levi Barent Cohen had dealt with Nelson and Sir Sidney Smith.[64]

But there was still no sign of the status the Montefiores were later to enjoy. In 1812, they travelled on the stage coach and, on one occasion at least, had to walk back from Kennington after visiting Mrs Montefiore.[65] In 1816, Judith wrote at Lyons: 'We see daily arrivals of English families of consequence, several going to Rome.'[66] She neither expects to meet them, nor identifies with them, in a period of rigid class distinctions, though of social mobility. Indeed, Moses always had an exaggerated respect for the great. A smile or a bow of recognition brought gratification.[67]

Moses and Judith Montefiore were insatiable travellers. From the time of their honeymoon trip in 1812, they took every opportunity to visit new places, whether for business or pleasure, or a combination of both. The end of the Napoleonic Wars made possible travel to the Continent, and they went in their coach in 1816 to France and Italy, following this with another trip to Italy in 1817–18.[68] Moses Montefiore was able to visit his birthplace at Leghorn for the first time and meet his relatives, though he was saddened that his great uncle Moses Racah was no longer alive to welcome him. Other holidays were spent in Cornwall and Scotland, and in 1823–4, he had the melancholy experience of visiting his dying brother in Italy, whence he had gone in the hope of recovery.[69]

His rising social status may be seen in the granting, on 28 January 1819, of his application for a coat of arms. He is described as 'Moses Montefiore of New Court, St Swithin's Lane, City of London and of Tinley Lodge, near Tunbridge, co. Kent, Esquire, Captain in 3rd Surrey Local Militia . . .'. The motto he chose was 'Think and Thank'. Nathan Mayer Rothschild had already obtained his coat of arms in February 1818, Moses Mocatta was to receive his in May 1819 and Joseph Cohen in July 1819.[70]

As for his prominence in the City, when Richard Dighton published a book entitled *City Characters* in 1824, included was a caricature portrait of Montefiore drawn and etched in June 1818.

But the routine of daily business in the City was to be his no longer. The story of his retirement at the age of forty is well known, as is the approbation of his wife and her comment: 'Thank God and be content.' His motivation is not so clear; perhaps he had been shocked by the early death of his brother; perhaps he wanted more freedom to promote his new business interests;[71] perhaps he realized that since he had the wherewithal to do and go as he pleased, he should no longer delay. He was a rich man. At his death he left a personal fortune of £370,000[72] and he may well have realized capital for various projects in the intervening years as well as continuing to invest soundly.

His desire to visit the Holy Land was, according to his wife's 1818 diary, first mentioned during their stay in Leghorn when they 'went in a boat to view two vessels that were going to Jaffa, Montefiore having a great inclination to visit Palestine, which enterprise I hope will not undertake.'[73] By 1827 her attitude had changed and she congratulated herself for having 'urged him to pursue the journey, even when his own ardour had somewhat abated and when I had to oppose my counsel to the advice and wishes of our companions.'[74]

Montefiore himself, at the end of his life, told a different story when asked by Leonard Montefiore, who was visiting him at East Cliff Lodge. He showed a ring he was wearing, a simple band of gold with the inscription *Koneh hacol*, possessor of all things! 'I wear that ring . . . as a reminder of the circumstances that first moved me to go to the Holy Land . . . it was a dream and nothing but a dream, that made me undertake my first pilgrimage to Palestine. We had been reading, Lady Montefiore and myself, the [hymn] *Eliyahu HaNabi* [Elijah the Prophet], on Sabbath night; and we were talking of the good news of which this prophet's appearance was to be the harbinger for Jerusalem. We both agreed that it would be a very interesting thing to visit Carmel and the scene of the Tishbite's exploit, and I promised that, if ever we had leisure, I would take Lady Montefiore to the East. That night I dreamed I saw in front of me a venerable man whom I knew to be Elijah the Prophet: he pointed to Jerusalem which I recognised in the distance, and said only those two words engraved upon my ring . . . I awoke, and then dreamt this a second time and then a third time, each time hearing only the words *Koneh hacol*. And the dream made so strong an impression upon me, that I resolved the very first thing I would do when I had time would be to go to the Holy Land.'[75]

Whatever the motivation, the visit proved a notable landmark in his personal life for on his forty-third birthday, on 24 October 1827, he wrote: 'This day I began a new era. I fully intend to dedicate much more time to the welfare of the poor and to attend Synagogue as regularly as possible on Monday, Thursday and Saturday.'[76]

The walk on Saturdays from Park Lane to Bevis Marks was a long one and he, often accompanied by his wife, had to leave home at 6 a.m. in order to be at synagogue for the beginning of the service. Besides the religious inspiration therefore, it must have been a practical relief when their own synagogue at Ramsgate, designed by David Mocatta, was dedicated in 1833,[77] and they could enjoy sabbath and festival services on home ground when they did not have to be in London. Not until the 1850s was the prohibition of a synagogue within six miles of Bevis Marks removed and Sephardim in the West End were at last able to establish a branch synagogue, first in Wigmore Street and then in Bryanston Street.[78]

At the Ramsgate synagogue, the wishes of the founder prevailed. Thus Moses Montefiore was *Hatan Torah* (Bridegroom of the Law) every year, and the congregation, which included the local Jewish traders and their families, as well as visitors to the town and guests of the Montefiores, were invited to breakfast every *Simhat Torah* (Festival of the Rejoicing of the Law). Since Lady Montefiore celebrated her birthday on Shabbat Bereshit (though she was reputedly born in February 1784), it was indeed a festive period.

The Montefiores had acquired East Cliff Lodge in 1831, though they had tried unsuccessfully to buy it earlier, to replace Tinley Lodge as their country home. They had liked Ramsgate ever since they had visited the town on their honeymoon journey, and the house and grounds satisfied all their requirements for a country estate. The house, built in the 1790s, was about half a mile from the town and had about twenty-four acres of land planted on the verge of the cliff. 'The building forms a quadrangle and encloses a paved courtyard in which is a well of fine water. The summit is embattled and the entire building may be considered a specimen of the modern Gothic. The residence stands upon a commanding eminence, from the principal front of which there are interesting views of East Kent, the Downs, the British Channel and the Coast of France ... The dining room is the most elegant specimen of Gothic domestic architecture in England.'[79]

The Gothic library was designed by Pugin and faced west. 'It is panelled throughout,' wrote the *Jewish World* on 24 October 1884, 'ceiling and all, in dark stained oak, and is said to be an unrivalled specimen of Gothic chamber architecture.'

The Montefiores soon became involved in county and local life, although it was not until 1843 that Moses Montefiore was inserted in the commission of the peace for the County of Kent. In 1844, he was nominated High Sheriff of Kent.[80]

The possession of East Cliff Lodge was the cause of the Montefiores meeting the Duchess of Kent and the Princess Victoria. The royal ladies were spending a holiday in Ramsgate and accepted the Montefiores' invitation to use the gardens of East Cliff Lodge, a golden key being specially cut for their use.[81]

By this time the Montefiores were on visiting terms with many members of the aristocracy, but it would still have enhanced their prestige when they received marked attention from the Queen's mother at a function given by the Duke of Sussex at Kensington Palace on 30 May 1838.[82] It was also Montefiore's good fortune that his year of office as one of the two Sheriffs of London coincided with the accession of Queen Victoria and her first visit in state to the City. To mark the occasion she knighted the sheriffs, who would otherwise not have expected to be so honoured. The year was fully occupied with official and social engagements, but unlike David Salomons, who had been sheriff in 1835, Sir Moses had no ambition to climb the steps of the City hierarchy. Instead, no sooner was his year of office completed than he was on his way to the Holy Land to plan a programme which would make the Jews there less dependent on charity by providing them with opportunities to practise agriculture.[83]

Such plans, and his relatively frequent visits, enabled him to evolve a philosophy regarding the role of the Jews in the Holy Land which he expressed in an interview given in Pesth in 1863 to a correspondent of the *Allgemaine Zeitung des Judenthums*, and reproduced in the *Jewish Chronicle* on 19 June of that year:

The answer which he gave to my question, whether he really entertained any hope of a future national restoration of the Israelites in the Holy Land, truly characterises the man. With a smile which lighted up his countenance, he replied: 'Of this I am quite certain; it was my constant dream, and I hope will be realised one day when I shall be no more.' And to the objection how it would be possible to gather in the Israelites scattered in all corners of the globe, he replied: 'I do not expect that all Israelites will quit their abodes in those territories in which they feel happy, even as there are Englishmen in Hungary, Germany, America or Japan; but Palestine must belong to the Jews, and Jerusalem is destined to become the seat of a Jewish empire.' And he poured forth a stream of eloquence in the description of the Holy Land, which, as he said, indeed flowed with milk and honey. His eyes sparkled as he spoke thus, and I believed to see before me a God-inspired prophet. I will not enter on a discussion of either the value or practicability of this idea; but its existence, fostered and nurtured amidst the vicissitudes of a long life, speaks for the heart of the man. In this feature, too,

I believe I can discern the Englishman, in whom the practical tendency of real
life is often joined to a certain enthusiastic abstract direction, especially in
questions partaking of a religious nature.

Two initiatives by Montefiore in the decade after his retirement
illustrate his desire to be accepted by intellectuals and patrons of
scholarship.

At the beginning of the nineteenth century, gentlemen's clubs
were being founded to cater for what today would be called special
interest groups. They were the successors of the eighteenth century
coffee houses where men would congregate to meet acquaintances,
gossip, transact business and read the newspapers, but unlike them,
they were restricted to members who paid an annual subscription
to belong. In 1824, on the initiative of John Wilson Croker, a committee was formed to found a new club,[84] and at its meeting on
1 March resolved 'that persons eligible to the Club shall be individuals
known for their scientific or literary attainments, Artists of eminence in any of the Fine Arts and Noblemen and Gentlemen distinguished as liberal patrons of Science, Literature or the Arts.' The
Club was the Athenaeum, whose early members included Sir Humphry
Davy, then President of the Royal Society, the Rt Hon Robert Peel,
Lord John Russell, Sir Thomas Lawrence, Francis Palgrave and the
Duke of Wellington. Isaac Lyon Goldsmid was a founder member.
Neither humble birth nor religion were a bar to membership pro-
vided the aspirant had the intellectual qualifications.

After using rented premises for a time, part of the land formerly
occupied by the now demolished Carlton House was acquired and
the architect Decimus Burton commissioned to design the elegant
building which still stands on the right hand corner of Pall Mall and
Waterloo Place above the Duke of York steps.

In 1830 all was ready, but the Club had a debt of £20,000 (even
after its reserve funds had been used). Accordingly, since the existing
members would not agree to raise the subscription, it was decided to
elect another two hundred members, one hundred of whom would
be chosen from the existing waiting list by a special selection committee, the other hundred to be elected by the membership from
candidates proposed and seconded before midnight on 1 June. Moses
Montefiore was not on the Club's waiting list (i.e. in the Candidates
Book 1824–9)[85] as were Thomas Babington Macaulay, John Stuart
Mill, and Thomas Barnes, the editor of *The Times*, who were duly
elected by the first procedure. But he evidently decided that he
wanted to become a member of the Athenaeum, or it may have been
suggested that he take advantage of the opportunity, for during
June, Nathan Mayer Rothschild wrote round on his behalf:[86]

I shall feel particularly obliged by the Favor of your Vote and Interest in favor of my Brother in Law Moses Montefiore Esquire of Park Lane who is a Candidate for the Athenaeum.

> I am
> > Dear Sir
> > Yours Truly

His application was successful. He was elected, but was ninety-second in the ballot, whereas Francis Goldsmid, Isaac Lyon's son, was fourth.[87]

Members of the Athenaeum in the mid-nineteenth century included writers such as Dickens and Thackeray, Darwin among scientists, and Palmerston among politicians. In the early years, a *conversazione* was held on Monday evenings, to which members could bring a guest (a gentleman of course).[88] The Athenaeum was a place where the great and the famous in every walk of life were proud to be seen.

Moses Montefiore's other ambition, to be a Fellow of the Royal Society was achieved in 1836. His application was signed by, among others, his brother-in-law, Benjamin Gompertz, the celebrated actuary.[89] This was a period of transition for the Royal Society,[90] when it was moving towards excluding gentleman fellows and adopting the present system of electing only distinguished practising scientists. But the Society seems to have been convinced by the sponsors' claims that Montefiore was 'much attached to Science and its practical use' and that he was 'likely to prove a valuable and useful member', and he was duly elected.[91]

Thus by 1840 his acquaintance included royalty and the aristocracy, politicians, foreign dignitaries, financiers, industrialists, and intellectuals. He was *persona grata* with the leaders of British society and he was the spokesman of Anglo-Jewry. The events of that year were to cast him in a new and unique role in which he would occupy the centre of the stage for the rest of his life.

NOTES

1. *The Times*, 23 October 1883, 24 October 1884.
2. *Jewish Chronicle*, 16 November 1883.
3. Sonia L. Lipman, 'Judith Montefiore — First Lady of Anglo-Jewry', Transactions of the Jewish Historical Society of England, vol. xxi, 1968.
4. *Jewish World*, July/August 1885.

5. R. D. Barnett, 'Sources for the Study of Sir Moses Montefiore', *Sir Moses Montefiore — A Symposium*, edited by V. D. Lipman (Oxford Centre for Postgraduate Hebrew Studies and Jewish Historical Society of England, 1982).

6. For the Italian background see Lucien Wolf, *Moses Montefiore, A Centennial Biography; Diaries of Sir Moses and Lady Montefiore*, edited by Dr Louis Loewe, 1890. A facsimile edition was published by the Jewish Historical Society of England and the Jewish Museum in 1983.

7. Paul Goodman, *Sir Moses Montefiore* (Jewish Publication Society of America, 1925).

8. Gedalia Yogev, *Diamonds and Coral* (Leicester University Press, 1978), p. 124.

9. *Jewish World*, 17 October 1884.

10. *London Gazette*, 7 November 1760.

11. R. D. Barnett, 'Samuel Vita Montefiore's Diary' in *Explorations*, edited by Mindlin and Bermant, 1967.

12. *Diaries*, i, p. 153.

13. R. D. Barnett in *Explorations*.

14. *Survey of London*, vol. xxvi.

15. Rate Books of St Mary Lambeth 1795—1801 at Minet Library, Lambeth. In March 1801, the houses in Kennington Terrace were valued at £32 and the Poor Law Rate was £1.12s. 0d. Moses Mocatta's house was valued at £36 and his payment was £1.16s. 0d. He also had a field valued at £18 with a payment of 18s. In June 1800 the Rate Books showed the house at 3 Kennington Terrace as 'empty'.

16. Information on Joseph Elias' addresses comes from Directories, and from the Land Tax records in Guildhall (Series 6015 and 11316).

17. *Diaries*, i, 9. I am indebted to Mr J. M. Ross, formerly of the Home Office, for confirming that Moses Montefiore, as the legitimate son of a British-born father, was himself British by birth.

18. Public Record Office, Middlesex, 1789, Macham 605.

19. PRO, Middlesex, 1812, Oxford 185.

20. PRO Middlesex, 1800, Adderley 132.

21. Moses Mocatta (1768—1857), translator of Isaac b. Abraham Troki's *Hizzuk Emunah* and *The Inquisition and Judaism*, a Portuguese inquisitorial sermon and the reply to it. In communal affairs he was especially concerned with education.

22. *Diaries*, i, 12.

23. N. Hans, *New Trends in Education in the Eighteenth Century*, 1951.

24. Ibid.

25. *Jewish World*, 31 July 1885.

26. Samuel W. Cooper, *Think and Thank*, (Jewish Publication Society of America, 1890, reprinted 1946).

27. The neighbour at Kennington Terrace (to which the Montefiores had just moved in 1800) was William Johnson. There are a number of Robert Johnsons in the directories, but no connection is made with the firm Johnson McCulloch which had a relatively short life at 19 East Cheap.

28. PRO, Apprenticeship Records.

29. *Jewish World*, 31 July 1885.

30. Stock Exchange Records, Guildhall; for a full account, see P. L. Cottrell, 'The Business Man and Financier', below.

31. *Diaries*, i, 13, 20.

32. *The Times*, 22 October 1883, 29 July 1885; *Graphic*, 15 August 1885.
33. PRO, Surrey, 1804, Heseltine 52.
34. PRO, Middlesex, 1824, Erskine 676.
35. PRO, T64/273, CUST 5/1A, 5/1B; E. B. Schumpeter, *English Overseas Trade Statistics 1697–1808*. The average annual values of imports from Italy were: 1781–5, £386,000; 1786–90, £747,000; 1791–5, £729,000; 1796–1800, £208,000.
36. *Diaries*, i, 11.
37. Goodman; I am grateful to Dr R. D. Barnett and Miss Miriam Rodriques Pereira for this information from the Bevis Marks archives.
38. Rothschild Archives, T42/13. I am grateful for the opportunity of consulting the Archives and thank Dr Gershom Knight, the archivist, Mrs Yvonne Moss and Mr David Hodge for their help.
39. *Diaries*; letter in the possession of Professor Raphael Loewe.
40. PRO, W013; J. W. Fortescue, *County Lieutenancies and the Army 1803–14* (London, 1909); Cecil Sebag Montefiore, *A History of The Volunteer Forces from the earliest times to the year 1860*, (London 1908) By December 1803, Volunteers of all ranks numbered 380,000.
41. PRO, W013.
42. Fortescue.
43. PRO, HO/51/44.
44. PRO, HO/51/44.
45. *Jewish World*, 31 July 1885.
46. PRO, W013.
47. Act of 43 George the Third C.96, section 58.
48. Sonia L. Lipman, 'Judith Montefiore. . .'.
49. Chaim Bermant, *The Cousinhood*, 1971.
50. Rothschild Archives, T27/13, Letter from Selig Cohen to N.M.R.
51. Richard Davis, *The English Rothschilds*, (Collins, 1983), p. 26.
52. Ibid.
53. *Diaries*, i, 16.
54. Lucien Wolf, 'Lady Montefiore's Honeymoon', in *Essays in Jewish History*, edited by Cecil Roth.
55. Rothschild Archives, T(a)7.
56. Sonia L. Lipman, 'Judith Montefiore . . .'.
57. Cardozo and Goodman, *Think and Thank*, 1933.
58. *Jewish Chronicle*, 9 January 1863.
59. Joseph Mayer, Nathaniel Mayer, Charlotte and Louisa.
60. *Diaries*; Sonia L. Lipman, 'Judith Montefiore . . .'.
61. Rothschild Archives, T42/1.
62. Ibid, T27/260.
63. Davis, *The English Rothschilds*, p. 37.
64. *Diaries*, i, 3.
65. 'Lady Montefiore's Honeymoon'.
66. Sonia L. Lipman, 'Judith Montefiore. . .'.
67. There are many examples in the *Diaries*.
68. See Sonia L. Lipman, 'Judith Montefiore . . .' for excerpts from Judith's diaries of the tours.
69. *Diaries*, i, 28; for a full account see Amalie Kass' contribution below.
70. *Anglo-Jewish Notabilities*, pp. 88, 109, 116.
71. See P. L. Cottrell, 'The Business Man and Financier' below.

72.   Calendar of the Grants of Probate and Letters of Administration, 1885, at Somerset House. Montefiore's fortune was re-assessed in May 1886 at £374,421-2s-5d.
73.   Sonia L. Lipman, 'Judith Montefiore . . .'.
74.   Ibid.
75.   *Jewish World*, 14 August 1885. *Koneh hacol* — possessor of all — a divine attribute mentioned in the first paragraph of the *Amidah* prayer, recited by the pious Jew thrice daily.
76.   Cardozo and Goodman, *Think and Thank*, p. 7.
77.   Ibid.
78.   A. M. Hyamson, *The Sephardim of England*, 1951.
79.   Cardozo and Goodman.
80.   *Diaries*, i, 319.
81.   *Diaries*, i, 94—6.
82.   *Diaries*, i, 138—9.
83.   Judith Montefiore, *Notes from a Journal*.
84.   *The Athenaeum: Club and Social Life in London 1824—1974* (Heinemann, 1975).
85.   I am indebted to Miss M. Webb, librarian and archivist of the Athenaeum for information from the Club's records.
86.   Copy letter in the Rothschild archives.
87.   Athenaeum records.
88.   *The Athenaeum: Club and Social Life in London 1824—1974.*
89.   I am indebted to the Royal Society for supplying a photocopy of the application.
90.   R. N. Salaman, 'The Jewish Fellows of the Royal Society', Miscellanies V, Jewish Historical Society of England.
91.   Application. His work for the Imperial Continental Gas Association proves him to have been a pioneer of the use of gas.

2

The Business Man and Financier

P. L. COTTRELL

During the first half of the nineteenth century, Sir Moses Montefiore was a stockbroker, while from the mid-1820s, he was a director of a number of important companies. Jews had been an important minority element in the institutions of the developing London capital market since the beginning of the eighteenth century[1] and so Montefiore's career as a man of affairs and financier was in no way unusual.

He was born into a particular segment of London Jewish society, the congregation of Spanish and Portuguese Jews.[2] Earlier members of this particular group had, individually, taken large holdings in the stock issues of the 1690s, 1700s, and 1720s, although collectively their subscriptions were small, less than those of the London Huguenot community.[3] The Sephardi Jews were accordingly well established in London by the 1780s, with the wealthiest living in the City, and their position and social standing were secure, in contrast to the majority of the Ashkenazim, who arrived in London in numbers from the 1750s and generally set up house and shop in the poorer districts such as Whitechapel, Houndsditch, and Mile End. The latter often formed part of the lowest strata of the lower orders, the submerged and transient population of the casually employed, which probably constituted an eighth of London's population by the end of the eighteenth century.[4]

The Montefiores were initially only at the edge of the rich Sephardi community. Moses Haim Montefiore had made the journey to England with his brother Joseph, possibly lured by the successful business activities of relations of their mother, in particular Sir Solomon de Medina, who in 1709 held £16,000 of Bank stock and had subscribed for more than £5,000 of East India stock as well.[5] Moses Haim used the expertize at his fingertips by becoming an Anglo-Italian merchant, and over twenty years rose to affluence. His fourth son, Joseph Elias, when trading on his own account, imported such Italian goods as Leghorn straw bonnets and Carrara marbles, possibly from his eldest brother Judah, who had remained at Leghorn with the Montefiore grandparents. Two other brothers, Eliezer and Jacob, in partnership, became

merchants, first in the City and then in the West Indies.[6] Joseph
Elias' marriage to Rachel Mocatta was a further part of the process of the Montefiores' integration with the rich Sephardi congregation. The Mocattas had been established in London since the
1690s and by the 1790s were major bankers and bullion dealers,
having acted for the Bank of England almost from the latter's foundation.[7] That Moses Montefiore in his turn chose to become a stockbroker may have been due to the influence of his maternal uncle
Moses Mocatta.

It has been put forward that Moses' uncles purchased the right for
him to practise as one of the twelve Jewish brokers in the City at a
cost of £1,200.[8] This, however, is not supported by the surviving
documentary evidence. Although Moses did become a member of
the London Stock Exchange in 1803, his application to be a subscriber being supported by M. V. J. Ellis, James Pulley, and his
uncle Moses Mocatta,[9] he was not admitted as a sworn Jewish
broker of the City of London until 1815. This was in no way unusual, as the Acts of 1697 and 1708 with respect to stockbroking,
had been treated with little respect almost since their passage through
Parliament. Mortimer, in 1761, estimated that only a third of stock-
brokers were sworn brokers. Under the 1708 Act the City of London's
monopoly to admit brokers was confirmed, the income from entry
fees and annual subscriptions reimbursing the City for the loss of the
office of Garbler and Spices. The Act of 1708, unlike the 1697
statute, left the process of regulation largely in the hands of City
officials, but they decided both to restrict the number of Jewish
brokers to twelve, as previously, and to hold the number constant
through not admitting a new Jewish broker until a vacancy occurred
as a result of death or retirement.[10] Between 1787 and 1815 fifteen
new Jewish brokers were admitted, and of particular interest here
are Joseph Cohen in September 1797, Moses Mocatta in September
1806, and Moses Montefiore in December 1815.[11] Moses Montefiore's
application was backed by Lord Mayor Samuel Goodbehere, who
had supported Moses Mocatta earlier, and Sir John Eamer. It would
appear that Abraham, Moses' brother, provided the surety for the
bond.[12] Therefore, with respect to Montefiore's start, what is more
likely is that Moses' uncles provided the necessary capital for their
nephew to set up as a stockbroker. There is also a possibility that
Moses' decision may have been influenced not just by Moses Mocatta
but also by paternal relations, as both H. J. Montefiore, giving an
address of Boulogne sur Mere, and H. Moses Montefiore, of Norvenos
Gate, Park Lane, were subscribers to the London Stock Exchange in
1802.[13]

Moses Montefiore entered the London Stock Exchange at a time of transition in the institution's history. Until 1773 the market had centred on the coffee houses of Exchange Alley, in particular Jonathan's. In 1773 a group of brokers acquired their own building, called for the first time the Stock Exchange, but admission was open to anyone who paid sixpence a day. In 1801 it was turned into a subscription room, but not smoothly, as there was friction between the proprietors and users, and complaints from former users who failed to be elected to the reconstituted institution. Peace did not reign until a new building was opened in Capel Court a year later, which did establish a Stock Exchange on the basis of elected membership, although not without challenges in the 1810s. It was owned by an unlimited joint stock company consisting of 550 members, but its management was vested in a Committee of General Purposes of thirty, elected annually by the general body of subscribers.[14]

Within the unique division of the market on the London Stock Exchange between jobbers and brokers, still not quite established by 1800, Moses Montefiore was a broker, buying and selling for clients. Initially he operated from coffee houses, in 1804 John's Coffee House, and then from 1805 until at least 1809, Grigsby's Coffee House, and he worked alone, having no partner and employing no clerk.[15] In 1806 he failed, as a result of a transaction in August with J. E. Daniels. The reasons for this occurrence are far from clear, but the business was considered by the Committee for General Purposes in October and December 1806 and twice in January 1807.[16] The house was then run largely informally, with no rule book being issued until February 1812,[17] and Montefiore, despite being ruined, was able to continue as a broker, for instance asking the Committee on 21 January 1807 for an arbitrator to adjust some disputes which had arisen from a transaction with a Mr Baumer involving bargains made 'in Tickets pending the Negotiations for the 1st Lottery 1806'.[18] His failure, however, made a deep impression on him and was largely, it would seem, the result of the duplicity of others. Twice in his diary he recorded the anniversary of the occasion, attributing it in August 1823 to N.N. who 'robbed me of all and more than I had',[19] while in August 1831 the entry was 'J.E.P. robbed me of all I possessed in the world and left me deeply in debt.'[20] It took until February 1815 for Moses Montefiore to repay his creditors and the complications of the case required his appearance before the Committee of General Purposes:

Moses Montefiore came to the Committee and stated that he wished to pay to his Creditors the balances due to them on account of the loss sustained by Elkin Daniels: that he had paid some of his Creditors in full and wished to have the opinion of the Committee respecting his paying the Balances due to J. Fernandez and James Flater Fall.

The Committee are of opinion that Moses Montefiore's conduct has done him great honour and that the same sense of attitude which prompted him on this occasion will direct him in the proper distribution of the Money, they therefore advise him to follow the dictates of his own mind in that distribution.[21]

It can only be surmised that Moses Montefiore had a difficult time on the London Stock Exchange during the 1800s. What is evident is that his fortunes changed from 1812, when he married Judith Barent Cohen, which probably provided Moses with substantial dowry and gave him a connection with Nathan Mayer Rothschild. Further, in the same year, or the following, he formed a stockbroking partnership with his brother Abraham. There is some slight evidence of greater solidity even before the conjunction of these three events, as by February 1812 Moses had an office at 9 Birchin Lane. During the same month his brother became a subscriber to the Stock Exchange, recommended by Moses and Moses Mocatta.[22] The partnership continued until 28 November 1816,[23] and from 19 June 1815[24] it employed the youngest of the brothers, Horatio Joseph, as a clerk. Horatio joined the Stock Exchange in his own right in 1817, being recommended by his two elder brothers,[25] and remained a subscriber, despite a rather bumpy career, until the 1860s.[26]

The capital available to the partnership with Abraham was probably substantially augmented by Moses' marriage to Judith. In the case of Nathan Mayer Rothschild, who in 1806 had married Hannah, Judith's eldest natural sister, it has been suggested that he received a dowry of £10,000[27] and that the opening of the first permanent Rothschild office in London at 12 Great St Helens was due to his wife's inheritance, resulting from the death of her father in 1808.[28] Whatever capital Moses Montefiore obtained as a result of his marriage to Judith apart, it certainly gave him a major business connection with Nathan Mayer Rothschild. Not only did he act as Rothschild's stockbroker, but also the business relationship was underpinned by a warm friendship.[29]

By becoming Rothschild's stockbroker, Moses Montefiore was able to benefit from the emergence and development of one of London's major merchant banks. Nathan had originally come to London, to Levi Barent Cohen, to gain commercial experience.[30] He quickly applied that training by opening an office in Manchester in May 1799 in order to buy direct from the cotton manufacturers' sale rooms, so by-passing the intermediation of English agents on the continent.[31] Even when he established his London house, Nathan Meyer continued to be involved in merchanting activities, but at the same time, and very rapidly, the banking side of the business developed, involving credit and bullion transactions and ultimately the flotation of loans.

Unfortunately only a fragmentary picture can be established of the relationship between Moses Montefiore and Nathan Mayer Rothschild. Loewe's extracts from Moses' diaries indicate that in 1813 the two men were working closely together in the difficult financial environment of the Napoleonic wars and that Nathan was providing advice with respect to the movement of the foreign exchanges and international flows of bullion.[32] In the spring of 1814 Moses, with Judith, visited Paris, being entertained by Salomon Rothschild. However the main news that Moses had for Nathan in London was the small chance of doing anything in Russian paper, the price of which was sustained by speculators from Frankfurt and other European financial centres. It was this Russian speculation that had brought Moses to Paris, but the only chance that appeared likely was the possibility of buying £2,000, if the price should fall to 90. Actually, Moses wanted to get back to London 'to be once more in the bustle of the Stock Exchange', although, according to Rothschild, business was very dull in the English capital. Montefiore, however, remained optimistic:

A new loan, will, I flatter myself soon set us to work again with redoubled energy; but should the Minister defer it for a month the funds must rise considerably, at any rate they cannot fall much: you will get 25 for your emission or I shall be greatly disappointed.[33]

In 1815, as a result of business with Nathan Mayer, Montefiore went to Dunkirk and Yarmouth, being able to make these trips, as in 1814, because of his partnership with Abraham. The following year, on the way to France and Italy, Moses undertook Rothschild business, starting when he and Judith landed at Calais on 2 May.[34] During the visit to France, Italy, and Germany in 1817 and 1818, Montefiore was anxious by February 1818 that there would be a loan operation which would necessitate his earlier return to England. In his absence Rothschild stock exchange transactions were being handled by Abraham Montefiore, the aim being to look for a fall in security prices, with Moses writing to Nathan:

I am very happy to learn you make as good a Bear as you formerly did a Bull, you must have had some difficulty with my brother, indeed it is quite a new character for both, it has one great advantage that while consols continue at or above 82 there can be very little to fear; you have beaten your antagonists so frequently that I am surprised there are any so hardy to be found in the Stock Exchange to oppose you in any considerable operation.[35]

At the same time, and in return, Rothschild handled Montefiore's fortune while the latter was absent from London, and indications are that Montefiore's wealth was quite considerable by 1818. For the European tour of that year the London banker was instructed to sell Montefiore's holdings of Navy five per cents to cover his bills of exchange drawn on Rothschilds.[36]

Loewe has stated that Montefiore gave up his counting house on 30 October 1820.[37] He was certainly in a position to do so, having £20,000 in Bank Stock alone in 1818.[38] But whether Moses Montefiore began to retire from business as early as 1820 is far from clear. He remained a subscriber to the London Stock Exchange until the business year ending on 25 March 1845,[39] while in 1820/1 he employed James Bagnall as a clerk.[40] It is more probable that with his move from New Court to Green Street in 1825, this side of his business life ceased to be very important. One supporting indication is that his visit to the Stock Exchange on 17 February 1824 was the first for more than a year.[41]

By the mid-1820s there were a number of Montefiores operating on the London market in addition to Abraham and Horatio Joseph. Abraham Junior (son of Samuel Montefiore by his marriage to Grace Mocatta, and therefore Moses Montefiore's cousin) became a subscriber in 1818, being recommended to the Committee by Jacob Mocatta and William Morgan.[42] Abraham Senior's business was doing well enough for him to employ a clerk, Thomas Bruce, between 1818 and 1822,[43] while in the latter year he was elected to the Committee for General Purposes.[44] It would seem that the whole Montefiore family, including female members, were speculating as bulls for a rise in government stocks during the feverish boom of the mid-1820s. Their activities led to resentment, which culminated in an unpleasant scene between Abraham and B. Carr in the Committee Room of the Stock Exchange. It resulted in Carr being reprimanded by the Committee and seems to have had its origins in Carr having 'suffered very severely by six persons who had been introduced to the Stock Exchange by Montefiore'.[45]

The younger members of the Montefiore family who were subscribers to the Stock Exchange, were not so successful in their business as Moses and Abraham. Abraham Junior failed on 3 March 1823[46] and was forced to leave the market for two years. He was readmitted for the year ending 25 March 1826, being recommended by Jacob Mocatta and William Morgan with the support of Abraham Junior's creditors, led by W. Greenway and Aaron Mocatta.[47] Similarly, Horatio failed in March 1823, but as a result of the non-payment of debt to him. He was forced to sell his plate and raise loans from friends to generate 'a sufficient sum to effect a general settlement with his Creditors in full'[48] and so was able to continue on the Exchange. Abraham Junior failed again on 14 October 1826 with debts of £350, but despite their relatively small size was unable to continue on the London market.[49] Three months before, Moses Montefiore Junior (another son of Samuel and Grace Montefiore) had become a subscriber to the Exchange, with J. M. Belisario and Abraham Lindo Mocatto providing the necessary sureties for the first two years of Moses' trading on the market.[50] However, his career was short, as he had left the Stock Exchange by the end of the decade. How difficult a career it could be on the market is illustrated by the experience of Horatio Joseph who failed in 1826, 1827, 1828, and again in 1832.

More members of the Montefiore family joined the Stock Exchange during the mid-nineteenth century, with Joseph becoming a subscriber in 1845 after acting as Horatio Joseph's clerk for the previous year.[51] However, by the end of the 1860s the family's presence on the London market had been reduced to Benjamin Montefiore, Horatio Joseph's son. But he had a sizeable firm, as it employed three clerks including E. Mocatta, who was permitted to trade on the floor of the market.[52] In the same way that he had received support from his uncles, Moses Montefiore assisted the start of the careers of his relations and friends of the family, providing one of the sureties for Abraham Lindo Mocatta in 1822,[53] along with John Capel, and recommending Benjamin Mocatta in 1833.[54]

Although Moses Montefiore remained a member of the London Stock Exchange until 1845,[55] from the early 1820s he was probably more a financier than a stockbroker. As with his previous career as a stockbroker, the connection with Rothschild was of considerable importance, because this allowed him to employ his wealth as an underwriter for Rothschild's loan flotations. Montefiore was, for example, one of the original subscribers to the Russian loan issue of 1822.[56] By 1819 Rothschild was well established as a successful merchant banker and had clearly demonstrated his forte in marketing government securities. Six years later some of the earlier brashness had gone, so that in the mid-1820s Rothschild was the leading spokesman among London financiers for conservative investment and marketing policies, having totally displaced Barings in acting for European governments.[57] The gains to be made from loan contracting were potentially substantial, with the Austrian chargé d'affaires in London estimating in 1824 that Rothschild, Reid & Irving, and Baring would collectively secure a profit of between £100,000 and £300,000 from the issue of the Austrian loan of that year.[58]

English overseas investment during the first half of the nineteenth century probably reached a peak during the boom of the mid-1820s[59] and Montefiore not only acted as an underwriter for Rothschild flotations, but also used his particular knowledge to speculate. In October 1822 he took at least £9,350 of Rothschild's Russian loan[60] and in April 1824 bought £25,012 more of the same issue.[61] At the same time, near the peak of the boom, he took a large position in French rentes, buying £81,606, and made a very small transaction in 'New Spanish' stock, buying £1,020 nominal on 12 April for £205 and selling the same for £211 in May. In April 1825 he sold a small parcel, amounting to £4,600, of the Columbian loan which had been issued the previous year, a transaction of some prudence as the new South American republics were quickly to default on their foreign debt.[62] Counterbalancing such activities, he held sizeable amounts of far less speculative securities, such as £50,000 South Sea stock and £10,000 Indian paper on which he drew dividends amounting to £1,400. His last dabble on the market during the boom of the mid-1820s would appear to have been a small transaction in Greek scrip,[63] arising from the loan of 1825 issued by Ricardos.[64] Thereafter until the end of the 1830s his account with Rothschilds only indicates occasional transactions in British government securities and the receipt of dividends on the same stocks.[65] However, most of his account from the mid-1820s is concerned with transactions arising from his domestic household and his travels abroad.

Side by side with Montefiore's transactions in foreign government securities in the mid-1820s were market operations in shares of newly formed companies of which he was a director. The most important of these concerns was the Alliance Assurance, formed in 1824, and in which Nathan Meyer Rothschild had a considerable interest. There are a number of versions of the origins of the Alliance. The company's official historian has attributed its inception to a casual meeting between Moses and Nathan Mayer, when the latter was on his way to draw some dividends arising from insurance company shares that he held. The two friends talked over the state of the British insurance industry, realized that their circle of acquaintances would make a useful clientèle, and Montefiore put forward that what was required was a company with a larger share capital and a more influential board than existing concerns.[66] Hyamson, following Wolf, has cast this story in rather a different mould, emphasizing two factors, one general and one particular. The first was that on one hand Jews had difficulty in obtaining insurance in the 1820s, with existing fire offices discriminating against them in the policies that they issued; while on the other it was not then appreciated generally that Jews were a better life risk in that they lived longer. In particular, Wolf and Hyamson have claimed that the Alliance was founded to give employment to Benjamin Gompertz, Moses' brother-in-law, who had failed to secure the post of actuary to the Guardian Office[67] and this particular point has been retold by Clapham, but with some cynicism.[68] It is difficult to find particular evidence with which to either rebut or confirm this story. Montefiore had had an interest in insurance since at least 1821 when he dined with directors of the Atlas Fire Assurance Company, a corporate connection he maintained until at least 1827,[69] while Gompertz, after following a career on the Stock Exchange including a partnership with Horatio Joseph in 1818,[70] had written an important paper on 'Life Contingencies' in 1820.[71] However, Gompertz did not join the Alliance until March 1825. The Montefiore-Rothschild group, therefore, had a growing particular interest in insurance from the beginning of the 1820s, but they may have been encouraged to take the matter in hand by the general boom in company formation in the mid-1820s and in particular the twenty per cent rise in insurance shares between October 1823 and October 1824.[72] In 1824 there were twenty-five insurance companies in existence, many of which had been formed during the first decade of the century, but during 1824 and 1825 a further fifteen companies were successfully established, while prospectuses were published on behalf of ten others.[73] For Rothschild the formation of an insurance company was not only a way to participate in the flotation profits of the mid-1820s company formation boom, but also allowed diversification of his interests in an institution which was complementary to the activity of his private bank.[74] The same considerations probably also carried considerable weight with the other banking founders of the Alliance, Francis Baring, and Samuel Gurney — the Quaker and head of the most important bill broking firm in London. The combination of these houses with Montefiore and John Irving made for a considerable force, called by contemporaries 'that mass of wealth which has been put in motion on this occasion' and 'nothing could be more respectable or substantial than the security [of the promoters]; the Bank of England could not be better.'[75] However, despite their wealth, their particular interests, and the generally favourable economic and financial climate, the Alliance was to have a difficult time for the first years of its existence, being forced to hive off its marine underwriting to a separate company, and experiencing both liquidity shortages and difficulties in expanding its business.

Montefiore was present at the first meeting of the Alliance's promoters, held on 12 March 1824 at 4 New Court. They approved the company's prospectus, made themselves its presidents, and allocated 2,000 £100 shares to each person present out of the 50,000 to be issued. Further, they reserved 2,000 shares more for themselves and a week later agreed to take up any of the 32,750 shares to be issued to the public that were not subscribed, so constituting themselves as an underwriting syndicate.[76] Montefiore not only became one of the company's presidents but was also appointed as its stockbroker,[77] carrying out the president's decision, made on 1 April 1824, to invest the company's capital in consols, rentes, and American, Austrian and Russian securities, together with putting £120,000 out at interest.[78] Actually, Gurney acquired the first parcel of rentes and the consols,[79] but Montefiore bought a further parcel of French government stock, the Russian stock, and in September 1824 more consols for the company.[80] In addition, as a president, he automatically became a member of all the five committees established on 1 April 1824 to supervise the various branches of the company's business; while two days earlier, along with Gurney and two directors, he had been charged with appointing the company's firemen.

Before the company could come into full active existence it had to be determined whether it could legally undertake marine underwriting in addition to life and fire business. Marine underwriting had not been mentioned in the company's prospectus, as under the 1720 Bubble Act no company or partnership could undertake it other than the Royal Exchange or London Assurances.[81] The presidents referred the question to a solicitor to see whether parliamentary action was necessary 'to abrogate [these] peculiar privileges'[82] and the advice was that a public Act was necessary to overturn the legislation of the previous century. On 5 May Montefiore, as a president, joined the special committee 'for the superintendence of Parliamentary Proceedings' and within eight weeks the necessary bill had reached the statute book. The bill in fact had a relatively easy passage with formidable support in Parliament, including favourable interventions by the Prime Minister, the Chancellor of the Exchequer, and the President of the Board of Trade.[83] The company subsequently gave a piece of plate worth £200 to S. Fowell Buxton, MP, for his effort in the House in carrying the bill.[84] By 30 August 'a plan of Marine Assurance' had been decided upon by the board, but in October the marine business had to be transferred to a separate company. This was the result of an injunction brought by the Lord Chancellor as a result of an action begun by W. R. F. Natusch, a shareholder but also an underwriter at Lloyds, who objected to signing the Alliance's deed of settlement which constituted it as an unincorporated company.[85] Montefiore, together with Rothschild and Gurney, took counsel's opinion but there was no other avenue but to separate the concern.[86]

The deed of settlement of the Alliance British and Foreign Life and Fire Assurance Company had been drawn up on 4 August 1824. It credited John Irving, Francis Baring and N. M. Rothschild as the progenitors of the company while Montefiore, as an executor and administrator for Rothschild, became a president. He took 2,000 shares in the concern, his presidential prior allotment, while his uncles Eliezer and Jacob subscribed for forty and seventy shares respectively.[87] The public issue was not totally successful as the presidential underwriting syndicate in November 1824 had to take up 2,150 unappropriated shares at a price eventually agreed of £15 each. In the case of the separate marine company, a deed of settlement was not drawn up until June 1825. Montefiore was one of the prime movers of the document and took 1,500 shares, with his uncle Eliezer signing the indenture for 100 shares.[88] Moses Montefiore began selling his shares in the original Alliance Company from 6 January 1825: between then and 28 January he sold 352 shares of which 130 went to members of the London Stock Exchange. In addition he transferred fifty shares to his mother, Rachel Montefiore. In contrast, uncle Eliezer bought a further five shares from David Salomons of the Stock Exchange.[89] Other family transactions were the free transfer of 300 shares by Montefiore to Henrietta, his brother Abraham's widow,[90] while between March and September 1825 Jacob Montefiore sold seventy shares of which ten were acquired by Joseph Barrow Montefiore, who, in turn during the same period also sold fifty shares, twenty of which were acquired by Horatio Joseph Montefiore.[91] At the beginning of 1826 Joseph Barrow Montefiore sold a further ten shares, with five going to Moses' wife,[92] while in July 1827 Horatio Joseph Montefiore, as a stockbroker, was responsible for the transfer of twenty-five shares.[93] Moses Montefiore worked his own position in the Alliance shares also through a joint account with Rothschilds by which he appears to have made £15,000 in October 1824 alone,[94] although this may have been subsequently transferred to the credit of the marine company.

Montefiore, when he was in England, was an assiduous member of the Alliance's board to the extent that during the late 1820s he largely ran the company in conjunction with Samuel Gurney. In both 1828 and 1829 Moses frequently chaired board meetings. The minutes of those meetings are largely anonymous and so it is difficult to establish the exact influence of Montefiore upon the decision-making process of the board. It is clear that he both brought business to the company and was entrusted with particular tasks. In February 1825 Montefiore, together with Howard, a director, nearly acquired the fire assurance for Kemp Town, Brighton,[95] but despite long discussions the arrangement could not be completed with Mr Kemp.[96] The company worked initially from a room in Rothschild's bank, paying £200 in rent.[97] This was a result of its being difficult to find suitable premises. Montefiore, with Gurney and Irving, investigated one property in April 1825 but it proved to be unsatisfactory.[98] However in June 1826 Montefiore, with Gurney, arranged for the purchase of the premises in Bartholomew Lane of Sir Peter Pole & Co., a bank which had collapsed in December 1825 during the financial crisis of that autumn and early winter. The Alliance obtained the property for £8,950,[99] a sum below the valuation of its own surveyor, and, once the necessary conversion building work was well under way, Montefiore joined the committee which superintended the furnishings of the new office.[100] Other domestic duties included reviewing the clerks' salaries along with Gurney, Richardson and Bowden.[101] During the early years of the company's existence, obtaining business proved to be difficult given the competition from other new companies as well as existing concerns, and as early as October 1824 shareholders were asked to procure life and fire business. Agents were particularly difficult to supervise and monitor, and in April 1825 Montefiore was asked to tour the country, with two other directors, 'with the view of increasing the efficiency of this Department as soon as convenient, with the full powers granted to them by Board Minute 19 January'.[102] The board gave its services freely to the company for 1825, but for 1826 it was decided that each of the five presidents should receive £225 per annum and the directors £150.[103] By 1829 Montefiore's fees, as one of the presidents, had only risen to £233. 5s. 2d.[104]

At the same time as Montefiore was involved with the formation of the Alliance Assurance, he was also concerned with the establishment of the Provincial Bank of Ireland. Just as the foundation of the Alliance had required the abrogation of the privileges of chartered companies formed a century before, so the setting up of the Provincial Bank necessitated the restriction of the monopoly of the Bank of Ireland. However, whereas the promoters of the Alliance had had to bring in their own private bill, in the case of the Provincial Bank the government had begun in 1821 the process of circumscribing the monopoly of corporate note-issuing banking held by the Bank of Ireland. But although it has been claimed that Lord Liverpool's ministry had the aim of securing greater financial stability in both England and Ireland through the introduction of commercial joint stock banking and started to tackle this general problem by experiments in Ireland, it is clearly evident that the framers of the 1821 Irish Banking Act were more concerned with the government's need to fund £0.5 m. of short term debt than the liberalization of banking law. While, by an amendment to the 1782 Act, the 1821 Act allowed note-issuing banks with more than six partners to be established outside of a fifty miles radius of Dublin, it did not repeal the legislation of 1756 which not only necessitated that any such 'new' banks would have to act in the names of all their partners, including listing them on all notes and receipts, but prevented any new institution having any partner engaged in overseas trade. These cumbersome provisions were only repealed in 1824, largely as a result of the successful attempt by Belfast merchants and bankers to form an unlimited bank in their city to meet the needs of the growing linen industry. At the same time a group, which had at its centre a number of Roman Catholics excluded from the direction of the Bank of Ireland, established the Hibernian Bank through a private act, in order to conduct deposit banking in Dublin. These two new banks were not concerned with the south and west of Ireland which had suffered considerably from the effects of the financial crisis of 1820 that had particularly affected the small, weak private banks in that region. This was the chosen area of operations for the Provincial Bank, whose promoters aimed at introducing banking on the Scottish system to Ireland — namely well managed branch banking supported by capital and a central metropolitan board.[105]

The founders of the Provincial Bank, a group of Irish MPs, had been heavily swayed by the ideas of Thomas Joplin, who in the early 1820s campaigned through pamphlets for the introduction of joint stock banking into England in order to overcome the chronic financial instability of the economy south of the border. In 1822 he had proposed a joint stock bank for Tyneside, his local area, while four years later he tried to set up the same type of bank in London.[106] Joplin, a Newcastle banker accustomed to handling Scottish notes, was conscious of the apparent greater stability of banks north of the border which, he argued, was due not to 'anything different in the nature of . . . money transactions . . . but the nature of their respective banking establishments; the Scotch banks being Joint Stock

Companies, while the English banks are private partnerships'. Actually, Joplin's pamphlets were polemics and while he referred to thirty-two banking companies in Scotland with deposits of over £200 m., his main remarks appear to be largely concerned with only four particular institutions. What seems to have been at the forefront of Joplin's mind were three public banks in Scotland which had been formed by charter, of which two, through holding large bullion reserves and investing largely in government stocks, acted as quasi-central banks and policed the system. Far more numerous were the provincial banks which were either private partnerships, like their southern and Irish counterparts, or moderately sized co-partnerships and by no means of the stature that Joplin implied. Actually, only nineteen of the forty-five provincial banking companies formed in Scotland between 1747 and 1836 had mōre than thirteen shareholders. These concerns were nearly as failure-prone as English and Irish private banks, with one-fifth meeting this fate before 1830, compared with a third in the case of England.[107]

While Joplin's arguments were not as well founded as they may have appeared, they did convince the promoters of the Provincial Bank. However, despite the legislation of 1821 and 1824, there were also some legal issues which still had to be resolved before the bank could appeal to the public for capital. These were threefold, of which the first stemmed from the lack of clarity in the existing legislation. It was implied that only Irish residents could become co-partners in the new banks, which would prevent the introduction of English capital. Further, the promoters wanted to issue notes in Dublin and desired to protect shareholders in their projected bank by establishing it as a full corporation with the privilege of limited liability. These latter considerations were the subject of discussions between Joplin and the board of the Bank of Ireland, but the publicist for commercial joint stock banking was unable to make any headway with regard to these issues.

Accordingly in March 1825, nine months after the bank scheme had been initiated, T. S. Rice for the promoters brought in a private bill at Westminster.[108] It would appear that it was during the preparatory stages for parliamentary legislation that Montefiore became involved in the Provincial Bank scheme, as he did not attend a board meeting of the institution until 11 February 1825.[109] The private bill, however, only received a first reading, being supplanted by legislation introduced by the government. The Liverpool ministry's bill was influenced by the objects of the promoters of the Provincial Bank, its overall aim being to remove any doubts arising from the 1824 Act and, specifically, to encourage the introduction of British capital into Ireland. It quickly went through the House, and received royal assent on 10 June 1825.

Two months later the deed of settlement, establishing the Provincial Bank as an unlimited note-issuing joint stock bank, was signed. Nearly two-thirds of the bank's shareholders were Londoners, most of whom had large individual holdings.[110] As the capital of the bank was accumulated, during the summer of 1825, Montefiore, together with two other directors of the bank — its accountant and its solicitor — toured Ireland in order to prepare for the opening of the bank's branches. The first to conduct business was the one at Cork which opened on 1 October 1825, and eight days later Montefiore, with the others who had visited Ireland, received a vote of thanks from the bank's London board. By the end of 1825 two further branches had been opened; in 1828 the bank had fourteen branches, and by 1845 it had achieved its aim of having outlets in all the main Irish towns.[111] The Provincial Bank's directorate remained in London, but the conduct of each branch, as in Scotland, was in the hands of a manager and an accountant, whose work was overseen by local directors. One of those managers, J. W. Gilbart, who was responsible for the Kilkenny and Waterford branches in the late 1820s, subsequently became the general manager of the London and Westminster Bank, and an important figure in the joint stock banking world through his writing and acting as spokesman for the Association of Joint Stock Banks. Whereas the London and Westminster, from 1833, introduced Scottish banking practice in London, the Provincial Bank, by paying interest on deposits and giving advances by cash credits and by its mode of branch management, initiated Scottish banking methods in Ireland.

There was some interlocking of the boards of the main companies that Montefiore became involved with from the mid-1820s. Blount of the Provincial Bank, who had accompanied Montefiore on the tour of Ireland in 1825, joined the board of the Alliance Assurance in March 1827,[112] whereas Thomas Joplin was the managing director of the Imperial Continental Gas Association between 1830 and 1832. The founder of the gas company was the inventor, Major-General Sir William Congreve, who had toyed with the idea of establishing gas works in European towns from 1814. As an equerry to George IV, as well as being the King's personal friend, this growing authority on the nascent gas industry was well placed to obtain continental concessions through his contacts with ambassadors and other foreign dignitaries at Court. He turned over the problem of financing his scheme to a small group consisting of Matthias Attwood, a director of the Phoenix Fire Office, a partner

in the Birmingham bank of Spooner, Attwood, and a close associate
of Joplin; Isaac Lyon Goldsmid, a partner in Mocatta and Goldsmid;
and Moses Montefiore. This wealthy triumvirate chose to pursue the
same method of floating Congreve's company as that used by the
promoters of the Alliance Assurance Company. Fifty-four per cent
of the shares of the Imperial Continental Gas Association were reserved for distribution amongst the concern's presidents, directors
and auditors, who then issued a circular to their relations, friends
and business acquaintances. Not surprisingly, given this method of
distribution, 2,795 out of 6,996 shares issued were held by directors
and officers of the company.[113] The same procedure of retaining
shares for the board and its acquaintances was used on subsequent
occasions when the company increased its capital. Consequently, in
1858, Montefiore was one of seven shareholders who held individually
more than 500 shares of the Association, and this group actually
controlled the company. In the case of the Imperial Continental, the
board were both the executive of the company and its principal
shareholders. Even in 1878 Montefiore was the second largest shareholder after the Goldsmid family.[114]

Initial subscriptions for shares of the Imperial Continental Gas
Association came into Montefiore's hands on the same day as the
deed of settlement of Alliance Assurance was drawn up.[115] The
company to begin with had a large proprietary, with some 850
shareholders besides the Association's presidents, directors and other
officials.[116] However, the 1825 crisis brought the company formation boom of the middle years of that decade to an abrupt end
and with the collapse of speculative euphoria the number of 'outside'
shareholders in the Alliance fell rapidly. The gas company had its
own particular problems (marked publicly by no dividends until
1831) which were the result of a number of factors. These were the
technical difficulties of beginning operations, low quality middle
management, and the competing claims for the time of the Association's directors and presidents.[117] Montefiore did visit the company's plants in Europe, and in December 1831 insisted that the
Association should not either purchase or rent any new gas plants
whatsoever until the company had paid a dividend.

Montefiore's firm resolution was probably in part due to an
inquiry conducted by Joplin in 1829 on behalf of the Association's
'outside' shareholders. In this investigation Joplin, with Attwood,
had visited the company's works at Ghent and Rotterdam and maintained in his subsequent report that these assets had been acquired
at above their true value. As a result of his pungent criticisms and his
claim that he could conduct the Association's affairs better than the

existing manager, Joplin became the Association's executive director in 1830 at a salary of £200. He was active until 1832 when his involvement in the inception of the National Provincial Bank diverted his energies elsewhere. Joplin ceased to be an executive director in 1832, and failed to be re-elected to the Association's board in 1837.[118]

The affairs of the gas company turned the corner during the early 1830s and from 1831 it began to earn profits. One measure of the disarray of the Association's first years was that it was by no means clear who was a member of its board, given the large number of absentees from directors' meetings. A new list of presidents and directors was drawn up in 1832; this included Attwood and Montefiore as presidents, and Horatio Montefiore and Moses Mocatta as directors. Moses Montefiore remained a president until his death, while during the middle years of the nineteenth century Nathaniel Montefiore was a director. The board received little in direct compensation for the services that it rendered to the Association. Directors' fees of £50 per annum were introduced in January 1833, together with fines for non-attendance at board meetings.[119]

In the mid-1820s Moses Montefiore went on to the boards of at least four other companies formed during the joint stock flotation of the decade. Two were South American mining companies and as such were typical of the speculative activity of the period[120] — thirty of these were formed during the closing months of 1824, all supported by City names, West End wealth, and even pamphlets from the pen of Disraeli, then a broker's clerk. Fortunes were made and lost as their shares first rocketed up and then plummeted down. Only eight survived the boom and only two, of which one was Montefiore's Imperial Brazilian, had by the 1850s made substantial dividend payments to their shareholders.[121]

From the mid-1820s Montefiore's business life was largely made up of attending board meetings and furthering the interests of the companies with which he had become associated, although he played some part with Rothschild in the flotation of the Slave Emancipation Loan of 1833 which added £20 m. to the British National Debt.[122] His brother-in-law died in 1836 and this may explain to some extent Montefiore's retreat from an active business life. However, his continuing connection with the Rothschild bank may have been responsible for Montefiore becoming briefly a director of the South Eastern Railway Company during the autumn of 1845. Equally, his short connection with the railway company could have stemmed from his role as a local dignitary at Ramsgate. Montefiore replaced Sir John Kirkland on the South Eastern's board and became a member of the company's Finance and Audit Committee, but only attended two board meetings before resigning on 4 December 1845.[123] Kirkland had been responsible for involving the South Eastern with one of the promotion groups headed by Lafitte which was seeking the concession for the French Northern Railway and which, with the South Eastern, was building the Amiens-Boulogne line. In July 1845 Lafitte and the French Rothschild group came together while Kirkland retired from the project. Therefore it may well be that Montefiore's task was to hold a limited watching brief over the South Eastern for the Rothschilds.[124]

All the indications are that Moses Montefiore became a wealthy man between 1812 and the mid-1820s. One plausible explanation would be that his marriage not only gave him capital but also a connection with Nathan Mayer Rothschild who, when he died in 1836, had a fortune of about £5 m. Stock market operations in conjunction with Rothschild seem the most likely reason for Montefiore's accumulation of wealth. To go further stretches reasonable explanation beyond conjecture into speculation, but a suggestion would be that both Rothschild and Montefiore benefited from the considerable medium-term appreciation of government securities from the end of the Napoleonic wars until the late 1820s, by when Montefiore had become a company director rather than a stockbroker. As a wealthy man Montefiore was typical of his age, since it was finance and commerce which generated large fortunes in the British economy of the nineteenth century, and these occupations were centred in London. Jews were an important element of the wealthy in nineteenth century British society, but this was largely due to their involvement with metropolitan finance and commerce rather than their religious background, though the synagogue was a node of a business self-help network, often reinforced by marital ties.[125]

NOTES

1. P. G. M. Dickson, *The Financial Revolution in England* (1967), pp. 514–6.
2. P. Goodman, *Moses Montefiore* (Philadelphia, 1925), p. 11.
3. Dickson, pp. 259, 269, 282.
4. G. Rude, *Hanoverian London 1714–1808* (1971), pp. 7–8, 83.
5. Dickson, p. 263; L. Wolf, *Sir Moses Montefiore. A Centennial Biography with Extracts from Letters and Journals* (1884), p. 5. It is Wolf who gives two dates, 1744 and 1758, for the arrival of the Montefiore brothers in London.

6. Wolf, pp. 7–8, 13; see also Loewe (ed.) *Diaries of Sir Moses and Lady Montefiore* (1890), pp. 7–8 and A. M. Hyamson, *Moses Montefiore: His life and times* (1951), pp. 5–6.

7. Sir J. Clapham, *The Bank of England. A History* (Cambridge, 1944, repr. 1970), I, pp. 132, 137, 138, 139, 141, 219, 221.

8. Wolf, p. 17; Loewe, p. 13.

9. Guildhall Library, London (hereafter Guildhall); Records of the London Stock Exchange, Ms 17, 957/2.

10. Dickson, pp. 494, 516–7; see also D. Abrahams, 'Jew Brokers of the City of London', *Jewish Historical Society of England. Miscellanies III* (1937).

11. City of London Record Office (hereafter CLRO), Guildhall, London: 62B, Brokers Admissions, II, 1787 to 1815.

12. CLRO: Birch, Rep 219, 1814–15, ff. 173–6; 4891, Bonds of Moses Montefiore, 21 January 1815, for Broker; 6213 Index to Brokers' Bonds, I–Z. Both Loewe and Goodman do point out that Moses did not obtain his broker's medal, the badge of a sworn broker, until 1815. Loewe, p. 20; Goodman, p. 31.

13. Guildhall: MS 19,1311, I, Subscribers to the London Stock Exchange 1802.

14. Dickson, pp. 490–3, 506; E. Victor Morgan and W. A. Thomas, *The Stock Exchange* (1962), pp. 68–72; see also W. J. Reader, *A House in the City* (1979) and W. R. Cope, 'The Stock Exchange Revisited', *Economica*, XLV, 1978.

15. Guildhall: MS 17,957/3–10.

16. Guildhall: Minutes of the Committee for General Purposes, MS 14,600/5; October 1806, ff. 238–9, 24 December 1806 f. 246, 7 January 1807; 21 January 1807.

17. Morgan and Thomas, p. 75.

18. Guildhall: MS14,600/5; 21 January 1807.

19. Loewe, p. 28.

20. Goodman, p. 32.

21. Guildhall: MS 14,600/8, 21 February 1815, ff. 97, 99.

22. Guildhall: MS 17,957/11; see also MS19,312, Admission Lists for 1811 and 1812.

23. Guildhall: MS 17,957/12–15; MS 14,600/8, 5 December 1816 f. 251.

24. Guildhall: MS 17,957/13–15; MS 14,600/8, 19 June 1815 f. 130.

25. Guildhall: MS 17,957/16.

26. Guildhall: MS 17,957/58.

27. Wolf, p. 20.

28. [S. D. Chapman], *N. M. Rothschild 1777–1836* (privately printed, 1977), p. 19.

29. Wolf, p. 22.

30. [Chapman], p. 5.

31. B. Williams, *The Making of Manchester Jewry, 1740–1875* (Manchester, 1976), pp. 17–19.

32. Loewe, p. 20.

33. Rothschild Archives (London) (hereafter RAL), Letters T42/1, 18140309; see also T42/2, n.d. (? March 1814), Judith to Hannah.

34. RAL, T42/3, 18160502.

35. RAL, T42/3, 18180210; see also T42/5, n.d. (? 10 February 1818) Judith to N. M. Rothschild.

36. RAL, T42/6, 18180312; see also T42/7, n.d. (? 12 March 1818) Judith to Hannah.
37. Loewe, p. 26.
38. RAL, T42/4.
39. Guildhall: MS 17,957/43.
40. Guildhall: MS 17,957/19.
41. Loewe, p. 28.
42. Guildhall: MS 17,957/16.
43. Guildhall: MS 17,957/17–20.
44. Guildhall: MS 14,600/9, 15 April 1822, f. 273.
45. Guildhall: MS 14,600/10, 9 June 1823, ff. 13–14.
46. Guildhall: MS 14,600/9, 3 March 1823, f. 331.
47. Guildhall: MS 17,957/24; see also MS 14,600/10, 19 March 1825, f. 183.
48. Guildhall: MS 14,600/9, 4 March 1823, f. 332; 7 March 1823, f. 334.
49. Guildhall: MS 14,600/10, 14 October 1823, f. 323.
50. Guildhall: MS 17,957/25.
51. Guildhall: MS 17,957/43–44.
52. Guildhall: MS 17,957/68.
53. Guildhall: MS 17,957/21.
54. Guildhall: MS 17,957/32.
55. He did not make an application to be a member of the Exchange for the year ending 25 March 1846; see Guildhall: MS 17,957/44.
56. [Chapman], p. 21.
57. R. W. Hidy, *The House of Baring in American Trade and Finance* (Cambridge, Mass.), 1949, pp. 46, 55.
58. K. F. Helleiner, *The Imperial Loans* (Oxford, 1965), p. 174.
59. See H. English, *A Complete View of the Joint Stock Companies during the years 1824 and 1825* (London 1827), and P. L. Cottrell, *British Overseas Investment in the Nineteenth Century* (1975).
60. RAL, Account Current Books Private, XV/2/1, f. 23.
61. RAL, XV/2/2, f. 88; see also, Ledger, VI/10/10, f. 349.
62. RAL, VI/10/11, f. 403.
63. RAL, Cash Books VII/Smith Payne Smith, 14–40.
64. On the Greek loans, see L. H. Jenks, *The Migration of British Capital to 1875* (1938, repr. 1971), pp. 50–1.
65. RAL, XV/2/3, ff. 204–5; XV/2/4, f. 87.
66. Sir W. Schooling, *Alliance Assurance 1824–1924* (1924), p. 1.
67. Hyamson, p. 8; Wolf, p. 26.
68. Sir J. Clapham, *An Economic History of Modern Britain*, I, *The Early Railway Age 1820–1850* (Cambridge, 2nd edn. 1930, repr. 1964), p. 287.
69. Loewe, p. 26; RAL, XV/2/3, f. 204.
70. Guildhall: MS 17,957/17.
71. Schooling, p. 22.
72. B. Supple, *The Royal Exchange Assurance* (Cambridge, 1970), p. 104; A. D. Gayer, W. W. Rostow, and A. J. Schwartz, *The Growth and Fluctuation of the British Economy 1790–1850* (1953), I, p. 373.
73. English, *passim*.
74. See D. S. Landes, 'The Old Bank and the New: The Financial Revolution of the Nineteenth Century', *Revue d'Histoire Moderne et Contemporaire*, III (1956); *idem*, *Bankers and Pashas* (1958), ch. 1.
75. Quoted in Supple, p. 199.

76. Guildhall: MS 12,162 A/1, Alliance, Director Minutes, 12 March 1824 and 19 March 1824.
77. *Ibid.*, 22 March 1824.
78. *Ibid.*, 1 April 1824.
79. *Ibid.*, 5 April 1824.
80. *Ibid.*, 9 April 1824, 15 September 1824.
81. Supple, p. 198.
82. Guildhall: MS 12,162 A/1, 14 April 1824.
83. Supple, p. 198.
84. Guildhall: MS 12,162 A/1, 23 June 1824.
85. Schooling, pp. 77–8.
86. Guildhall: MS 12,162 A/1, 27 October 1824, 10 November 1824.
87. Guildhall: MS 12,160 H/1, MS 12,160 H/3, Alliance, Deed of Settlement.
88. Guildhall: MS 14,085/1, Alliance Marine, Deed of Settlement.
89. Guildhall: MS 14,077/2, Alliance, Share Transfers.
90. Guildhall: MS 14,077/3.
91. Guildhall: MS 14,077/1, 3.
92. Guildhall: MS 14,077/4.
93. Guildhall: MS 14,077/5.
94. RAL, VI/10/10, f. 185.
95. Guildhall: MS 12,162 A/1, 23 February 1825.
96. *Ibid.*, 1 June 1825.
97. *Ibid.*, 15 June 1825.
98. *Ibid.*, 6 April 1825, 13 April 1825.
99. *Ibid.*, 14 June 1826.
100. *Ibid.*, 29 November 1826.
101. *Ibid.*, 4 April 1827.
102. *Ibid.*, 6 April 1825.
103. *Ibid.*, 8 March 1826.
104. *Ibid.*, 22 April 1829.
105. G. L. Barrow, *The Emergence of the Irish Banking System, 1820–1845* (Dublin, 1975), pp. 61–81.
106. B. L. Anderson and P. L. Cottrell, *Money and Banking in England* (1974), pp. 223–7, 270–1, 276–9; S. E. Thomas, *The Rise and Growth of Joint Stock Banking* (1934), pp. 72–7.
107. See S. G. Checkland, *Scottish Banking: a History 1695–1973* (Glasgow, 1975), and C. W. Munn, *The Scottish Provincial Banking Companies 1747–1864* (Edinburgh, 1981).
108. Barrow, pp. 75–8.
109. Loewe, p. 31.
110. Barrow, p. 78.
111. Loewe, p. 32; Barrow, pp. 78–9.
112. Guildhall: MS 12,162 A/1, 21 March 1827.
113. N. K. Hill, 'The History of the Imperial Continental Gas Association, 1824–1900', (Univ. of London, Ph.D. thesis 1950), pp. 1–6.
114. *Ibid.*, pp. 45, 92, 158.
115. Loewe, p. 29.
116. Hill, p. 6.
117. *Ibid.*, p. 33.
118. *Ibid.*, pp. 35–40; see also H. Withers, *National Provincial Bank, 1833 to 1933* (?London, 1933).
119. Hill, pp. 36, 38, 175.

120. See A. W. Randall, *Real del Monte: A British Mining Venture in Mexico* (1972).
121. Jenks, pp. 54–5, 56–7.
122. Wolf, p. 28; Hyamson, p. 8.
123. Public Record Office, Kew, London (PRO): RAIL/635/20, 9 October 1845, 16 October 1845, 30 October 1845, 20 November 1845, 4 December 1945.
124. PRO: RAIL/635/18, 4 December 1844, 19 December 1844, 21 December 1844, 9 January 1945, 17 April 1945, 1 May 1945, 31 July 1845. See also O. S. Nock, *The South Eastern and Chatham Railway* (1961); F. Caron, *Histoire de l'Exploitation d'un Grand Reseau* (Paris, 1973); H. Pollins, 'The Jews' Role in the Early British Railways', *Jewish Social Studies*, (1953).
125. See W. D. Rubinstein, 'Modern Britain', in W. D. Rubinstein (ed.), *Wealth and the Wealthy in the Modern World* (1980); see also W. D. Rubinstein, 'The Victorian Middle Classes: Wealth, Occupation and Geography', *Economic History Review*, 2nd ser., (1977).

3

The Uneasy Victorian:
Montefiore as Communal Leader

ISRAEL FINESTEIN

F. W. Hirst wrote a well-known biography of his friend John Morley. Reviewing it, S. K. Ratcliffe quoted Balfour as saying that 'biography should be written by an acute enemy.'[1] As far as I know, Montefiore had no acute enemies, certainly none who would have been ready to try his hand at a full-scale biography. Indeed, there has been a surfeit of friends, acute and otherwise.

Every segment of the Anglo-Jewish community, Orthodox and Reform, and at all levels of society, including recent immigrants, had their own reasons — whether self-esteem, grateful recollection, or a prudent regard for Jewish fashion or for Jewish—Gentile public relations — to share in the uncritical pietistic estimates with which his character and achievements were measured.

Not surprisingly his three immediate successors as President of the Board of Deputies were his favourite nephews. The first was Joseph Mayer Montefiore, his eldest nephew and close associate in commercial enterprises, who had served as President for two periods, mainly when his uncle was abroad. The second, who became President in 1880, was the notable commercial lawyer, Arthur Cohen. The third, who succeeded in 1895, was Joseph Sebag, a leading stockbroker who changed his name by leave of the Queen to Sebag-Montefiore and who inherited his uncle's estate at Ramsgate. Of the last two, each had at some time accompanied Montefiore abroad, and each gave the aid of his name to the Choveve Zion movement, as Montefiore himself would certainly have done. They were opposed to political Zionism, unlike Montefiore's great-nephew, Francis (through another line), whose utility to the Zionist movement was associated with his name, which Weizmann described as 'legendary — in Jewry'.[2]

A century after his death Montefiore is entitled to a just appraisal as a communal figure. The uniqueness of his place in Jewish history is assured. His undoubted larger-than-life quality should not deter the modern examiner from a proper evaluation. When Lucien Wolf in 1922 described Montefiore as 'essentially a business man',[3] it was a phrase which, even in its complimentary context, would have been deemed inappropriate in earlier years. He certainly had the pragmatism of the cautious business man, as well as the tough persistence in pursuit of his espoused causes. He expected obedience. His courteous manners only accentuated the impact of his tall and impressive appearance. His Jewish philanthropy was avuncular rather than imaginative.

When Wolf observed in 1892 that 'the world still requires ... a final picture of this interesting personality,' he stated better than even he then probably knew. For all its reference to controversial matters, Wolf's famous essay in 1897 entitled 'The Queen's Jewry 1837–1897' retains much of the hagiographic approach, at times reminiscent of certain conventional accounts of the Court of Victoria and Albert. From Wolf's aseptic narrative of events at the Board in 1853, no-one would have gathered the degree of personal bitterness, communal disharmony and long-term discord engendered by Montefiore's autocracy. He was concerned to exclude from the Board four members of the West London Synagogue of British Jews who had been elected by provincial orthodox congregations as their Deputies. At one meeting of the Board on that issue, the uproar was such that the President fled the hall and police were called lest the heated dissension end in violence.[4] Neither the community nor its press was then in any mood for hagiography, whose day had not yet dawned.

Montefiore does not belong to a single age. This precursor of Zionism was a man of the eighteenth century. Yet there is in this combination an element of consistency and continuity. In the communal life of Anglo-Jewry in the eighteenth century there was a deeply ingrained inward-looking habit. The comparatively quiescent spirit of the Sephardi leadership in public relations had many historical sources. It was felt that as long as the Jews remained peaceable and law-abiding, they had nothing to fear. Many of the legal discriminations under which they laboured were shared by non-Anglican Christians. The sudden flare of anti-Jewish sentiment in the streets in the wake of the Naturalization Act of 1753, was a warning of the danger of a too-forward Jewish profile. Many were alive in Montefiore's thirties who had heard tell of the virtues and wisdom of the quiet life, and it became an inherited strong presumption. The widespread social acceptance in London and the Provinces of the ever-expanding Jewish middle classes, and the prominence of Jews in banking and commerce, resulted in a sedate view as to the civic and political aspirations of individual Jews. The urgency of the need to present a case for the collective Jewish community was not self-evident. The civic honours of individual Jews in the City of London, the entry of Jews into the county magistracy and Montefiore's own knighthood, tended in some minds to confirm and not to erode the wisdom of that view.

Unless one bears in mind these considerations and assumptions, the main features of Montefiore's communal stance cannot realistically be assessed. In 1821, Lord Stowell, the notable ecclesiastical lawyer and judge, declared of the Jews that 'though native subjects under the protection of the general law they are in many respects governed by institutions of their own and particularly in the (*sic*) marriages.' Differences of opinion within the Jewish community on the approach to the English law of marriage and divorce often reflected a diversity of opinions and outlook within the community over the status of the Jew in society in a changing world.[5] Montefiore would have preferred the civil law to permit Jews to marry within their own rules as to prohibited degrees of consanguinity and affinity. He would also have wished the law to recognize rabbinic divorce as entitlement to remarriage without civil dissolution of marriage. Such proposals were not likely to commend themselves to men of the stamp of Sir David Salomons or the Goldsmids.

In 1857 Montefiore, as President of the Board, and with the Chief Rabbi's eager support, procured from the Government the inclusion of a clause in the Matrimonial Causes Bill of that year which would have exempted Jews from its provisions for civil divorce. The Committee whose report prompted the Bill had been appointed in 1851 when Montefiore was given a promise — which he noted in his diary — by its Chairman, Dr. Stephen Lushington, to recommend the clause. It was highly contentious. Salomons, supported by Lionel de Rothschild, secured the withdrawal by the Government of any such clause. Salomons considered that Jews, as Englishmen, should be bound by the law's requirements, while at the same time, and within that framework, also comply with their own religious restrictions.

Yet for some, the distinctiveness of the Jews and their long-standing character as 'the Jewish nation', strengthened their retention of the insignia of their separateness. In Montefiore, considerations of tradition and public policy converged. As a leader whose enthusiasm for change was temperamentally dependent upon the pressure brought to bear, he was likely to experience great strain in the new age and to arouse in others impatience and at worst animosity. Like many a benevolent despot, Montefiore was flawed in his despotism. The price of his long tenure at the Board — he was President with short intervals for thirty-nine years — was that his obdurate personality and strong self-will failed to win the day on some important issues. By holding on to office he marred the growth of new cadres of leadership and delayed the development of adequate communal machinery for the expanding, multi-faceted and increasingly diversified community. In instinct and policy he was out of accord with the later generations through which he lived.

Yet he anticipated, albeit unwittingly, an epoch when greater attention was given by Jews to the inner state of communal life and to the springs of survival, and when there came to the fore the notion of the immediacy of practical national restorationism as a major item for the public agenda of practical men of affairs in communal office. Emancipation had progressed on the premise of the continuing expansion of the liberal spirit[6] and on the politics and philosophy of individualism. Montefiore lived into the new age of a resurgent romantic and xenophobic nationalism, which was reinforced in its effects by various forms of conservative opportunism.

However, he did not and could not reasonably have foreseen the nature and extent of the injurious impact which the new politics and their related emotions were to have upon the civic condition and status of the Jews in Europe. Any similarities which may be detected between his incipient Zionism on the one hand and elements of the 'New Judaea' outlook from the 1890s onwards on the other hand, are attributable to the instincts and the heightened self-consciousness of a pious Jew as he looked out upon the new opportunities and the daunting challenges of a new world.

Whatever his concern over the potential danger to Jewish practices and Jewish cohesion arising from the full acceptance of emancipation, he swam with that tide, even if he did so at his own pace. His involvement with the development of Jewish life in the Holy Land, for all its emphasis upon self-help, was essentially a matter of philanthropy and welfare. It was in tune with high social fashion, imperial interest and intellectual speculation, as well as reflecting Jewish kinship, a sense of Jewish religious duty and the acknowledgement of the place of Jerusalem in Jewish history. He was a child of the times into which he was born and during which he first came to public prominence. He was so, as much in his contradictions as in his consistencies, yet he bestrode the ages uniquely, incalculably and, for us, tantalizingly.

Montefiore was not to know that he lived into an entirely new and fateful age in Jewish history. His efforts and eminence, which belonged to an expansive era of optimism and liberationism, proved to be an encouragement to those of the succeeding generation who saw political Zionism as a danger and who invested their hopes for Jewish amelioration in the rationality of persuasion and in patience and faith under stress. They had a common strand in the memory of his career. This writer is of the opinion, so far as such hypotheses have meaning, that Montefiore would in fact have followed Herzl's star, and would have expected British support for an initiative with the Sultan over Palestine.

In communal administration, Montefiore was the archetype amateur. It was part of the paternalism of the wealthy. It was an extension of the charitable impulse. It facilitated the presentation to the wider society of the best face of the Jewish community. It was as though the interests of the Jewish community were a family matter requiring personal attention. It was the exercise of a personal authority. This was imperturbably applied even when the *ancien régime* of a one-time compact community was visibly and irretrievably in dissolution.

Montefiore delayed over-long the appointment of a Secretary to the Board of Deputies, whose role and potential were quickly changing. He long failed to appreciate the need for a standing committee to advise and assist him. Its value was urged upon him as a means for formulating policy and for the effective execution of decisions, and (even in connection with those very purposes) for procuring a wide and safe basis for his leadership. In spite of the adoption of a Constitution for the first time in 1835, the Board remained an informal body, a loose assembly of congregational notables from the main synagogues in London and, intermittently, from some provincial communities, meeting as occasion was thought to require or as the President might arbitrarily decide.

Montefiore's personal attention to communal issues differed from the close grasp of detail which was a feature of Lionel Louis Cohen's administration in congregational and charitable affairs. Cohen brought to bear a rare expertise in organization and in the dispatch of business. Nor can Montefiore's administration be compared to Francis Goldsmid's personal involvement in public relations during the campaign for Jewish emancipation. Goldsmid was a skilled pamphleteer, and he and his father were particularly gifted and admired lobbyists. Nor would Montefiore by temperament or aspiration have been able to anticipate or emulate Salomons' style of bringing public pressure to bear in forcing the pace of the law. Salomons saw himself as a vindicator in his own career of the reality and justice of the Jewish case. Montefiore was not so much a vigorous protagonist on behalf of his Jewish fellow-citizens, as their representative and exemplar in his religiosity, his well-advertised domesticity and his extra-denominational benevolence. Such palpable qualities may have been shared by other Jewish communal leaders but were in his case held to be symptomatic of a distinctive and fashionable way of life which was his public image.

Disraeli's ideas on the social responsibilities of status and the public duty of the landed interest were connected with characteristic elements in English history which survived far into the nineteenth century, attenuated, but still socially and politically significant. For a man of Montefiore's stamp and temperament, such features were part of the natural order and, within the Jewish community, were to him as consonant with good sense, sound morality and wise authority as in the wider society. 'England', wrote Leslie Stephen in 1866, 'is still an aristocratic country ... because the whole upper and middle, and a great part of the lower, classes have still an instinctive liking for the established order of things; because innumerable social ties bind us together spontaneously, so as to give to the aristocracy a position tolerably corresponding to their political privileges.'[7] Quite apart from any party or political implications, Montefiore lived and acted in accordance with the spirit of that description. In spite of his readiness to accept change when it proved inescapable, he expected that those whom he sought to serve within his community would share the inherited approach. The community was a voluntary association, free from State intervention. It was neither a *gemeinde* nor the constituency of a *consistoire*. Its inner arrangements were its own. Its so-called system of government was typically English, resting upon the pragmatism of personal authority progressively amended by historical evolution. Montefiore's approach to his self-imposed tasks within it was essentially that of an Englishman of his era and rank.

New forces were at work. A deferential society had to accommodate itself to the self-assertiveness born of the social, economic and ideological transformations of the late eighteenth and early nineteenth centuries. Montefiore was himself part of the upper middle classes who were leading the whole wide 'middling class' towards a degree of political power reflecting their economic position. Industrial and commercial expansion brought forward new types of political personality and social prominence. Like his father-in-law, Levi Barent Cohen, and his brother-in-law, Nathan Mayer Rothschild, Montefiore was in the van of the Jewish wing of the new mercantile class. Long before he moved from the station of commercial affluence to the rank of aristocracy, he had come to enjoy within the Jewish community all the attributes of aristocracy. He failed to perceive that the 'middling class' was gaining strength within his own community and that the redistribution of power in society as a whole had its analogy, if somewhat stifled, in that community.[8]

'The middle classes', observes Professor Harrison, 'did not aim to destroy the landed interest; they undermined its power while deferring to its political and social leadership.'[9] That comment aptly applies to the Jewish community. A conventional paternalism was pervasive in synagogal administration, the government of Jewish welfare agencies, and the relationships within the social hierarchy of the community. A moralizing high-minded personal entrenchment was allied to an inertia of system. The reactions to this combination gave birth to unease and anxiety among those who ruled the established institutions.

Despite the definition of powers and duties in the new Constitution of the Board and the increasing regularity of its meetings, Montefiore hardly regarded the new formulations as fettering his personal authority. This attitude increasingly aroused adverse comment. A letter to the *Voice of Jacob* on 16 February 1844 signed H.F. (undoubtedly Henry Faudel)[10] made a renewed call for meetings of the Board to be open to the press. '. . . the seed of enquiry is already abroad,' wrote that sagacious communal critic. Abolition of secrecy would save the Board, he added from 'many reproachful observations to which they are now subject . . .' Criticisms of arbitrariness and apparent inactivity were mingled with concern over the marked independence of the President from people and movements imbued with the spirit of change.

The charge of apparent inactivity was over leadership of the campaign for emancipation being left to individuals, notably Salomons. This undercurrent of complaint was also connected with the contention that the Board and the community's leaders did not respond at all, or with sufficient public effect, to the periodic slanders upon Jews. Indeed, on 31 January 1851, the *Jewish Chronicle* severely upbraided 'leaders' (editorial inverted commas) who 'have ensconced themselves behind the most impregnable of all fortresses, *indifference*' (editorial italics). The editor noted that this was not the first time that that newspaper had called on 'those who are placed in a prominent position by their wealth and station which providence . . . has placed in their possession and who thereby claim, and justly so, to be considered leaders in Israel, to defend themselves and their brethren against insinuations in the press of antisocial behaviour by Jews.'

The Board belatedly appointed as Secretary in 1838 the talented solicitor, Sampson Samuel. The absence of a professional officer had certainly been one of the reasons for the Board taking no cognizance of the presentation and passage through Parliament of the Marriage Act of 1835.[11] It was only following its enactment — the measure was completed by the end of August 1835 — that its possible application to Jews was noted. It is first referred to in the Board's minutes more than six months later, the Board not meeting between June 1835 and March 1836.

It is desirable to place into its historical context Montefiore's statement in his diary on 9 July 1837 that he was 'most firmly resolved not to give up the smallest part of our religious forms and privileges to obtain civil rights.' With the enthusiastic support of most Deputies, he had become engaged in the promotion of a Bill to exclude Jewish marriage from the Marriage Act of 1835. He was intensely disappointed when Dr Whateley, the Archbishop of Dublin, an influential advocate of Jewish emancipation, refused to launch the proposed measure in the House of Lords. Through lack of support, the Bill was dropped. It was also clear that the proposed Bill did not enjoy unanimous support within the Jewish leadership. Some critics were prepared to castigate the Board for its delay, while at the same time having reservations about the wisdom of pressing for amending legislation; the notion of a Jewish enclave in society should not be encouraged in the public mind. These sentiments prevailed: the Board and the Chief Rabbinate came to acknowledge the impracticability of obtaining exemption, and acquiesced in the measure.

In preparing the Board's constitution, the representatives of the major London synagogues resolved in 1835 that 'it would be of essential advantage to the interests of the Jews of Britain that in all matters touching their political welfare they should be represented by one body.' The immediate reason was that the efforts towards emancipation would be more efficiently directed and carry greater public weight if promoted by a single communal body, recognized by the Jewish community and by the political world as having that responsibility and the relevant authority. From the inception of the Board, in respect of Jewish representations to public bodies, the model was the arrangement previously made by the Protestant Dissenters for their own inner consultation through 'deputies' and the use of the latter as the forum through which representations were made for the Dissenters' civil advancement.

However impressed Montefiore may have been by the resolution of 1835, it is unlikely that it occurred to him that the 'body' thereby referred to would find itself engaged for a protracted period in public pressure upon governments and ministers. The advance of the Dissenters had been considerable. He was hopeful of early Jewish relief in similar directions, and regarded the utility of the 'one body' as resting upon its ability to speak authoritatively for the Jewish community and to move speedily. But he found himself before long at the head of an institution regarded by some as having the task of persistent, perhaps annual, political campaigning — on pain of being charged with neglect of duty, indifference to needs, or organizational lethargy and incompetence. Furthermore, he quickly found that what had always been essentially a standing conference of the major synagogues in the capital came to be a far wider assembly, in which the idea of representation was taken far more seriously as a practical matter than as a notional theme based upon the prestige and influence of prominent individuals.

The Goldsmids were to use the representative idea against the leadership of the Board. They asked, in particular, why the provincial communities, even those with members on the Board, should allow themselves to be spoken for by a few magnates in London. They did not regard the 'one body' system as justifying or requiring the silence of those who differed from the leadership or even from the majority at the Board. That way lay despotism, un-English and possibly unjust.

What gave the critics greater animus was that what had been defined as a body concerned with 'all matters touching their *political* welfare' had become an instrument for the exclusion of facilities for members of Reform, to which, as Jewish citizens, they claimed to be entitled.[12] The criticism ran as follows: while each marriage was to be given civil registration, the law left the solemnization of marriage to the religious principles of the parties. Yet the legislation was so administered by the Board that membership of an Orthodox synagogue became a condition of registration. In 1855 the Reformers sought legislation which would have ended the President's sole authority to certify. The divisions at the Board and within the community over what should be the Board's reaction were intense. Montefiore was in favour of resisting the proposed change. The issue was revived in 1856 in the form of a clause limited to the Reform Congregation. The Board decided not to oppose that special measure of relief, but only after further acrimony. It was a visibly reluctant decision. The announcement of the President's early next visit to Palestine did not wholly efface the embarrassment.

Although the Board appointed *ad hoc* committees occasionally, in respect of particular issues, it became widely accepted in the 1850s that there was no effective substitute for a standing, or watching, committee for general purposes, not least to advise expertly, with professional aid, on legal or parliamentary matters as they arose or might be anticipated. On 7 April 1854, in a trenchant leading article in the *Hebrew Observer*, Abraham Benisch, while complimenting the Board on recent 'infusion of new blood' from the middle classes, warned against the danger of leaving the burden of leadership upon one man, the President. Montefiore was ill at the time, and that fact added point to the article, but Benisch was concerned with the system. He described the President as 'physically unable to act, and prohibited to think'. He advocated the creation in London of a committee of 'regents' to act in emergencies, with a view to subsequent ratification by the Board, which should meet in extraordinary session whenever required. He supported his suggestion by the analogy of the practice of several Nonconformist bodies where 'it works very well'.

The creation by the Board in 1854 of a standing general purposes committee (the direct ancestor of the present Law, Parliamentary and General Purposes Committee) has a communal significance beyond its immediate context. It resulted from pressure in the Jewish press, the growing realization among Deputies that the Board had long ceased to be an extended family matter, and the sharp divisions within the Board in the 1850s.

Sampson Samuel, as Secretary, proposed to the Board on 20 September 1854, on the President's behalf, the appointment of this standing committee. His reasons represent a distinct stage in the evolution of the public life of Anglo-Jewry and in the forms of its leadership. He spoke of the 'undue' amount of 'responsibility and labour' falling upon President and Secretary. The proposal was readily acceptable to the Board.

The old-style government of the President was unacceptable, not merely on account of age — he remained President for another twenty years — but also because of the advantage of formal consultations before major decisions were taken. The serious disarray at the Board in 1853 brought to a head many issues, administrative and constitutional. The admission of the press to the Board from 1853 symbolized the new approach to authority and accountability. These changes afforded the rising Jewish professional classes and the newly self-conscious Jewish mercantile elements, the opportunity of making felt in a variety of spheres fresh nuances of liberalism and a broader democratic spirit than were contemplated twenty years earlier. Sampson Samuel skilfully steered his office through the pulls and counterpulls of opinion until 1854, when the pressures of his post caused him to resign.

Montefiore was often confronted at the Board with challenges to his authority and judgment. The laudatory welcomes on his re-elections contrast with the frequent criticisms by one group or another, and in the press. On 14 January 1838, the Elders of his Synagogue resolved that henceforth Deputies were to be elected by the Elders and Yehidim and from amongst the membership of either body. This extension of the franchise was part of the expression within Anglo-Jewry of an ever more widely defined popular opinion. At the first meeting of the new Board on 12 August 1838, Loewe noted from the President's diary that 'he appears to have apprehended some difficulty in managing' the new assembly.

In the 1850s the Board consisted of barely more than sixty Deputies, about one-half of whom represented provincial congregations. Most of those who sat for provincial constituencies were Londoners. It is remarkable that so small a body ranked so high in Jewish counsels: a reflection of the wealth and influence of the upper echelons of London Jewish society, the prestige and power of Britain, and the character and missions of the President. These circumstances often gave the debates the seriousness with which the participants endowed their own roles. By the same token, any alleged failures tended to attract commensurate concern. The President carried the burden. It was typical that the Board should be attacked in the *Jewish Chronicle* for allowing a state of affairs under which an MP (none other than the son of the late Sir Robert Peel) could tell the House of Commons on 24 February 1853 that he did not think the Jews felt any dissatisfaction at being excluded from Parliament. The editor accused the Board of being unresponsive to public opinion, citing a number of issues on which the initiative had been left to the Jewish press; and now once again the Board was over-detached. These criticisms were unfair. Peel's hostility to Jewish entry into Parliament was well known. Salomons was by now in the forefront of the campaign, conducting his own battles for all to see. The Board had given him consistent public support. But the Board was by-passed by Salomons' efforts, and its illustrious head was often a cheering spectator. This was thought to detract from the standing of the Board, and to give the campaign a misleading personal character. Montefiore was surely at greater ease in Zion than in the caustic purlieus of Anglo-Jewish politics.

As early as 1841, in the first issue of the *Voice of Jacob*, there was editorial reference to the burdens of lay office under the old dispensation. 'In most instances', wrote the editor, 'the direction (of communal bodies) is undertaken by benevolent gentlemen whose commercial and professional avocations frequently compel them to abandon the charge for months together to the very persons whom it is their office to supervise.' Even with Montefiore, long retired from active business, and served by the energetic Samuel, the community had by the mid-century wholly outgrown its earlier framework. Not only had the age of the senior executive secretary dawned, but so had the age of committees. Montefiore never acclimatized himself to the new constraints, or if he did, old habits broke through. The situation aggravated his sense of unease.

In October 1857 Montefiore informed the Board that 'advanced age and impaired health might some time since have reasonably resulted' in his retirement. He described himself as 'sensible . . . that (the Presidency) might well have been entrusted to younger and other hands . . .' He had earlier in that year proffered his resignation. In May 1862 he adopted the device of tendering his resignation to his Synagogue as one of their Deputies, but was prevailed upon to withdraw it. Four years later, after having delayed resuming office through illness following his return from overseas, he wrote in his Diary (11 May 1868) that he felt better and was 'reluctant' to refuse the proffered appointment of President . . . as perhaps it may be the means of promoting the general unity of all the Jews in England . . .' He added: 'I think our MPs should be *ex officio* members of the Board as the best means of expressing the sentiments of the Board in the House of Commons.'

Such inclusion would have brought into the Board the prominent Reformers, Francis Goldsmid and John Simon, who were regular spokesmen for Jewish causes in the House, particularly the rights of the Jews of Rumania. The anomaly of Jewish spokesmen in the House being perforce outside the Board was apparent. Loewe's view was that Montefiore wanted if possible a *rapprochement* with the Reform congregation, at least a working arrangement without prejudice to principle. In September 1870 he was invited by Simon Waley to the consecration of the new premises of that congregation. In reply Montefiore wrote that he felt 'a sincere and deep anxiety for the unity of the Jews' and that he wished to see unity before the consecration. He did not attend. Principles remained intact. The West London Synagogue of British Jews was first represented on the Board in 1886.

On the establishment of the West London Synagogue of British Jews, Loewe commented accurately that Montefiore acted out of a sense of what he deemed his duty. 'He did not interfere,' wrote that perspicacious observer, 'with the opinions of those who differed from him unless compelled to do so by actual duty.' When in his official position he was required to give an opinion on religious matters 'he invariably referred to the spiritual head of the community for guidance,' whose injunctions he obeyed 'at whatever cost to himself'.

How to deploy these procedures in the face of a *de facto* pluralism without at the same time recognizing as at least potentially valid what his own system held to be invalid and subversive, presented

Montefiore at a most inopportune moment with questions whose modernity was the very vice he feared. The inopportune nature of the moment was threefold. His 'guide' was Hirschell, between whom and the lay leadership there was a mutual dependence, which, given his age and frailty and their sense of crisis and responsibility, induced all concerned to resort to peremptoriness. Secondly, the Anglo-Jewish community was unaccustomed to sudden change, theological debate, or philosophical enquiry. The argument thus proceeded on questions of authority and power — they were indeed the bed-rock issues, but the approach to them was uncushioned. Thirdly, the campaign for emancipation was at its high point. What was done by Montefiore and his immediate colleagues was in the glare of gentile interest and in the path of the campaign, whose leaders saw analogies which they found discomforting. Montefiore wrestled with the question for forty years.

The contentions over the Reformers stimulated, but were not the cause of, a recurring *malaise* in his Presidency. His repeated indications of readiness to step down (apart from the occasions of his foreign travels) were not always, if at all, formalities. Among his firmest supporters were Louis Cohen, his nephew and a banker, and Henry Harris, a solicitor who wielded over his own synagogue in Maiden Lane the control which Montefiore would have found congenial at the Board. Ranged against him on the issues of 1853 were some prestigious figures, among them Lionel de Rothschild, and influential aspirants to public office, including Benjamin Phillips (merchant, and in 1865, Lord Mayor of London). The opposition tended to consist of an assortment of grandees, supporters of liberal Whiggism, rising businessmen attracted by the 'Nonconformist conscience', and some provincial spokesmen who shared the radical and/or utilitarian outlook of leaders of their cities or their brand of libertarianism.

In an article on the Board in the *Jewish Chronicle* of 8 February 1856, the editor regretted the passing of the times when 'the meetings chiefly partook of the nature of friendly conversations.' In those days, he added, 'the deputies met in the home of the President, enjoyed his hospitality, were in some measure treated as guests . . .'. Now, with the expansion of the Board, this was not so. That journal was by tradition an advocate of a more broadly-based representative body. What in reality the editor bemoaned was that the new type of assembly was unruly and unwieldy, and the President seemed unable to assert in debate the power of the chair. A chairman who allows excessive latitude in debate may prove to be a somewhat arbitrary President. No wonder that Montefiore's offers to retire were usually accompanied by genuine references to ailing health.

When Montefiore returned from his spectacular, and to a significant extent successful, mission to the East, his personal prestige was
immense at home and abroad. It was inevitable that the leading Jews
in London should wish to pay tangible personal tribute to their
most celebrated figure. It was perhaps equally inevitable that there
should be a difference of opinion over what should be done. There
were those who wanted to satisfy the much-discussed current need
to provide for the training of a native Ministry and for the endowment of higher Jewish learning. The more influential view was that
the occasion could be satisfactorily met by a public presentation to
the returning *shtadlan*. The debate continued after his arrival home.
The aged and infirm Chief Rabbi, Solomon Hirschell, is not known
to have taken part. He little comprehended the demands of the new
age of *haskalah*, emancipation and Anglicization. Neither its opportunities nor its pitfalls bestirred him.

One of the earliest public advocates of 'the establishment of a
college for the training of a regular Jewish Ministry' was the author
of a well-argued brochure entitled *What is due from the Jews on the
success of the Mission to the East?* The title is highly indicative. It
is an unsigned publication from the pen of a well-informed and gifted
writer and probably belongs to 1841. He deplores 'the negligence
with which so excellent an undertaking has long been allowed to lie
dormant in the minds of our municifent and enlightened brethren.'
He relates the provision of 'a thoroughly educated clergy, gifted with
the requirements of our faith and of our age', to several ends. It
would counter conversionism, help rebut 'the Gentile decrying of
Judaism', limit communal dissension and assist in the restoration of
unity. He called upon Sir Moses personally to take a lead, in view of
what the writer deemed to be the urgency of these considerations
and the educational value of the proposal short term and long term.
The writer's opinions coincided with those of Morris Raphall and
Abraham Benisch, either of whom could have been the author.

The brochure cited approvingly a yet more powerful plea from
one 'F', in an address which appears to have been circulated in
December 1840. The author was Jacob Franklin. Both works expressly relate their call to the opportunity afforded by the recent
creation of the Montefiore Testimonial Fund. Franklin's publication
requested the community 'to render (Montefiore's) return the occasion for such a foundation', namely 'a College to train young men
of the higher classes for the Ministry'. The author refers to a 'lamen-
table dearth of spiritual information' together with an 'indifference
and laxity of observance which are the reproach of the greater portion of our community, while the rest are taunted as mere zealots,

unable to justify their unenquiring adherence.' He adds: 'With a few honourable but partial exceptions the gentlemen styled reverend by courtesy are selected for their vocal capabilities exclusively. Can it be wondered at that our places of worship are deserted when the service is so conducted, and bereft of any exposition of Judaism?'

The *Voice of Jacob*, from its inception by Franklin in 1841, was a regular advocate of the cause. On 30 September 1842, it noted with dismay that during the recent High Festivals only three congregations had the advantage of sermons, namely Liverpool (David Meyer Isaacs), Birmingham (Morris Raphall) and the Western Synagogue in London (Henry Abraham Henry). The leaders of the community were 'unequal to the requirements of the day', and their 'do-nothing policy' was denounced. Although these strictures were directed at the Chief Rabbinate and were concerned with a number of 'ecclesiastical' questions, a central feature of the indictment was the general lack of effort to set up ministerial training facilities and encourage recruitment. The thrust of the charge extended to the lay leadership.

By this time the chances which had been opened up in connection with the Montefiore Testimonial had gone by. In November 1842 at Windsor, Messrs B. Mortimer and Hunt of Bond Street showed to the Queen and the Prince the elaborate silver plate structure which they had been commissioned by the Montefiore Testimonial Committee to fashion for presentation to her esteemed subject; they approved the work, whose ceremonial delivery to Montefiore was delayed by Hirschell's death until the expiry of the prescribed thirty days of mourning.

The *Voice of Jacob* made, and continued to make, a series of alternative proposals which would have involved native candidates for the Ministry seeking part of their training abroad. It was as though for the time being there was a sense of resignation due to lack of response from those who had been urged to lead the movement for the creation of a College.[13]

The public requests for a 'ministerial college' were resumed. In a notable letter in the *Voice of Jacob* on 15 November 1844, the pseudonymous writer, probably Benisch, pointedly contrasted the scale of money contributed towards the relief of poverty with the failure to endow the training of a Jewish Ministry. He adopted the argument, of which Faudel was then the main advocate, that money devoted to relief had a pauperizing effect upon the recipients in the prevailing disorganized state of distribution. He invited 'a few pious-minded philanthropists' to support selected young men for training at a university or *yeshiva* abroad as a preparation for service in Anglo-Jewry.

When Nathan Marcus Adler assumed office as Chief Rabbi in 1845 he was under no illusion as to the need for a trained Anglo-Jewish Ministry in the modern community, or as to the strong body of opinion in its favour.[14] On 4 January 1852 Montefiore presided at the public meeting convened to consider the scheme which Adler had propounded. It was clear that the lack of progress was the result of divergent opinions. Adler said as much in his address at the inauguration of the College on 11 November 1855. He spoke of 'the numerous difficulties', adding that 'some regarded (the scheme) as unnecessary, nay injurious to the progress of the community . . . others were in favour of one leading principle but against another . . . those whose support was expected left the project to its fate.' Often he had 'despaired of its attainment'. The episode is a commentary upon the limits to even Montefiore's power on vital communal concerns, and upon the consequences of the earlier failure to set a scheme in motion. The College came into being at least a decade after its due time and was deprived of the advantages of the association with it of men who went abroad for lack of training and opportunity in England, or who had cut themselves adrift from the ministerial vocation. The loss of 'native talent' was a frequent cry in the intervening years.

The apparent complacency of the communal leadership was frequently attacked in the sharpest terms. When Morris Raphall left England for New York in 1849, his departure was taken as a sign of communal lethargy in the serious patronage of learning. Scholar and publicist, Raphall was Minister for eight years of the Birmingham Hebrew Congregation and the most influential Jewish preacher in the land, save possibly for Adler. The *Jewish Chronicle*, in an editorial philippic, on 19 October 1849 accused the leadership of lack of appreciation, and of being 'with but few exceptions . . . not yet alive to the value of the mind', despite being 'a class numbering in their ranks men of wealth, station and influence . . . !' One of Raphall's most striking successes and failures in England was his production of the still impressive *Hebrew Review and Magazine of Rabbinical Literature* for eighteen months between 1834 and 1836, before it succumbed through communal neglect, despite his pleas and warnings. 'We are depressed', wrote Benisch in the *Hebrew Observer* on 28 January 1853, 'by the conviction that the orthodox party are in a perfect state of quiescence, and are culpable to a degree for shutting their eyes to the requirements of the age.' He had in mind in particular the long delay in the fructification of plans for the College at a time of growing need. 'The children of the wealthy', he added, 'seldom hear (Jewish teachings) from preacher or precentor.'[15]

For the immigrant and the poor, the Jewish day school was a useful agent for Anglicization. For the settled English Jew, 'desegregation' was the self-respecting corollary to civil rights, even, and perhaps especially, in matters touching upon degree training. Salomons' letter to Adler of 13 February 1852 dissociated his contribution from the proposed day school and from the funds of the old Beth Hamedrash, and expressly limited its use to the education of 'Jewish fellow-subjects for the Ministry'. Almost every phrase reflected his compromise and Adler's agony.

It is remarkable that the published diaries are silent as to Montefiore's reactions to the public pleas for the creation of a Jewish day school for the middle classes, although they contain much concerning public ceremonial. This may reflect Loewe's belief that his readers would find interest in that detail. Jews were not alone in that regard. It may also have reflected Montefiore's undoubted personal interest in protocol, formal dress and hierarchy. It is inconceivable that he was unaware of educational proposals which became matters of communal controversy. Whether he inscribed his views thereon in his daily journal is unknown: in the published selections there is little reference to Jews' College, and no reference to the day school in Finsbury Square which Adler founded in 1855 as a recruiting centre for the College, which was formally opened at the same time. To Adler, that day school was of vital significance, not only as a feeder to the College, but as a provider of Jewish education to the growing anglicized community living away from the older residential areas.

Montefiore gave his patronage and financial support to the College and the school, but on an eleemosynary scale not commensurate with their needs or Adler's conception of the potential. The closure of the school in 1879 had a deeper cause besides the fact that Jewish families were leaving the area for west and west central London. Financial support was inadequate. Those sections of the community for whom the school was principally designed lost their tenuous interest in such a venture. The opposition of the 1840s and 1850s to the creation of a Jewish day school had become conventional communal policy by the 1870s and was shared by such diverse leaders of opinion as Hermann Adler, Samuel Montagu and Simeon Singer. That opposition was reinforced by the provisions of the Education Act of 1870, since increasing numbers of Jews found it natural to avail themselves of the public elementary education prescribed by the Act out of rates and taxes. Montefiore cannot carry the responsibility for communal fashion. His alliance with Adler was firm and lasting on many fronts. One is driven to the conclusion that it was a matter of priorities and perception, as well as the formidable trends of opinion.

Frequent references were made in the press to the more affluent Jewish families sending their children to Christian foundations or Christian-orientated schools. To Salomons, this presented no draw-back, provided the Jewish children were not given Christian instruc-tion. Their Jewish education would be left to special tuition at home or elsewhere. To Adler, such an arrangement involved at best edu-cational minimalism and at worst so scanty a Jewish education as to spell danger to the Jewish child in the Christian environment. There were increasing numbers of private Jewish schools of varying degrees of competence and fashion. Adler wanted to reinforce the system by providing his own school. At the same time he was successfully en-gaged in the reorganization of the Jews' Free School, the strengthening of its curricula, the encouragement of the education of girls, and improving teaching skills. He sought to extend these developments to the other 'charitable' schools by example and direction. He was sharply aware of the contrast between the communal attention to those schools and the readiness in the better-off elements of Jewish society to abide by a more limited set of Jewish educational standards for themselves.

It was to this that the *Hebrew Observer* alluded on 15 December 1854 when it wrote of the needs of the children of 'our higher and middle classes' and called for a remedy from those 'with the will and the power of endowing (proposals) with substantial reality'.

In 1830 a Society for the Cultivation of the Hebrew Language and Literature was founded in London. It was a society of *maskilim*, attracting some moral and practical support from interested laymen. Montefiore attended at least one of its meetings. It was short-lived. The society 'died of inanition', commented A. L. Green in the *Jewish Chronicle* on 22 October 1869, in an illuminating review of Jewish literary effort in his life-time. Perhaps its initiators — Michael Josephs, Hyman Hurwitz and others — made the error, as Green contended, of not first creating the taste. Be that as it may, neither the elected leaders of the community nor those in the forefront of the campaign for emancipation gave any significant support to the effort, or to the periodic attempts by comparable elements in the community, to stimulate an active interest in Jewish literary works.

The continental Jewish scholars who came to England to explore the Hebrew manuscripts and printed works in the British Museum and at the ancient universities, were often surprised at the polite lack of enthusiasm by the men at the head of the community. For example, it fell to Raphall to raise private subventions as best he could for the wherewithal of Hirsch Edelmann , the Russian Jewish pioneer in the examination of medieval Hebrew manuscripts at the Bodleian. Among Edelmann's publications was *Ginzei Oxford*, jointly edited by him and Leopold Dukes, the Hungarian Jewish scholar, and translated into English in 1851 by Marcus Bresslau, himself a well-known figure in Anglo-Jewish journalism and a frequent critic of communal neglect of cultural endowment. Raphall was assisted in his fund-raising by David Barnett, a jeweller and leading member of the Birmingham synagogue, and M. H. Simonson, a scholarly *shochet*, in Manchester.

Writing in the *Jewish Monthly* in September 1947 on literary patrons in Anglo-Jewry, Cecil Roth archly observed: 'Men like Moses Montefiore and the Rothschilds of the second generation . . . could generally be relied upon to provide a few pounds for any deserving cause, even literary, or to subscribe to a few copies of any new book in the sphere of Hebrew studies. But either these benefactions were on a modest scale, or else English Jews preferred to conceal the scale of their generosity . . .'. Lady Montefiore's youngest sister, Esther, married Samuel Moses Samuel, whose younger brother, Denis, married the youngest daughter of Mr. and Mrs. Samuel Moses Samuel. Denis and his son, Arthur, provided the financial backing for the publication of some of Edelmann's works.

To illustrate further Montefiore's relationships with other Anglo-Jewish leaders, and his outlook and stance on public issues, it is helpful to consider his role in the campaign for Jewish emancipation. In 1828 and 1829, Montefiore was party with Isaac Lyon Goldsmid and Nathan Mayer Rothschild to the sounding out of opinion in politically influential circles on the prospect of legislation for the abolition of religious disabilities.[16] On 26 June 1828, Montefiore and Goldsmid met prominent non-Anglican Protestants and Roman Catholics. Their discussion was clearly concerned primarily with the movement for the lifting of civil disabilities from Christian non-Anglicans. The liberalizing legislation of 1828 did not extend to the Jews, who were expressly excluded by the Act of that year from the rights it granted to Protestant Dissenters. That ironic outcome was the immediate cause of the campaign for comparable legislation to relieve the Jewish subjects of the Crown, save that it was always understood that any public campaign should in prudence await the success of the continuing movement for Catholic emancipation.

In April 1829, the Lord Chancellor, Lord Lyndhurst, reflecting the Prime Minister's concern as well as his own, advised Rothschild and Montefiore that the Jewish leaders should be guided by public opinion. Such advice was also related to the need to let the Catholic question settle first. Montefiore for the present continued to assume that if there was to be a Bill in respect of the Jews it ought to be for the general abolition of their disabilities. Whether to press for full abolition, including the right to sit in Parliament without Christian oath, or to press for some lesser target — such as the opening of the municipalities — had not arisen for consideration.

Later in April 1829, the sympathetic Lyndhurst suggested to Rothschild, Montefiore and Goldsmid, in response to further representations for guidance, that they should present a Petition to the House of Lords and await the reaction. If it was received 'quietly', then 'they could immediately bring in a Bill . . . In the event of it occasioning any unpleasant feeling, they would not attempt to advance farther than session, more particularly as the public and even the King himself were not yet reconciled to the measure of that year in favour of the Catholics.' The Lord Chancellor advised against calling on the vocal and liberal parliamentarian, Lord Holland, as he 'would make some sensation'. They approached a friend of Rothschild, Lord Bexley, who was recommended by Lyndhurst. Basing himself on Montefiore's diaries, Loewe describes Bexley as a friend who 'appeared to be doubtful of their obtaining all the privileges that year.' In the event it proved impossible to secure the services of any member of the Upper House to present a Petition.

In May 1829 Bexley told the three Jewish spokesmen that he 'thought that everything would be granted to the Jews except seats in Parliament.' All soundings pointed to the wisdom of leaving further efforts until the following year. In 1830 the agitation for parliamentary reform gained momentum. Partisan acerbity in Parliament mounted. Resistance to change was thereby sharpened. In this atmosphere, the Jewish claims were viewed with greater reserve than before. They were regarded even by some friends of the Jewish cause as better not pressed for the time being. Yet others (including some Christians as well as Jews) thought it proper to urge the Jewish claims without delay, as part of the transformation of the political scene then clearly in progress. Most Jews had no wish to promote further political dissension. None wished to provoke radical agitation. A difference of approach and emphasis developed within the leadership. Loewe indicates that in February 1830 Montefiore recorded in his diary that Goldsmid was 'greatly against' the proposal to defer calling upon Wellington for his views in the new year, and that those whom Goldsmid had consulted shared his opinion.

The three leaders did indeed see Wellington during that month. He expressly refused to commit his Government on the Jewish question, advised a postponement of any application by them, and warned them that it would be at their own risk if they proceeded. Montefiore 'thought the answer on the whole favourable' in that 'the Duke had no determined prejudice' against the removal of the disabilities. 'Should the Commons suffer it to pass quietly, Mr. Montefiore had no doubt that the Duke would take no part against them.' Sir Robert Grant presented the Jewish Petition to the House of Commons, where it was 'tolerably well received'. In the Spring, Grant, not surprisingly, in the light of what had gone before, enquired whether the Jews would refuse all offers short of total abolition, that is to say the opening of Parliament to them. 'It was Mr. Montefiore's opinion that they should take what they could get.' reports Loewe. Rothschild reported to Montefiore that Goldsmid had stated his preference for losing all rather than 'to give up Parliament'. Montefiore wrote in his diary: 'I decidedly differ from him: we should accept all we can get.' The Bill of 1830, which was on Goldsmid's lines, and would have placed the Jews on the same terms as the Catholics after the Catholic Emancipation Act of 1829, was defeated in the House of Commons. In 1833 a similar Bill passed the Commons and was defeated in the Upper House.

Before the Reform Act of 1832, which increased the prospect of securing a majority in the House of Commons, there were indications of a continuing divergence. The immediate question was whether to postpone any further attempt. Clearly this was the advice of those members of the Government who had been consulted, including Lyndhurst. The opinion of Dr Stephen Lushington, the leading ecclesiastical lawyer, and for many years a consultant to the Board and to individual Jewish public figures on legal issues, was that there should be no delay. He also shared Goldsmid's view that the Jews should accept nothing less than a general Bill for total abolition. When he was visited in 1831 by Montefiore and Goldsmid, he told them as much, whereupon Montefiore informed him that 'he was sure' that the Deputies would 'gladly accept' anything the Government might offer. Holland was in two minds, but following a conference with Goldsmid he declared himself in favour of Lushington's advice. It was in connection with these exchanges that Montefiore inscribed his well-known entry in his diary to the effect that Goldsmid was 'greatly displeased' with the Deputies and had threatened to establish a new synagogue with the aid of young men and would alter the form of service along the Reformist lines of the new synagogue in Hamburg.

It was inevitable that following the Act of 1832 there should be a further Jewish Bill. Its passage through the House of Commons in 1833 certainly pointed to the accord which existed between the liberality of the Jewish cause and the reforming spirit of the Whig-Radical-Utilitarian combination in the new House. The strength of Toryism and Church opinion in the House of Lords continued to bar a Jewish measure, whether whole or partial. In 1835, in response to the special case of Salomons, Parliament opened to professing Jews the office of Sheriff in the City of London. This development strengthened the hands of the gradualists, but did not diminish the instinct for the wider claims.

The Jewish differences came strikingly to the Government's attention in 1844. Salomons' career had by this time projected sharp public attention on the general exclusion of professing Jews from municipal government. It was evident that Salomons' advancement in the municipal life of the City was impeded only by the restrictive state of the law. The pragmatic mind of the Prime Minister, Sir Robert Peel, was not attracted by the likelihood of an embroilment with City sentiment, which was preponderantly in favour of Salomons' claim and the Jewish submissions. When in February a deputation from the Board, headed by the President, waited upon him, he confided to them that he had been considering 'some measure' to place before his colleagues, but he had not proceeded because of the Jewish differences. He explained that he had been told in a letter from Goldsmid that the Jews would not be satisfied with any relief less than the whole. Peel may have been favourably persuaded by the practical benefit to the State from harnessing the energy of Jews aspiring to public office, and by party advantages, but he was naturally reluctant to be seen to enter into the arena of Jewish dissension. He made it clear to Montefiore and his fellow Deputies that he would renew his active consideration. He stated that he knew they would feel 'as well satisfied with a part and that they should not thereby be precluded from hereafter getting more.'

The Act of 1845, introduced by Peel's Government and enthusiastically promoted by Lyndhurst, who was again Lord Chancellor, greatly eased the Jewish argument in favour of the opening of Parliament. The success of the Act placed a considerable burden of proof upon the opponents of the Jewish case. Yet the opposition remained strong within the Tory Party and the Church of England. Montefiore and the Board gave consistent support to the movement, but the initiative remained firmly with Salomons until, largely through the latter's efforts, the House of Commons was opened in 1858.

What were the elements of difference between the schools of Montefiore and Goldsmid? Temperament played a part. Montefiore had neither Salomons' spur of public ambition on the national stage nor Goldsmid's spur of hurt to self-esteem occasioned by the sensibility of a reduced form of citizenship. Montefiore had serious doubts as to whether he should accept nomination as Sheriff of the City, when this was offered to him in 1837. Would he be able to reconcile the office with Sabbath observance and the dietary laws? Would the duty interfere with his many public and communal commitments? Family and friends persuaded him to accept the proposal. His knighthood in that year and the public honour accorded him by the Queen on his return from his Mission to the East and on other occasions, gave him intense satisfaction; but this gratification was different from that involved in the holding of contested political office. Such was never central to his test of equality. He was possessed in this connection of an old-worldliness which was more easily satisfied and less demanding. He supported the cause of Jewish emancipation as the fulfilment of citizenship, and as a model and an encouragement to other lands and to Jewish communities therein. But he showed few signs of treating it as the central theme of Jewish public effort. Nor could he free his thoughts from the price which success might entail in terms of Jewish attachment in general and Jewish observances in particular. He was guided by an older set of priorities.

The comparative conservatism of religious Reform in Anglo-Jewry did little to allay his concern when he considered the nature of Reform in Germany and the United States. But that was not the whole of his anxiety. It was the encounter by Jews, within whatever grouping, with the new opportunities and the new scientific learning, which strengthened his wish to move slowly and circumspectly. Attitudes to the Act of 1835 and to the proposed Jewish Bill were only symptomatic and were not at the heart of the matter. His observations probably reflected in part his own sense of guilt and regret that the Board did not act in time during its passage through Parliament.

Isaac Lyon Goldsmid was a more sophisticated politician than Montefiore. Goldsmid's involvement with the establishment of the University of London demonstrated a keen sense not only of justice to those excluded from the ancient universities or from their degrees on religious grounds but also of the leverage which Jews could exert on public opinion. That Jews of talent should wish to seek higher secular education was a natural concomitant to their entry into the wider society. That his son, Francis, should present himself to the Benchers of Lincoln's Inn for call to the Bar without Christian oath or declaration was in accord with the approach of father and son to the developing role of the Jew in public life. The admission of Francis

Goldsmid to the Bar in 1833 — the first professing Jew called to the English Bar — was an event of considerable significance in its day. The Goldsmids shared the growing self-consciousness of being British, indeed English, in an increasingly Anglicized Jewish community, which at that time was probably mostly of native birth. The Mendelssohnian outlook on life was of sufficiently recent vintage to exercise an intellectual and consciously philosophical influence. The widely-read, much-travelled and less inhibited younger men were likely to be affected. German patterns were infectious.

Montefiore was a natural ally of conservatism. By instinct, disposition and responsibility, he evinced those 'conservative tendencies' which Disraeli attributed to Jews as people. His support of the Whigs and Liberals as the party of emancipation gave way in later years to his inclination to vote for the Conservatives, in which he followed the example of Lionel Louis Cohen and not that of Arthur Cohen, who became Tory and Liberal MPs respectively. The Goldsmids were closely allied to the reformist section of the Whigs and to the Liberal Party which emerged therefrom. Montefiore respected establishments and was an assiduous participant in the panoply of social standing. Quite apart from his belief that the statutory recognition of the Board by Parliament in 1836 was a communal good in that it tended to uphold rabbinic authority, there was an affinity of spirit between himself and the centralized authority with which that recognition endowed the Board and its President.

By choice, and ultimately by force of events, Montefiore accepted a life of strenuous service to his people. In some fields he was a man of wide imagination and bold initiative. Nearer home his steps were at times abrupt, at times, halting, and were often concealed by his fame and the sincerity of his purpose. There was not and never can be another man like him.

NOTES

1. *The Observer*, 30 January 1927. The scurrilous pamphlet on Montefiore, *Megillat Setarim*, by the Hebrew bibliographer and author, Ephraim Deinard (1846—1930) was published in New York in 1928 in an edition limited to 50 copies [VDL].
2. *Trial and Error* (1949), p. 64. Montefiore's baronetcy was by royal leave revived for Francis.
3. Cecil Roth (ed.), *Essays in Jewish History* (1934), pp. 233, 311—62, 335—6, 388.
4. Israel Finestein, 'The Anglo-Jewish Revolt of 1853', *Jewish Quarterly*, vol. 26, Nos. 3—4 (1979), 103—13. On 8 December 1853 the four were

by resolution of the Board declared to be disqualified from membership. The motion was carried only by Montefiore's casting vote. The principal advocates of exclusion were Louis Cohen, the banker kinsman of the Rothschilds, and Henry Harris, a prominent solicitor. They were close allies of the President, who had exerted himself to dissuade congregants from voting for the four in the constituencies. The leading opponents of the motion were David Salomons and Lionel de Rothschild. The resolution disqualified from membership any member of a congregation which did not conform in religious matters to the ecclesiastical authorities of the Board as enshrined in its constitution, namely the Haham and the Chief Rabbi. Montefiore's 'liberal' critics regarded this test as analogous to the contentions whereby professing Jews were excluded from Parliament.

5. Israel Finestein, 'Anglo-Jewry and the Law of Divorce', *Jewish Chronicle*, 19 April 1957; and 'An Aspect of the Jews and English Marriage Law During the Emancipation: the Prohibited Degrees', *Jewish Journal of Sociology*, vol. VII, No. 1 (1965), 3—21.

6. That spirit was allied to an optimism which sprang from the mid-Victorian belief in progress, providence and the eradicability of prejudice through the diffusion of knowledge and through the improving of social conditions by technological changes. These assumptions and convictions may be detected in Montefiore's hopeful reply to information from Gerson von Bleichroeder, Bismarck's banker, concerning the growth of anti-semitism in Germany and elsewhere in Europe. The reply is dated 13 June 1880 and appears in the *Diaries*. See also Montefiore's letter of 24 May 1881 therein to Arthur Cohen supporting the latter's acceptance of the Foreign Office's opinion as to the unwisdom of making *official* representations to the Russian Government in respect of the pogroms. The communal debate between 1879 and 1882 on these issues (see Israel Finestein, 'Arthur Cohen Q.C. 1829—1914', *Remember the Days*, ed. J. M. Shaftesley (1966), pp. 279—302), reflects the undoubted inception of the modern period in Jewish history.

7. Cited by Asa Briggs in *Victorian People* (1955), Sec. 5 of Ch. 9.

8. When Montefiore left for Palestine in 1855 and again in 1857, Isaac Foligno was elected President of the Board. Lionel de Rothschild had declined the office. The years 1853 to 1856 saw considerable dissension at the Board. Montefiore contemplated his departures for Jerusalem with relief. The *Jewish Chronicle* made the significant comment, albeit in the language of the day, that by the appointment of Foligno, a businessman, the Presidency 'for the first time has passed from the ranks of the aristocracy to those of the people.' Montefiore had inherited the Presidency from his maternal uncle, Moses Mocatta, in 1835.

9. J. F. C. Harrison, *The Early Victorians 1832—51*, (Panther, 1973), p. 123.

10. Faudel (1809—63) was a Director of the Union Steam Shipping Co. and of the Southampton Docks. He was typical of the able younger men whose assessments of communal needs and performance marked them out for leadership, but who remained critics and proposers. Some of these men found a place in the Anglo-Jewish Association (founded in 1871), including a number of leading figures in Reform who were excluded from the Board.

11. The prohibited degrees prescribed in this measure did not coincide with those in Jewish religious law. The question arose as to whether the Act applied to Jews. See note 5.

12.   The Registration Act of 1836 required the Registrar-General to supply
      marriage registers to every person as the President of the Board shall
      certify to be 'the Secretary of a Synagogue . . . of persons professing the
      Jewish religion'. In effecting the civil registration of marriages solemnized
      in the Synagogues, the Secretary was agent for the Registrar-General.
13.   See in particular, *Voice of Jacob*, 2 September 1842, where Franklin refers
      to his having 'learned from bitter experience that the time is not yet ripe
      for that unity of purpose' required to establish a ministerial training
      college in Anglo-Jewry.
14.   The proposed remodelling of the old Beth Hamedrash of the Ashkenazi
      community in 1841, contemplated by its Trustees, had not been pursued.
      To create a seminary to provide 'a profound theological training and a
      modern university career' became 'one of the principal objects' of Adler's
      Chief Rabbinate: Isidore Harris, *History of Jews' College*, Jubilee Volume,
      (1960), p. iv. Within his first year, his enquiries were sufficiently advanced
      to enable him to call a first formal meeting of communal notables. See
      also A. M. Hyamson, *Jews' College, London, (1855–1955)*, (1955).
15.   One of the earliest references in the Jewish press to the need for a Jewish
      day school in the interests of the Anglicized community was a letter to
      the *Voice of Jacob*, on 17 February 1843 from John Braham, optician
      and synagogue leader in Bristol. His letter was prophetic in calling for a
      training college for ministers and teachers, with the Chief Rabbi (no-one
      was yet appointed) at its head, and with a Jewish day school attached. He
      clearly envisaged that during the interregnum the lay leadership would
      take the initiative. He also boldly, and with long foresight, proposed a levy
      on synagogue seat rentals throughout the country to help finance the
      scheme, to which he returned in the press from time to time.
16.   Save for the chronicle of Montefiore's activities in Palestine, no part of the
      published Diaries is more particularized than his engagements in connec-
      tion with the possibility of legislation for removing Jewish civil disabilities.
      For the campaign generally and Jewish and general public opinion, see
      U. R. Q. Henriques, *Religious Toleration in England, 1787–1833*, (1961);
      V. D. Lipman, 'The Age of Emancipation 1815–1880', *Three Centuries
      of Anglo-Jewish History* (1961); Israel Finestein, 'Anglo-Jewish Opinion
      During the Struggle for Emancipation', *Trans. JHSE* XX (1964); M. C. N.
      Salbstein, *The Emancipation of the Jews in Britain* (1982).

4

Friends and Philanthropists: Montefiore and Dr Hodgkin

AMALIE M. KASS

In the Anglican cemetery in Jaffa, a tall obelisk of polished Aberdeen granite marks the grave of Dr Thomas Hodgkin. The obelisk was placed there on behalf of Sir Moses Montefiore to commemorate his forty years friendship with Hodgkin.[1] Hodgkin's professional skills were the basis of their acquaintance; from 1823 onward he was physician to several members of the Montefiore family. At least as compelling a bond was a shared concern for the oppressed, a concern that led to joint philanthropic activities in England and overseas and to five journeys together for the relief of suffering Jews. It was on the last of these that Hodgkin died unexpectedly in the Holy Land.

Montefiore's pre-eminence among nineteenth-century Anglo-Jewish philanthropists has been well established, the length of his years adding lustre to the notoriety of his deeds.[2] Though primarily remembered as a physician, in his lifetime Thomas Hodgkin too was recognized as an outstanding philanthropist. 'Few men were more beloved than Dr. Hodgkin; his truly Christian charity, his unostentatious piety, his utter self-negation, won and kept the love and esteem of all who knew him', said the *Lancet* at the time of his death.[3] 'His strong sympathy with his fellow men of all climes and colours rendered Dr. Thomas Hodgkin's name familiar to high and low; and his hand was ever held out to aid those who were least capable of returning his generosity', wrote one of his friends.[4]

Outwardly the two men were quite different. Montefiore's heritage as a Sephardic Jew, his limited formal education, his successful career in business and finance, and the honours bestowed upon him by worldwide Jewry and by the English Government present a decided contrast to Hodgkin's background and experiences.[5] Hodgkin's ancestors were members of the Society of Friends or Quakers, and had risen from the English yeomanry to become provincial wool staplers, brewers and coal merchants. A grand-uncle, also Thomas Hodgkin, set an intellectual pattern for subsequent generations when he abandoned trade to become a schoolmaster. Hodgkin's father, John, was a renowned calligrapher and tutor to daughters of fashionable families in and around London. His mother, born Elizabeth Rickman, was well educated for her day and had been a governess to the Gurney family of Norwich before her marriage. He and his brother, John Jun., were educated at home in the classics, mathematics and languages. In 1814, the family moved to Tottenham where a circle of prosperous, energetic Quakers, well experienced in science and philanthropy, nurtured the boy's interests in both fields. Luke Howard, the pioneer meteorologist, and William Phillips, the geologist, were among those whose scientific activities captured his youthful enthusiasm.

Thomas served as private secretary to William Allen, the Quaker chemist and philanthropist, and was then apprenticed to an apothecary firm in Brighton. At the end of two years there, he decided to study medicine. He walked the wards of Guy's Hospital in London, then studied medicine formally at the University of Edinburgh and in Paris, where he was influenced by the work of Laennec. Hodgkin received his medical degree from Edinburgh in 1823. Two years later he was appointed Lecturer in Morbid Anatomy and Curator of the Museum at Guy's Hospital. During the next twelve years he almost singlehandedly created the pathological museum at Guy's; one can still see many of his original specimens there, with descriptions in his meticulous handwriting. He introduced the use of the stethoscope, presented the first systematic lectures on pathology, and made significant observations with J. J. Lister (father of the distinguished surgeon), who had developed the achromatic microscope. His researches and descriptions of diseases included papers on carcinoma, retroversion of the aortic valves and cholera. Most well known is the paper 'On Some Morbid Appearances of the Absorbant Glands and Spleen' which later led Samuel Wilks to name this disorder Hodgkin's Disease, thereby fixing Hodgkin's name in modern day consciousness.

These medical accomplishments should have led to a promotion to Assistant Physician at Guy's Hospital. Hodgkin was a leading candidate when the position became vacant in 1837. However, he did not receive the appointment, primarily because of the personal enmity of the Treasurer of the hospital, Benjamin Harrison, who had been affronted by some of Hodgkin's Quaker practices and by his active participation in social reform. Hodgkin's efforts to protect Canadian Indians from the deleterious effects of the fur trade had been particularly offensive to Harrison, who was a member of the policy-making Committee of the Hudson's Bay Company, the prime target of Hodgkin's criticism.[6] Thereafter Hodgkin practised medicine privately, interrupted by a brief period on the staff of St Thomas's Hospital. He continued to publish on medical subjects, worked for reform of medical education and pioneered efforts to improve the health of the poor.

Hodgkin's appearance and personality also contrasted with Montefiore's. The latter was unusually tall, over 6 feet, 3 inches, at a time when average height was less than today, and he conveyed a sense of dignity and influence.[7] Hodgkin was short and wiry, exuding energy and motion. Whereas Montefiore was astute in financial matters, Hodgkin was often unwise about money. The physician made business deals that were financially disastrous to him, gave personal loans to unreliable acquaintances, and was diffident about collecting fees for his professional services. On one occasion he offended a wealthy patient with whom he stayed up all night, asking only ten pounds for his services and then telling the gentleman that he 'did not look as if he could afford more'.[8]

Montefiore moved easily at the upper levels of British society and delighted in entertaining and being entertained by English royalty and by foreign potentates. Hodgkin's Quaker ideology forbade ostentation and his more modest means necessitated a different life style, although his comfortable homes, first in the West End and later in Bedford Square, were frequently the site for meetings of his many philanthropic and scientific organizations. Though assertive when defending those whose cause he advocated, Hodgkin was personally retiring and self-effacing. He declined a fellowship in the Royal College of Physicians because it seemed to him to be 'an invidious distinction'.[9] In 1857, his friends started a testimonial subscription on his behalf, but Hodgkin would not accept the three hundred guineas they raised.[10]

Despite these differences, Montefiore and Hodgkin shared similar values and interests. Each came from a family in which religion was of paramount importance and each exemplified and perpetuated that commitment throughout his own life. As was not unusual among Jews or the Quakers, both Montefiore and Hodgkin were well read in Scripture and enjoyed quoting chapter and verse when appropriate. Montefiore carefully observed the Sabbath and Holy Days; the ceremonies for his installation as Sheriff of London were rescheduled so that they would not coincide with religious obligations on the Jewish New Year.[11]

Hodgkin did not deviate from the injunctions and obligations of the Quakers. He wore simple, unadorned clothing, forebore to doff his hat in public and used the traditional 'thee' and 'thou' in speech and writing. He was a regular attendant at Meeting for Worship and at the various organizational meetings of the Friends. In his later years, he overcame his natural reluctance and agreed to serve as

Clerk and as an Elder of the Westminster Monthly Meeting.[12] If the Meeting for Sufferings or the Yearly Meeting were addressing one of the social causes with which he was concerned, he worked tirelessly to prepare information. A great sadness of his personal life resulted from the Quaker rule forbidding first cousin marriages. Hodgkin was deeply attached to his own first cousin, Sarah Godlee, and wanted to marry her. He tried to have the rule of consanguinity revoked, but when that was refused he gave up Sarah rather than act contrary to his religion. When he was more than fifty years old, Hodgkin married another Sarah, a widow named Sarah Callow Scaife, who became a Friend before their marriage.

As Jew and Quaker, Montefiore and Hodgkin shared the common experiences of Englishmen outside the established Church. They belonged to small sects. The Jewish population in England in 1830 has been estimated between 25,000 and 30,000; the Quakers numbered about 16,000.[13] Though not themselves greatly victimized by extreme religious intolerance, each recognized the distinctions that remained in English society. When Hodgkin enrolled at the University of Edinburgh, neither Jews nor Quakers could receive degrees from Oxford and Cambridge. The creation of University College London in 1826 and the subsequent chartering of the University of London in 1836, opened higher education in England to non-Anglicans. The Jews had provided some of the financial backing for University College.[14] Hodgkin was one of the initial appointees to the Senate of the University of London and was an active member of the Senate for the rest of his life.

In medicine there were subtle discriminations caused by the reluctance of the Royal College of Physicians to accept for Fellowship medical degrees from universities other than Oxford, Cambridge or Dublin. Hodgkin's rejection of their Fellowship was in one sense a rejection of the exception they tried to make in his case. Neither Jews nor Quakers were fully enfranchised politically until 1828, when Quakers were admitted to Parliament, and 1858, when Jews saw the end of legal limitations on their political rights.

Jews and Quakers shared more than their Dissenter status. Many among them had become leaders of British industry and finance. Rothschilds, Montefiores, Cohens and Goldsmids were matched by Gurneys, Bevans, Lloyds and Barclays, to name only a few of the outstanding families.[15] Along with wealth in both sects came a deeply engrained sense of the need for charitable giving, a spirit which both Montefiore and Hodgkin epitomized. Montefiore's benefactions were legion and not limited to Jews. Money was given for the poor, for education, for hospitals, sometimes in response to requests, often without solicitation. His worldwide efforts on behalf of persecuted Jews followed from the same sources.

Hodgkin was equally representative of this commitment. His more limited finances did not allow large gifts, but many individuals who had suffered a loss received small amounts of money from him, along with recommendations to other potential donors. The constraints of the pocketbook were more than compensated for by his lifelong non-medical activities. His Quaker upbringing produced an early awareness of the tragic plight of the North American Indian and of the horrors of slavery, and resulted in a life-long desire to defend all peoples threatened by the obliterative aspects of Western civilization. He took the lead in the creation of the British African Civilization Society which supported the American colony of freed blacks in Liberia and he remained a loyal advocate of Liberia and of other plans to colonize American blacks in Africa.[16] He was one of the founders of the Aborigines Protection Society and its foremost spokesman, carrying on a voluminous worldwide correspondence about conditions in 'uncivilized' places and advising about protection of the natives. On their behalf, he drafted and presented memorials to the British government and wrote appeals for publication in journals and the Press. An interest in scientific study of the different races and cultures of mankind led him to participate in the formation of the Ethnological Society of London and in its researches, which were eventually opposed by blatantly racist theorists.[17] Hodgkin served for many years as Honorary Secretary and Honorary Foreign Secretary of the Royal Geographical Society. Montefiore was also a member of the Geographical Society though not an active participant.[18] The doctor was heavily involved with the British Association for the Advancement of Science — as a member of the Council, in various sub-sections, and as a speaker.[19] He also helped create the Syrian Medical Aid Association, which sent doctors to Beirut and Damascus to introduce Western medicine through free dispensaries which were open to all people.[20] Both Hodgkin and Montefiore, the Quaker and the Jew, held an unshakeable belief in the Biblical injunction to 'draw out thy soul to the hungry, and satisfy the afflicted soul.'

The origins of the Montefiore-Hodgkin friendship have an ironic twist. While studying medicine in Paris in 1821—22, Hodgkin made the acquaintance of Benjamin Thorpe, a clerk at the banking offices of the Rothschilds.[21] It is possible that they first met through business; Thomas's father had placed funds at Rothschild's for his son's use in Paris.[22] In any case, Hodgkin is known to have treated Thorpe for 'grave pulmonary disease' and to have travelled with him to England in the autumn of 1822.[23] Hodgkin spent the following academic year completing his medical studies at the University of Edinburgh; Thorpe, his health restored, returned to Paris and the Rothschild office, but he did not forget the young physician.[24] When the occasion arose, he recommended Hodgkin to Abraham Montefiore, Moses' younger brother, who was a consumptive. He had been seriously ill and was in Paris planning a recuperative journey to the south of France and/or Italy. Thorpe wrote in January 1823 that Abraham 'wants a friend skilled in medicine' to travel with him, and suggested that Thomas Hodgkin should become his *compagnon de voyage*.[25] Thomas hesitated, not only because his studies would not be completed until August, but also because he questioned the wisdom of such a situation. He wrote to his father:

Though I have always when conversing with my medical friends expressed a disinclination to be attached to a family in the capacity of travelling M.D. from an idea that one must in such a situation be too little one's own master to derive all the advantage of being in a foreign country yet I confess thee I feel very much disposed to accept the offer now made which I think may be productive of advantage to me both in the journey itself & in its consequences. Your fears as to the dangers of attending to a patient such as you have described may I think safely be set at rest when I say that . . . the contagious nature of some forms of consumption . . . I much doubt . . .[26]

There was also concern because Henrietta Montefiore was reputed to have a difficult personality. 'She is rather eloquent say the respondants,' John Hodgkin, Sen. reported, but these fears were temporarily allayed during her brief return to London when the Hodgkins met her on behalf of their son.[27] Thomas completed his medical education in late summer, and by the first week of September he had gone to Paris, met the invalid and was writing home for clothes and books he would need for the journey southward.[28] It was during these initial interviews in Paris that Hodgkin met Moses, who had left England with his wife Judith on 20 August for a pleasure trip to France, Germany, and Italy.[29]

On 16 September 1823 the Abraham Montefiore party set out — the sick man and his wife in one carriage, their children and governess in another, Dr. Hodgkin with the latter group or on horseback.[30] Abraham was unwell at the departure but withstood the rigours of travel over the French Alps and through the Piedmont to Pisa. Unfortunately, that city did not please him so they continued onward to Rome, where he suffered a relapse. 'There is great cause to consider his case as one of the most serious nature affording but slight ground for hope, though it is most likely to be a protracted one.'[31] Italian doctors were called in as consultants. They advised bleeding. Hodgkin disagreed with their recommendations but the Montefiores did not. Indeed, they viewed Hodgkin's treatment as too inactive. He preferred to 'try to make the patient suffer as little as possible but not do too much' since the outcome was inevitable.[32] Inevitable too was the tension between physician and patient and patient's wife. In addition to be rebuffed professionally, the young doctor felt constrained from enjoying the sights and society of Rome. He looked forward to the expected arrival of Abraham's brother, 'a very agreeable man whose presence at this painful period will I have no doubt be relieving'.[33] Upon their arrival Moses and Judith were distressed to find his brother so seriously ill and they decided to prolong their stay in Rome. 'The diametrically opposite character of MM often makes the days pass by no means unpleasantly', Hodgkin wrote to his parents early in January 1824. There was talk by Moses of an eventual trip to Greece, Constantinople, Palestine and Egypt and 'if his brother's indisposition does not set this journey aside it is possible that he will give me the offer of accompanying him'.[35]

Relations between doctor and patient continued to deteriorate. On 8 January, Abraham wrote Hodgkin a brief note of dismissal couched in phrases of concern for the young man's opportunities for travel.[36] The earnest physician was deeply wounded by Abraham's rejection, though he could not have been too surprised, since he had not been in the sick room for weeks and there had been unpleasant incidents between him and Henrietta.[37] He would have preferred to have been the one to give notice, but he consoled himself that:

I retain on the separation so much of the good will & good opinion to Moses Montefiore & other members of the family who are here, as will counteract any unfavourable report which may have passed respecting me to any of A.M.'s friends in England.[38]

In fact, Moses made him:

a handsome present of a pedometer which will be a very agreeable accompaniment to me should I make a part of my excursion towards home on foot.[39]

Hodgkin's parents and brother were equally concerned lest his reputation be damaged by the episode in Rome. John Jun. wondered why 'thy good friend Moses M.' did not advise Thomas to resign, thereby preventing any suggestion of unsatisfactory service.[40] But the rumours they feared do not seem to have surfaced. Moses returned to England in February to attend to business matters and to hire a ship on which to take his brother across the

Mediterranean to Jerusalem.[41] Thomas had given him a formal letter of introduction to the Hodgkin family and there were several pleasant meetings. 'We were indeed highly gratified by the encomiums which he and his amiable wife passed upon thee,' Thomas's mother proudly wrote him. Montefiore had assured them that their son's reputation 'stands high in the estimation of many at Rome who are capable of appreciating medical skills & other talents'.[42] Henrietta seems to have received most of the blame for the fiasco. Hodgkin wrote a letter home in Latin in which he minced no words. He admitted that Henrietta was a devoted wife who tirelessly cared for the sick man.

I have never seen anyone more affectionate than she. She looks after him almost by herself . . . She does without food and sleep, survives the cold and chill. She tolerates all this with almost superhuman vigour. But if her nature seems scarcely human she does not at all incline to the nature of angels for most of all I think she has got a most unfortunate and accursed power of causing trouble for other people . . . In no way do I need a poetic imagination to conjure up a Medusa and the hair styles which she loves to affect is just like snakes.[43]

Moses' continued esteem for Hodgkin was evident the following month. At the creation of the Alliance British and Foreign Life and Fire Assurance Company, he arranged for his friend to become one of the original shareholders. Perhaps Montefiore shared the Hodgkin feeling that the doctor had been wronged; perhaps it was his customary largesse. In any event, Montefiore made ten shares of Alliance stock available to Thomas at £10 per share; within the week they had reached £25 per share and were continuing to advance.[44] Montefiore wrote to Hodgkin that he 'was happy to do that which will be in yr. interest'.[45] Montefiore also intended to have his friend appointed physician to the new institution, a post which would certainly have advanced his career, but since Hodgkin had remained on the continent the position did not come to him.[46] Montefiore's patronage was evidenced later in the year when the Marine Assurance Company was organized and Hodgkin once more received ten of the original shares. He also acquired shares in the Imperial and Continental Gas Association, another Montefiore enterprise.[47] Hodgkin still owned these shares at the time of his death.[48]

Though Montefiore had expected to spend a brief time in England and then rejoin his brother for the sea voyage to the Holy Land, the demands of these business activities detained him. Meanwhile, Abraham left Italy and was travelling northward through France when he succumbed at Lyons on 28 August 1824.[49] Montefiore's *Diary* expressed his grief at Abraham's death and his remorse for not pursuing the original plans:

> Seize the transient hour
> Improve each moment as it flies —,
> Life is a short summer — man a flower
> He dies, alas! How soon he dies.[50]

When Thomas Hodgkin heard of Abraham's death he wrote from Paris of his 'respects & condolence to my excellent friend MM & also to such other members of the family as I have the pleasure of knowing.'[51] By then he had recovered from the disappointment of the experience in Rome. He replied to Benjamin Thorpe's apologies for having made the introduction to Abraham,

As to thy kindness in introducing A. Montefiore my sense of obligation to thee remains unalterably the same. I owe to this introduction the gratifying and valuable friendship of M. Montefiore & of some other members of his family.[52]

A gratifying and valuable friendship it remained.

Tradition has it that Hodgkin became Montefiore's personal physician at this time. One of the earliest Montefiore biographers stated 'For forty years he (Hodgkin) had been intimately associated with the Jewish philanthropist.'[53] Another biographer referred to Hodgkin as Montefiore's 'medical attendant for forty years'.[54] As mentioned above, the Hodgkin tombstone commemorated 'A Friendship of more than 40 years' so the supposition is not without foundation. However, the Hodgkin papers reveal nothing that directly substantiates the claim. Nor do the Montefiore *Diaries* identify the 'eminent physician' under whose care Montefiore placed himself in 1828, a physician who 'for a long time visited him almost daily . . . (and) would often accompany him on his way to the city'.[55] Hodgkin was just building his medical reputation at the time, was occupied with his duties at Guy's and was residing in New Broad Street, a good distance from Montefiore in Park Lane. It is possible that Hodgkin began to attend Montefiore in this period but we cannot be certain.

It is clear that Hodgkin did serve for a few years as physician to two Jewish Friendly Societies, the Society of United Israelites and the Society of United Sisters, probably through Montefiore's influence. Hodgkin's professional duties included care for 'upwards of a hundred poor Jews'.[56] He resigned these posts in 1831, but continued an informal association with similar patients. His niece recalled that Dr. Hodgkin 'was much beloved by the Jews in the East of London, and well known in the poor quarters where he continually attended them without any charge'. According to her reminiscence, 'the Aborigines and the Jews took the first place in his mind'.[57]

In any case, Hodgkin and Montefiore saw one another with some frequency. When Hodgkin 'had the pleasure of being at thy house' in 1836, he sought Montefiore's support for a scientific expedition to Canada to be led by Richard King, a surgeon who had been a colleague at Guy's and who had supplied Hodgkin with the information about the sorry condition of the Indians living under the aegis of Hudson's Bay Company.[58] When Hodgkin's promotion at Guy's was under consideration, Montefiore was asked to help promote his friend's candidacy. He responded vigorously. He promised to use his own influence with the Governors of the hospital and to ask his brother-in-law, Benjamin Cohen, and some of the Rothschilds to do the same. Montefiore wrote to John Hodgkin, Jun.,

The regard and esteem I have for your excellent Brother makes me feel most anxious for his success and it is a great satisfaction for me to be able to state his claims are to my mind very superior to those of any other Candidate and I am confident his Election will greatly promote the best interests of the Hospital.[59]

Unfortunately, Montefiore's efforts and those of many other Hodgkin advocates did not prevail.*

The failure to be promoted at Guy's marked a turning point in Hodgkin's life. Intensely disappointed, he suffered a prolonged depression and remained permanently embittered toward Harrison and the other officials of the hospital. He resigned the appointments he had held at Guy's and, when his health improved, he became increasingly involved with his various philanthropic and scientific interests. Hodgkin was approaching his fortieth birthday at this time. Montefiore was forty when he gave up his daily involvement with business — a coincidence, but one which would add to the sympathy and understanding each had for the other.

The closeness of the Montefiore—Hodgkin friendship is most clearly seen in the overseas journeys which they made together. Each was an experienced and enthusiastic traveller. Montefiore's reputation and his connections with the British establishment facilitated useful introductions to important foreigners. Hodgkin too had many friends abroad, from his holiday journeys, and from his many medical and scientific associations. His duties as Honorary Secretary of the Royal Geographical Society, coupled with his correspondence and activities on behalf of the Aborigines Protection Society and the Ethnological Society of London, provided him with information

---

*Samuel Gurney, Montefiore's associate in the insurance companies and a good friend of the Hodgkin family from the time when Elizabeth Hodgkin was his sisters' governess, was one of the prominent sponsors of Hodgkin's candidacy. See 'Statement on the pending appointment of Assistant Physician to Guy's Hospital', n.d., 33:56.

and contacts in many distant places. Evidently, Hodgkin took travel as seriously as he did all his pursuits. A nephew who accompanied him to the continent in 1846 noted the doctor's theory that travel was 'a kind of fever . . . (which) should be treated with low diet', but that 'my dear Uncle, who was . . . a little man with . . . great powers of endurance kept the party on the go all the time'.[60]

There were three early offers to Hodgkin to travel with the Montefiores. In June 1837, he declined an invitation to Cyrene, primarily because he feared 'the intense heat' would be harmful to him.[61] He was at that time in the midst of a prolonged convalescence from a debilitating fever. In November 1838, he chose not to join the Montefiores on their second journey to Palestine.[62] Sir Moses had been especially sensitive, suggesting that Hodgkin should join them at least as far as France and quit them whenever he should desire, but Hodgkin was still suffering from the effects of the Guy's episode and unable to accept. Two years later, he decided not to join one of Montefiore's most dramatic missions, the trip to Egypt and Constantinople during the 'Damascus Affair'. Hodgkin must have struggled with this refusal, for he recognized that the journey presented a 'task of no small difficulty and self denial . . . a noble and benign enterprise'.[63] Perhaps there were other invitations not recorded in the Hodgkin papers. Sir Moses and Lady Montefiore continued their travels in response to appeals from overseas.

In 1857 there was a significant change when Hodgkin accompanied the Montefiores to the Holy Land. The chance to be in that part of the world surely must have been interesting to one so intimately familiar with the Old and New Testaments. Apart from its religious connotations, his involvement with the Syrian Medical Aid Association during the 1840s had given him some insight into conditions there. The weaknesses of the Turkish political regime, coupled with the poverty and degradation of the inhabitants, aroused his interest and concern long after the Syrian Medical Aid Association became defunct.[64]

This was the fifth visit by Sir Moses and Lady Montefiore to the land so dear to them, and was undertaken to check on the projects already begun and to provide more aid where needed.*

Hodgkin and the Montefiores left England on 25 February 1857 and were away for five months. Hodgkin's letters provide a picture of their activities. In Southern France, Sir Moses spent the Sabbath at Lyons but thoughtfully urged Hodgkin 'to go to Nismes (sic) where he might spend First Day with Friends'. In Marseilles, 'Sir M. was much engaged with gas works belonging to Continental Gas

*See 'The Saga of 1855' below.

Co.'[65] While passing through Italy, Hodgkin had time to explore the antiquities and observe geological formations. He made sketches of those things he thought of particular interest.[66] Following a stop-over in Malta, he wrote to his colleagues in the Senate of the University of London urging closer connections between the University of Malta and the University of London. He also described the care which Sir Moses took to avoid embarking on the Sabbath.[67] The group reached Alexandria on 5 May and proceeded to Cairo on a train engaged for Lord Elgin. Hodgkin rejoiced to see the ancient marvels which he had read about as a schoolboy.[68]

When the party arrived in Jaffa, Sir Moses was gratified to learn that conditions had improved.[69] Escorted by the former Governor of Jerusalem, Ahmed Agha, and his horsemen, plus the British Consul of Jerusalem and the Vice-Consul of Jaffa,* the group proceeded by horseback to Lydda where they camped 'in a beautiful vineyard'. Sir Moses ordered two sheep cooked for Ahmed Agha's men who 'after sunset, made a great feast, and were very merry'. The ride onward to Jerusalem was extremely perilous, due to darkness and the difficult terrain, and Lady Montefiore was 'remarkably frightened'.[70] Hodgkin subsequently suggested improvements for the road.[71]

Although the Montefiores were greatly pleased to be in Jerusalem once more, Hodgkin was not favourably impressed by the city or its inhabitants. Modern Jerusalem, he noted, is a 'poor and miserable place'. The dirty streets, poor houses, excessive use of tobacco, and idleness induced by the Turkish pipe, distressed him.[72] His observations provide interesting details while revealing his own Victorian cum Quaker attitudes.[73]

Jerusalem & other places with which there is so much sacred & historical connection with a large amount of fabulous & superstitious addition producing confusion & doubt can scarcely fail to produce disappointment & pain. The moral & physical condition of the inhabitants tends to increase rather (than) remove these feelings. The Jews especially are in a deplorable state. We know that formerly their sufferings were mainly owing to intolerance & persecution but both of these evils are I trust at present greatly mitigated and are still abating. Their existing evils are very much produced by unfortunate circumstances essentially connected with themselves. Numbers flock to Jerusalem either in

*The British Vice-Consul in Jaffa was Assad Yacoob Kayat, an acquaintance of Hodgkin's from the Syrian Medical Aid Association. Kayat trained in surgery at St George's Hospital, London, and became a member of the Royal College of Surgeons in 1846. See *List of the Fellows and Members of the Royal College of Surgeons of England*, 31 August 1846. He subsequently went to Jaffa, where he served as British Vice-Consul from 1847 until his death in 1865. See Foreign Office List for 1856, p. 30 and FO 78/1874, H. A. Kayat, 23 Nov., 1865. Hodgkin and Montefiore had to straighten out some tangled financial problems for Kayat while in Palestine. See 13:117.

advanced age expressly to die there or still young & in the vigour of their age for
the purpose as they term it of 'Serving the Lord' which really means doing
nothing but reading the Talmud & going to the Synagogue. They do not even
take sufficient bodily exercise to preserve their health & have their food brought
to them. Their means of subsistence as far as I could learn are derived from
presents & from collections made amongst their more industrious brethren in
different parts of the world. Though the sums raised in this way are considerable
they are inadequate to furnish comforts to the large & increasing numbers augmented by early and improvident marriages which aggravate the evils which I
have already mentioned. Till very lately the children had little or no instruction
but schools have recently been established for girls by Sir M. Montefiore & for
boys by a fund bequeathed by a German Jew. The language used by the Jews of
Jerusalem is as peculiar & degenerate as their habits being a mixture of Spanish,
Arabic, German, Polish & Hebrew. Those who esteem themselves learned Hebrew
scholars are in other respects most ignorant men & quite unfit to act as leading
Rabbis if appointed to foreign Synagogues. I have gathered these facts from the
representatives of Jews who understand & deplore this state of things.

Hodgkin also gave a picture of the Christian population in Jerusalem.

The Christians of Jerusalem are much divided & those places which are mis-
named Holy & have long been the strong attraction of the fanatical & superstitious are in a state of disgraceful delapidation deplorable in an archeological
point of view. There are some excellent men connected with Missionary societies
with whom I was greatly pleased & interested but I am decidedly of the judgment that associations & Societies professedly formed & supported for the purpose of converting the Jews are a great mistake in principle & practice.*

The Montefiores pursued their multitudinous projects with no dis-
cernible loss of dedication. The dispensary, weaving establishment
and the girls' school received their careful attention and there were
many conferences about the proposed hospital and the windmill that
Sir Moses wished to have installed outside the walls of Jerusalem.
Evidently he and Judith enjoyed good health and their physician was
asked to serve them in several other capacities. Hodgkin was sent to
Jaffa to investigate the financial condition of a small agricultural
enterprise which Montefiore had sponsored; he reported that it was
not doing well. Farms at Safed and Tiberias had also been unsuccessful. The physician acted as Montefiore's amanuensis, responding to
the many petitions and letters his renowned friend received, and he
helped draft plans for a railway from Jaffa to Jerusalem.[74]
On his own initiative, Hodgkin petitioned the Turks to remove
'some of the heaps of dirt which accumulate in the narrow streets',

*Hodgkin was familiar with the Society for the Promotion of Christianity amongst the
Jews. He was not sympathetic to their endeavours and was greatly displeased when one of
the doctors sent to Beirut by the Syrian Medical Aid Association transferred his allegiance
and became an agent for the conversionists. See Hodgkin to the Secretary of the Society for
Promotion of Christianity amongst the Jews, 1844 May 2, 18:23.

and when the Pasha pleaded lack of funds, 'a subscription list was opened and the novel work was commenced at once.'[75] Hodgkin also convened a meeting of the Europeans in Jerusalem to whom he proposed formation of a mechanics institute where principles of improved transportation, sanitation and agriculture might be disseminated. He 'had the gratification . . . to see the meeting unite in the resolution to make the attempt' to carry out his suggestions. Hodgkin had become an advocate of this form of adult education twenty years earlier when he had lectured at the Spitalfields Mechanics Institute on improved health for the poor of London.

What emerges from all this activity is the belief shared by Montefiore and Hodgkin that in addition to providing direct aid for improved sanitation, medicine and education, it was essential to encourage 'self-help' projects, especially in agriculture and handicrafts. The projects Montefiore supported and Hodgkin abetted were similar to those which Hodgkin had habitually recommended to people in non-industrial, non-Westernized places. With hindsight, their endeavours seem overly ambitious, whether due to poor planning and insufficient financing or to the complexities and problems often inherent when 'out-siders' try to impose solutions. Mechanics institutes may have been appropriate for the poor of London or Manchester but were not necessarily applicable in Palestine. Nonetheless, both Hodgkin and Montefiore persevered in their determination to establish those institutions in which they confidently believed. That they sought to transpose those things which seemed to them to work well in England is understandable and not unlike other European reformers of the same period.

The Montefiore party left Jerusalem on 7 June 1857 and was soon back in Alexandria, where they enjoyed the elaborate hospitality of the Pasha. Hodgkin's journal reveals a charming picture of Lady Montefiore, who, he said, accompanied her husband whereever 'proper and desirable'. She visited the harem and her subsequent description

very much compensated for our inevitable exclusion from that part of the court. Though Moslem Lords do not allow their ladies to go into society we had repeated proof that they do not object to come into society where ladies take a conspicuous part. At Alexandria Kourcheed Pasha the Governor & at Cairo Zoulficor Pasha the President of the Council dined with Sir M. and sat beside Lady M. at the head of the table.[77]

Unfortunately Hodgkin did not repeat Lady Montefiore's description of the harem for our edification.

Even the Montefiores were impressed. Their diaries tell of 'elegant repasts served by thirty attendants' and a breakfast 'magnificently served in truly regal state; not less than thirty-two servants were in attendance'. Less elegant were the 'millions of mosquitoes and their innumerable associates' which forced the party to abandon their bedrooms and spend a night on chairs in the adjoining gallery.[78]

Recrossing the Mediterranean, they travelled overland. Hodgkin dined with some of the Montefiore relatives in Vienna. While on the train *en route* from Vienna to Prague he experienced a severe urticarial attack (hives), which caused him serious though temporary discomfort.[79] Hodgkin's wife had seriously considered meeting the doctor in Germany, but decided against it. As she explained to her brother-in-law, her husband 'acted most judiciously ... remaining with Sir M. until they arrive in England, being remunerated for his services ... he is not quite at liberty to do as he pleases.'[80]

For the Montefiores the journey gave the satisfaction of further accomplishments in their self-imposed mission.* From Hodgkin's mind and pen a variety of productions ensued. Despite his belief that 'I have far less poetry than most persons & therefore observe in a very matter of fact way', he was eager to publish his observations.[81] His longstanding interest in geology led to detailed, illustrated descriptions of formations in the places he had visited.[82] Exposure to a non-European culture had further stimulated his interest in ethnology and he prepared a paper about the Bedouins of Egypt and Palestine for the 1857 meeting of the British Association for the Advancement of Science.[83] Hodgkin prefaced his observations with the assertion that

a more full & complete knowledge of Ethnology in which the genius, intellectual characteristics & prevailing dispositions of different Nations should be included (is) most important to the adoption of a sound & successful policy in our intercourse with other nations.

He described the physical differences among the people he had observed, including negroes present in the area. With characteristic Anglo-Saxon aplomb, he expressed confidence that the Bedouins need not be feared and that they could be 'domesticated' if the correct measures were taken.

There would probably be much difficulty & frequent failure in any serious attempt to bring the Bedouins of the desert into honest industrious & settled life — if ultimate success were not obtained I believe it would be more attributable

---

*The *Diaries* and the Hodgkin papers give no hint that there was serious opposition to Montefiore's schemes. However, dispatches from the British Consul in Jerusalem to the Foreign Office suggest that 'fanatical, obscurantist' rabbis did not want schools, agriculture or industrial projects promoted among the Jews. See FO 78/1383 (Pol. No. 1), 1 January 1858, in Hyamson, *British Consulate*, I, pp. 257—60.

to imperfection in the plan & to want of tact than to the unalterable nature of
the Bedouin character.

His proposal for the formation of a mechanics institute in Jerusalem
received public notice in England, accompanied by an appeal for
contributions in the form of apparatus, models and books.[84] To Sir
Moses, he sent elaborate plans for a new almshouse, to be built
instead of the hospital, and for other construction in Jerusalem.*[85]
Hodgkin also published two articles opposing construction of a canal
at Suez. Since Sir Moses had declined to invest in that enterprise
when de Lesseps offered him a part in 1855, and was still partial to
eventual construction of a railway in the area, it is not surprising that
Hodgkin should argue in favour of an eastward connection for the
Cairo-Alexandria Railway. His proposals met with sharp criticism in
The Railway Times.[86]

In the spring of 1859, Sir Moses and Lady Montefiore, again accompanied by Hodgkin, hurried to Rome on an urgent mission to
Pope Pius IX. Some months earlier they had learned the terrifying
story of the abduction by papal police of a seven-year-old Jewish
child, Edgar Mortara, from his family home in Bologna. The explanation of the Church was that a servant of the Mortara family
had baptized the child six years earlier when he was critically ill and
in danger of dying without the possibility of salvation. The servant's
recent confession of the baptism to her priest had led to the child's
forced removal from his family and his placement in a Dominican
monastery where he was to be raised as a Catholic. Outrage swept
the Jews of Europe and America; many Christians were equally
incensed by the kidnapping and the violation of the parents' rights.
Jews in the Kingdom of Savoy appealed to the British Board of
Deputies which requested Sir Moses to intercede personally and to
present the family's case to the Vatican, a task he immediately
accepted.[87] For Hodgkin, it was a welcome challenge undertaken for
the 'satisfaction . . . of promoting Religious Liberty'.[88]

Unfortunately we do not possess any correspondence from Hodgkin
about the Mortara affair. The Montefiore *Diaries* describe the frus-
tration which Sir Moses endured because of the refusal of the papal
authorities to consider the case or to hear his own presentation.
Despite the support he received from British and French diplomats
in Rome, he was denied an audience with the Pope. The Papal
Secretary, Cardinal Antonelli, initially refused even to receive him,

---

*Montefiore had reluctantly abandoned his plans for a hospital because one had been
donated by the French branch of the Rothschild family. See the article by A. Schischa
'The Saga of 1855' below.

but finally granted an interview which produced no change in the stand of the Church.

The delays and anxiety inherent in the futile negotiations were temporarily alleviated by one social event. The Prince of Wales was in Rome and invited them to dinner and a musical soirée. 'A most lively and agreeable party', remarked Sir Moses, a man well accustomed to galas and feasts.[89] Dr. Hodgkin was also present, but for him the evening may have been less familiar. The Hodgkin papers contain few references to 'delights of the palate' or entertainments, other than exotica in foreign lands. As a pious Quaker he would have looked askance at the wines, liqueurs and rich foods which were undoubtedly served for the pleasure of the Prince and his guests. Lady Montefiore who was 'weak and poorly' did not attend. Indeed, she was not well for most of the trip. Her poor health added to Montefiore's distress and ultimate disappointment with what was the only admitted failure of his philanthropic career.*

This was not the first reference to Judith's poor health. Several *Diary* entries in 1857 and 1858 note her unsatisfactory condition, consultations with 'eminent' physicians such as Sir Charles Locock** and Dr Canham, and a winter in Italy for the more agreeable climate. She continued poorly after her return from the Mortara mission and throughout 1860 the story was the same.[90] In July, Hodgkin wrote to Sir Charles Locock 'at the request of our friend Sir Moses Montefiore', who was considering another trip to Palestine but was concerned about the effect of the journey on his wife whom he would not leave behind. Hodgkin pointed out that although she bore travel well, they would be 'in the east under tents in the autumn' and she was 'between 70 and 80 years of age'.[91] Locock indicated his approval nonetheless, but the plans were abandoned. Instead, Sir Moses decided to go to a 'place on the Mediterranean as recommended by . . . (Hodgkin) and Sir Charles Locock' and

---

*Despite Montefiore's valiant efforts and the outcry from many places, Edgar Mortara remained a personal ward of the Pope. He took the name Pius Mary and became a novice in the Order of Canons Regular of the Lateran at the Canonica of St. Agnes. He was ordained a priest in 1873 and gained a reputation as a saintly, pious, tireless worker, a preacher of distinction whose sermons 'breathed fire and passion'. He was sent on missions to many countries including the U.S. and England and died in Belgium in 1940. His parents, who had tried desperately to regain their son, did see him on several occasions, but apparently he was satisfied with his Catholicism. See Korn, op. cit., note 90.

**Sir Charles Locock (1799–1875) was physician-accoucheur to Queen Victoria, physician in Westminster Lying-In Hospital, President of the Royal Medical Chirurgical Society, 1857. See *Dictionary of National Biography*, XII, 55–6; Russell Maulitz, 'Metropolitan Medicine and the Man Midwife: The Early Life and Letters of Sir Charles Locock', *Med. Hist.*, xxvi (1982), 25–46.

in September he invited his doctor/friend to accompany them. Hodgkin accepted, but the patient's condition worsened and the trip was postponed. Hodgkin shared the anxiety felt by his 'attached friend', expressing to him his 'sincere desire that Providence may guide our course for the best'.[92] Throughout the winter there were further consultations and plans to avoid the severe English weather. In April the decision was made to cancel any trip for that year and instead Judith was taken from their London home to Ramsgate in an 'invalid carriage'.[93] Unfortunately for Hodgkin, he had rented his own home in anticipation of being absent for the winter months, so spent them temporarily housed by family and friends.[94]

Judith alternated between Ramsgate and London during the remainder of 1861 and the first eight months of 1862, returning to Park Lane in September. Again there was talk of going to Nice for the coming winter. Sir Charles Locock continued to favour it. Hodgkin was less optimistic.[95] His fears were borne out. Despite a temporary improvement, on 19 September, Lady Montefiore 'was seized with a very serious form of sickness & though she seemed for a time to be rallying from the attack she did not survive quite a week'.[96] 24 September was the eve of *Rosh Hashanah*, the Jewish New Year. Evening prayers were said near her bedroom so that she could hear the service. Afterward she and Sir Moses exchanged blessings as they had done on Sabbath and Holy Days for fifty years. Sir Moses was at the dining table with other members of the family when Dr. Hodgkin called him to the bedside. Both were present when she died.[*][97]

I accompanied Sir Moses to Ramsgate whither he had the corpse conveyed by a special train on seventh day night (Saturday). During the remainder of the night & early part of the following day the grave was dug by Israelites who being unaccustomed to the work found the excavation of the chalk tedious & laborious. The funeral was very largely attended by Jews from a distance & the Chief Rabbi a German from Hanover & another distinguished preacher amongst the Jews made suitable addresses on the occasion. Whatever may have been the prevailing opinion amongst the Jews in former times as to a future state it was very evident that the belief in such a state is fully entertained by their teachers as well as by Sir Moses himself. He had been most attentive & devoted to his wife & her loss at his time of life is a shock & change the effects of which are to be feared.[**]

[*]The death certificate for Judith Montefiore suggests that she died of an abdominal malignancy complicated by an intestinal obstruction. See Sonia L. Lipman, 'Judith Montefiore — First Lady of Anglo-Jewry', *Trans. Jewish Hist. Soc.*, xxi (1966), 287–303.

[**]Both men had no children. Like Montefiore, Hodgkin was deeply attached to his various nieces and nephews. His brother, John Hodgkin Jun., had eleven children and it is from him that the distinguished Hodgkin family descends.

After her death Sir Moses distributed mementoes of his wife among their friends and relatives. To Sarah Frances Hodgkin he sent a 'little souvenir' and the touching letter which begins:

My dear Madam,

It cannot, I trust be otherwise than pleasing to you to be assured by me of the very sincere Friendship and esteem entertained by my dear departed wife for Dr. Hodgkin as well as for yourself — a feeling also which for my part I shall ever cherish. And it is not indeed merely in the light of a most valued personal Friend that we have been called upon to regard your excellent and dear Husband, for superadded to his ordinary claims upon our own friendship so thoroughly established and confirmed on the occasion when we were fellow travellers together to the Holy Land — the recollection of which circumstances has always afforded us much pleasure, we have had reason to feel most grateful to him for the invaluable professional aid and services which his great experience and eminent skill and judgment enabled him to render with such true kindness and especially to dear Lady Montefiore in her last illness.[99]

During the period of Judith's decline, both Montefiore and Hodgkin were engaged together in a cause that seems as real today as it did then. In July 1860 news reached England of massacres in Syria. Sir Moses learned that more than 3,300 Christians had been killed and 151 Christian villages destroyed by Druse fanatics; 20,000 refugees were homeless. Outraged, he hastened to the City to do something about the situation. He published a letter in *The Times*, suggesting the formation of a committee to solicit funds and he made the initial contribution of £200.[100] His gesture met with immediate response from men of wealth and political importance and the British Syrian Relief Fund was organized. Dr. Hodgkin was a member of the Committee.[101] Even before they were fully operative, he drafted an appeal for funds. He drew up lists of medicines which would be needed and sought first-hand information from his friends in Syria.[102] The Committee raised large sums for distribution by the British Consuls in Damascus and Beirut. Their efforts added to the general alarm felt by Christians throughout the world.[103] Montefiore also used his influence with the Foreign Office to make certain Jews in the area did not suffer by being falsely implicated in the massacres.[104] Eventually order was restored by intervention of the European powers.*[105]

There is evidence that before her death Lady Montefiore asked

---

*The British government sent Lord Dufferin to Beirut to investigate the situation and protect his country's interests. His dispatches to the Foreign Office show a change in the original assessment of the massacres. 'However criminal may have been the excesses into which the Druzes were subsequently betrayed, the original provocation came from the Christians ... they are themselves in a great measure responsible for the torrents of blood which have been shed.' FO 78/1628, Beirut, 24 Feb. 1861, Lord Dufferin to Sir Henry Bulwer.

Dr. Hodgkin to promise to accompany her husband on future travels.[106] If so, the promise was faithfully kept. Early in 1863, Montefiore and Hodgkin set out for the east, intending to secure concessions from the Turkish government 'necessary for the proper working and expansion of institutions for our poor brethren'.[107] A new sultan was on the throne in Constantinople and Montefiore wanted to secure a reaffirmation of the privileges he had previously received. He expected to continue on to Palestine afterwards.

Hodgkin's medical skills were in demand on this journey, for Montefiore was in poor health and still suffering from the loss of his wife. There were frequent stops *en route*. Hodgkin had time to send letters to England discussing not only his friend's 'colds and weakness', but the great variety of issues which occupied his own thoughts: the small number of Friends in southern France, the 'great and rapid improvements which are going forward in every place which we have visited . . . (with which) we in England are not keeping pace', and the appointment of examiners at the University of London.[108] There were extensive comments on the current rebellion in Poland and an urgent appeal to Friends in England to send 'a thoroughly respectful yet fervent Christian appeal' on behalf of the Poles to the Russian Emperor. Sir Moses was reported to share Hodgkin's concern about the Polish crisis and to offer suggestions of a similar nature.[109] Montefiore's personal interview with the previous Czar in 1848 had apparently persuaded him that reasonableness could succeed in St Petersburg. Such a view accorded with Hodgkin's Quaker pacifism, though history was to prove both wrong.

Hodgkin had time to visit medical museums in Genoa and Florence.[110] Sir Moses spent the Passover holiday in Pisa and visited Leghorn. Hodgkin requested that information be sent him about Biblical sites such as Rebecca's Well and Laban's house, in the event they should continue on to Damascus.[111] They took the train by slow stages from Venice to Trieste to Budapest, continually uncertain as to the wisdom of continuing onward. Hodgkin worked hard 'keeping pace with my duties', but he managed to appreciate the 'convenience and better view afforded by rail travel'.[112] The museum in Larsbach gave him a chance to see 'specimens illustrative of ethnology from the Pacific Ocean and different parts of Africa.[113]

Finally, they reached Constantinople. Montefiore's health improved; Hodgkin in turn was temporarily ill.[114] Sir Moses was received by various ministers of the Sultan but forced to wait three weeks for an audience with the latter.[115] The time was not lost, however. Sir Moses made many charitable contributions in memory of Lady Montefiore.[116] Hodgkin developed detailed plans for a lying-in charity and presented a copy of his proposal for a Mechanics Institute in Jerusalem to the Local Association for the Promotion of Social Science in Turkey and Greece.[117]

Having in connection with the duties of my profession . . . been accustomed to pay attention to the circumstances which affect the health & general well being of towns I have naturally been induced, when travelling, to look to these subjects & on some of these occasions I have had the presumption to communicate the results of my observations to some of the influential residents. A case of this kind occurred when, in company with my excellent friends Sir Moses & Lady Montefiore I was at Jerusalem about six years ago . . . The idea of a Mechanics Institute having occurred to me as offering a sort of neutral ground on which all classes might harmoniously combine, whatever may be their causes of separation elsewhere . . . being suited to the poor & labouring portion of the population as well as to the rich & middle classes.

Hodgkin's additional suggestions for improvements in roads, sanitation, housing and his comments on economic development were not different from those he had made in the Holy Land.

The interview with the Sultan was finally granted 'at the Sweet Waters of Europe above the extremity of the Golden Horn. I accompanied Sir Moses and the Dragoman of the British Ambassador acted as interpreter.'[118] The Sultan, only thirty years old, was praised for his vigour, ability and interest in promoting change. He confirmed all privileges hitherto granted to his Jewish subjects and the concessions given Sir Moses for land and construction in Jerusalem. Hodgkin's concern for his patron's health forced an abandonment of the plans to continue on to Jerusalem and they returned directly to England. Montefiore wrote to express his gratitude for 'your friendship and anxious attentions to me during our long and somewhat difficult journey to the Turkish capital'.

Hodgkin continued to see Montefiore and other members of his family over the next several months. Mrs Sarah Goldsmid, Sir Moses' sister, was his patient at the time.[119] On 11 November 1863 Hodgkin was surprised to learn that Sir Moses 'wishes me at Dover on second evening so that we can take the first boat on third day morning'.[120] Six days later Montefiore left England for Morocco. 'I had also the privilege of forming one of the party', wrote Hodgkin

and as an old and attached fellow-traveller and friend, took a pleasing interest in endeavouring to maintain the health and strength of the venerable leader of the expedition, hoping that my exertions during a long journey, unavoidably attended with fatigue, difficulty, and not altogether without risk, would afford some satisfaction to Sir Moses' anxious relatives; besides which my own feelings were warmly engaged in the undertaking.[121]

Hodgkin's part in the Moroccan expedition is generally better known than is his role in the earlier journeys because his impressions were subsequently published. *A Narrative of a Journey to Morocco in 1863 and 1864*, dedicated to Sir Moses, appeared posthumously in 1866. The *Narrative* gives a complete account of the trip, including weeks in France, Spain and Gibraltar prior to and following the time spent in North Africa. Probably Hodgkin's current role in the Royal Geographical Society provided the impetus for the account. He gave careful descriptions of geology, antiquities, constructions, water systems, agricultural methods, even the horses and camels. Although his letters and journals on previous travels contained the same sort of data this was the only publication in book form.[122]

The most unusual feature of the book is four lithographs made from Hodgkin's original drawings. He was not a creative artist, but his eyes and hand, trained for pathological observation and notation, give a charming and an accurate representation of the scenes. 'The Quadrangle of the Palace at Morocco where the Sultan Received Sir Moses Montefiore' shows an immense courtyard, surrounded by high walls with arched gateways, hundreds of soldiers lined up on foot and horse, the small band of Europeans in Western clothing and the Sultan on a magnificent steed. There is an elaborate state coach to one side. 'The Encampment' gives a sense of the barren desert with low hills in the distance. In the foreground are seen the tents of Montefiore's expedition, with the British banner high upon the flagpole, and horses, camels, bearers, guides and servants busily engaged in the activities of the camp. Again, Montefiore had used personal diplomacy and moral persuasion to remedy the plight of the Jews. For Hodgkin, the experience reinforced his faith in reasonable and peaceable conduct by nations as well as by men. Both were naïve about the permanent effect of their mission. In the short run, the support Montefiore had from the British government assured success.

One has to be impressed by Montefiore's stamina and determination. He was nearly eighty years old, Hodgkin a mere sixty-five. He was besieged by delegations of Jews with requests for aid and sympathy and he tirelessly visited schools, synagogues, and other religious institutions. His personality and reputation had a strong effect on everyone with whom he came in contact. A poignant description of the octogenarian's reception by the French Emperor, Napoleon III, comes from Hodgkin's pen.[124]

On this occasion I accompanied him & was much gratified with having the opportunity of being in company with so remarkable a man. The interview was short but perfectly agreeable. The Emperor showed marked attention to

Sir Moses, placing a chair for him with his own hand & during the conversation was cheerful and smiling.

Perhaps Hodgkin, fluent in French, assisted the interview.*

Both the Montefiore *Diary* and Hodgkin *Narrative* contain descriptions of the exotic culture they found in Morocco. The magnificence of the Sultan's palace was especially impressive. The extensive gardens were abundantly planted with orange, lemon and olive trees and contained irrigation canals and two pools of water with a working model of a steam boat in one of them. The Sultan forbade any intrusion into the interior of the palace, but the gifts bestowed on the travellers and the feasts and public displays in their honour were lavish. The traditional hospitality of the Moroccan people, even those living poorly in the desert, was appreciated by the foreigners.

Hodgkin could be critical, too. Some of the Sultan's troops resembled

a sort of degraded European army ... Few, if any of the men had shoes or stockings ... their old cloth jackets were indiscriminately of red, blue, or green ... These troops had very much the appearance of prisoners clothed in left off soldiers' garments.[125]

The frequent lack of cleanliness and industriousness and the neglect of education offended him. Nonetheless, Hodgkin was eager for England

to have more intimate and more extensive intercourse with Morocco, and its present relations should be somewhat modified, although even now ... our relations with the Government are of the most friendly and cordial kind ...[126]

He appended extracts from other travellers' accounts to his *Narrative*, hoping to add further information to his countrymen's knowledge of Morocco. He also included a speech which he had delivered in Tangier at the conclusion of the journey, exhorting the citizens to make those changes which he thought would benefit their community. He especially stressed education for all classes and recommended adoption of mottoes such as 'Knowledge is Power' and 'Virtue is Happiness'.[127]

The Moroccan journey provided another opportunity for ancillary benevolences, again reflecting both Montefiore's and Hodgkin's confidence in the benefits of education and medicine. In Tangier, Montefiore donated £300 in Lady Montefiore's memory for the

---

*Montefiore wrote, 'Dr. Hodgkin went with me to the Palace and the Secretary of the Emperor kindly informed him that my Physician was with me he said he might enter this circumstance gave me much pleasure.' See Montefiore to Joseph Sebag, Paris, 1.4.1864, Sebag-Montefiore MSS.

establishment of a school for Jewish girls, similar to the one he and his wife had inaugurated in Jerusalem, and similar to one Hodgkin had tried to encourage for African girls in Liberia.[128] Both displayed an interest in education for girls long before that was a generally accepted idea. After he returned to England, Hodgkin sent a parcel of schoolbooks for the children in Mogador. Although the books were published by the British and Foreign School Society, designed primarily for Christians, Hodgkin assured the recipients that 'many Israelite children have satisfactorily attended schools where they have been used'.[129] In Mogador, Montefiore contributed money to start a hospital and Hodgkin joined in wishing success.[130] Throughout the journey, the physician responded to persons who sought his professional advice.

When Montefiore and his associates were ready to depart from Gibraltar, the Jews held a leave-taking ceremony. Speeches were made and gratitude expressed. Hodgkin felt he should contribute a few words.[131]

... poor speaker as I am, I could not remain silent, and as the only Christian present, I felt ... excited on the spur of the moment to give expression to some of the feelings which had impressed me during the course of the mission.

The words of my dear friend, Sir Moses Montefiore, recalled to mind the almost parental solicitude which, during the forty years of our acquaintance, I had experienced from himself and the late Lady Montefiore, kindness which I could not remember without emotion. Independent occasions of a professional character, during an equally long period, had brought me into more than ordinary intercourse with the Children of Israel, and I could not be insensible to the respect and kindness which they had invariably evinced towards me.

He paid homage to 'our leader' for his perseverence in obtaining the Sultan's edict, but he suggested that

it would require continued vigilance, care and caution that its object not be lost ... The Israelites of Morocco are a people who might render the greatest benefit to the country in which they live.

I alluded to the remarkable fulfilment of the prophecy that the Israelites should be as it were 'sifted amongst the nations'; but I also remembered another prophecy to the effect that 'they should be as dew from heaven', and I believed that that also would be verified in such a manner as would prove acceptable both to Jews and Christians.

Despite the pleasure and sense of accomplishment which the journeys with Montefiore provided, Hodgkin's prolonged travels were impinging on his medical practice. 'Repeated & lengthened absence from home is of course injurious to practice & I am in consequence increasingly obliged to look for income from other quarters', he told a friend in 1864.[132] His health was deteriorating also. Throughout his life he experienced periodic nervous episodes, the exact nature of which is not clear. He also suffered from a chronic intestinal disorder, and had a serious attack in 1864.[133] Hence, when he learned that Sir Moses was contemplating still another visit to Palestine, Hodgkin wrote to his brother

I do not want to absent myself from England this season for many reasons though to avoid an English Spring & go southward is always agreeable to my bodily feelings, but if I do go it may afford me the opportunity of seeing much which I missed on my first visit as well as make me of service in carrying out some plans of a public & lasting utility.[134]

Among the plans he was promoting at that time were one for the supply of medicines to Hebron and Safed and another for improvement of the water system in Jerusalem. Montefiore was also involved with the latter scheme.[135]

The proposed trip was a response to a dire situation in the Holy Land. The region had been simultaneously attacked by drought, locusts and a cholera epidemic. Relief funds were raised throughout the British Empire and Montefiore, now more than eighty years old, was asked by the Board of Deputies to administer them.[136] Hodgkin's promise to Lady Montefiore and his sense of duty took precedence over any personal hesitation, and together with Dr Loewe and Mr and Mrs Joseph Sebag, (he was a nephew to Montefiore), they left England on 27 February 1866, travelling via Paris, Marseilles and Alexandria to Jaffa, which they reached on 19 March. They expected to proceed to Jerusalem the following day, but were detained because Hodgkin was seriously ill. Contrary to the hopes he had expressed to his brother, the Mediterranean climate was not beneficial. He found the weather in Alexandria oppressive and by Jaffa he was 'in almost ceaseless agony, delirium, tenesmus, gasping'.*[137] Sir Moses provided more of the story.[138]

Being most reluctant to leave him, I remained with him up to the latest moment, until it became absolutely necessary to depart for Jerusalem, in order to arrive there in time for the Passover holidays . . . While at Jaffa I had frequently expressed my strong desire to remain there with my lamented friend, to take him with me to Jerusalem or to relinquish my journey thither, and return with him to Europe; but all my friends assured me that it would be most imprudent for Dr. Hodgkin to travel at that time, and that the best and only advisable course was to let him remain in the house of Mr. Kyat,** the British Consular Agent,

---

*Hodgkin's description and those of others present suggest he suffered from dysentery or cholera.

**Son of Assad Yacoob Kayat, appointed Vice Consul in Jaffa on the death of his father. See Great Britain, Public Record Office, FO 78/1929, Consular No. 13, British Consulate, Jerusalem, 12 May 1866.

under the most [sic] kind and watchful attendance of that gentleman and his family, with whom he had been staying since our arrival at Jaffa. Advice so earnestly urged, I could not but follow. Accordingly, on Sunday the 25th of March, having previously secured the professional services of Dr. Sozzi, the physician of the Lazaretto,* and left my own English servant, and likewise engaged another, to be constantly in attendance on my esteemed friend, I reluctantly quitted Jaffa for Jerusalem, after paying a farewell visit to my friend, in the full hope of being soon rejoined by him, and having for this purpose left for his convenience the Takhterrawan (sedan chair) which the Governor of Jerusalem had kindly sent to Jaffa for my own use. This hope, however, was not destined to be realized.

Hodgkin's last letter, dictated to his wife, evidences the twin themes of love and duty which had characterized his life, and adds his appreciation of Sir Moses' efforts during these days.[139]

I wish in the shortest terms to say all that is loving, grateful, and affectionate to thee; to thank thee for thy great kindness, and to excuse all my deficiencies.
Thou knowest how intensely I love my brother & his family but I must only send love, & say how much I have thought upon them. My dear love to all my friends; I lament the little service I have done and entreat all to (love) and serve their Lord and Master.
. . . Dear Sir Moses was obliged to leave me to go to Jerusalem, but he has been boundless in his kindness, and spared nothing for my relief.

Montefiore remained apprised of the situation in Jaffa and when he realized that, contrary to his expectations, the danger had increased he asked Captain Henry Moore, brother of the British Consul, and Dr Thomas Chaplin to hurry down to Jaffa to tend his dying friend. Dr Chaplin, a doctor assigned to the region by the Society for the Conversion of the Jews[140] described Hodgkin's final days in a letter to Mrs. Hodgkin.[141]

His sufferings were very great, but it will be some consolation to you to know that every thing that *could* be done to alleviate them was done. Nothing could exceed the kindness & solicitude of Sir Moses Montefiore . . . He (Hodgkin) prayed much & spoke often to me of the state of his mind. He said differences of religious persuasion need not separate believers — 'We are brethren in Christ, and Christ is not divided.' . . . I asked him if he would like the English clergyman from Jerusalem to visit him, he said No . . . 'If my omnipresent Lord is with me that is all the comfort I need.' He entrusted to me a package of books, relating to the Society of Friends wh he wished to remain in Jerusalem & to be lent to any one who wd like to read them. He said 'the little sect to wh I belong has been much spoken against & supposed to hold garbled doctrines, with reference to Christianity & I would like to do something however little towards removing this false impression.' Also he gave me six pairs of spectacles & some scissars (sic) for poor Jews . . . The funeral . . . was a sad & solemn scene. The mist was just clearing off the gardens, and the morning breeze came laden with the perfume of the orange flowers, as we laid him to his rest.

*Quarantine station.

Sir Moses received news of Hodgkin's death on the night of 5 April. His sorrow was profound. Apart from the death of Judith, there is no one mentioned in the *Diaries* whose death so deeply grieved him.* 'The sad event . . . overwhelmed me with sorrow and cast a gloom over me which I sought vainly to dispel.' He was unable to conduct his affairs as usual 'partly by the grief I acutely felt at the loss of my late friend, Dr Hodgkin'. On the return from Jerusalem 'I would not proceed into Jaffa until I had first visited the place which enclosed the mortal remains of my dear friend'.[142] He began to plan for the permanent grave marker. When he was back in England he purchased the granite column 'as a mark of my respect and esteem' and it was suitably engraved:

> Here rests the body of
> THOMAS HODGKIN, M.D.
> of Bedford Square, London
>
> A Man distinguished alike for Scientific
> Attainments, Medical Skill
> And self-sacrificing Philanthropy
> He died at Jaffa, the 4th of April, 1866
> In the 68th year of his Age
> In the Faith and Hope of the Gospel
>
> This tomb was Erected by
> SIR MOSES MONTEFIORE, BART.
> In Commemoration of
> A Friendship of more than 40 years
> And of Many Journeys taken together
> in Europe, Asia and Africa

A latin inscription, chosen by John Hodgkin, was included, *Humani nihil a se alienum putabat.***[143] In 1875, on his seventh and final journey to Palestine, Montefiore went immediately to 'the tomb of my much lamented friend, Dr Hodgkin', a visit he repeated before departing from the country. He ordered that 'for the better preservation of the ground, a suitable railing should be made round the monument. It was a melancholy occasion . . .'.[144]

Montefiore's estimation of his friend, 'one so guileless, so pious, so amiable in private life, so respected in his public career, and so desirous to assist with all his heart in the amelioration of the human race' reflected 'a long and intimate association with me, and with my late dearly beloved wife'.[145] Hodgkin might easily have used similar words about Montefiore, for the Jewish financier and the Quaker

*Since the original diaries were largely destroyed and what we have was edited by Dr Loewe, one can not say for certain how Montefiore felt about his friends or relatives.

**'He thought nothing of humanity was alien to him', based on the words of Terence.

physician were 'kindred souls'. Each felt compelled to effect improvements in the lives of others and each had confidence in his ability to
do so. One might say that they did not differ from any English
philanthropists of the nineteenth century whose eagerness to 'do
good' led to a proliferation of societies for the benefit of the poor,
diseased, illiterate and oppressed.[146] The support which Montefiore
received from the British government, the moral and financial re-
inforcement of the Anglo-Jewish community, the traditional philanthropic commitment of the Quakers — all these had a part in their
attitude and their actions. Yet these two were willing, indeed eager,
to extend themselves far more than most people. They had a genuine
passion for philanthropy. It is this which each recognized in the
other. Their fervent sense of duty characterized their individual
lives and forged their friendship.

NOTES

1. The Hodgkin-Montefiore friendship has been commented upon by many
   writers, most recently Alex Sakula, 'Dr. Thomas Hodgkin and Sir Moses
   Montefiore Bart. — the friendship of two remarkable men', *J. Roy. Soc.
   Med.*, lxxiv (May, 1979), 382—7; E. S. Stern, 'Dr Hodgkin's Relationship
   with his Distinguished Friend and Patient, Sir Moses Montefiore, Bt FRS',
   Med. Hist., xi (April, 1967), 182—5.
2. The primary source used for Montefiore is the *Diaries of Sir Moses and
   Lady Montefiore*, ed. Louis Loewe (2 vol., London, Griffith Farrer Okeden
   and Welsh, 1890: reprinted 1983). The standard biographies used are Paul
   Goodman, *Moses Montefiore* (Philadelphia, Jewish Publication Society
   of America, 1925); Lucien Wolf, *Sir Moses Montefiore, A Centennial
   Biography with Selections from Letters and Journals* (New York, Harper
   & Bro., 1885). Also, Paul H. Emden, *Jews of Britain* (London, Sampson
   Low, Marston & Co., 1943); Albert M. Hyamson, *Moses Montefiore, His
   Life and Times* (London, Jewish Religious Educational Publications, 1951);
   Cecil Roth, *Essays and Portraits in Anglo-Jewish History* (Philadelphia,
   Jewish Publication Society of America, 1962).
3. *Lancet*, I (April, 1866), 445—6.
4. Thomas Hodgkin, Obituary, *Soc. Sci. Review, Sanitary Review and Journal
   of the Sciences*, xxx (June, 1866), 534—9.
5. For Hodgkin's life and career, see Edward H. Kass and Anne H. Bartlett,
   'Thomas Hodgkin, M.D. (1798—1866): An Annotated Bibliography', *Bull.
   Hist. Med.*, cxv (Mar.—Apr., 1969), 138—75; Edward H. Kass, 'Thomas
   Hodgkin, Physician and Social Scientist', *Guy's Hosp. Rep.*, cxv (1966),
   269—80; Michael Rose, *Curator of The Dead, Thomas Hodgkin (1798—
   1866)*, (London, Peter Owen, 1981).
   The papers of Thomas Hodgkin, MD have been microfilmed and are on
   deposit at the Countway Library, Harvard Medical School, Boston. Citations
   hereafter made in this paper refer to the reel and item as catalogued under

the direction of Dr Edward H. Kass, Channing Laboratory, Harvard Medical School. The first nineteen reels of the Hodgkin papers, in the same order, are also on deposit at Friends House Library, London, where they are numbered MSS 178 to MSS 196. 'A Cursory Index to the Thomas Hodgkin Microfilms in the Library of the Society of Friends, London' was compiled by L. D. Pedersen, November, 1980.

6. Edward H. Kass, Anne B. Carey, Amalie M. Kass, 'Thomas Hodgkin and Benjamin Harrison: Crisis and Promotion in Academia', *Med. Hist.* xxiv (April, 1980), 192–208.

7. Goodman, op. cit., pp. 218–19.

8. *Lancet*, note 3 above.

9. Ibid.

10. Ibid.

11. Montefiore, *Diaries i*, pp. 108–9.

12. Westminster Monthly Meeting, *Minutes, Vol. 16 and 17*, Friends House Library.

13. Cecil Roth, *A History of the Jews in England*, 3rd ed. (Oxford, Clarendon Press, 1964), p. 24; Elizabeth Isichei, *Victorian Quakers* (London, Oxford University Press, 1970), p. 112. For nineteenth century Anglo-Jewry, see also V. D. Lipman, 'The Age of Emancipation 1815–1880,' in V. D. Lipman, ed. *Three Centuries of Anglo-Jewish History* (Jewish Historical Society of England, printed by W. Heffer, Cambridge, 1961), pp. 69–106.

14. Lipman, op. cit., p. 87.

15. Chaim Bermant, *The Cousinhood* (New York, Macmillan, 1972), pp. 423–8, points out the analogies between Anglo-Jewry and The Society of Friends.

16. Amalie M. Kass and Edward H. Kass, 'Martin Delany, Thomas Hodgkin, and the Black Nationalist Movement,' *N.E.J. Med.* 305 (17 Sept. 1981), 682–4; Amalie M. Kass, 'Dr. Thomas Hodgkin, Dr. Martin Delany and the "Return to Africa"', *Med. Hist.*, 27: 4 (Oct. 1983).

17. George W. Stocking, Jr., 'What's in a name? The Origins of the Royal Anthropological Institute (1837–71)', *Man*, vi (1971), 369–90.

18. *Journal of The Royal Geographical Society of London*, i, (1830–1), xvii; *Proceedings, Royal Geographical Society*, N.S. vii (1885), 616.

19. *Index to Reports and Transactions of the British Association for the Advancement of Science from 1831 to 1861 inclusive* (London, John Murray, 1864); See also the annual reports of the Association for Hodgkin on the Council and sub-sections.

20. *British and Foreign Medical Review*, xiii (Jan–Apr. 1842), 579–80; *Lancet*, (1842–3, vol. 1), 867; (1842–3, vol. 2), 454; (1943–4, vol. 1), 755, 764–6; *London Medical Gazette*, xxxi (1842–3) 905–8; The Ladies' Benevolent Association for Syria and the Holy Land Established in June 1844, for the purpose of co-operating with the Syrian Medical-Aid Association in affording Comfort and Relief to the Sick of ALL NATIONS, the aged, and the indigent blind, in Syria and Palestine (London: William Watts, 1845).

21. For Benjamin Thorpe, see *Dictionary of National Biography*, xix, pp. 795–96. Thorpe later abandoned banking and became one of England's outstanding Anglo-Saxon scholars.

22. See note 5 above. John Hodgkin Sen. to Thomas Hodgkin, 14 Oct. 1821, 3: 257.

23. John Hodgkin, Jun., *Autobiography*, unpub. mss., 13:232; John Hodgkin, Jun., to John Hodgkin, Sen., 19 Sept. 1822, 4:73.

24. Benjamin Thorpe to Thomas Hodgkin, 24 Nov. 1822, 8:90.

25. Benjamin Thorpe to John Hodgkin, Sen., 31 Jan. 1823, 8:93.

26. Thomas Hodgkin to John Hodgkin, Sen., 4 Aug. 1823, 14:16.

27. John Hodgkin, Sen. to Thomas Hodgkin, 1 Aug. 1823, 14:19; John Hodgkin Sen. to Thomas Hodgkin, 24 Aug. 1823, 14:20.

28. Thomas Hodgkin to John Hodgkin, Sen., 6 Sept. 1823, 6:192.

29. Montefiore, *Diaries*, i, p. 28; Thomas Hodgkin to Elizabeth Hodgkin, 11 Dec. 1823, 2:202.

30. Thomas Hodgkin to Elizabeth and John Hodgkin, Sen., n.d., [Sept. 1823], 6:194.

31. Thomas Hodgkin to John Hodgkin, Jun., 22 Oct. 1823, 6:193.

32. Thomas Hodgkin to John Hodgkin, Jun., 12 Nov. 1823, 2:201.

33. Thomas Hodgkin to John Hodgkin, Jun., 29 Nov. 1823, 2–203.

34. *Diaries*, i, p. 28; 1824, 2:206.

35. Thomas Hodgkin to John Hodgkin, Jun., 29 Dec. 1823, 2–205.

36. Abraham Montefiore to Thomas Hodgkin, 8 Jan. 1824, 2:208.

37. M. A. Favell (?) to Thomas Hodgkin, n.d., 2:242.

38. Thomas Hodgkin to John Hodgkin, Sen., 11 Jan. 1824, 2:209.

39. Thomas Hodgkin to John Hodgkin, Sen., 24 Jan. 1824, 2:210.

40. John Hodgkin, Jun., to Thomas Hodgkin, 29 Jan. 1824, 14:36.

41. *Diaries*, i, p. 28.

42. Thomas Hodgkin to John Hodgkin, Sen., 25 Jan. 1824, 2:211; Elizabeth and John Hodgkin, Sen. to Thomas Hodgkin, 20 Feb. 1824, 14:38 and 25 Feb. 1824, 14:39.

43. 29 Dec. 1823, 2:204. I am grateful to Dr. Vivian Nutton, Wellcome Institute for the History of Medicine, for translating the Latin portion of this letter.

44. John Hodgkin, Sen. to Thomas Hodgkin, 13 Mar. 1824, 14:42; Prospectus for Alliance British & Foreign Life & Fire Assurance Co., to Thomas Hodgkin, 2:161; Certificate for Alliance British & Foreign Life and Fire Assurance Co., March 1824, 25:67.

45. 17 May 1824, 8:115.

46. John Hodgkin, Jun. to Thomas Hodgkin, 19 Mar. 1824, 14:42.

47. Prospectus addressed to Thomas Hodgkin, Esq., 2:173; John Hodgkin Sr. to Thomas Hodgkin, 26 Jan. 1825, 14:82.

48. John Hodgkin, Jun., S. Newham, & R. Godlee to Alliance British and Foreign Life and Fire Assurance, Co., 1872, 2:145; Thomas Hodgkin MD, deceased, Statement of Assets, 9:70.

49. Wolf., op. cit., p. 25.

50. *Diaries*, i, p. 80.

51. Thomas Hodgkin to John Hodgkin, Jun., 1 Sept. 1824, 6:199.

52. 20 April 1824, 2:230.

53. Wolf, op. cit., p. 238.

54. Goodman, op. cit., p. 218.

55. *Diaries*, i, pp. 55–6. Similar references to 'eminent physicians' appear in *Diaries*, ii, pp. 32–3, 37.

56. Thomas Hodgkin to the President, Treasurer and members of The Society of United Israelites, 25 Sept. 1831, 12:10; Aaron Hart to Thomas Hodgkin, 12 Oct. 1831, 4:332; Thomas Hodgkin to The President, Treasurer and Committee of The Society of United Sisters, n.d., 12:11; Thomas Hodgkin to H. Drummond, n.d., 12:109.

57. Mariabella Hodgkin Fry, 'Personal Recollections of Dr. Hodgkin', n.d. [1919], 10:73.
58. Thomas Hodgkin to Moses Montefiore, 8 Dec. 1836, 12:65.
59. Moses Montefiore to John Hodgkin, Jun., 1 Sep. 1837, 8:5.
60 Thomas Hodgkin, D.C.L., *Autobiography*, MSS, n.d., 15:169.
61. Thomas Hodgkin to John Hodgkin, Sen., 7 Jun. 1837, 6:252.
62. Moses Montefiore to Thomas Hodgkin, 7 Nov. 1838, 25:45.
63. Thomas Hodgkin to Sir Moses and Lady Montefiore, 28 June 1840, 19:226.
64. Thomas Hodgkin to n.n., 1 May 1849, 13:48.
65. Thomas Hodgkin to John Hodgkin, Jun., 11 March 1857, 2:255.
66. Thomas Hodgkin to John Hodgkin, Jun., 18 April 1857, 7:256.
67. Thomas Hodgkin to John Hodgkin Jr, 3 May 1857, 7:258; Thomas Hodgkin to Sir J. Clark, 3 May 1857, 13:116.
68. John Hodgkin, Jun. to Thomas Hodgkin, 14 June 1857; 4:259.
69. For Montefiore's account of the journey, see *Diaries*, ii, pp. 63—71.
70. *Diaries*, ii, p. 66.
71. Hodgkin, *Journal*, 26 May 1857, 13:117.
72. Ibid., 14 June 1857.
73. Thomas Hodgkin to Hudson Gurney, 28 July 1857, 13:123.
74. Moses Montefiore to E. T. Rogers, Esq., 3 June 1857, 9:2, draft by Hodgkin. For the British Consul's view of Montefiore's railway scheme, see James Finn to The Earl of Clarendon, FO 78/1294 (Pol. No. 23), in Hyamson, *British Consulate in Jerusalem, loc. cit.*, No. 184.
75. E. Finn, Jr., 'On The Anglican Church and Consulate House at Jerusalem', 1:221; E. Finn, Jr., to [Thomas Hodgkin], 17 Nov. 1857, 1:215.
76. Ibid; *Journal of The Society of Arts*, 4 Sept. 1857, pp. 579—81.
77. Hodgkin, *Journal*, n.d. [June, 1857], 13:121.
78. *Diaries*, ii, p. 71.
79. Hodgkin, *Journal*, 6 July 1857, 13:121.
80. 9 July 1857, 23:21.
81. Thomas Hodgkin to Hudson Gurney, note 73 above.
82. Thomas Hodgkin, 'Some observations respecting certain Geological Appearances, which attracted my notice, in the course of my late journey', MSS, 1:222; 1:220.
83. 13:119. The *Reports of the British Association for the Advancement of Science* show that this paper was not read at the 1857 meeting. However, the Minutes of the Council of the Ethnological Society of London state that a paper on the Bedouins was read by Dr Hodgkin, 25 Nov. 1857.
84. *Jrl. Soc. Arts*, note 76 above.
85. 13:122.
86. *Literary Gazette and Journal of Archaeology, Science and Art*, No. 2126 (17 Oct. 1857), 1005; *Br. Assoc. Adv. Sci. Rep.* Pt. II (1857), 199; *Diaries*, i, p. 31; *The Railway Times*, xx, No. 39 (19 Sept. 1857), 1354—5.
87. *Diaries*, ii, pp. 86—7; Cecil Roth, op. cit. p. 271; Bertram Wallace Korn, *The American Reaction to The Mortara Case 1858—1859* (Cincinnati, American Jewish Archives, 1957), *passim*.
88. John Hodgkin Jun. to Thomas Hodgkin, 17 Feb. 1859, 4:277; Thomas Hodgkin to John Hodgkin, Jun., 1 Mar. 1859, 10:59.
89. *Diaries*, ii, pp. 91—2.
90. *Diaries*, ii, pp. 74—6, 108, 111, 112, 115.
91. 12 July 1860, 13:149.

92. Thomas Hodgkin to Sir Moses Montefiore, 5 Feb. 1861, 13:167; *Diaries*, ii, pp. 116, 121.
93. *Diaries*, ii, pp. 127—8.
94. Thomas Hodgkin to Leonidas Dracachis, 7 Feb. 1861, 18:330; Thomas Hodgkin to Hudson Gurney, 3 April 1861, 13:171.
95. Thomas Hodgkin to John Hodgkin, Jun., 6 Sept. 1862, 7:293; *Diaries*, ii, p. 136.
96. Thomas Hodgkin to W. A. Gurney, 19 Oct. 1862, 13:194.
97. *Diaries*, ii, p. 138.
98. See note 96 above.
99. Nov. 1862, 14:125.
100. *Diaries*, ii, pp. 112—14; Great Britain, Public Record Office, FO 78/1549, Sir Culling Eardley Eardley to Lord John Russell, 1 Aug. 1860.
101. 'Resolutions of Meeting of General Committee', 19 April 1861, British Syrian Relief Fund. I am grateful to Mr. Robert Sebag-Montefiore for enabling me to use the Montefiore material related to the British Syrian Relief Fund and other Montefiore manuscripts.
102. 13:149; Thomas Hodgkin to M. Spartali, 1 Sept. 1860, 18:308; Thomas Hodgkin to Leonides Dracachis, 2 Feb. 1861, 18:330.
103. *Lancet* (1860, vol. ii), p. 442; Correspondence with Syria, British Syrian Relief Fund, February—March 1861, Montefiore MSS.; Charles H. Churchill, *The Druzes and The Maronites under the Turkish Rule* (New York, Arno Press Reprint, 1973); Francis Lenormant, *Les Derniers Evenements de Syrie* (Paris, Ch. Douniol, 1869); n.n., *The Massacres in Syria* (New York, Robert M. DeWitt, 1860).
104. Great Britain, Public Record Office, FO 78/1551, Sir Moses Montefiore to Lord John Russell, 16 Oct. 1860; Sir Culling Eardley Eardley to Lord John Russell, 20 Oct. 1860; Foreign Office to Sir Moses Montefiore, 26 Oct. 1860; Sir Moses Montefiore to Lord John Russell, 30 Oct. 1860; *Diaries*, ii, pp. 117—21.
105. Great Britain, Public Record Office, FO 78/1497, 1498, 1499, 1624, 1626, 1628, 1629 contain dispatches and correspondence regarding British intervention in the Syrian crisis and the transfer of sums by the British Syrian Relief Fund to the affected areas. See also *Diaries*, ii, pp. 125—6, 132, and 'Resolutions of the Meeting of the General Committee', note 101 above. The Syrian Relief Committee was anxious to promote cotton cultivation in Syria as a scheme which would also relieve the cotton shortage caused by the American Civil War. Hodgkin had supported similar schemes in Africa, see note 16 above.
106. Sarah Frances Hodgkin to John Hodgkin, Jun., 4 June 1866, 9:57.
107. *Diaries*, ii, p. 141. For Montefiore's account of the journey see *Diaries*, ii, pp. 141—3.
108. Thomas Hodgkin to Jules Paradon, 1 Feb. 1863, 13:200; Thomas Hodgkin to Peter Bedford, 13 Feb. 1863, 13:263; Thomas Hodgkin to Sir James Clark, 8 April 1863, 13:207.
109. Thomas Hodgkin to John Hodgkin, Jun., 25 Feb. 1863, 13:204; Thomas Hodgkin to Thomas Young, 18 April 1863, 13:208.
110. Thomas Hodgkin to Dr Beke, 20 Mar. 1863, 13:206.
111. Thomas Hodgkin to John Hodgkin, Jun., 6 May 1863, 7:298.
112. Thomas Hodgkin to Dr N. Shaw, n.d. [1863], 13:210.
113. Thomas Hodgkin to Leon Halperson, 25 May 1863, 13:213.
114. Thomas Hodgkin to Joseph Sebag, 28 May 1863, Sebag-Montefiore MSS. Once again Hodgkin acted as amanuensis for Montefiore.

115. *Diaries*, ii, pp. 142—3.
116. Thomas Hodgkin to Dr Foote, 20 May 1863, 13:215; Thomas Hodgkin, notes, 13:213.
117. Thomas Hodgkin to Hudson Gurney, 6 June 1863, 13:216.
118. 3 July 1863, 9:80.
119. Thomas Hodgkin to Vito Sonsino, 13 Aug. 1863, 13:228; Thomas Hodgkin to Joseph Sebag, 1 January 1863 [1864], Sebag-Montefiore MSS.
120. Thomas Hodgkin to John Hodgkin, Jun., 7:295.
121. Thomas Hodgkin, *Narrative of a Journey to Morocco* (London, T. Cautley Newby, 1866; also reprint, New York, Arno Press and New York Times, 1971), p. 4.
122. Hodgkin, *Narrative*, *passim*. See also Royal Geographical Society of London, *Proceedings*, ix (1865), 24—7 for Hodgkin's report; 'Dr. Hodgkin on some Geological appearances in the Northwest of Morocco', *British Assoc. for the Adv. of Sci.*, 1864, 58; 'Dr. Hodgkin on the Growth of desert in Morocco', ibid., 191.
123. For Montefiore's account of the Moroccan journey, see *Diaries*, ii, pp. 146—6.
124. Thomas Hodgkin to T. F. Reade, n.d. [1864], 18:171.
125. Hodgkin, *Narrative*, p. 79.
126. Ibid., p. 127.
127. Ibid., pp. 153—7.
128. Thomas Hodgkin to J. J. Roberts, 19 Aug. 1861, 19:31; Thomas Hodgkin to Rev James Payne, 22 July 1862, 19:67.
129. Thomas Hodgkin to J. L. Yuly Jun., 17 Oct. 1865, 19:157.
130. Sir Moses to n.n., draft by Thomas Hodgkin, n.d., 19:180.
131. Hodgkin, *Narrative*, pp. 106—7.
132. Thomas Hodgkin to n.n., 4 June 1864.
133. Thomas Chaplin to John Hodgkin Jun., 12 May 1866, 23:28.
134. Thomas Hodgkin to John Hodgkin, Jun., 25 Jan. 1866, 19:169.
135. Thomas Hodgkin to Daniel Hanbury Jun., 6 June 1864, 19:109; Thomas Hodgkin to Sir Henry James, 19 Aug. 1865, 8:143; Sir Henry James to Thomas Hodgkin, 28 Aug. 1865, 8:273; *Diaries*, ii, p. 166.
136. *Diaries*, ii, pp. 169—73.
137. Thomas Hodgkin to Sarah Frances Hodgkin, by Habib Kayat, n.d. [March, 1866], 15:168.
138. *Diaries*, ii, pp. 172—3.
139. See note 137 above.
140. W. T. Gidney, *The History of the London Society for Promoting Christianity amongst the Jews from 1809 to 1908* (London, The London Society for Promoting Christianity, etc., 1908), p. 325.
141. 17 April 1866, 23:46.
142. *Diaries*, ii, pp. 180, 187—8.
143. Sarah Frances Hodgkin to John Hodgkin, Jun., 4 Aug. 1866, 9:60.
144. *Diaries*, ii, 274; *An Open Letter addressed to Sir Moses Montefiore, Bt., . . . together with A Narrative of forty days sojourn in the Holy Land by Sir Moses Montefiore on his return from his seventh pilgrimage to the Land of Promise, 9 Ellul 5625, 9 Sept. 1875* (London, Wertheimer, Lea & Co., 1875), pp. 60, 68.
145. *Diaries*, ii, p. 173.
146. David Owen, *English Philanthropy 1660—1960* (Cambridge, Harvard University Press, 1964), pp. 3—5.

5

Louis Loewe: Aide and Confidant

RAPHAEL LOEWE

A great—grandson who endeavours to address himself in an academic manner to the achievements of his ancestor is liable to find the edge of his scholarship blunted by *pietas*. Dr Louis Loewe died some thirty-one years before my own birth, and although I heard much about him from his son, my grandfather, and others, the natural veneration of his family for his memory in effect made him for me as legendary a figure as was Sir Moses Montefiore himself. In the following attempt to record, and assess, his share in their co-operative endeavours I rely almost entirely on documents: a few items of oral tradition that seem to me pertinent are marked as such.

In order to appreciate Louis Loewe's supportive role in Montefiore's work, it is necessary to sketch briefly his own background and early life.[1] He was born (Eliezer Ha-Levi Loewe) in Zülz, now called Biala, south-east of Breslau near Oppeln (Opole) in what was Prussian Silesia, in 1809, the son of Marcus (b.) Jacob Löwe (Mordecai Ha-Levi), the local rabbi; and he received a rabbinical education in his home town, at Lissa, Nikolsburg and at Pressburg (Bratislava), where he was one of the pupils of Moses Sopher (Schreiber),[2] who is generally known by the title of his posthumously published *responsa* as the *Ḥatham Sopher,* the bastion of traditionalist reaction against incipient reform in Judaism. With this foundation he then pursued his secular studies at the universities of Vienna and Berlin, where he obtained his doctorate. He possessed remarkable talents as a linguist. It is recorded that in 1840 he addressed a crowded synagogue in Galata, across the water from Istanbul, in four languages, and he is credited with competence in no less than thirty-nine; he enjoyed a contemporary reputation of being one of the foremost linguists in Europe. An invitation to catalogue a coin collection in Hamburg led him to develop an interest in oriental numismatics, and it was the desire to pursue research in the rich oriental manuscript holdings at Oxford, Cambridge, and the British Museum that first brought him to England in 1835. It was then that he met the Montefiores in London and was entertained by them in Ramsgate.[3] He was requested by Montefiore to draw up a plan for travels in Palestine, and the holograph letter of thanks for his having done so is reproduced in Loewe's edition of the Montefiore *Diaries*. He was also introduced to the Duke of Sussex,[4] an uncle of the future Queen Victoria, whose literary interests had led him to Hebrew — in which he acquired some modest ability — and to the encouragement of semitic scholarship as pertinent to biblical studies. The Duke of Sussex and Sir Sidney Smith,[5] who had defended Acre against Napoleon, financed Loewe to travel widely in the eastern Mediterranean and the Nile valley, studying languages, ethnology, and Egyptian antiquities,[6] and during these journeys he occasionally corresponded with Montefiore. On his return to Europe early in 1839 he chanced to encounter the Montefiores in Rome *en route* for Palestine,[7] and they persuaded him to accompany them as Montefiore's secretary. Presumably it was during that visit that their friendship was cemented in such manner as to lead Montefiore to invite Loewe to return with him to England, where he had some scholarly standing both by virtue of his reputation and as 'orientalist' to the Duke of Sussex. One has to assume also that Montefiore gave him some assurance of financial viability, though not definite employment, for at the beginning of his own diary for the 'Damascus' journey of 1840, Loewe wrote on 7 July, 'Sir Moses engaged me for the Mission to act in the quality of Secretary and Interpreter of Oriental and Modern languages.'[8]

That the relationship of the two men ripened through a sense of interdependence into one of close friendship and confidence is reflected between the lines of the *Diaries* in many places and particularly in the account of Sir Moses' last days.[9] It is also attested in a large collection of holograph letters from Montefiore to Loewe in my possession, dated between *c.* 1844 and 1879, in which he regularly addresses Loewe as 'Dear Doctor'. It is therefore pertinent to consider what led Montefiore quickly to appreciate that Loewe could prove a particularly valuable assistant and collaborator in carrying out the projects that he nurtured for philanthropic work directed towards Jewry in general and the Jews of Palestine in particular, and the defence of his people against prejudice and calumny wherever they might occur.

Obviously, Loewe's linguistic range — which included Arabic, Turkish, and, one may surmise, also Russian — was a primary consideration: Montefiore himself commanded Italian and French, but was innocent of Yiddish, and the fact that he regularly addressed his letters to 'Dr Löewe' surely indicates that he did not know any German either. But personal qualities also played a part. The terms of the invitations to dine in Park Lane or to stay at East Cliff Lodge in Ramsgate, frequently extended by Moses or Judith Montefiore

to the Loewes, make it clear that the two couples found each other's
company congenial. The *Dictionary of National Biography* records
that Loewe was of a retiring nature, and averse from public life; and
Montefiore, whose diary makes it clear enough that he himself
relished cutting a figure on a prominent stage, was perhaps glad to
have as his colleague someone who, whilst accepting substantial
delegated responsibility, was in no way concerned to steal the lime-
light. Thirdly, there was a congruence in attitude towards the polity
no less than the politics of Jewry: in politics, a pragmatism that gave
priority to integration as the route to Anglo-Jewish emancipation,
rather than the assertion of claims to emancipation as a right, on
doctrinaire grounds of political philosophy (although in due course
Montefiore ungrudgingly recognized the achievements of the pro-
tagonists of this approach).[10] As regards the internal polity of
Anglo-Jewry, both men maintained a conservative respect for rabbinic
institutions that would not countenance the programme of would-be
reformers. Already, at the time of Loewe's first visit to England,
Solomon Hirschel, rabbi of the Great Synagogue in London, perhaps
jealous of a young rabbinic scholar's abilities and suspicious of his
western academic qualifications, had written to the *Ḥatham Sopher*
asking whether Loewe's credentials were in order, and whether he
was likely in any way to lend himself to the endeavours of the reformers; and the fact that the *Hatham Sopher's* answer, which is not
preserved, was apparently reassuring, did not deter Hirschel from
trying again.[11] One would much like to know what advice Loewe
gave Montefiore (it seems inconceivable that they would not have
discussed the matter) in 1853, when Montefiore, as president of the
Board of Deputies, gave his casting vote against the admission of
deputies to represent the Reform Synagogue;[12] unfortunately
neither the *Diaries* nor the letters in my possession throw any light
on this.

A few other biographical details remain to be noted as relevant to
Loewe's work with Montefiore. In 1844 he applied for the Chair
of Hebrew at University College London, and although his appointment was recommended by the committee of academics to whom
applications were remitted, it was not implemented. The college
records make it clear, between the lines, that Loewe's appointment
was not acceptable to Sir Isaac Lyon Goldsmid, whose wishes as a
founder and benefactor of the College had to be taken into account,
and a contributory factor may well have been Loewe's sponsorship
by Montefiore: he and Goldsmid took opposing views regarding
emancipation, and were not on the most cordial of terms.[13] Loewe
thereupon started a private boarding school at Brighton, later

transferred to Broadstairs, which he maintained alongside his work for Montefiore until the latter's death, except for the three years (1855—58) during which he was the first Principal of Jews' College — or, strictly speaking, Headmaster of Jews' College School that was the first phase of its foundation.[14] Even when the Judith, Lady Montefiore College opened in Ramsgate in 1869 with Loewe as the Principal, he continued to run the Broadstairs school. The significance of these aspects of Loewe's affairs lies in the circumstance that he was not, apparently, ever a full-time salaried official in Montefiore's employ, even though much — one may suspect most — of his time was devoted to work for Montefiore. One can only guess at the reasons — possibly a wish on one side to preserve independence, and on the other to respect it. The effect, so family tradition has it, was that Loewe never quite knew where he stood financially.[15]

The Montefiore *Diaries* are frequently suggestive of the kind of services for which Sir Moses needed Loewe, but Loewe's reticence naturally tended to suppress his own part. There are also Loewe's own diary for 1840[16] and Montefiore's surviving letters to him. The number of times that Loewe is asked in these letters to meet Montefiore in London — mostly at the office of the Alliance Assurance, where Montefiore could apparently entertain guests to dinner — indicates that there will have been much that was unrecorded in their exchange of ideas; so that one ought not to assume, from the absence of letters on certain topics, which will certainly have interested both men, that the subjects were never ventilated. Conspicuously lacking, for instance, is reference in the letters to Anglo-Jewish affairs (see above, n. 10). Moreover, that advice was asked on many topics and about many people and their proposals and solicitations is attested by the tradition (passed to me by my Father) that Loewe was frequently regarded as Montefiore's *éminence grise*: the reason being that, when Montefiore wished to refuse a request with minimum embarrassment, his usual formula was: 'I will first ask Dr Loewe.'

A major area for which Loewe was responsible was the handling of Montefiore's voluminous foreign correspondence. A great many of Montefiore's own letters refer to enclosures requiring draft replies, or acknowledge receipt of such and indicate that he has signed and despatched them. (It would seem that a kind of 'diplomatic bag' travelled between London and Brighton or Ramsgate, presumably by rail rather than simply through the Post Office.) Loewe wrote a very fair European hand, and his rabbinic Hebrew script, like his Arabic, was exquisite. Many of the letters that Montefiore received

enclosed remittances for Palestine — sometimes of quite small sums,
less than £10 — from the United Kingdom, from eastern Europe and
from America, and it would seem that Montefiore let it be known that
he was willing to be used as a collecting agent. One letter, dated 10
April 1856, encloses £10 to be forwarded to those who devote themselves 'to the study of the Law at Tiberias'. Montefiore had received
this from Sir Francis Palgrave,[17] the historian (1788–1861), himself
an apostate from Judaism, with strict instructions that the money was
to be transmitted anonymously. Loewe had the task of preparing the
necessary papers for sending the money, through Rothschilds', to
Beirut, and he must have found it irksome and sometimes frustrating,
as the following letter from Montefiore indicates:

Grosvenor Gate Park Lane
19 June 1850

Dear Doctor
   This morning I received a letter from Warsaw, containing a Bill drawn at
Vienna for Piastres 36815 payable at Constantinople I am at aloss [sic] to
know   how I should act I must not remit it to M Roquerbe & Co at Beirout,
as they made on the last occasion, a very large and heavy charge on giving
money for a similar Bill. I have but one way of remitting that is to say to give
the Bill to Messrs Rothschild in London, they will say how much sterling money
they can give for it and for that amount they will give an order on Beirout but I
am sure there will be a heavy loss on the transaction and the poor instead of
getting 36815 Piastres will only receive perhaps 10 per cent less
   I had hoped that the good people of Warsaw would have seen the desirability
of sending a Bill on London instead of Constantinople which I think you desired
them to do in future
   I will endeavour to see some of the Turkish merchants & to find out if it be
possible to get an order on Beirout for the Bill on Constantinople on allowing
them a Commission . . . . I hope to have the benefit of your advice in the matter —
I am very anxious that you be so good as to prepare a letter to Warsaw in reply
to their communication repeating to them, the difficult position that I am
placed in by their Indirect remittance from neither Banker or Merchant and
cannot expose myself to risk, or what I consider still worse the possibility of
acting not in accordance with their Wishes . . .

Or again, on 3 June 1856:

I have just received the large packet of letters you have so promptly written for
my signature for remittances to the Holy Land and acknowledgments to the
Parties who remitted the money if it were not that I well know the deep interest
you take in the prosperity of our Brethren in the East I should wish you might
have a little rest and that no fresh Bills would come to disturb you for sometime
[sic] but I believe this would not give you pleasure as you devote yourself to
the happiness of others.

   A counterpart to Loewe's handling of the foreign correspondence
was his accompanying Montefiore on most of his foreign missions,

the exception being the Morocco visit in 1863. In a fragmentary letter, probably written in November 1863, which details his travel plans and the members of his party, Montefiore writes to Loewe: 'I regret very much you cannot accompany me on this Mission.' The sort of lynx-eyed counsel that Loewe could afford him is well illustrated by an incident in the 'Damascus' mission of 1840, recorded (in Loewe's words, not Montefiore's) in the *Diaries* at 29 August,[18] when he was shown the final draft of the Turkish statement regarding the victims of the blood—accusation, and noticed that it contained the word *afu,* meaning *pardon.* Despite chancery rejoinders that the word was not univocal, Loewe insisted on having it emended to read 'honourable release'. He sent Munk (who, though a distinguished Arabist, did not know Turkish) with the Arabic version to alert Montefiore and Crémieux to the unacceptability of the draft as it stood, but Munk went to Crémieux only. 'Monsieur Crémieux (Loewe wrote, editorially, in the *Diaries*) being probably anxious to see the misleading word removed . . . came at once . . . without informing Sir Moses . . . The Pasha . . . ordered that the word "*Afoo*" should be taken out, and the words "*itlak ve Tervîhh*", signifying "an honourable liberation", substituted . . .'. Crémieux, much to Montefiore's annoyance, thus attained the semblance of priority and so the primary credit for eliciting from Mehemet Ali a document in acceptable form.[19] Loewe's private diary is less circumspect:[20]

Negeb Effendi . . . wanted to argue that similar expressions might be used even without it signifying the word *pardon*. Mr Munk, however, as well as myself, said that we certainly would not suffer such an expression. I mentioned several expressions where the word originally had no other meaning than *to pardon*, and I requested Mr. Munk, as I wished to wait for the Turkish copies and also for the Firman, to go home and to inform Sir M. of all which had taken place. Mr. Munk had with him an Arabic translation of the Turkish order which was made for him at the Palace (as he does not understand Turkish), and I certainly expected that he would show it to Sir Moses . . . . On my entering the room of Sir Moses I found Messrs Harris, Bell and Mr. Stephens (the latter who writes for *The Times*). All of them knew that I was at the Palace and all expected to see the happy instrument of the liberation of the Jews. I, however, thought it prudent not to mention a word about the displeasing term, as I was sure Sir M. would rather sacrifice the prisoners than declare those who had already fallen victims of their innocence, as being guilty. About this I had gained the most powerful conviction a few days before, when Sir Moses and Lady Montefiore had a violent dispute with Mr. and Mrs. Crémieux, the latter actually wishing to accede to an arrangement by which the surviving prisoners might have been set at liberty and the suspicion of guilt cast on the dead. I simply stated that I had brought the copy of the Pasha's order, translated it before them, but took care not to note that expression. A few minutes afterwards I ordered my dinner to be brought into my room and then asked Sir M. to come in for a few minutes, when I communicated to him the above-mentioned facts. I was surprised to learn that Mr. Munk never called on him. Sir Moses immediately told me to proceed to the Pasha for the alteration of that term. And whilst we were speaking on the subject Mr. Crémieux rushed in praising and congratulating himself on his own successful work.

Extracts from Montefiore's letters indicate the wide range of matters on which he turned to Loewe for advice, occasionally on personal matters as well as public ones. To begin with a family matter, a Mrs Cohen — presumably of the family into which Montefiore had married — had written to him in distress about the intention of her daughter R to marry a gentile. On 5 February 1878 Montefiore forwarded her letter to Loewe:

I wish you would be so kind as to sketch for me an answer to Mrs Cohen's letter and express my concern with some sympathising expression on my part . . . say all you can to comfort Mrs C but you cannot avoid the expression of my feelings on the intended marriage pray excuse the trouble I am giving you, but I know no person, who could better guide me on this occasion half so well [sic] as yourself . . .

Writing on 4 December 1844 Montefiore alluded to Nathan Adler's recent appointment as Ashkenazi Chief Rabbi (he had been one of the reception committee when Adler had arrived at Dover on 1 July (*Diaries,* i, p. 324); in his correspondence with Loewe he regularly refers to Adler as 'our excellent Chief Rabbi'):

I sincerely hope with you that the Election of Rabbi Adler may restore peace to our Congregations and promote the welfare of our Community I truly believe he is the most likely of the three[21] candidates to obtain the confidence of all Parties in England and thus I trust will be able to work for the good of all
   I should much like to write him a letter in a delicate style of congratulation on his success in a manner congratulating rather our Congregations on his Election but this may also be left till I see you.

The situation of the Jews of Damascus long preoccupied Montefiore. When accusations against them were renewed in 1847 he was entreated to go to France and protest their innocence before Louis Philippe, and having resolved to do so he wrote on 6 July to alert Loewe (see *Diaries,* ii, pp. 19—22):

Dear Doctor
   I have received a Despatch from Viscount Palmerston for His Excellency the Marquis of Normanby at Paris, and I think with the Blessing of God to leave London on Friday to pass the Sabbath at Ramsgate and to cross the Channel on Sunday Morning I hope you will not be inconvenienced for the short time, you have to prepare for the Journey we can arrange the papers as we travel as I believe with you, there is not a moment to be lost . . . If please God we are successful, we may be back in a week.

His failure to secure the removal of the inscription in the church of the Capuchins at Damascus attributing to the Jews the death of Father Thomas continued to haunt him (*Diaries,* ii, pp. 19–22; 115). On 31 January 1850 he wrote:

I shall ask Lord Palmerston to grant me an interview after next week, pray give me your advice as to what I should say to him & what to ask him for

1st Damascus	The lying stone in the Convent
	Qu^y about schools there
2 Jerusalem	Missionaries
	Mr Finn [22]
	Russian & Polish Jews

in fact I wish you to give the matter some consideration and favour me with the result.

Again, on 22 December of the same year:

You have with your accustomed kindness and despatch sent me the address which you have written in a manner that entirely Coincides with my idea of the stile that is likely to prove most efficacious, I shall endeavour to impress every word of it on my memory and if possible, in the event of my obtaining an audience of the President repeat it to him . . . I . . . pray that . . . God . . . will bless my exertions in the cause of our Brethren at Damascus and incline the heart of the President to accede to my petition . . .

On Russia, one has to bear in mind that whilst over a period of more than fifty years Montefiore was concerned, to the point of anguish, at the plight of Jews in eastern Europe, he deluded himself (as subsequent history showed) as to his own effectiveness in achieving any significant improvement in their condition, as opposed to the raising of their morale — for which his visits and his interest worked wonders. Impressed — not to say flattered — by the cordiality of his reception by Nicholas I and his ministers (who had an eye on the possible advantage to themselves of Montefiore's Rothschild connections), he overestimated his success in moderating the Tsar's repressive policy towards his Jewish subjects. [23]

A letter written from London in Montefiore's firm, early hand, and dated merely 'March 7th' presumably belongs to 1844: [24]

Will you dine with me to day, . . . I am most desirous of settling at once the letter to Count Kisseleff I should like to read it over with you I will then take it to Baron Brunnow [25] for his approval before despatching it to St. Petersburg

Pray do not forget that Mrs Loewe and yourself are to dine with us to-morrow . . .

When, in 1851, the Jews of Surami in Georgia were victimized because of some false accusation (not, it seems, the blood-libel)

and Montefiore received appeals to intervene (*Diaries*, II, p. 23), he contemplated journeying to Tiflis himself; on 14 January he wrote to Loewe:

I can think of little else than the unhappy situation of our poor Brethren at Suram and what can possibly be done to rescue them from their dangerous position, I am anxiously looking for your advice. Suram is I think at the extremity of the Black sea two or three days Journey from Teflis the Capital of Georgia, it is terribly distant from London, nevertheless that would not deter me from going there, if you could go with me, if the Journey was recommended by Baron Brunnow & Lord Palmerston I have not yet had any reply from our excellent Chief Rabbi, but hope to get it tomorrow as yet nothing has been done, for which I reproach myself very much, but patience God help them poor Souls . . .

An undated note, presumably of 1873, relates to the Russian reply to the Board of Deputies' address on the Duke of Edinburgh's engagement to the Grand Duchess Marie Alexandrovna (*Diaries*, ii, p. 258):

Dear Doctor
    As you twice accompanied me to Russia and as the Emperor was exceedingly courteous to you, perhaps you would like to show to Mr Tait the Despatch I received from St Petersburg in reply to the address of the Board of Deputies I send you herewith the Original . . . also . . . a Copy of the Persian Report and also your translation of the Shah's letter . . .[26]

Not surprisingly, Montefiore's interest in Palestine bulks very large in the correspondence. In an undated letter written no later than 1854[27] he asks about distress at Safed:

You have not informed me of the cause of the disturbances in the vicinity of Safed, which obliges the Jews to remain within their houses, or the cause of the great poverty of the people, almost to starvation, do pray let me know all about it, and what remedy you recommend me to adopt, Write by all means an answer for me, at any rate expressing my deep sympathy for their sufferings, and my willingness to render them any assistance in my power . . .

Before then, in 1844, Montefiore was endeavouring to introduce western weaving techniques in Jerusalem, and he arranged to send a man from Preston to train an initial cadre of three (*Diaries,* i, p. 23, ii, pp. 48, 66f., 77); the enterprise was wound up in 1857. Presumably he had machine-weaving in mind, but in view of the absence of water-power and of coal at Jerusalem he will not have envisaged a Lancashire-type mill. Others on the spot apparently had grandiose ideas, as the following letter of 27 June 1845 makes clear. Its paternalistic — perhaps even imperious — tone is unmistakable; no doubt Montefiore's need to keep under control the many calls made on him explains it.

I have received the enclosed letter from Mr Behrens,[28] it has given me much pain to find our Eastern people have been corresponding with people at Manchester asking advice of them . . . I most certainly shall give them no Introduction to any one at Manchester

As to Spinning Machines and Power looms they will get none from me

Pray give them some good advice, if they understood english I should write them instantly myself, and open their eyes if possible to their real position . . .

In 1845 Montefiore received, through Baron James de Rothschild in Paris, a letter from the French Consul in Jerusalem[29] alleging that Dr S. Fränkel (whom Montefiore had appointed) was in fact charging for medicines, exercising favouritism in making available his medical services, and generally behaving in a reprobate manner. Though himself suspecting the French of mischief-making intrigue, he wrote (probably in 1844)[30] making clear that the charges could not be allowed to go by default:

I assure you this letter has given me much pain and has caused me serious uneasiness, I wish to have your opinion as to what had best be done under the circumstance I am very loath to believe the french Count I do not forget Ratti Menton's[31] lies, and this I hope will prove a similar deception, nevertheless a searching enquiry must be made as to Frankel's conduct at Jerusalem the difficulty is to know, how best to obtain the information. I am certainly but ill satisfied with the tenor of Frankel's letters to You and me . . .

Again, on 8 October 1846 he wrote:

Dear Doctor

I think I hear you say shall I never be at rest, letters, more letters, but so it is, the Mail from the Holy land is arrived, and brought the enclosed; I am surprized that Dr Frankel has not written, nor any person at Jerusalem . . . Pray oblige me, by looking over all the letters you have of mine & prepare answers, to such as you think require it . . .

On 14 December 1849 (adding also the Hebrew date) he wrote:

I have had the pleasure to receive this Morning a letter from Cincinnati Ohio with a remittance of £25 for the relief of our Brethren in the Holy land. I trouble you with it enclosed, and beg of you to write a Hebrew letter in which I will enclose the Money for the Holy land, pray use the strongest language, that the money may be distributed, in the manner its Donors direct and for them to return me a receipt that I may forward it to Cincinnati . . . I have so much to say to you respecting the Affairs of the East . . . & Colonel Gawler's[32] intended Publication, that I am most anxious to pay you a visit . . .

The following letter is of interest as being the sole example in the correspondence reflecting a difference of view between the two, and the terms in which Montefiore almost apologises for this emphasize the strong bond that existed between them. There is no date, but internal evidence earlier in the letter[33] points to 1857. It would

appear that Loewe had been pleading in vain to protect the employment of some person retained by Montefiore in Jerusalem who had
forfeited his trust:

I am afraid I was not so patient last night as I should have been, but had you
witnessed all I did on the unfortunate subject and heard from the mouths of
at least eight persons all present at the same time, headed by the Haham Bashi,
you would I am perfectly sure come to the same conclusion I have done, that
is, the man cannot remain in our employment, indeed the paper which has
disappeared in so mysterious manner (*sic*) and which was presented to me with
great formality, fully confirmed the unfortunate reports that were current in
the Holy City It is most painful to me to differ in opinion with you, but on this
point I regret we are not I fear ever likely to agree unless the document witnessed by the Haham Bashi should again appear I am going to the Chief Rabbi
who will I have no doubt be good enough to see you regarding the answers to
the letters and believe me

your very truly
MM

In February 1857 Montefiore left on his fifth visit to Palestine,
Loewe not being on this occasion a member of his party. On 14
April he wrote to him from Rome:

. . . it is with much pleasure I learn the success of the experiment you recommended of the purchase of grain during the summer for the benefit of the poor
at Jerusalem and I hope a similar result has taken place at the other Holy
Cities . . .

In 1860 detailed plans were being made regarding the Touro almshouses (*Mishkenoth Sha'ananim*: was it perhaps Loewe who proposed
this name for them?)[34] into which enterprise Montefiore had channelled his earlier ideas of building a hospital (*Diaries,* ii, pp. 109–
111). The intention was to accommodate equal numbers of Ashkenazim and Sephardim; and true to his quintessentially English
notions of paternalism where philanthropy was concerned, he took
it for granted that the inmates were to be subject to discipline
(*Diaries,* ii, p. 177). That explains the following, dated 17 August
1860:

on the subject of the Alms Houses It has at length been agreed after many
Conferences to adopt the suggestions of the Chief Rabbi I am therefore compelled to request you to make the required alterations in your letters & I must
also beg of you to make a Copy of the regulations in the square Hebrew Character that the Portuguese may understand them I must have them printed . . .

When Moses Montefiore died in 1885 the government, and the
administration of the endowment of the Judith Lady Montefiore
College in Ramsgate passed to the Elders of the Spanish and Portuguese

Jews' Congregation in London, who at first entertained the notion of amalgamating it with their own almost defunct *Medrash 'Eṣ Ḥayyim* (conventionally transliterated *Heshaim*) in such a way as to revitalize the latter. Loewe was confirmed as Head of the College, having in fact received the emoluments of that appointment from Montefiore himself up to September 1888; in November of which year he died, having meanwhile removed to London. Dr Moses Gaster had been appointed *Haham* in 1887, and, quite apart from Loewe's advanced age, it would seem that Gaster not unreasonably wished to gather the direction of the College into his own hands.[35] Loewe had completed the edition of the *Diaries of Sir Moses and Lady Montefiore* six months before his death, and one may surmise from some unevenness in the work that he felt, in his seventy-ninth year, that he was writing against time. Montefiore and he had each identified in the other the complement to his own powers and opportunities for the realization of projects and ideals that they held in common. Montefiore depended on Loewe's linguistic range, his scholarship, and, as his chief staff officer, frequently also on his judgement. Loewe lacked both personal ambition in regard to Jewish leadership and the material resources for philanthropic enterprise that Montefiore not only commanded from his private pocket but which, by his personal example and magnetism, he was able also to elicit from others in a position to give. Loewe seems to have appreciated that as Montefiore's *aide* he could promote the growth of the Jewish community in Palestine and support the cause of Jewish scholarship (he was himself a member of the *Ḥovevey Ṣiyyon*,[36] and on the committee of the *Meqiṣey Nirdamim*,[37] a society concerned with the publishing of rabbinic manuscripts), and that he could also make a valuable, if unspectacular contribution to the relief of Jewish suffering and the removal of Jewish disabilities generally. In his description of Montefiore's last days and his funeral (*Diaries,* ii, pp. 340f., 348) he records how, when Montefiore knew he was dying, he begged Loewe not to leave him, and how, mindful of that request, he stood by the grave until it was covered and then placed two lighted candles at its head. In paying that farewell tribute, my great—grandfather was unknowingly writing his own epitaph.

NOTES

1.　Articles on Louis Loewe will be found in the *Dictionary of National Biography*, 34, p. 68 (G. Goodwin); *Jewish Encyclopedia*, 8, p. 149 (H. Hirschfeld, his son-in-law); briefly in the German *Encyclopaedia*

Judaica, 10, 1143 (C. Roth); the English *Encyclopaedia Judaica*, 11, p. 448 (G. Elkoshi), with bibliography; S. Wininger, *Grosse Jüdische National-Biographie*, 4, p. 158.

2.   *Encyclopaedia Judaica*, 15, 77; *Jewish Encyclopedia*, 11, p. 110.

3.   *Diaries of Sir Moses and Lady Montefiore*, ed. L. Loewe, 1890, i, pp. v, 101—2.

4.   *Dictionary of National Biography*, 2, p. 257 (T. F. Henderson).

5.   *Dictionary of National Biography*, 53, p. 162 (J. K. Laughton).

6.   He published his *The Origin of the Egyptian Language* in 1837 (J. F. Champollion's decipherment of hieroglyphics began in 1821).

7.   *Diaries*, i, p. 154.

8.   Published by Herbert Loewe (his grandson) in *Yehudith*, I (Ramsgate, 1940), p. 15.

9.   *Diaries*, ii, pp. 340f.

10. *Diaries*, ii, pp. 9 f., 21, 78.

11. Two letters published by Solomon Schreiber, *'Iggeroth Sopherim* (1929), ii, pp. 80—83, translated by L. I. Rabinowitz, 'Three Letters of Anglo-Jewish Interest', *Miscellanies* of the Jewish Historical Society of England, 5, (1948), pp. 135—41. Moses Sopher's reply to neither letter is printed, but the terms of Hirschel's second letter imply that the *Ḥatham Sopher* had nothing untoward to say about the pupil to whom he had granted the *Attereth Baḥurim* (in place of the usual rabbinical diploma, since Loewe was then still a bachelor).

12. Cf. *Diaries*, i, pp. 301 f. (1841: there is nothing printed for the year 1853). See I. Finestein, 'The Anglo-Jewish Revolt of 1853', *Jewish Quarterly*, (December 1978), pp. 103—113.

13. S. Stein, *The Beginnings of Hebrew Studies at University College London* (1951), p. 24, n. 24. Inspection of the report and of the relevant minute books makes it clear that Goldsmid used his influence in the background in effect to veto the appointment; but it would ill become the incumbent of a chair that was denied to his great-grandfather to spell out the details.

14. See A. M. Hyamson, *Jews' College, London 1855—1955*, (1955), pp. 22 f., 25, 27; *Jewish Encyclopedia*, 7, p. 185; *Encyclopaedia Judaica*, 10, 98. I. Harris in *The Jewish Chronicle*, Supplement, 1 June 1906, p. iii, says that Loewe resigned because he found the remuneration inadequate. The same writer, as editor of the *Jews' College Jubilee Volume* (1906), p. xiii, records that on his retirement the Council paid tribute to Loewe's work as Head of the College and college school.

15. My grandfather told me that whenever one of his siblings (including himself, eight survived into adulthood) became engaged Montefiore would send a monetary present, but that their father was constrained to point out that it in fact represented his salary cheque. Montefiore's reputation for generosity is in no sense here impugned, but the procedure suggests an arbitrariness which coheres with other items of oral tradition. In his will, of which Loewe was executor, Montefiore bequeathed him £1000 (*Diaries*, ii, p. 349) — in effect, a retirement pension.

16. See above, n. 8.

17. See *Dictionary of National Biography*, 43, p. 107. The identity of 'Sir Fr P' referred to in Montefiore's letter to Loewe is substantiated by a separate slip (apparently in Montefiore's hand) with the name in full. His son, Francis Turner Palgrave (1824—97), the editor of the *Golden Treasury*, cannot have been the donor, since he was never knighted.

18. *Diaries*, i, p. 252.

19. See Ursula Henriques, 'Who killed Father Thomas?' in *Sir Moses Montefiore: A Symposium*, ed. V. D. Lipman (1982), p. 67.

20. *Yehudith* (see n. 8), p. 26.

21. There had been four candidates in all, the others being Benjamin Auerbach of Darmstadt, Hirsch Hirschfeld of Wollstein, and Samson Raphael Hirsch, then of Emden.

22. James Finn, British Consul in Jerusalem, was alleged to have been missionizing.

23. See Benjamin Jaffe, 'Sir Moses Montefiore in Russia', in *Sir Moses Montefiore* (see n. 9), pp. 76–81.

24. See *Diaries*, i, p. 317; on 6 June 1844 Montefiore was anxiously awaiting an answer from Brunnow. By 7 March 1846 he was already in Europe, *en route* for St Petersburg (p. 325). He did not meet Count Kisseleff, the member of the Russian government who dealt with Jewish affairs, until 10 April 1846 (p. 334).

25. The Russian ambassador in London.

26. Presumably the reply to the address that Montefiore presented to the Shah on his visit to England. It is printed in *Diaries*, ii, p. 256.

27. It refers to C. 'H.' Parness of Vilna (i.e. Ḥayyim Naḥman Parnas, see *Encyclopaedia Judaica*, 13, 124). On his visit in 1839 Montefiore was aghast at the dire poverty of the Jews of Safed; *Diaries*, i, p. 168.

28. Either Sir Jacob Behrens (1806–89), the textile magnate of Bradford, or his brother Louis Behrens (1811–84).

29. Printed in A. M. Hyamson, *The British Consulate in Jerusalem*, I, pp. 66 ff.

30. Written from Maidstone, no doubt during Montefiore's official presence there as Sheriff of Kent.

31. Rattimenton was the French Consul at Damascus in 1840; *Diaries*, ii, pp. 243 f., 259, 285.

32. George Gawler (1796–1869), Christian Zionist; *Encyclopaedia Judaica*, 7, 338 (G. Kressel). It was Gawler who interested Montefiore in promoting Jewish agricultural settlements in Palestine.

33. There is reference in it to Holman, of Canterbury, with whom Montefiore made an agreement to erect the windmill in Jerusalem; *Diaries*, ii, p. 63.

34. The *Diaries* (ii, p. 111) state that the name was adopted at a meeting held by Sir Moses with Kursheedt and Loewe at the Brighton home of Chief Rabbi (Dr. Adler) on Tuesday 10 July 1860 and that the name ('the dwellings of those that are at ease') was adopted 'to avoid hurting the feelings of the inmates by calling the buildings almshouses'; but the extract from Montefiore's diary does not specify who suggested the name. Mr A. Schischa has drawn my attention to D. de Sola Pool, 'Some relations of Gershom Kursheedt, and Sir Moses Montefiore', *Publications of the American Jewish Historical Society*, 37 (1947), p. 219, who (whilst quoting the foregoing passage of the *Diaries*) states positively that the name was adopted on the advice of Adler and Loewe: but Pool is imprecise regarding his source material.

35. D. A. J. Cardozo and Paul Goodman, *Think and Thank*, pp. 147–151.

36. *Encyclopædia Judaica*, 8: 463 and 16, 1038; *Jewish Encyclopedia*, 4, 46; *Diaries*, ii, p. 325.

37. *Encyclopaedia Judaica*, 11, 1270, *Jewish Encyclopedia*, 8, p. 447.

6

Montefiore and the Visual Arts

HELEN ROSENAU

The celebration of Sir Moses Montefiore's anniversary affords an opportunity for reassessing his personality and allows for an appreciation of his contribution in the field of the visual arts. It is not so much the making of new discoveries that is important but the attempt to understand Sir Moses in the context of his time as a patriotic Jewish Victorian.[1] It has been suggested that it was Lady Montefiore who stimulated his artistic purchases;[2] at any rate, both the Montefiores bought sculptures of a neo-classical style in Carrara and in Rome in 1839 and, probably, also the laver in Italian marble still to be found in their own Ramsgate Synagogue, completed in 1833.

Both Louis Loewe in his edition of Sir Moses and Lady Montefiore's *Diaries* as well as Judith Montefiore in her *Private Journal* and *Notes from a Private Journal* mention a number of neo-classical but by no means distinguished artists whom they patronised. They also purchased copies of paintings by old masters, inexpensive works, although the scale of his wife's purchases in Carrara, according to her *Notes from a Private Journal*, might have 'ruined' Sir Moses in 1839. If this is to be regarded as no more than a jest, it nevertheless expresses Montefiore's lack of formal interest or commitment to the arts, while a religious interest was evident when he commissioned a Torah Scroll and Mantle in Rome.[3]

In accordance with prevalent taste, Judith Montefiore admired the Renaissance, especially Raphael, as is clear from the quotations of poetry that enliven her *Notes*. In Florence, she quotes Samuel Rogers (p. 105) on Raphael and Michelangelo. She also quotes Lord Byron's *Childe Harold's Pilgrimage* in this connection (pp. 113 ff.), beginning with Santa Croce and ending with Canova (*Canto* iv, liv and lv) and also in connection with the Lake of Thrasimene (p. 118: *Canto* iv, lxv). In Rome she feels inspired by the verses on Egeria (p. 168 ff.) in *Childe Harold* (*Canto* iv, cxv) and especially (p. 127) Milton's *Paradise Regained*, beginning with 'Great and glorious Rome, Queen of the Earth' (Bk. iv, verses 44 ff.). She quotes from Samuel Rogers again (p. 144) with regard to Naples (Samuel Rogers's collection of poems, *Italy*, had numerous editions and an illustrated one in 1830).

Mrs Lipman has drawn attention to the fact that Judith Montefiore was proficient in languages. As she was privately educated, her lessons would have included some teaching of music and the arts. A governess was to impart a sound English education with French, music and singing, dancing and drawing. The situation was more critically assessed by Charles Dickens when he told John Foster in 1844 about the 'brimful of cant' uttered about the arts in Italy.[4]

The influence of Raphael and the Renaissance in general was paramount in English art of the early nineteenth century.[5] Judith Montefiore was patriotic and particularly rejoiced in encountering the work of the English sculptor John Gibson in Rome (*Notes*, p. 175). She savoured rather indiscriminately works of a wide variety of styles, from Herculaneum and Pompeii, to St Peter's in Rome, and St Maria in Cosmedin (known to her as 'St Maria belonging to the Greeks').

Judith Montefiore bought a number of cheap genre paintings; among them a *Mandolino* by an otherwise unknown painter, Cavalleri, and a piece by the expatriate German, Pietro Rittig, representing *Students in the Academy of Painting* (Loewe i, p. 155). Her religious conviction did not preclude her from admiring a *Virgin and Child* by Murillo in Florence (*Notes*, p. 110). She evidently kept her religious and cultural activities in separate compartments and showed no unconventional commitment in either field.

Judith Montefiore was, presumably, influenced by her husband when she complained about the high prices of mosaic tables (*Notes*, p. 97). Both the Montefiores may have felt that expenditure on the arts was rather frivolous and less meritorious than practical acts of charity. Judith Montefiore therefore commissioned copies, among them one after Carlo Dolci (1616–86), a fashionable painter known for his maudlin and sentimental style, based on Raphael. She was, evidently, unable fully to appreciate the difference in quality between a copy and its original.

Sir Moses was not primarily interested in the arts, as his main concerns were religious and charitable, but even in this field his strong sense of decorum and concern with formal hierarchies and distinctions reveal an aesthetic and personal approach. A telling example of his attitude is found in a passage from the book of *Reminiscences* of 1902 by Frederick Goodall (1822–1904), the Victorian painter.[6] He relates that according to Sir Joseph Sebag-Montefiore, nephew of Sir Moses, his uncle's favourite painting represented the unusual scene of *King David on his Death-Bed* with Abishag in attendance, whilst Bathsheba knelt before the King imploring him to grant the succession to their son, Solomon (I Kings 1:15–31). This is not the

popular scene of David discovering Bathsheba at her toilet: it is a subject of non-sexual significance, involving the royal succession and
evoking deep emotions, perhaps related to Sir Moses' own lack of children. Unfortunately, Sir Moses did not identify either the artist or the
location of the painting, but the description so impressed Goodall
that he proceeded to paint the scene himself for Sir Joseph.

Solomon was David's youngest son and, therefore, the claim of
the elder Adonijah to the succession was stronger, even if the laws
of primogeniture did not fully operate at the time. One is reminded
of Isaac blessing Jacob rather than Esau and Joseph blessing Ephraim
before Manasseh. It should also be noted that Aaron was the elder
brother but Moses became the charismatic leader.

A painting best fitting the description by Sir Moses formed part
of the private collections of Laporte, and later Sieck, in Hanover.
In 1863 it was in a collection in Söder, near Hanover, and has recently been acquired by the Narodni Gallery in Prague. As Montefiore
visited Hanover for several days at the end of July 1872, he would
have had ample opportunity to see this picture, which is the work of
Barendt van den Eeckhout, the well known disciple of Rembrandt.[7]
The picture includes a fourth figure: the prophet Nathan in attendance. A signed drawing by the same artist, in the Metropolitan
Museum, New York, shows an identical composition. Furthermore,
there exists a slightly retouched drawing by Rembrandt, the master
himself, in the Chatsworth collection,[8] to be dated *c.* 1645 because
of the concentration on the figures and the Baroque motifs. This
was possibly a preliminary study for a lost, or non-executed, painting
and shows the four figures also seen in van den Eeckhout's painting
and drawing. The scene is rarely depicted and therefore Moses
Montefiore's favourite painting was doubtlessly inspired by a composition that was by, or derived from, Rembrandt. This makes
Montefiore's intuition remarkable. He sensed the greatness of
Rembrandt as an interpreter of the Bible.

By contrast, Rembrandt was not particularly appreciated by the
Victorians, although they studied Dutch realistic works, among
them those of Gerard Dou and other small-scale masters of the
Rembrandt School. Rembrandt himself, however, was almost forgotten.

The great exception in England was the writer and painter William
Hazlitt, who admired Rembrandt's 'genius' and singled out for
praise *Jacob's Dream* in the Dulwich College Art Gallery, revealing
what Hazlitt calls Rembrandt's 'gorgeous obscurity'.[9] However, the
painting bears the signature of Aert de Gelder, a disciple of Rembrandt,
who also painted other Jewish subjects.

To return to Goodall: at the moment, the location of his painting cannot be traced, but Mr. Denzil Sebag-Montefiore remembers seeing it as a child in Ramsgate at East Cliff Lodge. Some idea can be formed with regard to its style and colouring. The Victorians believed that by meticulous realism of detail they could evoke the spirit of a place or make a biblical event seem present, and Goodall was a typical Victorian.

He had visited Egypt twice, in 1858–9 and in 1870–1. Goodall was an admirer of Sir Edmund John Poynter, whose *Israel in Egypt* was exhibited at the Royal Academy in 1867. However, Goodall had dealt with oriental themes even earlier, as seen in his *Early Morning in the Wilderness of Shur* of 1860, and in his submission for the diploma of the Royal Academy of *Song of the Nubian Slave* in 1864. His *The Ploughman and the Shepherdess, The Time of Evening Prayer* with a motto culled from Lord Byron's *Don Juan* was exhibited at the Royal Academy in 1897 and presented in 1898 to the National Gallery. It is now in the possession of the Tate Gallery.

Goodall should not be under-rated; he had a delicate sense of colour and the luminosity of the rising sun in his *Early Morning in the Wilderness* is remarkable. The harmonious and detailed colouring of the tribe's rugs is also worth noting. However, his main concern was with exactness — an unromantic approach, found also among other Victorian painters attracted by the Orient. Goodall refers to Sir Joseph's procuring of brocades from 'the Synagogue' (presumably hangings or curtains from Bevis Marks). At the same time Mrs Goodall 'ransacked' London for colourful materials and a wild lion's skin. Furthermore, Goodall consulted a publication by Austen Henry Layard on *Nineveh and its Remains* for details of ivory carvings. His concern was with historicity rather than religious commitment.[10] So Goodall's painting of *King David on his Deathbed* cannot have shown much similarity to the Rembrandt composition. He was more interested in oriental scenes than in the text of the Bible.

For a fuller understanding of the taste of Sir Moses Montefiore in relation to the painting centred on David and Bathsheba, it is helpful to consider a photograph showing him seated before the portrait of his deceased wife — a diagonal composition of baroque character. He is seen, as it were, in adoration and this is similar in spirit to some of the funerary sculpture of the Victorian period. He is holding the edict of 1864 by the Sultan of Morocco. The portrait, by an unknown artist, was in East Cliff Lodge at Ramsgate and shows Lady Montefiore in an elaborate costume far removed from the precepts of simplicity advocated by the author of *The Jewish*

Manual Written by a Lady (probably Judith Montefiore). This photograph is also an illustration of the concern of Sir Moses with iconographic, as opposed to formal, values — a concern which, it may be suggested, is typical of the Jewish attitude towards the visual arts. It would also help to explain the interest of Sir Moses in architecture, which is of a non-figurative character and in keeping with the Second Commandment forbidding pictorial representation.

It is usual to show male sitters at a desk in Victorian art, but in the case of Sir Moses there is a special emphasis on the documents. The interest in such documents on the part of Sir Moses Montefiore is founded on the struggle for emancipation of the Jewish people coupled, no doubt, with a desire for personal recognition.

Sir Moses' favourite painter seems to have been Solomon Alexander Hart (1806—81) with whom he shared a similarity of outlook, as Hart prided himself on being an Englishman as well as remaining a conscious and loyal Jew.[11] There are two representative portraits by him of Moses Montefiore; the first being the well known one in Lieutenancy uniform (see *Journal of Jewish Studies* (1979), Pl. III, fig. 3) of 1848, in which he holds the *Firman* from the Sultan of Turkey; the second being a hitherto unpublished portrait, now in the Public Library of Ramsgate, initially commissioned for its Town Hall and exhibited at the Royal Academy in 1869. Hart was not a particularly outstanding painter, but he caught the mood of his sitter — first as an exponent of Victorian society and, in the second example, as a culturally arrived patriarch surrounded by important but unidentified papers. The neo-classical inkstand is a successful example of Hart's painting, Hart evidently being better at rendering inanimate than animate motifs.

Of a different nature is the posthumous portrait by Frederick Goodall exhibited at the Royal Academy in 1890, two years after his picture of King David with Bathsheba. The original painting is now on indefinite loan from Mr. Harold Sebag-Montefiore to the Embassy of Israel in London. The work is signed, but an unsigned copy in the Spanish and Portuguese Synagogue in Lauderdale Road, Maida Vale, London, is attributed to 'Frank Goodall', a non-existent painter. It is, probably, a copy by the master himself, a fact not uncommon among Victorian artists.[12]

Moses Montefiore on at least one occasion expressed his appreciation of the Renaissance. During his visit to the Synagogue in Pisa in 1858 — a building of the late Renaissance style — he expressed regret for not having built his Ramsgate Synagogue after this model, a typical Victorian attitude towards historicism. A further example of Moses Montefiore's interest in the arts is attested by Holman

Hunt, who recalls how Montefiore and Guedalla helped him in Jerusalem to find Jewish models for his paintings.[13]

In 1843 a *Testimonial* was presented to Sir Moses by the Congregation of Spanish and Portuguese Jews. It was a token of appreciation and commemoration, recalling the *Firman* of 1840 that granted protection and equal rights to Jews throughout the Turkish Empire in answer to the Blood Libel, the so-called Damascus Affair of 1840.[14]

The *Testimonial* in wrought silver serves no utilitarian purpose, but it is of high quality design and workmanship. It is now on permanent loan to the Victoria and Albert Museum, which also has a sketchbook or Album containing drawings by the sculptor, George Hayter. They include portrait sketches of Sir Moses, with and without top hat; these were used in the composition of the central panel, showing the interior of Bevis Marks with Sir Moses and other worshippers and a realistic rendering of the *Ner Tamid*, also to be found in the sketchbook. The style of the reliefs is neo-classical and the novel iconography glorifies the achievements of Sir Moses. The arms of Sir Moses, including supporters with banners inscribed *Jerusalem* in Hebrew lettering, are also to be seen. It is remarkable that the *Testimonial* was conceived as a monument surmounted by the scene, in the round, of David conquering a lion in order to rescue a lamb (I Samuel 17:34).

On the other hand, Moses Montefiore commissioned portrait busts of Archbishop and Mrs Tait and also of Sir Austen Layard, but never of himself or his wife due to the respect he felt for the prohibition of 'brazen images'. It will be remembered that Sir George Hayter had sketched Sir Moses for the testimonial purpose and for this reason the gift cannot have come as a complete surprise. Montefiore appears to have raised no objection to portrait medals, among them the famous one of 1864 of himself and Judith by Charles Wiener. Sir Moses deliberately eschewed sculpture in the round, so far as realistic portraits of Jews were concerned. On the other hand, he tolerated symbolic figures or figures that were susceptible of a symbolic interpretation, such as Moses, Ezra, a Jew in chains and a Jew released, Sphinxes, and David adorning the *Testimonial*.

If Montefiore sat for the sculptor Henry Weekes, during the latter's terminal illness in Ramsgate in 1877, it was an act of charity, not of patronage.[15] The sculptor Aristide Fontana showed a bust of Montefiore in 1884 at the Exhibition of the Royal Academy. However, this was a tribute, obtained without sittings, for the centenary of Montefiore's birth and may be associated with the numerous small plaster busts commemorating Sir Moses' hundredth birthday.

Montefiore never purchased his own bust: in this he acted very differerently from Sir David Salomons, the first Jewish Lord Mayor of the City of London, who sat for a handsome neo-classical bust by Jozsef Engel in 1857.[16] It is also significant that no bust exists of Judith Montefiore.

Montefiore's love of architecture was as abiding as his affection for Jerusalem; his settlement, the *Mishkenot Sha'ananim*, was far more than an almshouse. It was accompanied by a windmill, still to be found on a commanding site. A synagogue was placed at each end of the elongated building, one for Ashkenazi, the other for Sephardi Jews, extending tolerance to living, but not to praying, in one community. The inspiration was not formal but practical, far removed from the ghetto mentality, a settlement *fuori le mure*. With its crenellations and its later awnings, Montefiore had built the nucleus of a new town outside Jerusalem. That the settlement was easily adapted to a different modern use as a luxury guesthouse is a sign of the flexibility of the design and one of its most outstanding qualities. The theme was appreciated by Conrad Schick, the famous missionary, when he planned the *Montefiorieh* adjacent to, and following similar concepts to, the *Mishkenot*.[17]

Montefiore's principles inspired the foundation of the *Judith Lady Montefiore College* in Ramsgate in 1866, not far from the Synagogue and the Mausoleum built by Sir Moses. In neo-Tudor domestic style and initially planned for ten scholars, it was surrounded by greenery and built in a crescent shape, an unusual plan for an isolated college but frequent in town development. The College was transferred to London; the Ramsgate building was sold to the Kent County Council and eventually pulled down in 1961.

It is possible to throw further light on the architecture of the Judith Lady Montefiore College with the help of some unpublished designs in the archives of the Spanish and Portuguese Synagogue in Lauderdale Road, London. It was planned with the utmost care; four cottages were pulled down to clear the site in Hereson. The architect, Henry David Davis (1838–1915), was specially concerned with the quality of the brickwork and similar details.[18]

Davis was a well known Jewish architect who with his partner, Barrow Emanuel, was outstanding for his many charitable and educational buildings. Among them were the Kent Street, Portsea Schools of 1874 in the neo-Tudor style. They built the West London Synagogue, completed in 1870, and the Spanish and Portuguese Synagogue in Lauderdale Road in 1896.[19]

The architectural commissions of Sir Moses show the catholicity of his taste. In the restoration of East Cliff Lodge, he employed

Burton, who was also commissioned by Sir Isaac Lyon Goldsmid at Furze Hill, near Brighton. Burton was a Classicist renowned for his work at Regent's Park.[20] It was in a similar tradition that Mocatta erected the Synagogue and Mausoleum in Hereson. Whilst the *Mishkenot* in Jerusalem can be described as a piece of rural England translated to the Holy Land, in the Judith Montefiore College at Ramsgate a totally different style is apparent, the Tudor Revival. These variations exemplify the flexibility and breadth of Moses Montefiore's architectural taste. As long as the purpose of the building was clear, the stylistic trimmings were for him of secondary importance. He was little concerned with form, but rather with the meaning and programme of a building.

To return to Ramsgate, the College with its almshouses evoked town or village planning. The arrangement of the scholars' or almshouses was in the shape of a crescent, probably the idea not of the architect but of Sir Moses himself, as Davis was not known for his interest in town planning. Montefiore would have been familiar with many an English city including such a feature as a crescent.

Temple Cottage, the home of the brothers Myers, was included in the plans of 1866, echoing the neo-Tudor style of the College. It was, unfortunately, pulled down in 1891. A separate garden for 'Mr Myers' is also indicated. On the other hand, the plan for Mill House, erected in 1901 and seen in the simplified sketch of *Think and Thank* (p. 14), is naturally absent in 1866. The College had as its central feature a Library, indicated on the plan as a Museum, so expressing the ancient connection of reading and collecting, still alive in the British Museum and Library today. The irregular site is reminiscent of Trafalgar Square, for which an architectural competition had earlier taken place.[21]

It is remarkable also that Montefiore envisaged a square or a crescent for further planning at Jerusalem outside the city: the crescent had become a typically English motif; the square, although derived from the Renaissance, was frequently found in ghettos, but also in Millstadt as described in Disraeli's *Coningsby*, of which Montefiore possessed a copy. It will be remembered that Sir Moses was to have laid the foundation stone for ten new houses in a crescent in *Meah Shearim* in 1875,[22] a contributing factor for further extensions of Jerusalem. Montefiore's wide ranging architectural taste is confirmed by the choice of his London residence, now 99 Park Lane, a tall house, substantially changed and renovated but still of recognizable outline. The view from the upper rooms, overlooking Hyde Park, combined the advantages of town and country, standing for new developments, clearly exemplified in some parts of the Grosvenor Estate.[23]

Montefiore was not a great patron of the arts, but he deserves an honourable place in the history of art for his individual approach and originality of taste. By contrast, Judith Montefiore was better educated with regard to the arts, but less original in her approach.

In conclusion, it might be added that the Jews are not the only people to have an iconoclastic attitude towards figural representation. The acknowledgement of a compelling numinous presence in the arts led to realization of their danger and, in the case of the Jews, the prohibition in the Second Commandment. Thus, the prohibition is an indirect affirmation of recognition and respect.[24] Moses Montefiore was exceptionally sensitive in the field of iconography and his creative preoccupation with architecture and planning singles him out, not only as a representative Jew, but also as a representative Victorian.

NOTES

1. Louis Loewe, *Diaries of Sir Moses and Lady Montefiore*, (London, 1890), i, 153 ff.; also facsimile edition, indexed by Walter Schwab (London, 1983). For a survey of the literature on the subject, see my articles in *Journal of Jewish Studies*, XXX No. 2 (1979), pp. 233 ff. and *Journal of Jewish Art*, VIII (1981), pp. 60 ff.

2. Sonia L. Lipman, 'Judith Montefiore — First Lady of Anglo-Jewry', *Transactions of the Jewish Historical Society of England* XXI (1968) pp. 287 ff.; relevant also are *The Jewish Manual Written by a Lady* (1846), perhaps by Judith Montefiore (see below); and *Private Journal of a Visit to Egypt and Palestine*, (London, 1836).

3. *Notes from a Private Journal of a Visit to Egypt and Palestine by way of Italy and the Mediterranean*, (London, 1844; 2nd ed. 1885), pp. 175 and 97. Also, *Diaries* i, pp. 154 ff., especially p. 153. In Rome Montefiore allowed himself a rare flutter when he purchased a statue of a negress, probably not an *Abundantia* as suggested by Loewe (i, p. 53). On the background of such works, see F. M. Snowden, *Blacks in Antiquity* (Harvard U.P. 1970). On Italian artists of the time see A. R. Willard, *History of Modern Italian Art* (London, 1900).

4. S. L. Lipman, 'Judith Montefiore' (see note 2); Josephine Kamm, *Hope Deferred* (London 1965), p. 170. John Forster, *The Life of Charles Dickens*, ii (1873), p. 142.

5. Thomas Sherrer Boase, *English Art 1800—70* (Oxford, 1959).

6. Frederick Goodall, *Reminiscences* (London, 1902), pp. 182 ff.

7. Werner Sumowski, *The Drawings of the Rembrandt School* (New York, 1979), especially III; also Gustav Friedrich Constantine Parthey, *Deutscher Bildersaal* (Berlin, 1861—4); James A. Montgomery, *Critical and Exegetical*

Commentary on the Book of Kings in *The International Critical Commentary*, ed. Henry Snyder Gehman (Edinburgh, 1951), pp. 74 ff.

8. Andor Pigler, *Barockthemen* (Budapest, 1956), i, pp. 158 ff.; Hans Martin Rotermund, *Rembrandt's Handzeichnungen und Radierungen zur Bibel* (Stuttgart, 1963), pl. 114; *Rembrandt after 30 years* (Chicago Institute of Arts, 1960); J. W. von Moltke, *Govaert Flinck* (Amsterdam, 1965); Theodor Ehrenstein, *Das Alte Testament im Bilde* (Vienna, 1923), p. 787. Ehrenstein is right about the painting in Dresden by W. de Poorter. It represents Esther, not Bathsheba, as made clear by the King's sceptre. For a different opinion see Pigler, p. 158 f. *Rembrandt, the Complete Edition of his Paintings* by A. Bredius (numerous editions), revised by Hans Gerson.

9. The references to Rembrandt in the works of Hazlitt are numerous. See the centenary edition of the *Complete Works of William Hazlitt* by P. P. Howe (London and Toronto, 1930 etc.); see also William Hazlitt, *Table Talk, Essays on Men and Manners* (World Classics, 1901). Also *Selected Essays 1778–1830*, ed. Geoffrey Keynes, especially pp. 642, 673. I owe the references to Hazlitt to Professor K. Tillotson. See also Peter Murray, *The Dulwich Picture Gallery, a Catalogue* (London 1980), No. 126.

10. Goodall, pp. 165 ff.

11. Solomon Alexander Hart, *Reminiscences*, ed. A. Brodie (London, 1882), p. 141.

12. Jeremy Maas, *Victorian Painters* (London, 1967).

13. On Pisa, Attilio Milano in *La Rassegna Mensile d'Israel* (1974), pp. 167 ff.; Brian de Breffny, *The Synagogue* (London, 1978), p. 103 f.; *Pre-Raphaelitism and the Pre-Raphaelite Brotherhood*, (London, 1905), i, pp. 403 ff. and ii, pp. 4 ff., quoted by Alfred Rubens, *A Jewish Iconography* (rev. edn. 1981), p. xviii.

14. *Journal of Jewish Studies* (1979).

15. Henry Weekes, *Lectures on Art etc.* London 1880, p. 9.

16. Malcolm Brown, *David Salomons' House, Catalogue of Mementoes* (privately printed 1968), No. 39.

17. Y. Ben-Arieh, *A City Reflected in its Times, New Jerusalem* (Jerusalem, 1977). See my article in *Journal of Jewish Art* VIII (1981), pp. 60 ff.

18. David Abraham Jessurun Cardozo and Paul Goodman, *Think and Thank*, (Oxford, 1933); *The Builder*, 9 July 1915, pp. 26 ff.

19. See note above and A. S. Diamond, *The Building of a Synagogue* (n.d.), obtainable from the West London Synagogue.

20. On Burton, see the Catalogue by Philip Miller, *Decimus Burton, His Life and Work* (London 1981), p. 47 f.

21. Helen Rosenau, *The Ideal City* (3rd edn., 1983), pp. 144 f.

22. Moses Montefiore, *A Narrative of Forty Days Sojourn in the Holy Land* (London, 1875), pp. 106 and 146 f.

23. *Survey of London*, Vol. 39 (Athlone Press, University of London, 1977).

24. Louis Jacobs, *What does Judaism say about . . .* (New York, 1973). Also *inter alia* Solomon Bennett Freehof, *Modern Reform Responsa* (Hebrew Union College, 1971), pp. 184 ff. See for the background the still unsurpassed work of Rudolf Otto, *The Idea of the Holy* (many editions). Also Mary Douglas, *Natural Symbols, Explorations in Cosmology* (London, 1978) and H. Rosenau, *Vision of the Temple, the Image of the Temple in Judaism and Christianity* (London, 1979).

I wish to thank Dr R. D. Barnett, Dr V. D. Lipman, Mrs S. L. Lipman and Professor R. Loewe for valuable suggestions. I also wish to thank Mr Peter Slater, the Slide Librarian of the University of London, for his assistance, and the staff of the Reference Library in Ramsgate for their generous help in my research. I am indebted to the staff of the Royal Institute of British Architects for assistance and, as always, to the authorities of the British Library for providing an intellectual home. I also record my thanks to the Authorities of the Niedersächsisches Landesmuseum, especially its Director, Dr H. W. Grohn, and Professor Kathleen Tillotson for her identification of poetry quotations. I also wish to thank Mrs Marian Rickards and Mr K. E. Wilson for assistance in the preparation of the manuscript.

SELECT HANDLIST OF PORTRAITURE OF MOSES AND JUDITH MONTEFIORE

Painting

Goodall, Frederick: *Moses Montefiore*, exhibited Royal Academy 1880, Israel Embassy. 2nd version, Spanish and Portuguese Synagogue.

Hart, Solomon Alexander: *Moses Montefiore 1848*, Spanish and Portuguese Synagogue.

———— *Moses Montefiore 1868*, Arthur Sebag-Montefiore.

———— *Moses Montefiore 1869*, intended for Ramsgate Town Hall, now in Ramsgate Public Library.

Richmond, George: *Moses Montefiore 1875*, Sun Alliance Insurance Group, Board Room.

Weigel, Henry: *Moses Montefiore 1881*, National Portrait Gallery.

———— *Judith Montefiore*, Spanish and Portuguese Synagogue, London.

———— *Judith Montefiore*, formerly at East Cliff Lodge, Ramsgate.

Caricature

Dighton, Richard: *Moses Montefiore, 1818*, etching.

Drawings

Hayter, George: *Sketchbook, 1842*, Victoria and Albert Museum. Numerous sketches of Moses Montefiore and perhaps one of Judith Montefiore.

Medals

Wiener, Charles Henry: Busts of Moses and Judith Montefiore, 1864, two years after Judith Montefiore's death, British Museum.

———— *Moses Montefiore*, struck in London by Loewenstark and Sons, 1881, British Museum. *Moses Montefiore*, struck in Corfu, 5645, British Museum.

For further reference consult:

R. D. Barnett: *Catalogue of the Permanent and Loan Collections of the Jewish Museum*, London, 1974.

Catalogue of the Anglo-Jewish Historical Exhibition, London, 1887.

Montefiore Album, Central Zionist Archives, Jerusalem.

Rosenau, Helen, in *Journal of Jewish Studies*, Autumn 1979.

Rubens, Alfred: *Jewish Iconography* (rev. edn.), London, 1981.

PART II

Foreign Affairs

1

'The Year of the Pride of Israel'
Montefiore and the Damascus
Blood Libel of 1840

TUDOR PARFITT

In his *History of the Jews* the historian Graetz (1817–1891) wrote:
'An unforeseen event, insignificant at the beginning – but of vast
importance in its results, exposed and punished the false prophets
and quack doctors and bound together the members of Judaism in
an indissoluble bond'.[1] The 'unforeseen event' (which, it must be said,
was hardly without precedent) came to be known as the Damascus
Affair. As Graetz indicated, the entire chapter was of considerable
significance in the history of the Jews in the nineteenth century, did
much to foster an interest in the plight of the Jews internationally,
and gave rise to a new spirit of co-operation and even 'unity' among
the various Jewish communities of the world.[2] The 'false prophets
and quack doctors' were, however, to make a swift recovery.

Briefly stated, for the facts are well-known, the blood libel hinged
on the disappearance on 5 February 1840 of Father Thomas, the
superior of a Capuchin house in Damascus, and his servant Ibrahim.
It is still not known what happened to the priest and servant. A
number of witnesses claim to have last seen them in the Jewish
Quarter, which housed some 6,000 Jews out of a total population
of perhaps 75,000 Muslims and 14,000 Christians.[3] The Jews of
Damascus were almost immediately accused of killing Thomas and
Ibrahim with the intention of using their blood for making Passover
matzot. Why this charge was taken up, if not instigated, by local
Christians in an area which had no prior record of blood libels, is
unclear.[4] Father Thomas had come under the jurisdiction of the
recently appointed French consul to Damascus, the Count of Ratti-
Menton, who gave his support to the charge against the Jews. Ratti-
Menton was given every support by the Egyptian Governor of
Damascus, Sherif Pasha, but it is unlikely that the libel or the subsequent persecution were instigated by the Egyptian ruler, Mehemet
Ali, who had conquered Damascus in 1831.[5] The Egyptian ruler did,
however, condone the proceedings against the Jews, probably out of
a desire to avoid displeasing the French, whose Consul was to play

such a prominent role in the whole affair,[6] at a time when French support was vital to his ambitions in the area. In any event several Jews were arrested and tortured. During the trial, which went on for several months, some of the Jews died under torture and others were forced into making 'confessions'.

The case was first brought to the attention of the Western world by a letter from the elders of the Jewish community in Constantinople dated 27 March 1840, addressed to Messrs de Rothschild in London. Because of the Egyptian invasion of Syria, the Constantinople Jewish community had no means of exerting any influence on behalf of the Damascus Jews through its normal channels and so outside help was sought. The letter, along with supporting documents from Damascus, was passed on by the Rothschilds to Moses Montefiore, who by this time had become known for his involvement with the Jews of Syria and Palestine.[7] The matter was put to the Board of Deputies and others at a meeting held at Montefiore's Park Lane home on 21 April 1840. The minutes of this meeting report that the acting President of the Board of Deputies, Joseph Henriques, concluded that 'the meeting had been specially summoned to take into consideration the means of staying the persecutions under which the Eastern Jews are now suffering.'[8] Subsequently, a meeting of the Board of Deputies held at the New Synagogue, Great St. Helen's on 15 June decided that 'Sir Moses Montefiore, from his high moral character, his influence and zeal, is particularly fitted to be the representative for such purpose of the British Jews at the Court of the Pasha of Egypt and the defender of our persecuted brethren in the East.'[9] Eventually, a mission headed by Montefiore and Adolphe Crémieux went to Alexandria to intercede with Mehemet Ali who, in due course, conceded the innocence of the imprisoned Jews and ordered their unconditional release. Subsequently the activity of Montefiore was at least partly responsible for the promulgation of the Firman Hatt-i Hümayun of 6 November 1840 by the 17-year-old Sultan Abdul Mejid.[10]

Ignorant people believe that the Jews are in the habit of making human sacrifices in order to use the blood in the (Passover) wafers. The Jews of Rhodes and Damascus, victims of this belief, subjects of our empire, have been persecuted by men of different faith. The calumny invented against the Jews, as well as the renewed violence to which they have been subjected, have come to the attention of our Imperial Throne. However it is not long since Jews of Rhodes, called to Constantinople for judgement, have been found innocent of the accusations which had been levelled at them. Moreover after investigations made by competent persons in the religious works of that nation it is clear that not only do Jews not use human blood but they also do not use the blood of animals. One can conclude, then, that the violence to which the Jews have been subjected, result from calumny and no more. The love that we have for our subjects extends equally to the Jewish nation ... we wish them to enjoy the advantages and privileges accorded to our other subjects by the *Hatti-i Serif* of Gülhane.

The 'investigations made by competent persons' seem to refer to material emanating from the London *Bet Din* and Chief Rabbi Solomon Hirschel which had been sent by Montefiore to the Porte.[11]

Montefiore's profound concern for the Jews of the area is un-disputed. His interest here, clearly, was to rid the Near East of this odious accusation and given that public recognition was accorded the fact that the Jews of Damascus had been wronged, his mission was crowned with a certain success. As we shall see, this success must be qualified.

In the context of the recent history of the Jews in Syria the Damascus Blood Libel was not a particularly surprising event. If the blood libel itself was virtually unknown in the Ottoman Empire, it should be remembered that anti-Jewish persecution of different sorts was a commonplace. When Burckhardt was in Syria some years before, he stressed that Muslim intolerance of Jews and Christians was particularly noticeable in Damascus: 'Damascus continues to be the seat of fanaticism.'[12] A little later, in 1823, Joseph Wolff was in Damascus and heard

the news that the high priest of the Jews, Joseph Abulafia and R. Farkhi, prime minister to the Pasha, both of whom I knew at Aleppo, with twelve others of the principal Jews at Damascus, were put in prison by express orders of the Sultan from Constantinople. It is left to them either to pay 40,000 bourses of piastres or to lose their heads. A renegade was appointed prime minister instead of the Jew, and the Turks began to shout, saying with smiles, Praise be to the Lord! a curse upon Raphael their Khakham! a curse upon all the Jews, their fathers, their mothers, grand fathers, grand mothers, their children, and their children's children.[13]

This is not the place to deal with the complex relationship between Jews and Muslims and Christians in the Middle East at the time.[14] It can be assumed, however, that the fact that the finances of the *vilayet* of Damascus were in the hands of a Jew over a considerable period (as they had been in the Pashalik of Acre some time before) did nothing to ingratiate the Jews in the affections of the common inhabitants of the land.[15] But it is also important to recall that during the Egyptian occupation of Syria and Palestine (1831—1840) the position of the Jews improved dramatically. In some ways, then, the events of 1840, and the general support that the persecution of the Jews was given by the Arab population at large, can be seen as a whiplash reaction against the various reforms introduced by the

Egyptians and in this sense is not dissimilar to the anti-Christian riots
which marred the 1860s in Damascus.[16]

No matter how relatively commonplace such persecution of the
Jews was in the Syria of 1840 (there had been worse 'pogroms'
against the Jews in nearby Safed in 1834 and 1838) it nonetheless
became a *cause célèbre* in the west and outraged western public
opinion. Throughout 1840 the case prompted the active participation
of Palmerston, Peel, Metternich, Queen Victoria (who gave Montefiore
the use of an official state vessel to cross the Channel on the first leg
of his voyage), John Forsyth, the American Secretary of State, and
Czar Nicholas of Russia. Public support in the USA had been courted
by public meetings in New York and Philadelphia and a meeting in
London's Mansion House on 3 July 1840 had demonstrated the
whole-hearted support of a wide cross-section of influential public
opinion. How can this massive interest be explained?

In the first place, the genuinely philanthropic instincts of men
such as Montefiore were brought to bear in an effective way. At the
same time a great deal of Jewish support was undoubtedly motivated
by a keen desire to prevent the spectre of the blood libel once again
haunting European Jewry and perhaps snatching away the newly
acquired fruits of (partial) emancipation. But in addition, Great
Britain had a declared interest in the Jews of the area. The year
before the Damascus Blood Libel, in January 1839, Palmerston
had instructed the first British Consul in Jerusalem, W. T. Young,
'to afford protection to the Jews generally'[17] and this policy was
subsequently extended to British consular officials throughout the
Ottoman Empire. Clearly it was to British advantage to have a
group in the Sultan's domains through which influence could be
exerted; France and to a lesser extent Austria had traditionally
posed as protectors of the local Latins, Maronites and Melkites,
while Russia saw itself as protector of the Greek Orthodox and
Armenian communities. There was, in addition, a powerful group
of people in England at the time who, influenced by millenarian
and other broadly evangelical considerations, had the warmest
sympathies for Jews in general, and particularly for those of the
Holy Land. One such was Lord Shaftesbury, Palmerston' stepfather-
in-law.

The immediate involvement of the French Consul in the case,
and the subsequent involvement of the Austrian Consul in Damascus
had the effect of drawing in the French and Austrian governments,
both of which, under Thiers and Metternich respectively, gave unqualified support to their consular representatives. Thus this relatively small incident in a remote place almost from the beginning

started to invoke and reflect political and other considerations from the stage of European affairs.

We know less than might be imagined of the Damascus libel itself, largely because the critical documents from the French side were removed from the normal consular correspondence in the French Foreign Ministry Archives in Paris and were gathered separately in the 'classified' section. They were there collected together under the title *Le Dossier du Père Thomas*. The three files that make up this dossier are entitled:

1. Dossier de l'affaire du Père Thomas de Damas assassiné par les Israelites indigènes
2. Affaire du Père Thomas assassiné par les Israelites indigènes
3. Dossier Ratti-Menton.

The dossier has been the object of considerable curiosity over the years and more than one Jewish scholar or institution has attempted to gain access to it. The Alliance Israélite Universelle made official requests to see the file in 1909 and 1913 but these requests were refused. In 1931 S. Posener, the then Secretary General of the Aid Committee for Russian Writers and Scholars in France and author of one of the standard texts on the Damascus case, applied to see the material and was refused. A memo of 1931 inserted in the file for the attention of M. la Boulaye — the then Director of Political and Commercial Affairs in the Foreign Ministry, read as follows:

More than ever today after the recent events in Palestine it appears inappropriate to draw the attention of the world to an affair which has provoked the most lively passions and whose memory, according to our agent in Beirut, M. Saint René Taillandier, has remained very alive in the Levant ... In any event, the agitation which would result in the mandated countries (Syria and Palestine) could have the gravest consequences and could trouble these regions for a long time to come, as here racial and religious conflicts are particularly acute.

An unsigned note of 7 March 1931 urged that the dossier should remain closed.

In view of these considerations, the department of political and commercial affairs believes that the refusal ... to open up the dossiers concerning the said affair of the Jews of Damascus must be maintained, the arguments which in 1909 and 1913 notably, gave rise to this decision have not lost their validity: indeed on the contrary, France is now directly interested in maintaining public order in the Levant where our Mandatory status creates its own responsibilities ... and this as much in regard to the local populations as to Foreign Powers. The bloody troubles which have been provoked in Palestine in 1929 — the bitter conflict between Zionists and Muslims — provide a striking example of the excesses which racial or confessional passions can bring about in the region.

During the Second World War the German authorities in occupied Paris made photocopies of the Father Thomas files which were sent

to Berlin along with similar material from the archives of the Alliance
Israélite Universelle in Paris and, indeed, 'antisemitica' from the rest
of occupied Europe.

In a letter dated 21 October 1952 the Jewish historian, Szajkowski,
wrote asking if he could see the file and added that he had found a
part of the copy of the Dossier in Berlin in July 1945.

In a departmental note of 17 December 1952 an unnamed French
official of the Foreign Ministry Archive service observed:

> M. Szajkowski/Frydman has let us know that he was able to procure photocopies
> in Berlin made by the Germans between 1940 and 1944. He presents 3 of these
> photocopies but refuses to reveal their number — simply stating that he does
> not believe he has the whole dossier.
>
> He notes that the dossier presents the role of Ratti-Menton and the Govern-
> ment of Louis Philippe in an unfavourable light. In the confidence that other
> documents would allow M. Szajkowski to correct his conclusions in the favour
> of France he requests permission to see the rest of the file.

Szajkowski's ruse failed and his application, too, was turned
down. In an article subsequently published in *Tziyyon* he claimed to
have 1,000 pages of photocopies from the dossier but he barely
quoted from the material and concluded that it was better not to use
the German copy but to await the possibility of examining the
original file.

It goes without saying, perhaps, that the files were closed to non-
Jews as well. Thus the anti-semite Albert Monniot wished to consult
the documents when he was 'researching' *Le Crime Rituel chez les
Juifs* but was not granted permission. The British anti-semite and
fascist A. S. Leese, author of *My Irrelevant Defence: Meditations
Inside Gaol and Out on Jewish Ritual Murder* (London, 1938)
concluded in respect of these files 'that the secrets of the Jew are
well guarded.' Clearly there were no Jewish 'secrets'. The only reason
for classifying this material for so long is the poor light shed on
the French Government and particularly on its consular staff in the
area.

It is perhaps worth recording that in the reorganization of the
Foreign Ministry material which took place in 1965, the titles of the
three files were retained: i.e. two files are still officially marked 'The
assassination of Père Thomas by the local Jews in 1840'. What is
more, a slip is inserted in the first file recommending any interested
reader to consult what is described as the authoritative book on the
subject — entitled *L'assassinat du Père Thomas et le Talmud* by Jean
Drault, published by the anti-semitic *La Vieille France* in the 1920s.[18]
Needless to say, the book expresses the most virulently anti-semitic
views. It is also worth recording that certain dispatches written between

March 1840 and April 1840 have been removed from the classified files and are not to be found elsewhere.

In the file there is a great deal of material which adds somewhat to our knowledge of the events surrounding the trial of the Jews, the role of the Pasha, and the day to day activities of the various European Consuls.

Unfortunately the files fail to solve the enigmatic question of what actually happened to Thomas and his servant. There is nothing to support the explanation given by Graetz and others since, that in fact Thomas and Ibrahim were killed by a Muslim merchant who had observed a heated argument between Thomas, Ibrahim and a Muslim muleteer. Nor is there evidence, here, or elsewhere as far as I know, to support Rosambert's claim that 'des Turcs — on le sut plus tard — étaient les assassins'.[19] Nor is there any support in the French archives for the account recently published by the noted historian of the Middle East, A. L. Tibawi, and based on the writing of a more or less contemporary Christian Arab chronicler Mīkhā'īl Mishāqa which, as the following quotation indicates, suggests that certain Jews were responsible for the murder of Thomas and Ibrahim but that the charge of ritual murder was a fabrication:

The disappearance of the padre was connected with the belief then common in the Near East, as it had been common in medieval Europe, that the Jews murdered Christians in order to mingle their blood with the unleavened bread of Passover. Details of the case, which assumed international significance, have often been related and need not be repeated here. But the crime was one of robbery followed by murder of which a Jewish barber and his assistant were accused, duly tried and condemned. The British consul Werry, himself sympathetic to the Jews, testified that the promptness of the Egyptians in taking action saved the Jewish community in Damascus from a general massacre.

According to Mīkhā'īl Mishāqa, a respectable Christian physician then resident in Damascus, who personally knew the padre and some of the Jews questioned, the leaders of the Jewish community made the mistake of overpleading the innocence of a few scoundrels in their community. In this way they compromised themselves and brought unnecessary accusations and suffering on themselves. Mishāqa adds that Sir Moses Montefiore was so moved as to seek an audience of Muḥammad 'Ali. He is reputed to have given him a present of 60,000 purses and 3,000 purses to the secretaries, in return for obtaining a pardon for the Jewish leaders but not a declaration of their innocence.[20]

In certain respects the French material makes the question more rather than less complex. We learn a little more about the *dramatis personae*. Thus Ratti-Menton, an aristocrat of Italian extraction, does not emerge entirely as described by Ursula Henriques in her recent article: 'Perhaps a sort of Himmler without the large-scale technology of destruction'. Ratti-Menton had been in Damascus for three months before the disappearance of the priest. During this period his dealings with the Jewish community indicate that his attitude towards the Jews was not particularly malevolent. The two relevant dispatches concern petitions by Jews to the consul on the subject of marriages. One reads:

Signor Mehir Sultan, an Algerian Rabbi who is here in Damascus with several of his Algerian co-religionists has given me a petition (enclosed) which he begs me to forward to your Excellency. As this petition is in Hebrew I had the petitioner explain it to me. The object is to secure the agreement of the King to the marriage of his son Moses aged 18 to a young Israelite of Damascus — I have promised him that I will do my best to obtain from your excellency the permission he asks for.[21]

Another similar request:

Sr. Mousa, an Algerian Jew aged 23 who like his father works in Damascus as an artisan, begs his Majesty's permission to marry a young Muscovite of the Jewish Faith who has been here in Damascus since she was a child. This young girl is an orphan and it is in order to assure her a fate less awful than the state in which she now finds herself that Sr. Mousa's father desires this union.

I believe, Minister, that there would be no difficulty in according authorization for him, especially as it coincides with an act of humanity.[22]

It should perhaps also be noted that, unlike most anti-semites, Ratti-Menton was not inclined to tar all Jews with the same brush. In a number of reports he stressed that it was only a handful of initiates in Damascus who knew of the 'tradition' of ritual murder. Subsequently, in a report to Thiers (no. 19, 24 March 1840), he claimed to receive some 'consolation' from the fact that 'civilized' European Jews had no knowledge of 'these acts of repulsive fanaticism' and in the same report he talks of his principles in connection with 'the emancipation of this portion of humanity' (i.e. European Jewry). All this, it must be admitted, does not add up to a great deal, but it perhaps might suggest that Ratti-Menton's motivation was not one of Jew hatred.

A further report from Ratti-Menton dated 21 December 1839 (no. 12) casts new light on one of the other principal figures in this drama, Father Thomas:

Father Thomas, a Franciscan [sic] priest has come to explain his position to me and ask, through my good offices, that the Government of the King help him in his old age.

Father Thomas, who is almost 70 years old, came to Syria 30 years ago after being promised by Cardinal Fech [probably Fesch who was the then French representative at the Holy See] that the imperial Government would provide for him. It is certain that this promise was never kept and that the priest in question has extremely limited resources.

From information I have gathered from M. Beaudin which concurs with that from our Lazarist monks here, Father Thomas has always been a peaceful man, fulfilling his priestly duties without fanaticism, and he has won the regard and the affection of Christian and Muslim alike. But one fact which in my opinion makes him deserving of benevolent support of the King's Government is the introduction of vaccine which the population of Damascus owes to him and which he has propogated with a praiseworthy zeal. He pins more hope on his request for a pension given that his advanced years will not allow him to enjoy it for very long. I must add that he is almost blind and that the presence in Damascus of a mission of Terre Sainte monks deprives him of the income which he would otherwise have had as French chaplain (*chapelain de la nation*).

What we learn of Thomas in this dispatch does not tally with later accounts. According to Pieritz, a Jewish convert from Jerusalem who visited Damascus not long after Thomas' disappearance, Thomas at 'about sixty years old was yet in full vigour, of a tall stature, and a hot temper'.[23] Where is the gentle priest described by Ratti-Menton, who has not long to live and is virtually blind?

Thomas' medical work in Syria was not unusual. W. M. Thomson, author of *The Land and the Book* spent some time in Damascus on a medical mission and reported:

The European renegades in the (medical) service are very little better, with a few exceptions. The monks that practise medicine as a profession have a very fair knowledge of simples, and compound their own medicines, and employ a good many recent chemicals and modern ingredients in the European *Materia Medica*; but their knowledge of acute diseases is necessarily limited.[24]

A Syrian Christian wrote of 'Italian or other quack medical professors, who are harsh in their treatment of the sick, unconscionable as to charges, and in any real case of difficulty seldom, if ever, successful'.[25] What sort of physician was Thomas? Pieritz wrote of him: 'He used particularly to vaccinate children, both of the Jews and others, by which he amassed a tolerable sum of money.'[26] This clearly contradicts Ratti-Menton's contention that Thomas was indigent. In addition how can we account for the presence in the priest's room on the day of his disappearance of the very considerable sum of 119,000 piastres mentioned by Ratti-Menton in a dispatch of 17 March, with the explanation that the money was handed over to Thomas' successor, Père François?[27] The little that we have to go on is sufficient to indicate that perhaps Thomas was not the most straightforward of priests and that there was a connection, previously unremarked, between Thomas and Ratti-Menton, before Thomas's disappearance. Why should Ratti-Menton have asked for a pension for Thomas if the latter was in comfortable circumstances and robust health?

Let us return to Ratti-Menton. What sort of a man was he? Born in Puerto Rico in 1799, he started his diplomatic career as Vice-Consul in Genoa in 1822, went on to Naples, Chili, Tiflis and Gibraltar before he was made Consul (*Première Classe*) in Damascus in 1839. On 5 March 1841, shortly after the conclusion of the affair, he was made a Chevalier of the Order of St Maurice and St Lazare. On 21 September 1842, Guizot wrote to Louis Philippe making reference to the recent budget and to the changes in the diplomatic staff which it necessitated:

Ref. to consulates created by recent budget changes in diplomatic staff:

In proposing the Count of Ratti-Menton for the new consulate at Canton I wished to reward his firm probity in Damascus. He knows English well. He is a man capable of conducting affairs on his own — which is an indispensable factor at this distance. Canton will become a very important post.

While he was in Canton he came under suspicion of corruption in a smuggling racket — but nothing came of it and he moved on shortly afterwards to Calcutta. In 1855 he was appointed Consul General in Havana, where again his name was connected with corruption in the tobacco trade. A note made by a French Foreign Ministry official dated July 1862 defended his honour in the following terms:

Ratti-Menton comes from an aristocratic family. His father was a captain of the regiment of the Dauphin. He joined the consular service in 1822.

It was in Damascus, where we find him in 1839, that his probity was put to the test from which he emerged intact. If it were not for the fact that his probity was being contested today I would not have recalled this incident. At Easter time a Latin monk, Father Thomas, disappeared and Ratti-Menton, under whose protection he came, soon acquired the proof that he had been assassinated by certain fanatical Jews. He demanded their punishment from the Muslim authorities and did not let himself be sidetracked from his duty by the attempts that were made to corrupt him and achieve his withdrawal from the case. A Jewish banker from Damascus, Farḥi, offered him, on behalf of the Chief Rabbi, the chance to help himself to the treasures of the synagogue.

By this time Ratti-Menton was a senior diplomatic officer: the year before he had been appointed an officer of the *Légion d'Honneur*. Nothing came of the allegations made against him in Havana and on 16 March 1862 he retired from the diplomatic service. The support that Ratti-Menton received from his government throughout his career was remarkable. According to the files no-one in the French Ministry of Foreign Affairs ever appears to have doubted the guilt of the Jews in the Damascus Affair, or to have suspected his involvement in any way despite the numerous occasions throughout his career when his 'probity', to say the least, was suspect. In none of the documents, including Ratti-Menton's personal file, is there any condemnation of his actions.

It seems quite probable that Ratti-Menton was involved in a conspiracy of sorts against the Jews. His subsequent history would suggest that he was in all probability corrupt. His earlier connections with Thomas and the rather mysterious contradictions about the latter's age, health and financial status would perhaps suggest that Thomas, too, might have been involved in the conspiracy. If the motive was financial gain then there would have been many a wealthy Christian who might have been happy to see the destruction of the community which contained his greatest rivals. We also know that Beaudin, the *chancelier* at the French consulate, who played a thoroughly discreditable role in the affair, acted as an agent for a number of foreign merchants in their dealings with Jewish merchants of Damascus.[28] As one of his functions in this respect was debt collection, extortion as a possible motive cannot be ruled out. Was Thomas given a generous sum of money and sent off to a retirement of comfortable obscurity? Did Ratti-Menton enrich himself in Damascus (despite his frequent protestations to the contrary), as he apparently tried to do later in his career? As Ratti-Menton himself was the author of the greater part of the material in the *Dossier du Père Thomas*, it would be surprising indeed if the answers to these questions were to be found in the French Foreign Ministry Archives.

Why did the French government support Ratti-Menton's 'conspiracy', if such it was? When the news of the blood libel broke in Paris in February, Thiers had just come to power. He had always defended French interests overseas with a particular insistence. An alliance with the Egyptians, now masters of Palestine and Syria, seemed to offer glittering opportunities. Throughout the correspondence, Ratti-Menton is careful on his side to stress the key position played by the Egyptian governor of Damascus in the case. Thus, by supporting Ratti-Menton the French government was also supporting the Egyptians. It seems probable that the Egyptian governor became as involved as he did at least partially through a desire to avoid offending the French, in the person of their Consul. Thus Ratti-Menton was allowed a free hand. It is impossible to know what Thiers' views were on the accusations against the Jews. He knew little about Judaism and less about the Jews of Syria. But he was certainly ready to exploit the blood libel to further French interests in the area.

Whatever Ratti-Menton's private reasons were for prosecuting the case against the Jews with such vigour, if indeed he had private reasons, his public position *vis-à-vis* the French authorities was that he was defending French interests and French honour. From the French point of view thus defined, the affair rapidly became part of a struggle for influence in Syria. The traditional right of the French to the protectorate of Catholics in the Ottoman Empire was being questioned. The French viewed the British and the Austrians as vying with each other for the right to protect Jews. In July 1840, Ratti-Menton wrote to Thiers:

In my letter no. 30 I had occasion to mention in passing the tendency of the Cabinet in Vienna to exploit 'l'affaire juive' to the advantage of Austrian interests . . . . Such protection of the Jews would have the immediate effect of rallying the Jews of Asia to Austria and to give to the principle (of protection) a strength which it fundamentally does not have but which would be an incontestable means of influence. A subsequent result would be to assure the Austrian Government of the gratitude of European Jews and consequently to facilitate loans.[29]

In a later dispatch Ratti-Menton made it quite clear that he was perfectly aware of the special interest that Britain had in the Jews which has been alluded to above. Writing to Thiers, he noted

that the English consul in Damascus has received orders to take particular and special interest in the affairs of the Jews and to give them assistance whenever possible. Lord Ponsonby [Ambassador to Constantinople] finished his letter telling Mr. Werry [British consul in Damascus] that the English and Austrian governments were agreed on this point.

In addition to this information which I think it is useful to pass on to His Majesty's Government is a further communication which I have hesitated to send for some time as it is the result of an indiscretion which although I did not provoke it, seemed to me of a confidential nature. It has to do with a letter written by the English Vice-Consul in Jerusalem to the English Consul in Damascus last March containing a copy of a paragraph of a letter from Lord Palmerston. Well before the assassination of Father Thomas, this minister ordered Vice-Consul Young, whenever possible, to seize any opportunity which might present itself to protect *ra'aya* Jews in his area.[30]

Thus the 'firm stand' he was taking against the Jews of Damascus was shown to be a stand against the machinations of Albion. Similarly, in an earlier report Ratti-Menton had presented the murder of Thomas as a calculated Jewish outrage against the prestige and honour of France.

For 32 years Father Thomas has gone around all the quarters of this city without danger pursuing his ministry of charity; but three months after a consulate of the King is established here the Jews attack immediate protégés of the Consulate!

It is a challenge to the tutelary action of His Majesty's Government and as such as well as because of the outrage to human society of these fiendish sacrifices, it is advisable to impose a salutory terror upon the Jews . . .[31]

Thus Ratti-Menton was able to present his prosecution of the Jews in such terms as it seemed a logical consequence and extension of

French policies in the area. Whatever Thiers' views on the blood libel might have been, he was prepared to support the Consul to the hilt, not on the merits or demerits of the idea of the accusation of ritual murder, but in his own words:

> As he [Ratti-Menton] has been opposed by all the foreign representatives, I have considered it my duty to support him, and I shall continue to uphold him until his errors, if any have been committed, shall have been proved . . .[32]

Ratti-Menton and others have suggested that it was the local Christians of Damascus who first hurled the charge of ritual murder against the Jews. Ratti-Menton's account of the first hours of the Affair shows that on the evening of 6 February, Thomas was to dine with a certain Dr Massari and various other foreign *réligieux.*

His absence at this meeting made even more remarkable by the simultaneous disappearance of his one domestic servant could only be explained by the supposition that Father Thomas had gone to neighbouring villages to vaccinate children. Informed of what had happened I went to the convent where the street was blocked by a multitude of Christians of all sects who were shouting that Father Thomas had been immolated by the Jews.[33]

It may indeed be that the initiative behind this attempt to undermine the position of the Jews in Damascus came from the local Christians. Relations between Christians and Jews in Damascus, as elsewhere, had for generations been aggravated by socio-economic rivalries. Christians and Jews had traditionally vied with each other for positions in the various branches of the Ottoman administration and in many cases there were fierce personal rivalries between Jewish and Christian merchants and artisans. An example of such rivalry is the fierce competition that existed between the Jewish family of Farḥi and the Christian family of Bahri in the administrative services of Syria. The local Christians had much to gain from attacking the Jews and it is probably no coincidence that some of the richest Jewish families in Damascus were implicated in the case. The Jews of Damascus, at any rate, seem to have held the local Christians responsible for the Affair. As soon as the Turks entered Damascus on 28 January 1841, after the Egyptian withdrawal, the Jews fell on the Christians with unrestrained fury.[34]

But it is unlikely that the specific allegation of ritual murder came from the local Arab Christians. There is very little evidence to suggest that in modern times there had been blood libels in the Middle East before 1840. As Crémieux put it:

Almost 1250 years ago Islam raised its standard in the Orient, in the city of Damascus. Never during this period have the Jews had this stupid accusation levelled at them. Christians are starting to make their influence felt in these lands and all of a sudden Western prejudices come to life in the Orient! What a sad subject for contemplation![35]

We do not know who first accused the Jews of Damascus of ritual murder. Ratti-Menton rather glosses over this point in his reports. The Christians he met outside Thomas's house were shouting (according to his report) that Thomas had been *immolé* by the Jews. While the French word has the sense of sacrifice (specifically by burning) it has the more usual, general sense of 'slaughter' and this, it appears, is what the word means here. Who first made the suggestion of ritual murder is unclear. Perhaps it was Ratti-Menton; perhaps it was the foreign priests of Thomas's convent which Wolff, the famous traveller, had found somewhat anti-semitic when he had stayed there some years before.[36] What does seem fairly apparent is that foreign monks played an active role in spreading news of the blood libel by distributing tracts containing quotations from supposedly Jewish sources which purported to demonstrate the truth of the libel. Pieritz wrote:

The monks have been very industrious in distributing these quotations in Arabic throughout the country, accompanied with the most malignant calumnies and misrepresentations of the affair at Damascus. I found some of these extracts in Arabic in Tyre (Sour). In Beyrout there is scarcely a person without them; and in Alexandria, I find them equally common in the Italian language.[37]

It is certain that within a short space of time the story of the accusations against the Jews of Damascus was well known in the Middle East, particularly among Christian groups and Turkish officials.[38]

Although the blood libel was virtually unknown in the Middle East in the period prior to 1840 it had been known in Turkey in the fifteenth and sixteenth centuries.[39] But there is little evidence for the presence of blood libels in Syria and Palestine and the surrounding areas in the centuries preceding the Damascus Affair. Such evidence as there is consists of two legends which were current in Jerusalem during the nineteenth century, both of which involve the supernatural salvation of the Jewish community of Jerusalem from destruction following the accusation that children had been murdered for ritual purposes. It is probable that these tales reflect a collective memory of European blood libels of the past; clearly they do not constitute historical evidence for our purposes.[40]

Blood libels became frequent throughout the entire region after the Damascus Affair. In the vicinity of Damascus there were nine blood libels between 1840 and 1900. In Palestine there were blood libels in 1847, 1848, 1870 and 1871. In 1844 there were two cases of blood libels in Egypt: one in Cairo, instigated by Muslims, and the other, in Alexandria, instigated by the Greek Orthodox;[41] in 1866, in Hamadan in western Iran, eighteen Jews were massacred following a ritual murder accusation — two more were burnt alive while the rest of the community only managed to escape the fury of the mob by converting *en masse* to Islam;[42] there were further libels in Alexandria in 1870,[43] in Smyrna in 1871,[44] and Damanhur (Egypt) in 1871 and 1873, initiated by Muslims[45] and again in Smyrna in 1873.[46] In 1875 there was a blood libel in Aleppo, as a result of which the Pasha of Aleppo had to send troops to guard the Jewish quarter.[47] In 1876 there was another blood libel in Smyrna[48] and one in Constantinople,[49] while 1877 saw libels in Damanhur and Mansura, where the local Muslims accused the Jews of kidnapping a Muslim child and killing it in order to use its blood for *matzot*.[50] In 1879 an official of the *Alliance Israélite Universelle* lamented:

Il n'est guère d'années où cette accusation odieuse ne se renouvelle surtout à l'approche de la Pâque, dans quelques régions de l'Orient. Elle s'est produite cette année à Metelin, près de Smyrna, à Kustendil, près de Salonique, à Alexandrie d'Egypt . . .[51]

H. H. Jessup, who spent fifty-three years in the Middle East and was one of the chief figures of the American Presbyterian church in Beirut, had an intimate knowledge of the local Arab churches. He wrote as follows on the relations between the local churches and the Jews:

They are hated intensely by all the sects, but more especially by the Greeks and Latins. In the gradations of Oriental cursing, it is tolerably reasonable to call a man a donkey, somewhat severe to call him a dog, contemptuous to call him a swine, but withering to the last degree to call him a Jew.

The animosity of the nominal Christian sects against the Jews is most relentless and unreasoning. They believe that the Jews kill Christian children every year at the Passover and mingle their blood with the Passover bread. Almost every year in the spring, this senseless charge is brought against the Jews . . . the Jews of Beirut and Damascus are obliged to pay heavy blackmail every year to the Greek and Latin 'lewd fellows of the baser sort' who threaten to raise a mob against them for killing Christian children . . . and not only do they regard them as children of hell but would rejoice to send them there if they could.[52]

In 1881, Joseph Sebag, the Vice-President of the London Committee of Deputies of British Jews, wrote to Earl Granville, the Secretary of State for Foreign Affairs:

On the 26 March last the London Committee of Deputies of the British Jews and the Anglo-Jewish Association had the honour to invite Your Lordship's attention to the terrible 'blood accusation' which annually, at the approach of Easter, is circulated in the East, principally among the ignorant classes of the Greek

Church — an accusation which in the present year threatened the Jewish inhabitants of Alexandria with most dangerous consequences.[53]

So, forty years on, the Board of Deputies was facing the same problem as it had in 1840. But never after 1840 was there such a magnificent and concerted effort by Jews and others to achieve justice and redress. In this sense the Hamburg Jews who presented Montefiore with a gold medal in recognition of his great work for the Damascus Jews were right to mark it *Shenat Geon Yisrael* (The Year of the Pride of Israel), the last two words having the numerical value of the Hebrew date of the Damascus Affair (5601). The Jews, as Thiers himself grudgingly conceded, had much to be proud of; and Montefiore more than any other. But in the long term, Montefiore's activity did nothing to stop the blood libel in the Middle East. Indeed, it could be argued that the unprecedented publicity that the Affair generated, did something to disseminate this form of Christian anti-semitism in the Arab world. In 1847 Beaudin, still in Damascus, was responsible for a further accusation of blood libel against the Jews. Montefiore again took the matter up and personally interviewed Louis-Philippe and Guizot, his foreign minister. Montefiore was able to extract a letter from Guizot, specifically condemning the outrage and assuring him that French consular staff would be instructed accordingly. But in the Middle East, western influence was increasing apace and as far as the blood libel was concerned, Pandora's box had been opened. In this sense 'the false prophets and quack doctors' had the last laugh.

Nonetheless, this only slightly detracts from Montefiore's great work — the importance of which lay elsewhere. The fact of the matter is that the Damascus Affair is one of the great examples of intercession by Jewish notables in the Jewish interest. The publicly acknowledged success of this intercession on the official level outweighs its failure to exorcize the spectre of the blood libel from the Middle East.

NOTES

1. H. Graetz, *History of the Jews* (London, 1901), v, p. 676.
2. There is general agreement on this. Thus in a recent work: 'The Jewish reaction to the Damascus Affair is justifiably regarded as a turning point in the history of Western Jewry in the nineteenth century': *A History of the Jewish People*, ed. H. H. Ben-Sasson (London, 1977), p. 848. See also e.g. B. Mevorah, 'Ikvoteiha shel 'alilat damesek be-hitpathutah shel ha-'ittonut ha-yehudit be-shanim 1840—1846', *Tziyyon*, 23—24, 1—2, p. 46.

3. There are no available statistics for the populations of Middle Eastern cities at this time. But see: J. Wolff, *Missionary Journal and Memoir*, (London, 1827), ii, p. 184, and J. L. Porter, *Five Years in Damascus*, vol. i, p. 139 (based on M. Bulad, 'who had access to the Government registers').

4. See below p. 143.

5. J. B. Levinsohn, *Efes Dammim*, tr. L. Loewe (London, 1841), p. xii.

6. Ibid.

7. See T. Parfitt, 'Sir Moses Montefiore and Palestine' in *Sir Moses Montefiore: A Symposium*, ed. V. D. Lipman (Oxford, 1982), pp. 31–42.

8. Board of Deputies: Minute Book, 3, 1838–August 1840.

9. Ibid.

10. An admirable account of Montefiore's activity is to be found in U. R. Q. Henriques, 'Who Killed Father Thomas?' in *Sir Moses Montefiore: A Symposium*, pp. 50–75.

11. A. Galanté, *Documents officiels Turcs concernant les Juifs de Turquie* (Stamboul, 1931), pp. 214–220.

12. J. L. Burckhardt, *Travels in Syria and the Holy Land* (London, 1822), p. 322.

13. Wolff, pp. 180–81.

14. I have dealt with this subject at length in *The Jews in Palestine before Zionism* (The Royal Historical Society, London, in press).

15. Cf. C. L. Irby and J. Mangles, *Travels in Egypt and Nubia, Syria and Asia Minor in 1817 and 1818* (London, 1823), p. 165.

16. See M. Ma'oz, 'Changes in the Position of the Jewish communities of Palestine and Syria in mid-19th century', *International Seminar on the History of Palestine and its Jewish Settlement during the Ottoman Period* (Jerusalem, 1970). See also J. Bowring, *Report on the Commercial Statistics of Syria Addressed to the Right Hon. Lord Viscount Palmerston, Parliamentary Papers*, 1840 (27B), 21, p. 136 'the political equality to which the other sects have been raised by the present government of Syria, creates a sort of religious disaffection towards their rulers.'

17. F.O. 78/368, J. Bidwell to W. T. Young, Foreign Office, 31 January 1839.

18. There is a considerable literature on the Damascus Affair. See especially: Z. Szajkowsi, 'Goral ha-Tikim be-Ministerion ha-Hutz ha-Tzarfati ha-Noge'im la-'Alilat Damesek', *Tziyyon*, xix, 3–4, 167–70; B. Mevorah, 'Ikvoteiha shel"Alilat Damesek"'; S. Posener, *Adolphe Crémieux* (Paris, 1933), i, 198–247, 259–60; N. M. Gelber, 'Oesterreich und die Damaskus Affaire im Jahre 1840', *Jahrbuch der Jüd. Lit. Gesellschaft*, xviii (1927); J. Meisl, 'Beiträge zur Damaskus Affaire', *Festschrift zu S. Dubnow 70-em Geburstag* (Berlin, 1930); A. Laurent, *Relation Historique des Affaires de Syrie depuis 1840 jusqu'au 1842* (Paris, 1846); G. W. Pieritz, *Persecution of the Jews at Damascus* (London, 1840); L. H. Loewenstein, *Damascia* (Rodelheim, 1840); L. Loewe, *The Damascus Affair* (Ramsgate, 1940); A. M. Hyamson in the *Transactions of the Jewish Historical Society of England*, vol. XVI (1952), 47–71. See also U. R. Q. Henriques, 'Who killed Father Thomas?' in *Sir Moses Montefiore: A Symposium*.

19. A. Rosambert, *Crimes Rituels* (extrait de la Revue Lorraine d'Anthropologie, 1931–32), p. 14.

20. A. L. Tibawi, *A Modern History of Syria* (London, 1969), p. 90.

21. Affaires Etrangères, Correspondence Commercial, Damas, no. 11, Damas, 21 Dec., 1839, Ratti-Menton to S. E. M. le Maréchal, Duc de Dalmatie, Ministre et Sécretaire d'Etat Aux Affaires Etrangères.

22. Ibid.
23. G. W. Pieritz, *Persecution of the Jews at Damascus*, p. 3.
24. Habeeb Risk Allah Effendi, *The Thistle and the Cedar of Lebanon* (2nd edn., London, 1854), quoted on p. 377.
25. *The Thistle and the Cedar*, p. 378.
26. Pieritz, p. 1.
27. A.E., Dir. Comm. 18, 17 March 1840, Ratti-Menton to Thiers.
28. A. Laurent, *Relation Historique des Affaires de Syrie Depuis 1840 jusqu'au 1842*, 1, p. 226 ff.
29. A.E. no. 33, Ratti-Menton to Thiers, 27 July 1840.
30. A.E. no. 34, Ratti-Menton to Thiers, 17 August 1840.
31. A.E. no. 16, Ratti-Menton to Duc de Dalmatie, 29 February 1840.
32. S. Posener, *Adolphe Crémieux* (Philadelphia, 1940), p. 103.
33. A.E. no. 16, Ratti-Menton to Duc de Dalmatie, 29 February 1840.
34. A. Laurent, *Relation Historique des Affaires de Syrie*, i, p. 259.
35. A. Crémieux, *Journal des Débats*, 8 April 1840.
36. Wolff, p. 196; H. H. Ben Sasson, p. 847: 'His fellow monks spread a rumour that he had been murdered as part of their religious ritual'; unfortunately no reference is given.
37. Pieritz, p. 15.
38. A. R. Malakhi, *Perakim be-Toledot ha-Yishuv ha-Yashan* (Tel Aviv, 1971), p. 83.
39. U. Heyd, 'Ritual Murder accusations in 15th and 16th century Turkey', *Sefunot* v (1961), pp. 137—44. See also H. L. Strack, *The Jew and Human Sacrifice* (London, 1909), p. 266.
40. See M. M. Raysher, *Shar'arei Yerushalayim* (Lemberg, 1866), p. 110; A. R. Malakhi, *Perakim be-Toledot ha-Yishuv*, pp. 79—80; J. E. Hanauer, *Folk-Lore of the Holy Land* (London, 1935), p. 77.
41. J. M. Landau, *Jews in Nineteenth Century Egypt* (London, 1969), p. 30.
42. Alliance Israélite Universelle (AIU) *Bulletin* (1866), 5.
43. AIU (Archives) l.B.i., D. Robino to AIU, 29 May 1870.
44. AIU *Bulletin* (1871), 4.
45. J. M. Landau, op. cit., 43, 199.
46. AIU *Bulletin* (1873), 95.
47. AIU *Bulletin* (1875), 13.
48. Ibid. (1876), 7.
49. Ibid.
50. J. M. Landau, op. cit., 39, 199.
51. AIU *Bulletin* (1879), 41. See e.g. J. M. Landau 'Alilot Dam u-Redifot Yehudim be-Mitzrayim be-Sof ha-Meah ha-19', *Sefunot*, 5, 1961, 415.
52. H. H. Jessup, *Fifty Three Years in Syria* (London, 1910), ii, 424—5.
53. Board of Deputies Archives 132/9/16 (Cases of Blood Libel) letter from Joseph Sebag to Earl Granville, 22 Sept. 1881.

2

A Diary that Survived: Damascus 1840

R. D. BARNETT

In a recent article[1] I drew attention to the senseless and virtually total destruction in the 1890s at Ramsgate of the considerable archives of Sir Moses Montefiore, especially of his diaries and correspondence, on the orders of his heir and successor, Sir Joseph Sebag-Montefiore. Lucien Wolf, who reports and comments bitterly on the incident, says there were till then in existence 'hundreds' of diaries of Sir Moses. However, Dr L. Loewe in the Preface to his edition of the *Diaries*[2] mentions having had the use of only eighty-five, though he does not say whether that number was all that existed.

In the same article I mentioned that among the very few surviving diaries was that covering the period in 1840 of Sir Moses' famous mission to Alexandria in connection with the 'Damascus Affair', which is preserved in the archives of the Spanish and Portuguese Jews' Congregation of London. The bicentenary of Sir Moses' birth seemed a fitting moment to transcribe and publish this record.[3]

The diary in fact consists of two pocket notebooks, containing entries in pencil. The books are $7\frac{1}{2}$ inches × $3\frac{1}{2}$ inches, bound in red morocco, each with a pair of loops designed to hold a pencil. The spines bear in gold lettering the words: 'Penny's Improved Patent'. Each booklet contains forty-six pages with cash ruling. A label on the end-paper describes them under a version of the royal coat of arms as 'H. Penny's/Improved Patent Metallic/Books/*warranted*/ if written on with his/prepared *pencils/to be* as plain *and durable* as *Ink*' and adds 'They will be found of great advantage to Travellers and all persons who wish to preserve their writing'. The stationer, W. T. and J. Mabley, of 9 Wellington Street North, Strand, adds his advertisement on a small label.

Would that Mr Penny's prophecy had been true! Perhaps Sir Moses did not use the right sort of pencil. The writing in the first notebook is small, neat and careful but at times exceedingly faint and hard to decipher; the second booklet is almost totally illegible (it is described more fully below). We are thus here concerned only with the first. Both booklets passed into the possession of Mrs. Cecil Sebag-Montefiore[4] (probably from her father-in-law, Sir Joseph Sebag-Montefiore), who presented them in 1936 to the Records and

Treasures Committee of the Synagogue through the kind offices of
the Revd D. B. de Mesquita, stating that it had been the particular
wish of her son Owen Sebag-Montefiore (d. 1935) that they should
be in the possession of the Synagogue.

It cannot be claimed that this diary adds any important historical
information to all that which was already known about the 'Damascus
Affair' and Sir Moses' mission. Indeed, there is one rather curious
omission — Sir Moses' diary makes no reference whatever to the
letter which the British Ambassador to the Porte procured from the
Sultan of Turkey's Grand Vizier, addressed to Mehemet Ali and
recommending Sir Moses and his party to him. This letter is published by Dr Loewe in the *Diaries* on p. 227 under the date of 8
August. Perhaps Sir Moses preferred not to present it, fearing lest it
might do more harm than good to his cause and prove an embarrassment.

But what the diary does contribute are two valuable things. First,
it discloses to us at last a little more of the real man, the lack of
which I much lamented in my article,[5] since it gives it to us in his
own *ipsissima verba*, written only for himself. Secondly, it shows
us clearly how Dr Loewe used the material at his disposal, altering
it and omitting a great deal as he thought fit. I have marked with a
vertical line in the side of the transcribed diary those sections or
paragraphs which also appear in Dr Loewe's book. It is thus easy to
see at a glance how much and what type of material he chose to
alter or omit. No doubt he was forced to do much of this by the
exigencies of space and time. Nevertheless, he was clearly not concerned to record those rather small or often droll details which show
us Sir Moses and his wife as very normal, very human beings with
whom we immediately feel an affinity — he loses his carpet bag
(8 July) and on 17 July his 'handsome' travelling-cap. He hates the
sea and sea travel: he and Judith are distinctly 'bad sailors'. He dislikes and distrusts Crémieux, who rubs him up the wrong way from
the start. But he can admire the beauty of nature and is not insensible
to the charms of a pretty girl (31 July), albeit he is a constant and
sincerely loving husband. His grammar is not always flawless, and he
displays a majestic indifference to the correct spelling of people's
names. But his piety and sincere orthodoxy are manifest. Each day
is headed with the praise of God (*Laus Deo*); many conclude with a
prayer. The name of God is usually spelt incompletely in deference
to the views of the strictly orthodox.

The complicated organization of the journey is not specifically
described, but can be pieced together from incidental information.
After Justina's eye operation (6 July) and a series of farewells,

mainly to members of the family, came the official send-off at London Bridge next day. At the offices of the Alliance Assurance Company, Sir Moses and his party meet their servants, who have brought their five carriages from Ramsgate. The carriages are put on board and all sail to Gravesend. Here Sir Moses and his party leave the boat and travel overland to Dover, cross the Channel to Calais, and catch up with the carriages at Boulogne. In them they are escorted by Delport, the Rothschild courier, from Calais as far as Lyons,[6] they then cross France to Marseilles; here the carriages are left and sent home with most of the servants. Lady Montefiore's maid, Harriet Rogers, left her at Paris. Two manservants remain with them: Robert Buck and (possibly) Ed. Bell Stephens; and a Mr and Mrs Edrehi, whose function is not clear — he may have been a *shomer* (ritual food inspector), embark with them (21 July) on the *Minos* to Malta.[7] On 2 August, 'Raphael', evidently a cook-cum-slaughterer, is mentioned. At Malta, after a stop of a mere twenty-four busy hours (27—28 July), they transfer to the *Eurotas*, arriving after a pretty rough voyage at Syra in the Cyclades on 1 August, where they transfer finally to the *Tancrede*, reaching Alexandria on 4 August. Sir Moses' own party consisted of his wife, the indispensable Dr Loewe, Dr Madden as medical adviser and observer, and Mr Wire, representing non-Jewish City opinion. The Crémieux had Solomon Munk.

The journal in this diary ends abruptly on 9 August. However, Sir Moses remained at Alexandria till 17 September. What took place between those dates may be followed in Dr Loewe's own diary[8] or in the official *Diaries*.[9]

The second pocket notebook is identical in size and appearance with the first. It contains mostly roughly jotted pencil notes, apparently some being raw material for the account in the first notebook, and covers the period 10—27 July. These notes were, however, all effaced with indiarubber and are now virtually illegible. A sketch of the town of Syra, and others of some travellers, are recognizable.

In our transcript of the diary, spelling is left exactly as in the original, but punctuation, largely absent, has been added, often involving some subjective interpretation.

NOTES

1.   'Sources for the Study of Sir Moses Montefiore', in V. D. Lipman ed., *Sir Moses Montefiore, a Symposium* (Oxford, 1982).

2.   *The Diaries of Sir Moses and Judith, Lady Montefiore* (London, 1890).

3.   I am obliged to the Wardens of the Spanish and Portuguese Synagogue

for permission to publish. (Since this was written, my attention has been called by Mrs David Franklin to the existence of a typescript transcript of this diary in The Department of MSS and Archives of the Hebrew National University Library. This transcript, apparently made many years ago, contains inaccuracies.)

4. Née Amy Raphael, d. 1942; m. Cecil (1873–1923), youngest son of Sir Joseph Sebag-Montefiore.

5. See note 1 above.

6. Information from Sir Moses' accounts at back of diary.

7. Information derived partly from Sir Moses' accounts (see note 6) and from lists of passengers' arrivals and departures, in *Il Portafoglio Maltese*, No. 118, Monday, 5 August 1840, pp. 981–2, to which my attention was kindly drawn by Mr D. R. Davis; a copy of this journal is in the Public Record Office.

8. 'The Damascus Affair' (transcript by Herbert Loewe of the diary of Dr L. Loewe) in *Yehudith*. (November 1940, Ramsgate).

9. See note 2 above.

Laus Deo, 6 July 5600/1840

Park Lane
Marine Office[1]

Rode to the City, called on Sam[1] de Symons,[2] took leave of him and his Wife; on Mrs. Em[1] Lousada[3] — she was most friendly; on Mrs. Ab. Henry[4] — visit of Condolence; on Dr. Stebbings;[5] 12 attended Cmd (?) ... B ... (?)[6] Oliver Farrer offered to take the Chair for me during my absence; called at Marine Office. Dr. Herschel[7] came to me, Isaac[8] and Louis Cohen,[9] Horatio.[10] I called on J. M. Pearce[11] in New Court;[12] at 2 o'clock Ben. Cohen[13] went with me to Sam[1] Gurney.[14] I took leave; we then rode to Mr. Freeman's,[15] Spring Gardens, where we met Justina Cohen,[16] with her Justina and Abby Gompertz.[17] Soon after came Aston Key,[18] Mr. Travers,[19] Mr. B. Cooper[20] and Mr. Liston;[21] they consulted together & decided in favour of the operation to remove little defect in Justina's eye; it was determined to have it done immediately. Mr.

F.2 Liston performed the Operation; she bore it with much fortitude. I returned to   F.2
the City to New Court; Isaac Cohen called with me at Freeman's Court,[22] but S. M. Samuel[23] came late. We then went to Park Lane; he took some dinner with us. Jud[24] and I went & took leave of Sally Montefiore,[25] called also at S. M. Samuel's — he was gone to the City to see us. [9] [This means 9 o'clock R.D.B] S. M. Samuel; S. B. Worms[26] had been there. We soon were visited by Mrs. de Rothschild[27] and Louisa,[28] Dr. Herschel and his son and grandson, Mr. and Mrs. Wire,[29] Isaac Cohen, Louis Cohen, Horatio and Joseph Sebag,[30] Dr. Loewe.[31] They remained late with us, Joseph Sebag all night. I was employed writing letters & making out accounts, although extremely fatigued; my dear Jud went to bed at midnight. I remained up. May the Almighty God of our Fathers Abraham, Isaac and Jacob Bless with complete Success our Mission and bring us in Peace and Safety back to our friends.

Laus Deo, Tuesday, 7 July

Marine Office
Dover The Ship Hotel

I was engaged writing letters, &c, till ½ past 3; I then reposed for half an hour on the sopha at 7 p.4; my dear Jud and I accompanied by Dr. Loewe, Horatio and his Joseph,[32] also Joseph Sebag, who had remained all night with me. We proceeded to the London Bridge Whf, where we were met by the Bedin[33] both of the German and Portuguese Congregations, and very many of our Brethren — Mr. Aaron Joseph,[34] Louis Cohen and I. Hillyer's father and brother A. Haliver.[35] I should think there were more than 100 Jews waiting to see us set off, all giving us their Blessing and wishing us health, success and safe return. They came on Board the Boat with us & shook hands with me on taking leave of us; this mark of kindness on the part of so many of our Brethren was most cheering to us. May the Almighty hearken to their Prayers and grant their Petitions.

The weather was very cloudy and threatening, blowing very hard from the West. Horatio, his Joseph, Louis Cohen and Joseph Sebag remained on board to accompany me as far as Gravesend. We were rather hurried in getting on board, it being very late before our Servants came to the Alliance [&] the Carriages were on board. In the Evening was much fatigued with writing and want of my natural rests, and my feelings were much excited by the scene I witness[ed] on the Whf and on Board the Boat — so great a number of kind

& good people leaving their beds at an unreasonable hour to offer us their good wishes and Blessings; well knowing how undeserving I am of such honour, I can only pray to the God of my Fathers to crown my Mission with success for the Glory of his Holy Name and for the peace of his children, the people

F.3   of his Choice and of his Covenant.   F.3

It was blow^g very hard when we reached Gravesend. We determined to land, which was not effected without some difficulty & inconvenience; both Jud and Mr. Wire got very wet. Horatio, his son, Louis Cohen and Jos Sebag left us immediately, returned to town by the $\frac{1}{2}$ p 8 Boat. We breakfasted at the Falcon, then proceeded in a Landau to this place Dover. We arrived at 6 — much fatigued; the weather is more moderate, but there is a heavy sea & to-morrow's Boat to Calais will leave at 8 from the Bay & must land the passengers in Boats at Calais, which I do not like and shall not go unless it be pretty Calm.   We wrote to our Mother and Horatio.

Laus Deo, Wednesday, 8 July

Dover, The Ship Hotel
Calais, Hotel Quillacq

The morning was cloudy & the weather threatening, but the Barometer had risen half a degree during the night; nevertheless, the sea was agitated & the wind blowing very fresh & squally from the West; the Boat had to leave the Harbour and lay out in the Bay for the arrival of the Mail & would have to land the Bags & passengers from the Roads in Boats. I was rather undetermined about going to-day; the Sailors said it would be squally; we at length determined on going and went on Board the Arrow, Capt. Smithet, a little before 8; at that hour she left the harbour. I went into the Bay about $\frac{1}{2}$ p 8; the Mail and several passengers were brought on board & we started; blowing hard with a heavy sea; we reached the French coast before eleven o'clock. Boats came alongside, the Bags and some few passengers were with difficulty put into them, the weather being squally & a heavy sea. We and many others would not venture, the Captain deeming it more prudent for us to remain on board till the vessel could enter. We came to an anchor and remained rolling about to about 4 o'clock; my poor Jud dreadfully sick, Dr. Loewe not much better, Mr. Wire and myself tolerably well. Thanks to the God of Israel, we entered the Harbour and landed

F.4   in safety/about $\frac{1}{2}$ p 4, a few minutes after the French steamer left it for Dover,   F.4 but Capt. S. said she would be obliged to land the Mail at Ramsgate. We took up our Quarters at the Hotel Quillacq as usual & sent for Mr. Rothschild's Courier Delport and agreed for his going with us to Paris. Before — indeed it was at the minute of our leaving Dover — I received a letter from Louis Cohen with a fine piece of Roast Beef & a Goose, Tongue & letters from David Salomons & Benjn Cohen, Joseph Sebag & Horatio.

We dined on some excellent Fish, also Louis Cohen's Beef. In the evening I wrote to our dear Mother, David Salomons,[36] Benjn Cohen, Louis Cohen,

F.5   &c. I received a note from Lady Barnard Neale[37] requesting me/to take   F.5 charge of a letter for Mrs. Lyons[38] at Alexandria. $\frac{1}{4}$ to 11 — I have just discovered that my Carpet Bag has not been brought to the Hotel. I am in great distress for it; perhaps it may still be on board the Steam Boat or at the Customs House; should it be lost, I know not what I shall do. The night is very wet.

Laus Deo, Thursday, 9 July 1840

Calais

Soon after six I had the pleasure to hear that my Carpet Bag had been brought from the Customs House. We breakfasted and left Calais ¼ to 9; the weather was less windy than yesterday, though still blowing fresh.

We found our Carriages & Servants all well at Boulogne & ready for us. Mr. Van Oven,[39] Mr. Aloof[40] and his Son, also Abby Lindo[41] paid us a visit at the Hotel des Bains.

F.5[v]   We took some refreshment, then proceeded in our Carriages to Abbeville,   F.5[v]
where we [stopped] near 2 hours to Dine. We slept near 2 hours.

Laus Deo, Friday, 10 July

Paris

We travelled all night, the weather mild & agreeable. We breakfasted at 8 o'clock at Baumont, and with heartfelt thanks to Almighty Gd arrived in safety at Paris at 37 m after 12, Hotel Maurice. Charlotte de Rothschild[42] came to us in a few minutes & begged of us to go with her to the Country. Baron Anselm came & spent an hour with us, Charlotte also; we breakfasted at ½ p. 2.

F.6   The heat has been great [deleted]./Dressed & prepared for the Sabbath [line   F.6
deleted]. Mr. Wire accompanied Jud, I (*sic*) & Dr. Loewe to Synagogue; we dined at 8 o'clock.

Laus Deo, Saturday, 11 July

Paris, Hotel Maurice

Jud, I, Dr. Loewe & Mr. Wire attended Synagogue this morn[g]. We we[re] caught in a heavy shower on our return to the Hotel. I left a card at Lord Granville's,[43] & Mr. Bulwer;[44] called on Anselm de Rothschild; we dined at ½ p. 6; Nath. Montefiore[45] dined with us, also Mr. & Mrs. Cremieux.[46]

Laus Deo, Sunday, 12 July

Paris

Went to P[illeg.]; was detained from 8 till one. At 4, Jud, I, Dr. Loewe & Mr. Wire went to S[illeg.] Mrs. Solomon de Rothschild,[47] Charlotte & Anselm, Mr. Wire Dr Loewe & Mr Cremieux [line illeg.]
[written across] Dr. Madden[48] arrived.

Laus Deo, Monday, 13 July

Paris

Attended ½ p 8 at Anselm de Rothschild's a Meeting of the Consistoire de France.[49] Mr. Cremieux, Dr. L & Mr. Wire were also present; the result was satisfactory. I drew £200 for my own account, and £300 f. the Fund. I wrote several letters.

We dined at 6. N. Montefiore dined with us — Jud, I & Mr. Wire, Dr. Loewe & Dr. Madden.

Laus Deo, Tuesday, 14 July

Paris
Auxerre

We left Paris 4 m 25, breakfasted at Villeneuve & reached Auxerre 7.10 after a pleasant day's Journey. We dressed, then dined. I wrote to J. M. Pearce.[50]

Laus Deo, Wednesday, 15 July

Auxerre
Chalons

We left Auxerre $\frac{1}{2}$ p 4, breakfasted at a miserable Hotel, where they charged extravagantly.

Arrived at Chalons after a delightful day's journey through beautiful country, $\frac{1}{2}$ p 8. We had a good supper.

F.7ᵛ   *Laus Deo, Thursday, 16 July*   F.7

Chalons
Lyons

We left Chalons at 6; breakfasted at Macon, reached Lyons Hotel de l'Europe $\frac{1}{2}$ past 6. Weather has been oppressively hot — th. 81. I am dreadfully fatigued, but must be off to-morrow mornᵍ before 4. Beautiful country, nearly all the wheat cut. Crops appear thin but of good quality.

Laus Deo, Friday, 17 July

Lyons

We were all up at 3 this morᵍ, but some of our party were complaining. Dr. Madden had been frightened out of his bed by rats & had taken refuge on the Sopha [*sic*] in the Sitting Room; all agreed the Hotel de l'Europe a most extravagant & dirty house. We rode to the Rhone & embarked on board the

F.8   L'Aigle; she started $\frac{1}{2}$ p 4 precisely. 5 Carriages & my passengers/other pʳˢ —   F.8 reached Valence 10.30. The heat has been great all day, th. 88 in the carriage at $\frac{1}{2}$ p 3. My handsome travelling cap blew overboard & was lost. Thanks to Almighty Gd we reached Avignon in safety at 5.20, and walked to the Hotel du Palais Royal. We dressed, read our Prayers, were much vexed to find our dinner was not Kasher [In Hebrew in original], through Mr. Cremieux to write [*sic*] to say our Host was a Jew and we should have everything we wished.

Laus Deo, Saturday, 18 July

Avignon, Hotel du Palais Royal

My dear Jud, Dr. Loewe & I went to the Synagogue this mornᵍ $\frac{1}{2}$ p 7, accompanied by a gentleman who came for us. I carried & was called to the Sepher; several ladies were there & accompanied us to the Hotel. The Synagogue is going rapidly to decay, about 40 Jewish families, not strict & little devotion. I was very weak & layed nearly the whole day on the Sopha [*sic*]. Several Jews with some ladies called on us & we all went at 2 to Synagogue. Dr. Madden & Mr. Wire visited the places most worthy of notice. We dined at 5, dinner Kasher [Hebrew], precisely at 10M. Cremieux arrived from Nimes & we left Avignon $\frac{1}{2}$ p 10, Dr. Madden & Dr. Loewe outside our carriage, Mr. Cremieux & Mr. Wire in the open one. My stomach was dreadfully out of order all night; I was in much pain. We felt the heat of the weather (?) terribly oppressive; our host & hostess were extremely civil.

Laus Deo, Sunday, 19 July

Marseilles, Hotel Beauven

F.9   We reached this place at $\frac{1}{2}$ p 9, dreadfully fatigued & very weak, my bowels   F.9
being out of order./ We breakfasted, several persons paid us visits, Mons. & Mad^{me} Cremieux, Mr. Cohen & his father the Grand Rabbin.

We went on board the Minos to see our Cabins, those reserved for Jud & I (*sic*) very bad, Mad^{me} Cremieux having secured very good ones for herself & party. We dined at 6, Kasher [in Hebrew in original]. Mr. Salomons. We are at a great loss for a ladies' maid.[51]

Laus Deo, Monday, 20 July

Marseilles

Dr. Madden, Mr. Wire & Dr. Loewe went this morn^g to Mons. Cremieux & expressed surprise that the Choice of Cabins had not been made to me & insisted on its being given to Jud & I (*sic*). Mr. Turnbull, the British Consul, called
F.9^v   on me. I left cards at Mr. Cohen,/the Grand Rabbin, Monsr A.   F.9^v

I called on Messrs Roux de Fraissinel & Co., presented my letter & drew £300 at 3 days' sight. Int 25/20 cent, $\frac{1}{2}$%. Went to the Gas Manufactory.[52] We dined at 5.

F.10   *Laus Deo, Tuesday, 21 July*   F.10

Marseilles
At sea

Soon after 6 this mor^g, my dear Jud, I & Dr. Loewe rode to Synagogue & prayed to the Gd of our Fathers the Almighty maker of Heaven & Earth for the Safety & Success of our Mission, on our return. I remained all day in the Hotel.
$\frac{1}{4}$ to 6. May the Almighty Gd of Israel pardon all our sins & conduct us in Safety, peace & happiness to the fulfilment of our Mission and to our return in health & felicity to our friends in England; bless & preserve my dear, dear Wife. Amen, Amen.

We dined at 3, having sent the baggage & Servants on Board; we followed at $\frac{1}{2}$ p 4. Mr. Palmer[53] accompanied us to the Boat; we met there Mr. Tailor, the Engineer, who being acquainted with our Captain, came to submit his Civility to us; the Capt. of the French Boat that took us last year from Civita Vecchia to Malta[54] paid us a Visit on Board; it was more than $\frac{1}{2}$ p 5 when Mr. & Mrs. Cremieux came on board; the evening blew very fresh when we first started, but the evening was fine.
.1^v   Mr. Moore, a Queen's Messenger, Mr. Doyle of the Chronicle[55]/   F.11^v

Laus Deo, Wednesday, 22 July

At Sea

The night was fine, the sea smooth, the wind NE, contrary. I am most grateful for a good night's rest. Weather dreadfully hot; we dined on our Kasher

[in Hebrew in original] Meat. I remain on deck till after Midnight. I was so ill all the day that I could do nothing either reading or writing; all on board most civil to us.

F.11^v   *Laus Deo [Thursday, 23 July]*

Leghorn

The Blessed Gd of our Fathers, Ab^m, Isaac & Jacob, has in his great mercy & goodness brought us in Safety & peace again to my native City. O, may he protect and guide me to the end of my life, to the Success of my Mission & to my happy return to England.

The Boat came to an Anchor at 7; it was after 8 when we landed. Lazzaro Montefiore[56] & a nephew of Mr. Bensaqueen[57] came on board to invite us to take up our residence at their houses, but as usual we went to the Hotel Globe. Mr. & Mrs. Cremieux took themselves to the Shore some minutes before us. We had many Visitors as soon as we were on Shore; a Deputation from the Syna-

F.12 gogue. I requested they would be so kind as to have Minha said soon after 12,/   F.12 at which hour I went there. My dear Jud had paid a Visit to Leon Montefiore[58] & his wife; they accompanied her to the Synagogue with Mr. Bensaqueen; we said Minha[59] & afterwards the Haham[60] said a Prayer for the Success of our Mission. The Haham opened the Hehal[61] before he said the Prayer for our

F.12^v Success, Safety and happy return to our friends and home./Mr. & Mrs. C[remieux]   F.12 came before prayers were finished from the Synagogue were [sic] the Parnassim[62] attended us. We immediately after Prayers returned to our Ship, but we only started at 20 m after 4. May the Almighty guide us in peace. Weather beautiful, fine weather but very hot; before leaving Leghorn I wrote to our dear and honoured Mother, also to Lionel de Rothschild,[63] enclosing one to the Com-mittee.

The night was calm & starlight; we passed very close to the Isle of Elba. I retired early, being much fatigued & my Ancles [sic] greatly swolen [sic].

Laus Deo, Friday, 24 July

Civita Vecchia

The Gd of our Fathers brought us in peace & Safety to this Harbour ¼ before 10; the Anchor was dropt at Leghorn, it was recommended to us not to land here, as there had been some little movement against the Israelites occasioned by the writings of a priest called Meyer, a converted Jew; soon after our arrival I had a visit from Mr. Scala[64] & Mr. Samuel Alatri,[65] a Deputation from Rome; their account was very unfavorable as to the opinion of the Papal G^t & murmurs

F.13 low but deep/were heard in Rome; they wished to be informed of the News   F.1 from the East directed to Mons. Sabato Alatri à Livourne.

They strongly recommended our going from Malta in an English Steam Boat to Egypt; as they observed several Jesuits in our Company, they related an incident that happened a few days ago which gave them much uneasiness; a hebrew woman was delivered by a Christ^n midwife of a daughter, which she immediately Baptised & the authorities would not give us [sic] the Child to the Mother.[66] I very much fear that Mr. Lehren's[67] & Mr. Cohen's[68] apprehen-sions are not without foundations. At Leghorn, just before Passover, a woman lost a child & accused the Jews of stealing of it, but the Governor put her in prison & said she should remain there till the Child was found. This had the

F.13^v desired effect, the Child was/found the next day, the incident was kept as quiet   F.1

as possible. Jews begged of me not to mention it. I wrote to our dear Mother also a letter which I shall send on Shore to-morrow to Charles de Rothschild,[69] as I shall not be able to go on Shore. We left Civita Vecchia 3.10, extremely hot, not a breath of air. I went to my berth & prepared for Sabbath, Washed, Shaved, read our Prayers.

Laus Deo, Saturday, 25 July

Naples

The last night was beautifully star light [*sic*], smooth sea, but Therm. 81 in our Cabin. This morning read our Prayers, Parasa,[70] &c; we came to an Anchor in the Harbour of Naples at [blank]; a few minutes afterwards the two eldest sons of Baron Charles de Rothschild came on/Board to invite us to his house, it being Sabbath we would not avail ourselves of his Kindness, all our party went on shore. Mons & Mad^me Cremieux went with the Cap^n to Pompeii. Baron Charles sent us a present of 2 fine live Turkey [*sic*], a dozen of Old Hock & a box of sweetmeats; he came himself at 3 o'clock with his eldest son & a letter from the Baroness. I had a long conversation with him on the subject of our Mission. He recommended the most conciliatory means to speak with the French Consul & indeed with every one that might be useful to us, appealing to their humanity & to assure them that it mainly depended on them [for] my success. Baron Charles said his Father had often taught him, when he had occasion to apply to an inferior or a man who had little/power to assist him in carrying an object he had in view; he spoke with the person as if the whole depended entirely on him, though perhaps he knew he had but the smallest possible influence in the business. Baron Charles said he would go to Rome & endeavour to obtain from the Pope an introduction for Dr. Madden, he being a Catholic, to the Church authorities in Damascus & Syria. I begged of him to try to get my Name included. Dr. M. & Mr. Wire had been with Baron Charles; he accompanied them to the Pope's Nuncio & to Mr. Temple;[71] with much persuasion they both visé in all their Names & Seals of Office Dr. Madden's letter from the Archbishop of Dublin. Baron Charles wished me to write him/under Cover to the English Consul at Naples, Mr. Galloway. He remained with us till dinner was announced, when he took leave with many expressions of friendship; at six o'clock he sent me afterwards by Mr. [blank] a letter of introduction to Mr. Laurin[72] at Alexandria; it was 9 when our Captain & his companions came on board. We started immediately, a beautiful star light [*sic*] night and hope with the Blessing of Heaven to reach Malta in safety & peace on Monday next. During the evening & till after midnight I remained on Deck; tho' there was no wind, there was a rolling sea. Mr. Wire wrote to our dear Mother & to Lionel de Rothschild[73] for me.

Laus Deo, 26 July 1840

At Sea

I did not leave the Deck till near one this mor^g. The small window or Bulls eye in our Cabin had been left open, a Sea broke in & filled our Berths. I was obliged to call up one of the Men & had the beds & clothes changed. fortunately my dear Jud had the moment before left the bed & thus escaped severe Wetting. We passed a most disagreeable night, the Vessel rolled so much — tho' no wind — we passed very close to Stromboli at 3 o'cl; it was smoking, but no flame visible; the sea became much smoother, the Sun set at 7 most beautifully; we had a fine view of Etna & entered the Streights [*sic*]. of Messina before it was quite dark; the night lovely starlight, much less damp. Th. 80.

Laus Deo, Monday, 27 July

At Sea

I did not leave the Deck till after 12 last night; the air was cooler, the sea smooth & we rested to mor^g. I rose at 6; we were still around the coast of Sicily. We have on board Mr. Moore, Queen's Messenger, Mr. Lancaster, the gentleman who prepared the Plan for the New Church at Malta;[74] he is returning from a Mission to Queen Caroline, who has promised to visit Malta next April or May with the Bishop of London to be present at its Dedication. The Jews appear under the greatest alarm in Italy, at Leghorn I should believe without much reason; at Rome I fear they have great cause. Mr. Scala said both the Pope & his Government were extremely against the Jews & had expressed a belief of the Murder of Father Tommaso. The Pope had refused to confirm two Bulls issued by previous Pontiffs when similar charges were brought against the Jews;[75] he said the Great Powers had taken up the enquiry & he would not interfere; the Christians seem to believe if the Jews [are] innocent, then the

F.16^v Christians must be guilty of conspiring against them. God help us./ F.16

12 n^o. A fine breeze N.W. running (?) 8 Knots − $\frac{1}{2}$ p 2 & Malta has been seen, a brave breeze carrying us rapidly through the Water. We entered the Harbour of Malta − Blessed be the Almighty Gd of Israel − in safety at 5 of clock. We soon landed, went to Dunsford's Hotel. I paid my respects to the Governor[76] at the Palace with Mr. Wire, also Sir Hector Grey,[77] who was most kind and came with us to the Hotel to see Judith. Capt. & Mrs. Copeland[78] soon came to us, remained a Couple of Hours. I was greatly fatigued but wrote to our dear Mother.

Laus Deo, Tuesday, 28 July

Malta (Th[ermometer] 83)

My dear Jud and I rose at 5; Dr. L[oewe] went with us at 6 to the Synagogue, where we said our prayers. I was very sorry to find that M. Abeacis[79] had written a story respecting having put our Names on the Curtain at the Achol.[80]

F.17 We left our Cards afterwards at the Palace at Sir Hector Grey,/Mr. & Mrs. F.1
Pariente,[81] Mr. & Mrs. McGill,[82] Sir Hector Grey. I find Mr. & Mrs. Cluyt[83] are at Florian[84] & Mr. Frere[85] at Corfu.

Mr. Christian[86] paid us a Visit. I drew £240 & £260 at 30 days' sight on N. M. R[othschild] & Sons on account of the Damascus Fund. My dear Jud and I with Dr. Loewe and Mr. Wire went on Board the Eurotas, Capt. de Reaudeau at $\frac{1}{2}$ p 11. Dr. Madden came afterwards. May the Almighty Gd of our Fathers, the Gd of Israel conduct us in peace & comfort to the desired port of our voyage, without the inconvenience of too much Wind or Sea. Oh, may he in his Great mercy grant us health & a happy Voyage, Amen, Amen.

The weather is fair, but it is blowing very hard − NNW. We left the harbour of Malta at one o'clock; we found a very rough Sea outside, which was terribly

F.17^v disagreeable./Those who have the happiness of remaining at home, can have no F.1
idea of the miseries of the Sea; but I confide in the Gd of Israel for protection & consolation. I trust the Sea will subside at the Sun goes down; my dear Jud is very unwell. I am not much better.

Laus Deo, Wednesday. 29 July, 5600

At Sea

F.18   I was lying on the Deck last night till after 12, when Dr. Madden came & persuaded me to go into my Cabin & assisted me below. I did not take my Cloths [*sic*] off; my dear Jud was on the floor of the Captain's Cabin on the Deck. The same weather continued to-day,/blowing very fresh N with a most disagreeable rolling Sea. Wind favourable but fresh; there is a most annoying smell on board this boat — bilgewater or bad oil used in the Engine. I feel most uncomfortable this morning, but my Trust is in Gd; about 2 in the aft. the weather became more moderate; an English steamer is in sight, I imagine going with Mr. Moore[87] to the Admiral at Vourla near Smyrna. At $\frac{1}{2}$ p 6 we had some heavy squalls of rain. While my dear Jud was on the Deck sitting on a Stool, a lurch of the vessel threw her down backwards with great force, both she &

.18ᵛ   I were much alarmed but thanks to Heaven she was but little/hurt, though frightened. The weather continued very rough, a most rolling sea. I remained all night in my Clothes in one of the little Cabins near the Wheels of the Engine on Deck, as the smell of the bilge water was unbearable below; my dear Jud, in the Captain's Cabin, much lightning.

F.18

F.18ᵛ

Laus Deo, Thursday, 30 July

At Sea

.19   The Night was very rough, with a terrible rolling Sea & this morᵍ the weather is no better. I fear we are making but little way, as the Vessel rolls so much. Oh, may I never forget my total helplessness at this moment, but to the Gd of my Fathers, the great Gd of Israel I rely for help & to calm the troubled ocean. Oh, the miseries of the Sailor's life no tongue can express. About one o'clock we first got sight of land — Cape Koron[88] [*sic*] in the Morea; the sea became less agitated and most grateful I am for it. Mr. Cremieux had suffered much from sea sickness. We passed Cape Matapan, then the Island of Serigo,[89] and entered the Greek Archipelago. Thanks to the Almighty, the night was fine, calm and star light.

F.19

Laus Deo, Friday, 31 July 1840

At Sea

9ᵛ   Last night I had my old quarters in the little Cabin on Deck; without taking off my clothes I slept pretty well & rose at 5; being Rosh Hodesh, said the Halel &c; it is now $\frac{1}{4}$ p 7./

A lovely morning, smooth sea, light breeze. We are close in with Falkner's Island[90] to the north of us, and the Island of Milo[91] to the ESE. How different are our feelings this morning to those of yesterday; how can I be sufficiently thankful to the Almighty for the happy change!

Among our agreeable companions is a young woman the wife of the French Minister in the Brazils, the Baroness de Rouane;[92] she is going to her Parents at Athens for her health, speaks English well. A Miss Payne, rather an elderly lady of Birminᵐ, friend of Mr. Attwood;[93] she was formerly a Companion of Mrs. Attwood's parents, named Marshall. Miss Payne had under her charge a young lady named Gee, very pretty, mild & amiable in her manners.[94]

$\frac{1}{2}$ p 9. Lovely morᵍ, deep blue sea, soon after eleven the heat of the sun compelled me to take refuge in the Cabin, where I wrote a few lines to our dear

F.19ᵛ

Mother, to be sent from Syra. We have found our Commandant, Monsr de Reaudeau, most civil & attentive. Mr. Southgate & Lady, an American Clergyman, a Missionary to Persia. Mr. Davids,[95] one of our Deputies & the Baroness with several others as well as Miss Payne and Miss Gee we take leave of when we reach Syra; also Mons. & Mad^m Nestorhole,[96] an Artist going to Egypt.

Mrs. Harriet Thorn goes to Vourla to meet her husband, an officer in the Navy. The appearance of the Islands is mountainous* & very barren; the fine clear sky makes them ('gives me' deleted) an interesting [blank]

F.20^v The town [of Syra]** has a very/handsome appearance, built on the side   F.20 of a high hill, that part called the Old Town on the Summit, with a Church on the Top, the New Town runs down to the Water's edge.

¼ before 5 o'clock we had the happiness to Cast Anchor in the Bay, pretty close to Syra. Praise be to the Almighty Gd of Israel for protect^g us and conducting us in Safety & peace to this place. The water here is extremely blue, but so clear that we could see the bottom 60 feet deep.

We had prepared everything for going immediately on board the Vessel

F.21   that was to take us to Alexandria, but/we learned with regret that she had not   F.21 yet arrived from Athens. We were consequently compelled to remain on board the Eurotas. I shaved and prepared for Sabbath; my dear Judith, I & Dr. L. read our prayers together after Dinner; most of the passengers went on shore to the [sic] see the town. Dr. Loewe remained with us; at night the town had a fairy-like appearance, thousands of lights sparkling to the summit of the hill.

Laus Deo, Saturday, 1 August 1840

Syra

A lovely morning but very hot; we read our prayers, Parasa,[97] &c., at ½ past 12; we left the Eurotas & went on board the Tancrede, which arrived in the

F.21^v Night from Athens in 7½ hours, Capt. T. Alliez./ May the Almighty Gd of   F.2 Israel grant us a safe & pleasant Voyage. It was ½ p 2 when we weighed Anchor. We had most interesting prospects of the several Islands in the Morea, [sic][98] particularly of Neros.[99] The sunset was the most splendid I had ever seen; we read our Psalms with Dr. L & Eve^g prayers. We have very few passengers besides our own party; a brother of Count Capo Distria[100] — he had been imprisoned 8 months & now sent our [sic] of Greece; a boat with soldiers remained close to the Steamer, till we left Syra. The night was beautifully clear — young moon & Stars. I slept in my dear Jud's Cabin, took a blue pill on retiring, by Dr. Madden's advice.

Laus Deo, Sunday, 2 August

At Sea

6 n 0 (?) Th[ermometer] 83. In sight of Candia near Cape Solomon,[101] fine, most pleasant breeze, all sail set, wind NW ½ p 12. The Almighty is most merciful to us, a magnificent day, cool air, brave breeze, 10 knots per hour [sic], a lively sea, but most of the party well & in good spirits, dear Jud as active & studious as ever. The sun made a golden set 10 m before 7, but not so rich as yesterday.

F.22^v Raphael[102] killed a sheep this mor^g, but it was Trepha [in Hebrew in original].   F.

*Dr Loewe read this wrongly as 'monotonous'.
** Added in ink.

Lovely scene, Moon & Stars but too much Sea. The wind, however, droped [*sic*] when the sun went down. I retired at 10.

Laus Deo, Monday, 3 August 1840

[At Sea]

Thanks to the Almighty for a good night's rest. The weather is fine, this morning a fair Wind but a rolling Sea, which impedes our way, otherwise we might have reached Alexandria this evening. I rose soon after 5; eleven o'clock we have a lovely day, lively dancing Sea, which gave us good spirits; at 12 o'clock we were 45 miles distant from Alexandria; the wind continued blowing very fresh & the sea rose considerably; we had considerable expectation of reaching Alexandria before sunset, but we lost that hope at 6, not having got sight of land. As soon as the sun set $\frac{1}{4}$ before seven, the sails were all taken in, the steam nearly all let off & the Ship's head turned off the land. The Moon & Stars were brightly shining, yet there was a very rolling sea & we tossed about very much. I turned in about 11.

F.23 [left margin] / F.23 [right margin]

Laus Deo, Tuesday, 4 August

At Sea

How just are thy mercies, O Lord! I rose at 5 after passing a very uneasy night; about midnight it began to blow from the N, which continues with a heavy Sea. 6, grace à Dieu, Sight of Land and of Alexandria, but blow^g and rolling terribly. $\frac{1}{4}$ past 7. Fell in with the Pilot Boat, furled all sails. We dropt the Anchor in the Harbour of Alexandria $\frac{1}{4}$ to 8: the harbour is filled with Ships of War, Turkish & Egyptian — Marmoudie (130 guns, two of 68). Dr. Loewe went (illegible) us help on shore to get us apartments at the Hotel, to see the Haham & Mr. Bell.[103]

O give thanks unto the Lord for his mercy endureth for ever. Laus Deo — Think & Thank.[104]

[Folios 24 to 33vo are given over to keeping accounts of petty expenses from Sunday 5 June to Thursday 17 September. Fos. 34 to 36^v are blank. The narrative is resumed on fos. 43 to 37, the book being reversed.]

.43^v [left margin]

At 10 I walked to Col. Hodges,[105] who received me most politely, said he wished to over the whole business with me, it had assumed a political character. I should find Mons. C[ochelet], the French Consul, very plausible but very firm. Mr. Laurin[106] was charged with [illegible]. Altogether, Col. H. recommended me to keep free from all parties, but he was going to breakfast & I am to call in 2 hours. Col. Hodges had seen with much satisfaction Dr. Herschel's letter[107] & had read it to Mahamad Ali.

F.43^v [right margin]

$\frac{1}{2}$ p 12. Col. Hodges accompanied me to French Consul, M. C[ochelet], and met there Mons. Cremieux; afterw^d to Austrian Consul,[108] met there Prussian Consul;[109] called on Russian,[110] he was asleep.

.42^v [left margin] *Laus Deo, Wednesday, 5 Aug^t*   F.42^v [right margin]

Alexandria

It was near 2 hrs mor^g before we retired. I rose soon after 5; a little before 8, Colonel Hodges called to accompany us to the Palace. I was dressed in my Uniform, Mr. Wire in a Court dress, Dr. Madden in his Official Dress as an employé of Government, a blue uniform trimmed with red. Mr. Thurburn[111] and Mr. Galloway[112] lent their Carriages for the use of the Party. I rode with Col. Hodges & read to him the Petition I had to present to His Highness the Pasha of Egypt; he said he approved of it & hoped it would be granted, but he did not by his manner appear to believe that it would.

F.42 · On our arrival we were immediately ushered into the Hall of Audience. · F.42
Mohamed Ali was seated at the same spot where I first saw him.[113] Col. Hodges presented me, saying he had the pleasure of presenting me as an Old acquaintance of His Highness; he made me a very gracious smile & bowed; he afterwards introduce the others.

Col. Hodges then said I had to present a petition to His Highness, which his Government had desired him to express to His Highness their desire to be granted. I then asked leave to read it to His Highness, to which in a gracious
F.41ᵛ · manner he assented. I read it very, very distinctly, he kept his eyes on me the · F.41ᵛ
whole time. When I had finished I requested his Drogaman [sic] might be permitted to read it to him in Turkish; the Pasha said it was long, that it should be translated, he would read it and give me an answer. I then begged that the heads of the petition might be read to him; he repeated [erased] it was long, it was long, should be translated. I then stated that the petition was respecting the Jews of Damascus; he said he knew it. Dr. Madden then presented to him an address of thanks from the Society for the Abolition of Slavery: he appeared pleased to be able to turn the conversation from my petition & he spoke for a considerably [sic] on the subject of slavery. I tried through Colonel Hodges to bring back my business, but ineffectually. I made the attempt three or four times, Col. Hodges saying to leave it to him. Before taking leave I told His Highness that the English people were looking to his answer with great anxiety & that I would wait on H.H. the day after to-morrow for it; he said Consul (?)
F.40ᵛ · I will give it, said it was an/affair of Justice, that I had brought a French advocat · F.40
[sic] this could not be permitted. Col. Hodges said Mr. Cremieux though an advocate came only from motives of humanity & was himself a Jew.

Nothing could have been less satisfactory than the Interview, very different from my previous ones, he did not speak a single word to me; in my former interviews he was most friendly & chatty.

I found Mons. Cochelet was with him last eveᵍ for an hour and a half. God of
F.40 · Israel, help and protect us poor Jews — we are not likely to have any other./ I · F.40
was much out of spirits all day. We had many visitors; Capt. Lyons, &c.

Laus Deo, Thursday, 6 August

Alexandria

We had many visitors — the Captains of two English Steamboats of War were of the Number, with Capt. Lyons.[114] We recᵈ a message from Col. Hodges that the Pasha was going on the Delta early to-morrow morᵍ. I went to the Consul; he read the letter he had sent to the Pasha on the subject of the Jews of Damascus — it could not have been stronger. I discovered on going to the Pasha it was nearly 9 when we entered the Palace — his reception was most affable and kind, very different to that of yesterday. I said I had heard he was going away; he replied he should be back on Friday & would see me & give me an answer.

In an adjoining Hall, they [sic] Officers & Servants were singing their prayers & frequently bowing low to the Earth. Mr. Bell[115] lent me his horse to go to the
F.39 · Palace. Mr. & Mrs. Bell took tea with us./ · F.3ᵉ

Laus Deo, Friday, 7 August

Alexandria

Mr. Galloway lent us his Phaeton.[116] We took a ride before breakfast. Mr. Laurin sent a Message that the Pasha had told him that he would grant our request. I wrote to London. Col. Hodges called on me.

Dressed and prepared for Sabbath, and we dined at 7, Mr. & Mrs. Bell & Mr. Galloway with us.

Leus Deo, Saturday, 8 August

Alexandria

.38ᵛ   My dear Jud, I and Dr. Loewe walked to Synagogue at 7; prayers were/   Fo.38ᵛ
finished ¼ before 9. The Service was read with devotion. Mr. Munk[117] was there — all the others or nearly so natives. I opened the Achol[118] & was called the 7th to the Sepher.[119] I called on Mr. Cremieux; he said he was not quite well. Col. Hodges was there with him. We had many Jews visited us — Capt. Lyons, Mr. Briggs,[120] &c, &c.

We dined at 8. We took our fast at 6 [*sic*].[121]

Laus Deo, Sunday, 9 August

Alexandria

Dr. Loewe and I went a little before 7 to Synagogue, were out ¼ to 10. Mr. Laurin paid us a visit. I called on Cremieux — he was very well.

Colonel Hodges & Mons. Laurin paid us long visits; at 5 Dr. L & I attended Synagogue. I opened the Achol & was called first to the Sepher; we broke our fast at 7 o'clock, very thankful to Almighty God for all his goodness to us.

Mr. & Mrs. Cremieux with several others came in as we were consuming our breakfast — he said he intended to turn Jew as soon as we were on our way to Beirout & to continue so till we had visited Jerusalem. I said I hoped he would always be so; he replied it would not be convenient to him to submit to such an engagement.

[The journal in this volume ends here. The petty expenses, 5 June to 17 September (when he left Alexandria to sail to Constantinople) include such items as Dr. Loewe's spectacles £3. 10s. 6d. The chief item of interest, however, that I notice is under 19 July — 'M. Cremieux's passage [from Marseilles] to Alexandria, 3,744 Fr.', suggesting that Sir Moses paid for Monsieur Cremieux to come, a fact that Mehemet Ali seems to have discovered (above, 5 August). Some items however (charity, &c.) are marked 'p', perhaps for 'personal', suggesting that the rest were charged to the Damascus Fund.]

NOTES

1. The Marine Office of the Alliance Assurance Company. Its full title was the Alliance, British and Foreign Fire and Life Assurance Company; Sir Moses regularly used its offices for his correspondence and business purposes when in London. The minutes of the meeting of Directors on 6 July show that Sir Moses was present but did not take the chair.
2. Samuel Lyon de Symons (1788–1860), son of Baron Lyon de Symons. Communal worker.

3. Emmanuel Baruch Lousada, Jr. (1783—1854), of Sidmouth, Devon, was appointed a magistrate of Devonshire (James Picciotto, ed. Finestein *Sketches*, p. 390). He married Jane, daughter of Abraham Goldsmid, in 1807. The inference might be drawn from Sir Moses' remark that she was not usually so very friendly.

4. Abraham Henry (1789—1840) was a member of a family prominent in the little Jewish community at Ramsgate. He married in 1816 Emma Lyons, a poetess, the first English Jewess to be known as an authoress; while living in London he became Treasurer of the Hambro Synagogue. He retired on account of ill health to live in Ramsgate; he died there on 21 April, 1840, and was buried in the local Jewish cemetary. Picciotto, pp. 282—307; Cardozo and Goodman, *Think and Thank*, p. 357.

5. Possibly Dr Henry Jones Stebbings (1799—1883), poet, preacher and historian.

6. Illegible passage: possibly 'attended Bd First Bk'. Sir Moses was a founder and director of the Provincial Bank of Ireland in 1825. Oliver Farrar was also a director.

7. Dr Solomon Hirschel (1762—1842), Chief Rabbi of the Ashkenazi Great Synagogue. On his letter addressed to Mehemet Ali concerning the Blood Libel, see note 107 below. Dr Hirschel's son was Rabbi David Berliner Hirschel, who settled in Jerusalem and devoted himself to the affairs of the *Perushim* Synagogue.

8. Isaac Cohen (1791—1866), brother of Judith, Lady Montefiore.

9. Louis Cohen (1799—1882), Stock Exchange merchant, warden of the Great Synagogue, member of the Board of Deputies and son of Lady Montefiore's half-brother, Joseph.

10. Horatio (1798—1867) was Sir Moses' youngest brother.

11. John Meriscoe Pearce, Bank director; pro-Jewish organizer of petition to Parliament on behalf of Jewish rights, 1829—30. See *Diaries*, i, 61, 65—7, 80. He is mentioned again on 14 July.

12. New Court, St. Swithin's Lane, contained the City offices of N. M. Rothschild and Sons; but apparently J. M. Pearce also had an office there.

13. Benjamin Cohen (1789—1867); married to Justina, Sir Moses' sister.

14. Samuel Gurney (1786—1886); Quaker, philanthropist and banker. Gurney seconded Sir Moses' nomination to be Sheriff of London and Middlesex in 1837. He was associated with him in many charitable causes.

15. Joseph Freeman, MRCSE, of 21 Spring Gardens, was a general practitioner.

16. Sir Moses' sister (1800—1873), married to Benjamin Cohen. See Note 13.

17. Abigail, Sir Moses' sister, married to Benjamin Gompertz (1779—1864).

18. Charles Aston Key, MRCSE (1793—1849), surgeon.

19. Benjamin Travers, FRCSE, surgeon, of Bond Street.

20. Brandsbury Blake Cooper, MRCSE, surgeon, of Guy's Hospital.

21. Robert Liston, MRCSE, surgeon.

22. Freeman's Court, 33 Cornhill, was the business office of S. M. Samuel. See Note 23.

23. Samuel Moses Samuel (1779—1873), brother-in-law of Lady Montefiore.

24. Sir Moses' pet name for his wife. Her pet name for him was 'Mun'.

25. Sarah, wife of Horatio Montefiore. See Note 10.

26. Salomon Benedict de Worms (1801—82), nephew of N. M. Rothschild; created Baron of the Austrian Empire in 1871.

27. Presumably, Mrs Lionel de Rothschild (1819—84) is meant.

28. Louisa, née Montefiore, Sir Moses' niece, married to (Sir) Anthony de Rothschild (1810—76).
29. Mr D. M. Wire was Under-Sheriff of the City of London when Sir Moses became Sheriff in 1837, and he became his great friend; later he became Lord Mayor.
30. Joseph Sebag (1822—1905) was the son of Sir Moses' sister Sarah, and Solomon Sebag. As Sir Moses and Lady Montefiore had no children, Sir Moses eventually made Joseph, who was his favourite nephew, his heir, subject to changing his name to Sebag-Montefiore.
31. Dr Louis Loewe (1809—88), Orientalist and traveller, employed by Sir Moses as his secretary, became his life-long *confidant*, adviser and friend.
32. Eldest son of Horatio. See Note 10.
33. Corruption of Heb. *Bet Din*, lit. 'House of Judgement', i.e. a rabbinical court of justice, plural *baté din*. In his edition of this part of the diary, Dr Loewe substitutes 'Ecclesiastical Courts'. *Diaries*, i, 220.
34. Aaron Joseph (d. 1875), supporter of charities in the Holy Land. *Jewish Chronicle*, 29 October 1875.
35. Abraham Haliva (1790—1853), Dayan of the Spanish and Portuguese Jewish Congregation; his brother had evidently changed his name to Hillyer.
36. Sir David Salomons (1797—1873), banker, civic and Jewish commercial leader. First Jewish Lord Mayor of London.
37. Lady Burrard Neale, widow of Admiral Sir Harry Burrard Neale, Bt. (1765—1840), who was C.-in-C. Mediterranean, 1832.
38. Presumably the wife of Capt. Lyons, RN, who is mentioned on 6 and 8 August. See *Diaries*, i, 227, and below Note 114.
39. Dr. Barnard van Oven (1796—1860), writer on the subject of Jewish rights.
40. Judah Aloof (1793—1859), warden of the Spanish and Portuguese Congregation, 1841—2. The family came from Gibraltar to London.
41. Abigail Lindo (1803—1848), authoress of a *Hebrew and English and English and Hebrew Vocabulary* (1837).
42. Charlotte de Rothschild (1807—59), wife of Baron Anselm de Rothschild (1803—74), who entered the Paris house of the firm.
43. Earl Granville (1773—1841), British Ambassador in Paris, 1821—41.
44. Sir Henry Bulwer (1801—72), Second Secretary and Chargé d'Affaires in Paris, 1839—40.
45. Dr Nathaniel Montefiore (1819—83), FRCSE., son of Sir Moses' brother Abraham by his second wife, Henrietta, née Rothschild: traveller, writer and chemist, Ch. Bermant, *The Cousinhood*, pp. 313—14.
46. Isaac Adolphe Crémieux (1796—1880), French advocate and Jewish communal leader. Crémieux had already visited London in June 1840 to attend the meeting of protest. Later he founded the *Alliance Israélite Universelle*.
47. Mrs Salomon Mayer von Rothschild, mother of Baron Anselm. See Note 42.
48. Dr R. R. Madden (1798—1886), non-Jewish writer, traveller and newspaper correspondent; campaigner for abolition of slavery. See *Diaries*, i, 226.
49. Representative body of French Jewry set up by Napoleon in 1808. Monsieur Crémieux was its Vice-President.
50. See above Note 11.
51. Sir Moses' accounts (at the end of the diary) showed payment under 13

July 'Harriet Rogers, Lady's maid, £10'. Evidently she left their service in Paris.

52. Sir Moses was a director of the Imperial Continental Gas Association, and was keenly interested in its affairs.

53. Mr G. H. Palmer (d. 1855) was an official of the Imperial Continental Gas Association. *Diaries*, ii, 101.

54. This refers to his journey to Palestine of 1838—9. He left Rome on Friday 12 April, embarking on Sunday 14 April, on the *Sesostris* for Malta. See Judith, Lady Montefiore, *Notes from a Journal* (1841), pp. 180 ff.

55. Mr [A.] Doyle of the Chronicle was apparently one of the special correspondents in the Eastern Mediterranean on the staff of the *Morning Chronicle*, an important London daily paper, which ran from 1770 to 1862. His initial is supplied from *Il Portafoglio Maltese*. See Introduction, note 7.

56. Eliezer Montefiore (b. 1783), first cousin once removed of Sir Moses.

57. Benzaken or Benzaquen; an eminent Moroccan family.

58. Judah Leon Vita Montefiore (b. 1786), brother of Eliezer Montefiore. See Note 56 above.

59. Afternoon Prayers.

60. i.e., Chief Rabbi.

61. i.e., the Ark of the Law.

62. Wardens.

63. See below, Note 73.

64. Prominent leader of the Rome community. *Diaries*, i, 222, 291—2.

65. Samuel Alatri (1805—89). Italian politician, communal worker and head of Rome Jewish community. (*Jewish Encyclopedia*).

66. This seems to have been an anticipation of the somewhat similar but more publicized Mortara case (1858) at Bologna, in which Sir Moses attempted officially, but unsuccessfully to intervene.

67. The exact significance of this remark, in the absence of Sir Moses' correspondence, is not clear. Probably Zvi Hirsch Lehren (1782—1853), Dutch merchant and commercial leader, is meant. He had joined in protests about the 'Damascus Affair'. *J.E.*, vii, p. 689; *Diaries*, i, 87—8.

68. Which Mr. Cohen is intended is not clear.

69. Baron Charles de Rothschild, otherwise Freiherr Karl Meyer von Rothschild (1788—1855), fourth son of Mayer Amschel Rothschild and head of the Italian branch; resident in Naples.

70. The weekly portion of the Pentateuch, read publicly in Hebrew in the Synagogue to seven persons, or privately at home.

71. Hon. Wm. Temple, British Ambassador at Naples.

72. Austrian Consul at Alexandria. See also Note 106.

73. Baron Lionel Nathan de Rothschild (1806—79), international banker, leader of the Anglo-Jewish community.

74. Richard Lankersheer (1803 ?—41), Head Superintendent of the Department of Civil Artifices in Malta, prepared plans for the Anglican Cathedral at Valetta, but these proved so faulty that they required modification by William Scamp. Lankersheer died next year, it was thought possibly by suicide. Queen Adelaide donated £8,000 for building this church. Lady Montefiore, *Notes from a Journal*, p. 187. Sir Moses' reference to Queen Caroline is, of course, a slip of memory.

75. Reference is to Bulls of Gregory IX, Innocent IV and the report of Cardinal Ganganelli, afterwards Clement XIV. C. Roth, *Ritual Murder — Libel and the Jew* (1935).

76. General Sir Henry Bouverie, KCB (1783—1857), was Governor and C.-in-C. in Malta the previous year. *Diaries*, i, 156.
77. Sir Hector Grey, Secretary of Government, Malta. Sir Moses had met him also in Malta during his visits to that island the previous year. *Diaries*, i, 156, 204.
78. Capt. Copeland, RN, of the *Mastiff*, and Mrs Copeland had visited Sir Moses and Lady Montefiore at Alexandria in December 1827, and conveyed them to Naples. *Diaries*, i, 49, 51—2.
79. Leading member of the small Jewish community of Malta; possibly a journalist.
80. i.e., Ark of the Law in the Synagogue.
81. A large Sephardi family represented at Gibraltar, Alexandria, Tangier and elsewhere. This family was resident in Malta and became close friends of the Montefiores on their previous visit to Malta. The family's name is given only as P———. Lady Montefiore, *Notes from a Journal*, p. 191.
82. Mr. McGill was the Superintendent of the silk farm at Boskett, which proved a failure. *Notes from a Journal*, p. 184.
83. Not identified.
84. i.e., Floriana, a suburb of Valletta.
85. John Hookham Frere, uncle of the Indian administrator, Sir Bartle Frere, *Diaries*, i, 156; another acquaintance of the previous year, *Notes from a Journal*, pp. 193—5. He possessed a house and a fine garden at La Pietà.
86. Not identified.
87. The Queen's Messenger, carrying dispatches. see note 55.
88. i.e., Cape Akritas, by Koroni.
89. i.e., Cerigo (Cythera).
90. Now called Falconera.
91. i.e., Melos.
92. Baroness de Rouen. See *Il Portafoglio Maltese*. See Introduction, note 7.
93. Mathias Attwood, MP, non—Jewish supporter of Jewish emancipation (1829), who had proposed Sir Moses for freedom and livery of Merchant Taylors' Company (1835); a director of Imperial Continental Gas Association (1842). *Diaries*, i, 61, 97, 113, 146, 306—7.
94. Miss M. 'Lazzarita' Jee, according to *Il Portafoglio Maltese*. See Introduction, note 7.
95. Mr. Joel Davis, who travelled on with Sir Moses to Malta and from Malta to Syra.
96. Sir Moses evidently refers to Nestor l'hôte (1802—42), a distinguished Egyptological artist, who was sent out by the French first in 1839 to record Egyptian monuments and inscriptions. See J. Vandier d'Abbadie, *Nestor l'hôte 1802—1842* (Leyden, 1982).
97. See above, note 70.
98. The Morea is the Peloponnesus. The Cyclades are perhaps meant.
99. Antiparos (formerly known popularly as Niaros) is meant.
100. Count John Capo d'Istria (1780—1831), president of the Greek republic after the battle of Navarino, assassinated 1831.
101. Cape Salmone on the east coast of Crete. At that time the name Candia — the name of the town now called Heraklion — was often given to the island as a whole.
102. See Introduction, p. 151.
103. Apparently a prominent resident of Alexandria. *Diaries*, i, 247.
104. Sir Moses' motto.

105. HBM Consul-General at Alexandria.
106. The Austrian Consul at Alexandria.
107. Dr Hirschel's letter (see note 7) to Mehemet Ali on the subject of the Blood Accusation is referred to in *Diaries*, i, 261.
108. See above, note 106.
109. The Prussian Consul was Monsieur de Wagner. *Diaries*, i, 261.
110. The Russian Consul was Count Medem. *Diaries*, i, 261.
111. Apparently a prominent resident. *Diaries*, i, 240—1, 246, 261.
112. British Consul at Naples (see above, under 25 July).
113. i.e., on his first visit to Alexandria in 1827.
114. See above, note 38.
115. See above, note 103.
116. A light four-wheeled open carriage with one or two seats.
117. Salomon Munk (1803—67). French orientalist, who accompanied Monsieur Crémieux.
118. i.e., the *Echal* or Ark of the Law.
119. The Scroll of the Law (Pentateuch), a portion of which is read consecutively to seven persons in the Sabbath service (see above, note 70).
120. A wealthy British merchant. See Dr. Loewe's *Diary* (*Yehudith* 1940) p. 22. He seems to have held a special place in the affairs of Mehemet Ali, and had already personally intervened in the 'Damascus Affair' while at Damascus by writing a letter to the Governor. (See *Morning Chronicle*, 30 July, col. B). The statement might imply that Capt. Lyons and Mr. Briggs were both Jewish; this would be interesting, if it were so to be understood, but I own to great doubts about it.
121. In that year (1840) the Solemn Jewish Fast Day of the 9th Ab fell on Saturday, 8 August. It is the custom, when a fast happens to fall on the Sabbath, to postpone its observance till the following day (except in the case of *Yom Kippur*, the Day of Atonement).

Acknowledgement is gratefully made to the following persons for assistance: Mr A. St. J. Lambkin (archivist, Allied Irish Banks): note 6. The Librarian, *Jewish Chronicle*, Mrs R Silver: notes 23, 24. Wellcome Historical Medical Library: notes 15, 18—20. Dr V. D. Lipman, CVO: notes 37, 71. Mr D. R. Davis: notes 76—9, 81, 82. Mrs E. Eisenthal: note 74, and Miss M. Rodrigues Pereira.

3

Mission to Morocco (1863–1864)

DAVID LITTMAN

Two centuries before Sir Moses Montefiore landed at Tangier on 11 December 1863, Joseph Addison's father (chaplain to the English garrison in Tangier) observed that the condition of Moroccan Jewry was '. . . no other than a better sort of Slavery'.[1] Six years after Sir Moses' death in 1885, Budgett Meakin, editor of *The Times of Morocco* and probably the most knowledgeable expert on Morocco of his time, wrote:

It is seven-and-twenty years since the mission of Sir Moses Montefiore to Marrakesh obtained some slight concessions to the Jewish subjects of the Sultan, for which they have been ever thankful; but there is much more to be done. Bad as the position of the Moor himself is, under a rotten government, that of his Israelitish neighbour is much worse . . . .[2]

A glance at the long history of Moroccan Jewry will provide an introduction to their condition of degradation, which — notwithstanding the ephemeral rise to royal power of a few powerful families[3] — was to last into the twentieth century.[4] Montefiore believed that he might improve their wretched status. It was this hope and not merely that of liberating those unjustly imprisoned, which inspired him to undertake so hazardous a voyage in his eightieth year.

Whereas legend associates the first presence of Israelites in North Africa with the earliest settlements of the seafaring Phoenicians, their history in that region only really begins in Graeco-Roman times, about a thousand years before the Arab conquest of the late seventh century.[5]

During the subsequent half-millenium, the flourishing Christian population of the region was virtually eliminated.

The Jewish communities, however, did not represent a threat to Muslim power and were often considered economically indispensable on account of their onerous *jizya* (poll-tax) and their inestimable trading experience. They managed to survive successive conquests and dynastic upheavals, even the cruellest of destructions under the fanatic Almohads of the twelfth century when some of the worst persecutions occurred. As an example, the widespread catastrophe

which took place between 1145 and 1148 was described by the poet
Abraham ibn Ezra in a poignant elegy, and by the equally renowned
contemporary chronicler, Abraham ibn Daud, who wrote: '[The
Almohads . . .] had crossed the sea to Spain, after having wiped out
every remnant of Jews from Tangiers to al-Mahdiya [in Tunisia] '.[6]
During this period Maimonides and his family fled from Cordoba
(1148) and then Fez (1165), to Egypt, by way of the Holy Land.

It is still debatable whether, as claimed by Arab historians, at the
outset of the Muslim conquest the Jewish and Christian inhabitants
of the Byzantine provinces had generally welcomed the invaders.
It is certain, however, that specific discriminatory regulations af-
fecting non-Muslims were becoming systematized throughout the
Islamic territories by the eighth century. The *dhimma*, traditionally
considered a 'pact of protection', and also known as the Covenant of
Umar,[7] fixed the relationship between the dominant Muslim community (*umma*) and the subjected peoples of the revealed religions
(*dhimmis*) living under an Islamic regime. The resulting disabilities
and humiliations, of which the *jizya* was but one example, stigmatized both the individual and the community. The status of the
dhimmi was intended to be inferior in every respect to that of the
Muslim. So long as the *dhimmi* observed all the conditions of this
pact of toleration, he was entitled to protection from the *umma*,
generally within the framework of his community.[8]

With the gradual disappearance of the Christians from North
Africa, the Jews became virtually the only *dhimmis* of the region.
The Muslim historian of the Almohads, al-Marrakushi (d. 1224),
has left us a vivid description of the conspicuously ugly and discriminatory garments which they were obliged to wear throughout
Spain and North Africa towards the end of the twelfth century.[9]
(The constant renewal of these vestimentary regulations century after
century probably influenced the Catholic Church which, at the IV
Lateran Council of Rome in 1216, ruled that all non-Christians
residing in Europe — mainly Jews — had to wear a distinctive
badge.[10]) In spite of this, their numbers were increased by some of
the Jewish refugees fleeing from Christian Spain and Portugal at the
end of the fifteenth century who settled in the Maghreb, including
Morocco.

From the thirteenth to the nineteenth centuries, the persistence of
the *dhimma*, the *jizya* and the discriminatory vestimentary regulations
in Morocco (and elsewhere) is confirmed by innumerable Arab,
dhimmi and European sources.[11]

In his letter of 1841 to the French consulate at Tangier, the
Sultan Mulay Abd ar-Rahman characterizes the traditional status of

the Jews in mid-nineteenth century Morocco: 'Our glorious faith only allows them the marks of lowliness and degradation, thus the sole fact that a Jew raises his voice against a Muslim constitutes a violation of the conditions of protection.'[12]

Budgett Meakin, whilst acknowledging the concessions which some Jews living in the coastal towns had gained through European intervention, stressed the daily indignities of the Moroccan Jews in general, particularly those in the interior: 'From the day of his birth till all trace of his last resting-place has disappeared, the Hebrew of Morocco is despised and scorned.'[13]

The Moroccan scene and European politics

The Moroccan royal chronicler, evoking the prosperity and security of the country at the end of Mulay Ismail's long reign (1672—1727), employed a convincing quip: 'A woman and a *dhimmi* [i.e. a Jew] could go from Wajda to Wadi Nun without . . . [hindrance].'[14] This affluence is attributed by Captain Braithwaite — a member of the British embassy to the new sultan in 1728 — to Mulay Ismail's remarkable foreign policy. Whereas he considered himself at war with all Christian nations,[15] nonetheless European consuls, merchants and other foreigners could reside in the Moroccan ports in complete security, conducting their trade and business exactly as in peacetime.[16] A hundred years later this pragmatic policy had been completely reversed and scarcely more than a hundred Europeans resided in the two ports of Tangier and Mogador (Essaouira), where their presence was barely tolerated.

Morocco was already a useful commercial partner for England from the sixteenth century and eventually became a vital and regular supplier of fresh provisions to Gibraltar after its acquisition by the treaty of Utrecht in 1713. Following Nelson's victory at Trafalgar in 1805, Morocco's trade with Great Britain, mainly via Gibraltar, became paramount, whereas her contacts with Spain, France and other European countries were gradually reduced, mainly to negotiations relating to captives of their respective nations held hostage in Morocco. By 1844, the US consul at Tangier neatly summed up British policy as 'keeping Morocco at peace with Europe'.[17] This was however no easy task, for the sultan would not heed British warnings to cease aiding the Emir Abd al-Kader in his struggle against the French in Algeria. When the latter reacted strongly by bombarding Tangier and Mogador and by crushing the Moroccan army at Isly near Wajda in August 1844, it was only the British government's firmness which persuaded Louis-Philippe to settle France's differences with Morocco by negotiation rather than war. A treaty was forced upon the sultan who was traumatized by the first Moroccan defeat at the hands of a European army for more than two hundred years. Thereafter, it was no longer possible to ignore demands from European powers.

In 1845, John Drummond Hay was appointed British consul general in Tangier. By 1850 he had become, like his father before him, the sultan's adviser on foreign policy and he was to retain this unusually influential position of trust for thirty-five years, during which period he never ceased to uphold the principle of Morocco's political and territorial independence, a basic tenet of British policy. Drummond Hay's perseverance obliged the sultan to sign the Treaty of Commerce and Navigation between Morocco and Great Britain in 1856, compared by Miège to the 1842 Treaty of Nanking which opened up China to Western trade. Most European states adhered to the new treaty — thereby benefiting from the wide commercial and other opportunities it offered (including the sultan's responsibility for any treaty infractions by his subjects), but France and Spain desired its advantages, whilst retaining specific rights from earlier treaties. The rivalry between France, Spain and Great Britain was consequently heightened and, paradoxically, the treaty itself, which its architect had believed would contribute to Morocco's prosperity and development, became — for a number of economic reasons little understood at the time — one of the chief causes of its accelerated decline.

France's successful colonization of Algeria exacerbated Spain's traditional ambitions (her 'natural rights') regarding Morocco, especially in the Riff. The Darmon case had almost led to a Hispano-Moroccan war in 1844,[18] but it was the contemptuous refusal of the Moroccan government to grant an indemnity for a Spanish ship captured and pillaged in 1856 by Riff pirates — and their retention of seven Spaniards as hostages — which soon developed into a *casus belli*. National fervour and patriotism were aroused, rekindling sacred remembrances of crusading days against the Moors, in what was a serious affront to Spanish pride, particularly as French claims after a similar incident had been generously satisfied by the sultan. Grave internal problems were forgotten, all classes and parties rallied round the new government of the moderate General O'Donnell, supported by the Liberal Union, which was formed in 1858. France and Spain rapidly reached an agreement and most of the European powers sided with Spain against Morocco. The British government, thus isolated, preferred neutrality, as Spain had provided written guarantees that Tangier would not be occupied (thereby endangering Gibraltar) and that Spanish troops would be withdrawn from Morocco after an eventual treaty between the belligerents.

War broke out in September 1859, soon after the death of the sultan and the accession to the throne of his son, Muhammad IV. Tetuan — totally abandoned and pillaged by local tribes — was easily captured on 6 February 1860 by the Spaniards, whereas Tangier resisted with clandestine British aid after the departure of its European and Jewish inhabitants to Gibraltar and Algeciras.[19] Spain's limited objectives were rapidly achieved, but the cost of continuing the war was prohibitive, especially when the Mexican question required attention. On the Moroccan side, the loss of so important a town and the immediate transformation of its principal mosque into a catholic church was felt as a greater national disaster than the defeat at the hands of the French in 1844. The town's recovery became a *sine qua non* for the new sultan and the *makhsen* ('treasury', i.e. government).

Drummond Hay's good offices were now acceptable to all and a treaty was rapidly negotiated and ratified in May 1860. Its principal provision was the payment by Morocco of twenty million duoros (about £5,000,000) in exchange for Spain's evacuation of Tetuan. A commercial treaty followed in 1861, more favourable to Spain than that of 1856, particularly on the thorny question of local *protégés*. Tetuan was finally evacuated in 1862 under another convention, whereby Morocco — now virtually bankrupt — agreed to pay fifteen per cent of its war indemnity and the balance from customs' duties over a period of twenty-four years. Even this initial payment proved beyond the means of the Moroccan treasury and a loan of £500,000 was raised in London; it was guaranteed by the British government on condition that her vice-consuls and consuls were granted the same status in the ports — enabling them to collect their agreed share from the customs — as had been conceded to the Spanish *recaudadores* (customs' officials). The new French minister took advantage of the absence of Drummond Hay in August 1863 — when his country's good offices were solicited by the sultan — to conclude an even more favourable commercial treaty with Morocco.

The myth of Moroccan military force, inspired mainly by fear of Barbary pirates, had been shattered forever.[20] The victors' *recaudadores* and vice-consuls were omnipresent and every two months an appropriate quantity of coinage was despatched from Tangier to Spain in a Spanish warship. Permanent European residents in the port towns rose from 130 in 1820, to 350 in 1854, 600 in 1858 and reached 1,400 in 1864. The Moroccan chronicler, al Nasiri, acknowledged the extent of the national defeat and humiliation: 'The

Tetuan affair brought about a loss of prestige in the Maghreb and the invasion of the country by the Christians. Never had such a disaster fallen upon the Muslims.'[21]

The war gave Spain a dominant role in Morocco, yet it was Great Britain which became the principal beneficiary. By the autumn of 1863, Drummond Hay was again appreciated by the humiliated sultan. An Anglo-French *entente* developed when the almost daily quarrels between the Spanish and British representatives in the ports heightened Anglo-Spanish rivalry, which was to last throughout the sixties.[22] It was no secret that the Spanish minister in Tangier, Francisco Merry y Colom (1860–1872), haunted by the possibility of either Britain or France controlling Morocco, preferred the country to stagnate. Drummond Hay, on the contrary, aspired, like Stratford de Redcliffe in Constantinople, to be both the protector and reformer of Morocco.[23]

Montefiore, Britain and the Ottoman Reforms

In May 1863, Sir Moses Montefiore was received in private audience by the new sultan following a warm welcome at Constantinople by the British ambassador and by Turkish ministers. His social contacts with Britain's ruling classes, from prime ministers down, his important financial position, his close relationship with the senior Rothschilds by marriage and his presidency of the Board of Deputies of British Jews gave him a unique position of authority at home and abroad.

This was a period of imperial grandeur, but also of messianic aspirations in certain aristocratic and ecclesiastical circles. In an age of liberalism, the Jews were recognized as the heirs to a glorious past, and certainly worthy of commiseration, particularly where Britain had political and strategic interests.[24] As foreign secretary in 1839, Lord Palmerston had instructed Britain's first vice-consul in Jerusalem, 'to afford Protection to the Jews in general' (to the young Queen Victoria he even quoted the prophet Jeremiah: 'Judah shall be saved and Israel live in peace at home' — 23:6).[25] Montefiore may well have helped to develop this policy following the Damascus Affair of 1840.[26]

The *Tanzimat* Reforms in the Ottoman Empire had begun with the promulgation of the Gülhane edict (*Hatt-i Sherif*) on 3 November 1839. Sultan Abdülmecid, with British prompting, had granted a special *firman* to Montefiore on 6 November 1840, which explicitly confirmed for the Jews of the empire the 'equal rights' recently accorded to all his non-Muslim subjects. The more important imperial rescript of 1856 (*Hatt-i Humayun*) was issued under strong European pressure following the Crimean War.[27] Sultan Abdülaziz provided Montefiore in May 1863 with a confirmatory *firman* similar to his brother's of 1840.

In the Maghreb, the scandal over the Sfez Affair induced Napoleon III to despatch a fleet to Tunis, forcing the bey to concede a 'Pledge of Security', followed by a Constitution in 1860 — which was repealed in 1864.[28]

When Montefiore returned home in late June 1863, after an absence of six months, Lord Palmerston (also seventy-eight) was still prime minister, Earl Russell his dynamic foreign secretary and, at the Foreign Office, Henry Layard was under secretary and Edmund Hammond the permanent under secretary. Montefiore knew them all very well, through close collaboration on missions abroad concerning foreign Jews.

It is hardly surprising that once the news of the 'Moroccan atrocities' began circulating (involving Catholic Spain), Britain's diplomatic aid and prestige were available to Montefiore, after he had decided to undertake his mission. The appropriate Biblical reference was not forgotten: 'Whom shall I send and who will go for us?' (Isaiah 6:8) — and on his successful return, the *Daily Telegraph* could proclaim enthusiastically: 'What is Christianity, if not such deeds as his!' This was the spiritual and humanitarian mood of a part of the nation's élite before and after the Safi Affair.[29]

The Safi Affair and its antecedents

The London Board of Deputies of British Jews, under the official presidency of Sir Moses Montefiore, had established a Morocco Relief Committee to aid their coreligionists from Tetuan and Tangier who had fled to Gibraltar and Algeciras during the Hispano-Moroccan war. The committee's activities and the situation of Moroccan Jewry (including a correspondence with Drummond Hay) are detailed in the confidential report prepared in late 1860 by the Board's delegate, Moses H. Picciotto, after his return from a mission of enquiry to Morocco (Tangier, Tetuan, Rabat, Mogador) and Gibraltar.[30] In June 1861, Picciotto sent to Narcisse Leven, secretary of the recently-formed Alliance Israélite Universelle (AIU) in Paris, a precise plan for the foundation of a school in Tetuan. By the end of 1862, the first AIU school was ceremoniously opened with over a hundred pupils under joint French and British protection.[31]

The first news on the 'Safi Affair' to reach Sir Moses Montefiore, 'in the course of the latter holidays' (probably on Friday 1 October), was a letter in Spanish, dated 17 September 1863, from Moses Pariente, president of the Jewish *Junta Gobernatura* of Tangier (identical letters were addressed to Adolphe Crémieux, president of the AIU, the Delegates of American Israelites, and elsewhere). As the foreign secretary, Earl Russell, was in Scotland, Montefiore wrote from Ramsgate on Sunday 4 October, to the under secretary enclosing a copy with an English translation.[32] In the absence of Layard, Edmund Hammond, the permanent under secretary, replied on Monday and also sent a forceful telegram to Consul Reade in Tangier for clarification, stating: '. . . The story as represented affords a shocking instance of barbarous cruelty and you will press upon the Moorish authorities in the strongest terms the evil effect which such transactions must produce on the British government'. The next day, Earl Russell himself telegraphed Reade, who replied on the 7th, and at greater length on 10 October. These contacts continued throughout the month, and on the 27th Hammond sent an FO dispatch to Ramsgate and wrote again to Sir Moses on Saturday the 31st in reply to the latter's letter of 28 October.[33]

The Board of Deputies first met urgently on Thursday 8 October to discuss this affair, as well as a separate case concerning two Jews (Azuelos and Benattar), bastinadoed and imprisoned in Tetuan.[34] It is therefore incomprehensible that the narrative of these events provided by Hodgkin (1866), Guedalla (1880) and Wolf (1884) is described as having commenced with 'a packet of letters' (from the Jewish community in Gibraltar!), received by Sir Moses Montefiore on Saturday 31 October; and even Loewe (1890) relies on an entry from Montefiore's diary of 21 October concerning a packet thoughtfully sent to him at Ramsgate by A- (probably A.H. Layard at the Foreign Office), telling of 'the warm and generous efforts of Her Majesty's Government on behalf of the two unfortunate Jews now in prison at Safi'.[35]

The highly complicated and confusing 'Safi Affair' had originated three months earlier when Senor Montilla, the *recaudador* at Safi, died unexpectedly on 30 July after an illness of three to five days. The Spanish vice-consul had the man's servant arrested — probably before his colleague's death — and charged the youth with having administered poison to his master, in complicity with other Jews.[36] The fourteen or fifteen-year-old Jacob Benyuda (also referred to as 'Accan' or 'Akkan' — and, in some later publications, as Jacob Wizeman), a native of Mogador, was bastinadoed, in the customary manner, for lack of any proof. Constant flagellation, coupled with a promise of leniency from the Spanish vice-consul, elicited from him the desired 'confession', in which he implicated Eliahou Lalouche (also referred to as Elias Beneluz, or Lallas). The latter suffered an even harsher treatment (references are made to various gruesome

Sir Moses Montefiore in the uniform of the City Lieutenancy, painted by Solomon Alexander Hart in 1846

The Rothschild family in 1821 by W.T. Hobday (by courtesy of N.M. Rothschild & Sons Ltd)

Gershom Kursheedt, a trustee of the Touro bequest, who accompanied Sir Moses Montefiore to Jerusalem in 1855

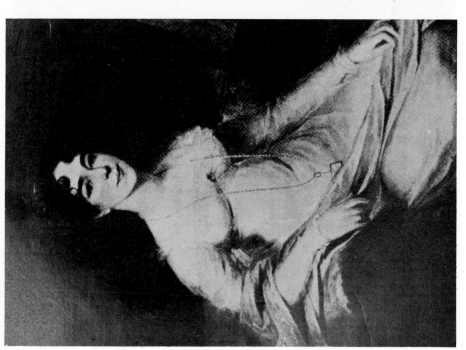

Judith Montefiore as a young woman

Dr Thomas Hodgkin (by courtesy of the Religious Society of Friends)

Dr Louis Loewe in 1842 (by courtesy of Professor Raphael Loewe)

Plan of the projected Jerusalem hospital, commissioned by Montefiore. The hospital was never built (by courtesy of Maxwell Whiteman)

Montefiore visiting the Sultan of Morocco in 1864, as illustrated by Dr Hodgkin

This portrait of Sir Moses at 100, 'drawn from life', appeared in the *Graphic* on 27 October 1883 (by courtesy of Roger and Anne Cowen)

East Cliff Lodge, Ramsgate, from the *Illustrated London News*, 3 November 1883 (by courtesy of Roger and Anne Cowen)

סיר משה מונטיפיורי ׀

רבו מגני ישרון בכל דור ודור בימי נדו. בארצות גלותו. אך אתה עלית על כלם. ככל מרי׳עי ישראל יצאת גם אתה לעזרתו. להושיעהו בצר לו בארצות עניו. אך יותר מהם פעלת לרומב את רוח עמך. רוח לאומו. אשר כמעט נדעך גם ממצוריקותיו. גם בחפשיו יחד.

אתה הראשין, אשר בעברך ארצות שונות להתיצב לפני מלכים ורוזני אר—ץ לישע עמך משכת אחריך את כל בני ישראל יושבי הארצות ההן. ותקשר לבות בני יעקב גרי ארצות שונות. שה פזורה ישראל היה לגוי אחד בכל ארצית נדחיו ושמך הנשא והמרומם על שפתי הגוי כלו היה לכב העם האחד ההוא.

אתה הראשין אשר עמת לבך לחונן את ציון ולקומם הריסמב ארץ אבותינו. ופעלתך היתה נר לרגלי בני עמנו הנאמנים לשים עין על תפארת עמם בימי קדם ולהשיב לו אחדותו הראשינה לימים יבאו.

על כן במלאת לך היום מאה שנה. הנה חג היום הזה לכל בני ישראל בכל ארצות תבל ומענה. חג לחובבי ציון, אשר שבוך למופת להם להחיית את עמם וארצם. ביום החג הזה ברכות עפות לך מכל פה. ושפתי כל איש ישראל תבענה תפלה לאלהי מרום לשלומך ולאורך ימיך. גם אנחנו. חברי אחת האגודות לקומם הריסות ציון אשר באדעססא, הננו נושאים לך. אדונינו השר. ברכתנו ממעמקי לבנו. כי אלהי ציון יחדש רוחך. יאמין כחך. יוכיף ימם על ימיך ואריך שנותיך בנעימים. ועיניך עוד תראינה בשלות אחרך בשוב ה״ את שיבת ציון. אמן ׀

Russian testimonial to Sir Moses illustrated by Isaac (later Leonid) Pasternak (by courtesy of the Montefiore Endowment Fund)

methods of torture, including being pressed in a wooden box, and the 'palo', probably the first stage of impaling) at the hands of the local Moroccan authorities and he too eventually 'confessed'. Both Benyuda and Lalouche recanted several times, only to 'confess' anew under the lash and worse, incriminating two other Jews — Makluf Aflalo and a certain Saïdo (or Shido). A pregnant woman, who sold milk daily to the *recaudador*, joined the accused in gaol for a time, as did those members of the families of the accused who had demonstrated forcefully in front of the mosque, crying out for justice. Lalouche escaped briefly at one stage and his father, mother, brothers and other Jews were imprisoned and flogged indiscriminately.

The various sources are not only confusing, but sometimes contradictory. The *recaudador* is successively described as being: 'very old and sick', 'over seventy', having left 'a widow and a son' (from Jewish sources); and 'about fifty, a former colonel, living alone' (from a Christian, living in Mogador). Moses Pariente's letter of 17 September shows that the Jewish community leaders were still awaiting 'a detailed report' on the whole affair — four days after Lalouche had been beheaded in the main market-place of Tangier! A private letter sent from Tangier to Gibraltar a few days later comments on this situation:

Do not depend on the gentlemen of this *Junta*. They do not possess the energy or unanimity so much required. They are full of dread lest they should come into collision with one or the other [representative of a European] government.[37]

One of the more interesting texts is also one of the most garbled. It is an eight-page, undated (end Sept. 1863?), scribbled translation from Spanish into French, being only an 'extract of an enquiry made under the auspices of the Jewish community of Tangier on the juridical murder of two Jews of Safi, in Morocco.'[38] The number of lashes administered to each of the four prisoners is recorded — from 150 to 500 blows, Shido receiving three times 300. Certain minor details are revealing: it is stated that 'Accan' had stolen a pistol and a watch from his master during his illness — because the latter had retained his wages; after the first scourging, being left alone in a room with Lalouche, he admits that through fear of more beatings he had 'confessed' and incriminated him. Lalouche replies: 'Is it not a sin to have implicated me, father of two children, and my own father now blind?' — thus confounding the vice-consul who steps out from his hiding-place. Lalouche is clearly referred to in this text as a 'British subject' who was handed over to the Spanish vice-consul by the French vice-consul (Gombaro), acting for the British vice-consul during the latter's absence from Safi. The narrative then becomes incomprehensible: it is the 'English vice-consul' who, returning to Safi from Mogador two days after the *recaudador*'s strange illness, but before his death, arrests 'old Makluf Aflalo' on suspicion of complicity in the alleged crime — simply because he had failed to greet the vice-consul. It is the same 'English vice-consul' who sends the accused men before the pasha for scourging. This must be an error in transmission, originating either in Safi, Tangier, or through the French translator in Paris who condensed the long report into an 'extract' — perhaps a confusion arose over the fact that the Spanish vice-consul had an English name: Butler. In this text, the Jews possessing European protections appeal to the pasha (via their consuls) 'to conform to the law of the country'; the pasha consults his wise son as well as the *cadi* (judge), who confirms that confessions obtained under torture are invalid, but that the sultan is certain to condemn the men to death in view of the Spanish request. A similar report in the *Jewish Chronicle* describes the Spanish minister's brutal opposition to the fair-minded *cadi* of Safi, and his precipitate message to the sultan demanding that the death sentence be applied forthwith. The newspaper's commentary is devastating:

> Now let the world see the contrast between this inhuman and barbarous Christian, Senor Merry y Colon, the Spanish Minister, and the God-fearing and conscientious Mohammedan Caddi, Mohammed Ben-abd-El-jaleck, the Moorish judge.[39]

Yet most of the letters from Morocco end with a general appeal to the British and French governments 'to relieve the Jews of Morocco from being oppressed by the Moorish authorities'.[40]

Useful data comes from other documents in Spanish, preserved in the AIU archives in Paris.[41] One is an undated copy of the attestation of Rabbi Saadiah Rebboh, the *dayan* of Safi. With two Muslim *adules* (notaries), he visited 'Accan of Mogador' in prison before his execution and declared that the boy explained how he had twice been forced to confess. 'The truth is that I have done nothing . . . but if they question me once more, I will say anything, as I am terribly afraid to be beaten again.' The rabbi appeals to the *cadi*, asking him, rhetorically, 'does the law of the *ulama* (religious scholars) of Morocco decree that all the Jews should die?' One letter, dated 8 October, is from David Serusi of Safi to Moses Pariente at Tangier: he explains that Benyuda had a good reputation in Mogador where he had worked for two years for a Senor Manuel Batto and that he had been in the *recaudador*'s service for no more than six weeks. The local pasha did not even allow him the chance of reciting the *shema* (declaration of faith in one God) with the assistance of a rabbi, before execution. He also refers to the difficulty of obtaining any signed attestations from the French and British (Carstensen) vice-consuls of Safi, because of instructions from Consul Reade in Tangier not to act without instructions from him. The third letter, dated 25 October, is from Pariente to Crémieux in Paris. It refers to Rabbi Rebboh's attestation and Serusi's letter (he is an 'Italian subject') and also mentions that the vice-consuls have certified that the 'very old and sick' *recaudador* was not poisoned; he also described in detail the more recent incident involving the flogging of two Jews in Tangier (Shalom Elcaim and Jacob Benharosh) by order of the Spanish minister.

It is strange that Lalouche's British connection was not stressed publicly by the Jewish communities in Morocco and England at the time. His father held an old passport issued in Gibraltar by a Mr Cardoza who had apparently acted as Tunisian consul. On these grounds, Frederick Carstensen, the British vice-consul in Safi (1858—1865), had granted British protection to the son. After Sir John Drummond Hay's return to Tangier, he endeavoured, in a long letter of 12 November, to reassure Earl Russell on this delicate point involving British honour, whereby an allegedly British-protected person could have been handed over to the Moroccan authorities — at the request of the Spaniards — and executed publicly in Tangier under the eyes of the European representatives. Firstly, it was difficult to refuse the Spanish requests; secondly, they did not then know what had actually taken place in Safi and what were the intentions of the Spanish government. Lalouche is here described as a man of bad character, a swindler, already convicted of theft, who treated his wife cruelly (Drummond Hay remained hostile all his life to what he called 'irregular protections'[42]). Sir John mentioned Butler's message to Carstensen, and Merry's formal letter to Reade, as being dated on 25 and 26 August respectively. Unless this is yet another error of transcription, it would seem to indicate, either that the *recaudador* died at the end of August (not July), or that the sequence of events as recorded elsewhere is flawed.[43]

Perhaps this seemingly minor aspect of the Affair, which appears to have rankled in London, might have further prompted the British government's decision — on humanitarian and political grounds — to provide Sir Moses with every possible aid for his forthcoming mission.

Although Reade in his 10 October letter to Russell quoted the words of Muhammad Bargash the Moroccan minister in Tangier stating that the two Jews had 'suffered death by order of the sultan in accordance with a decree of the *ulama*', he added:

I cannot however refrain from expressing to your Lordship, in the meantime, my conviction that the investigations of this horrible affair has been attended with much cruelty and injustice, as well as my extreme surprise and regret that such proceedings should have been enacted if not under the direct patronage of the Spanish Authorities, with at any rate, their apparent sanction.

He confirmed that no autopsy had been carried out by the Spanish naval doctors on the spot; that Benyuda was beheaded on 14 September at Safi (Carstensen considered him guilty) without a trial; that the same fate had befallen Lalouche, who was sent to Tangier at Merry's request and executed there on 13 September by order of the sultan (he proclaimed his innocence to the end, whilst pronouncing the *shema*). Makluf and Saido were expected to be executed, although 'these two had nothing approaching even to a trial — and yet they are sentenced to death.'[44]

Merry is again portrayed in the worst possible light by Sir John in a 29 October despatch.[45] Two young Jews of Tangier (Elcaim and Benharosh) had accidentally splashed the Spanish minister's Muslim servant with mud from a puddle and were rudely treated by him, at which they replied, 'Are you going to kill us as you did the Safi Jews?' The servant reported these words at the Spanish legation and one of the Jews was immediately bastinadoed and both imprisoned by order of Consul Rizzo.[46] On Merry's return from Madrid ten days later they were taken back in chains to the scene of the incident, and there received several hundred lashes on 25 October (instead of the 50 requested by Merry) under the window of two British subjects, who hastened to report the matter to the British consulate. The pasha confirmed to Consul Reade that Merry had insisted 'that the Jews who had been flogged shall not be set at liberty until they change their European attire for the costume of the country'.[47]

When Drummond Hay called on the Moroccan Minister Bargash, the latter referred to 'dark menaces made by Merry if blind compliance was not granted to their demands', and Sir John felt powerless to act unless the British government was ready to shield the Moorish authorities from Spain should they refuse Merry's dictates. He advised diplomatic action in Madrid. In his letter of 12 November to the foreign secretary he declared that the British vice-consul in Tetuan (Kirby Green) had confirmed the truth of a previous complaint of 18 September from the Jewish committee of Tetuan (see note 34), concerning 'an old cobbler' and 'a poor lad' (Abraham Azuelos and Jacob Benattar) who were still chained and imprisoned, having received from 600 to 800 lashes by order of the local authorities two months earlier at the request of the Spanish vice-consul.

A Spaniard had been robbed, one shoe was left behind by the thief in his flight and all the Jewish cobblers were summoned by the pasha to identify it; old Azuelos unaware of the incident, readily recognized his workmanship, but was unable to remember the client's name: 'I have made so many shoes'. On these grounds alone, he and the boy were arrested, imprisoned and bastinadoed.

All these events reached the British public through the newspapers, first in the columns of the *Jewish Chronicle and Hebrew Observer*, and in other articles of the national press.[48] The anti-Spanish tone was very strong and the language of the editorials unrestrained:

Would it not be sheer madness in a great nation just emerging from an un- paralleled state of prostration and barbarism, the consequence of the terrible crimes of the past of which it is now conscious [. . .] to rouse the indignation of the civilised world by misdeeds [. . .] and thus to alienate from it that public opinion which within the last few years began to veer round, and to believe in the extinction of the race of those delighting in the shrieks of men and women — aye of youths and maidens — expiring in the flames [. . .] If Damascus had its Ratti-Menton [. . .] why should not Tangiers be afflicted with a Merry, fol- lowing in the same bloody track . . .[49]

There seems to be a fatality about Spain compelling her, against her will, to act the part of Israel's evil genius [. . .] And now, when the fires of the auto- da-fes have ceased to cast their lurid reflection over the Spanish sky; when happily, the eyes of inquisitors can no longer feast upon the writhing forms of tortured tender maidens [. . .] It is as though the Spaniard had stood for cen- turies on his coast watching for an opportunity when he could conveniently cross the sea and complete beyond it the work of destruction commenced in his own land [. . . Spain] knows well enough that Morocco would not offer any determined opposition even if Senor Merry should require the whole Jewish population as a sacrifice, in order to pacify her wrath . . .[50]

Prompt, even heroic, action seemed necessary. By Friday 30 October, Sir Moses had informed his nephew, J. M. Montefiore, of his readiness to embark on the long journey, as he considered a general persecution of the Jews of Morocco, of which the actual outbreak was only a forerunner, as imminent; the Chief Rabbi of the British Empire, Dr Nathan Adler, in a letter sent to the Board of Deputies on 2 November, suggested that 'it needs but your solici- tation to induce our esteemed friend' to set out for Morocco and succeed 'in rolling off the foul reproach of murder from our nation'. On the 4th, J. M. Montefiore requested assistance from Earl Russell for Sir Moses' mission and Sir Moses wrote to his nephew the next day:

It is my earnest hope, that with the continuance and assistance to be afforded me in support of the mission, it may under God's Blessing be my happy privilege to become the instrument not only of accomplishing the liberation of the two

Jews now in prison under fearful imputations but also of establishing their innocence and of vindicating the honour of the Jewish community of Morocco.[51]

On the 11th, Sir Moses thanked Hammond the permanent under secretary for his letter of confirmation, adding, 'I propose to leave as quickly as I can and am only awaiting the letters [of recommendation for Madrid and Morocco] so kindly promised.'[52] He collected them himself the following day at the Foreign Office, called on the Lord Mayor of London and wrote from the Alliance Office for funds to be made available.

My dear Baron Rothschild,
Leaving for Morocco in 2–3 days. Request letters of Credit for £5,000 on Paris, Bayonne, Madrid, Cadiz, Gibraltar, Malta, Naples, Beyrout, plus letters of introduction to any persons at these places. Will call tomorrow at New Court.[53]

(Why Malta and Beirut, but not Tangier, one wonders?)

The editorial comment which appeared in the *Jewish Chronicle* of 13 November not only poured forth its literary wrath and anathema on Spain, but rose to new heights of hyperbole when describing Sir Moses:

. . . the most illustrious son of the patriarchs [who must] once more gird up his loins [. . .] a man verging upon eighty [. . .] we tremble for so precious a life [. . .] But since it [the mission] has arisen, let us confess that no coreligionist all over the globe is so well qualified for it as Israel's veteran champion.[54]

Prayers were offered up in all the synagogues, and on 17 November Sir Moses left Dover for Madrid accompanied by Haim Guedalla,[55] Sampson Samuel, solicitor to the Board of Deputies, Dr Hodgkin[56] and two attendants.

Madrid and Tangier

The Montefiore party arrived in Madrid after a week. Aside from spending the Sabbath in Bayonne, his only other recorded rest was at Bordeaux where Montefiore found time to inspect the local installations of the Imperial Continental Gas Association of which he was president.[57] The British ambassador in Madrid, Sir John Crampton, was on friendly terms with the liberal ruling circles and had instructions from the Foreign Office (Montefiore himself was carrying one such letter) to provide every assistance to the octogenarian. Within twenty-four hours of his meeting with Crampton, Montefiore was received by the Spanish prime minister, the Marquis of Miraflores, who was most co-operative: in fact, a stay of execution for Makluf and Saido had already been granted eight weeks earlier, after Baron James de Rothschild (youngest brother of Nathan Mayer) had interceded with the government of Madrid through the Spanish embassy in Paris.

Montefiore's six days in Madrid show him skilfully practising his usual style of diplomacy. Apart from the prime minister, whom he saw twice and from whom he obtained an official letter of introduction to the Spanish minister in Tangier, he also met Generals Prim and O'Donnell (the Duke of Tetuan), as well as various ambassadors and other distinguished personalities. His contacts were facilitated by the British ambassador whom he met regularly, by the Rothschild letters of recommendation, and also thanks to Mr W. Weisweiller (described as a friend and relative) who occupied an influential position in Madrid as a financier and lavish consul of foreign countries.[58] He remained an extra two days in order to have a private audience of the Queen of Spain and the Prince Consort who assured him 'of their respect for all religions'.

The party continued on the long journey south by train and diligence to Cordova and then Seville. There, introduced by a letter from Weisweiller, he met Merry's father (Don Antonio Merry y Colon), the acting consul for Russia and Prussia. He obtained from him a personal letter of recommendation to his son in Tangier, where he arrived early on 11 December from Cadiz, twenty-five days after his departure from Dover.

Success in Tangier

The old man was carried ashore in a princely manner on a portable couch, whilst a great number of Jews, led by Moses Pariente, enthusiastically welcomed him. Dr Hodgkin noted 'the peculiar sound uttered by the Jewish females in Morocco when they wish to give expression to their joyful greetings with distinguished honour.'[59] The same Friday Montefiore received various deputations and communications from Jewish communities throughout Morocco, before resting on the Sabbath.

He met the British minister and Consul Reade on Sunday and delivered Earl Russell's letter of 12 November, which instructed Drummond Hay 'to afford to him all such assistance as you can with propriety', not only regarding the Safi prisoners, but also 'in the hope of improving the condition of the Jews [of Morocco]'.[60]

In a letter to Russell dated 15 December, Sir John described Montefiore's rapid success in obtaining the immediate release of the two youths (Elcaim and Benharosh) who had been imprisoned in Tangier for two months and publicly bastinadoed on 25 October, as well as the assurance that the two Safi prisoners would soon be released (doc. 1). In a separate letter, he related how Montefiore had been directly responsible for his own reconciliation with Merry (doc. 2). This was not just a note of courtesy, for he sent a private letter the next day to Hammond in which he lavishly praises 'the good old man', who had not only achieved so much for his co-religionists, but had been of great personal service to him; his bad relations with the Spanish minister — a matter of serious concern to the Foreign Office — were now ended. As for Montefiore's intended voyage to thank the sultan at Marrakesh, Sir John wrote: 'It is a great undertaking for a man of 78 [*sic*] to travel in Morocco' and suggested that Carstensen accompany him on the visit.[61] Montefiore asked for Reade, an old friend, and this wise preference was accepted (doc. 3).

In his report of 18 December to the Board of Deputies, Montefiore referred to the liberation, through his intervention, of a Moor imprisoned on suspicion of killing two Jews[62] and his having been introduced by Drummond Hay to the European ministers at their respective legations: he also alluded to the lecture given by Dr Hodgkin (translated into Spanish) to the 'male and female members' of the leading Jewish families of Tangier, which was 'followed by the exhibition of philosophical experiments'. His long discussions with the *Junta* led to the opening in 1864 of an Anglo-French school for the children of the 7–8,000 Jews of Tangier, which was administered jointly by the Board of Deputies and the Alliance Israélite Universelle — the first AIU school of Tetuan having proved a big success in less than a year.

The determination of the Spanish government to be cleared of the accusation of launching an anti-Jewish 'crusade' is evident from the circular of 20 December (doc. 4) sent by Merry to the Spanish consuls and vice-consuls in all the port towns. This circular — almost certainly prepared in Madrid — and an exchange of letters between the minister and Montefiore were published in the *Gibraltar Chronicle* (28 December), the daily London newspapers (5 January) and the *Jewish Chronicle* (8 January). Spain's public act of contrition required a suitable response from the London Jewish weekly which was forthcoming: 'let us perform an act of justice, and repair in an hour of cheerfulness the wrong committed by us in an hour of gloom'. The warm reception given to 'Israel's champion' in Madrid and the withdrawal by the Spanish government of all proceedings against the two unexecuted Safi Jews convinced its editor (probably on instructions!) that — 'we were in error'. The *Gibraltar Chronicle* had refrained from involving the Madrid government (see *supra*, note 46) and was 'glad to see that the Spanish Government have now taken the best and most effectual means of removing the erroneous opinion . . .'.

The London *Morning Advertiser*'s commentator, however, remained doubtful about 'the personal solicitude of Donna Isabella for the Jews and all other people who are not under the teaching of the Romish priests', and even referred sarcastically to the queen's 'favourite devotion to the Virgin of Atocha and the directions of her overtaxed confessor', going so far as to suggest that the same circular in favour of the Jews of Morocco should be reissued 'to prevent acts of cruelty on the part of the Spanish authorities against the *Protestants*.'[63]

Gibraltar – Mogador – Marrakesh

On 22 December Montefiore and his party crossed over the straits to Gibraltar and were ceremoniously received by the Jewish community, whilst the guard on duty presented arms. Sir William Codrington had been particularly helpful to the Jewish refugees from Tetuan and Tangier four years earlier; both he and his brother (Admiral Codrington), and his father, were acquainted with Sir Moses. On this occasion the governor not only invited the Montefiore party to dinner, but also – and for the first time – some of the leading Jews of the colony. The *séjour* on the Rock in sunny weather, awaiting suitable transport to enable Montefiore to reach first Safi (symbolically) and then Marrakesh, lasted a fortnight.

Five days later, the Admiralty – under instructions from Earl Russell – 'despatched the frigate *Magicienne* from Malta to Gibraltar to convey Sir Moses Montefiore to Morocco'.[64] The British warship left for Safi on 6 January, Montefiore generously lodged in the captain's cabin, the latter in his saloon, whilst Dr Hodgkin and Mr Samuel had their hammocks slung between two guns near the captain's door. Although the sultan's escort was awaiting them, rough weather prevented the party's disembarkation for two days – with the exception of Montefiore's faithful courier, Ferrache, who got ashore during a calm moment. After the customary exchange of gun salutes and the reception by signal flags of a message from the authorities indicating that Makluf and Saido had been released on the very day that the *Magicienne* had set sail from Gibraltar, they continued south to Mogador, arriving there on 10 January.

The eventful sea and land voyage to Marrakesh has been vividly described by Dr Hodgkin, as well as by Montefiore in his letters and diary. Captain Armitage's unpublished official report is a useful complement.[65]

The preparations for the inland journey lasted a week, during which the whole party, including Consul Reade (who had now joined

them), Captain Armitage and two of his officers were 'hospitably
entertained by Mr Abraham Corcos [US consul at Mogador since
1862], one of the most opulent of the Jewish merchants at this
port.'[66]

The departure of the sultan's guests took place on Sunday 17
January. A caravan of fifteen camels, several baggage mules, and up
to one hundred servants, followers and soldiers set off on the arduous
110 mile journey. The governor of Mogador and his officers accompanied this impressive company for an hour, whereas Abraham
Corcos and some leading rabbis and members of the community
remained with them for the first day and night. Montefiore had been
provided with a *chaise à porteur* by the Portuguese minister in
Tangier, which was harnessed to a mule in front and another behind,
thus reducing the old man's hardships. Few Europeans before him —
other than foreign embassies — had received an authorization, let
alone an escort, to penetrate as far inland as the sultan's desert
capital. The following Friday, a group of wealthy Jews from
Marrakesh, led by Abraham Corcos' cousin, welcomed them and the
whole caravan rested for the entire Sabbath period. A guard of
honour met them at the entry to the town on the 25th and brought
them to a disused palace, surrounded by a garden, which had been
especially furnished for their *séjour*.[67]

Guests of the sultan

The sultan's hospitality and extreme consideration for his guests
lasted throughout the next fortnight at Marrakesh, until their return
to the coast at Mazagan. There, they boarded HMS *Magicienne* — a
month after their arrival at Mogador — for the return journey to
Gibraltar. This privileged treatment of a Jew by a sultan of Morocco,
who claimed direct descent from the Prophet Muhammad, can only
be explained by the exceptional political and economic conjuncture —
and especially by Britain's official patronage of the mission.
Drummond Hay had already hinted at this in his letter to his friend
the Vizier Yamani, written after Montefiore's initial success in Tangier
(referred to in doc. 1). The stamp of total British backing was amply
demonstrated by Montefiore's arrival on board a British warship
(Merry had come to Safi on a Spanish warship to demand Benyuda's
public execution four months earlier and to bring Lalouche to
Tangier for execution) and the uniforms of his British escort to
Marrakesh.[68] This patronage was amply confirmed to the *makhsen*
by Consul Reade's letter to the vizier (doc. 6) and by Montefiore's
own petition. In England, admiration was expressed in the House
of Commons, as well as in the daily press.[69]

Nothing was wanting on the part of England to give this Mission a semi-official character. An English man-of-war, in the company of an English Consul [only for the return journey], conveyed him to the coast of Africa and back again to an English possession; an English naval officer and the same English Consul accompanied him on his journey to the Court of the Sultan, and the latter, as a deputy of the English Government, presented him to the monarch; and again, it was the English Minister at Tangier who opened the path for him to the person of the Prince. The Sultan thus, in some measure, stands pledged to England [on the subject of the *dahir* or edict], the only Christian Power from which he knows he has nothing to fear and much to hope, and whose interest it is to support his throne.[70]

The original instructions from Russell that Drummond Hay should give Montefiore 'all such assistance as you can with propriety' had grown into a diplomatic *cause célèbre*, with its own momentum, 'under the shadow of England's mighty protection'.

Consul Reade was taken by surprise when, on their arrival in Marrakesh, Montefiore showed him the petition he had prepared in Gibraltar and which he intended submitting to the sultan. His letter of 7 February to Drummond Hay explains the reasons why he felt that he had no alternative but to support strongly this initiative, so that the mission would not fail.

Reade emphasized the following points (doc. 5):
1. The sultan had to believe that it was a 'political necessity' for him to grant the petition.
2. It must be demonstrated that his 'personal interests' would benefit from its acceptance.
3. Montefiore was petitioning for the rights of Jews and Christians, but the latter were in no need of such intercession and he would not press this aspect.

To the vizier he emphasized (doc. 6):
1. The long-standing friendly relations between Britain and Morocco;
2. The British government's interest in Montefiore's mission, as he came 'in the name of the Hebrew Community of England and . . . on behalf of the civilized world'.
3. The solicitude of the 'Governments of Europe and America' for the Jews in Muslim countries. The 'protections' extended to them by these powers might be reduced if the Jews of Morocco were placed 'on an equal footing' with the sultan's Muslim subjects (see *supra*, note 42).
4. Turkey had been saved from Russia during the Crimean war by England and her allies because the Ottoman sultan 'had given repeated proofs of the just and tolerant spirit by which he was animated.'
5. Sir Moses Montefiore had presented to the Ottoman sultan a similar

petition in 1840 to the one he was now submitting to the Moroccan sultan. Its acceptance would promote the welfare and happiness . . . of mankind in general and would also be in the sultan's interests.

The sultan's ceremonious reception for the embassy took place early on 1 February. Montefiore speaks of soldiers in serried rank 'of great variety of hue and accoutrements'. Hodgkin noted that the soldiers were not dressed or armed in the old Moorish style, but had become 'a sort of degraded European army [. . .] These troops had very much the appearance of prisoners clothed in left off soldiers' garments'. But, as the party passed the avenue into the vast plain, the massed cavalry and foot soldiers (about six thousand) afforded a most impressive sight. The ministers came forward to greet them, white stallions with rich saddles were led past as well as the royal carriage covered in green. Trumpets heralded the monarch, riding a fine pure-white horse — a symbolical sign of esteem and welcome (a white horse also preceded Montefiore's sedan). The short public audience was said to have been one of the most grandiose ever given by the sultan. He expressed his pleasure at receiving subjects of the Queen of England, and referred to the close friendship between the two countries, adding a few kind words to Montefiore. The latter, standing before the mounted monarch wearing his uniform of the City Lieutenancy, declared that he came on behalf of his brethren and the English people. He presented a sealed petition (Memorial) in Arabic 'on behalf of the Jewish and Christian subjects of his empire'.

The vizier entertained all members of the English embassy at his palace the same evening and discussed a number of subjects with Montefiore, including the extension of the *mellah* of Mogador and the acquisition of a house to serve as a hospital at Tangier. Montefiore had decided not to leave without a royal edict (*dahir*) and this, he notes, was 'placed in my hands' on 5 February. It is clear, however, from Reade's narrative (doc. 5) that the *dahir* was not delivered to Montefiore, but — on the sultan's strict instructions — into the hands of the British consul. Reade made a copy and then sent the original to Montefiore.

The sultan received his guests two days later with the same honours as the first time, but more intimately, seated on an impressive divan. He reiterated to Montefiore his intention of protecting his Jewish subjects, conversed through interpreters (Reade and Nahon) and then had the party guided through his extensive royal gardens for several hours, Montefiore in his sedan, the others mounted.

A tour of the Jewish quarter followed. Ten days earlier, Montefiore had met numerous deputations, comprising up to four hundred visitors. Now, led by the sultan's guards, he was welcomed in the *mellah* with such vociferous enthusiasm by virtually the whole population (about ten thousand) that his sedan could hardly advance through the narrow, dirty streets to the largest and oldest synagogue, which Sir Moses found to be 'a very humble structure' and Dr Hodgkin 'a small rudely decorated room', as well as to the houses of the wealthy Corcos and Nahon families.[71] Their impressive departure the next day once more found the streets everywhere thronged, with many poor Jews seeking a last gift from their adored benefactor and being mercilessly beaten back by the guards, so as to allow a passage out of the town.

The triumphant return

The party reached Mazagan eight days later, considerable hospitality being offered them all along the 120 mile route by the district governors, amidst joyous manifestations from the Jewish village populations. The only disagreeable incident was the customary malediction of a local Moor who, oblivious to the imposing entourage, spat into the old man's sedan before he was arrested, undoubtedly considering that its occupant had no more rights to such honours than would a local *dhimmi* Jew.[72]

The habitually variegated and vociferous crowd of Jews met them at some distance from Mazagan and their numbers increased as they entered the town.[73] Montefiore went straight to the synagogue and gave thanks for the success of the mission and their safe return. The group partook of a great feast the same evening, increasingly pressed by Captain Armitage to embark, which they did the following morning, whilst Mr Moses Nahon spent the entire night satisfying the claims of the countless attendants. Gibraltar was finally reached on the 17th, six weeks after HMS *Magicienne* had set out for the Moroccan coast.

There followed a much-needed rest for the 'champion of Israel' who caught up on his correspondence and prepared diligently for his return journey. A month later, he was once more received in private audience by the Spanish royal couple at Madrid, this time presenting to them a copy of the *dahir* and its Spanish translation. Then Paris, where the British ambassador arranged a private audience with Napoleon III on 31 March, at which Montefiore handed to the Emperor a copy of the sultan's edict and its French translation. Finally to Ramsgate, where on 5 April, twenty weeks after leaving, he sent his final letter to the Board of Deputies.

The mood in the country towards the octogenarian, particularly amongst the Jewish community, could fairly be described as reverential awe, and its manner of expression overwhelmingly gushing. A month before his return, the *Daily Telegraph* in a leading article had referred to '. . . what one good old man had done to wipe away tears from streaming eyes and cause oppression to cease . . .', before concluding on a moral note:

> Fatigued and feeble with travel, the venerable suppliant has returned with the blessing of a population and the admiration of honest men accompanying him to his English home. His last of many such noble works is his greatest, and cannot fail to be followed by justice and amity along the shores of Africa . . . Honour to the good grey hairs of the aged baronet! we say; and may those who differ from him in 'faith' show, with their gold and influence, 'works' but half as bold and heroic as those of Sir Moses Montefiore.[74]

Thousands of messages poured in from all over the country — and the world.

Intentions and achievements of all the parties

The British government had once more given its official support to a Montefiore mission on behalf of foreign Jews. The means displayed and the firmness adopted might suggest that — as in Palestine — their aims were not solely humanitarian. Britain's desire was to keep Morocco at peace with Europe by reducing the opportunities for direct foreign interference and to guarantee regular provisions for Gibraltar, as well as maintaining her long-established and privileged economic position. There is no indication of a policy — either then or later — to use the plight of Moroccan Jewry as a stepping-stone to direct control of the country. The opposite is true. Britain did not want another European country to have an excuse to intervene.

As a young man, Drummond Hay had observed: 'With Moors and Chinese you must be kind, but very firm, or the end would be great guns.'[75] Reade's letter to Yamani (doc. 6) is a perfect example of this method of diplomacy. He was aware, as he explained to his minister in Tangier, of the difficulty of achieving the Ottoman-type reform which Montefiore was seeking, 'opposed as it was to the religious and deeply rooted prejudices of a fanatical people' (doc. 5). Drummond Hay knew this situation as well as anyone. He had joined his father in Tangier at sixteen (1832) and, in a noteworthy publication, described a journey from Tangier to Larache in 1839 to obtain blood horses for the young Queen Victoria; there, he observed that the condition of the Moroccan Jew ('the slave of slaves') was worse than that of the black Muslim slave.[76] On succeeding his father as British consul general in 1845, he was shocked (as well as humiliated) that his Jewish official interpreter, David

Sicsu, in the time-honoured *dhimmi* tradition, automatically removed his shoes whenever he passed near a mosque. He reminded
Sicsu that the privileges of a British subject dispensed him from this
humiliating act.[77] Now, twenty-five years later, he felt that the
'increase of trade and the general progress of civilization'[78] would
modify these 'fanatical feelings . . . more especially of the inhabitants
of the inland Towns' (doc. 7), and informed Russell in London that
he was glad that 'a more direct interference on the part of Her
Majesty's Government and myself' had not been required in order to
obtain the important concessions contained in the *dahir*.[79]

Montefiore's initial aims were clearly described in his letter of 5
November to his nephew, the acting president of the Board of
Deputies, as 'the liberation of the two Jews now in prison' and 'the
vindication of the honour of the Jewish community of Morocco' —
essentially the same aims as were adopted for the Damascus
Affair.[80] But in 1840 he had been able to follow up the initial
success by obtaining an imperial *firman* in Constantinople which
exonerated the Jews from the accusation of ritual murder and
specifically confirmed their rights throughout the Ottoman Empire
on the lines of the *Tanzimat* reforms. Because the Jews of the
Orient had kept a low profile and had not flaunted their 'equal rights'
with Muslims, they had been spared in the violent backlash of 1860
which struck the Christians, particularly in Damascus and the
Lebanon, leading to European intervention.[81]

As 'he considered a general persecution of the Jews of Morocco . . .
as imminent', Montefiore probably envisaged, from the outset of his
mission, an appeal to the Sultan of Morocco along the lines of this
firman — reconfirmed to him by the new Ottoman sultan in May
1863 — even though he did not divulge his intentions until the last
moment in Marrakesh for fear of losing British support.[82] He was
obviously aware of the actual situation in Morocco from relatives
and from the recent reports (both written and verbal) emanating
from the Morocco Relief Committee founded in 1859. He had seen
with his own eyes the misery of the Jewish population and the
ambiguous situation of a few wealthy families. In his first letter from
Marrakesh (26 January) to the Board he referred to the obligation
for all Jews without distinction to walk barefooted in the streets of
the town, adding that these 'degradingly distinctive marks' (the
discriminatory clothing as well) were common to all the towns and
villages of the interior. Six days before his meeting with the sultan,
he was not sure if there 'is the remotest possibility of success',
consoling himself with the thought that he would nonetheless have
done his utmost and that whatever the outcome his visit would

provide his co-religionists with a moral boost. Yet a month later, writing from Gibraltar to Earl Russell on 23 February (whilst transmitting in all directions countless copies of the *dahir*), he expresses his hopes that the edict 'will be of immediate benefit to the Jews of Morocco, and tend to secure their future welfare'. To the Board of Deputies, the next day, he was even more optimistic, declaring his belief that 'this degrading distinction [walking barefooted], together with every other will, I trust, now be speedily removed'.[83]

There was a natural tendency to exaggerate somewhat and to consider hopes and dreams as achieved before the results were actually confirmed. It is revealing in this respect that in his letter to Russell from Gibraltar, Montefiore restricted himself, for obvious reasons, to the condition of the Jews, although in all published letters and declarations — before leaving London and after returning home — he often referred jointly to the 'Jews and Christians' of Morocco. Clearly, the Christian residents of the Moroccan sea-ports, as fully-protected nationals of European powers, were in no need of the traditional Islamic toleration conceded to the *ahl al-dhimma* in accordance with the Pact, or Covenant of Umar. However, public opinion in England and Europe would be more sensitive to a universal humanitarian plea. The demographical importance of Moroccan Jewry was also magnified. An initial estimate of 200,000 in November 1863 soon reached 500,000, whereas the actual Jewish population of Morocco was then probably not more than 100,000 persons — any estimate in excess of 150,000 was a pure figment of the imagination.[84] On the other hand, this exaggeration also might have been dictated by the desire to impress once again liberal public opinion with the magnitude of the injustice.

But there was a point where such aims and hopes foundered on the rock of reality. There seems to have been an inability to grasp the basic difference between the contemporary situation in the Ottoman Empire and that of Morocco. Reforms such as those initiated in the eighteenth century and extracted from Turkey in the preceding generation — in the teeth of a popular and traditional refusal to recognize the *dhimmi* as an equal — were inconceivable in a country such as Morocco (which was similar to Yemen and Persia[85] in this respect), where the *ulama* were powerful, the people fanatical, and the ruler's authority tenuous. This is expressly indicated by the terminology which effectively divided the country: *bled al-makhsen* ('lands of the treasury', i.e. the area controlled by the sultan); and *bled al-siba* ('lands of freedom' — virtually autonomous regions).[86]

Moroccan opinion on the event is summarized by the court

chronicler, al-Nasiri. Although chronicled probably twenty years afterwards, we find here the principal elements — except its origins, the Safi Affair — from an Islamic standpoint. The humiliation of the war with Spain (Tetuan), the problem of 'protections', the desire of the Jews for 'emancipation', the important position of 'Rothschild' in England, the latter's appointment of his relative (Montefiore) to head a delegation and the English government's backing are all recounted. The sultan, not wishing to send Montefiore away as a failure (he had brought gifts), granted the *dahir*, which merely provided 'a clear statement of the Religious Law . . . upholding the pact of protection.' Nasiri explained how the *dahir* had been granted in favour of 'the respectable Jews and their poor', but other Jews (especially those in the ports) had become 'arrogant and reckless'; another *dahir*, 'clarifying' the first one, was soon after circulated.

The closing paragraph of the *dahir* of 5 February 1864 refers to the fact that nothing new is being promulgated, merely what is 'already well established, well known, and recorded'. There can be no doubt that the 'Pact of Umar' is implied here, as well as its corollary, the traditional *dhimmi* condition. The language was elegant and sounded magnanimous to European ears, for it was not fully realized that the key to the text was the significance of the words 'justice' and 'injustice', which might mean one thing in Europe, but quite another in Morocco when applied to *dhimmis*, in a strict Islamic sense. 'Emancipation' was never envisaged and Nasiri is categoric that the (*dhimmi*) Jews were not to be granted the same rights as the (foreign) Christians in the ports. He regretted that the first *dahir* had even been issued and warmly approved its nullification (he was a deputy judge of Salé at the time).[87] His ill-humour was similar to that of much Muslim reaction in the aftermath of the promulgation of the Humayun edict of 1856 (and in Tunisia after the 1857 Pledge of Security).[88] The explosion of a huge store of gunpowder, which ravaged an area of the town two days before Montefiore's arrival in Marrakesh, was considered as a sign of ill-omen. Be that as it may, explosions of wrath — both from the populace and from many local governors — towards the Jews of Morocco, guilty of 'arrogance' and 'recklessness' for attempting to avail themselves of the *dahir*'s explicit protection (intended 'to strike fear into those who would commit aggression against them'), were not slow in multiplying.

However, the pomp and circumstance of Montefiore's reception and the noble imperial edict were highly appreciated in London. Layard, at Question Time in the House of Commons, praised the sultan's great generosity, and the expression in the edict, 'that not

even a fractional portion of the smallest imaginable particle of injustice shall reach any one of them [the Jews]' seemed equitable,
even if this example of 'the exaggerated style of Oriental decrees'
drew a laugh.[89] At the public meeting held in the London Tavern
a month later on 13 April, it was resolved to send an official vote of
thanks through the British government to the sultan for his 'noble
conduct'. A particularly eloquent speaker suggested that if a new
subject for a Westminster Palace fresco were required, why not this
mission — Sir Moses presenting his petition for 'equal rights to Jew
and Christian alike' and the sultan granting it. Yet another speaker
'hardly knew whom to admire most — Sir Moses Montefiore, the
champion of a great cause, or the Emperor of Morocco who gave
him so gracious a reception'.[90] The possibility that the imperial
edict might become a 'dead letter' was also raised, but immediately
dismissed as virtually impossible — 'it bears the character of a semi-
international treaty'.[91]

But local realities were quite another matter. A memorandum of
complaints from various Jewish communities of the interior had
reached the *Junta* in Tangier, who in turn alerted the British minister
in Tangier and also wrote to London, Paris and elsewhere. Drummond
Hay acted promptly and firmly by sending (20 April) a strong
circular to all British vice-consuls in the country (doc. 9) and on
2 May wrote to Russell in London (doc. 8) enclosing a copy of both
the circular and a translation of the memorandum. In another
letter he advised the British government 'to defer, for the present,
communicating to the Sultan the sense entertained by the meeting
at the London Tavern'.

Montefiore wrote an ornate, diplomatic, letter to the Vizier Yamani
on 1 June recounting how he had handed a copy of the *dahir* to the
Spanish and French monarchs, adding: 'The Imperial Edict of his
Sheriffian Majesty has obtained a world-wide celebrity, and has
everywhere received the eulogies to which it is so eminently entitled.'
He told of 'sad tidings' having reached him that some governors and
officials were disregarding the sultan's instructions and implored him
to keep aglow the 'beam of light' (the edict), so that 'anticipations
of a brighter future' (for the Jews of Morocco) and 'fond hopes' may
not become 'a vain shadow' and 'a delusive dream'. Two months later
he received an eloquent reassurance from Yamani, who stressed that
'injustice' is forbidden for 'people professing our religion' and likewise for 'people professing any other religion', and that the sultan
had ordered that the Jews of his empire should be treated with kindness 'and strict justice'.[92]

The memorandum referred to events in Salé, Azemmour, Mogador,

Fez, Meknes, Dar al-Baida (Casablanca) and Demnat, but other complaints some trivial, others horrific, were received.[93]

One of the most revealing and moving reports is from Chechuan (doc. 10), which portrays the drab everyday life of misery which the Jews of this village of fanatics accepted with resignation. Twenty years later, the explorer Charles de Foucauld, disguised as a Jew, described Chechuan (south of Tetuan — in the *bled al-siba*) as 'renowned for its intolerance' and the Jews as suffering the worst treatment, including regular stoning. Foucauld remarked that he and his companion were cursed by every Muslim who passed them with the formula: 'May Allah assure that the father who gave you birth shall burn for eternity, Jew!'[94] On this same voyage, Foucauld singled out the towns of Sefrou and Demnat, where he found the Jews to be 'the happiest' whom he had seen in Morocco. Yet, in early 1864 the Jews of Demnat were so harrassed that they petitioned Montefiore and Reade during their visit to the sultan and redress was promised, but to no avail. They were forced to work on the Sabbath and Holy Days, many of their houses had been confiscated so that a mosque might be built (the Muslim version states — because the houses were too close to the existing mosque's source of water), the men had found refuge in a Muslim sanctuary but were not allowed food, whilst their wives and daughters 'suffer the most brutal outrages from the caïd and his servants'. Six months later, on 4 August, a Foreign Office letter informed Sir Francis Goldsmid that the British, French, Italian, Portuguese and United States representatives had intervened with some effect, but Drummond Hay felt that any attempt to compel the sultan's officers 'to carry into effect the Edict . . . might place in jeopardy the lives of the Jews'. However, he was optimistic 'that the gradual progress of civilization and commerce, and the influence of the agents of the European Gov^ts must be looked to for improving the state of the Jews in Morocco rather than any sudden reforms imposed upon an ignorant and fanatical people'. Twenty years later (1884—5), the year after Foucauld's visit, many of the six to seven hundred Jewish inhabitants of the town were once again undergoing unbearable persecutions by the governor, although 'they are on very good terms with the Arabs'. By the turn of the century, Budgett Meakin was writing that, 'until many of them were driven, by persecution, to the capital [Marrakesh], it was the home of a large number of well-to-do Jews, but now the mellah is the scene of poverty and filth alone'.[95]

All these complaints show that, paradoxically, the *dahir* might have had the opposite effect from that intended. As an observer noted in 1876, the *firman* was drawn up in too vague a manner to

have any practical value (doc. 12). In view of the ever-worsening
climate, Drummond Hay had — like the sultan but for different
reasons — circulated a second message to the British vice-consuls
restricting their interference on behalf of Jewish plaintiffs to cases
where extreme cruelty was employed, advising that the utmost
caution was to be used where individual Jews might have behaved
in a provocative manner. In London, Hammond, on instructions
from the foreign secretary, forwarded a copy of this circular and
another despatch of 7 August from Tangier to Montefiore. The
latter, greatly disturbed by the implications of the new circular,
wrote immediately to Earl Russell on 7 September enclosing a
diplomatic letter for eventual forwarding to Drummond Hay, as well
as a draft of his proposed address to 'The Rabbis, Elders and Congregational Authorities of the Jews of Morocco' (doc. 11). He hoped
thereby to convince the foreign secretary of his own good faith, of
the mistaken policy being adopted by the British representatives and
of the general pacific qualities of the Jews of Morocco. Montefiore's
direct influence is evident in Russell's letter, dispatched on 10
September to his minister in Tangier, now advised to 'reconsider the
terms of your circular with a view to relieve the apprehension which,
in its present terms, it is calculated to excite in the minds of the
Jewish population in Morocco and of their friends in this country'.
The form of the draft letter was carefully modified by a second,
authoritative, hand (Russell, Layard or Hammond?) so as not to
offend Drummond Hay, and the last, most revealing, phrase was
added — 'and of their friends in this country' (i.e. Jews and non-
Jews).[96]

Queen Victoria received Montefiore in audience on 20 June 1864
(he arrived at Windsor Castle on the same day as the Turkish ambassador, Mustapha Pasha) and three months later, whilst resting at his
favourite retreat, Smithembottom, he optimistically confided in his
diary:

> I have great cause for thankfulness. Since I was here in November last, I hope
> that by Divine blessing, I have been of some use to my fellow-creatures, both
> Jews and Christians, and, I believe, I may add, 'Moors'. To God alone, who
> helped and sustained me, be honour and glory.[97]

Two weeks later, near to his eightieth birthday, he was honoured
by the Lord Mayor in a moving ceremony at Guildhall as 'a distinguished member of the Hebrew community' who in a lifetime
of altruistic effort had alleviated 'the sufferings and miseries of
people of all creeds and denominations (Cheers)' and he handed Sir
Moses a resolution of thanks on behalf of the Common Council.

The pomp and circumstance in London was a continuation of that of Marrakesh — manifestations of the best intentions, but quite irrelevant to the realities of the situation. The condition of the Jews, based on religious dogma, could not be changed by 'fond hopes' or the magic wand of foreign individuals or governments — this was indeed 'a delusive dream'!

The Moroccan reality

The contemporary official Moroccan viewpoint has already been observed. A recent Moroccan historian, Abdallah Laroui, confirms Nasiri's assertion that the purpose of those Jews living in the seaports, in contact with Europeans, was to abolish the *dhimma*; whereas the *ulama*, and the people in general, were determined to maintain the pre-eminence of Islam which required the humiliation of the *dhimmis*.[98] He shows how in 1837 the religious authorities had advised against allowing the Jews of Fez even the authorization to build a public bath in their own *mellah*, for this precise reason: the possibility that they might thereby escape from their providential inferiority, through cleanliness. Laroui emphasized that this period witnessed a renewed interest in the works of the fifteenth century theologian, Muhammad al-Maghili (d. 1503), whose opinions on the *dhimmis* and the strict application of the *dhimma* (Pact of Umar), were copied and distributed in large quantities, being twice lithographed towards the end of the nineteenth century.[99] The force of Maghili's argument in the fifteenth century had been astutely turned against the rich and influential Muslims, guilty of employing 'the worst enemies' of the Prophet, instead of maintaining them in their natural state of humiliation. The significant distribution of the tracts during this period was clearly in reaction to the 'emancipation' of a small number of Jews in the seaports of Morocco, a situation which, paradoxically, probably reached its culmination with Montefiore's visit, after which a strong reaction on all levels developed to maintain the traditional norm.

For ample proof of the lack of progress in the changes predicted by both Montefiore and Drummond Hay, it is enough to recall, not only the increased numbers of murders and incidents involving Jews over the next generation, but also the deteriorated situation of those living in the interior of the country.[100] The respected orientalist Joseph Halévy, who had already been on missions to Ethiopia and southern Yemen,[101] has left us a graphic description of the unchanged condition of misery and humiliation endured by the Jews of Marrakesh a dozen years after the sultan had granted the famous *dahir* to Montefiore, whose efforts had 'roused so much legitimate applause amongst all men of generous spirit' (doc. 12).

The reality, clear in 1876, should have been as clear to someone of Montefiore's experience in 1864. Yet, relying on his instincts, his strength of purpose, his diplomatic skills and an extraordinary stamina, the octogenarian was determined to succeed, as he had in the past (except in the Mortara Case of 1859 concerning the papacy). The ostensible success of the mission — to the general applause of liberal European opinion[102] — gave it a symbolic aura which gainsaid any criticism, then or later, during the hero's lifetime.

When on 3 December 1880 at the time of the Madrid Conference, the London *Jewish World* published an article on the Montefiore mission by 'an Englishman' (dated Gibraltar, 10 November), the sixty-five-year-old Guedalla took up his pen to defend his ninety-five-year-old uncle in a forty-page refutation, which was printed within two weeks of the incriminating text's appearance:

> It is difficult to account for the object of this dastardly attempt to substitute falsehood for truth [. . .] It makes one's blood boil to read such attempts to detract from eminent service, as will be seen from the perusal of the risks encountered on the mission by the venerable baronet, to say nothing of the enormous expense incurred.[103]

The article errs on many details concerning the Safi Affair itself and Montefiore's intentions and achievements, giving a somewhat garbled and even tendentious version.[104] However, some of the statements quoted 'from a most respectable resident' of Marrakesh (perhaps a Corcos or a Nahon) have the ring of authenticity and the anonymous writer's own contemporary conclusion is most incisive.

The Vizier Yamani (Tiebi Bouarshrin) is supposed to have asked the leading Jewish notables of Marrakesh what answer might be given their distinguished English co-religionist's petition to the sultan on their behalf, and was told by them, 'write anything you like', as anyhow *they* would make sure it became a dead letter after Montefiore's departure. The author's confidant added, seventeen years after the event: 'Sir Moses did not bring any guns or regiments behind him; he came to beg, and we all can play at that game.' The notable added that he himself (a favourite at the sultan's court, then and now) had walked barefoot on the very day Montefiore had left Marrakesh (see doc. 13 for the same situation in 1911).

The anonymous — yet courageous — 'Englishman' writing from Gibraltar deplores this lack of moral courage, but, with a profound understanding of the psychological motifs behind such behaviour, he concludes thus — in 1880!:

Yet, we must make allowances for their weakness, produced by years of oppression, and the fact of the Jewish bodies who possess influence in Europe allowing themselves to be cajoled by mellifluous words and 'chats over' matters which are not only of national importance, but concern the existence and freedom of their brethren from cruel oppression in a land not very far away.

Two years after Sir Moses Montefiore's death in 1885, the orientalist, Dr Louis Loewe, who had accompanied his friend on nine of his missions abroad (but not to Morocco) gave his own thoughts on the subject:

Some readers who have attentively perused the narrative of Sir Moses' Mission to Morocco, will perhaps say that since the issuing of the Sultan's edict twenty-three years ago, His Sheriffian Majesty's commands contained therein do not seem to have been very strictly adhered to. The Moors say, and apparently with good reason, 'To promise is not the same as to perform'. Their observation seems just, when we find that, notwithstanding the promises made by the Sultan to Sir Moses, he continued to receive complaints from almost every Hebrew community of the oppression and ill-treatment to which they had been subjected.[105]

Aftermath and Conclusion

It was too early to expect a voluntary change of attitudes from the *ulama*, the people, the ruling classes or even the sultan; and Montefiore had not come with either 'guns or regiments', nor would he have considered such an eventuality.

Half a century later, on 30 March 1912, the sultan Abdul-Hafiz signed a treaty with France establishing thereby the French Protectorate over most of Morocco, the Spanish Protectorate being confined to a small area in the north of the country. This followed a decade of intense internal revolt and disorder, including French intervention, since 1907. During this period the situation of the Jews became particularly precarious — scores of them were killed and hundreds of women and children were abducted for ransom, mainly in Taza, Settat and Casablanca. On 17 April 1912 the sultan's mutinous troops, joined by a civilian mob, attacked Europeans — principally French — in Fez, and then turned on the defenceless population of the *mellah*. Throughout three days and nights — 'Assassination, rape, fire, looting — nothing was spared this unfortunate Jewish community'. More than sixty men, women and children were killed, fifty wounded and 10,000 left homeless, of whom 2,000 found a welcome shelter and safety on the first evening in one of the sultan's courtyards adjoining the menagerie and stables.[106]

The director of the Alliance boys' school at Fez had sent his vivid description of this catastrophe to Paris. Scarcely fifteen months earlier he had advised the president of the Alliance Israélite Universelle not to intervene with the Moroccan authorities on behalf of Rabbi Vidal Sarfaty. The old man had bitterly complained that all Jews still had to go barefoot when entering the palace courtyard on community matters. Amram Elmaleh, like Drummond Hay and Montefiore before him, declared his faith in 'the passing of time and the penetration of modern ideas into the Muslim world' (doc. 13).

But the guns and the regiments had come to stay for forty years. New laws were passed and customs adopted. Soon, it no longer mattered whether the Moroccan Jews wore European attire, nor shoes or *babouches* outside of their quarters in all the towns and villages of the interior, even in front of the sultan. Like their Muslim compatriots, they entered upon a new era in which for them the shackles of the past − the *dhimma* − would no longer keep them rigidly in a condition of inferiority.[107]

Unfortunately this era did not begin in 1864 after Montefiore's peace mission, but only in 1912 under foreign rule.

Yet Moroccan Jewry's destiny was not to take place in Morocco, where 2,500 years earlier their ancestors had settled. Paradoxically, messianic aspirations within some British circles had coincided with Britain's political interests in the Eastern Mediterranean, and these circumstances provided the basic conditions for modern political Zionism to flourish in Palestine. Montefiore himself had laboured philanthropically throughout his life in the Holy Land, mainly in Jerusalem. He could not have been unaware of the messianic dreams of Moroccan Jewry,[108] but never could he have imagined that one hundred years after his mission to Morocco the greater part of the descendants of those whose honour he wished to vindicate in 1863 would have gathered together in a massive exodus towards their ancestral homeland.[109]

MISSION TO MOROCCO: DOCUMENTS

1

*British Minister Drummond Hay (Tangier) to Foreign Minister
Earl Russell (London)*

Your Lordship's Despatch marked 'Separate' of the 12th ultimo [November] was delivered to me by Sir Moses Montefiore, who arrived here from Cadiz on the 11th instant.

Sir Moses called on Mr. Merry and obtained from him a letter to the Moorish Minister, declaring that the Spanish Government withdrew from further prosecution of the two Jews [Makluf and Saido] now imprisoned at Saffee on a charge of being concerned in the alleged murder of a Spanish subject, and requesting that the Sultan would give orders for their liberation.

At Sir Moses' request I presented him to the Moorish Minister Seed Mohammed Bargash and supported both verbally and in a letter I addressed the Minister for transmission to the Sultan, the petition of Sir Moses Montefiore.

Seed Mohammed Bargash has assured me that he is persuaded the Sultan will give orders that the prisoners be released, now that the Spanish Government has withdrawn from further prosecution of this case.

It is Sir Moses' intention to go to Saffee, and thence he will proceed to the Moorish Court at Morocco to thank the Sultan. I have written to the Moorish Oozeer [the Vizier 'Seed Taib Ben Yamany'] to request that a kind reception be given by His Majesty to Sir Moses Montefiore.

I have given also to Sir Moses Montefiore letters of recommendation to the British Vice Consuls and to the Moorish Authorities at the Western ports which he intends to visit.

Sir Moses has also obtained the release of the two Jews [Elcaim and Benharosh] who had been bastinadoed and imprisoned at Tangier, at the demand of Mr. Merry, on account of some dispute with his servant.

PUBLIC RECORD OFFICE (LONDON)
(F.O. 99/117, Drummond Hay to Russell, N° 15, Tangier, 15 Dec. 1863)

2

Through the good offices of Sir Moses Montefiore a reconciliation has taken place between the Spanish Minister, Mr Merry and myself, and all matters of discussion between us have been mutually and amicably dropped.

PRO
(F.O. 99/117, Drummond Hay to Russell, N° 14, Tangier, 15 Dec. 1863)

3

Sir Moses Montefiore (Tangier) to Sir John Drummond Hay (Tangier)

It being my intention D.V. to carry out my projects of a visit to the Sultan to thank him for his liberation of the prisoners at Saffi, and to solicit the continuance of his humane protection of his Jewish subjects, I shall esteem it a very great favor if you will give your permission to Consul Reade to accompany me.

The companionship of a gentleman possessing so much intelligence and justly occupying so influential a position in this country cannot fail to be of the utmost utility to me, and I shall also be truly delighted to have this pleasing opportunity to enjoy the society of so old a friend.

To you Sir John, I can but reiterate my gratitude for your efficient aid and constant attention.
PRO
(F.O. 99/117, Montefiore to Drummond Hay, 17 Dec. 1863)

4

Merry y Colon to Spanish consuls and vice-consuls (Morocco)

The Government of Her Majesty the Queen has seen with much displeasure the gross calumnies which have been written against Spain, in the belief that the Spanish Consuls in Morocco have undertaken a crusade against the Israelites established in this empire.

Such calumnies must not in the least influence your feelings, nor ought they to occasion any alteration in the proceedings of the agents of Spain in Morocco, regarding the Israelites, as relates to aiding and protecting them.

On the contrary, the best mode of successfully combating such calumnies is increasing your solicitude for this race, which is so sadly circumstanced in this country.

Thus you will avail yourselves of every opportunity which may arise to prevent acts of cruelty on the part of the Moorish Authorities against the Israelites, and also in cases of notorious injustice, and when it is the question to inflict the punishment of the lash, in order to extort confession, in any case you will resolutely interpose your influence with the local authorities to prevent the commission of such act of barbarity.

(Extract from a circular by Spanish Minister (Tangier), Merry y Colon, 20 Dec. 1863 — the above translation is from Guedalla, p. 37, slightly different from that published in the *Jewish Chronicle*, 8 Jan. 1864)

5

Consul Thomas F. Reade (Marrakesh) to Sir John Drummond Hay (Tangier)

Before leaving this city, which we purpose doing tomorrow, I think it my duty, to dispatch to you, by express courier, the following brief sketch of the proceedings and results of Sir Moses Montefiore's mission to the Sultan's Court, since our arrival here on the 25th ultimo.

Up to the latter date, I had been given to understand that the object of Sir Moses' mission was simply to thank the Sultan for the liberation of the Jews in prison at Saffi, as well as to solicit that His Majesty's Hebrew Subjects might in future be treated with more mercy and justice than, as a body, they have hitherto been. The support required from me, as an officer of Her Majesty's Government, would, in such a case, have been little more than nominal, and my course of action clear and simple.

To my surprise, however, I learnt from Sir Moses, on our arrival at Morocco [Marrakesh], that it was his intention to submit to the Sultan a petition, which he had drawn up at Gibraltar, subsequently to his visit to Tangier, and which he shewed to me for the first time, praying that, in all matters connected with the administration of justice in this country, Jews and Christians might be placed on an equal footing with Mohamedans.

The attainment of a reform so important as that which Sir Moses was desirous of bringing about, opposed as it was to the religious and deeply rooted prejudices of a fanatical people, would, under any circumstances, have appeared to me a difficult matter. I felt, however, that Sir Moses had seriously enhanced the difficulties of our task by starting upon his mission, without submitting his petition, in the first place, to your consideration, and obtaining from you a stronger representation in support of it than the letters of recommendation to the Oozir with which you had provided us.

I was, at the same time, aware that, unless the Sultan could be brought to regard as a political necessity the concessions sought for, the mission upon which we had come would prove a failure.

To ensure success it was necessary to shew by argumental demonstration that His Majesty's personal interests were consulted in the negotiation as much as those of his Hebrew Subjects.

Under these circumstances, and in my inability to await a reference to Tangier, I thought it my duty to back Sir Moses' petition, by addressing to the Oozir a strong representation in its support. Of that representation I beg herewith to inclose a translation.

In all my communications with the Oozir, on the subject of Sir Moses Montefiore's Petition, I carefully abstained from all allusion to the treatment of Christians, as, although Sir Moses' demands purported to be on behalf of Christians as well as Jews, the former did not stand in need of any such intercession in their favour, the privileges they enjoy in this country being even greater than those accorded to Mohamedans.

On the 1st instant, our first audience of the Sultan took place. His Majesty received Sir Moses Montefiore, Captain Armytage, and the rest of our party, with much kindness and courtesy, and spoke in the most friendly terms of the Queen of Great Britain and the British Government and nation. During the interview, Sir Moses presented to the Sultan his petition; and His Majesty graciously received it, and promised to favourably consider it.

Four days afterwards, an Imperial Edict, of which the inclosed is a translation, was brought to me by an Officer of the Sultan's body guard, who had been instructed to deliver it into no other hands but mine. After taking a copy of the original document, I delivered the latter to Sir Moses Montefiore, who has expressed to me his intention of conveying it himself to Her Majesty's Secretary of State for Foreign Affairs.

We had another audience of the Sultan, this morning, when we took leave of His Majesty and thanked him for the very gracious and satisfactory reply he had given to Sir Moses' petition. His Majesty expressed himself to us in the same friendly terms as on the former occasion.

PRO

(F.O. 99/121, Reade to Drummond Hay, 7 Feb. 1863. Inclosure N° 1 in Drummond Hay's Despatch N° 16 of 20 Feb. 1864)

6

Consul Reade (Marrakesh) to Moroccan Vizier Yamani (Marrakesh)

The friendly relations which so happily subsist between the British Government and that of His Majesty the Sultan, are, as Your Excellence is aware, of long standing, sincere, and durable. It is under the inspiration of those friendly relations that I have been directed by Sir John Hay Drummond Hay, H.B.M^s Minister at Tangier, to accompany the Baronet, Sir Moses Montefiore, to the Exalted presence, and assure His Majesty of the deep and lively interest that is taken by the British Government in the object of that gentleman's mission. He comes to express, in the name of the Hebrew Community of England, and, I may add, on behalf of the civilized world, his acknowledgements to the Sultan for past acts of favour done to his coreligionists in this country, and more especially for the late gracious liberation of the two Israelite prisoners at Saffi. He comes also to pray that His Majesty's favour may continue to be extended to the Hebrews of this country, and that the latter may be placed on an equal footing with their Mussulman neighbours, in as far as their personal protection and claims for justice are concerned.

The social condition of the Israelites who dwell in Mohamedan countries has long been a subject of solicitude with the Governments of Europe and America; and in Morocco, or rather in certain parts of Morocco, their position has been found to be one of peculiar hardship and degradation. It is this circumstance, more perhaps than any other, which has influenced the Agents of Foreign Powers to extend, of late years, the protection of their respective flags beyond the limits of Treaty Stipulations; and thus the Sovereign attributes of His Majesty have been infringed upon, and his authority materially weakened.

For this state of things, however, there is a remedy; and a better one cannot be found than that of graciously acceding to the terms of Sir Moses Montefiore's petition.

The philanthropic disposition of the Sultan is well known to us, as also the facilities which, under His auspices, are so happily accorded to persons of every denomination and creed to dwell in this country, engage in mercantile pursuits, and observe the rites of their religion. We are therefore convinced that it will also be His Majesty's pleasure to ordain, that the remaining vestiges of the intolerance of former administrations in this country shall be effectually wiped away, that no humiliating badge shall remain to mark a distinction between one class of His Majesty's Subjects and another, and that equal justice shall henceforth be meted out to Mussulman and Israelite.

His Majesty will thus not only more closely and lastingly cement His alliances with the Sovereigns or Potentates of other countries, but he will remove the principal, if not only, cause that is, or can be, assigned in justification of the abuses that are from time to time perpetrated by some of the Foreign Representatives, with regard to the protection they accord to Subjects of these Dominions.

The Israelites are essentially an industrious and loyal class. Raised to a higher social position, they would become even more useful, as has been seen in other countries where some of them have become great public benefactors.

Not many years ago, the independence, and I may add the very existence of the Ottoman Empire were seriously menaced by the grasping schemes of Russia, when England, France and Sardinia, tending a helping hand to the injured Sultan, broke, in the Crimean war that followed, the aggressor's power, and secured the future peace and tranquillity of Turkey. Now, this would not have been the case if the late Sultan Abdul Mejid had not given repeated proofs of the just and tolerant spirit by which he was animated. A singular manifestation of this spirit took place in 1840, when he acceded to a petition of a similar nature to the one we are now treating — which petition was, as on the present occasion, submitted to His Imperial Majesty by the distinguished Baronet Sir Moses Montefiore.

His Majesty the Sultan will, I am sure, do all in his power to promote the welfare and happiness, not only of the whole of his subjects, but of mankind in general. And it is this conviction, as well as that that [sic] a compliance with Sir Moses' present petition would tend largely to advance His Majesty's interests, which has emboldened me to address to Your Excellency the preceding remarks. I beg that they may be submitted to the favourable consideration of His Majesty. Peace.
PRO
(F.O. 99/121, Reade to Taib Ben Yamany, 28 Jan. 1863, Inclosure N° 2 in Drummond Hay's Despatch N° 16 of 20 Feb. 1864)

7

Sir John Drummond Hay (Tangier) to Foreign Minister Earl Russell (London)

Sir Moses Montefiore and Mr Reade returned from the Moorish Court on the 17th Instant, in Her Majesty's ship 'Magicienne'.

I have the honour to inclose, herewith, the copy of a report addressed to me by Mr. Reade from Morocco, inclosing the copy of a Note he had delivered to the Moorish Oozeer, Seed Tayeb El Yamanee, urging The Sultan to accede to the Petition, which had been made to His Majesty by Sir Moses Montefiore in behalf of his coreligionists in this Country, — and, further, a Translation of a Firman or Edict, issued by the Sultan to his Governors and Officers, ordaining that the Jews be treated with lenity and justice.

Taking into consideration the fanatical feelings of the Mohamedans of Morocco, more especially of the inhabitants of the inland Towns, I am of opinion that The Sultan could not have granted greater concessions, than he has done in this Edict, for alleviating the grievance of his Jewish Subjects without endangering his own position, and indeed, the safety of the Jews themselves.

The residence and intercourse of Europeans with the Mohamedans, the increase of trade and the general progress of civilization will, I trust, gradually tend to bring about modifications in the system of government, and also in the general conduct and feelings of the Mohamedan population towards Christians and Jews. There is no doubt that the present Sultan and his Chief Minister, Seed Tayeb, are far more enlightened and advanced in liberal ideas than the

Moorish Governors or other officers of state or of the Mohamedan population in general.

Sir Moses Montefiore has spoken very highly of the important services rendered to him by Mr. Reade, in aiding to bring to a successful issue the object of the mission. I have signified to Mr. Reade my approval of his conduct, and of the prudence and tact he has shewn in the peculiar position in which he was placed, and in having succeeded in inducing The Sultan and his Ministers to make such important concessions without a more direct interference on the part of Her Majesty's Government and myself. [. . .]
PRO
(F.O. 99/121, Drummond Hay to Russell, 20 Feb. 1864, N° 16 – reached the Foreign Office on 3 March)

8

Sir John Drummond Hay (Tangier) to Foreign Minister Earl Russell (London)

I regret to inform your Lordship, that the Elders of the Jewish Committee at Tangier have reported to me several acts of tyranny and cruelty, which are alleged to have been recently perpetrated, by the Governors of the Interior upon the Jews.

It appears, that the Edict delivered by the Sultan to Sir Moses Montefiore had caused considerable dissatisfaction amongst the Mohamedan population and especially the fanatical Governors and Chiefs of the Interior, and that the Sultan had not ventured to send copies of the Edict to all his Officers, but is said to have merely addressed letters to some of the Governors and Chiefs, recommending that the poorer class of Jews should be kindly treated. On the other hand, the Jewish population, naturally elated by the success of Sir Moses Montefiore's mission to the Sultan, had assumed a more independant manner in their dealings with the Mohamedans and had, on several occasions, refused to submit to such arbitrary acts of the Governors, as were supposed to be at variance with the wording or spirit of the Edict.

I enclose a translation of the various cases of cruelty and tyranny, which have been reported to me by the Jewish Elders, but of which, I have not as yet received any confirmation from the Consular Officers at the Ports. On receiving the first report, of the tyrannical conduct of a Governor of Algarb towards some Jews, I wrote a private letter to the Prime Minister, Seed Tayeb El Yamanee, expressing my surprize, that any Governor should venture to disobey the Sultans Edict, and requesting that immediate steps should be taken to prevent a repetition of such tyranny. The Minister in reply, sent me the report of the Governor of his proceedings, which was at variance with the Jewish account.

I learn from the Jewish Elders, that at Morocco [Marrakesh] the Sultan had severely punished some Mohamedans of that city, who had been accused of ill-treating the Jews, showing that though the Sultan has the will and disposition to act humanely, His Majesty has not sufficient power or authority over his people in the Interior to enforce his wishes.

Whatever may be the cause of the present reaction and revival of the persecution of the Jews by the Mohamedan Governors and Chiefs, I could not remain a passive spectator of such acts of tyranny and fanaticism, and allow the step, which the Sultan has voluntarily made, in favour of religious tolerance, to be retraced. I have therefore addressed a circular to the British Vice Consuls at the Ports, directing them to act in concert with their Colleagues in checking acts of tyranny or cruelty, and if it be necessary to take temporarily under their protection any innocent Jew or family, who are persecuted by the Mohamedans. The Circular has been drawn up more especially with the view of having an effect on the minds of the Mohamedan Authorities — I have sent an Arabic translation to the Vice Consuls, in order that they may communicate it to each Governor — I have also communicated a copy to Seed Mohamed Bargash, and have told him distinctly, that the British Government and people will lose all confidence in the Moorish Government, and cease to take the same interest in the independance and welfare of this Country, they have hitherto felt, if such barbarities are allowed to be perpetrated.

In adopting the course I have done, I think it may tend to support the Sultan's liberal intentions, and lead the Moorish Officers at the Ports to understand that by further acts of cruelty, they may not only incur the displeasure of the Sultan, but bring about the direct interference of European Governments in behalf of the oppressed Jews.

Several of my Colleagues have acquainted me, they have adopted a similar course — Monsieur de Tallenay, The French Chargé d'Affaires, has assured the Jewish Elders, he has reported to his Government these occurrences, but that he cannot take any step, until he receives instructions, as the French Government had not taken any notice of the late persecutions of the Jews at Saffee who were accused of the murder of a Spanish Subject.

7th May
P.S. Monsieur de Tallenay has informed me that he has addressed a Circular to the French Consular Officers at the Moorish Porte regarding the ill treatment of the Jews.
PRO
(F.O. 99/121, Drummond Hay to Russell, N° 26, Tangier, 2 May 1864)

9

Sir John Drummond Hay's circular (Tangier) to British vice-consuls, etc.

The object of the mission of Sir Moses Montefiore to the Moorish Court, and the success that attended his representations to the Sultan in behalf of his coreligionists in this country, have no doubt come to your knowledge. The liberal and benevolent sentiments manifested by the Sultan in the instructions issued to his Governors and Officers in the late Edict which he delivered to Sir Moses Montefiore regarding the Jews, have received the approbation of Her Majesty's Government, and, of the civilized world and have tended generally to create a more favorable feeling and lively interest towards the Sultan of Morocco, and this Country than had hitherto been entertained.

Under such circumstances I have felt the deepest regret and dissatisfaction on learning that various recent cases of arbitrary and cruel treatment of the Jews have occurred, shewing that, though the Sultan — Seed Mohamed — is a wise and benevolent Sovereign, his Officers are not worthy to serve so excellent a master and that, whilst His Majesty is seeking to promote civilization, and Commerce and to act with justice and humanity towards all persons in his realms, there are Officers in His Majesty's employment who through their ignorance, cruelty, and venality will bring the Moorish Government, not only into disrepute, but even place in jeopardy the peaceful relations of European Powers with the Moorish Government.

The days of persecution and intolerance towards persons of different creeds have passed away and must not be allowed to return in Morocco. The Sultan of Turkey and the Princes of other Mohamedan Powers have enacted laws placing Christians and Jews on an equal footing with the Mohamedans in the eyes of the law; in fact, granting that reciprocity of rights which has long been given to Mohamedans in Great Britain and by other nations of Europe and America. [A very important point.]

The Christian Governments of the world, whilst they applaud

these reforms and have drawn more closely the ties of friendship and alliance towards those Mohamedan Powers who have shewn a spirit of liberality, will not remain silent should the Edicts that have been issued or the Laws that have been enacted become dead letters, and the old persecution of religious sects be revived.

My predecessors as well as myself have on several occasions given instructions to British Consular Officers in Morocco to use their good Offices in behalf of any Jews or Mohamedans who might be tyrannically and cruelly persecuted by the Moorish Authorities, but at the same time, to avoid, as far as it was possible, the appearance of an undue interference with the rights of the Sultan's Officers to govern Moorish subjects.

You are also acquainted with the opinions I entertain regarding irregular protection being afforded to Moorish subjects by Consular Officers, and, with the steps I have taken, and continue to take, in supporting this Government in checking like irregularities; but I have to desire that you take an opportunity of stating distinctly to the Local Authorities at the Port of your residence that, acts of tyranny and barbarity towards the Jews, or others, cannot be tolerated, and that I shall be compelled to report to Her Majesty's Government and to the Governments of Austria, Denmark, and the Netherlands, which I have the honour to represent, if I learn that acts of cruelty and tyranny towards the Jews continue to be perpetrated. You will further state that, I am convinced that orders will ultimately be given, not only to myself, but to the Agents of all the Governments represented in Morocco, to restore protection in its fullest sense when it becomes manifest that confidence can no longer be placed in an impartial administration of justice by the Moorish Authorities. I trust, however, that the future conduct of the Morocco Authorities towards the Jews, and indeed towards all persons under their jurisdiction, may be such as to render it unnecessary, for me, or other Representatives of Foreign Powers, to make an appeal to our Governments.

In the meantime, as the Representative in this country of several civilized Powers from whom I have recently received strong instructions regarding the interest they take in the Jewish race, and the signification of their approval of the late Edict of the Sultan, I cannot allow that the Officers under my jurisdiction should remain passive spectators of the cruel acts of Governors or other Officers who appear to have set at naught the Sultan's Mandate. I have therefore to direct that you, not only continue to use your good Offices in behalf of the Jews as heretofore instructed, but I authorize you to join with your Colleagues in remonstrating with the Moorish

Authorities against any persecution or cruel treatment of the Jews, in contravention of the orders in the Sultan's Edict, of which I inclose a copy and translation. Should no attention be paid to your remonstrances by the Moorish authorities you are authorized to take temporally [*sic*] under your protection, or if you find no other Colleagues disposed to act with you, under the protection of the Consular Representatives of Great Britain, Austria and the Netherlands, any innocent Jew or Jewish family who may be cruelly persecuted by a Moorish Authority. You will at the same time be careful to collect such evidence as may tend to substantiate your right of interference in accordance with my instructions and the dictates of humanity. You are of course desired not to interfere with the course of Moorish justice when properly administered, or to take undue notice of the complaints of Jews in trivial cases.

I send you a translation of this letter into Arabic to enable you to communicate it to the Governor or other Authorities at your Town.

The Consular Officers of Great Britain, Austria and the Netherlands will keep copies of this Circular and its inclosures. You are at liberty to give a copy of the Arabic translation of this letter or of any document it contains to the Authority who may wish to possess them. Under any circumstances you are to cause the translations to be read to the Governor at your Port, so that, he may not declare hereafter he ignored the line of conduct you are instructed to adopt. You may further freely communicate this Circular to any one of Your Colleagues.

I further inclose a list in English and Arabic of the outrages which the Jewish Elders of Tangier allege to have been committed since the Sultan issued his Edict.

PRO

(F.O. 99/121, Drummond Hay to British vice-consuls & Austrian & Danish consular Offices at the Western Ports of Morocco, 20 April. Inclosure N° 2 in Drummond Hay's Despatch N° 26 of 2 May 1864)

10

Jewish Community of Chechuan (24 March 1864)

Chechuan is a small village surrounded by Arab tribes whose members are given to permanent feuding and the anger generated by their constant failures often rebounds on us. Moreover, all government in this region is, so to speak, purely nominal and powerless.

Here, the feeling of being trapped grips us in the day as well as at night; lucky are those who manage to get away, never to return.

As for the rest of us, we have almost abandoned any hope other than in the power of God the Almighty.

To give you an idea of what we have to endure, we will proceed to relate some incidents which punctuate the drabness of our daily life.

Upon leaving the Jewish quarter we have to take off our shoes and fully expect to be hit by stones aimed at us, as we cross the Arab part of the village. Nobody will ever come to our assistance. Before the judge one argues, 'It's a Jew.' Thefts are committed openly here: 'An Arab buys something from a Jew but, instead of paying tells him: 'I have already paid you, O Jew, son of a dog!' It is better for the poor, luckless wretch to keep quiet. The Jewish quarters are frequently entered surreptitiously. In the daytime they infiltrate under the very noses of the abetting and indifferent guards by whatever means offer themselves. Any house found unlocked is entered and, having thoroughly looted it, the intruders leave again, not without having ill-treated any child or woman they find on the way. At night they get into the houses by breaching their walls.

Since all this can be done with impunity, they go even further. Finding a Jewish woman in the street they make so bold as to tear away her head-scarf, frightening her out of her wits so that she hardly knows what to do. It happens that Jews from the interior come to live in this town but, finding life here no improvement, prefer to convert to Islam. This happened last year. A married Jew with several children tried to escape martyrdom by becoming a Muslim. As usual this had grave consequences for us.

This renegade wanted to take his wife and children along but they refused to follow him, whereupon he sent some Arabs to track them down. However luckily, or perhaps unluckily, someone managed to spirit the family away from the howling mob to Tetuan. When the Arabs heard of this they threw all of us into jail the day after Passover, compelling us to track down and deliver the fugitives into their hands. We had to do this although those in Tetuan had refused to return the family.

After three days they were sent back to us, and managing once again to hide them from the Arabs, we had to raise 300 douros at an exorbitant rate of interest to allow the affair to be forgotten without the family actually being handed over.

This occurs so frequently and to such an extent that we have long ceased to worry about our material misery.

We should also speak about the condition of the Jewish quarter. This is a street of about 20 tumble-down houses in an advanced state of disrepair which we leave very rarely. All in all, we are about 64 families with about 60 boys and 50 girls.

Of these 64 families, only about 10 can afford to give their children some kind of instruction; the others are obliged to take their children early to work and these are even more to be pitied than the rest of us.

Please let us know what you can do for us.

This ends our report and we hope, as always, that God will improve our lot in the future.

(Archives, *AIU*, Maroc, IVC 11)

Letter in Judeo-Arabic, dated 16 Adar 5624 (24 March 1864), from the Community of Chechuan, sitting in council and signed Aserruya, sent to Mr Carmona, 'for the Alliance Israélite Universelle (Paris)'. Trans. David Littman (into English from the original French translation of 1864)

11

Sir Moses Montefiore's Circular (Ramsgate) to the Jews of Morocco

Throughout the World, a chief characteristic of the Jews, is that of being loyal obedient, and peaceful Subjects of their Sovereign — From what I have seen and know of my Brethren in Morocco, I feel assured they are not exceptions to this universally admitted truth. The precepts inculcating this conduct are enforced on us by the sacred Scriptures and by the wise exhortations of our Sages.

Unless due respect be paid to the just exercise of legally constituted authority, there can be neither order nor safety. Happily, the Imperial Edict of your August Sovereign is intended to sustain the cause of justice and humanity throughout the Moorish Empire and though it may be that in some places the subordinate authorities abuse the powers with which they are entrusted, let it not be said that their severity or wrongdoing is attributable to any manifestation of disrespect on your part. You must never for a moment forget the loyalty, the affection and the respect, due to your Sovereign, on whom you must rely, and to whom in case of need, you must appeal for protection against oppression, and redress for injury.

Let neither actions nor words from you induce your fellow countrymen of the Mahomedan Faith to suppose that you are in any way unmindful or regardless of your duties, as Subjects of His Imperial Majesty, but on the contrary, that it is your ardent desire and most anxious wish, to testify your love and obedience towards him, and also to cultivate the esteem and good-will, of your fellow countrymen.

It is by conduct such as this we may hope that under the Almighty's Blessing, the hearts of those who would molest or injure you, will be softened, so that should injustice be done, it will be speedily and surely punished.

Most ardently and most anxiously do I desire your welfare, to promote this I have laboured with intense anxiety. I know full well that these my words are conveyed to willing listeners, to those who fully recognize their truth, and I feel sure that you will to the utmost of your ability, seek and give effect to my wishes.

Over the poorer and less educated classes of our Brethren in Morocco, let your watchfulness be exercised, so far as in you lies — so that they pay due obedience and respect to the constituted authorities — let them be patient under small annoyances but firm and reliant on their August Sovereign who will not fail to punish those who abuse his commands, disregard his Edict or venture to impose serious wrong upon his Jewish Subjects.

I trust and believe that in such cases the ear of your August Sovereign will ever be open to your cry.

May it be the will of God to remove from you all further suffering, to inspire your rulers with the spirit of humanity and justice, and to grant to your August Sovereign a long and happy reign.

PRO

(F.O. 99/123, Montefiore (signed in English and Hebrew) to the Rabbis, Elders and Congregational Authorities of the Jews of Morocco. Draft letter 6 Elul 5624 (7 Sept. 1864), sent to Earl Russell with letters of 7 Sept. 1864 to him and Drummond Hay)

12

Marrakesh in 1876 — twelve years after the dahir

On entering the town, I was not able to distinguish the different groups of the population in the midst of the crowd that gathered through curiosity around my little caravan; but as I advanced the crowd divided itself into two parts, each recognizable from its attire. On one side, men of an aggressive expression, clad in magnificent burnooses with rich edgings, their heads covered with large turbans neatly folded and their feet shod with beautiful yellow sandals, largely embroidered with gold and silver filigrane; on the other side a shy and shoddy crowd, whose only headgear was a blue kerchief with black spots, carelessly knotted around their necks, carrying in their hands rustic sandals while continuing to walk barefoot, despite the sharp stones in the road. Need it be said that the latter were the Jews, for whom it is prohibited to wear a turban, which is the only sure protection for the head against the rays of the tropical sun, and who cannot, thanks to a cruel refinement, even wear shoes outside of their quarter, the Mellah. It is impossible to imagine the sufferings of these wretches, who, amid the jeerings of the Muslim population along the road, jump and cringe with pain, their feet torn and their nails crushed by the stones. (pp. 50—51)

In the course of my conversations, I was not a little surprised to learn that the condition of our coreligionists in Morocco [i.e. Marrakesh] has in fact worsened since Sir Moses Montefiore's visit to the former sultan. The venerable baronet's philanthropic action, which had roused so much legitimate applause among all men of good will, had resulted in a *firman* (i.e. *dahir*), whose terms were too vaguely formulated to be of any practical use. (p. 52)

The Arab system has always aimed at dominating the mass of the people by a small number of privileged individuals dependent on the government. This tendency has brought about within the population of the *mellah* the formation of quite a powerful oligarchy which the authorities quite openly favour and which, through fear or gratitude, always collaborates with the administration in order to stifle the voice and complaints of the population. This group of *gebirim* (i.e. notables) is made up of ten families who have become rich by trading with the money which the sultan lent to them some years ago. They reside in spacious houses which are sumptuously furnished; their table is well garnished with meats and even wines from Europe, but upon leaving their houses they are assimilated with the others and subjected to the same discriminatory laws as the least commoner [. . .] Caught between the fear of the Arabs and the hardly disguised animosity of their fellow Jews, the *gebirim* of the Mellah appear to me rather to be pitied than envied. Their life is torn between the need to survive and remorse, so much so that they have little time left to enjoy their riches. (pp. 54—55)

Our coreligionists in Meknes believe that their brethren from Morocco [Marrakesh] are better off than is the case. The edict of the late sultan remains a dead letter throughout the kingdom and the better situation of the Jews living in the sea-ports is entirely due to [the presence of] the representatives of the European powers. (p. 69)

Joseph Halévy, Archives (*AIU*), France IX A 73, and also *Bulletin*, *AIU*, 1st. Sem. 1877. (Text of his detailed report on his mission, July 1876, prepared in August 1876)

13

Muslim conception of the Jews of Morocco (Fez, 1911)

[. . .] It is my opinion that it would be impossible to obtain an order from the sultan to allow Jews to enter the palace with their shoes on.

It is a concession which his pride would not permit, and one quite contrary to the Muslim conception of the relative positions of the Jews and themselves [. . .] In itself, the matter is neither serious nor urgent: with the passing of time and the penetration of modern ideas into the Muslim world, as well as the increase in the number of protected persons, this mark of servitude imposed upon the Jews will eventually disappear; those able to adopt European dress would rid themselves of it immediately.

Archives (*AIU*), Maroc XV E 246. Letter, 30 Jan. 1911 from Amram Elmaleh (director, AIU, Fez boys' school) to president, AIU, Paris. Full text translated in Littman, *Jews . . late 19th century*, 28, n.s. 35/36 *WLB* (London, 1975), 75–76. See n. 4.

NOTES

1. Lancelot Addison, *The present State of the Jews, more particularly relating to those in Barbary* (London, 1675), p. 7. He was 'Chaplain to His Majesty in Ordinary' during the first seven years of the English occupation of Tangier (1662–1683), acquired from Portugal by Charles II as part of Catherine de Braganza's dowry. The celebrated essayist was his eldest son. On Addison's comparison, see Budgett Meakin's more precise appreciation: 'their position [the Jews'] is in some respects even worse than that of negro slaves, who being Mohammedans, may benefit at law from certain rights denied to those who spurn their prophet.' (Article 'Morocco', *The Jewish Encyclopedia*, ix (New York & London, 1901–1916); 27. See note 76 *infra*.

2. J. E. Budgett Meakin, 'The Jews of Morocco', *The Jewish Quarterly Review* iv (1892), 369. In his many books on Morocco, Meakin frequently refers to the Jews, particularly in *The Moors* (London, 1902), pp. 425–487. For an interesting reference to Montefiore's visit, see *The Moors*, pp. 427–8.

3. See Samuel Romanelli's vivid description (1787–1790) of these Jewish *sahab al-sultan* (friends of the sultan), in his *Massa Ba'arav* (*The Oracle of Arabia*) (Berlin, 1792), English trans. in H. Z. Hirschberg, *A History of the Jews in North Africa* (Leiden, 1974), vol. i, pp. 290–291. The late David Corcos, scion of a famous Moroccan Jewish family of merchants, repeatedly stressed the crucial role of these *gebirim* (notables) in shielding the Jewish masses. See, particularly, his last article, 'Trois documents inédits sur les relations judéo-musulmanes dans le vieux Maroc', *Michael* V (Tel Aviv, 1978), 94. This apologetic viewpoint is in contradiction to the descriptions of Romanelli, of Joseph Halévy in 1876 (See document 12, *infra*) and cannot stand against the overwhelming documentary evidence.

4. David Littman, 'Jews under Muslim rule in the late nineteenth century', *Wiener Library Bulletin* 28 n.s. 35/36 (1975), 65–76; 'Jews under Muslim rule II: Morocco 1903–1912', *WLB* 29 n.s. 37/38 (1976), 3–19; Norman Stillman, 'L'expérience judéo-marocaine: un point de vue révisionniste',

in *Judaïsme d'Afrique Du Nord aux XIXe—XXe siècles* (Jérusalem, 1980), pp. 5—24.

5. H. Z. Hirschberg, vol. i, pp. 1—25; André Chouraqui, *Between East and West: A history of the Jews of North Africa* (Philadelphia, 1968), pp. 2—9.

6. Abraham ibn Daud, *Sefer Ha-Qabbalah (The Book of Tradition)*, trans., G. D. Cohen (London, 1967), p. 96.

7. Traditionally attributed to Umar I (634—644) but by most orientalists to Umar II (717—720), or later. See A. S. Tritton, *The Caliphs and their non-Muslim subjects: A critical study of the Covenant of Umar* (London, Reprint 1970).

8. Bat Ye'or, *Le Dhimmi: Profil de l'opprimé en Orient et en Afrique du Nord depuis la conquête arabe* (Paris, 1980). The revised English edition (with an enlarged document section) is announced for 1984, under the title, *The Dhimmi: Jews and Christians under Islam* (New Jersey & London, 1984). See, *inter alia*, Tritton; Eliyahu Strauss (Ashtor), 'The social isolation of *Ahl adh-Dhimma*', in *P. Hirshler Memorial Book* (Budapest, 1949) pp. 73—94; Antoine Fattal, *Le statut légal des non-Musulmans en pays d'Islam* (Beirut, 1958); Bernard Lewis, 'L'Islam et les non-Musulmans', in *Annales* no. 3—4 (Paris, mai-août 1980), 784—800.

9. al-Marrakushi, *Al-mu'jib fi talkhis akhbar al-maghrib (Histoire des Almohades)*. Trans., E. Fagnan (Algiers, 1915), pp. 264—265. English trans., doc. 12, Bat Ye'or, *The Dhimmi* . . . .

10. Louis Gardet, *La Cité musulmane: Vie sociale et politique* (Paris, 1954), p. 348; Robert Brunschvig, *La Berberie orientale sous les Hafsides* (Paris, 1940), vol. i, p. 404.

11. Documents are to be found in English (as well as a useful bibliography) in Bat Ye'or, *The Dhimmi*; and in Norman A. Stillman, *The Jews of Arab Lands: A History and Source Book* (Philadelphia, 1979). See also André Chouraqui, *La condition juridique de l'israélite marocain* (Paris, 1950). Georges Vajda, *Un recueil de textes historiques judéo-marocains*, Hespéris 12 (Paris, 1951) provides Moroccan Jewish chronicles from the sixteenth to the nineteenth century: some of these texts may be found in English in H. Z. Hirschberg, vol. ii (1981), pp. 191 ff; Bat Ye'or, *The Dhimmi*, documents 97, 101.

12. Eugène Fumey, *Choix de correspondance marocaine (50 lettres officielles de la Cour chérifienne)* (Paris, 1903), p. 15 (letter 18). English trans. in Bat Ye'or, doc. 63.

13. Budgett Meakin, 'The Jews', *Jewish Quarterly Review* (London, 1892), 380 idem, *The Moors* (London, 1902), p. 431.

14. H. Z. Hirschberg, vol. ii, p. 254. Wajda is in the north-east of Morocco; the estuary of the Wadi Nun reaches the Atlantic south of Agadir. It is noteworthy that the Muslim woman is mentioned before the *dhimmi*. This extraordinary situation resulted from the great fear of the sultan.

15. This might well be a reference to the traditional *jihad* (holy war), a fundamental Islamic conception which divides the peoples of the world into two irreconcilable camps: that of the *Dar al-Harb*, the 'Territory of War', which covers those regions controlled by the infidels, and the *Dar al-Islam*, the 'Territory of Islam', the Muslim homeland where Islamic law reigns. See, *inter alia*, E. Tyan 'Djihad', in *Encyclopaedia Islam*[2] 2 (1965); Majid Khadduri, *War and peace in the law of Islam* (Baltimore, 1955); Rudolph Peters, *Islam and Colonialism: The doctrine of Jihad in modern history* (The Hague, 1979).

16. John Braithwaite, *The History of the Revolutions in the Empire of Morocco*

upon the death of the late Emperor Mulay Ishmael (London, 1729), p. 449, in Jean-Louis Miège, *Le Maroc et l'Europe 1830–1894,* 4 vols. (Paris, 1961–65), vol. ii, p. 25, n. 6. Miège's remarkable study (the 5th volume, containing an invaluable index, appeared in 1969 under the title, *Documents d'histoire économique et sociale marocaine au 19e siècle*) has been used extensively for the subsequent brief summary on Morocco.

17. Miège, vol. ii, p. 197.

18. Victor Darmon, a Tunisian Jew, was the Spanish consular agent at Mazagan. His execution in January 1844 was followed by a Spanish ultimatum. The crisis was only overcome by the Hispano-Moroccan convention of 6 May 1845.

19. Nearly five thousand Jews from Tetuan and Tangier sought refuge in Gibraltar, and others in Algeciras. In 1860 a committee was set up by the Board of Deputies of British Jews to aid these refugees. See *infra,* n.30.

20. Barbary corsairs had been active from the 16th century, beginning with Khayr al-Din Barbarossa. When the Sultan Mulay Ismail died, aged ninety-three, his harem contained 1400 concubines, many from European nations; he also used innumerable Christian captive-slaves for his vast building projects. This traditional system of piracy was ended in Algeria after the British naval attack in 1816 and the European ultimatum to the Dey of Algiers of 20 November 1818; Christian slavery was ended in Morocco at the same period, but tribute money continued to be paid by Denmark and Sweden until 1845.

21. al Nasiri, *Kitab el Istiqsa . . . History of Morocco* (Cairo, 1894), vol. ii, p. 238, quoted in Miège, vol. ii, p. 387.

22. Drummond Hay left for England on 17 June and only returned in October. Thomas Reade, consul in Tangier since 1859, replaced him during absences. The French minister Béclard observed that 'the dominant trait of Reade was his pronounced animosity against Spain and particularly the officials of the Spanish Legation in Tangier'. (*Archives Générales,* Rabat, AA 31, Tangier 1-7-1863, in Miège, vol. ii, p. 392, n. 3).

23. Miège, vol. iv, p. 203, quoting A. J. P. Taylor: 'British policy in Morocco 1886–1902', *English Historical Review* 66, no. 260 (London, July 1951), 342. Before succeeding his father as consul general in Tangier, John Drummond Hay had been posted, aged 24, to Constantinople (1840–1845), where he greatly admired Sir Stratford (de Redcliffe) Canning. There he came to know the 25-year-old Henry Layard, fresh from his extraordinary discoveries at Nineveh, and now under Canning's wing.

24. Bat Ye'or, *Le Dhimmi* (French), pp. 81–83.

25. FO 78/368 (No. 2), dated 31 Jan. 1839, in Albert M. Hyamson, *The British Consulate in Jerusalem in relation to the Jews of Palestine: 1838–1914,* 2 vols (London, 1939–1941), vol. i, p. 2 (and Introduction); *idem,* 'British projects for the restoration of the Jews to Palestine', *Publications of the American Jewish Historical Society,* 26 (New York), 134 ff. Meir Verete, 'The Restoration of the Jews in English Protestant Thought, 1790–1840', *Middle Eastern Studies,* 8, no. 1 (1972). On this subject, see the interesting letter (and proposition) from Charles Henry Churchill to Sir Moses Montefiore, 15 Aug. 1842. Minute Book (MB), BD (Board of Deputies), MB5 May 1841–Feb. 1846, f. 144. See also A. A. Bonar and M'Cheyne, *Narrative of a Mission of Inquiry to the Jews from the Church of Scotland in 1839* (Edinburgh, 1842), pp. 321–2.

26. On the Damascus Affair, I know of no earlier reference, since the nineteenth century, to the grotesque 'Ratti-Menton version' of events, published by a member of the Oriental Society of Paris, Achille Laurent, in vol. ii (pp. 407) of his *Relation historique des Affaires de Syrie depuis 1840 jusqu'en 1842; Statistique générale du Mont-Liban et Procédure complète dirigée en 1840 contre des Juifs de Damas à la disparition du père Thomas, etc.* (Paris, 1846). See study by Tudor Parfitt in this volume.

27. Bernard Lewis, *The Emergence of Modern Turkey* (Oxford University Press, 1961; paperback 1968), ch. 4; Moshe Ma'oz, *Ottoman Reform in Syria and Palestine 1840—1861* (O.U.P., 1968); for the full text of the 1856 edict, see Stillman, *The Jews*, pp. 357—60 (and also pp. 95—100 for the background).

28. Samuel (Batto) Sfez, a Tunisian Jewish carter, was accused in 1857 of insulting Islam and executed within twenty-four hours. Armed bands attacked the Jews, who barricaded themselves in their *hara* (quarter); the Europeans prepared to defend themselves. Since 1856 the British and French consuls advised the bey to apply or adapt the Ottoman reforms to Tunisia. See Jean Ganiage, *Les Origines du Protectorat Français en Tunisie*, pp. 71—88; Hirschberg, vol. ii, pp. 112—115.

29. *Jewish Chronicle*, 13 Nov. 1863, p. 4; 11 March 1864, p. 7, reproducing 'a leading article' from the *Daily Telegraph*.

30. Moses H. Picciotto, *Jews of Morocco* (London, 1860); see also Narcisse Leven, *Cinquante Ans d'Histoire: L'Alliance Israélite Universelle*, 2 vols (Paris, 1911—20), vol. ii, p. 12; André Chouraqui, *L'Alliance Israélite Universelle* (Paris, 1965), p. 152; Hirschberg, vol. ii. pp. 306—7.

31. Leven, vol. 2, pp. 12 ff; Chouraqui, *L'Alliance*, pp. 152—3. 'Fifty years later about 50,000 boys and girls were receiving an education from 1500 teachers at approximately two hundred primary and vocational schools in nearly one hundred towns throughout the Ottoman Empire, Persia and the Maghreb.' (See D. G. Littman, 'A General Introduction to the Archives on Oriental Affairs of the Alliance Israélite Universelle (1860—1920) and a selection of fourteen unpublished letters from Morocco', *Int. Conference on Jewish communities in Muslim Lands 31 March—2 April 1974* (Hebrew University, Jerusalem, 1974).

32. *Public Record Office (PRO) London*, FO 99/119 (4 Oct. 1863 with letter of 17 Sept.); *Alliance Israélite Universelle* (Paris), Maroc VIII B (17 Sept. 1863).

33. FO 99/116 (5 Oct. 1863); FO 99/117 (6, 7, 10 Oct. 1863) and FO 99/119 (27, 28, 30 Oct. 1863). See also translation of letter from Pariente to Drummond Hay (Tangier), 27 Oct. 1863, FO 99/117.

34. *Jewish Chronicle*, 16 October 1863, p. 5; and FO 99/119, 9 Oct. 1863, including letter from Moses Bentala, President Jewish committee Tetuan.

35. Thomas Hodgkin, *Narrative of a Journey to Morocco in 1863—1864* (London, 1866), p. 1; Haim Guedalla, *Refutation of an anonymous article in the 'Jewish World', entitled: 'Secret History of Sir M. Montefiore's Mission to Morocco in 1863—4'* (London, 1880), p. 5; Lucien Wolf, *Sir Moses Montefiore: A centennial biography* (London, 1884), p. 214; Louis Loewe, *Diaries of Sir Moses and Lady Montefiore, comprising their life and work as recorded in their Diaries from 1812—1883*, 2 vols. (London, 1890), vol. ii, p. 145 (facsimile 1 vol. edn., 1983).

36. The name of the Spanish *recaudador* and his alleged date of death are given by Miège, vol. ii, p. 561, and p. 564, n. 4; he refers, *inter alia*, to

Archives Générales, Rabat (AGR) AA 31, Tanger, 27/9/1863 and *USA Foreign Affairs (UFA)*, 1863–1864, pp. 416 ff. Documentation on the Affair and its aftermath is also available at the PRO (London), scattered in FO 99/116–123; *Alliance Israélite Universelle (AIU)*, Maroc VIII B, Maroc IV, C11 (Tanger); and various newspapers, particularly the *Gibraltar Chronicle*, and (from 16 October) the *Jewish Chronicle*, as well as a few issues of national newspapers, such as the *Morning Advertiser*, the *Daily Telegraph*, etc. The descriptions up to 31 October which are referred to in the above-mentioned published works (*supra*, n. 35) are repetitive summaries, obviously based on incomplete reports. These 'preliminaries' were considered of little importance compared to the mission itself.

37. Letter (22 Sept. 1863) from S. Benhayon and Haim Labos (Tangier) to Judah de Azar Serfaty (Gibraltar), in *Jewish Chronicle*, 16 Oct. 1863, pp. 5–6.

38. *AIU*, Maroc IV C11 (Tangier). This 'enquiry', originating probably in Safi, was posterior by about a fortnight to the *Junta*'s letter of 17 Sept. The latter showed that, after the first two executions, 'Shido and Mocluf' were still in danger of death; whereas, in the last line of the 'enquiry', mention is made of a stay of execution as a result of an intercession having been made with the Spanish government. This seems to be a reference to the 'démarche' made to Madrid by Baron James de Rothschild, via the Spanish ambassador in Paris (*Jewish Chronicle* editorial of 16 Oct.), probably as a result of the letter of 17 Sept. which had also been sent to Crémieux at the AIU in Paris.

39. *Jewish Chronicle*, 6 November 1863, p. 6.

40. FO 99/119 Hammond to Sir F. Goldsmid (Auckland House, Farington) and to Drummond Hay (Tangier), 9 Dec. 1863. See also translation of letter from Pariente to Drummond Hay, Tangier, 27 Oct. 1863, FO/117.

41. *AIU*, Maroc VIII B, of 8 & 25 Oct. 1863.

42. Drummond Hay's visit to the sultan at Fez (12 April 1863) was intended to resolve a few differences and double the yearly supply of cattle to Gibraltar (from 3,000 to 6,000 head). Once again he expressed his views against the system of 'protections', which hardly benefited Britain's import trade (from Manchester) with Morocco, but was indispensable for France and other European states engaged in Morocco's export trade. *PRO* FO 99/117, 12 April, 1863; FO 99/176, and Miège, vol. ii, pp. 318–320, pp. 401–407, pp. 553 ff. See also, letter signed 'Veritas', in *Jewish Chronicle*, 20 Nov. 1863, p. 6.

43. FO 99/117, 12 November 1863.

44. FO 99/117, 10 Oct. 1863.

45. FO 99/117, 29 Oct. 1863.

46. This incident was also recorded by the *Gibraltar Chronicle* in an article (reprinted in the *Jewish Chronicle*, 11 Dec. 1863, p. 8) which concluded by stating that these various injustices should not be considered as a policy of the Spanish government, but the mistakes of its agents. In his memorandum of 26 Oct. (FO 99/117), Consul Reade noted that, 'Consul Rizzo is Merry's evil genius'. Miège indicates that Felipo Rizzo was later dismissed from the Spanish Legation for embezzlement (vol. ii, p. 392, n.2).

47. The Spanish minister was still in Spain when this conversation took place and Consul Rizzo was in charge at the Legation. This reference is an interesting confirmation concerning the situation at that time in Tangier,

the first town of Morocco where Jews, who did not have European protection, adopted European dress as a form of liberation from their discriminatory garb . . . and status. This was not appreciated by the Moroccan authorities, nor, so it is suggested here, by the Spanish consul and his minister (and certainly not by their Muslim groom). See Hay and Brooks, *A Memoir of Sir John Drummond Hay* (London, 1896), p. 132: 'It is only within the last thirty years that Jews in Morocco — not foreign employés or protected subjects — have been allowed to assume the European dress, or to wear yellow slippers or red caps when in native costume. Formerly they were compelled to confine themselves to black slippers and the Jewish gaberdine.'

48. *J.C.*, from 16 Oct. 1863 onwards; first article in *Morning Advertiser* of 18 Oct. 1863.
49. *J.C.*, 16 Oct. 1863.
50. *J.C.*, 9 Nov. 1863.
51. Board of Deputies (BD), Letter Book (LB), MB9 1859–1864, f. 279. I thank Dr R. D. Barnett who drew this letter to my attention — and also those referred to in notes 53, 58, the penultimate reference in note 25, and the last reference in note 82.
52. FO 99/119, 11 Nov. 1863.
53. NMR, 12 Nov. 1863. Montefiore was one of the founders of the Alliance Assurance Company in 1824. This was his City office.
54. *J.C.*, 13 Nov. 1863.
55. Haim Guedalla (1815–1904) had married Montefiore's niece Jemima. The Guedalla family was from Mogador and a 'Ben Guidilla' is mentioned by a shipwrecked American captain in 1815 as one of the four richest Jewish merchant families of the town (with Macnin, Abitbol and Zagury), who, altogether, covered half of the humiliating *jizya* poll-tax payable by the Jewish community. (James Riley, *Loss of the American Brig Commerce – August 1815* (London, 1817), p. 440). Montefiore had other Moroccan connections. The daughter of his uncle Samuel had married Judah Guedalla (Haim's father) and one of Samuel's sons, a Hatchevell or Hajwal. His aunt Sarah had married an Abraham Israel of Gibraltar and their son married a Bendahon. Sir Moses' grandmother (Esther Hannah) was the daughter of Massahod Racah, described as 'a Moorish merchant of Leghorn'. His own sister Sarah married Solomon Sebag (1783–1831) who had been sent to London from Mogador in 1799; their son Joseph (1822–1903), Jemima's brother, inherited Montefiore's Ramsgate estate in 1885. It was this same Sarah, his eldest sister, Mrs Goldsmid (after the death of her husband she had married Moses Asher Goldsmid), who died towards the end of December in Nice whilst Montefiore was in Gibraltar preparing to leave for Mogador; Guedalla left with Montefiore's faithful travelling attendant, Charles Oliffe, to handle the post-funeral arrangements of his deceased mother-in-law.
56. The most complete accounts of the journey are in letters from Sir Moses to J. M. Montefiore, president *pro tem.* of the Board of Deputies in the *Jewish Chronicle*, 1 Jan. 1864; 8 Jan. (letter of 18 Dec. M.M. to J.M.M.); 19 Feb. (letter of 26 January, M.M. to J.M.M.); 11 March (letter of 24 Feb., M.M. to J.M.M.); and Guedalla, particularly pp. 33–34 for letter of M.M. to J.M.M. of 5 April 1864. See also bibliographical references in note 35, *supra*; as well as Israel Davis, *Sir Moses Montefiore: A biographical sketch* (London, 1884); J. Weston, *Sir Moses Montefiore, the story of his*

life (London, 1885); Paul Goodman, *Moses Montefiore* (Philadelphia, 1925); S.U. Nahon, *Sir Moses Montefiore: A life in the service of Jewry* (Jerusalem, 1965).

57. Montefiore had been one of the founders of the Imperial Continental Gas Association which provided gas lighting to the principal European cities. He remained its president until his death.

58. Weisweiller had been so helpful to Montefiore in Spain both in December and March that on Montefiore's stopover in Madrid on his way home — and before his second private meeting with the Queen — he wrote on 11 March from the Hotel de los Principes, Puerto del Sol to the Board of Deputies, 'I wish the Board to understand that we are under very great obligation to him'. (MD, BD, MB9, Jan. 1859—March 1864, f. 305).

59. Hodgkin, p. 24; Guedalla, pp. 12—13.

60. FO 99/116, 12 Nov. 1863 (draft).

61. FO 99/117, 16 Dec. 1863; FO 99/116, 23 and 31 Dec. 1863.

62. The assassination of Jews in Morocco — often those travelling between towns — was a common occurrence. A detailed list of 307 Jews murdered by Muslims in Morocco between 1864—1880 (it did not include the whole country, i.e. Marrakesh, etc.) was prepared by the Alliance Israélite Universelle at the time of the Madrid Conference of 1880 (*Bulletin AIU* 2 (2e sem. 1880): 17—18). It was difficult to obtain justice, as the oath of a *dhimmi* was not valid in an Islamic court of law and it was extremely rare for a Muslim to testify against another Muslim when a Jew was involved. Monetary compensation was more likely to be obtained for the widow and orphans when the victim had the 'protection' of a European state. See letter in Spanish dated 20 Oct. 1863 in the Archives (Maroc VIIIB) of the *AIU* (Paris), from Isaac Benros of Larache to Adolph Crémieux (Pres. *AIU*), describing the assassination of three Jews, the disappearance of their bodies (often they would be cut into pieces and thrown down disused wells) and a demand for justice. It is interesting that Montefiore had hardly delivered Merry's letter to Bargash abandoning all charges against the imprisoned Safi Jews, when on returning to his lodgings he found the deputation of fifty Moors requesting his intervention with the minister in favour of one of their tribe.

63. In 1851, Spain had signed a Concordat with the papacy recognizing the Catholic religion as the sole authorized faith of the country. Six months after Montefiore's second meeting with Isabella II (March 1864), General Narvaez returned to power at the head of a strongly Catholic and reactionary government. The reference to her 'overtaxed confessor' was not mere slander. Donna Isabella (1830—1904) became queen when she was three, was declared of age under Narvaez's rule in 1843, and was married to her cousin Francis, Duke of Cadiz, at sixteen. By 1868, at the time of Narvaez's death, the scandals involving the queen's name were ruthlessly exposed in the Spanish press by the liberals, particularly after she made her latest favourite — a cook's son and an actor — minister of state. During this revolutionary movement the queen fled and was deposed.

64. FO 99/123, Admiralty letter of 4 Jan. 1864 to Hammond for Earl Russell, confirming his instructions; same date, from Montefiore to Russell thanking him for all assistance: 'the influence and power of our own loved country, are never better nor more gracefully exercised than in the cause of humanity and justice.'

65. FO 99/123, Report of 17 Feb. 1864 from Capt. Armitage to Capt. (soon to be Admiral) Ommaney, senior naval officer, Gibraltar. Enclosure in Admiralty letter to Hammond of 15 March 1864.

66. Guedalla, p. 23, and Loewe, vol. ii, p. 152.

67. See Hodgkin's graphic description, especially on the extremely cold nights with only 'the kitchen chafing-dishes to give us a little warmth in the evening.'

68. This British backing was the prime 'influence at the palace', rather than any efforts by Abraham Corcos, as suggested in the article, 'Corcos', *Encyclopaedia Judaica* v (Jerusalem, 1971), 962.

69. Layard, replying to a question in the Commons, stated, 'The Foreign Office felt sympathy in his mission and did all they could [. . .] to support his representations', and he emphasized that, 'having had the honour of acting with him on various occasions', he could bear testimony to Montefiore's spirit of humanity and philanthropy, 'which extended to the people of every nation who were suffering wrong or injustice (Cheers).' Reported in London daily papers of 8 March and reprinted by *Jewish Chronicle*, 11 March 1864, p. 7.

70. *Jewish Chronicle*, 11 March 1864, p. 4.

71. The services rendered by both families should not be underestimated. Moses Nahon, vice-president of the *Junta* at Tangier accompanied the group from Mogador, dealing directly with all 'arrangements' and acting, whenever necessary, as interpreter.

72. References to this normal and traditional behaviour in Morocco are numerous. See *infra*, n. 94.

73. The Jews of Mazagan, as of virtually every Moroccan sea-port (and throughout North Africa to Tripoli), formed 20 per cent to 30 per cent of the town's population.

74. Reprinted in *Jewish Chronicle*, 11 March, p. 7.

75. Drummond Hay, *Journal of an expedition to the Court of Morocco* (Cambridge, 1848).

76. John Hay Drummond Hay, *Western Barbary: its wild tribes and savage animals* (London, 1844), pp. 1, 66; idem, *Journal*, p. 98; Hay and Brooks, *A Memoir*, p. 125. See *supra*, n. 1, and Riley, p. 455.

77. *A Memoir*, p. 132.

78. It is extraordinary to find him using the same arguments — almost the same words — in 1880 at the Conference of Madrid. He was then more determined than ever (he failed) to end the system of 'irregular protections', whilst recognizing, sixteen years after Montefiore's visit, that the Jews were still very much persecuted. *The Jewish World*, 26 Nov., 3 Dec. 1880.

79. Reade's skilful handling of a difficult situation probably helped his appointment as consul at Cairo on 3 June 1864, Horace Philip White replacing him in Tangier.

80. See *supra*, n. 51.

81. Ma'oz, pp. 202—9. Montefiore intervened twice on this occasion: by a dramatic humanitarian appeal on behalf of the Christian community of Damascus (over £20,000 was raised in England), and later through an official appeal to the foreign secretary on behalf of the Jewish community of Damascus, victimized by the surviving Christians, 'by reason that they have been murdered, plundered and maltreated, whereas the children of Israel were left uninjured'. See *The Times*, 12 July 1860; Montefiore to Lord John Russell (enclosing letter from the heads of the

Jewish community at Damascus to Montefiore), 16 October 1860, in *Parliamentary Papers*, 1861, (2800) lxviii, pp. 193–5. The last two letters appear as doc. 51 in Bat Ye'or, *The Dhimmi*. An account (24/9/1860) sent by the Prussian consul in Damascus to his ambassador in Constantinople is published in Stillman, *The Jews*, pp. 403–4.

82. See Montefiore's conversation on Friday 30 October with his nephew, J. M. Montefiore — referred to in meeting of Board of Deputies, Tuesday 3 November (*J.C.*, 6 Nov. 1863); see doc. 5, Reade to Drummond Hay, 7 February 1864. Montefiore had already tried without success to obtain a special edict from the Sultan of Morocco in 1845. After the Prince de Joinville's fleet had bombarded Mogador in August 1844, the neighbouring Kabyle tribes ruthlessly pillaged the town, killing some and raping many. The Jews, who formed one-third of its population (their importance can be gauged by the fact that this chief port of the empire was totally in-active on Sabbaths and Jewish holy days) appealed to their brethren in London. A Committee was formed which raised £2,500 to help them in their 'destitution and misery'. Montefiore, who had family connections with Mogador (*supra*, note 55), was delegated by the Committee to write to the foreign secretary, requesting him to transmit an address to the sultan, through the British consul in Tangier. The aim was to obtain an imperial *firman* in favour of Moroccan Jewry, 'that they shall be protected and defended; that they shall possess the same advantages and enjoy the same privileges as my Brethren who live in the Turkish Empire'. The Earl of Aberdeen accepted Montefiore's request and the address was trans-mitted to the sultan by Drummond Hay. In his reply, Mulay Abd ar-Rahman's vizier, Ben Idriss, explained to Montefiore that: 'The Hebrew nation enjoy throughout the whole of His Empire all that particular protection which can be obtained under the Shadow of Justice and Truth [. . .] How therefore can we now grant them other privileges more com-plete than those which they already have.' See FO 99/29, 9 Jan. 1845 (M.M. to E. of A.), 21 Jan. (draft reply), as well as copy of address to the sultan and his vizier's reply (dated 16 *Safer* 1261).

83. *J.C.*, 11 March 1864. This was wishful thinking. On the day he left Marrakesh, all the Jews continued to walk barefooted in the streets (*Jewish World*, 3 Dec. 1880) and they continued to do so in all the towns of the interior (with the exception of Meknes) until the French Protec-torate fifty years later (see docs. 12 and 13).

84. Charles de Foucauld, *Reconnaissance au Maroc: 1883–1884* (Paris, 1888), pp. 401–3, provides detailed but incomplete statistics (number of families) by region, which would point to a total population of under 50,000 twenty years afterwards. Even allowing for emigration, this is far too low, yet 200,000 is far too high for 1864. The figure was probably in the region of 70,000–100,000 then.

85. On the situation of the Jews in the last half of the nineteenth century in Persia, see David Littman, 'Jews under Muslim Rule: the case of Persia', *Wiener Library Bulletin*, 32 n.s. 49/50 (1979), 2–15.

86. De Foucauld, *ibid*. (Appendice: 'Les Israélites au Maroc'), pp. 395–402. Foucauld's invaluable description of the Jews of Morocco at that time is flawed by his inveterate antisemitism. As an officer, at St Cyr and Saumur, the future mystic had been the close friend of the notorious Marquis de Morès (Michel Carrouges, *Foucauld: Devant l'Afrique du Nord* (Paris, 1961), p. 149).

87. For a biography of Nasiri by his two sons (1921) see *Archives Marocaines* 30 (Paris, 1923), pp. 1—26. For the *dahir* and all other relevant documents from Al-Nasiri, see his *Kitab al Istiqsa*, vol. ix (Casablanca, 1956), pp. 112—14. English translation in Stillman, *The Jews*, pp. 371—3.

88. Bat Ye'or (*The Dhimmi*) has devoted two chapters of her study (French and English editions, part I, ch. 3 and 4) to the problems of the emancipation of the *Dhimmi* peoples, in relation to the *dhimma* on the one hand and European imperialism on the other. Ma'oz, p. 202, refers to the reflections of the Ottoman historian, Ahmed Cevdet Pasha (d. 1895); Stillman, *The Jews*, p. 361, gives the complete text of Cevdet, translated by Bernard Lewis (which Stillman spells 'Jevdet'); see also Lewis, *The Emergence*, pp. 123—8. After a rebellion, the Tunisian Constitution of 1860 which followed the earlier 'Pledge of Security' was repealed (30 August 1864) by the Bey of Tunis, Muhammad al-Sadiq. Paradoxically, this suited the French. It was not desired that 'equal rights' should automatically end 'foreign protections'; see Jamil M. Abun-Nasr, *A History of the Maghreb* (Cambridge, 1971), pp. 263—8.

89. *J.C.*, 11 March 1864, p. 7 (copying daily papers, 8 March). Layard here refers to the figure of '500,000' Jews of Morocco to be found in Montefiore's letter to Drummond Hay of 23 February (FO 99/123).

90. *J.C.*, 22 April 1864, p. 5. G. J. Goschen, MP (included in the Cabinet in in 1865) felt that, 'The Emperor of Morocco has taught the world at large a most valuable lesson respecting the value of civil and religious liberty'. Whilst Gladstone was meeting with Garibaldi on 12 April and was amongst the crowd pressing to welcome him at the Opera on the 14th, it was the Chancellor of the Exchequer's brother who seconded Sir Anthony Rothschild's resolution at the Tavern meeting of 13 April. See John Morley, *Life of Gladstone*, 3 vols. (London 1904), vol. ii, pp. 108—13.

91. *J.C.*, 11 March 1864, p. 4. Drummond Hay's circular letter to British vice-consuls of 20 April (doc. 9) stated that the 'Christian Governments of the world' will not remain silent should law reforms or edicts 'become dead letters and the old persecution of religious sects be revived'. In a letter of 31 May 1864, Sir Francis Goldsmid appeals to Earl Russell to do all he can to prevent the *dahir* 'becoming a dead letter' and check the 'fresh outbursts of persecution'. (FO 99/123).

92. Loewe, vol. ii, pp. 159—61.

93. The translation (Tangier) of the Memorandum sent by Drummond Hay to Russell on 2 May 1864 is dated 25/4/64. See also *Archives* (AIU), Maroc IVC11, IC1, VIIIB, etc. (March—August 1864); FO 99/123, Goldsmid to Russell (31/5/64), Russell to Goldsmid (3/6/64), Goldsmid to Russell (22/7/64) enclosing documents received from AIU (Paris), etc.; *USA Foreign Affairs*, vol. iii, p. 352, in Miège, vol. ii, p. 568, etc.

94. de Foucauld, *Reconnaissance au Maroc* (Paris, 1939 – in 1 vol.), p. 5. See *supra*, note 72; Meakin, *The Land of the Moors* (London, 1901), pp. 318—19.

95. For 1864, see Memorandum, *supra*, p. 196 and n. 93; the letter of Nahon (French vice-consulate, Tetuan), in *Archives* (AIU) Maroc IV C11, 24 June, 1864, etc.; FO 99/123 (documents received from AIU) via Goldsmid (*supra*, note 93), summary of contents relating to persecutions (Jews of Demnat), with the phrase: 'the Emperor of Morocco has himself very recently given orders that the Jews are to be treated with extreme rigour, in consequence of which new atrocities are daily being perpetrated'; and

FO (draft) letter to Goldsmid, 24 August 1864. For the 1884–1885 period, see AIU letters published in Littman, *WLB* 28, n.s. 35/36 (London, 1975), 73–74 (reference to Montefiore's visit) and particularly the brochure published in Tangier on 25 August 1884 by the director of the newly-founded *Times of Morocco*, Budgett Meakin's father (copy in *Archives* (AIU), Maroc IVC11 (Tangier)); also Meakin, *The Land of the Moors* (London, 1901), p. 348. For a useful (restricted) Moroccan version of these events, see Ahmed Toufiq, 'Les Juifs dans la société marocaine au 19e siècle: L'exemple des Juifs de Demnate', in *Juifs du Maroc* (Paris, 1980), pp. 153–66.

96. FO 99/120, no. 20 (draft) 10 Sept. 1864 to Sir John Drummond Hay.
97. Loewe, vol. ii, p. 164.
98. Abdallah Laroui, *Les origines sociales et culturelles du nationalisme marocain* (Paris, 1980), pp. 310–14.
99. Ibid.; and for al-Maghili himself see Georges Vajda, 'Un traité maghrébin "adversus Judaeos"', in *Extraits des Etudes d'Orientalisme dédiés à la mémoire de Lévi-Provencal* (Paris, 1962), vol. ii, pp. 805–13.
100. See *supra*, note 62; and, for texts in English, Littman, *supra*, note 4 and Bat Ye'or, *The Dhimmi*, docs. 64–80.
101. His 'Etudes Sabéennes' were published in the *Journal Asiatique* (the result of his voyage to southern Arabia under the auspices of the French Académie des Inscriptions et Belles Lettres) before his mission to Morocco for the Alliance Israélite Universelle, which had sent him eight years earlier to Ethiopia regarding the Falashas. See *supra*, doc. 12.
102. 'The western world was in one of its generous moments . . . a liberal Europe was then a force and not a dream'. Morley (on the London reception of Garibaldi the same week), vol. ii, p. 109.
103. Guedalla, pp. 3 and 39.
104. Jacob Benyuda is here referred to as 'Jacob Wizeman' (executed at *thirteen*). A wealthy Mr Joseph Sriki, 'knowing that Sir Moses was on his way to Madrid', is alleged to have offered 'his whole fortune' as bail for Lalouche in exchange for three days of grace. As Lalouche was executed on 13 September and Montefiore first knew about the Affair more than two weeks later, this is probably Sriki's *post hoc* interpretation of events. Sriki (or Eshriquy) was the interpreter for Great Britain, Sweden and Norway until his brother Moses replaced him in 1865. On Montefiore's arrival in Tangier, he had dedicated a newly-finished synagogue 'for the benefit of the poor', in commemoration (as to one-half of the structure) of Montefiore's visit. See Hodgkin, p. 28; *Jewish Chronicle*, 8 Jan. 1864, p. 5; Miège, vol. ii, p. 561, n.3.
105. Loewe, vol. ii, p. 165.
106. Archives *AIU*, Maroc, letter (22 April 1912) from Amram Elmaleh to pres. AIU, Paris. See also his reports of 22 Nov. 1912 and Oct. 1913. English translations in Littman, *WLB*, 29, n.s. 37/38 (London, 1975), 16–19.
107. The 'dawn' was a long one. The French government preferred the maintenance of traditional institutions, improving them where possible, rather than inaugurating a totally new régime. The result was that (in 1950) 'Even though their situation has progressively improved since the establishment of the French Protectorate, the Jews are still *dhimmis*, politically-speaking.' (Chouraqui, *La condition*, pp. 121 and 71). On 23 May 1948, after the massacre of Moroccan Jews by mobs in the towns of Oujda,

Jerada and Petitjean (Morocco was still under the French Protectorate), Sultan Muhammad V issued a proclamation which stated, *inter alia*, that the Jews of Morocco still retained 'a special status which had always been granted to them since the Muslim conquest'. They were ordered not to back the 'Zionist aggression or manifest their solidarity with it; because in so doing they undermined both their special rights and their Moroccan nationality'. These 'special rights' are evidently the traditional rights of toleration and protection under the Pact of Umar. (Ibid., Annex, ch. 2.)

108. It is curious that a few years before Montefiore's visit, a Prussian orientalist visiting Morocco spoke to Jews in Tetuan who asked him with emotion if it was true that 'Rothschild' was about to buy back Palestine from the Ottoman sultan which would then become a new Jewish kingdom. Heinrich Freiherr von Maltzen, *Drei Jahre im Nordwestern von Afrika: Reisen in Algerien und Morokko*, 4 vols. (Leipzig, 1863), vol. iv, p. 68. See his most interesting description of the Jews of Marrakesh, vol. iv, pp. 199—204.

109. In 1948, they numbered nearly 300,000. Over the next twenty years, three-quarters of this population left for Israel (others went to Europe and the Americas), and in 1984, 120 years after Montefiore's mission, barely 15,000 remained in Morocco. Those in Israel and their children constitute today almost fifteen per cent of its Jewish population — between 400,000 and 500,000 souls.

4

Journey to Romania, 1867

U. R. Q. HENRIQUES

I

In 1867 Sir Moses Montefiore was eighty-two years old. He was still saddened by the loss of his wife in 1862 and at times suffered from ill health. Yet he had not lost his old passion for travelling and was ready to go anywhere to intercede for persecuted Jews. Rich and generous, his great reputation rested above all on these journeys which were interspersed with visits to Palestine in a lifelong effort to re-establish independent self-supporting Jewish communities in the Holy Land.

Sir Moses' method of going about these rescue missions was well-established. He prepared the ground by making contact with as many representatives and important ministers of the country concerned as could be reached. He then secured promises of support from the rulers of other European powers. Next he obtained letters of introduction (readily granted by successive British Foreign Ministers) to the British ambassadors and consuls in the area. Finally he collected a band of fellow travellers, and set out. Invariably he went straight to the top. He sought and obtained interviews with the Sultan of Turkey, with Mehemet Ali the rebellious Pasha of Egypt, Nicholas I of Russia, Louis Napoleon in Paris and Queen Isabella of Spain in Madrid en route to Marrakesh, where he was formally entertained by the Sultan. One of the few crowned heads who refused access was Pope Pius IX. A secondary object of his visits was to make contact with the local Jewish communities, to whose schools and charities he would distribute largesse. Before returning home he would coax from the ruler concerned a formal declaration that his Jewish subjects would henceforth receive complete equality with all his other subjects of whatever religion, and that their persons and property would be protected by the law. These declarations he would cause to be distributed to the Press and sent to the rulers of the Great Powers, together with his courtly thanks for their assistance. Montefiore's journey to Romania in 1867 was the last of these rescue missions. Despite the deplorable destruction of his diaries after his death, enough material remains to attempt some assessment of whether or not his method was effective.

II

In 1867 Romania was still in the process of being formed from the union of the two Danube principalities, Walachia and Moldavia. The principalities were only now emerging from centuries of Turkish rule. In the eighteenth century they had been misruled by Greeks appointed from the Phanariot district of Constantinople by the Sultans, but in the early nineteenth century they had become increasingly subject to Russian influence, and this culminated in a Russian invasion and temporary occupation between 1828 and 1834. Under the government of the Russian Prince Kisselev they had obtained their first twin constitution, the *Réglements Organiques*. But after the Crimean War, Russian influence had waned, and by the Treaty of Paris in 1856 the principalities, still nominally under Turkish sovereignty, became the responsibility of the European Powers. Under the distracting influence of Great Power rivalry and intrigue the union of Walachia and Moldavia and the independence of budding Romania advanced in slow and irregular stages. The union was more or less achieved by the election of Prince Cuza to be ruler of both countries in 1857, and was confirmed, after Cuza's fall from power in 1865, by the election of Prince Carol of Hohenzollern-Sigmaringen (generally known at the time as Prince Charles) at the instigation of France and with the tacit consent of the other Powers. Formal independence of Turkey and of the Powers had to await the Peace of Berlin in 1878.[1]

The struggle for the emergence of the new State, squeezed between decaying Turkey and expanding Russia, and under the spasmodic and disunited tutelage of the kingdoms of western Europe must have affected its governments and leading politicians. Like other Balkan countries, it was economically and socially backward. Its population of about five million consisted mostly of peasants, emerging from legal serfdom into financial and economic subjection to the landowners, or boyars. Its soil was very fertile, and its main product was grain. It had almost no industries. Its few towns and large villages were mostly trading points, in Walachia built up by Greeks and Bulgarians, in Moldavia by Jews. A small native middle class of officials, traders and shopkeepers, just beginning to emerge, was bitterly jealous of these 'foreigners', while itself treated with suspicion by the boyars. Secure under franchises which excluded the peasants and ensured that their interests predominated, the boyars themselves tended to divide into family factions, some of whose politicians protected Jews and foreign traders against the challenge of the Romanian middle class. Others (many educated abroad) sought the votes of the Romanian bourgeoisie and professed

political radicalism. The drive for independence and the need for
union to achieve it had bred among the politically conscious, especially the radicals, an acrid and aggressive nationalism. They hated
the tutelage of foreign powers, often exercised patronisingly and
without tact. It was no exception, for instance, for the British
Consul—General at Bucharest to seek an audience with the reigning
prince, and tell him what mistakes he was making in governing his
country, subsequently reporting the interview to the British Foreign
Secretary.[2] One of the curious customs inherited from the Turkish
empire was that of foreign 'protection'.[3] Many of the wealthier
foreign merchants and bankers held Russian or Austrian passports
and were protected from the jurisdiction of the Romanian courts
by the consuls of the powers concerned. This gave Russia and
Austria a handle for intervening in Romanian affairs, and was hated
by the Romanian authorities. As it was, or seemed to be, a protection from the corruption and prejudice of the Romanian local
courts, foreign jurisdiction was sought by wealthy Jews. The economic and political weakness which necessitated constant dissimulation
in order to achieve national ends, bred in Romanian politicians an
impressive capacity to say one thing and do another. High sounding
declarations of political principle were affirmed and ignored. The
country was full of laws and lawlessness, and scapegoats for the
failings of government were constantly sought among foreigners,
and especially the Jews.

III

A small number of Jews of Sephardi origin and well assimilated into
the population had lived in Moldavia for centuries. They were subject to some religious or scriptural anti-semitism emanating from the
Eastern Orthodox Church, but it would seem not seriously menaced
by it. During the eighteenth and early nineteenth centuries many
Jews from Russia and Galicia fled from wars and persecution across
the Danube. Although consistently overrated by their enemies, the
total Jewish population was not large, even if it grew quickly. An
official estimate gave some 10,000 Jews in Moldavia in 1803. By
1834 a census showed 50,000 in Moldavia and 5,000 in Walachia.
In 1859 there were about 119,000 in Moldavia and 15,000 in Walachia.
In 1899 there were 269,000 Jews in Romania in a total population
of nearly 6,000,000.[4] The proportion of Jews to Romanians never
exceeded 5 per cent, although it appeared larger because of the con-
centrations of Jews in the towns, where they sometimes constituted
half the population. Here they formed a shopkeeper and artisan class

which seemed to stand between the unskilled immigrant peasant labourers and the élite of traders and officials. In the countryside there were far fewer of them, but they were either travelling salesmen and pedlars, or resident tenant farmers of large estates, or inn and tavern keepers. As farmers they stood between the boyar landowners and the peasants. The boyars were accused of employing them as rent and tax collectors because they were 'less accessible to pity' than the natives.[5] As innkeepers they administered the boyar monopoly of the drink trade, and might add money-lending on the side. As travelling salesmen they supplied the peasants with small luxuries otherwise unobtainable, but incurred the animosity of the uncompetitive Romanian traders. Everywhere their means of livelihood or their commercial talents offended some class of the population. The more conservative of the boyars defended them half-heartedly, provided they did not aspire to political equality. It has been said recently that they formed part of the boyars' means of hindering the growth of a middle class, while successive governments kept them out of the productive functions of a real bourgeois class.[6] Then they were blamed for keeping the country backward. The most positive contribution made by any of them to the economy was probably as bankers, some very rich and with international connections.

While the excuse for persecuting the Jews was religious, the real motives were social and economic. They were by far the biggest religious minority in a predominantly Russian Orthodox country. One estimate gave 134,168 in 1866, to about 54,000 Roman Catholics and small numbers of other minorities including Protestants and Muslims.[7] They were conspicuous not only through difference of religion, but through differences of custom, language and dress. Organized, with their own institutions, including schools and hospitals, they represented to the extreme nationalists both a parasitic growth on the economy and a nation within the nation.

Romania was not the only state where anti-semitism flourished. It was common in other Balkan states with sizeable Jewish populations, especially Serbia, where conditions were similar. There the Jews, accused of under-selling Serbian traders, were forbidden to settle in the country, and herded into a ghetto in Belgrade, under the guns of the Turkish fortress. In both countries there was a flourishing anti-semitic press. The Jews were accused of fleecing the peasants and debauching them with drink. In Serbia, where the national enemy was still Turkey, they were accused of favouring the Turks. In Romania, which feared the Russians, they were accused of being Russian agents. In Moldavia they were supposed to

support the separatist party which wanted to dissolve the union of
Moldavia with Walachia, even while they were blamed for the economic depression of Jassy, the ancient capital which had lost its
government institutions and much consequent employment as a
result of the union.

Restrictive legislation against Romanian Jews went back into the
eighteenth and very early nineteenth centuries, when they were forbidden to reside in villages or trade in agricultural products. Many
restrictive measures then and later betrayed Russian influence.
Kisselev's *Réglement Organique* for Moldavia forbade foreigners to
enjoy political rights, which included the right to own real property.
His *Réglement Organique* for Walachia forbade any but Christians
to acquire Walachian nationality, and with it the right to own real
property. As Walachia and Moldavia gradually united, the disabilities
of foreigners and non-Christians came together to prevent Jews from
acquiring Romanian citizenship and property rights. Old Jewish
families and recent immigrants were confounded in a sort of state-
lessness, except where it suited the Romanian authorities to recognize
them for certain unpopular purposes, such as conscription. The
restrictive legislation continued sporadically, but on the whole with
increasing intensity, throughout the nineteenth century. It was fit-
fully enforced and there were ways round most of it. The laws against
farming inhabited lands or keeping inns were aimed against the
boyars as much as the Jews, and could be circumvented by 'protection' or bribery. Middle-class Jews acquired Austrian passports
and the protection of the Austrian courts (as did some Romanians).
They were able to acquire land and houses under the names of a
third party. The older and wealthier Jewish families kept a 'low
profile' and suffered comparatively little. The lower classes suffered
most from creeping legislation which sought out and prohibited
their special means of livelihood. From the 1830s this was comple-
mented by sporadic expulsions of those without means of livelihood
from village to town and district to district. Huddled into the ghettos
of the larger towns, they became despised as dirty and insanitary, a
menace to public health, ready victims for government 'sanitary'
measures or sanctions against 'vagabonds'.[8]

IV

The growth of political liberalism in mid-nineteenth century Europe
seemed to promise well for the Balkan Jews. In Britain, France and
Prussia it brought about political and partial social emancipation. In
Romania, however, the young radicals, mostly educated in western

Europe, were active nationalists and also dependent on the votes of Romanian traders and shopkeepers against the leaders of the conservative boyars. So expressions of enthusiasm for natural rights and political equality in the revolutionary year of 1848 somehow managed to leave out the Jews. In 1848 an attempt in Walachia, where the Jews being fewer in number were less unpopular, to set up a constitutional assembly to devise a constitution granting equal rights to all came to nothing. In 1856 the Treaty of Paris, tidying up the aftermath of the Crimean War, proclaimed for Moldavia and Walachia equal liability to taxation and equal right to public employment. But equal political rights were guaranteed only to Christians, with a permission to extend these to the Jews at some later date. The reign of Prince Cuza (1859—66), who was trying to gain the approval of the European powers to the formal union of Moldavia and Walachia, provided a breathing space — nearly a decade of comparative toleration for the Jews. Restrictive laws were not enforced, or were even reversed. In 1865, Jews born in now united Romania, or resident for ten years, were allowed to naturalize. Jews were even allowed to join the National Guard.[9] The radicals, although demanding a foreign prince (who might be manipulated by themselves rather than by conservative boyar families), behaved with circumspection, hoping the European powers would accept the *de facto* union and would persuade Turkey to accept *de facto* Romanian Independence.

In 1866 Prince Cuza was deposed by a radical coup, and with French help Prince Carol of Hohenzollern-Sigmaringen was offered the throne. The newly elected chamber met in Bucharest to devise a constitution for Romania, inspired by the principles of liberty, equality and fraternity. The liberal tide was running strongly, and it seemed to hopeful European Jews a golden opportunity to secure Jewish emancipation in Romania. So Adolphe Crémieux, well-known French republican politician, and leader of the French Jews, came to Bucharest to address members of the Chamber and encourage them to include in the new constitution a clause granting full social and political rights to the Jews. What happened was described by Consul-General, John Green, in a dispatch to the British Foreign Secretary, Lord Clarendon, on 12 July. What he called the 'advanced revolutionary party' received M. Crémieux in a committee room of the Assembly, where he addressed the Deputies on the rights of man in general and the rights of Jews in particular. Then an article was inserted in the Project of a Constitution declaring that all men are equal irrespective of religion. The declaration 'gave great offence to the Christian shopkeepers of Bucharest, who are prefectly aware that they are not equal to the Jews in financial transactions, and fear their competition in the field of politics'. A crowd gathered outside the Assembly, and when the radical leaders Rosetti and Bratianu tried to address it they were hailed as 'The Rabbi', and 'Judas'.[10] Prince Ghika, leader of one of the great political families, asked if they had no confidence in him, and received the reply, 'Not the slightest'. The Deputies then withdrew the clause from the Project of a Constitution, saving their faces by declaring that the decision to do so had been taken some days earlier. The mob, elated with success, rushed to a new and handsome synagogue which had just been built, and attacked it with hatchets and crowbars until disturbed by a few men of the National Guard. A riot ensued, in which Jewish shops were smashed and property damaged and looted. Although nobody was actually injured the incident was a portent of things to come. It showed how shallow was Romanian liberalism. Romania was about to celebrate its union and its independence by turning on its Jews.

V

During the spring of 1867, Jewish leaders in Britain, and the British Foreign Office, were preoccupied with events in Serbia where, for several years, there had been more active and lawless persecution of the Jews than in Romania. Murders of Jews went unpunished while the government of Prince Michael of Serbia re-enacted earlier legislation expelling Jews from the interior of the country, denying them the right to own land and houses, bequeath property, or start new business enterprises. The ghetto in Belgrade was reduced by the guns of the Turkish fortress to rubble, and the inhabitants to destitution. Lord Stanley, Foreign Minister of the new Derby-Disraeli government, although unwilling to make Serbian independence conditional on a guarantee of good treatment of the Serbian Jews, was generally sympathetic. The matter was ventilated in the House of Commons on 30 March by Sir Francis Goldsmid.[11] Montefiore was in constant communication with the Foreign Office about it through his friend Layard. In the spring of 1867 Montefiore was probably contemplating a journey either to Belgrade or to Persia, from whose Jewish communities came cries for help against vexatious laws and arbitrary taxes. Then on 23 May news arrived of serious trouble in Jassy.[12]

There had been nervousness among the Jews of Jassy, where unemployment and depression prevailed, during the Bucharest riots of 1866. But the troubles of 1867 were deliberately induced by the Romanian government. Ion Bratianu, French educated and in Prince Cuza's time a leader of the radical opposition, was now Minister of the Interior under Prince Carol.[13] Still nominally a European radical, imbued with liberal ideas, he had been duly converted by the Bucharest uprising against Jewish emancipation, which showed very clearly what kind of policies the shopkeeper voters wanted enforced against the Jews. Early in May he had dispatched two circulars to the prefects of districts and the mayors of towns in Moldavia. One referred to Article 50 of the *Réglement Organique* for Moldavia (1834) prohibiting Jews from farming estates and owning or managing inns and taverns, and ordered that it should be strictly observed. The other ordered that all Israelites, whether or not under foreign protection, who were incapable of earning their livelihood, should be termed vagabonds. The authorities should then seize them and send them back under escort whence they came. Bratianu himself came to Jassy to encourage the good work, and reinforced it with a public letter to the Mayor complaining of the filthy state of the Jewish hospital, and saying that it must be cleaned, and all Jewish children compelled to attend the state schools.[14]

The Minister's initiative met with an enthusiastic response. Immediately the local police began arresting Jews in the streets, chaining them and dragging them off to prison. Self-constituted tribunals organized house-to-house searches, then tried the prisoners and sentenced them to deportation. As usual, the rich were able to buy their freedom, and the brunt of the hardship fell on the poor. The antisemitic press, directed by a group of unemployed teachers, began inciting the Christian population against the Jews, saying the Jews had ruined them and stolen their property, and should be banished. Many Jews, fearing a massacre, invaded the British consulate and asked for protection. Their communal leaders telegraphed and wrote to everyone they could think of who might help them; to Crémieux, Baron Lionel de Rothschild, Sir Francis Goldsmid, Sir Moses Montefiore and Lord Stanley. The Chief Rabbi of Jassy sent a telegram to Lord Stanley saying that upwards of 20,000 families at Jassy were in danger of their lives and about 300 already ruined. He begged the English government to instruct the consul to take them under his protection.[15]

To extend official protection (which implied putting the Jews under the jurisdiction of the consular court) was one thing the British government would not do. But Lord Stanley telegraphed Green at Bucharest ordering him to make strong representations to Prince Carol and his government and to desire St Clair to do the same to the local authorities at Jassy.[16] The Austrian and Russian Consuls at Jassy spontaneously joined him in protest.[17] In Paris the old republican Crémieux sought an interview with the Emperor Napoleon

III and persuaded him to send a strong telegram to Prince Carol. The
Emperor could not believe that the enlightened government of His
Highness imposed 'measures so contradictory to humanity and civilization'.[18] At Jassy, St Clair was genuinely shocked that such an order
could emanate from a disciple of Mazzini.[19] He had to be restrained
from extending British protection to the Jews. The arrests even
aroused some internal opposition. Fourteen leading boyars of Jassy
petitioned Prince Carol to stop the persecution,[20] and the higher
courts later reversed some of the verdicts of the unofficial tribunals.[21]

    To this international outcry Prince Carol and his ministers res-
ponded with surprised innocence. They knew of no persecution.
Bratianu affirmed that the circulars were intended solely to cope
with the problem of vagabondage and as sanitary measures in the
face of an outbreak of cholera at Jassy (for which by implication he
blamed the Jews). He promised St Clair that measures would be
taken to prevent wrongful arrests, and then left the town without
giving any further instructions. When Prince Carol visited Jassy to
see conditions for himself, the Jews were prevented from approaching
him, but a torchlight procession which had gone out to greet him
hunted them in the streets and set fire to their beards. A pregnant
woman who tried to protect her husband was wounded in the arm
with a bayonet.[22]

                                    VI

Because of the troubles in Jassy, Sir Moses Montefiore decided to go
to Romania. On 31 May he wrote to the communal leaders of the
town offering to do anything he could to ameliorate their position.
He would 'not be deterred from the fulfilment of this duty by any
amount of self sacrifice'.[23] But the London Committee of the
Board of Deputies, albeit more or less his personal fief, was in no
hurry to send him. At a meeting on 28 June some members suggested
that the reports from Jassy were exaggerated, those from France
being of a more favourable tendency. They wanted combined action
with the French Alliance Universelle. The Board expressed admiration
of Sir Moses' resolution to go to Romania, but because of his age and
the dangers of the journey it would not commit itself by proposing
it.[24]

    In July, news arrived in London of a *noyade* at Galatz. The first
party of Jews condemned for vagabondage at Jassy, ten or eleven of
them, had arrived at this Romanian Danube port on 14 July. They
were immediately put in a small boat, rowed across the river, and

dumped on a deserted marshy island. They were found by Turkish border guards, who, seeing they had no passports nor papers, rowed them back again. By order of the Mayor of Galatz, soldiers of the garrison returned them once more to the Turkish side where they spent a mosquito-ridden night in the mud of the marshes. When, the following morning, they once more appeared in an exhausted state in a boat rowed by three soldiers, the Romanian soldiers refused to let them land, lined them up on the river bank, and forced them into the water, with bayonets. The Turks rowed off as quickly as possible (some accounts hint that the boat was fired on by the Romanian soldiers), and two of the 'passengers', a very old man and a boy, who had clung to the boat were carried into deep water and drowned. The Romanian soldiers made no attempt to save them, but eventually they were forced by the growing agitation of the crowd which had assembled on the river bank to let the survivors scramble ashore. They were taken away to the Jewish hospital.[25]

The news of the *noyade*, which reached the Alliance Universelle at Paris and Baron Rothschild in London on the 17th, and Montefiore on the 18th, caused the outcry against the Romanian government to be redoubled. The Alliance now demanded the immediate dismissal of Bratianu, and began a press campaign against the Romanian government. Prince Carol thought it politic to send a personal secretary, one Émile Picot, who had obtained his Romanian appointment through the influence of a friend of the Emperor, (apparently his *soeur de lait* or fellow participant in refreshment from his wet-nurse), to Paris to make contact with the Alliance and explain to its members how greatly the Prince sympathized with the Jews.[26] In response to further dispatches about the barbarities being practised in Jassy, the Board of Deputies had overcome its doubts about the wisdom of Montefiore's journey and decided to support him.[27] News of the *noyade* made his mission more urgent, and on 19 July he wrote to Lord Stanley asking for letters of assistance to the British consuls in Romania.[28] However, such a mission could not be arranged quickly. As well as instructing its representatives in Romania, the Foreign Office agreed to endorse requests for letters of support from the rulers of Prussia and Russia (which cost Bismarck and Gortchakov nothing, although Russia's treatment of its Jews was worse than Romania's). An interview was arranged with Napoleon III *en route* through France. Then the journey had to be organized and financed through the various European Rothschild banks. Montefiore travelled with a considerable equipage. On this occasion he took with him his nephew Arthur Cohen QC, MP, Captain Henry Moore of the Bombay Staff Corps (one of a succession of non-Jewish officers who accompanied Montefiore on his travels, no doubt as a kind of chief of staff), his personal doctor, James Daniel of Ramsgate, his *shochet* (or ritual slaughterer), his personal attendant Albertine and, last but not least, his secretary and biographer, Louis Loewe.[29] Although remote and uncivilized, Romania was not too difficult to reach, as the party could take a river steamer from Vienna down the Danube. The main discomfort would be the great heat of central Europe in late summer.

Meantime the row over the *noyade* burgeoned. The accounts differed with the sources. The Galatz Jews reported four drowned. The Romanians held an enquiry and admitted two drowned who, they said, had been thrown out of the boat by the Turkish soldiers. They refused to take part in the Turkish enquiry, which blamed the Romanians for all that had happened. Consul Ward at Galatz, writing indignantly to Green, confirmed two lost in the river off Galatz, but reported the additional loss of an old man overnight in the mud of the Turkish marshes.[30] On 15 July the Consuls of Austria, France, Britain, Italy, Prussia and Russia, wrote a joint protest to the Prefect of Galatz which evoked an angry repudiation from him. The Jews were said to be spreading copies of the consuls' protest round the cafés, and foreign boats lying in the port.[31] The climax came when it was known that a Jew in the Galatz prison had been shot, according to the Romanian authorites, while trying to escape. The news evoked a bitter letter from Crémieux to Picot, now back in Bucharest. 'This frightful dispatch', wrote Crémieux, 'proves two things: the first that Jews are detained in Galatz prisons, the second *c'est qu'on ne se contente pas de les noyer, on les fusille'*.[32] This time international, especially French, pressure was to lead to the resignation of Bratianu, although not to the cessation of his influence. Also, the next party which arrived in Galatz for deportation was released.[33] But before that Montefiore had set out on his journey.

VII

Encouraged by prayers in all the British synagogues, Sir Moses and his party left Dover on the morning of 30 July 1867, and arrived in Paris the same evening. Here the British Ambassador, as asked, had arranged an audience with Napoleon III. The Emperor shook Montefiore warmly by the hand and promised his support for the mission.[34] On 6 August the party resumed their journey, travelling through Strasbourg, Stuttgart, Donauworth and Ratisbon to Vienna, where they arrived on 14 August. Montefiore, together with Arthur Cohen and Louis Loewe, called on the British Ambassador, Lord

Bloomfield, only to find that the Austrian Emperor, the Foreign Minister and the Russian Ambassador were all away. In the next two days Montefiore sustained a double blow. News arrived from England of the death of his brother Horatio, and Arthur Cohen was summoned home by his wife. But although complaining of weakness, Montefiore was anxious to proceed. On Sunday 18 August the diminished party boarded an Austrian river steamer and on the 22nd they reached Bucharest.[35]

Just before starting out on his journey, Montefiore had received a letter from a Monsieur A. Halfon, banker and president of the Bucharest branch of the Alliance Universelle. Halfon begged him to stay at home. Not only was he too old to fatigue himself with such a journey, it was feared that his coming would wound the *amour propre* of the prince, the government and the Romanian people. The indication was that the support of their fellow Jews in Paris, London and Vienna, reflected in the journals, would help to prevent further persecution. Sir Moses should stay at home and use his influence from a distance. Assuming that the wealthy Bucharest Jews who, according to Consul-General Green, had little to complain of, were trying as usual to keep out of trouble and distance themselves from the poor immigrant Jews, Montefiore ignored the letter.

Despite this warning, Montefiore was welcomed with the utmost courtesy and respect by the Jewish community and the Romanian government alike. The Jewish leaders came to his hotel room to hold a Saturday morning service, since the heat was too great for the old man to walk to the synagogue.[36] They were followed by numerous deputations from Hebrew schools and charities, attracted no doubt by Montefiore's reputation for wealth and generosity. But there also came the Foreign Minister and two secretaries of Prince Carol, one of them Émile Picot, with whom Montefiore had a long talk. Prince Carol himself was most amiable and invited Sir Moses to dine with him on 29 August.

It probably smoothed Sir Moses' path that Bratianu had resigned the week before he arrived, following the President of the Chamber, Cretulescu, and it was not yet apparent that the government being formed under Stefan Golescu would be no more tolerant to the Jews than its predecessor. Montefiore, as always, behaved with great tact and dignity. 'He was anxious to avoid giving the slightest umbrage to the Romanian government by alluding to the immediate events which induced him to undertake his Journey', reported Green to Stanley. 'His object is to restore confidence among his co-religionists here, and to be able to assure those in England and elsewhere that Jews in the Principalities will in future be treated with justice and toleration'.[37] Green was enthusiastic about the dignified and modest language in which Sir Moses pleaded the cause of his co-religionists; he thought that 'both the Prince and his ministers had brought themselves to expect words of a very different import'. In other words, Montefiore, a natural conservative, did not vapour about Natural Rights nor demand immediate political equality for the Jews, nor threaten adverse publicity if they did not get it. He combined the manners of a gentleman with limited demands, and he was evidently being compared with Crémieux, to his credit. The Prince received him 'with that genial politeness which is natural to him, but from which no inference can be drawn'. But Green, while taken with Sir Moses' charm, was sceptical about the long-term effect of his visit.

Not everyone was as pleased to see Montefiore as the Prince. Even while Sir Moses was busy composing a petition entreating Prince Carol to give 'positive orders' for the protection of the Romanian Jews, Green received news of money being distributed among the mob to attack the party. The violently nationalist journal *Natinuea* carried a long article proposing an anti-semitic petition, to attract mass signatures, of which the main burden was a demand for the expulsion of all immigrants since 1848 who were without industrial occupation, the retention of Crown lands by the government (possibly to keep them out of the clutches of the Jews — or the boyars), and an end to Hebrew immigration. The tone was possibly more violent than the content, but the Government received it coldly, forbade signing of the petition except indoors, and supplied Montefiore with a police guard on his visits to Jewish and Christian charities. The nationalists responded by placing tables bearing copies of the petition for signature outside Montefiore's hotel and immediately under the window of the first floor suite in which he was staying. The day after the royal dinner party, Montefiore, returning from a long day talking to Green and touring charitable institutions, found a large crowd gathered round the tables under his window. Some of the other hotel residents rushed into his room crying, 'They want to take your life!' Not a bit daunted, he flung the window wide open, stood in the middle of it with Loewe beside him and addressed the mob. 'Fire away if you like', he shouted; 'I came here in the name of justice and humanity to plead the cause of innocent sufferers.'[38] The crowd shouted and bayed, but did nothing and eventually dispersed. In the evening M. Halfon came with tears in his eyes, crying, 'We shall all be massacred!' Montefiore was not in the least deterred. 'Are you afraid?' he asked Halfon; 'I have no fear whatever.'[39] He ordered a carriage with two lights on the front so that he could be clearly seen, and with an apprehensive Louis Loewe by his side he drove around Bucharest while its citizens lined the streets. When they had left the town centre and the crowds behind and were travelling down a dark and lonely road, Loewe was alarmed to find that a carriage without lights was following close behind. At his suggestion they stopped to question the occupants, when a gentleman jumped out and rushed up to Montefiore. It was an interesting moment – but the gentleman only besought Montefiore to intercede with Prince Charles to continue his privilege of lighting Bucharest with oil lamps . . . [40]

On returning to the hotel they found a 'lady' and an 'officer' who said they had come to talk to Sir Moses on political subjects, and had to be induced, with much difficulty, to leave.

The visit had a few more days to run. So far it had all the appearance of a success. But Montefiore was not blind to realities. 'I am', he wrote, 'most anxious, weak, out of health and vexed to the heart . . . Political factions strive to create confusion by my presence in this place.'[41] He was cheered by the arrival of a kind and conciliatory letter from Prince Carol.

> Comme j'ai eu l'occasion de vous le dire de vive voix, les voeux que vous formez pour vos coreligionnaires sont déjà accomplis. Les Israélites sont l'objet de toute ma solicitude et de toute celle de mon gouvernement et je suis bien aise que vous soyez venu en Roumanie pour vous convaincre que la persécution religieuse dont la malveillance a fait tant de bruit n'existe point. S'il est arrivé que les Israélites fussent inquiétés, ce sont là des faits isolés, dont mon gouvernement n'entend pas assumer la responsabilité. Je tiendrai toujours à l'honneur de faire respecter la liberté religieuse et je veillerai sans cesse à l'exécution des lois qui protégent les Israélites comme tous les autres Roumains dans leur personne et dans leurs biens . . .[42]

Here was Montefiore's seal of endeavour and proof of success. In a sense the remainder of the visit was but aftermath. He went on a further round of visits, including another to Prince Carol, during which he showed the Prince some of the threatening letters he had received. He was told that the Prince also received – and ignored – them. On 1 September he said farewell to the Prince and then visited representatives of the Hebrew community to ascertain what foundation the editor of *Natinuea* had for his 'pretended dread that Bucharest would be converted into a second Jerusalem'. After hearing about all the synagogues, charities, hospitals, colleges and schools, to which he distributed his customary largesse, he understood the editor's reason, while not sympathizing with his sentiments. He would rejoice in the appellation.

> The more Synagogues, the more prayers are offered up for the preservation of the life of the reigning monarch and the prosperity of the country; the more colleges for religious instruction, the more efficient the promulgation of the law of God: 'Thou shalt love thy neighbour as thyself' . . .; the more charitable institutions, the more aid, comfort and consolation for the poor and suffering. 'Jerusalem' is the emblem of peace, as the word *Shalom* indicates, and Bucharest, nay, the whole country under the sway of His Serene Highness, the reigning Prince, would become renowned as an abode of peace for all his loyal subjects, without distinction of creed or nationality.[43]

According to Loewe, 'the street was now thronged with thousands of his co-religionists, and many houses presented the appearance of an impromptu illumination.'[44]

VIII

Carrying with him a portrait of the Prince, brought to him as a present by Picot, Montefiore and his companions left for Giurgevo on the Danube. They did not go to Jassy. Loewe had secretly visited Green to show him a collection of the threatening letters, tell him about the uproar outside the Hotel Otteliano, and doubtless inform him also of the strange people who persisted in wandering into Montefiore's suite despite the official police guard. Green vetoed Sir Moses' visit to Jassy. Not only would he incur danger himself, he would imperil the Jews of Jassy by producing a riot. Reluctantly Montefiore changed his plans. At Giurgevo he received further deputations on the upshot of the mission. It was not happy about the hired a steamer and travelled up the Danube, shooting the dangerous rapids by the Iron Gate and admiring the Roman monuments on the Serbian bank. Something of a holiday atmosphere prevailed. After a sabbath rest by the riverside they boarded another steamer and on 8 September arrived at Budapest. Thereafter the journey home became a kind of triumphal progress. In Vienna Montefiore called on Lord Bloomfield and the Austrian Minister of Foreign Affairs and received deputations from Austrian Jewish communities. Letters of thanks were dispatched, including one to John Green for his kind attentions. Flowery missives from the German and Portuguese congregations at Bucharest awaited Montefiore at Ramsgate. The party reached home on 20 September.

Montefiore could scarcely wait to proclaim the success of his mission. Already on 31 August he had telegraphed the Board of Deputies: 'By the blessing of God I am happy to say that my endeavours have been crowned with success.' J. M. Montefiore promptly passed it on to *The Times* with a covering letter, where it was published on 5 September. Once in England, Montefiore went to London to report on his journey to Lord Stanley. In his official letter of thanks to the Foreign Secretary he was sure Lord Stanley would share his gratification that 'the objects I sought to obtain have been fully accomplished . . . I have every reason to hope that the laws of the country which provide for the protection of the Jews as well as of all the other inhabitants of Rumania, will be carried out in their full integrity.'[45]

The Board of Deputies received a report and copies of all the correspondence, including Montefiore's letter to Green in which he expressed his deep regret that the state of his health 'with other considerations' had prevented him from going to Jassy.[46]

For the next few weeks Montefiore was wrapped in a cloud of public adulation. The Board of Deputies passed resolutions appreciating the great anxieties 'to which its venerated colleague must have been subjected'.[47] The *Daily Telegraph* wrote that he had been entirely successful in the merciful object of his journey.[48] *The Times* on 21 September published in full his correspondence with Prince Carol. The *Jewish Chronicle*, normally a sober paper, stretched the resources of the English language in writing about Sir Moses. Back in July it had produced a fulsome leader about the 'youthful fiery heart beating under a head crowned with venerable snowy hair'.[49] On 4 October it had a long piece about 'our revered champion' who had set out 'to fight the battle of his race . . . of humanity, freedom and religion'. But it also included some more sober reflections on the upshot of the mission. It was not happy about the phrase in Prince Carol's letter calling the calamities *des faits isolés*, for which his government could not assume responsibility. But it concluded that it was a triumph that the letter had been obtained, and believed its influence would be felt far beyond Romania.[50] Montefiore basked in an aura of publicity and recognition. He had hopes of a peerage on the recommendation of the famous philanthropist, Lord Shaftesbury, but neither political party, when in power, would give him one.

The very day after the *Jewish Chronicle*'s adulatory leader news arrived of renewed persecution of the Romanian Jews. *The Times* reported that a mob had broken into the synagogue at Galatz and injured a number of worshippers.[51] Soon, further details were made known by Sir Francis Goldsmid, who had received them from the Galatz committee of the Alliance Israélite Universelle.[52] The Prefect of Galatz was organizing the expulsion of Jews from the surrounding villages. He was ignoring the opposition of the local boyars and cajoling and threatening the heads of the villages into carrying out the expulsion orders. Nobody took any notice of Prince Carol. The round of mobs and judicial injustices, of protests and complaints to the consuls began all over again. The British Foreign Office, as usual, offered its good offices, but sent strict orders to Consul Ward at Galatz not to treat any Jews as British-protected persons. The Jews arrested at Galatz were released, probably on orders from Bucharest, but Consul Ward noted as a new feature a reluctance of endangered Jews to seek the help of foreign consuls. Several had been driven from their homes despite being under Austrian or French protection.[53] And the mob violence quickly broke out again, fomented by a revival of the old blood libel. The district of Berlad had failed to obey Bratianu's circular, and had been comparatively free from troubles. Yet by January 1868 expulsions were proceeding there on a large scale, and the Chief Rabbi of Berlad was writing anguished letters to Montefiore begging him to come and save them.[54] Montefiore wrote a letter of expostulation to the Foreign Minister, Stefan Golescu, and Golescu replied, politely enough, but claiming not only that the reports were greatly exaggerated but that, according to an enquiry already held, 'It was his co-religionists who had occasioned if not invited the movement concerned.'[55] Montefiore sent the letter unexpurgated to *The Times*,[56] a blunder which Green in Bucharest did not fail to notice with consternation.[57] In February 1868 Bratianu was back in office and the persecutions intensified. In April Montefiore was offering to go out again to remind Prince Carol of his promises, if it would do any good. But his friend Edmund Hammond[58] at the Foreign Office plainly thought he could do no more than Green was already doing.

From 1868 the persecutions in Romania, albeit always sporadic, tended to intensify. Restrictive laws were renewed or initiated. The Jews now became subject to conscription into the army, although debarred from commissioned rank. Quite how serious these developments were was difficult to assess. Green remarked that they operated as indirect taxation, since the Jews were used to bribing their exemption, although when they could avoid their effects they did so loudly.[59] The mobs and the expulsions were no idle threat, although the numbers expelled may have been exaggerated. The British and other consuls (especially Count Eder, Consul-General for Austria) continued, with exemplary compassion, to do their best for the persecuted, with ill-concealed contempt for the Romanians. The Gladstone government of 1868—74 was sympathetic, but like the Conservative administration before it, would not take the Romanian Jews under its protection. But in any case, such protection was becoming ineffective as Romanian independence and defiance of the Powers increased. Resort to foreign jurisdiction only aroused the hostility of Romanian nationalists to the 'foreigners' in their midst.

By the end of 1867 at the very latest Montefiore must have known that his attempt to gain toleration for the Romanian Jews had failed. Indeed, he probably realized it when he was actually in Romania and observed the activities of the political factions. Why he was so anxious to claim complete success on the basis of assurances of a government which had already proved its untrustworthiness must be a matter for speculation. Montefiore was a very vain man, if also a sincere one in his desire to help the Jews. He had no love for Disraeli who refused him the coveted peerage, and whom, in his heart of hearts, he must have considered a traitor to Judaism. Yet when Disraeli himself insisted at the Congress of Berlin in 1878 that formal recognition of Romanian independence must depend on a clear promise of social and political equality for the Jews, written into the Treaty, Montefiore was on the platform at Charing Cross Station to welcome him home.

Thereafter, independence secured, successive Romanian governments balked at fulfilling the Treaty. By the turn of the century Romanian Jews were emigrating by the hundred to America, only too often to be refused entry. In the First World War Romania joined the right, i.e. the Allied side. As a reward she obtained Bessarabia, Bukovina and Transylvania and became much bigger, if of more regular shape. The new territories contained large populations of Hungarian-speaking Jews as well as other religious minorities. Persecutions were renewed and redoubled. If there was never a holocaust on the German scale it was because Romania was anarchic and ineffective rather than uniform and efficient; not because of good will.

IX

It remains only to consider two questions. Did Montefiore do any good at all; and could he have done more?

There is evidence that in the 1860s foreign intervention exercised some restraining influence on Romanian government campaigns against the Jews. In April 1868 Jon Bratianu opposed a proposal for heavier legislative restrictions on the Jews because it would give the Powers the right to protest, containing as it did some provisions 'contrary to the sentiments of the civilized world'.[60] He hinted that all necessary persecution could be carried on in the name of expelling vagabonds. In such influence Montefiore played a part, although the part was, perhaps, more conspicuous than effective. In retrospect it seems that the Romanian ministers treated him with polite contempt. The attitude of Prince Carol is more problematic. Possibly he was weak rather than villainous, not without good will, at least towards Sir Moses himself. But he was entirely dependent on the votes of the commercial middle class, collected on an anti-semitic ticket. His secretary, Émile Picot, was friendly with the men of the Paris Alliance Israélite Universelle, but after Prussia defeated Austria at the battle of Sadowa, Prince Carol turned towards the rising sun of Germany and Bismarck, and Picot was replaced by a German secretary, Friedlander, as his counsellor.[61] Montefiore's technique of persuasion was wasted on an insecure prince who was himself the captive of internal faction and of international forces he could not control.

Montefiore was probably more successful, at least temporarily, in raising the morale of the Jews themselves. Here was a man of venerable aspect and courtly bearing who hobnobbed with royalty and yet proclaimed himself one of them. Nor was he afraid to face mobs nor challenge the authorities, as were their own leaders. They saw a Jew who could stand up, rich, generous and courageous. Poor Halfon showed up badly by comparison. Yet Montefiore went home and they were left with Halfon; recollecting, perhaps, that it is not too difficult to be brave for a fortnight. Halfon lived in Romania and Montefiore did not.

It is a mistake to think of Montefiore as a solitary individual, operating entirely on his own. He was, in effect, a member of an uncoordinated and inharmonious team. The team was the small body of rich and prominent Jews who tried to protect their threatened brethren all over the world.[62] With the support of the Jewish middle class, where there was one, they operated largely by putting pressure on their own, more or less friendly governments to take action against the persecutors. In this respect Montefiore was less important and influential than Adolphe Crémieux, his old colleague and rival of the Damascus blood libel trials of 1840. Crémieux's Alliance Israélite Universelle, with its local committees, schools and charities all over Europe was a far larger and more successful organization than Montefiore's Board of Deputies of British Jews.[63] Crémieux had at least as much influence on Napoleon III and his Foreign Minister, Drouyn de Lhuys, as had Montefiore on Lord Stanley. He was succeeded by Bismarck's great Jewish banker, Gerson Bleichröder, prompted by the Rothschilds, who tried so hard to get his Prussian master to force the Romanians to accept and implement the terms of the Treaty of Berlin.[64] Up to 1870 France had more influence on Romania, whose union and independence it had supported in the councils of the Powers, than did Britain, which sat on the fence.[65] Crémieux even succeeded in getting Bratianu temporarily dismissed, while in 1868 the leading German Jews, with the help of the press, succeeded in preventing the enactment of even harsher anti-semitic laws.[66]

Inside Britain, Montefiore, by 1869, although better known, was less influential than Sir Francis Goldsmid. Goldsmid was the channel through whom news and views of the Alliance Israélite Universelle reached British Jews and the British government. He was Liberal MP for Reading, and had been a pamphleteer and campaigner for Jewish Emancipation since his youth. He was also a founder of the religious Reform movement, which met with Sir Moses' strong disapproval. In 1870 he was to help to start the Anglo-Jewish Association as a rival to Montefiore's Board of Deputies (although the two had a Conjoint Foreign Committee from 1878).[67] Then there was Baron Lionel de Rothschild, with his riches and his international family connections. The British Foreign Office, with commendable patience, kept them all informed on Jewish matters abroad, and carried on multiple correspondence with all three, and sometimes with Joseph Mayer Montefiore, Sir Moses' chairman pro tem of the Board of Deputies as well. At the height of the ascendancy of European liberalism, the British Foreign Office, its representatives abroad as well as successive foreign ministers, were generally sympathetic towards the Jews, and contemptuous of those who persecuted them. They responded to pressure up to the point at which it might draw them into entanglements and embarrass British foreign policy. Disraeli, with his powerful Jewish self-identification, had additional motives for his response. But his strong interest in the Jewish question proved something of a snare to him. When news came in 1876 of the Turkish massacres of the Bulgarians he took it too lightly. Disraeli and the Foreign Office officials were more accustomed to hearing of the Balkan Christians persecuting the Jews than of the Turks persecuting the Christians.

If the Jewish leaders had worked more closely together they might have been more powerful than they were, or were made out to be. But it is unlikely that they would have succeeded in their common object. In any case, it is improbable that Montefiore would ever have consented to play second fiddle, especially to Crémieux (with whom he had uneasy relations on the Damascus Affair mission in 1840).

He did his best in the way he knew best, not sparing himself in the cause. If he had little success, no one else succeeded in making headway against that sullen rising tide of anti-semitism in Romania.

Note on sources

Because of the loss of Montefiore's own diaries much of the account of the events of the journey to Romania has of necessity been based on *The Diaries of Sir Moses and Lady Montefiore,* vol. ii by his secretary and devoted companion, Louis Loewe. Although his accuracy cannot always be depended on, Loewe was at least an eyewitness of all that happened.

For the events leading up to the journey, as they appeared in the correspondence, between the British consuls in Romania and the Foreign Office, as well as the relations between the Foreign Office and Sir Moses Montefiore and other leading British Jews, the main source is Parliamentary Accounts and Papers (41) 1877 No. 89, correspondence respecting the condition and treatment of the Jews in Serbia and Romania. The letters in this large volume were taken out of the Foreign Office files covering British relations with Serbia and Romania. The letters appear in a confidential printed volume in the PRO at Kew, obviously collected for the subsequent Parliamentary Paper. Unfortunately, when the collection was made most of the original letters were destroyed, and with them any personal or unofficial comments which may have been written in the margins.

NOTES

1.   T. W. Rike, *The Making of Roumania* (Oxford University Press, 1931), *passim*, R. W. Seton-Watson, *A History of the Roumanians* (Cambridge University Press, 1934), ch. VII, IX, XI, XII.
2.   E.g. the interview of the British consul general at Bucharest, John Green, with Prince Carol, in which he told the Prince that he had committed serious blunders in mobilizing frontier guards, trying to establish the use of paper money, allowing agitation against the Jews, etc., etc. John Green to Lord Clarendon, 10 July 1866. Public Record Office, Kew, Foreign Office 78/1921. Lord Clarendon (4th Earl of Clarendon 1800—70) was Foreign Secretary in Gladstone's government from 1868 to 1870. He had been Lord Lieutenant of Ireland from 1847—52 and Foreign Secretary from 1853—8 and 1865—7. John Green (1808—77) was consul-general for the United Provinces of Moldavia and Walachia from 1867—74. He was knighted in 1874.
3.   The result of 'capitulations', i.e. treaty agreements between the Porte and

various Western powers giving the nationals of these powers, including those they chose to protect, the right of trial in their consular courts.

4. Francis Rey, 'La Question Israélite en Roumanie', *Revue general de droit international public*, x (1903), 513—14. Seton-Watson gives figures for 1859 as 118,000 in Moldavia and 9,200 in Walachia. *History of the Roumanians*, p. 348. He accepts uncritically the official Romanian anti-semitic slant on the effects of the Jewish population, especially in the towns where Jews were sometimes an actual majority.

5. Rey, 'La Question Israélite', p. 462.

6. Carol Iancu, *Les Juifs en Roumanie 1866—1919* (University of Provence, 1978), p. 25.

7. *L'Occident et la persecution israélite en Roumanie*, (Paris, 1870), p. 124. The anonymous author took his figures from Jean Petresco, *Statistique Administrative de Roumanie* (Bucharest, 1866).

8. Rey, 'La Question Israélite', pp. 461—5.

9. *Ibid*, p. 465.

10. P.R.O. F.O. 78/1921. According to Seton-Watson, *History of the Roumanians*, p. 349, Crémieux offered to raise a low interest loan of 25,000,000 francs in return for guarantees of political rights for the Jews. Consul Green says nothing about any loan in his letters.

11. Report in *The Times*, 30 March 1867.

12. Dr L. Loewe, ed. *The Diaries of Sir Moses and Lady Montefiore* (London, Griffith Forman & Co., 1890), ii, 192—3. Cf. telegram communicated to Hammond at the Foreign Office by Goldsmid from the Jewish community at Jassy, P.P. 1877, 89:106.

13. Ion Bratianu, French educated and temporarily exiled to Paris after 1848. Political journalist and leader of radical party with his brother Dmitrie, and Constantine Rosetti. Largely responsible for downfall of Cuza and accession of Prince Carol, who was very dependent on him. Temporarily retired 1868, implicated in a republican plot 1870, yet Minister of Finance in 1876, and with near-dictatorial powers from 1880—8. Adept at 'managing' the restricted Romanian franchise. Later secured Romanian alliance with Bismarck. Increasingly reactionary and unpopular until forced from office.

14. Iancu, *Les Juifs en Roumanie*, p. 69. Copies of the circular were enclosed with a detailed account of events by St Clair, British consul at Jassy, in a despatch from Green to Stanley on 27 May. P.P. 1877, 89: 170—2.

15. P.P. 1877, 89: 166. Edward Henry Stanley, 1826—93, later 15th Earl of Derby, and son of Disraeli's Prime Minister; a liberal-minded Conservative. Foreign Secretary 1867—9 and 1874—8, eventually resigning in protest at Disraeli's aggressive policy towards Russia in the Balkan crisis. Colonial Secretary under Gladstone, 1882—5; ended as Liberal-Unionist in the Lords. Too open-minded and indecisive to make a top rank party politician.

16. Hammond to Goldsmid, 25 May. P.P. 1877, 89:167.

17. St Clair to Green, 21 May, P.P. 1877, 89:167.

18. Iancu, *Les Juifs en Roumanie*, p. 71.

19. St Clair to Green, 21 May, P.P. 1877, 89:172.

20. Copy of boyars' petition to Prince Carol, P.P. 1877, 89:177.

21. Goldsmid to Hammond, 4 July 1867, P.P. 1877, 89:181—2.

22. St Clair to Green, 28 June 1867, P.P. 1867, 74:535.

23. Sir Moses Montefiore to the Jewish community of Jassy, 31 May 1867. P.P. 1877, 89:168.

24. *Jewish Chronicle,* 28 June 1867. Sir Moses' nephew, Mr J. M. Montefiore, referred to as 'President pro tem', was in the chair.
25. Telegram from Galatz sent via Orsova to Sir Moses Montefiore and communicated by J. M. Montefiore to Edmund Hammond at the Foreign Office on 19 July 1867. P.P. 1877, 89:184.
26. Iancu, *Les Juifs en Roumanie,* p. 74.
27. *Jewish Chronicle,* 25 July 1867.
28. Montefiore to Stanley, 19 July, P.P. 1877, 89:183—4.
29. *Diaries* ii, 197; *Jewish Chronicle,* 4 Oct. 1867.
30. Ward (British consul at Galatz) to Green, 9 Aug. 1867, forwarded by Green to Stanley, 10 Aug. P.P. 1877, 89:297.
31. P.P. 1877, 89:197—9.
32. Iancu, *Les Juifs en Roumanie,* p. 76.
33. Ward to Green, 9 Aug. 1867; Green to Stanley, 10 Aug. 1867, P.P. 1877, 89:202.
34. *Diaries,* ii, 197.
35. Ibid., ii, 198.
36. Ibid., ii, 205—6.
37. Green to Stanley, 24 Aug. 1867. P.P. 1877, 89:208.
38. *Diaries,* ii, 205.
39. Ibid., ii, 206.
40. Ibid., ii, 207.
41. Ibid., ii, 207.
42. Ibid., ii, 209.
43. Ibid., ii, 210.
44. Ibid., ii, 210.
45. Montefiore to Stanley, 20 Sept. 1867, P.P. 1877, 89:215.
46. *Jewish Chronicle,* 4 Oct. 1867.
47. Ibid., 4 Oct. 1867.
48. Ibid., 27 Sept. 1867.
49. Ibid., 12 July 1867.
50. Ibid., 4 Oct. 1867.
51. *The Times,* 5 Oct. 1867.
52. Goldsmid to Egerton, 1 Nov. 1867. Enclosure of 18 Oct. P.P. 1877, 89: 219—20.
53. Ward to Green, 9 Dec. 1867, forwarded by Green to Stanley 14 Dec. P.P. 1877, 89:221.
54. Isaac Tauber, chief rabbi of Berlad to Sir Moses Montefiore, 7 Jan. 1868, forwarded by Montefiore in a letter to Hammond at the Foreign Office on 29 Jan.; P.P. 1877, 89:223—4.
55. Stephan Golescu to Sir Moses Montefiore, 7 Feb. 1868, P.P. 1877, 89: 235—6.
56. *The Times,* 29 Feb. 1868.
57. Green to Stanley, 10 March 1868.; P.P. 1877, 89:238. Loewe omitted the offending sentence from Golescu's letter when he reprinted it in the *Diaries.*
58. Montefiore to Hammond, 10 April 1868; P.P. 1877, 89:244. Edmund Hammond was Montefiore's chief link with the Foreign Office in the Romanian question. Eton, Harrow and Oxford educated, he was permanent under secretary at the Foreign Office from 1854—73; created a baron in 1874 and died in 1890. According to Boase, *Modern English Biography,* vol. i, he was chiefly distinguished for assuring Lord Granville on 27 June

1870 that the world was profoundly at peace. The Franco-Prussian war broke out on 15 July. In the light of his courteous correspondence with Montefiore this comment seems at the least an over-simplification of Hammond's abilities.

59. Green to Lord Clarendon, 13 May 1869; P.P. 1877, 89:299.

60. Green to Stanley, 10 April 1868; Enclosure. P.P. 1877, 89:253.

61. Iancu, *Les Juifs en Roumanie*, p. 82. Carol compensated the Bucharest Jews out of his own pocket for the loss of their synagogue in the 1866 riots. But he was said by his biographer to consider the Jews 'undesirable aliens who by their superior industry and their inferior morals were exploiting his people'. Fritz Stern, *Gold and Iron: Bismarck, Bleichröder and the Building of the German Empire*. (Alfred A. Knopf, New York, 1977), p. 357. Stern was quoting from the four-volume *Aus dem Leben König Karls von Rumanien. Aufzeichnungen eines Augenzeugen.* (Stuttgart, 1894—1900), 1:257. The author of this work, who himself took the official Romanian view that the Jews were a social and economic menace, attributed the same sentiments to Prince Carol.

62. Stern, *Gold and Iron*, pp. 355, 369.

63. S. Posener, *Adolphe Crémieux, (1796—1880)*, (Paris, Librairie Felix Alcan, 1933) ii, 140—4.

64. Stern, *Gold and Iron*, pp. 351—93. Stern describes how Bismarck manipulated Bleichröder into trading finance for the building of the Romanian railways in return for a blind eye on Romania's failure to fulfil the pledges of Jewish emancipation in the Treaty of Berlin.

65. Rike, *The Making of Roumania, passim*.

66. Stern, *Gold and Iron*, p. 357.

67. I am indebted for this information to Dr V. D. Lipman.

5

The Visits to Russia

CHIMEN ABRAMSKY

To understand fully the reasons for the decision of Sir Moses Montefiore, at the age of sixty-two, to make the arduous journey to Russia to intercede with the Tsar Nicholas I on behalf of the Jews there, it is necessary first to summarize the principal policies of Nicholas I towards the Jews.

From the start of his reign in 1826, the Tsar was convinced that the Jews were barbaric enemies of Christianity and aliens in Russia. As Russia could not get rid of them it was important to drag the Jews out of medieval darkness, which was first and foremost due to their adherence to the Talmud and Rabbinic Judaism, and to try by all means, foul and persuasive, to convert as many of them to Christianity as possible. At the same time, for those determined to remain Jews — the majority — life had to be made as harsh as possible.

During his reign there was a vast amount of legislation concerning Jews. First came the obligatory acquisition of surnames, which was modelled on the policies of Prussia and Austria. Then in 1827 he ordered the recruitment of Jews to the army. Each district of the Pale of Settlement, excluding the Kingdom of Poland, had to supply a number of recruits, who would have to serve twenty-five years. As Jews did not have experience of army service, children of twelve to eighteen would have to undergo six additional years of preliminary training to become proper soldiers. The recruitment was left to the Jews themselves and it became known as the Cantonist system, based on the Swiss Cantonal system of recruitment.

The majority of these juvenile recruits were the children of the poor, who were kidnapped from their homes by Jews, known by the Yiddish word *Khappers* (kidnappers). This led to a sharp polarization in the Jewish community between the poor and the better-off.

No open opposition could manifest itself for fear of more severe repression from the Tsarist Government. This method of recruitment lasted throughout the reign of Nicholas I, until his son, Alexander II, ascended the throne in 1856 and abolished it. The majority of the children thus recruited either converted or perished, while a minority who survived adhered heroically to the Jewish religion.[1]

From 1840, the Tsar was determined to abolish the communal organization, the *Kahal,* which was responsible to the Government for taxation, and the management of all community affairs — the appointment of clergy, the provision of Jewish education, and other aspects of Jewish life in a closed society.

The problem of secular education in Government-run schools for Jewish children became a central concern for the Tsar and his Minister of Education, Count Sergei Uvarov. It aroused conflicting views among Jews. The orthodox were opposed to secular education replacing traditional Jewish religious education. The *Maskilim* (those under the influence of European Enlightenment) were enthusiastic for the plans of Uvarov. The former suspected also conversionist aims in the Tsar's approach to secular State schools. The Tsar and Uvarov denied this, while the *Maskilim* closed their eyes to the danger.[2]

As a corollary of all these policies minor decrees ordered that orthodox Jews, particularly the Hasidim, should change their traditional garb and wear European clothes. In 1844 the *Kahal* was abolished and Jews were taxed as individuals. This briefly is the background to Moses Montefiore's first visit to Russia in 1846.

Russia and Poland, unlike Germany, France and England, lacked a Jewish periodical press up to 1860, but Montefiore had become famous throughout the Jewish world as a result of his intervention in the Damascus Blood Libel of 1840. A number of Hebrew and Yiddish books were immediately published glorifying the part played by him in rescuing the Damascus Jews, so that his role was far more strongly emphasized than that of Adolphe Crémieux.

Of the publications issued, the most important was by the Vilna writer Mordecai Aron Ginsburg,[3] the leading *Maskil* of Lithuania, who also, in 1843, translated and published the diary kept in German by Dr Loewe on his visit with the Montefiores to Safed in 1838.[4] The Damascus affair thus made Montefiore the great hero of the Jewish people and the most prominent Jew in the world, to whom Jews in trouble could turn for help, and he retained this pre-eminence until his death in 1885.

In December 1840, the Tsar appointed a Committee under the chairmanship of Count P. D. Kiselev to plan measures to reorganize radically the lives of the Jews of Russia, with State secular education as the programme's main plank. For this purpose, Count Uvarov, the Minister of Education, whose ambition was to foster 'orthodoxy, autocracy and (Russian) nationality', devised a plan for enforcing secular State education on Jews and abolishing the traditional religious schools (like *Hadarim* and *Talmud Torahs*).

Uvarov appointed a young German Reform Jew, Max Lilienthal, to be the principal co-ordinator of the scheme. Lilienthal was entrusted with visiting the most important Jewish centres to convince their leaders of the benevolence of the Tsar, so that the Jews should agree to his educational plans.

Lilienthal met opposition from many orthodox Jews, while receiving enthusiastic support from the minority of *Maskilim*. The Government then decided to convene a conference in St Petersburg with the famous Rabbis, including Yitzhak, the son of Chaim, the Head of the Yeshiva of Volozhin, and Menahem Mendel Schneurson, the leader of the Hasidim in White Russia, together with Bezalel Stern, the Galician leader of the *Maskilim* in Odessa, and Israel Heilpern, the banker from Berdichev; and thereby impose its views on the reluctant Jews.[5]

How Montefiore came to be invited to Russia is not entirely clear, nor whether the idea came from the Russian-Polish Jews themselves, from German Jews, or from Lilienthal. The evidence is confused.[6] He certainly did not accept Lilienthal's invitation and resolved to choose his own time. This he did at the beginning of 1846, inviting Dr Loewe to accompany him. He began his preparations in December 1842, after he had a long discussion with Baron Brunnow, the Russian Ambassador to the Court of St James's.[7] The Ambassador advised him to 'proceed in the first instance to St Petersburg and speak with the Emperor himself, and not to go as I had intended to the several cities in Poland previously to my going to St Petersburg'.

The meaning of Brunnow's advice was clear. The Tsar did not wish Montefiore to be influenced by Jewish representatives in the Pale and in many ways wanted to curb his travels in White Russia, Lithuania and Poland.

Simultaneously with trying to encourage the Jews to accept Uvarov's education scheme, the Tsar ordered at the end of 1843 the deportation of Jews from the border areas with Prussia, which would have ruined 100,000 Jews who earned their livings as innkeepers, distillers, or craftsmen operating in the rural economy as locksmiths, blacksmiths, carpenters and glaziers. A minority were engaged in smuggling goods across the long border. Brunnow ignored the fact that the vast majority of Jews were hard working and blamed the decree on the few Jewish smugglers, explaining to Montefiore:

He [Brunnow] believed the Minister of Justice thought it was an act of mercy to remove the Jews from the temptation of smuggling of which crime many had been guilty, and no doubt the Emperor was of that opinion, which was the cause of the order.[8]

Already from London, before proceeding to Russia, Montefiore had pleaded with the Ambassador to influence the Tsar to cancel the Ukase. In this he did not succeed, but he did obtain a promise of trying to postpone its execution for a few years. In June 1844 the Tsar arrived in London for a short visit. Montefiore worked hard to obtain an audience with him and attempted to enlist the aid of Lord Aberdeen and the Prime Minister, Sir Robert Peel, but the Tsar did not find the time to see him. However, he did postpone carrying out the decree of expulsion from the rural areas.

Montefiore continued to have discussions with Brunnow about his proposed journey to Russia, and the Ambassador advised him to go in his personal capacity rather than as the representative of the Board of Deputies, though he expressed serious doubts about the purpose of the journey itself.[9]

The reason is clear: to avoid public criticism of the Tsar's policies towards the Jews, and the Tsar's objections to interference in the internal affairs of Russia. Lord Aberdeen had already hinted at this when he told Montefiore in 1841: 'All the European Powers were extremely jealous of any interference on the part of England.[10]

At last, on 10 March 1846, Montefiore and his entourage set off for Russia. The roads in Russia were appalling by Western standards, railways did not yet exist, and Montefiore was sixty-two years of age. In March the ice begins to melt, the roads are frequently impassable and rivers difficult to cross because of the thinness of the ice. Within ten days he reached the small Jewish community of Mitava (present day Soviet Latvia) and told the local Jewish leaders that 'he wished to travel as privately as possible'. He made the same request to the Jews in Riga.[11]

After a most arduous and hazardous journey the group reached St Petersburg on 2 April. The Foreign Minister, the veteran diplomat, Count Nesselrode, received him on 5 April, and Montefiore told him that the chief purpose of his visit was to influence the Tsar to repeal the decrees for the expulsion of the Jews from the rural areas, to have discussions on the establishment of Jewish schools, and to attempt to settle a number of Jews on the land.

Nesselrode repeated the Tsar's arguments that his aim was 'to raise the Jews and make them more useful members of society', that the Russian Jews were on a far lower level than Western Jews who were 'the cream of the Jews' and that Russian and Polish Jews 'were engaged in low traffic and contraband pursuits'. Montefiore was not aware that these views were not Nesselrode's alone, but those of the Tsar. This showed a certain naïvety on his part.[12]

Next day he and Dr Loewe were received by Count Uvarov, the powerful and influential Minister of Education. Uvarov was of the opinion that all Western Jews were like the Reform Jew Lilienthal and would be amenable to the view of the Tsar that Russian Jews were barbarians and ignoramuses. Uvarov delivered the following diatribe:

The Jews of Russia were different from Jews in any other part of the world: they were orthodox and believed in the Talmud, which he considered false. They were ignorant of their own religion and he was obliged to force them to study Hebrew their own language.

It would appear that Uvarov's attack on the Talmud was expected, and Loewe had prepared a long apologetic reply, quoting at length what Christian scholars, such as Reuchlin, Muenster, Selden, Buxtorf and others had written favourably about the importance of the Talmud.[13] They also contended that Jews knew Hebrew very well and had written and were writing important books in that language.

Three days later the Tsar himself received Montefiore in a private audience, and the latter presented him with an address imploring the Tsar 'to give your most humane consideration to the conditions of my co-religionists under Your Majesty's sway', and 'to alleviate to the utmost extent which Your Majesty's justice and wisdom may think fit, all such laws and edicts as may be proved to press heavily on the Israelites'. To which the Tsar replied that he should be assured that he and his Ministers 'were most desirous for the improvement of their situation in every way possible'. The interview lasted twenty minutes.

Their stay in St Petersburg concluded with a long session with Count Kiselev, the Chairman of the special Commission which was examining the situation of the Jews in Russia. Kiselev was brutally frank with Montefiore. If five or six hundred thousand Jews wished to leave Russia 'he [Kiselev] did not wish to keep them'. He added sarcastically: 'Sir Moses might, if he liked, take ten thousand or more to Palestine or elsewhere'. If the Jews failed to master a trade they would be punished as vagrants.[14]

The meeting with Kiselev should have cleared Montefiore of any hopeful illusions he entertained of improving the lot of Russian Jews. The remarks about a large number of Jews having to emigrate were uttered thirty-five years before the wave of pogroms of 1881, and the mass immigration to the West. But Montefiore and the Jews themselves continued to pin their hopes on the benevolence of the Tsar. It seems that apart from attending prayers at the small Soldiers' Synagogue, Montefiore did not meet local Jews in St Petersburg except for four who came specially from Vilna to pay their respects to him. It is not clear from his diaries where Montefiore and his party celebrated Passover. They made preparations for their journey to Vilna — the Jerusalem of Lithuania, the principal centre of both *Haskalah* and learning in the Pale of Settlement.

Montefiore received the necessary travel documents, letters of recommendation to the Governor and other high officials, and on 21 April they set out on the road to Lithuania, travelling via Rejitsa and Dvinsk (present day Daugavpils in Soviet Latvia). On 29 April they arrived to a tumultuous welcome in Vilna, with a special Committee of leading Jews in the town to receive them. What Montefiore and his group were not aware of was that they were under constant surveillance by the Secret Police, who listened to all their conversations and watched their every movement.[15]

Their stay in Vilna has been described in great detail by a number of Hebrew writers of the time.[16]

Montefiore had a series of meetings with the leaders of the Jewish community of Vilna, both spiritual and lay, who acquainted him with the real situation of the Jews in Russia, and who replied in a very frank and courageous manner in a memorandum written in Hebrew to all the arguments of the Tsar, Uvarov and Kiselev against the Jews.[17]

The English guests spent eleven days in Vilna and were extremely busy from early morning till late at night. The scholar, Zvi Hirsch Katzenellenbogen, described in letters how Montefiore arranged a private daily *Minyan* (a quorum for prayers) in his hotel, in which Katzenellenbogen participated regularly. On Saturday, Dr Loewe delivered a sermon in the Great Synagogue. During the week the guests went to pay homage at the tomb of Elijah, the Gaon of Vilna, where they offered prayers.[18]

Montefiore gave charity to the value of five thousand gold roubles — a vast sum for those days. The writer enumerated in detail the different amounts he gave, to synagogues and Talmud Torahs, as well as to well-known Hebrew writers of the time: thus, for example, to Mordecai Aron Ginsburg, five half-imperials; to Shmuel Yosef Finn, five half-imperials; to the brother of the writer of this letter four half-imperials; to the poet S. Salkind(son) three half-imperials, and so on. The charities Montefiore distributed were the largest ever given by a single individual at one time.[19]

The memorandum submitted to Montefiore by the leaders of the Jewish community of Vilna was divided into six short chapters:
1. the character of the inhabitants of Vilna
2. the situation of the city at that time

3. hunger and death in the city
4. the hospital in the city
5. craftsmen in the city, and finally
6. the requirements of the city.

According to the document, the number of Jews in Vilna was approximately 40,000. The majority knew Russian and Polish, and among them were famous scholars and writers. In the past, Vilna Jews had been prosperous, but now the harshness of the Government's policies had caused deep impoverishment. This was due mainly to the form of recruitment to the army, the destruction of their livelihood: 'the children taken to the army, the majority of whom were forced to convert and leave their parents in a permanent state of mourning. We are treated as slaves, harsh decrees follow one another.'

Jews were driven out of Christian streets and forbidden to live in many parts of the city. Jews were forbidden to own distilleries — in the past thousands had earned their living from them.

The Karaites had succeeded, with the help of the Government, in expelling the Jews from Troki (a town near Vilna mostly inhabited by Karaites). Because of the removal of Jews from many quarters of Vilna, hunger had increased and mortality had risen considerably. Many people were homeless. The Jewish hospital had been taken over by Christians, and there was sharp discrimination against Jews who were sick.

The Government accused the Jews of being idlers and parasites. 'We have many craftsmen among us': masons, silversmiths, painters, bakers, musicians, coopers, tinkers, fur capmakers, tailors, carvers, cobblers, glaziers, braziers, candleholder makers, locksmiths, chimney sweeps, suede makers, watch makers, polishers, nurses, cotton wool makers, apothecaries, teachers, scribes, brush makers, blacksmiths, midwives, weavers, printers, engravers, candle makers, dyers and students (the memorandum is in Hebrew; the list is in Yiddish).

A few had even acquired land to till. Some were porters, carters, water-drawers, and there were no criminals among them. Not one Jews was in prison for burglary or other crimes.

The memorandum proudly declared that 'we have in Vilna some of the foremost Talmudic scholars of the country and very famous writers'.

The memorandum pleaded with Montefiore not to abandon the Jews 'in the land which is so hostile to us and to demand their rights'.[20]

From Vilna, Montefiore journeyed to Warsaw, but on the way stopped for a day in Kovno, meeting many Jews who told him facts similar to those that he had heard in Vilna.

In Warsaw he received a number of Jewish delegations, including one from Cracow (which at the time belonged to Austria). 'The accounts which Sir Moses continued to receive from the Jews of their position in this country, were most distressing,' wrote Loewe in the *Diaries*. [21]

Among the delegations Montefiore received in Warsaw was one of Hasidim (spelt peculiarly *Khaseedim*): 'they were headed by Mr Posener, a gentleman who had done much for the promotion of industry in Poland'. He informed Montefiore that he would carry out the Government decree of wearing European clothes instead of the traditional Hasidic garb. 'His example would have a most favourable effect upon others.' [22]

After Montefiore had learned of the economic position of the Jews in Warsaw and the surrounding cities, he and his group returned to London, and prayers were recited in gratitude for his journey. [23]

In November 1846, Montefiore sent two long memoranda on the Jews in Russia and Poland to Count Kiselev, and a short memorandum to Uvarov. [24]

Montefiore answered systematically every accusation levelled against the Jews by the Tsar, Kiselev and Uvarov, presenting a remarkable defence of the Jews. The memoranda were obviously based on the material gathered by Montefiore and Loewe during their travels. They dealt with the economic restrictions on residence, on occupations, on the difficulties of mobility outside the Pale of Settlement, and the so-called Jewish idleness, stressing the willingness of many Jews to do even the most menial jobs for less pay than the regular rates just to be able to earn a living, the desire of the Jews to work on the land and the denial of land to them.

Montefiore once again rejected the accusations against the Talmud, and refuted the Tsar's arguments that the Jews were taught by the Talmud to cheat the Gentiles, quoting extensively from Joseph Karo's *Shulchan Aruch* and Maimonides' Code (this part was obviously written by Loewe). He pointed out the large number of craftsmen among the Jews (based on the Vilna memorandum).

Kiselev and Uvarov politely acknowledged receipt of these documents and promised to present them to the Tsar and the special Committee on the Jews, and assured Montefiore that the Tsar 'has been pleased to express once more the interest he takes in his Israelite subjects, whose welfare and moral advancement will not cease to be the object of his constant solicitude'.

With this the matter rested. The persecutions continued till Nicholas I died at the end of 1855. After the death of the Tsar, Baron Guenzburg reported to Montefiore 'that the Emperor had issued a Ukase permitting Jewish youths to attend the public colleges, and to absolve themselves from school on Sabbaths and Festivals'.[25]

Montefiore again became preoccupied with the Jews in Palestine and in the East, and Russia disappeared from his horizon. In 1872 Russia celebrated the bicentenary of Peter the Great. Major celebrations were arranged in St Petersburg and Montefiore was honoured by Alexander II, who invited him to come and participate. The old man of eighty-eight undertook the journey, and was granted a long audience with the Tsar, who treated him with the utmost courtesy. Politically it was of little consequence to the Jews, though by comparison with Nicholas I, Alexander II did improve their economic position.

In 1879 there was a blood libel in the Caucasian town of Kutais, where a number of Jews were accused of killing a Christian child for ritual purposes. By that time Montefiore was in his ninety-fifth year, yet he dispatched a telegram stating 'that he was ready to start for the Russian capital to plead the cause of the accused before the Emperor'. One cannot but admire the courage and the steadfastness of a man of such an advanced age. Fortunately the accused were freed before he ventured on his journey. Montefiore received a warm letter of thanks from the famous advocate, L. Kupernick, who, though converted to Christianity, remained a fervent defender of the Jews.[26]

Montefiore lived until after the assassination of Alexander II, the wave of pogroms which followed, and the first stream of mass immigration to the West and America, as well as the launching of the Jewish National Movement, the Hovevei Zion (Lovers of Zion). At the age of ninety—seven he was still willing to go to plead the cause of the Jews, but he was dissuaded from considering such an enterprise by Arthur Cohen, the President of the Board of Deputies at the time.

Lord Granville, the Foreign Secretary, advised caution. He told a delegation of the Board of Deputies 'that it must be remembered that all nations are jealous of interference in their national concerns and this is especially so with regard to the Great Powers of Europe'.

He told them further 'that I do not agree with those who have said that a strong representation from a foreign Government would strengthen the hands of the Russian Government ... if any representations are made, they should not be official representations, and moreover they should not be public'.[27] These sentiments fitted perfectly with the style advocated by Montefiore throughout his long life. Both Montefiore and Granville outlived their age. They belonged to the past. Montefiore was the last great 'medieval'

Shtadlan. New winds were blowing, bringing with them very powerful social forces and movements. Different responses would be
needed to the new problems and challenges that were facing the Jews
in Europe.[28]

Although Montefiore had outlived his age, the Hovevei Zion, at their
first conference in Katowice, honoured him by printing thousands of
copies of his portrait to sell to the many supporters of the movement,
to raise funds to help the first Jewish colonies in *Eretz Israel.* The
undertaking could be considered as naïve by modern ideas, but it
did express the profound feelings felt for Montefiore by the mass of
Jews in Eastern Europe.[29]

A German historian, writing of the time of Nicholas I in Russia,
summed up the feelings of the Russian Jews towards Montefiore:
'As to the poor Jews themselves they look upon him as, and actually
call him, the Messiah.'[30]

NOTES

1. On the Cantonist system and Nicholas' policies towards the Jews, see Salo
    W Baron, *The Russian Jews* (New York, 1974); S. M. Dubnow, *History of
    the Jews in Russia and Poland,* Vol. ii (New York, 1969); Louis Greenberg,
    The Jews in Russia — the Struggle for Emancipation, Vol. i (New York,
    1945), pp. 30—55; Saul Ginsburg, *Historishe Werk,* Vol. ii (New York,
    1937), pp. 3—22, iii, pp. 1—138; Isaac Levitats, *The Jewish Community
    in Russia 1772—1844* (New York, 1943); Michael Stanislawski, *Czar
    Nicholas I and the Jews* (Philadelphia, Jewish Publication Society of
    America, 1983), reference to Montefiore, pp. 78—9. E. Tcherikower,
    'He'Hamon Ha'yehudi, Hamaskilim Ve'Hamemshalah b'eyemei Nicholas I',
    Zion, Vol. iv, No. 2, pp. 150—169 (Jerusalem, 1939).
    The classic work on the period of Nicholas I is the Russian book by
    Julius Hessen, *Istoria Evreiskajo Naroda v Rossii,* two volumes (Leningrad,
    1925—27).
2. See David Philipson, *Max Lilienthal, American Rabbi, His Life and Writings*
    (New York, 1915), pp. 12—45, 133—158, 159—363; Michael Stanislawski,
    quotes the latest research on him.
3. 'Hamat Damesek', written in 1840. The Russian censorship forbade its
    publication. It circulated widely in manuscript. It was first published in
    Koenigsberg in 1860, fourteen years after the death of the author.
4. Mordecai Aron Ginsburg *Dvir* Part I (Vilna, 1844), pp. 1—48 (the censor-
    ship permit is signed, 21 December 1843). Originally the Diary was pub-
    lished in German in *Orient* (1839), see Joseph Klausner, *Historia shel
    HaSifrut Ha'Ivrit He'Hadasha,* iii (Jerusalem, 1953), p. 138.
5. See Ginsburg, pp. 32—6; Philipson, pp. 20—45; Baron, pp. 41—6;
    Stanislawski, pp. 75—82.
6. See *Diaries of Sir Moses and Lady Montefiore,* Vol. i, p. 311, dated 17
    October 1842: 'A petition was received from the Hebrew congregation

in Riga imploring Sir Moses to intercede on their behalf with the Emperor
of Russia'. Many others, from various places, on the same subject, followed. This in turn is followed by the entreaties of many communities in
Germany, France, Italy and America (!) asking him 'to accede to the
petitions of their brethren in Russia'. Montefiore was 'roused by that
sorrowful event . . . to render some service to the Jews in Russia' (that is,
the death of Chief Rabbi Solomon Hirschell), and in consequence obtained information from German and English travellers who had just
returned from visiting Warsaw and other important cities in the Tsar's
vast Empire'. On 12 November 1843, he recorded: 'and to some letters he
received from several trustworthy sources, giving disheartening accounts
of the state of the Jews in Russia' (p. 319). Then on 16 November 1844 he
wrote, 'A special delegate arrived from Poland to entreat Sir Moses in the
name of many thousands of his brethren to intercede on their behalf with
the Russian Government' (p. 324).

The reference above to Riga becomes clear from a letter written by
Montefiore on 22 September 1842, in reply to Max Lilienthal, in which he
acknowledged receipt of his letter of 30 July, inviting him in the name of
Count Uvarov to come to St Petersburg to participate in the proposed
conference dealing with the education of the Jews. Montefiore wished him
success in his work, but was cautious and avoided committing himself on
whether he would accept the invitation. (See Julius Hessen 'Letter from
Moses Montefiore to Max Lilienthal' in *Perezhitoye*, i (St Petersburg,
1908), pp. 27—8, in Appendix, Document section. The original is lost, but
the Ministry of Education preserved a Russian translation which Hessen
published. A garbled summary is given by Philipson, pp. 36—7; and
Greenberg i, p. 37. Cf. Montefiore *Diaries*, i, p. 312, entry dated 8 December 1842.

7.   *Diaries*, i, p. 312. Brunnow was Ambassador in London for well over
     thirty years. It seems that already in 1842 the communities of Vilna and
     Odessa asked him to participate in the 'Jewish Commission' that the Tsar
     was going to set up, and that his presence might favourably influence the
     members of the Commission towards the Jews. The petition was signed on
     behalf of the Vilna Jews by the writer and scholar, Shmuel Yosef Finn,
     and by Elijah Mordecai Werbel in Odessa (see Efraim Moshe Pinner *Mazevot
     Kivrot Ha'rabanim Ve'anshe Hashem* (Berlin, 1861), pp. 59—62, without
     giving exact dates; also Ginsburg, *Historishe Werk*, ii, p. 171, footnote.)
8.   *Diaries*, i, pp. 316—7.
9.   Ibid., p. 324.
10. Ibid., p. 304.
11. Ibid., pp. 326—7.
12. Ibid., pp. 330—1.
13. Ibid., pp. 331—2.
14. Ibid., pp. 332—5.
15. See S. Ginsburg, 'Moshe Montefiore in Russland', *Historishe Werk*, ii,
     pp. 177—80, and footnote on p. 177.
16. For a rhetorical description, see Mordecai Aron Ginsburg, *Dvir*, ii (Vilna,
     1862); Isaac Meir Dick, *'Ha'oreach'* (Koenigsberg, 1860). Both were
     written in 1846, but were not allowed to be published till much later,
     after the death of Nicholas I. A poetic description was written by David
     Mitzkun, *Kinor David* (Vilna, 1863). A very prosaic account was given
     in private letters by the well-known Vilna *Maskil* and scholar, Zvi Hirsch

Katzenellenbogen to his son-in-law, Yakov Katznelson, and written while Montefiore was still in Vilna. They were published by Saul Ginsburg in his *Historishe Werk*, Vol. ii (New York, 1937), pp. 98—106.

17. The full text of this remarkable document is in Saul Ginsburg, appendix 3, pp. 293—8.
18. Elijah Gaon of Vilna (1720—97), the foremost Talmudic and Rabbinic authority of the eighteenth century in Europe.
19. Ginsburg, pp. 100—5. Mordecai Aron Ginsburg (1795—1846) was the leading Hebrew writer of the early *Haskalah* in Lithuania. He wrote many books, among them a remarkable autobiography, *Aviezer* (Vilna, 1864); Shmuel Yosef Finn (1818—69), prolific author, who wrote an important Talmudic dictionary, *Ha-Otzar*, in 4 volumes; S. Salkind (son) (d. 1868), Hebrew poet, father of the famous missionary, Isaac Edward Salkinson, who translated the New Testament, some plays of Shakespeare and Milton's 'Paradise Lost' into Hebrew; Zvi Hirsch Katznellenbogen (1797—1868), scholar, author of *Netivot Olam* (on Methodology in the Talmud).
20. Ginsburg, pp. 293—8. This is a brief summary of the main points. It is remarkable for its courage in denouncing the bitterness of the oppression the Jews were suffering, and the exceptional details it provides of the economic situation of the leading Jewish community in Lithuania.
21. *Diaries*, i, pp. 349—50.
22. Ibid., pp. 354—5; on Shlomo Zalman Posener and Montefiore, see also Jacob Shatsky, *The History of the Jews in Warsaw* (New York, 1948), Vol. ii (Yiddish), pp. 86—9.
23. Ginsburg, appendix 5, pp. 301—3. A list of special prayers relating to Montefiore's journey to Russia in the Jewish Theological Seminary, New York, numbers eleven special publications.
24. *Diaries*, i, pp. 360—73; 374—9; 380—4. They were published for the first time in the *Diaries* in 1890.
25. *Diaries*, ii, p. 101, entry dated 20 May 1859.
26. *Diaries*, ii, pp. 291—2. On the Kutais blood libel, see Greenberg, i, p. 179. On Kupernick, see Saul Ginsburg, *Meshumodim in Tsarishn Russland* (New York, 1946), pp. 264—78.
27. *Diaries*, ii, pp. 298—9.
28. See on the whole period the excellent books by Jonathan Frankel, *Prophecy and Politics* (Cambridge 1981), and David Vital, *The Origins of Zionism* (Oxford, 1975).
29. *Diaries* ii, pp. 325—6; Vital, pp. 163—4.
30. See Theodor Schemann, *Geschichte Russlands unter Kaiser Nikolaus I* (Berlin, 1908—19), Vol. iv, p. 79, quoted in Salo W. Baron, *The Russian Jew under Tsars and Soviets*, p. 358, note 14. Warm sentiments were expressed many years later by Bertrand Russell in his *Autobiography*, i, p. 29.

PART III

The Holy Land

1

The Saga of 1855: A Study in Depth

A. SCHISCHA

I

The beginning of the year 5614 (late autumn and winter 1853—4) did not augur well for the inhabitants of the Holy Land. A severe outbreak of smallpox caused great anxiety but passed leaving the community unscathed. Sir Moses Montefiore's doctor[1] was reported to have vaccinated two hundred children and the epidemic claimed no Jewish victims.[2] The rainy season started very early, normally a welcome occurrence, but not so that year. Violent storms, accompanied by torrential downpours, wrought havoc in the fields causing 'total failure of the . . . harvest'.[3]

The first reports of '. . . the appalling misery of our starving brethren in Zion . . .' reached Sir Moses Montefiore by letter from Jerusalem dated Shevat 5614 (January—February 1854) and were followed by others from Safed, Tiberias and Hebron in Adar (February—March).[4]

Further misfortune befell the Yishuv (Jews of the Holy Land) when in October 1853 the Crimean War broke out between Turkey and Russia.[5] Jews of Eastern European origin — and they formed by far the largest group of the Ashkenazim (Central and East European Jews) in the Holy Land — were cut off from their main source of income. The charities that funded the *halukah*, on which they depended, dried up within weeks as the Russians prohibited all transfers of money to the Holy Land which, as part of the Turkish Empire, was enemy territory.

The situation in Palestine grew more and more desperate. James Finn, the British Consul in Jerusalem, reported in a dispatch: 'The price of all provisions is risen to unprecedented height, and great destitution in consequence. This is mostly felt in the Jewish quarters for the alarming diminution of their supplies from Russia . . .'.[6] Finn elaborated in *Stirring Times*: 'From all these causes[7] there was a universal amount of poverty and distress among the poorer Christians and Moslems, and very severe distress among the Jews who always suffer more than others in time of trouble and who were on this occasion deprived by reason of the war of a considerable portion of the charitable funds contributed by the Jews of the countries of their support.'[8]

The Sephardi community also had to bear the brunt of the war. Turkish Jewry could not be depended upon for the generous help they had provided for generations.[9] Jews in Turkey were called up to fight, business was drastically curtailed, and tax burdens cut their capacity to help. The poor of the 'Four Cities' were the first to feel the consequences. The *tzedakah* (charity) that arrived was not enough to meet even minimum requirements.

In desperation, the Sephardi Chief Rabbi of Jerusalem (*Rishon leZion*), Haham Itzhac Covo,[10] was asked to undertake a mission to Europe. Although eighty-five and in precarious health, he set out for England to plead for help. At Alexandria he was taken ill and died.

Sir Moses Montefiore was always ready to help Jewry wherever help was needed, and particularly when the call came from the Holy Land. He had learned of the worsening situation in January and February 1854, and later of the consequences of the war. However, he was prevented then from giving assistance. In February he was in Scarborough where he was struck down by serious illness, which kept him in bed for forty-seven days. He returned to London, still unwell and very weak, at the end of March.[11]

None the less, it was reported at the end of April that Sir Moses was planning a journey to Constantinople early in May, 'No doubt for the benefit of the Jews of the East'.[12] Preparations for the immediate 'amelioration' of the plight of 'our brethren in the Holy Land' were set in motion. Sir Moses had the full co-operation of the Chief Rabbi, Dr N. M. Adler, and presented a carefully prepared plan to him in a letter from Ramsgate dated 15 May 1854.[13]

In that letter Sir Moses suggested an urgent 'appeal' to the public for immediate help. He asked Dr Adler to enrol the support of his ministers by issuing a 'Pastoral Letter' in conjunction with the appeal. The religious and national press was to be asked to give wide publicity to the contents of both. Dr Adler answered in the affirmative on 18 May[14] and enclosed the proposed text of the 'Pastoral Letter'. This correspondence, the pastoral letter and the appeal, together with copies of some of the heart-rending letters Sir Moses had received from the Holy Land, were then printed as a special supplement to the *Jewish Chronicle* of 19 May; and reprinted as a booklet which was widely distributed.[15]

Sir Moses and Lady Montefiore were the first to contribute, giving £500. The *Jewish Chronicle* in the following months published long lists of contributors to the fund and their contributions: in a comparatively short time £19,887 was raised.[16]

The primary reason for the appeal was to provide immediate help in the acute famine, which raised prices catastrophically.[17] But it had been made clear that the fund was also to serve to remedy basic defects in the existing system of distributing charity in the Holy Land, by providing alternative means of earning a livelihood, which would have beneficial effects in the long term: as Dr Adler declared, '. . . by providing conditions that part of the Jewish population should earn its living by work'.[18]

Almost simultaneously with the news of the famine, there was an unexpected development which was to play an important part in the decisions subsequently taken by Sir Moses and Dr Adler. Judah Touro,[19] a native of Newport, R.I., and one of the richest and most respected citizens of New Orleans, died there on 18 January 1854. Hardly known outside his home town and his circle of personal friends, his attachment to Judaism, in spite of his orthodox background, was tenuous. Through the influence of Gershom Kursheedt,[20] another native of Newport, who also had made his home in New Orleans, Touro was persuaded to take a more positive attitude to Judaism. He contributed generously to Jewish charities and in the last years of his life was reputed to have observed the Sabbath and the dietary laws. He died a bachelor, at the age of seventy-eight. To those who knew him it was no surprise that he left almost the whole of his vast fortune to be distributed among a variety of charitable institutions.[21] Among the bequests were two very substantial sums to be used for the benefit of the indigent Jews of the Holy Land. Paragraph 24 of the will[22] stated: 'I give and bequeath to the North American Relief Society for Indigent Jews in Jerusalem, Palestine[23] (Sir Moses Montefiore their agent) Ten Thousand Dollars.' In paragraph 28, the testator gave clear instructions as to the purpose of the second bequest and who should be the final arbiter of his wishes:

It being my earnest wish to co-operate with said Sir Moses Montefiore of London, Great Britain, in endeavouring to ameliorate the conditions of our unfortunate Jewish brethren in the Holy Land and to secure to them the inestimable privilege of worshipping the Almighty according to our religion without molestation, I therefore bequeath the sum of fifty thousand dollars, to be paid by my executors for said object, through the said Sir Moses Montefiore, in such manner as he may advise, as best calculated to promote the aforesaid object; and in case of any legal difficulty, or impairment in the way of carrying out said bequest . . .

Touro admired Sir Moses for his humanitarian work[24] and he therefore wished him to be involved in the implementation of his last wishes. James Finn records, on the authority of Sir Moses, that the latter had never heard of the existence of the 'American Jewish Gentleman' before 'the legacy was announced to him'.[25]

The first mention of Touro's death and will in the Anglo-Jewish

press was a terse news item sent on 23 January 1854 from New
Orleans and published in the *Jewish Chronicle* of 10 February. It
is reported that among other legacies he left '. . . 10,000 dollars to
New York Relief Society for Indigent Jews in Palestine; also 50,000
dollars to the agent of the said society for ameliorating the conditions of the Jews in the Holy Land, and securing the enjoyment
of their religion . . .'. The report gave a somewhat garbled version of
the facts. It referred to an 'agent' and Sir Moses' name was not
mentioned.

The first intelligence that reached Sir Moses of the death of
Touro and the contents of the will, was contained in a letter from
the Revd Dr S. M. Isaacs of New York,[26] who wrote that Touro
'. . . had left the North American Relief Society $10,000 and a
further sum of $50,000 for the benefit of the poor Israelites of
Palestine; the latter sum subject to Sir Moses' control conjointly
with the executors'.[27] This would have given Sir Moses a subordinate
role: he might act only 'conjointly with the executors'. It ignored
the obvious meaning of the will, which stated unequivocally that
$50,000 be handed over to Sir Moses Montefiore to be spent 'as he
may advise' the executors. Indeed, Sir Moses accepted the assign-
ment 'on trust' and not as a mere adviser to the executors.

An official intimation must soon have provided Sir Moses with
the correct text of the will and, as Dr Loewe related: 'Sir Moses
immediately expressed his willingness to forward the remittance of
the North American Relief Society to the Holy Land, and to accept
the trust of the Touro legacy . . .'.[28] In other words, to act as 'their
agent'[29] for the North American Relief Society in respect of the
$10,000, and to act as a trustee — independent if need be of the
views of others — with absolute discretion and powers in respect of
the $50,000 legacy.

Although it was rumoured in London that Sir Moses was to
travel to Constantinople early in May 1854, this was premature.[30]
Instead, Sir Moses involved himself in the 'Public Appeal'. The daily
press and even members of the non-Jewish clergy took up the cause
of the starving Jews of the Holy Land, with laudable results. But
the question arises whether the Touro legacy might have been used
to feed the hungry.[31] This was impossible, because the money was
not yet available to Sir Moses and because the will's terminology,
by inference, stipulated that the funds should be used to provide
facilities which would create long term, or even permanent, benefits.

Sir Moses and Dr Adler had their own ideas of what should be
done with the money raised. The Chief Rabbi was the first to express his views. In the Pastoral Letter he wrote that, while the

primary purpose of the appeal was to feed the starving Jews of Palestine and help them with the utmost urgency, he aimed also to obviate the perennial problem of poverty in the Holy Land. Once the emergency was over, any surplus funds should be used '. . . to bring about a unity of action among the different congregations there, to purchase land, to establish farms and factories and to devote *part* of the money annually collected, as wages to those who will [work] . . . The time for the realisation of such scheme may not be remote, as the munificent legacy of the philanthropist Judah Touro was bequeathed for this very purpose,[32] which bequest will have an important bearing on the improvement of the Holy Land.'[33]

Sir Moses' letter to Dr Adler suggests the lines on which he was thinking: '. . . from indirect and direct sources, I learn that fathers in Israel — men profoundly learned in the Law, who, so that they may die near the graves of our forefathers, submit to live in the most abject poverty — are now impelled by the very love they bear their children to sell them to strangers. "So" to use their own words "that their offspring may be spared death" — death from starvation.'[34]

What Sir Moses was aiming at is clear. Jewish children were brought to the missionary hospital, which was well stocked with food and fuel, to be saved from starvation. This could be avoided only by providing a Jewish hospital, staffed by Jews and catering for the sick and convalescent in accordance with all Jewish requirements.[35]

On 5 August, Gershom Kursheedt, one of the four executors of the Touro will, who was destined to play a considerable part in the implementation of its terms, arrived in London 'to arrange with Sir Moses about the legacy of fifty thousand dollars left at his disposal for the purpose of relieving the poor Israelites in the Holy Land in such a manner as Sir Moses should advise'.[36]

'Sir Moses, at the first interview he had with this gentleman, suggested that the money should be employed in building a hospital in Jerusalem. Mr Kursheedt immediately assented, and Sir Moses gave him the plan and drawing made about a year before. He was most happy, as it settled the principal business he had in England; the co-executors had given him full power to agree to any plan Sir Moses should propose. A letter was prepared by a solicitor to that effect, which Mr Kursheedt signed.'[37]

Kursheedt's eager approval of the proposition fully justified Sir Moses' optimism and 'Letters were addressed to the Baroness James de Rothschild[38] in Paris and Baron Amschel de Rothschild in Frankfurt, to apprise them of the legacy of the late Judah Touro and of the manner in which it had been decided to employ it.'[39]

II

The need for a Jewish hospital in Jerusalem had long been recognized by both Montefiore and the Rothschilds.

The first academically trained medical practitioner to practise in the city was Dr Dalton, who was sent out by the London Society in 1824 as a medical missionary. The missionaries realized very early the great value to their cause of a free medical service in a society where no other medical help was available. They provided a free health service, which included free access to a doctor and free medicines. Nicolayson, a Dane, who was a lay member of the London Society, was sent to Jerusalem to assist Dr Dalton. He arrived early in January 1826, a few weeks before Dr Dalton died.[40] He was to spend the rest of his life in the Middle East, much of it in Jerusalem. His task was to widen the scope of missionary work in the area, a task very much in keeping with his organizational capacity.

There is evidence that the medical missionaries had some early successes, and this deeply disturbed Sir Moses.[41] When in 1842, Dr Ludwig Philippson of Magdeburg, owner and editor of the *Allgemeine Zeitung des Judenthums (AZdJ)* appealed in his columns for pledges to a fund for building a hospital in Jerusalem, Sir Moses and Lady Montefiore were among the first to pledge their support, and as Philippson proudly claimed, they did so without even being approached.[42] The venture was strongly supported by the Paris Rothschilds who offered 100,000 francs. This, however, was subject to the onerous condition that, together with the building of the hospital, a secular school system, modelled on Western European institutions, should be established and attached to it. The condition was unacceptable to the Yishuv. Sir Moses withdrew from the scheme, as he was not prepared to be a party to proposals rejected by the Rabbinate of Jerusalem.[43] As the Rothschild offer lapsed, Philippson's venture failed to get off the ground.

Even while it seemed to have a good chance of success, however, Sir Moses realized that it was at best a long-term plan and something had to be done immediately. News from Jerusalem had just reached him that three adult Jews had been converted by the medical missionaries.[44] The missionary historian Ayerst noted for the year 1842 '... the success of the medical department'.[45]

Accordingly, 'he [Sir Moses] made an agreement with a physician, Dr S Fränkel,[46] to allow him a salary for three years, to furnish the requisite medicines, and to pay his expenses to Jerusalem on condition that he should attend the poor gratuitously'.[47] Sir Moses immediately ordered 'from the Apothecaries' Hall drugs, surgical instruments, and fittings for the dispensary in Jerusalem' and 'he saw them packed and forwarded to the Holy City'.[48]

Dr Fränkel, who arrived in Jerusalem early in 1843, thus became the first Jewish physician in the Holy City. His appointment not only mitigated the dire medical problem of the Jewish population, but proved an antidote to conversion by the medical missionaries. However, Nicolayson, who was instrumental in having the Anglican Church built on Mount Zion, adjacent to the Jewish Quarter of the city, attached to his church a 'Jewish hospital'.[49] This was opened to the Jewish public on 12 December 1844 with another qualified physician, Dr MacGowan, in charge,[50] and it immediately attracted many Jews.

This enabled the missionaries to augment the already freely administered medical service and dispensary with a free hospital service, assuring a close and intimate contact with prospective converts when they, as patients, were least able to resist. The food provided was strictly *kasher*, free, and served by a Hebrew-speaking staff. A synagogue was available for those who wished to make use of it. Conversion was never overtly discussed, but a copy of the New Testament in Hebrew was placed unobtrusively next to the bed of every patient and under the bread plates at mealtimes.

This threat was met by 'the establishment of a Jewish Hospital in opposition to that of the mission',[51] which was put in the hands of Dr Fränkel. Thus, 'the Jews, thanks to Sir Moses Montefiore, have a hospital of their own at Jerusalem, as well as the conversionists.'[52] However, this venture did not come up to expectation. The reason was, says Ayerst, that '. . . the order and comfort prevailing in the latter [i.e. the missionaries' hospital] was so superior, and the confidence in Dr MacGowan's skill . . .'.[53] A leader writer in the *Jewish Chronicle* stated that Dr Fränkel was not able to gain the confidence of the Yishuv. Two weeks later the *Jewish Chronicle* demanded 'a full and diligent inquiry into the present state of the Jewish hospital with a view of improving conditions, and thus defeating the ends of conversion aimed at by the establishment of the Mission — the inefficacy of excommunications against those who have unfortunately to resort to that asylum, on account of the unsatisfactory state of their own establishment . . .'[54]

Although the initial agreement with Dr Fränkel was for an appointment of three years,[55] possibly as a stop-gap or trial period, he held the position for fifteen years, until 1858.[56]

Sir Moses was aware, as was everybody concerned, that a one-man medical team was not sufficient for the growing Jewish population in Jerusalem.[57] An attempt was made locally in Jerusalem to tackle the problem when in 1843 the *Perushim* (Ashkenazi Jews from Lithuania and Poland, followers of Elijah, Gaon of Vilna, 1720–97) sent an emissary to Hungary to collect funds.[58]

That plan foundered, as did the attempt of the Sephardim to join up with the Hasidim to establish a hospital in or about 1844.[59] They sent H. Israel Moshe Hazan, who spent some time in London, to raise funds,[60] but he left empty-handed. In a letter dated Tevet 5606 he wrote: 'The reasons that the sacred and national object of my mission has met with no favour, I cannot divine; yet so it is . . . .'[61]

In 1845 the *Bikur Holim* Society of the *Perushim Kolel* was founded, and a building was rented to be used as a hospital.[62] J. M. Pines stated in 1894 that it was not known exactly when it was founded but there is evidence that it was already functioning by 1847.[63]

In 1849 cholera struck the Holy Land. The first city to suffer was Tiberias, in January. From there it spread rapidly. Haim Guedalla published in the *Jewish Chronicle* an English translation of several letters received by Sir Moses from the Holy Land imploring him to send help immediately and set up a Jewish hospital there. Eight rabbis of the Sephardi community pleaded in a long and well reasoned letter the need for such an institution. The urgency was heightened by the steady growth of the Jewish population and by the indescribably degrading poverty which provided the right conditions for the work of the missionaries. The *Herem* (ban of excommunication) pronounced on anyone using a missionary hospital fell on deaf ears when life depended on immediate medical aid. The sick would resort to the hospital clandestinely, if not openly. The rabbis appealed to Sir Moses to gather together 'the wealthy inhabitants of England, the merchant princes of the House of Rothschild . . .' to build a hospital without delay.[64] Rabbi Shmuel of Dolhinovo[65] was even more outspoken: 'Many of us in spite of the *Herem* of the German and Portuguese ecclesiastics, will resort to the conversionist hospitals, and, alas in several instances follow the inducements held out, and forsake the religion of our fathers.'[66] Other letters followed from Sephardi and Ashkenazi congregations in Jerusalem,[67] all stressing the desperate need to offer physical as well as spiritual help.

The letters were published in the *Jewish Chronicle* in anticipation of Sir Moses' third journey to the Holy Land. He left England in May 1849,[68] in response to these and similar letters,[69] to dispense immediate help to victims of the epidemic. It was said that although the total raised by the public appeal fell short of £200, Sir Moses himself gave over £5,000. Colonel Gawler[70] accompanied Sir Moses, an indication that he was also intent on pursuing his long cherished wish to establish agricultural enterprises in the Holy Land. That the hospital was another reason for his journey we learn from an eloquent Hebrew poem and prayer of farewell composed by Leopold Dukes,[71] and printed in the *Jewish Chronicle* with an English translation:[72] The prayer repeats the points about the need for a hospital and the necessity for Sir Moses' journey: '. . . with intent to enquire after the welfare of Jerusalem and to bring healing balm to the afflicted and sick of thy people restoring them to light and gladness, and preserving them from spiritual perdition'.

Sir Moses returned to England without much evident progress having been made. The visit nevertheless kept the problem in the forefront of his thoughts. Dr Loewe noted that during 1851[73] Sir Moses was very much occupied with the Emancipation Bill, then before Parliament. Once voting on the Bill was over, Sir Moses

again turned his attention to the Holy Land and to a scheme which had been *occupying his mind* [for] *some considerable time.*

It had *long been his ardent desire* to establish a hospital in Jerusalem, and as such an institution necessitated considerable capital, he entered into correspondence with his friends on the subject, *spent several hundred pounds* in having proper plans drawn up by English and foreign architects, and consulted medical authorities in the large hospitals respecting various improvements which had been introduced. Count Pizzamano the Austrian Consul[74] in Jerusalem, also took a lively interest in the scheme, and promised to assist Sir Moses to the utmost.

In 1854 all seemed set fair to build the hospital with the Touro legacy, but that there were still more obstacles to be overcome became apparent within days of Kursheedt's assent. Dr Loewe continues:

Sir Moses, however, had soon to learn that Mr Kursheedt had been induced to alter his mind, and had withdrawn the consent he had given to the building of the hospital.[75]

Sir Moses was most unexpectedly confronted with Kursheedt's change of mind when on 15 August Kursheedt arrived at the appointed time at the offices of the Alliance Assurance Company to announce to the 'great surprise' of Sir Moses that he 'must decline' to accompany him on the arranged visit to the American Consul who was to be informed of the decision in respect of the Touro legacy. Furthermore, he, Kursheedt, 'could not sign the proposed memorandum'. There is no indication as to who 'induced' Kursheedt to alter his mind, nor why he should have done so. It is not on record whether Sir Moses went to see the American Consul. However, he asked for, and duly obtained, an audience with Lord Clarendon, the Foreign Secretary, on 22 August,

> ... to acquaint him with his desire to obtain a *firman* from the Sultan, giving power to purchase land for agricultural purposes, building, etc. as also to build a hospital in Jerusalem with a synagogue attached to it. His Lordship said he had written to Lord Stratford de Redcliffe, but there were great difficulties regarding the land; as to the hospital, he had heard that one for the Jews had been opened only one month since. This was the hospital to be known by the name of 'Rothschild Hospital'. Sir Moses informed his Lordship of the Juda Touro bequest, and received a promise that he should be assisted in his great work whenever necessary.[76]

It becomes obvious why Kursheedt did not accompany Sir Moses, and certainly it is not surprising that he withdrew his assent if he was already aware of events in Jerusalem. What is however significant is that the Foreign Secretary had the up-to-date information readily available. He knew, of course, that the Turkish Government still resisted any sale of land to foreigners.[77] His information on the Jewish hospital was supplied by James Finn,[78] in a dispatch dated Jerusalem, 27 July 1854, to his superior, Lord Stratford de Redcliffe, the British Ambassador in Constantinople, with a copy to the Foreign Secretary in London:

> I have the honour to report that yesterday a good Jewish hospital was opened in Jerusalem by a Mr Albert Cohn, President of the Israelitish Consistorial Committee in Paris, founded by the funds supplied by various members of the Rothschild families and under the particular auspices of the Emperor of Austria and his Government, His Imperial Majesty having subscribed personally to the object.[79]

Notwithstanding his reservation, Lord Clarendon was as good as his word. The British diplomatic representatives were advised of Sir Moses' projected journey to Constantinople and the Holy Land, and were ordered to assist him as and when their assistance was required. As it turned out, the official diplomatic assistance was of invaluable help to Sir Moses.

It would be surprising if Sir Moses was unaware of the inauguration of the Rothschild hospital by Albert Cohn or if he heard of it for the first time from Lord Clarendon. Loewe's narrative does not suggest any surprise on Sir Moses' part. Yet once he knew of the establishment of the hospital, why did he still insist on using the Touro legacy for building another?

III

The Rothschild Hospital[80] originated as a result of the visit of Gustave de Rothschild,[81] son of Baron James and Baroness Betty de Rothschild of Paris, to Jerusalem, in August 1853, in the company of a number of French officers. He arrived incognito to explore unobtrusively on behalf of his parents the possibilities of improving the lot of the Jewish population by providing facilities of long-term value. One Sabbath,[82] Dr Fränkel called on Rabbi Selig Hausdorf to inform him that Gustave, on the advice of the Austrian Consul, Count Pizzamano,[83] wished to meet him. Hausdorf was a leading member of the German–Holland *Kolel* and intimately aware of the problems and needs of the Yishuv. He was honorary dragoman[84] to the Austrian Consulate and trusted adviser on Jewish affairs to Count Pizzamano. On meeting Rothschild, Hausdorf was informed of the purpose of his visit. His advice was that a Jewish hospital was needed more urgently than anything else. He was asked to prepare a memorandum with his recommendations. Two copies were required, one for Baroness Betty.[85] It had to be prepared quickly as Gustave was leaving for home on Sunday morning. Hausdorf worked through the night and delivered the papers in time. In July 1854,[86] the *AZdJ* informed its readers that Dr Albert Cohn, the almoner of the Paris Rothschilds had hastily left Paris and was on his way to Jerusalem. At Alexandria, where he arrived on 2 July, he made contact with Hausdorf, who met him on arrival at Jaffa on 8 July.

Cohn spent three hectic weeks, from 9 July to 29 July (11 Tammuz to 4 Av), in Jerusalem.[87] Accommodation was found for him in a spacious house in the south of the city very near the walls, and with a fine view over the Temple area and the Western Wall.

In discussion with Cohn, Hausdorf repeated his advice to Gustave de Rothschild that a hospital must be the first priority. Cohn agreed, and assured Hausdorf that a hospital would be in existence before he left Jerusalem. As the building he was occupying seemed suitable for the purpose, it was decided to lease it.[88] Michel Erlanger,[89] Albert Cohn's companion on the journey, and Hausdorf, bought beds, bedding, linen and furniture locally to equip two wards to accommodate eighteen patients. A young physician, Dr Bernhard Neumann, who was in Jerusalem, accepted the position of Chief Medical Officer.[90]

On Rosh Hodesh Av (26 July), Cohn was ready to open the hospital with an impressive inaugural ceremony. It was named, in accordance with the wish of Baroness Betty, the 'Mayer de Rothschild Hospital' in memory of the founder of the Rothschild dynasty. All this was achieved within nineteen days of Cohn setting foot in the Holy Land.

While the operation was presented as an *ad hoc* decision, there can be no doubt that much detailed planning had been done in great secrecy before Cohn's journey. This is shown by the visit incognito of Gustave de Rothschild and Dr Cohn's hasty unannounced departure for Palestine; even the name of the hospital was pre-arranged. The reasons lie partly in Dr Cohn's character and the French chauvinism of this Austro-Hungarian Jew. Cohn was well provided with Rothschild money and had very wide terms of reference. He could act and spend as he saw fit, and he was obviously determined to get in first.

It is likely that on 6 August, when Kursheedt was told by Sir Moses of his plans, neither man knew of the totally unexpected development just twelve days previously. Sir Moses was of course aware of the French Rothschilds' previous interest and their thinking, on lines parallel to his own. Accordingly, he was eager to communicate his news to the Rothschilds, and in particular Baroness Betty, who seems to have been the moving force. The sudden retraction by Kursheedt, and his refusal to call on the US Consul,[91] are now understandable, since he, and probably Sir Moses, would have heard the news by 15 August. Cohn's action radically changed the situation.

If this reconstruction of the sequence of events is correct, it explains why Kursheedt thought there was no need to build a second hospital but not why Sir Moses persisted, as he did in his interview with Lord Clarendon.

Sir Moses' idea of a hospital in Jerusalem was certainly not an *ad hoc* adaptation of a disused school building, as is shown by the architects' plans drawn at great expense for him. Dr Ludwig August Frankl, who was shown a lithographed copy of these plans by Dr S. Fränkel in Jerusalem in 1856, described them as magnificent in every detail. The elevation, the internal arrangements, the general harmonious appearance were all just right 'for the hospital to be built'. He also evaluated the quality of the design as a doctor of medicine.[92]

Meanwhile, the leader writer of the *Jewish Chronicle* asked some pointed questions about Albert Cohn's visit to Palestine; he was equally not sparing in his criticism of Sir Moses' and Dr Adler's way of distributing the large sums at their disposal[93].

While Sir Moses' motives and actions were common knowledge and at all times impeccable, this cannot be said of Cohn. He was clearly motivated to get in on the act first. Hausdorf records details of a dialogue between himself and Cohn on the latter's arrival in Jerusalem. Cohn told him the objects he wished to achieve on this visit, among them to establish the hospital. Hausdorf commented:

Yes this is most important, we have heard enough about hospitals from visiting philanthropists who promise that on their returning to their homes they will give instructions to fill this desideratum. Yet, we have not perceived that they kept their promises. The reason for that is simple; as soon they are out of sight of the Holy City, the promises are forgotten . . . .[94]

This was an obvious attack on Sir Moses' credibility. However, Cohn in his reply assured him that this would not happen on his visit. Cohn gave full expression to his feelings in his inaugural address at the hospital on 26 July (1 Av), which he delivered in the presence of the whole Consular Corps, the local civic dignitaries, the representatives of the Rabbinate and indeed the whole Jewish population. Finn described the scene, and in particular Albert Cohn's behaviour, in a dispatch to his immediate superior, Lord Stratford de Redcliffe, the Ambassador in Constantinople:[95]

. . . a good Jewish hospital was opened yesterday 26th July 1854 by Mr Albert Cohn, President of the Israelite Consistorial Committee in Paris . . .[96] a good deal of pleasure was visible among the friends of Mr Cohn;[97] but I had to regret the use of the following expression used in his opening address, among others which may be overlooked in public oratory — 'Today we witness the first fruits in the East of European civilization' thereby ignoring the medical benevolence of . . .[98] also the Jewish hospital commenced a few years since . . .[99] but still more the benevolence of Sir Moses Montefiore who has for several years maintained here a Jewish physician for Jews with a valuable dispensary. All this was overlooked, as well as the very name of Montefiore which is so indelibly connected with Jerusalem, but the Rothschild name was everywhere.

There were other problems with which Jewish leaders had to contend. One was the legal disabilities of the Jews in the Turkish Empire. To be effective, it was of paramount importance that all representative Jewish organizations co-ordinated their activities *vis à vis* the civil authorities. In the wake of the Crimean War the Western powers made representations to the Sultan to remove the restrictions imposed on their nationals by the Muslim laws. They were successful, but that still left members of minority religions, and in particular the Jews of Turkish nationality, governed by grossly discriminatory legislation. The Consistoire of French Jews petitioned Napoleon III to intercede with the Sultan to extend to the Jews the rights granted to Christians. Sir Moses thought the time opportune for a similar approach by the Board of Deputies to the British Government; and an address was forwarded to Lord Clarendon.[100] In due course, Dr Albert Cohn, the President of the Consistoire 'deputed by Messrs Rothschild of Paris, in conjunction with Sir Moses Montefiore and the Rev Dr Adler, and the Jews in general' was received on 21 August 1854 by the Sultan in Constantinople. The audience was the subject of a leading article in the *Jewish Chronicle*.[101] Notwithstanding the melodramatic description[102] of his audience, the results were fairly satisfactory. The Sultan bade Cohn farewell with the assurance, 'When thou shalt return to Constantinople, thou wilt find thy co-religionists in a better condition, I promise thee.'

From contemporary press reports it appears that a *modus vivendi* was arranged also between London and Paris for the co-ordination of the Holy Land relief work. On 6 October 1854 Dr Cohn paid a visit to London. In a short news item the *Jewish Chronicle* extended a cordial welcome to 'the worthy philanthropist':[103]

We are gratified to state, that as regards the Jews in Palestine, he[104] has succeeded in bringing the efforts of the Messrs Rothschild of Paris and his own plans, in harmony with those of Messrs Rothschild, Sir Moses Montefiore and the Rev Dr Adler, the Chief Rabbi. These benevolent men now co-operate in regenerating the fallen position of our brethren in the Holy Land; whilst Dr Cohen [*sic*] on his accord and at his own expense has introduced the modern system of education amongst the Jews of Constantinople, Smyrna, Alexandria, etc. . . .

All seemed set fair and to augur well for a happier relationship in the future. However, the *entente cordiale* was at best only of short duration.

A quarto pamphlet[105] of eight pages in Hebrew, *Divrei Hayomim le Yisrael* appeared in Jerusalem bearing the date 15 Av 5615 (7 August 1854). No author is mentioned, nor does the text give any indication of his identity. It is a nauseating panegyric of the Rothschild benevolence to Jerusalem, and it makes extravagant claims for the meritorious work of Albert Cohn and his endless bounty. It contains some back-handed praise for Sir Moses:

Our great man 'Don Montefiore' who was the pioneer provider of the medical services of a doctor and a pharmacy, but what did he provide to guide orphans those who have no father or mother neither where to sleep? And what for the old, the lonely and the destitute? There is no one to wait on them, no one to take them to hospital.

The insinuation is clear: Sir Moses provided a physician but this is of no use as he has built no hospital or asylum. It repeats Hausdorf's quoted remarks and continues:

This is the day the L-d maketh wonders . . . he who is the G-d of *R. Abraham Albert of Paris* [who] declared to the multitudes here in the City of G-d, that he is the *messenger* to fulfil the important Mitsvah to further the cause of Zion, to let the poor know that the hearts of our brethren the house of Jacob [are set] to found[106] here in the City of Praise, a house of succor and help, an asylum *Hospital* . . .

It is not far-fetched to assume that this pamphlet was commissioned by Albert Cohn, though there is no proof. He distributed it and made sure it was in the right hands at the right time. Cohn sent one copy of the pamphlet to the editor of the *Jewish Chronicle* after he re-turned to Paris from his visit to London. The latter could not have received it earlier than 20 November 1854, that is, about four months after it was printed. During the summer the *Jewish Chronicle* published a number of news items and reports on Dr Cohn's ac-tivities: his visit to London, letters from him and to him — all sup-plied by Cohn, and all praising him and his actions. If the editor of the *Jewish Chronicle* could have had prior sight of that pamphlet, and judging by the effect it had on him, it is hardly likely that he would have printed all the material Cohn passed to him. Two long editorials[107] under the heading 'What has been done for the Holy Land?' were devoted to this publication, almost all of which was printed in translation. The writer expressed his deep disappointment that nothing had come of the agreement reported in the *Jewish Chronicle* on 3 November 1854, i.e. that the charity appeals organ-ized in London by Sir Moses and Dr Adler and the work of the Rothschilds in Paris should be co-ordinated. Such an arrangement would obviate duplication, it would also preserve funds and make sure that the funds raised were spent prudently. The editorial im-plied that Dr Cohn acted against the accord reached on his visit to London. In fact he acted, to quote Ludwig August Frankl's apt phrase: 'Es gibt eine Eifersucht des Grossmutes',[108] which was putting on Cohn's action a somewhat generous complexion. The Jewish Chronicle editorial writer had no such niceties in mind. After apportioning praise where praise was due he observed with undisguised cynicism after paraphrasing part of the pamphlet:

The brochure is composed in a style of oriental phraseology, replete with ex-pressions of gratitude for the kindness received from the Angel of Grace[109] who came to their[110] rescue when they were on the brink of destitution and starvation, and who saved the congregation of Israel in the Holy Land from utter destruction.[111]

There are even harsher words of criticism:

It appears strange enough that most of the societies and establishments [which] were according to information originally received by us, instituted by the joint and philanthropic effort of Dr Adler and Sir Moses Montefiore are claimed by Mons. Cohen [sic!] *who has handed us the brochure* printed in Jerusalem under the title of 'Chronicles of Israel' which sets forth the proceedings of Mons. Albert Cohen during his visit to the Holy Land, and munificent gifts he distributed and the highly useful establishments which he erected.

These are very serious charges, which reflect on Cohn's credibility and his lack of good faith and cast serious doubt on his integrity. But having said that, the leader writer even[112] casts serious doubts on the long-term viability of the much publicized achievements, factual and fictitious.

But whilst we and any well-wishers to that community[113] must be enraptured with these temporary measures of relief, the question irresistibly forces itself upon us — how long will these temporary measures remain in force? How long will the funds last? There being *no endowments*, no annual subscriptions, but only *momentary* gifts, what will be done when the funds are exhausted, which events must occur very shortly. In a word, what step has been taken for the permanent stability of any of the charities instituted?

The writer stresses the temporary palliative value of Dr Cohn's actions and also the generous distributions of Dr Adler. He then comes from the general to the specific, the one real achievement of Dr Cohn, the hospital:

Even the account of the Hospital, which we were given to understand was to be an endowed institution by the legacy of the late Juda Touro appears to us yet an *ad interim* affair.

This is a penetrating analysis. A hospital which had at its disposal no more than two converted rooms in a former infants' school building with facilities limited at any time to a maximum of eighteen in-patients, to serve the Jewish population which in 1839 was 5,500[114] and which had grown to 8,000 by 1854[115] and lacked any assured income to sustain it, could at best be no more than a short-term interim solution.

These views were shared by the Editor of the *AZdJ*. Philippson, in an editorial dated 1 September 1854,[116] ridiculed the sudden decision and the whirlwind 'foundation of charities tour' of Dr Albert Cohn. Dr Cohn, he accused unreservedly, had not the slightest intention of doing anything for the Jews of Jerusalem, until he, Philippson, came to Paris to rouse the attention of the Consistoire. Cohn was on his way to his country seat at Fontainebleau, but instead suddenly decided to go to Jerusalem with 50,000 Rothschild francs.[117] Suddenly decided and suddenly acted upon: on 2 July he arrived in Alexandria, six days later, on 8 July, in Jaffa, on the 9th in Jerusalem, on the 26th he consecrated the hospital there, then back via Smyrna to Constantinople, and on 25 August he already sends his letter from on board ship at Piraeus (near Athens) to the press. In such a hurry, no proper and convincing assessment of any situation is possible, nor can any creation produced thus be properly thought out.

This background history only amplified the severe strictures published in the previous issue, when he concluded a report on Cohn's hospital with a short footnote: 'For a Jewish population of 8,000, obviously a mere 18 beds is rather paltry!'

IV

During the rest of 1854 there was a steady clamour in the press for an exhaustive report of what had been done with the £19,887. 11s. 4d. produced by the Appeal and what was to be done with the surplus not required for immediate needs. Although Sir Moses was concerned with many other matters at home and abroad,[118] including the status of Jews of Turkish nationality and the Russian Jewish prisoners in Sheerness, the Holy Land and its problems were in the forefront of his thoughts.

Sir Moses had by that time turned seventy. A routine medical check-up showed a slight heart defect, some digestive disorders and 'poison in his blood'. But he still carried on with his communal work, and did 'not stop his preparations for another journey to the East'.[119]

The first indication of an impending journey was reported in the press early in 1855.[120] They were 'credibly informed' that Sir Moses and Lady Montefiore were to travel early in the spring to the Holy Land, '. . . for the purpose of personally supervising the proper application of the funds collected for the improvement of the state of the Palestinian Jews'. They were to proceed shortly, via Constantinople, to the Holy Land for the fourth time. Dr Loewe quotes from the first report of the trustees of the Appeal fund,[121] adding only that it was intended to find the extent[122]

. . . to which the temporary and provisional relief, already mentioned, had proved effective, and to organise the best means which might be devised for the appropriation of the remainder of the funds, with a view to the utmost benefit of the supplicants, and, at the same time, to the effectual accomplishment of the intentions of the benevolent contributors.

In a printed letter, Sir Moses informed his co-worker, Revd S. M. Isaacs, of his intentions:

Grosvenor Gate, Park Lane
February 5th 5616 — 1855
Rev. and Dear Sir:- I take the earliest opportunity of informing you that it is my intention, D.V., of proceeding to the Holy Land immediately after Passover, with the object of learning what steps can be practically adopted for improving the condition of our brethren there. I flatter myself that the information will afford you pleasure, and will equally gratify me, to receive from you any

suggestions that you may think will benefit the cause in which we are engaged. Accept the assurance of my esteem, and believe me,

    Rev and Dear Sir
        Yours faithfully
        Moses Montefiore
Revd S. M. Isaacs, New York[123]

The report suggests that the *only* purpose of the forthcoming visit to the Holy Land was to deal with the distribution and future allocation of the Appeal funds. Two items one would have expected are not mentioned: the hospital in Jerusalem and the Touro legacy. Both these were mentioned or alluded to in the original Appeal in May 1854. In another news item other objects of the journey are mentioned. When the preparations for the journey to the East were completed Sir Moses asked to see the Prime Minister to enlist his support for the mission. Lord Palmerston met Sir Moses on 25 March and gave him the opportunity to elaborate on his plans. He told the Prime Minister about '. . . his intentions of going to the East with the object of erecting a hospital at Jerusalem and encouraging the cultivation of land in Palestine . . . by the Sultan allowing Jews to purchase land.[124] The Prime Minister replied 'that the hospital was a desirable institution'. As to the purchase of land, he could hold out no hope but thought, as an alternative, long leases could be acquired. Lord Palmerston handed him letters of recommendation to Lord Cowley in Paris[125] and to Lord Stratford de Redcliffe in Constantinople. He also suggested that Lord Clarendon would provide Sir Moses with further letters addressed to the British representatives at embassies and consulates *en route* to the East.

It seems strange that while in the previous August Lord Clarendon had considered that the Rothschild Hospital made any other hospital superfluous, only eight months later Lord Palmerston should have thought Sir Moses' plan 'desirable'. He was even assured by the Prime Minister that he could count on Lord Clarendon's help. Even more important, Mr. Kursheedt and his co-executors of the Touro will had changed direction. A laconic entry in the *Diaries*[126] for 30 April 1855 reads:

Sir Moses had the satisfaction of receiving a further sum of about £3,000 in addition to the £5,058 of the Judah Touro legacy already remitted to him on 24 February . . . .[127]

Over a year passed between the first news of the Touro bequest in January 1854 and the arrival of the first instalment in February 1855. This delay may be explained by Kursheedt's refusal to support Sir Moses' consistent determination to build the hospital with the Touro funds. The executors were unwilling to part with the money under such conditions. Then, without explanation, £8,025 was transferred to Sir Moses without any apparent strings attached.[128] Next, Kursheedt suddenly arrived in England shortly before Sir Moses was to set out on his journey to the East with the intention of accompanying him; and, as Mrs. Guedalla noted in her Diary:[129] '. . . and [he] *was now, it appeared,*[130] in possession of full powers regarding the building of the hospital in Jerusalem'.

Kursheedt had come round to Sir Moses' way of thinking, even before he returned to America. The *New York Express*[131] reported in October 1854 that Kursheedt had returned recently from England where he had gone to discuss with Sir Moses Montefiore the future of the Touro legacy. 'They agreed to *build a hospital, large enough to accommodate one hundred patients.* Also [they agreed] to endow it sufficiently and assure the necessary pharmaceutical supply.' The hospital would contain a synagogue, and would be built in a garden setting. While Kursheedt was by then convinced of the need for Sir Moses' hospital, it took him time to convince his co-executors.

Dr Albert Cohn's visit to London in November 1854 had the express purpose of negotiating co-operation between Paris and London in all the relief work for the Holy Land. There is evidence that Dr Cohn had hoped that the running costs of his hospital would be financed by the establishment of an endowment fund from the Touro legacy.[132]

If this proposition had proved practicable, it would have provided both Dr Cohn and the New Orleans trustees with a credible alternative to Sir Moses' plan. There would have been the hospital, i.e. Dr Cohn's eighteen-bed institution; the Touro legacy would have been used as an endowment fund to ensure the maintenance of that miniature hospital for an almost indefinite time; and Dr Cohn would have been the true benefactor of Jerusalem's Jewry. However, Dr Cohn by his distortions and untruths, as displayed in the brochure, dissipated all the goodwill engendered on his visit to London. On reconsideration it was clear that the hospital which Cohn had founded, even if the Touro legacy were used as an endowment fund, would have been at best an *ad interim* affair. In other words, all that would have been achieved would have been the saving of Dr Cohn's credibility. The proposal, however, never got off the ground. Sir Moses' rather unflattering views of Cohn are reported by Finn in a Consular dispatch to Lord Stratford de Redcliffe:[133]

. . . but at length he explained to me his vexation at the proceedings of Mr Albert Cohn last July in Jerusalem on bringing some Rothschild money here for benevolent purposes.[134] [He] made improper use of Sir Moses' name, and went home proclaiming the ascendancy of French influence in this country,[135] with the decline of that of England. Sir Moses declares that no other object than that of contradicting by facts that unfounded assertion, would have brought him here at so advanced an age and in so enfeebled a state of health as he is.

Kursheedt who, by the time Cohn came to London, had already returned to New Orleans, was no doubt kept informed of the negotiations, as well as the outcome. He succeeded in convincing his co-executors to accept Sir Moses' plans. Once the agreement of all parties concerned was reached, the remittances started to arrive in London.

The, at times, brutally condemnatory views expressed in the *Jewish Chronicle* and elsewhere on the value of Dr Cohn's work, and the fact that the Touro executors, who provided the funds, sided with Sir Moses, were no doubt reported to the Prime Minister and Lord Clarendon. It is thus not surprising that their attitude changed to support the 'desirability' of a hospital.

With all the obstacles out of the way, Mr. Kursheedt accompanied Sir Moses Montefiore on his journey to the East — with no less than £12,000 to be spent.[136]

V

On Sunday 13 May, Sir Moses and Lady Montefiore set out on their journey. Sir Moses first called on 'the Warden of the Synagogue' — which synagogue is not specified — 'to take instructions as to their wishes on how the charity money they had entrusted to him should be distributed'.[137]

Sir Moses and Lady Montefiore were accompanied by Haim and Jemima Guedalla and by Gershom Kursheedt. They left Finsbury Square after an 'affectionate parting' from friends and were met at the station by Dr Adler, Joseph Sebag,[138] Uncle Benjamin and Aunt Cohen,[139] Mr Louis Cohen and sons, and others who came to see them off. They arrived late in the evening at Dover and spent the night at the Ship Hotel. Next morning, they were joined by Dr Loewe.[140]

On the following day, after a fairly rough crossing, they arrived at Calais, where they spent two nights to allow Lady Montefiore to recuperate from the sea voyage. On Thursday 17 May they took the train to Cologne where they spent the first Sabbath away from home. Early on Sunday morning they travelled to Hanover, arriving shortly after noon. Sir Moses 'before breakfast, went to see Mrs Adler', the nonagenarian mother of the Chief Rabbi.[141] He was accompanied by Mr Kursheedt and Dr Loewe and they spent nearly an hour with her. Sir Moses presented her with a valuable silver writing set.[142] The party dined at a restaurant 'where everything was well arranged and the dinner good', but 'very exorbitant in price'. The night was spent in the 'British Hotel' and 'whilst at breakfast, Mrs Adler . . . came in. She had not left her home for many months previously. Sir Moses would not go on eating, so she left shortly'.

The journey continued via Dresden to Prague where they arrived 'Pentecost Eve: we said prayers, and retired early'.[143] In the morning, the first day of Shavuoth, they 'went to synagogue — the one celebrated for its antiquity . . .' (the Alt-Neu Schul).[144] They were fêted all the time. A deputation from the City called upon Sir Moses 'which was a great mark of respect'.

All the synagogues sent deputations, and Sir Moses and Lady Montefiore were followed by the crowds wherever they went. On the second day of Shavuoth they were visited by various gentlemen, '. . . and among the first, Rapoport, the Grand Rabbi of the place'. Rabbi S. J. L. Rapoport, the spiritual head of the community, discussed the problem of the Jewish inhabitants of the Holy Land. After visiting seven synagogues, the old cemetery, and many antiquities, the fatigued couple went to bed at their hotel immediately after dinner, to be woken up by a serenade performed by the choristers of the new synagogue.

They left Prague the next day and stopped at Kollin, where the Sabbath (26 May) was spent. The Chief Rabbi, Dr Daniel Frank, 'a person of superior endowments, came and addressed Sir Moses and Lady Montefiore most impressively', Dr Loewe translated and Sir Moses and company were very impressed by what they heard. Sir Moses paid a return visit to Rabbi Frank's house on Sunday. They stayed till late afternoon so that Sir Moses could visit the Synagogue and School, and he was so impressed by what he saw that he 'presented fifty pounds for a medal to be struck so that it might form a yearly prize to the best boy and girl with the name of the Rabbi on it'.[145]

They next spent three days at Vienna.[146] Baron Anselm de Rothschild called immediately on their arrival and 'conversed with Sir Moses on the subject of the journey, and offered his services.[147] As usual the community paid its respects. The British Ambassador, Lord Westmorland, invited Sir Moses to dinner. There, as in Prague, 'solemn services were held in the Synagogue'.[148] The local poet, Emmanuel Stern, presented the Montefiores with a beautiful Hebrew and German 'welcome-to-Vienna' poem.[149]

They left Vienna by train and reached Laibach,[150] the southern terminus of the Austrian railway system,[151] after a hair-raising journey that same evening '. . . and now adieu to railway travelling'. From there they had to travel by coach. Friday and Saturday were spent quietly in the picturesque village of Adelsburg, famous for its stalactite grotto, which the company visited after the termination of the Sabbath.[152]

On Sunday 3 June, they set out by coach from Adelsburg at 11 a.m. and reached Trieste on the Adriatic coast by almost midnight. The journey over the magnificently beautiful Dolomites was an exhilarating experience.

They stayed in Trieste until Friday. On Thursday evening in a brilliantly lit synagogue,[153] 'the Chief Rabbi, a man approaching his eightieth year, delivered a sermon in firm tone'[154] in honour of Sir Moses and hoping for his success. The community 'printed a pamphlet ... in order to perpetuate the remembrance' of Sir Moses Montefiore's stay in the city. It contained a Hebrew and Italian prayer by Chief Rabbi Treves, and an 'elegant and expressive' sonnet by Signor Abraham Vita Morpurgo.[155] Before leaving Trieste Sir Moses was presented by the Chief Rabbi and notables with an address, which he answered in a letter.[156]

A touching episode concerned another member of the ancient Morpurgo family, Rachel Morpurgo,[157] the famous Italian Hebrew poetess, who asked to be allowed to join Lady Montefiore's entourage as a domestic servant. She longed to be in close touch with Judith and also had the ultimate aim of settling in the Holy Land. This request could not be accepted and the disappointing message was conveyed to her by Dr Loewe. She expressed her feelings in a beautiful sonnet published a year later.[158]

On Friday 8 June the party embarked on the *Germania en route* to Constantinople. The weather was at first pleasant and Friday and Sabbath were much enjoyed. By Saturday night the weather turned stormy, causing great discomfort to some of the passengers. Sunday evening, 11 June, the ship dropped anchor in the harbour of Corfu, much to the relief of all. Mrs Guedalla was excited by the 'glimmer of millions of stars that are shining . . . .'.[159]

When the boat 'anchored off the Harbour a little crowd had come wonderingly to us and exchanged friendly greetings.' And, word soon reached the small Jewish community of the identity of the distinguished passenger on board the *Germania*. 'Several deputations came on board from the Jews, and the Rabbi's Lady [wife of Israel Moshe Hazan][160] sent Lady Montefiore a splendid bouquet, half a yard in length and of a conical shape.' While Sir Moses paid a visit to the Governor, Sir John Young, other members of his entourage made a sightseeing tour. The boat left Corfu after re-stocking with fresh provisions.

On the 13th they reached Piraeus — Athens and went ashore for a sightseeing tour. There was a further short stop-over at Smyrna on 15 June and finally, to quote Mrs Guedalla, on Sunday the 17th, 'We have to be thankful to the A-mighty for having caused us to reach this far-famed city of Constantinople in safety'.[161]

VI

Exactly five weeks after leaving London, Sir Moses and his party reached the halfway stage of their itinerary, Constantinople. The success of the mission to Jerusalem depended largely on the outcome of his discussions at the Porte and his ability to convince the Sultan of the desirability of his projects, so that the Sultan would grant him, on behalf of the Jews of the Holy Land, rights denied to them for centuries: to build a hospital, to buy land, to till the land with Jewish labour.

As soon as the boat arrived off the coast on 17 June, 'Mr. Camondo[162] came on board to receive Sir Moses and Lady'.[163] Abraham Camondo, later Baron Camondo, one of the richest Jews of Constantinople, was very active in Jewish communal affairs and influential with the civil authorities. The party was taken to the palatial Camondo home in Galata (the fashionable suburb of Constantinople), which was put at Sir Moses' disposal for as long as he needed it.[164] A description of the Camondo family, the household, the style of life and the truly oriental hospitality of the family is given by Jemima Guedalla, as is also the scene in Constantinople, the impassable roads, the unbearable heat and the constant plague of insects of all kinds.

Sir Moses, never one to waste time, within hours of landing delivered 'his letters,[165] and called on Lord Stratford de Redcliffe,[166] Ali Pasha,[167] the Grand Vizier, Rechid Pasha[168] and Rifaat Pasha . . .'. The extensive preparations made in London proved of great help, especially Palmerston's letters and the fact that Lord Clarendon had already in 1854[169] sent Lord Stratford de Redcliffe a 'private communication' about the purpose of Sir Moses' intended visit. Official 'instructions' had been sent from the Foreign Secretary in at least three dispatches: 26 January 1855, 28 March 1855[170] and 7 April 1855,[171] the last being conveyed by Sir Moses personally to Lord Stratford de Redcliffe.

FO/78/1062
Draft[172]   F[oreign] O[ffice]
Lord Stratford   7 April 1855
'Separate'
My Lord,
This dispatch will be delivered to y[our] E[xcellency] by Sir Moses Montefiore who is proceeding to the East with a view to the amelioration of the condition

of Jews in the Holy Land, by the cultivation of the soil, and the erection of a
hospital; and I have to instruct y[our] E[xcellency] to afford to Sir Moses
Montefiore all the assistance and facilities in your power in the furtherance of
his undertaking. See M. Montefiore March 28.[173]

Before 25 June one of the dragomans of the British Embassy, Mr
Etienne Pisani[174] informed Sir Moses that an audience with the
Sultan had been arranged for Thursday the 28th;[175] and the dispatch
already sent by Lord Stratford de Redcliffe to London on 20 June
(three days after Sir Moses' arrival) showed the degree of assistance
accorded personally by the Ambassador and his staff.

FO/78/1081   Constantinople
No. 450   June 20th 1855

My Lord,
Sir Moses Montefiore, who arrived here a few days ago, has requested my assistance to procure permission for him to build a hospital at Jerusalem for the
accommodation of invalids professing the Jewish Religion. He has also a wish to
obtain for the Jews of Palestine the privilege of holding land with a view of
affording them the means of subsistence independent of charity.

Concerning that on grounds of humanity in one case, and on those of policy
on the other the plans and intentions of Sir Moses are worthy of favourable
consideration, I have no hesitation to recommend them to Fuad Pasha,[176] and
to request that Sir Moses may be allowed to pay his respects in person to His
Majesty the Sultan, as well as to his Ministers at the Porte.

I am happy to say that the most friendly assurances have been given to me
by the Ottoman Secretary of State. The hospital, to be built out of funds in
Sir Moses Montefiore's possession, may be considered as granted; the Sultan
will also grant him the desired audience, and it is by no means impossible that
even the question of land may be arranged in a satisfactory manner.

I have the honour to be, with the greatest respect, My Lord, Your Lordship's
most Obedient Servant
                              Stratford de Redcliffe

This dispatch is endorsed in Clarendon's handwriting in pencil on the
reverse:

Rec'd London 2 July
Learn with satisfaction that he has been able to arrange these matters which
formed the subject of private communication to him ... asked Ld Ponsonby ...[177]

It was arranged that on the Thursday Pisani would accompany Sir
Moses, to act as translator and general factotum. The day before the
audience a completely unexpected message informed Sir Moses:[178]
'that the Turkish Ministers, being desirous of showing me some mark
of the high esteem they entertain for me, expressed the desire of
conferring upon me the honour of the *Medjidjeh*'.

The next day (28 June), at two o'clock in the afternoon, Sir Moses,
in the company of Mr Pisani and Dr Loewe, was received by the
Sultan. On Sir Moses being presented by Mr Pisani, the Sultan

'graciously said that he remembered me very well, and was happy to see me again'. (The Sultan had seen Sir Moses in 1840, and had ensured that the Rhodes blood libel case was stopped before there was any danger to life.)[179] Sir Moses then presented his request to

His Majesty to grant me his countenance and support, and in compliance with my petition to the Porte. His Majesty replied that it was his happiness and duty to do all in his power to promote the welfare of his subjects; that he would grant my request, and was happy to do so for my philanthropy and humanity.[180]

Sir Moses thus achieved what he had set his heart upon: permission to build *his* hospital in Jerusalem and to acquire land for the purpose, as well as for agricultural pursuits. He was anxious to have the *Firman* in his possession, duly executed, sealed and signed, as quickly as possible, and 'entreated' Mr Pisani to obtain it by Monday (2 July). On Friday (29 June) Sir Moses and Lady Montefiore were received by the Ambassador and Lady Stratford de Redcliffe in whose company they spent two hours. 'His Lordship has been informed of all that has passed at my audience with the Sultan and was pleased with the result'.

On Sunday (1 July) Sir Moses, accompanied by Mr William Dorea, another member of the Embassy staff (with his Kawass) and Dr Loewe, proceeded to the Porte to see Ali Pasha: 'His Excellency confirmed in the most flattering manner all that His Majesty the Sultan promised me', and said the *Firman* should be ready in two to three days. 'Ali Pasha is a mild and agreeable man, and expressed much pleasure in assisting my philanthropic efforts.' At the request of Sir Moses, Reshid Pasha promised to write letters of introduction to the Governors of Beirut and Jerusalem.

Sir Moses noted with obvious delight in his diary on 3 July that he had been informed by Mr Pisani that he '. . . had received the Firman for the building of the hospital, and also that for myself, which according to the usual practice he had forwarded to the Ambassador for transmission to me'. Pisani also informed Sir Moses that 'the Sultan was pleased to confer upon you the *Medjidjeh* of the second class.[181] Jemima Guedalla, though more concerned with events and scenery than political developments, noted the same day: 'The good news came this morning of the *Firman* being in the hands of the Ambassador'.[182] However, this news proved slightly premature.

The next day, Wednesday (4 July), Sir Moses took a day for sightseeing. He, Lady Montefiore, Dr Loewe and Mrs Camondo, Sen. visited two hospitals in Therapia. They also walked to see Lord Stratford de Redcliffe at the Embassy, which was in that district. Lord Stratford de Redcliffe took this opportunity to tell them that the *Firmans*[183] were ready and 'should be sent to the British Consul at Pera for me [i.e. Sir Moses] as was usual'.

Lord Stratford de Redcliffe presented him with the Order which the Sultan had conferred upon him: 'He would ... inform the British Government of it in his dispatches ...' and would 'add his wish that Her Majesty the Queen would allow Sir Moses to wear the Order of the Sultan'.

That Sir Moses appreciated the support he received from the Ambassador can be gauged from his diary:[184] 'I feel deeply indebted to Lord [Stratford de] Redcliffe, who has by his great kindness aided my endeavours to assist my co-religionists in Palestine! May G-d reward him, Amen.'

Thursday (5 July) was supposed to be the last day of the visit to Constantinople. Jemima Guedalla, who much enjoyed the stay, but suffered from the natural environment, confided to her diary with undisguised relief that she 'woke — that morning — with the delightful impression that our last night here has passed'. The luggage was packed and stowed on board ship. But then, to her utter disappointment: 'We found Sir Moses had not received the papers and he declared nothing would induce him to start [the onward journey] without them.' They were near despair.

However, all turned out well. The dispatch rider arrived with the 'papers'. Jemima exclaimed excitedly, 'They are come — they are come. Happy words to our ears. The *Firman* is here.'[185]

VII

Late that afternoon (5 July) Sir Moses and Lady Montefiore and their party sailed on *l'Imperatrice*, 'a very fine vessel' with 'good cabin facilities'. Sir Moses had the *Firman* to build the hospital, vizirial letters to buy land and property in the Holy Land, and letters of recommendation from the British Ambassador and the Turkish authorities to their counterparts and subordinates in the Holy Land.

There were, however, a further twelve days on board ship, some of them on rough seas, others enlivened by lesser incidents like the excitement caused by a rumour of a pair of sharks closely following the boat.[186] Among the passengers were a desperately sick Turkish woman, and an English soldier wounded in the Crimea, who were tended by Dr Loewe who gave them palliatives to lessen their pain.[187] A group of fifteen Jews from Constantinople were going 'to *end their days* in Jerusalem'; and in Alexandretta, 'an infested village',[188] they were joined by 'a very respectable family from Baghdad. . . to *go and live* in the Holy Land'.

At various ports of call, they had to put up with onerous quarantine regulations, which were rigorously enforced to prevent the spread of the cholera epidemic.[189] Nevertheless,[190]

Wherever practicable Sir Moses went on shore to acquaint himself with the state of the Jews in the locality, but at others that was impossible, deputations came on board and presented addresses. He thus had ample opportunities to ascertain the exact conditions of his brethren in Smyrna, Rhodes, Messina, Scadroon (Alexandretta), Latakia, Cyprus and Bayrout . . . .

In Latakia Sir Moses received the very welcome intelligence that 'all the things had reached Beyrouth safely',[191] meaning the papers sent from Constantinople to the British Consul via Beirut.

On 15 July, 'We are really at Beyrouth' and 'on ascending the deck a beautiful prospect presented itself . . . Alas! we have to remain here two days.' They were allowed to go ashore to enjoy the short stop-over but the scorching mid-summer heat prevented them from enjoying the countryside beyond the city. Ibrahim, 'the dragoman[192] of whose capabilities in former journeys Sir Moses and Lady Montefiore have spoken' was engaged by Sir Moses to 'go with us to Jerusalem'.

The landfall of the *l'Imperatrice*, midday Sunday 15 July 1855), was the beginning of what became — in retrospect — the most important of Sir Moses' visits to the Holy Land. After 'offering up a sincere prayer to the A-mighty for having brought us over the sea portion of our journey to Jerusalem', they landed at Jaffa where they spent the night. 'We went to an hotel kept by an Israelite; we have our beds put up; the sitting room is small and overhangs the sea'. Mrs Guedalla continues: 'We are so delighted to find ourselves on *terra firma*, that notwithstanding the poorness of our accommodation all seems charming.'[193]

Sir Moses, within hours of landing, spent an hour with Mr Khayat,[194] the British Consul in Jaffa. The next day was also spent in Jaffa and a number of deputations waited upon Sir Moses. Among the callers were the Governor of Jaffa and Ahmed Aga, who was to play an important part in enabling Sir Moses to achieve his aim.

On the following day, at 4 o'clock in the afternoon, the party set out for Jerusalem. Sir Moses and Haim Guedalla travelled in 'tachterevans',[195] Lady Montefiore, Jemima Guedalla, Mr Kursheedt and Dr Loewe were on horseback. Twelve mounted guards accompanied them 'as the road was reported to be unsafe'. They travelled through the night, stopping for short breaks at Ramleh, Abu Gosh, Latrun, 'where we entered a tent and had something to drink — no one who has not been in this country can imagine what a luxury a glass of water is'. All along the way they were met by village dignitaries and local governors with their attendants who 'pirouetted on their steeds and performed the most astonishing acts of horsemanship . . .';[196] or, as Finn put it, '. . . by the escort of horsemen who had been sent out by the Turkish authorities and who were careering around at Jeerad play, and were firing off their guns and pistols'.[197] As soon as the Holy City came into sight, the party stopped and 'all dismounted, as usual, for a short prayer'.

They were met by thousands of Jews as they were approaching Jerusalem.[198] The crowd was headed by the Haham Bashi, the heads of the *Batei Din* (ecclesiastical courts), and by the religious and lay leaders of the community.[199] Finn, in a dispatch to Lord Stratford de Redcliffe,[200] reported that they 'were received with much respect by the Turkish authorities, and needless to add, with enthusiasm by the Jewish people'.

The party was fatigued but delighted to be within sight of Jerusalem on that Friday 20 July.[201] They pitched their tents outside the City 'within sight of the Walls'; 'that is to say — our encampment is in the plains of Moab, outside the Jaffa Gate . . .; 'at the cornice nearest to the Wall. . .'[202] 'at the Terebinth tree on the corner of the Maidan nearest to the walls',[203] and on the same spot occupied by Sir Moses and Lady Montefiore on their visit of 1849.[204]

The encampment was rather dingy. The slightest winds made everybody apprehensive, and one of the tents, occupied by Mrs Guedalla, disintegrated even before it was put to use. Their love for the place was the only redeeming factor:

Were it not in this land, I should certainly have many fears in being so exposed and surrounded by such strange and fierce looking individuals, no protection against the entrance of animals . . . .[205]

The great terebinth tree provided some shade against the intense mid-summer heat of Jerusalem, but to protect themselves from the sand blown up by sharp desert winds, they had to take shelter under canvas.

Notwithstanding the strain of the night journey from Jaffa to Jerusalem — and the short stop-over at Jaffa was anything but restful — Sir Moses was at work almost from the moment of his arrival. Finn wrote in his private diary that when meeting them at the roadside as the Montefiore party stopped for prayers on the first sight of the Holy City, he and his wife Elizabeth 'were almost surprised to see the change six years had made in them both; they are very feeble with age'.

Before their arrival the Finns and Montefiores had been in communication. Mrs Finn offered their home in Jerusalem, but Lady Montefiore declined. They had, she wrote, decided to camp in tents.[206]

Information of Montefiore's pending arrival and the objects of his visit were forwarded from London to Consul Finn[207] at Jerusalem, and instructions from Lord Stratford de Redcliffe were dispatched to him from Constantinople.[208]

> Therapia
> July 4th 1855
>
> Sir
> Referring to your previous correspondence I have much satisfaction in sending you herewith Firman with an English translation, Authorising the Construction of a Synagogue in Jerusalem, as solicited by the Ashkenazy Jews.[209]
> .You will have the goodness to assist the parties concerned in obtaining a full execution of the Sultan's order in their favour.
> I have the honour . . .
> [Lord Stratford de Redcliffe]
> J. Finn Esq.,
> Jerusalem

Similarly, instructions were issued by the Turkish ministers at Constantinople and forwarded to the Governor of Jerusalem, Kiamil Pasha,[210] who was well disposed to Jerusalem's Jews. The Vizirial letter containing the instructions was brought by Sir Moses.[211]

In his official day by day notes of 20 July 1855, Finn wrote:

> Sir Moses Montefiore sent to the Consul the Dispatches, Vizireal letters, and Firman of which he was the bearer. One Viz[ireal] letter is for the encouragement of Jewish agriculture, the other for the creation of a Jewish hospital and the Firman is in re: Ashkenazi synagogue.

Sabbath (21 July — 6 Av) was spent quietly, mainly under canvas. On Sunday a further twelve soldiers were posted round the encampment 'on account of the unsettled state of things'. Monday the 23rd being the eve of the 'Black Fast',[212] Sir Moses did not want to receive Jewish visitors, but 'different Consuls called', as did Achmet Pasha,[213] his son and grandson. Consul Finn presented Sir Moses to the Pasha 'and the documents were read in Council'.[214] This terse statement is amplified by Finn's recollection of the event:

> On official presentation of Sir Moses with his documents to the Pasha, a Council of the City Effendis was necessary, and had been summoned for hearing the Sultan's Firman read. These worthies delayed their appearance, and we were told that they were at prayers. When they came, and after formal compliments, the Firman was read out by the Official secretary. The Pasha set the example (which the rest seemed inclined to have omitted) of standing, as usual while a Sultan's Firman was being read; and of making a salutation of respect at the close. His Excellency the Pasha was not wanting in any attention; and due ceremonial, with abundance of complimentary speeches, following the reading.[215]

After the ceremony was over Sir Moses and his party were invited to the roof of the barracks to view the Temple Courts; and after having seen the view paid a visit to the Commandant of the Garrison. 'On leaving the barracks a Guard of Honour was turned out and presented arms.'[216] The Commandant personally saw Sir Moses off and accompanied the party on foot, walking in front of them in the street 'as far as the arch of *"Ecce Homo"* under which the sedan chair was waiting'.[217] Finn attributed this great honour to the fact that Sir Moses was the bearer of 'the Nishan of Order of Mejeedieh'.

Tuesday 24 July was the Fast of 9 Av. All members of the party fasted and some walked to the Western Wall. 'Sir Moses and Lady Montefiore bear it wonderfully. It is a long and fatiguing day.'[218] As Finn noted — 'no business could be transacted on such a day'.

VIII

On Thursday 26 July (11 Av) Sir Moses took the most controversial step in all his seven visits to the Holy Land. It caused heart-searching problems for the Rabbinate of Jerusalem in their relationship with him. The delicate nature of the situation has been obscured by Dr Loewe, and is not even mentioned by Sir Moses' biographers. In consequence, even the fundamental facts are in dispute, dates were distorted and serious scholars specializing in the period misled.

For that day, Dr Loewe records one particular event. The cryptic text reads:[219] 'They received an invitation from the Pasha to see all the places held in veneration by Moslem, Christian and Jew.'

In the next paragraph Loewe relates that the Patriarchs of the Greek, Latin and Armenian convents extended similar invitations: 'Sir Moses however was not able to accept them all because to accept them would have diverted his attention from the objects of his journey.' Loewe continues with verbatim extracts from the Second Report of the Appeal Fund, published one year later in 1856,[220] and then mentions a meeting on 27 July. This is followed by the information that 'with the concurrence of the Rabbinate' Sir Moses and Lady Montefiore succeeded in founding a girls' school,[221] an event that took place on 17 August, three weeks later than the sequence of the narrative would suggest, since no date is given in the text. The next two and a half pages[222] consist of an excerpt from Miss Mary Eliza Rogers' *Domestic Life in Palestine*,[223] giving a very favourable account of her visit to the girls' school in May 1856.

It is most unusual for Dr Loewe to draw on outside sources, and, when doing so, he usually paraphrases. I am left with the impression that the reference to 26 July is deliberately obscured by the unexpectedly verbose five pages which follow and interrupt the narrative.

Indeed, one may ask what is the place that is venerated by Muslims, Christians and Jews, in that order? Loewe mentions 'places'. That this place (or places) is (or are) in Jerusalem may be assumed from the fact that the invitation came from the Pasha, the Governor of Jerusalem. In fact, it was an invitation to Sir Moses and his party to visit the Temple Mount and the Area of the Sanctuary that gave Dr Loewe good reason to be evasive about this episode.

For centuries Islam had jealously excluded all 'non-believers' from the precincts of the Hharam esh Sharief. Trespassers risked their lives. Only very recently had the rigidly enforced ban on non-Muslims been slightly relaxed. The first Europeans to enjoy the privilege of walking upon the hallowed ground were the Duke and Duchess of Brabant (later King Leopold II of the Belgians). He brought a *firman* granting permission from Constantinople. Its implementation by the Pasha involved a subterfuge to deceive and temporarily imprison the hereditary Guardian of the Hharam.[224]

While the Duke and Duchess of Brabant were admitted at their own request, Sir Moses was invited by the Pasha, an extraordinary and unprecedented distinction.[225] He accepted the invitation and on the 26th, he and his party, guided by the Pasha in person, entered the place where no Jew had stood for nearly two millenia, the *Har haBayit* and *M'kom haMikdash*. It was Finn's considered view that 'Sir Moses Montefiore acted wisely . . . in accepting the very high honour . . .' offered by the Pasha.

Haim and Jemima Guedalla were present and Jemima, the most reliable chronicler of day-by-day events, wrote:[226] Thursday 26th July — Rose at six to prepare for an early visit to the Mosque of Omar. We proceeded to the Governor's who received us most courteously; his name is Kramel Pasha,[227] and he escorted us to this spot, which so few besides ourselves have had the privilege to enter — so jealously has the Mussulman guarded it from the profanation of non-believers in the prophet — it is quite an event for us to be allowed to see it . . . It was a wonderful sight and never to be forgotten.'[228]

It did not occur to her that others might regard this excursion as a serious transgression of the *Halachah* (Jewish Law).

According to Mrs Guedalla the party consisted of Sir Moses and Lady Montefiore, Mr and Mrs Guedalla and Dr S. Fränkel. Consul and Mrs Finn, and Mr and Miss Rogers came at Sir Moses' invitation. Finn noted in his Consular Diary, 'Consul and the office accompanied Sir Moses Montefiore to the Hharam esh Sharief.'[229]

Gershom Kursheedt's name was omitted from Mrs Guedalla's list, but his presence is attested by Kursheedt himself in a letter addressed to his relatives in New Orleans.[230] Dr Loewe, also missing from Mrs Guedalla's list, is mentioned in the 'letter' in the *Wiener Mittheilungen*,[231] and also by Mrs Finn.[232]

Finn complicates matters, as he adds[233] 'Sir Moses and Lady Montefiore with their friends and attendants' to his own party, 'also the two Jewish interpreters, one attached to my Consulate, the other the official interpreter of the Chief Rabbi, both present out of respect for Sir Moses Montefiore'. His 'interpreter' was his Jewish dragoman,[234] Raphael Meyuhas.[235] Who filled that post at the Chief Rabbi's Office, I am unable to say, but there can be no doubt that he was an orthodox Jew, as was Meyuhas. As such, it is hardly feasible that either would have entered the Area of the Sanctuary, let alone a representative of the Chief Rabbi. It is strange that these two interpreters are not mentioned by Finn either in his Consular Diary or in his private diaries, nor by Mrs Finn.

The visit caused consternation in Jerusalem. How could a man who had the reputation of conforming most scrupulously even with the minutest requirements of the *Halachah*, have flouted so flagrantly the Holy Law? Rabbi Moshe Reischer, a resident of Jerusalem[236] at the time, wrote about twelve years later that Sir Moses 'acted against the wishes of the whole population of Jerusalem when he entered the *M'kom haMikdash*. They warned him he should refrain from doing so. In particular as all of us [i.e. Jews] are profaned by [the inevitable] contact with the deceased. It was just not right'. He is not correct when he states that Sir Moses was warned. The available evidence suggests that the population was rather surprised after the event to learn that the party *had* been. He is nevertheless correct when he says that Jerusalem's Jewry resented the action.

James Finn, who was closely involved, related that, notwithstanding Sir Moses' record as the roving ambassador of troubled Jewry, the saviour of the Jews in Damascus in 1840, and all that he had consistently done for the Holy Land since he first set foot on the holy soil in 1827:[237] 'Nevertheless, the bigots did manage to stir up ungrateful zealots,[238] some of whom even went to the length of pronouncing excommunications upon the good man, I believe in three synagogues . . .'.[239] He claimed to have good reason to believe these rumours as he had heard them from eye witnesses.

The continental Jewish press carried the news of Sir Moses Montefiore's expedition to the *M'kom haMikdash*, and commented on its merits (if any), and alleged consequences. Some editors and their correspondents agreed with Sir Moses, other opposed him.

Some saw the events as Sir Moses wished, others felt the retribution (*Herem*) to have been justified. Yet others denied the basic facts on which these various judgements were based; they claimed some events never took place. The *Jewish Chronicle* made no mention of it until 30 November 1855, by which time Sir Moses and his party were back in London.[240] And, even at that late date, it surfaced as a by-product of other news. It was reported that the poor of Jerusalem were not satisfied with Sir Moses on this fourth visit, because he entrusted the distribution of the money he brought for charity to the rabbis. The paper also quoted the opinions of two missionaries, Crawford[241] and Nicolayson (in an unnamed missionary journal appearing in London) on the reaction of Jerusalem Jewry to the trespass of Sir Moses and party on the *M'kom haMikdash.*[242]

On the value of this source, the quotations from which take up nearly two columns, the *Jewish Chronicle* commented:

> The real friends of Israel will perceive much that will rejoice their hearts, even among the distorted statements of a journal whose articles are evidently manufactured to order.

A typical extract read: 'The *zealots* had *further* reason to be dissatisfied with Sir Moses because of his "mortal offence" of entering into the Mosque of Omar which they still regard as in some sense the temple, and which they hold is unlawful for any Jew to enter as being contrary to both the written and oral law.'

Crawford went into much detail but made no mention of a *Herem* against Sir Moses though what he wrote comes very near to it: 'Indeed some of them openly remonstrated with Sir Moses against such profanity, and others said that they considered that by that very act he renounced his religion.'

Both Finn and Crawford were aware that the prohibition on entering the *Har haBayit* was an *halachic* axiom. Both reported that the 'Rabbis' argued the validity of the prohibition at the present time. Both were wrong on the basic facts. Yet, in stating that there were *halachic* disputations, they were correct.

IX

Another grievance caused adverse comment and resentment among a large section of the Jerusalem community and displeased Sir Moses and his party. His terms of reference limited the use he could make of the very large sums of money at his disposal. The Touro legacy was for the building of the hospital. Of the near £20,000 produced by the Appeal, £6,364 had already been sent to the Holy Land for the relief of the starving population.[243] Once the emergency had passed, the remainder of the Appeal Fund was to be used in compliance with the terms of reference:[244]

Besides the bestowal of the temporary assistance, the trustees have been from the commencement of their operations most anxious by stemming its very source, to prevent the recurrence of such frightful sufferings; an object the accomplishment of which might best be promoted by avoiding the evils of indiscriminate alms-giving, and by discouraging reliance on adventitious aid, so destructive to habits of forethought and industry.

This did not mean that the poor who were dependent on charity and, in particular, on the *Halukah*, were ignored.[245] 'A considerable sum [was] entrusted to the elders of the communities, to be distributed among the necessitous poor of Jerusalem, Hebrew, [*sic*] Jaffa and other congregations.[246] Only the method of help was altered. This, it was hoped, would discriminate in favour of the needy.

However, this change gave rise to an unpleasant reaction from those who rightly or wrongly felt disadvantaged. On 5 August Jemima Guedalla noted in her diary:[247] 'Hundreds of people have been here to solicit alms.' After jotting down the activities of the day and the various visitors who called, she wrote that evening:

A large body of very poor people have come up and have taken their position around the tents; they declare they will not leave till Sir Moses has heard their complaints against the Hahamim for getting possession of all the money and not relieving them with it ... Seeing they were not prepared to move, about eight Ibrahim[248] addressed them and said Sir Moses would not return for hours, upon which they agreed to depart and return the next day.

And that is exactly what they did. Early next morning when Mrs Guedalla rose she

found the plain covered with masses of people. The ringleader was discovered and placed by Dr Loewe[249] under a tree with coffee to regale him and two men to attend him; then the Doctor addressed the people they reiterated their complaints and said they were starving. A small sum was given to each, and an engagement formed with several who wished to enter their homes as agriculturalists. All progressed most harmoniously, when all at once the ringleader made a demand for meat and other things, and became so uproarious that our janissary and others tried to handle him, but he pushed the first down; four of the guards then took him in hand, and amid the shrieks and cries of the women and howlings of the men, he was carried off to the English Consul, who put him in Prison for his unruly conduct. This scene quite upset us all.

That these excesses were not the spontaneous expression of despair is shown by the intemperate demands for meat and the complaint against the Hahamim that they did not give them any money. Finn's consular diary complements the story. He noted on that day, 6 August:

'A Russian Jew (English subject) named [left blank] imprisoned for insult and violence to Sir M. Montefiore.'[250] Sir Moses nevertheless forgave him, as Finn wrote next day: 'The Jew released from prison by request of Sir Moses.'

The news travelled fast and far. The *Wiener Mittheilungen*[251] published in German translation parts of a Hebrew letter, dated Jerusalem 22 Av (6 August), that is, the day of the first rowdy demonstration outside Sir Moses' tents. The demonstrators wanted quick publicity. The anonymous Jerusalem writer says:

Sir Moses has aroused the displeasure of the local population. So far he has done nothing for the local poor. The large funds which were entrusted to him by benevolent donors for the purpose of giving succour to the needy, he misappropriated for other purposes. Yesterday, Sir Moses in the presence of the Rabbi[252] stated that there were no poor in Jerusalem! In response, the Rabbi acted to have a proclamation published in all the synagogues that all the poor should congregate at the tents of the Baronet 'to demonstrate as the living exemplars', with the result that 300 rag-covered wailing paupers laid siege to Sir Moses' camp. This is a strange way [to deliver] a stormy petition [it would be strange] in the Capital of Albion. Sir Moses and his companion Dr Loewe made themselves hated, because they dared to enter the *M'kom haMikdash* on the *Har haBayit*. The population of Jerusalem is waiting with impatience for their departure, but looks forward with anticipation to the arrival of the true philanthropist,[253] Herr Albert Cohn of Paris.[254]

We have seen in Mrs Guedalla's entry who the 'Rabbi' was: an unnamed Russian Jew, a rabble-rouser with the capacity to agitate an ungrateful crowd, an individual on whom Sir Moses never even set eyes.[255] It is of course not surprising that further disturbances occurred. Jemima Guedalla wrote in her diary:[256]

Tuesday 7 — rose at quarter past six. Prayers are said each day in the large tent. Alas! somewhat of the scene of yesterday was renewed; another man began haranguing and wailing, said he was starving and would not leave till he was relieved. Dr L. interfered and he was made to withdraw. Really if this annoyance goes on we shall scarcely be safe in our own tents.

On 3 September, above the defamatory 'letter from Jerusalem', the *Wiener Mittheilungen* printed a forceful denial of the *Herem* allegations which had appeared on 25 August in two separate non-Jewish newspapers, *Das Fremdenblatt* and *Die Morgenpost*.[257] A Mr Adutt[258] wrote (in German):

As I am very well informed, I am in a position to state with absolute certainty that the above allegations are without any foundation. Sir Moses Montefiore was received by the Jewish population of Jerusalem with enthusiasm[259] and what is more he enjoys the best personal relationship with the Rabbinate.

A news report similar in substance but different in tone and details was published in Philippson's *AZdJ*.[260] This was copied from the 'Preussische Correspondent' of an unnamed paper. It bears no overt bias against Sir Moses but is highly critical of the Rabbinate and the Jews of Jerusalem. The writer stated objectively the aims of Sir Moses, for what purpose the funds would be used, and also for what they would not be used. However, 'the local Jews prefer the dirty and demeaning existence of the idler, to that of the life of those who earn their living by the sweat of their brow.' Sir Moses was not prepared to dispose of the funds in 'hard cash' but wished to use them 'for the benefit of all'. However, by the course he had taken '. . . he made himself liable for a synagogal *Herem*'. But as this could not be presented as a convincing reason for such drastic action, the trespass on the *M'kom haMikdash* was 'used by the Rabbis as a pretence'. And the *Herem* was duly pronounced.[261]

Philippson's ostensible purpose in reprinting in full an earlier report from another paper[262] was to give space for a refutation. A *Privat-mittheilung* dated Hamburg 3 September 1855, by an anonymous writer was submitted to the *AZdJ*. In this, the writer categorically denied the report of the 'Preussische Correspondent' of Jerusalem, that the demonstrators in Jerusalem threatened Sir Moses with the *Herem*. 'We are authentically informed from Jerusalem that, to say the least, this does not accord with the truth.' It was nevertheless admitted that among the Jews of Jerusalem there was much consternation caused by the visit to the *M'kom haMikdash*, but he added that 'at no time was there a *Herem* pronounced . . .'. Sir Moses enjoyed as much respect as ever, as his munificence was welcome.

Philippson disagreed with this statement of the facts and rather unconvincingly tried to make out a case that a *Herem* was pronounced in secret,[263] which never came to the knowledge of Sir Moses. He did not seem to realize how ridiculous was this compromise theory about a *Herem*. For it is clear that the Jews of Jerusalem were, if anything, only too demonstrative and always ready to make sure that everyone knew their likes and dislikes; and what purpose could be served by pronouncing a *Herem*, of which the victim would remain in ignorance?

Philippson, however, identified, without naming, the author of the *Privat-mittheilung*, by indicating his identity with a sneer. The defender of Sir Moses and the Jews of Jerusalem was, he said, the 'Nassi de Erez Israel m'Altona'. The title of *Nasi* (prince) of the Land of Israel used to be bestowed by the Rabbinate of Jerusalem upon a person who had distinguished himself as a patron of the Jews in the Holy Land.[264] Rabbi Jacob Ettlinger, the Chief Rabbi of Altona,[265] known as the 'last Gaon of Germany' was given that distinction. He was a close collaborator of the *Pekidim v'Amarklim* of Amsterdam and he was, as the *Pekidim* were, an outspoken antagonist of Reform Judaism in all its aspects. Philippson had a long-running feud with the *Pekidim* and clashed on many occasions with their leadership. Nor had he any love for Sir Moses. This helps to explain his attitude.

So far evidence has been cited from people who were to all intents and purposes outsiders, the one exception being Rabbi Moshe Reischer. He however did not allude to a *Herem* ever being pronounced. So is there any evidence from the rabbis or from the population of Jerusalem that a *Herem* was indeed pronounced? If so, what was the local reaction?

The historian A. R. Malachi[266] remembered that when he was a boy in Jerusalem at the turn of the century, the *Herem* upon Sir Moses was part of local folklore. Eliezer Ben Yehuda, in an article published in 1884,[267] mentioned Sir Moses' visit to the *M'kom haMikdash* and the ensuing *Herem*. He added that 'when Sir Moses got to know what had happened, he asked for the names of those who pronounced the *Herem* upon him. Next morning when he was called to the *Sefer* (reading from the Scroll of the Law), he asked to have a *Mi Sheberach* (prayer) read for them, and rewarded them in recognition of their honest action.' Ben Yehuda omitted all dates.

Rabbi Samuel Weingarten[268] quoted another savant, and a native of the Holy Land, Rabbi Hayim Hirschensohn:[269]

When I was a child in Jerusalem, a boy of 11, I remember, Sir Moses Montefiore came for the sixth time to Jerusalem, in 1867.[270] I well remember having heard that he and his 'Rabbi'[271] Dr Loewe entered the *M'kom haMikdash*.[272] A Rabbi Moshe Yoseph Lissa when he heard of it, grabbed a Shofar (ram's horn) and excommunicated Sir Moses Montefiore in the streets of Jerusalem. When they, Sir Moses Montefiore who was a very G-d fearing man, and Dr Loewe, turned to the Rabbis to remonstrate that what they had done was done in all innocence, and that they acted in accordance with the ruling of the R'Abad [Rabbi Abraham ben David of Posquières],[273] the Rabbis of Jerusalem put their minds to rest: there was no need to take notice of Rabbi Moshe Yoseph Lissa as he was not of sound mind . . . .[274]

We cannot accept without some reservation his assertion that the *Herem* was pronounced in consequence of the entry to the *M'kom haMikdash*. Malachi however produced further important evidence, which perhaps could be faulted in some details, but nevertheless has the ingredients of a correct recall of the events by a major participant in the drama. Malachi discovered[275] an interview by Jacob Goldman,[276] a pioneer journalist of Jerusalem, with the Chief Rabbi,

Shmuel Salant,[277] in 1887. Goldman asked Rabbi Salant whether 'according to old inhabitants of Jerusalem, Sir Moses Montefiore and Dr Loewe were excommunicated because they entered the *M'kom haMikdash*.' Salant refuted this unreservedly:

The story of the excommunication is an absolute lie. It is true that tempers ran high in Jerusalem and Sir Moses enraged the feelings of the *Haredim* [strictly orthodox]. But no one had the resolve to tell them [Sir Moses and Dr Loewe] so. Haham Haim Nissim Abualafia[278] was the Haham of the Sephardim at the time and R Yeshaya Bordaki[279] the Rabbi of the Ashkenazim. Yes, they lacked the courage to rebuke them, and to tell Sir Moses of his misdeed. However, the next day when Dr Loewe had to call on me, I took the opportunity to castigate him. He was astonished by what I had to say, and referred me to the Rabad,[280] who, he asserted, was of the opinion that there is no sanctity attached [to the Precincts of the Temple] in present day conditions. I pointed out to him that he was mistaken and referred him to [the *Halachah* in] the *Shulchan Aruch*.[281] He replied: 'That is the view of Maimonides, but we may act according to the view of Rabad'. 'You are wrong again,' I replied, 'they both, Rambam and Rabad, agree that there is an absolute prohibition of entry to the *M'kom haMikdash*, and this is binding for all times. Where their opinions differ is only in the definition as to the class of transgression it fits into.'[282] Dr Loewe's sincere reaction was an admission: 'I am sorry, I made a mistake. However (he added), Sir Moses would not have accepted my advice not to enter.' My riposte was: 'You are again mistaken, Sir Moses would never have entered had his attention been drawn to the gravity of such a step.'

If the tempers of Jerusalem were seething against Sir Moses, Dr Loewe was much to blame. Here we have a clear account by one who took an active part in the events, recalling his own involvement; and he was absolutely sure that no *Herem* was issued in consequence of that particular event. However, was there one in another context?

Although decades apart, Ben-Yehuda and Hirschensohn mention that Sir Moses supposedly forgave those who excommunicated him and that he had a *Mi Sheberach* (prayer) read for them. There is no apparent connection between the two except that both seem to be using the same folklore sources.

Haim Guedalla was at Sir Moses' side during the whole of their stay in the Holy Land. He took exception to what was printed by Philippson and wrote to the Editor:[283]

London: My attention has been drawn to the report in no. 37 of your excellent publication. There I noticed your report written from Hamburg and bearing on our recent stay in Jerusalem. As I am aware of your dedication to the truth, I hasten to inform you that, when you say that we were excommunicated because of our visit to the Mosque of Omar, this is nothing but an invention. Not one single word was ever uttered on this subject, even though I was in daily contact with the rabbinical authorities.[284] I will ask you to publish this, my refutation, in one of your forthcoming issues.
                              H. Guedalla.

It is characteristic of Philippson, that in a postscript he side-tracked the issue, as he had done with the denial by Rabbi Jacob Ettinger. His prejudices were apparent.

To recapitulate, it seems that those who were personally involved were the most determined to deny that a *Herem* was issued because of the *M'kom haMikdash* episode. The contemporary propagators of the rumours are all quoted in the press as anonymous letter writers or correspondents, which is always suspicious and particularly when the sources are the *AZdJ* and, to a lesser degree, the *Wiener Mittheilungen*. The missionaries had their own reasons for believing the story, but their accounts cannot be accepted without serious reservations.

X

Sir Moses took a personal interest in a number of Jerusalem charities already in existence and to ensure their long term survival he gave them considerable subsidies. Some had been founded earlier by the Montefiores, for example, the *Bikkur Holim*, known as the 'Lying-in Charity', inaugurated about 1845 by Lady Montefiore,[285] and the Free Loan Society.[286] But Sir Moses was well aware that the Holy City badly needed schools for boys and girls.

He abandoned the idea of a boys' school very quickly. It was, he was told, not needed because boys' education was fully catered for in the existing Talmud Torah schools.[287] However, he persisted with the establishment of the girls' school. Mrs Guedalla noted as the last item for Wednesday 1 August:[288]

> With joy I hear that a school is going to be instituted for the girls. I could have desired it to include a few more branches than Hebrew and sewing but we must view this as a happy commencement, and *le bon temps viendra*, great objects must be attained by slow degrees. . .

What was a sign of great hope to Jemima Guedalla was the ominous harbinger of much trouble for many Jerusalemites, who saw it as a breach in traditional teaching methods.

On 2 August (Thursday), news of the impending establishment of a girls' school circulated and on Friday, Jemima Guedalla returned to the subject:[289] 'Hundreds of people have been here to have their children's names inserted for attendance in the school Sir Moses and Lady Montefiore are going to found'; and all that enthusiasm was shown even before a building was available to house the school.

However, finding the appropriate accommodation did not create any particular problem. On 7 August, Finn wrote in his private

diary:[290] 'Long interview with Sir Moses Montefiore in the town
house — unexpectedly, caused by the delay of the Effendi in writing
out the lease of the house he has taken.' When the Effendi finally
arrived,[291] 'Lease of large house for Sir M. Montefiore ratified to be
used for Jewish school.' Dr Loewe commented: 'Sir Moses was
fortunately enabled to secure for this establishment one of the best
houses in the Jewish Quarter.'[292]

Mrs Guedalla has been quoted on the purpose of the school. Dr
Loewe amplified this: 'With the concurrence of the Jewish authorities
in Jerusalem Sir Moses and Lady Montefiore succeeded in founding
a girls' school in which, in addition to other subjects necessary to
the daughters of Israel, instruction in dressmaking, embroidery, and
domestic occupations forms a prominent feature of the plan of
education.'

To prove the efficiency of Jewish labour, Sir Moses 'entrusted' to
thirty-five Jewish 'mechanics' the work of refurbishing the classrooms with all necessities. They '. . . completed the several contracts
in the most satisfactory manner . . .'.[293]

The engagement of local teaching staff was achieved with equal
ease. There was no shortage of talent. Dr Loewe continued:

... they had the gratification to find that on the next day after the establishment of the school had become known in the City, 144 girls attended,[294] and
the names of 400 girls, many of them belonging to the best and most pious
families were registered in the school books.

Dr Loewe, as so often, omits dates. It seems 'the next day' in the
above quotation refers to the day after the lease of the building
had been signed and sealed on 8 August (Wednesday).

To assume that all was well and going the way Sir Moses wanted
would be wrong. Mrs Guedalla as well as Dr Loewe enthused about
the spontaneity of the parents. There was however another reaction,
anything but gratifying. Finn in his private diary noted:[295]

August 3 — in the evening I was most pained to hear that the Rabbinical Jews
are getting up an excitement against Sir Moses Montefiore, that boys had thrown
stones after his Sedan,[296] and then from the tops of the houses had shouted
the cry which is customary of the funeral of an excommunicated person.

Finn did not associate this ugly outburst with any particular
cause, but the date is significant. 3 August was the day on which
the *Herem* ritual was hurled at Sir Moses. It is the first mention of
a definite date associated with the act of *Herem*.

To associate this event with the visit to the *M'kom haMikdash*
defies logic. That took place on 26 July and there is no good reason

why the repercussions should have been delayed for nine days. As for the 'alms-riots', they started three days later, on 6 August. Thus we can discount these two occurrences.

Only one event took place on 3 August: hundreds of parents wanted to enrol their children in the girls' school. Secular education was an emotive subject in the Holy City. It had produced more 'prohibitions' and 'excommunications', official and clandestine, over the years than any other controversial issue.[297] The enthusiastic reception by one section of the population brought forth violent rejection by another. The corollary, a *Herem*, could almost be expected.

This outburst of religious fury seems strange in view of Dr Loewe's claim that the girls' school was founded 'with the concurrence of the Jewish authorities'. However, Dr Loewe told only part of the story. The 'Jewish authorities' mentioned were those of the Sephardim, who were more amenable to secular education and perhaps also to external influences. To quote Nicolayson,[298] the girls' school was 'reluctantly admitted among the Sephardim,[299] but indignantly rejected and protested against by the Ashkenazim'. To Finn[300] the girls school was '. . . for instruction in reading, writing and needlework; this itself was a bold innovation upon *Oriental* Jewish principles and customs', which suggests that the school was designed mainly for the Oriental-Sephardi section. Indeed, this was more or less correct. Finn reported protests of the 'Rabbinical Jews', a term synonymous in his vocabulary with 'Ashkenazi Jews'.[301] Some Ashkenazim,[302] however, supported the introduction of secular education for girls, but the Rabbinate and the great majority of the community, in particular the *Perushim*, were implacably opposed to it.

The ferment did not abate; indeed it erupted again in another ugly demonstration a few days later. The despicable 'alms riots' were stirred up and added another 'cause', this time by deliberate trouble makers who took to the streets. The result of it was in Mrs Guedalla's words,[303]

Thursday 9 August — another circumstance occurred to pain us; there was a report that there had been a disturbance in one of the synagogues, and the Shofar had been blown out. Various reasons are assigned.

'Blowing out the Shofar' can have only one meaning in this context — a *Herem*[304]. Mrs Guedalla was aware of this but seems bewildered and unable to assign the action to any one definite cause. However, one may, with some caution, assert that the cause was the girls' school. The *Wiener Mittheilungen* on 12 November 1855 printed a long and laudatory report on Sir Moses Montefiore and his work on his recent visit to Jerusalem. The communication is dated 'Jerusalem, 6 Elul, 5615';[305] the writer is identified only by a capital letter 'H' printed in front of the date. The same report is printed in the *AZdJ* on the same date, 12 November 1855. This is no coincidence; it is an obvious press release, to be published in various newspapers simultaneously.[306] Whereas in the *Wiener Mittheilungen* the only indication of the author is the enigmatic capital 'H', the *AZdJ* indicates its source by a short introduction. It reads (in translation): 'Breslau, 5 November (Private communication). I would ask you to have the following letter which reached me from an *authentic* source printed in the *AZdJ*. M.H.' The 'H' as printed in the *Wien. Mitth.* is missing in the *AZdJ*, but the *AZdJ* has the formal 'Geehrtester Herr' introducing the letter, and concludes it with 'Ihr aufrichtiger Amicus'; both phrases are omitted from the *Wiener Mittheilungen*.

The purpose of the letter was the desire of 'H' to inform 'M.H.' '... of the various activities undertaken by the tender-hearted Sir Moses Montefiore in Jerusalem.' Most of the space is taken up by descriptions of two events that took place on Rosh Chodesh Ellul — 15 August: the official opening of the girls' school in the morning and the laying of the foundation stone of the hospital in the afternoon.[307] According to Mrs Guedalla the order of events should have been the other way round, but a technical problem at the last moment necessitated a change of programme.[308] The party assembled at ten in the morning. In the presence of many visitors, teachers, supervisors, and eighty-four girls, Dr Loewe opened the order of service with the recitation of solemn Hebrew prayers at 11 o'clock. He then addressed the assembled company in Spanish, explaining the aims of the new institution and, turning to the girls, he expressed the hope that the school would bestow upon them great benefits. He told them of the hopes of the founders and of the advantages the pupils would gain by serious and industrious work. The ceremony terminated with a recitation of prayers for Sir Moses' and Lady Montefiore's health, to which all present responded with a hearty 'Amen'. The formalities over, refreshments followed; and with the girls filing past the noble couple in pairs, the elated crowd happily dispersed.

It is strange that 'H' speaks of only eighty-four pupils having attended when, only days before, 144 enrolled, and it also seems peculiar that Loewe should have addressed the visitors and prospective pupils in Spanish. But there was a close link between the diminished numbers and the language of the oration. According to Mrs Guedalla, who was also present at the opening ceremony,

'... eighty-two pupils attended, all of the Sephardim Congregation, the others being prevented it is thought, by their ecclesiastical heads ...'.

'H' then devoted a paragraph to the afternoon's event and immediately following that he returned to the girls' school and the aftermath of the inauguration service. He told 'M.H.' that the new school, which was established in one of the best buildings in Jerusalem and was equipped with the most modern furniture and educational aids available, caused much worry to some of 'our very religious brethren'. They feared that the modern school could introduce the 'modern' reform ideology to Jerusalem. In their religious fervour they betook themselves to *one* synagogue and there pronounced the *Herem* on the founder of the school, Sir Moses Montefiore.

The governing body of the synagogue, and its head, Rabbi Yeshaya Bordaki, immediately nullified the *Herem*. Rabbi Bordaki also succeeded in calming down tempers and assuring everyone that the founder [Sir Moses Montefiore] who had sacrificed so much for the sake of their religion, would not allow any such principles to intrude into any of his institutions. The people thus fully pacified, dispersed and left quickly for their homes.

Dr Loewe showed them the constitution of the school which read:[309] 'A school to teach the daughters of the Jews to be able to read their prayers from the book, and to know the G-d of our fathers with heart and soul.'

This had the desired effect, as all were now fully convinced of the pure motives of the founder. Sir Moses next day at morning service — in appreciation of the sincerity of the protesters — had the *Mi Sheberach* (prayer) read for them. He also distributed alms among the poor.

Here we have the facts. Sir Moses Montefiore was indeed excommunicated by an unnamed person or persons. The *Herem* was pronounced in a synagogue whose Rabbi was Rabbi Yeshaya Bordaki, which indicates the venue: the Hurvah Synagogue. To use this particular synagogue for the action shows the utter insensitivity of the perpetrators. It was hardly four weeks since Sir Moses had brought from Constantinople the *Firman* for its rebuilding. However, in mitigation, one may assume that the culprit was Rabbi Yoseph Moshe Lissa, described by Hirschensohn as a scholar but of diminished legal responsibility.

To sum up: there is no contemporary witness who categorically states he was present at the alleged pronouncement of a *Herem* on Sir Moses Montefiore because of his trespass onto the Precincts of the Sanctuary, the *M'kom haMikdash*. Indeed, R. Shmuel Salant and H. Guedalla resolutely deny any such pronouncement took place. Mrs Guedalla's diary entry on 9 August could be construed as evidence that the 'alms-riots' contributed to the issue of the *Herem*. However, this is hypothetical; the only conclusive evidence for a *Herem* pronouncement is in connection with the school, but that evidence is irrefutable that it was the act of a person or persons who had arrogated to themselves a right to which they had not the slightest claim.

The atmosphere of Jerusalem in those three weeks caused Mrs Guedalla to write:[310]

> I have learnt a great deal of life in this journey.
> I find it in all places chequered alike.
> I long to see good done here, but alas the recipients
> do not enter into it.
> I long to see difficulties met quietly and dispassionately,
> but all remarks lead to discord.
> I long for this beautiful land to be as we read of it,
> but I see nothing but poverty.

How sad, how true.

Rabbi Jacob Saphir[311] a prominent member of the *Perushim*, in a long Hebrew panegyric poem[312] described the achievements of Sir Moses Montefiore on his 1855 visit:

Be thou blessed unto the Eternal, Yehoodith the lovely Princess.
Great is thy kindness to the daughter of Zion, a mother in Israel.
A school has thou established for them in order to teach them the knowledge of G-d.

In the explanatory footnote Saphir adds:

It is a great thing that they have established at Jerusalem a school in order to teach the daughters of Zion the Law of G-d, and those commandments necessary to be known by the daughters of Israel.
They are taught by G-d fearing women. They are also instructed in needlework and every other household duty which might be useful to them as wives.
May the Eternal bless them from Zion.

With such a curriculum even the *Perushim* could have found little fault. We have no personal knowledge of any of the teachers at the time of the opening of the school. A year later, in 1856, Miss Flora Randegger,[313] daughter of Rabbi Meir Randegger of Trieste, a very talented and truly G-d fearing teacher, instructed the girls for a while.

It seems that if the *Perushim* were pleased, the *Maskilim* ['enlightened' – modernizers] were up in arms. L. A. Frankl visited the

school in June 1856. He described a scene of pathetically undisciplined chaos, counting twenty-one girls, a few of whom busied themselves with sewing, while the others were fast asleep, as was the
teacher in an adjoining room, surrounded by another six sleeping
girls. Five teachers were on the payroll but none were in sight except
for the sleeper. To send the children to school, the parents had to be
bribed. He could not find one good word for the institution.[314]

By coincidence, on the day L. A. Frankl was approaching Jerusalem,
27 May 1856,[315] another visitor called at the Montefiore Girls'
School. Miss M. E. Rogers gave a full description of the school and
stated how impressed she was by what she saw. It may well be that
Dr Loewe quoted her verbatim in refutation of Frankl's religio-
politically biased views.

XI

In spite of other involvements, Sir Moses Montefiore did not neglect
the main purposes of his journey.

Of the two Vizirial letters,[316] one contained the right to acquire
land specifically 'for the erection of an hospital either inside or
outside the city,[317] as may be found desirable, the other couched
in more general terms for encouragement of Jewish agriculture'.

Sir Moses was well acquainted with the housing problems of
Jerusalem and therefore when submitting his request to the Sultan
he made sure that if necessary he would be able to buy land outside
the city walls. In his quest for a site, he enlisted the help of Finn
and the City Elders. Finn arranged that on 25 July 'we all were to
meet at the Seraglio to propose suitable sites.'[318] On that day Finn
noted in his private diary:[319] 'I rode with Dr Loewe over the Quarter
of the City called *BAB HHATTA* to look for a site for the hospital,
thence through the *Hharat el Mogharabi* to the site near the lepers'
houses . . .'. He and Dr Loewe also searched in other areas '. . . and
in particular examined that part of the City inside and near the
'Zion' or 'Nebi David' gate but could find no site suitable, which
would not involve enormous trouble and expense'.

Finn, in his dispatch to his superior, expressed his surprise at the
magnitude of Sir Moses' designs for his hospital. This may have
contributed to the difficulty of finding a suitable site within the
cramped confines of the City.

On 25 July, Finn told how M. Finzi,[320] the British Vice-Consul
at Acre, and Rab Arieh,[321] one of the most prominent members of
the community, had 'begged me to offer the Talbiyeh to Sir Moses
for the Jews hospital'.[322] Finn did not record his reaction to this
suggestion but obviously it was not taken seriously by him.

However, Jemima Guedalla noted on 29 July[323] that there were 'signs of the ground being obtained', and on 2 August,[324] 'Sir Moses, Mr Kursheedt and the Doctor went to see land for the hospital.'

On 1 August and again on the 2nd she recorded that Achmet Aga came 'to pay his respects to Sir Moses and Lady'. As an aside she added: 'he was Governor of this City when they were here sixteen years ago . . .'.[325] He had some land to sell, which — it seems — he had offered to Sir Moses. It therefore paid him to know what was going on.

On 9 August, Jemima wrote:[326] 'Sir Moses works unremittingly almost day and night, and Dr Loewe is *talking* and *planning*[327] eternally.' That suggests that there was already something tangible to talk about. Indeed, Dr Loewe recorded,[328] alas, again omitting the dates:

Having surmounted the difficulties and impediments which he had to encounter, Sir Moses eventually succeeded in purchasing a track [*sic*] of land to the west of the Holy City, adjoining the high road from Jerusalem to Hebron in the most beautiful and salubrious locality, and within a few minutes walk from the Jaffa and Zion Gates . . . The land was sold by 'Ahhmed Agha Dizdar [*sic*] who was Governor of Jerusalem during the reign of Mohammed Ali, and who since 1839 had stood in friendly relations with Sir Moses . . . .

The quaint bargaining went on for some days, the final agreement being arrived at after a day-long dialogue, reminiscent of Abraham's experience with Ephron, and with the same result. Ahmet Aga Dizdar, the friend of sixteen years, got his price. The dialogue, as Dr Loewe remembered it, runs:

When Sir Moses broached the subject of the purchase to him [i.e. Ahmet Agha Dizdar] his answer was:
'You are my friend, my brother, the apple of my eye, take possession of it at once. This land I hold as an heirloom from my ancestors. I would not sell it to any person for thousands of pounds, but you I give it without any money: it is yours, take possession of it . . . I myself, my wife, and children we are all yours! And this was his reply to Sir Moses day after day, whenever he was asked the price for which he would sell the said property.

After Dr Loewe had exhausted all his 'stock of Arabic phraseology' as interpreter between Sir Moses and Ahmet Aga Dizdar, the latter gave way:

You are my friend, my brother; by my beard, my head, I declare this is the case, tell Sir Moses to give me a souvenir of one thousand pounds sterling, and we will go at once to the Ckadi.

Once the price was stated to be £1,000, Sir Moses counted out that sum in golden sovereigns, in readiness to hand over at the right moment. It was decided that purchaser and vendor 'proceed[ed] to the British Consulate . . .' where[329]

The Witnessing sealing, etc. of the contract, that is to say the actual sale was performed in the British Consulate, but the registration was of course also made in the public Mahhkameh (or Moslem Hall of Justice).

It is tantalizing that Finn, like Dr Loewe, omitted the operative date.[330]

A copy of the purchase contract, which was discovered in a private collection, was recently published in full with a contemporary English translation. In 1981 Dr Ruth Kark transcribed the Arab date of this document as 9 August 1855, whereas the earlier published reproduction of the same document dated it 12 August.[331]

By 12 August Montefiore certainly claimed full rights to the site since Mrs Guedalla related:

. . . went at eleven to see the site of new hospital with all our party. Struck a tent there, very delighted with the locality about there. By a remark made by Dr Loewe, Sir Moses decided on having all our tents removed here, and as our gipsy life permits of these hasty removals the change was decided on.

It is difficult to understand what was Dr Loewe's remark that made Sir Moses decide, immediately to move the camp to the newly acquired land. It may have been no more than a suggestion to transfer themselves to the 'salubrious' air, and the delight of camping on one's own land. Perhaps they thought it was advisable to take immediate physical possession, as a legal safeguard, bearing in mind that the contract still needed the ratification of the 'public *Mahhkameh*'.

Finn's entry in his private diary for 14 August reads:[332]

I called on the Montefiores in their encampment, namely the ground purchased for £1,000 from Ahmad Aga Tuzdar for the hospitals, the gardens etc. etc.

Sir Moses came to town to have sealed and certified the deed of sale. This made in his own name ('tho not a Turkish subject) being intended for the institutions.

'The Hojet ratified of the land [*sic*] bought by Sir M. Montefiore' on the same day.[333] Finn wrote in *Stirring Times*:[334]

In this purchase the deed of sale was made out in his own name, 'though he was not a Turkish subject, and this was a signal favour conceded by the Ottoman Government, on the ground of the purchase being for the purposes of a permanent charitable nature'.

The fact that Sir Moses was the purchaser is stressed in the preamble to the sale contract.[335] It says the permission to buy the land was

given to Sir Moses Montefiore 'the honourable, one of the Mosaic
sect, an ornament of the tribe of Israel . . . who is a nobleman . . .
a piece of land for the establishment of an hospital for the benefit
of the Jewish Rayahs dwelling in Jerusalem.'

All this means that although the Vizirial letter to allow the purchase of land for the hospital was in the name of Sir Moses Montefiore,
it would not convey a title absolute to him. He was to hold the land
on behalf of, and for the benefit of, the indigenous and foreign Jews
of Jerusalem.

There is a remarkable difference in the wording of this text as
quoted in translation by Dr Loewe, and the official translation
printed by Dr Kark. Dr Loewe's version[336] reads: '. . . of establishing thereon an hospital for the poor of the Israelites who reside in
Jerusalem *and he* [i.e. Sir Moses] *does as he pleases*'.

This last sentence puts a completely different complexion on the
proviso. It states only that the first choice would be the hospital,
but that can be altered if the need arises, e.g. if other uses were
preferred. The only condition was that the utilization of the ground
would have to be for the benefit of the poor of Jerusalem. This
proviso was probably stipulated by Sir Moses, for the following
reason. It is widely accepted that the funds to purchase the land
came from the Touro legacy.[337] This belief is wrong. Equally wrong
is the belief that the purchase price came from Sir Moses' private
purse,[338] no doubt owing to the quoted preamble of the deed as
popularized by Dr Loewe. The truth is that the money spent on the
purchase came from the 'Appeal Fund'. In the Second Report of the
Fund published in 1856[339] the Balance Sheet states clearly that
£1,086 was spent to purchase the land in Jerusalem. The £1,000
represented the 120,000 piastres[340] purchase price, and £86 was
probably for incidentals and/or *baksheesh*. As Sir Moses was the
holder of the *Firman*, he wanted it to be made absolutely clear that
his holding was for the benefit of the poor.

The site was 66,225 sq. yards, large enough to accommodate not
only the projected hospital but also to realize Sir Moses' other
idealistic projects. Finn's official dispatch[341] reported that Sir
Moses '. . . succeeded in purchasing a piece of land in his own name,
outside but near the city, for the erection of an hospital, and employment of poor Jews in gardening'.

There was criticism of the quality of the land. L. A. Frankl[342]
summed up the various views, adding his own observations. Some
critics contended that £1,000 was too much to have paid, although
he admitted having been told that the broken rocks were worth almost as much as building materials. Others thought it wrong to

build a hospital outside the city walls, as it would be of no use in case of a sudden emergency after sunset. At that time the gates were closed at night and opened to no one until the following daybreak. Equally, the mortally ill could not be visited by relatives at a late hour, and it would be almost impossible for the seriously ill, even in daytime, to climb up to the hospital, particularly in the heat of summer. Moreover, when raids by roving Beduin were expected, the city gates were closed day and night. When the spread of a cholera epidemic was feared, the gates were almost permanently shut. In those circumstances the hospital would be completely isolated.

Frankl dismissed as questionable the claim that the site was in healthy surroundings. As a practising physician in Vienna, he stated authoritatively that its proximity to the Turkish cemetery, where the dead were buried only two feet below ground, caused serious contamination of the air. Events proved every one of his criticisms to be completely unfounded.

An anonymous 'Jewish Traveller', in a communication to the *Jewish Chronicle* in late 1857,[343] was highly critical of everything Sir Moses did and intended to do. *Inter alia*, he condemned the projected hospital as 'what I call folly'; and he assured the reader that it would be a failure, repeating Frankl's arguments. Moses Sachs[344] for once refuted much of Frankl's criticism in a single sentence. 'This place, with the finest garden, Sir Moses bought, in order to build a hospital there . . .'. As for the justification of the purchase, Mrs Guedalla's simple common sense assessment was more to the point than that of the sophisticated critics:[345] 'The Greek and the Armenian communities buy up all the land they can here; this piece escaped by miracle.' If they were paying for all the land they could get hold of, it could not be so bad. What the critics omitted was what could be done with the site. However, Solomon Hurwitz, a visitor from abroad, who arrived in Jerusalem in August 1856, wrote from Jerusalem in October 1856[346] that he took the opportunity to visit the Jewish institutions and '. . . especially the piece of ground which was purchased by Sir Moses, it is a beautiful plot. In my opinion there should be built on that piece of ground 500 alms houses . . .'.

On 13 August, Dr Loewe personally remeasured the land and borders. He finished this task with a beautifully symbolic action,[347] '. . . inscribing the initials of Sir Moses' name in large Hebrew characters on a piece of rock forming the angle of its boundary line upon the road the right side of which, when coming from the Jaffa Gate, leads to Beth Essefafa'.

Finn[348] found in these solitary Hebrew initials 'Mem Mem' a deeply moving message: 'And thus was a Hebrew possession once more appropriated in the Land of Promise, after an interval of many ages.'

XII

Once the legal formalities were settled, the time had come to start on the preparations for the hospital.

On the second day of Rosh Hodesh Ellul — 15 August, two great events were to take place. The 'first stone' of *the* Hospital was to be set early in the morning. Mrs Guedalla gives some guidance on the detailed programme:[349] '. . . Got up at five, thinking the stone for the hospital would be laid at six, instead of which nothing was ready for the ceremony, the stone having taken greater time to prepare than was expected.'

Rabbi Jacob Saphir[350] gives details of the unexpected difficulties that were encountered. On the south-east corner of the site a shaft was to be sunk in the ground, but the work took much longer than expected. A heavy boulder was to be hollowed out and then used as the foundation stone. This operation also turned out to be more time-consuming than planned.

As a result the inauguration ceremony of the Girls' School, which was scheduled for the afternoon, was brought forward to the morning.

A third project was scheduled in which Sir Moses was only indirectly concerned, but in which he was interested. Haim Guedalla had been instructed by his father, Judah Guedalla, to establish a *Yesheebah* in his name in Jerusalem. Jemima's diary is full of references to her husband's efforts to make arrangements and much of Haim Guedalla's time was taken up in discussing details with the Sephardi Hahamim who were to be the beneficiaries. It was certainly not an easy task: nothing could go smoothly in Jerusalem, not even dispensing charity.

The Hahamim who were to be the fellows of the 'Yesheebah', ('a place for reading the law') were assured of a regular stipend, to be paid twice annually out of the Judah Guedalla Trust which was to be set up in London.[351] The formal opening of the 'Yesheebah' was scheduled to take place between the two other ceremonies. Mrs Guedalla takes up the story:

We then proceeded to Mr Guedalla's Yesheebah, a place for reading the law . . . and went back fully inclined to do justice to the dinner that H[aim] ordered to be prepared; but suddenly H[aim] came in, took Lady Montefiore under his arm, and said we should leave immediately, as Signor Abolain[352] could not leave his house, being surrounded by poor people who said he should not eat whilst they starved, and that an answer must be sent to a petition they sent to

Sir Moses before he should leave the house. This act of intimidation so annoyed Sir Moses that he and H[aim] agreed not to open the Yesheebah that day.

The crowd thus prevented the venerable Chief Rabbi from appearing at the festive dinner to mark the opening of the 'Yesheebah'. It was the means, they thought, by which they could force Sir Moses to commit himself to meet the demands contained in their 'petition'. Jemima Guedalla does not mention the substance of the petition. This can, nevertheless, be ascertained as the document has survived.[353] It bears no date and the name of the addressee is not stated. However, the short note on the reverse of the document in the hand of Dr Loewe supplies the missing details.[354] It was handed to Sir Moses [in Jerusalem] on 15 Av 5615 (30 July 1855).

In it the signatories, seven Hahamim,[355] related in much detail the dire financial plight of the Sephardi community in Jerusalem, owing to the burden of £13,400 in accumulated debts. The debts were owing to local non-Jewish money lenders who were continually adding interest to the capital and charging interest on interest. There were also small debts, the minute savings of members of the community, of widows and orphans, who deposited their 'fortunes' to augment their *Halukah* share with the paltry interest earned on the capital. This was a satisfactory arrangement for the poor in normal times, but 1855 could not be termed normal. The poor needed every piastre of their capital to pay for the bare necessities of life. But the coffers of the community were absolutely bare, and the Hahamim could not meet their obligations.

Sir Moses was asked to consolidate the large debts and to replace them with a single loan raised on the money market in London. The terms were considerably lower in London than in Jerusalem and the more reasonable interest payments could be met from the annual income of the community. Obviously it was understood by all that an arrangement of this sort could not be made in Jerusalem. It would have to wait for Sir Moses' return to London. On the other hand the small loans borrowed within the community created problems which could not be deferred. A letter delivered to Sir Moses at half past nine in the evening of 14 August, contained demands that all these should be repaid without delay.[356] The communal leaders, and certainly the poor, had the full sympathy of Sir Moses, but he was not prepared to yield to the intimidation of their boycott of the opening of the 'Yesheebah'. When, after an hour's wait, an ultimatum was brought by a junior Haham and read out to them, Sir Moses and his party left to visit Dr Fränkel. The gesture, in obvious anger, was well understood by the Hahamim and before long the venerable Haham Abulafia arrived to implore Sir Moses to return to perform the opening of the 'Yesheebah'. He was unsuccessful, if for no other reason than that Sir Moses had to attend the main function of the day. 'We went back in the order of coming, and went to the site where the first stone was to be placed; the ceremony was interesting and the feeling of all concerned most spontaneous.'[357]

The inhabitants of Jerusalem gathered in their thousands, representing all religious groups, hours before the ceremony was to begin. Dr Loewe formally opened the proceedings with a Hebrew prayer he had composed for the occasion and with the recitation of appropriate psalms.[358] He continued with a sermon in which the need of a Jewish hospital in the Holy City was vividly demonstrated and the gratitude due to the one who had made that ideal possible, and to the founder, for his effort and devotion, was emphasized. 'G-d grant that the defunct Mr Touro may for his charitable thoughts be favourably remembered, also Sir Moses and Lady Montefiore for their good actions.[359] 'Sir Moses and Lady Montefiore in the presence of a numerous concourse of spectators of various religious denominations had the satisfaction to lay the foundation stone of the intended hospital.'[360]

Jemima Guedalla continued the story: 'A tin case was put in [the hollow of] the stone stating the year, the cause of the foundation and our names.' (i.e. the names of Sir Moses and Lady Montefiore, Gershom Kursheedt, Haim and Jemima Guedalla and Dr Loewe.) In fact, a copy of the purchase contract was put into the foundation stone and thus these names were recorded for posterity.

According to Rabbi Jacob Saphir,[361] who witnessed the ceremony, Kursheedt placed Judah Touro's signet ring in the foundation stone. Saphir probably was unaware of the true significance and human tragedy that prompted this gesture. Judah Touro had lost his father in 1783 when he was eight years old. His mother, with her four young children, moved to Boston where she joined her brother, Michael Moses Hays', household. Judah was apprenticed in his uncle's country home. He was very capable and was sent abroad by his uncle on various business trips. He was very fond of his cousin Catherine, and became engaged to her. The engagement was opposed by his uncle and broken off. It is assumed that it was for this reason that he left Boston and settled in New Orleans,[362] where he spent all his immensely successful business life, but remained a lonely man. However, Touro the bachelor remembered Catherine in his will almost fifty years after leaving Boston. He left her $5,000 'as an expression of the kind remembrance in which that esteemed friend is held by me'. It is sad to reflect that Catherine was never to know of this 'remembrance' as she, a spinster of near eighty, pre-deceased Touro by about a forthnight. She was buried in Rhode Island, where Touro also found his eternal rest. It was not Touro's signet ring that Kursheedt, Touro's trusted friend, placed in the cavity of the foundation stone; it was '. . . a gold ring of the lady to whom he was betrothed in early life, but did not, from circumstances marry.'

XIII

In spite of the excitement and physical strain which would have sapped the energy of a much younger man, 16 August was, to Sir Moses Montefiore, just another working day. The first callers came before breakfast. Haham Abulafia 'arrived on a donkey'; and several other Hahamim who were elected to be 'fellows' of Mr Guedalla's 'Yesheebah' arrived soon after. 'They came to apologize for the conduct yesterday'[363] to which Mrs Guedalla added a personal note, 'it was a great pain to me'. She obviously felt sorry for them.

The topic of discussion was the petition and letter sent to Sir Moses on 14 August, but to which he had not yet replied. They again implored Sir Moses to make available funds for the community to repay, in particular, the debts to the 'poor' lenders.[364] As the petition contained some serious allegations against the Ashkenazim, Sir Moses sent for their representatives to hear their views, as well as those of the representatives of other communities.[365] We do not know whether these interviews and discussions bore any immediate result. Sir Moses was deeply moved by the plight of the people, and took their petition with him to London to submit to his committee.[366] The committee's sympathetic response is in the Second Report of the Appeal Fund, which summarizes the petition. The committee's proposals for change are referred to by Dr Loewe[367] (but are not relevant here).

On Thursday 16 August all the differences between Sir Moses and Haim Guedalla and the Hahamim were amicably settled. Guedalla attended a morning service on Shabbat 18 August at his new 'Yesheebah', where 'he breakfasted with all the members, he came home rather *more than jolly* . . .'.[368]

The laying of the hospital foundation stone, though an impressive demonstration of intent was only a symbolic act. The plans drawn about 1852 for Sir Moses' Hospital were by two well-known English architects, Wyatt Papworth and Thomas Allason.[369] Lithographed copies of the architectural drawings were deposited with Dr Simon Fränkel in whose possession they were seen by L. A. Frankl in 1856.[370]

The first step in preparing the land was to surround it with a solid stone wall to protect it from predators, human as well as animal.

Haham Eliyahu Navon[371] and Rabbi Isaac Rosenthal,[372] one Sephardi and one Ashkenazi, were engaged to take charge of the newly acquired Montefiore interests in Jerusalem. They were to be paid[373] 'for your work in respect of the work and the workmen, the labour in the vineyard, and all the efforts connected with these pursuits . . .'. It was their responsibility to administer the funds forwarded to them, to pay all outgoings of the various enterprises, and to keep proper accounts. They were to be the link between the work in progress in Jerusalem and the administrative headquarters in England.[374]

The weekly salary was agreed at £1, a very considerable sum then in Jerusalem.[375] They were paid on 21 Teveth (30 December) 1855 for nineteen weeks in arrear, as from Sunday 19 August 1855, apparently the date their employment commenced. The salaries were to be paid in the future by the same arrangement, i.e. every nineteen weeks in arrears. One of the instructions to the supervisors was that to build the wall they were to hire Jewish labour.[376] Within days of the start of the building work, forty labourers earned their living there.

In the construction of the wall, only stones quarried on site were to be used. They still sparkle with a gold and metallic gleam when the sun's rays set on them, although some 'seven score and near ten' years have passed since they were laid in the wall.

It was Sir Moses' intention to visit Hebron as soon as his work in Jerusalem was finished, and members of the party began to pack in the early morning of 16 August. However, they were delayed, not only because Kursheedt felt unwell, but because Lady Montefiore was ill with a high fever, causing some concern. However, by Tuesday (21 August) with characteristic will power she was well enough to undertake the journey.[377]

Before leaving Jerusalem, Sir Moses managed to remedy another evil from which the Jewish Quarter had suffered for centuries. The Muslim slaughter house had been in the Jewish Quarter since the days of Caliph Omar. Blood, offal and obnoxious refuse had accumulated for centuries and were offensive and a constant health hazard. Sir Moses persuaded Kiamil Pasha of these 'noisome evils' and by order of the Pasha 'the slaughter house was removed without the walls of the city'.[378]

The rebellion of Sheikh Abd el Rahman,[379] who had long terrorized Hebron, had just been crushed by Kiamil Pasha, but to visit the town was still hazardous. Sir Moses wished to help the constantly oppressed small Jewish community, and to see on the spot what he could do. On the Muslim *Korban Bairam* festival, Sir Moses entertained the troops and officers magnificently, as well as the general population. To the elders of the two congregations, Sephardi and Ashkenazi, he gave £300 to be distributed among the Hahamim and the poor.[380] Sir Moses thought that since there was no medical service, the next best thing would be a dispensary, which should be of great benefit to the Jews and the general population. The land on which Sir Moses' party encamped was suitable and available for purchase. The Arab owner asked £50 and Dr Loewe was to put the proposition to Sir Moses, who, however, was tired and had gone to bed. Next morning, when the owner came, he increased his price to £500. Sir Moses, of course, refused and the land was not bought for the dispensary. On Friday morning the party left Hebron to make their way by stages to Jaffa. Sabbath was spent in an Arab village. On Sunday they moved on and, after stopping at Ramleh, they reached Jaffa late Sunday evening.

In Jaffa[381] 'some property was purchased, with a house and well, affording abundant supply of excellent water'.

The property had already been purchased before Sir Moses travelled to Hebron, the legal formalities being completed in Jerusalem, with the blessing of Kiamil Pasha, on 18 August.[382] Before leaving the Holy Land, Sir Moses made sure that 'A number of poor Israelites were at once engaged upon the land, which is known as "Biera" and situated near the estate of the Wurthemburg [sic] Templars . . .'.[383] Pardes Montefiore, as it became known, was the first Jewish owned 'pardes', i.e. orchard, in Palestine. In time it was incorporated into Tel Aviv.[384]

In Jaffa the party took rooms again in the same primitive hotel as on their arrival in the Holy Land.[385] They were seen off by many friends: Dr Fränkel, who had travelled with them from Jerusalem; Ahmet Aga and his family; Mr Kayat, the British Vice-Consul, who brought on board many letters which had arrived at Haifa and were waiting to be handed over. It is surprising that no mention is made of any Jewish deputation coming to Jaffa to wish Sir Moses and his party 'Bon Voyage!'

On Tuesday 28 August, at four in the afternoon, they boarded the ship which was to take them on the first lap of the homeward journey, to Alexandria.

As the boat carrying the party moved out of the rocky harbour of Jaffa, Sir Moses may well have allowed his thoughts to linger upon his experiences of the last few weeks, and his success in acquiring land for a purpose-built hospital in Jerusalem. It must have given him unqualified delight that he was the first foreign Jew able to purchase land in Palestine. He had done so for the benefit of his brethren and he had been privileged to lay the foundation stone for his hospital.

He could not have foreseen that within two years, on his next visit, he would be persuaded to abandon his long-cherished plan in favour of alms-houses. For the sake of communal harmony, he agreed to the change without demur.

Was it another failure? No! For nothing could change the fact that the stone Sir Moses laid on Rosh Hodesh Ellul in 1855 was destined to be the foundation stone of Jewish Jerusalem without the walls.

NOTES

I   1. Dr Simon Fränkel, see p. 274.
2. James Finn, *Stirring Times*, vol. i (London, 1878), pp. 435—6. The Moslem parents would not allow their children to be vaccinated and the epidemic claimed the lives of eight hundred children.
3. Chief Rabbi, Dr N. M. Adler, in his Pastoral Letter, *Jewish Chronicle* (J.C.), 19 May 1854; Lucien Wolf, *Sir Moses Montefiore, A Centennial Biography* (London, 1888), p. 169.
4. Printed *J.C.*, 19 May 1854, pp. 284—7, together with the Chief Rabbi's Pastoral Letter and translations of letters from Jerusalem, Safed, Tiberias and Hebron. Reprinted as: *An Appeal on Behalf of the Famishing Jews in the Holy Land* (London, [May], 1854), 8°, 16 pp.
5. It broke out in October 1853 between Turkey and Russia. England and France declared war on Russia on 24 March 1854.
6. A. M. Hyamson, *British Consulate in Jerusalem* (1940), vol. i, p. 222, dispatch no. 159, 27 May 1854.
7. The famine, hard winter, etc.
8. *Stirring Times*, vol. i (London, 1878), p. 436, chapter headed 'Corn at Famine Prices'.
9. *Stirring Times*, p. 436.
10. *J.C.*, 13 October 1854 reports the death of H. B. Itzhac Covo (without mentioning the name — just the Chief Rabbi), and his funeral on 17 August 1854, in Alexandria. His age is given as 86. The *Allgemeine Zeitung des Judenthums* (AZdJ) of 23 October 1854 published a *Necrolog* signed jointly by Moses Sachs and S. Hausdorf. James Finn mentioned the journey and death of Haham Covo (not mentioning his name) in *Stirring Times*, pt. 1, p. 79. Finn gave a letter of recommendation to the Chief Rabbi for his mission. The name is variously spelt as Cobo, Covo, Kobe, etc. For Hebrew sources see: Haham Isaac Badhav, *Atereth Zahav* (Yerushalayim, 1897), in particular the introduction; also many other publications by H. Badhav (a grandson of Haham Covo); Frumkin/Rivlin, *Toldoth Hahmey Yerushalayim*, pt. 3 (Jerusalem, 1929), pp. 276—9; M. D. Gaon, *Yehudey haMizrah b'Eretz Yisrael*, pt. 2 (Jerusalem, 1938), pp. 615—17; Abraham Yaari, *Shluhey Eretz Yisrael* (Jerusalem, 1951), pp. 703—4; Abraham Elmaleh, *HaRishonim le Zion* (Jerusalem, 1930).
11. *Diaries of Sir Moses and Lady Montefiore* ed. Loewe (1890) ii, pp. 32—3. No exact date is given nor is the reason stated for Sir Moses and Lady Montefiore's journey to Yorkshire.
12. *J.C.*, 21 April 1854. Lucien Wolf, *Biography*, p. 167, states that Sir Moses

Montefiore was particularly hard at work at that time, in the interest of
the Jews in the Turkish Empire; cf. also *Diaries*, ii, p. 37, which state that
he made representations to the British Government in their interest;
Lucien Wolf, *Notes on the Diplomatic History of the Jewish Question*
(1919), pp. 18–23.

13. Sir Moses Montefiore's letter is printed in full: *Diaries*, ii, pp. 31–2, but
the all-important date and place are omitted. Neither is the Chief Rabbi's
reply mentioned. All dates are quoted from *J.C.*, 19 May 1854.

14. *J.C.*, 19 May 1854.

15. *Appeal.* The donations were to be sent to the Chief Rabbi, also Sir Moses
Montefiore. The committee consisted of Henry Louis Cohen, S. L. de
Symons, Jun., Philip Lucas, A. J. Montefiore, Dr Loewe, and the Hon.
Sec., the Revd A. L. Green.

16. Analysis of these lists should be an interesting study in social and religious
participation. It would be interesting to see, e.g., whether any known
sympathizers of the missionaries were among the contributors.

17. *J.C.*, Second and Third Reports (see below); and *Diaries*, ii, p. 32.

18. *J.C.*, 19 May 1854, p. 283, col. 2; *Appeal*, p. 7.

19. Leon Hühner, *The Life of Judah Touro (1775–1854)* (Philadelphia,
1946).

20. b. Rhode Island, 1815–d. London, 1863. Lived most of his active life in
New Orleans. Married in London, 12 Jan 1861, Grace Guedalla (sister of
Haim G., d. of Judah G.). He had at that time a London address; the
wedding took place at the bride's home. (G. H. Whitehill, *Bevis Marks
Records*, vol. iii (London, 1973), p. 86 no. 352.) He died in 1863 and
had an extensive obituary notice (*J.C.*, 15 May 1863). His sisters en-
dowed a trust to keep some graves in order (probably of Gershom and
Grace) in 1884. cf. Laski, *Laws and Charities of the Spanish and Portuguese
Jews' Congregation of London* (London, 1952); Hühner, *The Life of
Judah Touro*; B. W. Korn, *The Early Jews of New Orleans* (Waltham,
1969); D. de Sola Pool, 'Some relations of Gershom Kursheedt and Sir
Moses Montefiore', *Publications of the American Jewish Historical Society*,
no. 37 (1947). See *Diaries*, Index, s.v. Touro, Guedalla.

21. For the full text of the Will, see Hühner, pp. 129–39. He bequeathed
money to many non-Jewish and Jewish charities.

22. Hühner, p. 67, discussing Touro's Jewish charitable work, states that 'he
contributed to early Palestinian colonisation projects and towards the
establishing of hospitals and almshouses'. His sources are given in notes
11 and 12 on p. 164 as Kohler, *Early American Zionist Project* and A. M.
Hyamson, *British Projects for the Restoration of Jews to Palestine*. In
Hyamson's paper there is nothing to support Huhner. As for the hospital
and the almshouses, the work was done by Sir Moses Montefiore, utilizing
Touro's legacy.

23. *Hevrat Terumat ha'Kodesh* was founded in 1824 at the initiative of Chief
Rabbi Solomon Hirschell. In or about 1853, the name was changed to 'The
North American Relief Society for Indigent Jews in Jerusalem', Palestine.
(I am indebted to Dr V. D. Lipman for this information, which he based
on MS AJHS, 1–33.)

24. Hühner, p. 67. No source given.

25. Hyamson, vol. i, no. 174, p. 234. James Finn to Lord Stratford de Redcliffe,
Jerusalem, 4 April 1854; Wolf, *Biography*, p. 169.

26. The Revd S. M. Isaacs and Sampson Simson were the founders of the

North American Relief Society. Isaacs was a frequent correspondent of Sir Moses Montefiore, mainly about relief.

27. *Diaries* ii, p. 31. The date of Isaacs' letter is not stated, but it may be assumed that it arrived at about the time the *Jewish Chronicle* published the news item.

28. *Diaries*, ii, p. 31.

29. Hühner, paras. 24 and 28 of will.

30. *J.C.*, 21 April 1854.

31. Sir Moses Montefiore was unjustly accused by many of holding on to the funds.

32. This is Dr Adler's interpretation of the wording of the will, which differs in part from Sir Moses Montefiore's interpretation. They also differed in the order of priorities.

33. *J.C.*, 19 May 1854, p. 285, col. 1; *Appeal*, p. 17. Dr Adler's suggestion, that the labour should be paid in part out of the annual collection for the *Halukah*, i.e. to 'rob the learned, the infirm, the widows and orphans' was rejected by the Old Yishuv whenever this notion was mentioned; the objections were justified.

34. Sir Moses Montefiore's letter of 15 May to Dr N. M. Adler, *J.C.* and *Appeal*.

35. Why was Sir Moses Montefiore so careful not to spell out his views in detail? Was he worried at this stage about the reaction in Government circles, who were partial to the views of the London Jews Society? It was probably because the 'Appeal' was to be distributed also among the gentile world, and many clergymen were actively helping, that he was so guarded.

36. *Diaries* ii, p. 38.

37. *Diaries* ii, p. 35.

38. b. Frankfurt, 1792—d. Paris, 1868. Founder of the Paris house of Rothschild.

39. *Diaries*, ii, pp. 35—6.

II   40. W. Ayerst, *The Jews of the Nineteenth Century* (London, 1848), pp. 392—398. On the early medical missionaries see also Ben Zion Gat, 'Mosdoth haRephua haRishonim b'Erets Yisrael', in *Jerusalem* (Hebrew), vol. v Jerusalem, 5713); *idem HaYishuv haYehudi b'Erets Yisrael* (Jerusalem, 5723), pp. 126 *et seq.*; Dr M. Eliav, *Ahavath Zion v'Anshey H'OD* (Jerusalem, 5731), p. 287. All but Ayerst suggest Bergmann and Gersheim were the first medical men in Jerusalem.

41. The news of three converts gave Sir Moses the impetus to act quickly (see footnote 44).

42. *AZdJ*, 19 November 1842: 'Sir Moses Montefiore London 70 Thal., Lady Judith Montefiore 70 Thal. Wir bemerken, dass diese beiden Gaben des verehrten Paares vorläufig und freiwillig, ohne unsere Aufforderung zugesichert worden ...'. However this statement is contradicted by *The Voice of Jacob*, vol. i (London, 26 August 1846), p. 191, which states '... about three years ago Dr Philippson, editor of the *AZdJ* formally proposed the hospital, under European superintendence. The brother of Dr P[hilippson], being about that time in England, enlisted the sympathy of Sir Moses and Lady Montefiore, as exemplified by their promise of £10 each.' The quotation from *The Voice of Jacob* is from an article, part of a vehement controversy between that paper, in its role as a supporter of Philippson's hospital fund, and the *Jewish Chronicle*. The editor of the *J.C.*, in his reply to the above article (as far as it bears in particular on our

point of interest), wrote 'large subscriptions *on paper*, and ephemeral prospects were trumpeted forth; but like all other proposals emanating from the speculative mind of Dr Ph. it was afterwards abandoned, not however, because the European influence prevailing in Jerusalem occasioned the hostility of the Perooshim, comprising the great bulk of the Ashkenazim body, but solely because these Persons *had no faith in the promises held out*, and naturally apprehended, that by joining they would involve themselves in difficulties endangering their subsistence, else these men would have been foremost in supporting a plan tending to their relief and benefit'.

43. See Sir Moses' letter to Haham Abraham Hayim Gaguin, 21 Tammuz 5604 (8 July 1844), published by Prof. B. Z. Dinaburg, *Zion* vol. i (Jerusalem, 1926), p. 88. Dinaburg seems to have missed the point of the letter.

44. See P. Grajevski, *Milhemeth haYehudim b'Mission* [Jerusalem] (Nisan, 1935). This important letter was recently photographically reproduced by Dr Israel Freidin, 'Bikur Holim Perushim in Jerusalem' (Hebrew), *Cathedra*, vol. xxvii, p. 123, March 1983. The purpose of the letter was to announce Dr Simon Fränkel's appointment as Sir Moses Montefiore's medical officer in Jerusalem.

45. Ayerst, p. 392.

46. Dr Fränkel was a native of Zülz, Upper Silesia, which was also the home town of Dr Loewe, almost certainly a factor in favour of Dr Fränkel's appointment.

47. *Diaries* i, p. 312.

48. *Diaries* i, p. 313, 26 January 1843.

49. Ayerst, p. 393.

50. Ayerst, p. 393.

51. Ayerst, p. 393.

52. *J.C.*, vol. i, No. 18, 16 May 1845.

53. Ayerst, p. 393.

54. *J.C.*, vol. i, No. 20, 13 June 1845.

55. Sir Moses paid his salary. See also Gat, *Jerusalem* (Hebrew), vol. iv (1953), p. 259, footnote 4, based on *AZdJ*, vol. xii, No. 3, p. 33.

56. MS in author's possession. After leaving Jerusalem in 1861/2 Fränkel was physician at the Rothschild Hospital in Constantinople (M. Sachs, *Hamagid* (Hebrew), vol. v, No. 16 (Lyck, 14 April 1862), quoted by G. Kressel, *Areshet* (Hebrew), vol. ii (Jerusalem 1960), p. 256). He was for some time in New York, L. A. Frankl, *Aus Egypten* (Wien 1860), p. 343. At some date Dr. S. Fränkel returned to Palestine and died in Jaffa in 1880 (Eliav, p. 230; footnote 9 on p. 296).

57. Dr S. Fränkel, in a letter in the *AZdJ*, dated Jerusalem, 31 December 1843, writes (as quoted in *The Voice of Jacob*, 12 April 1844), commenting on the lack of a Jewish hospital in Jerusalem: 'He [Dr Fränkel] says, that the fatal consequences have often resulted to the sick, from the want of a roof to cover them.' His letter contains also the information that because the missionaries could supply that need, a roof over the head of the sick, they had succeeded in converting ten Jews within the previous nine months.

58. Dr I. Freidin, pp. 121–2. In 1843 R. Meir Leb Reich was sent to Hungary to raise funds. The 2,500 grossos he collected were deposited with Rabbi A. S. W. Sofer, Chief Rabbi of Pressburg, to be forwarded via Amsterdam to Jerusalem.

59. R. Israel Back, the first Hebrew printer in Jerusalem and an ardent Hasid (follower) of R. Yisroel of Rhuzin, and Haham Israel Moshe Hazan, a

dayan of the Sephardim of Jerusalem, were the prime movers in this attempt.

60. *The Voice of Jacob* (London), vol. iv, No. 107, 17 July 1845 reported that 'he is now in London, seeking aid for the hospital there and for other pious objects'. The biographer of Rabbi I. M. Hazan, Dr. Jose Faur, *The Man and His Work* (Hebrew), (Haifa, 1978), p. 14—15, is unaware of the purpose of Haham Hazan's travels, as were R. Frumkin/Rivlin, *Toldoth Hahmey Yerushalayim* (Hebrew) part 3 (Jerusalem, 1929), p. 303, and Abraham Yaari, *Sheluhey Erets Yisrael* (Jerusalem, 1948), pp. 729—32. Sir Moses met H. Hazan in Corfu on his way to Constantinople, 11 June (see *Diaries* and Guedalla); and again on 18 June 1857 in Alexandria, of which he was then Chief Rabbi.

61. Cf. *J.C.*, 4 September 1846, p. 208; *Voice of Jacob*, vol. v (London), 25 August 1846. The feud between the two papers had nothing to do with the hospital projected by Back and Hazan.

62. Rabbi Moshe Reischer, *Sha'arey Yerushalayim* (Warsaw, 1868), p. 27, also Freidin, p. 124.

63. [J. M. Pines] *Ma'amar Heyd Harim* (Jerusalem, 1894).

64. *J.C.*, 28 March 1849, pp. 193—4. A letter dated Jerusalem, 25 December 1848. Even before the spate of letters arrived from the Holy Land in November 1848, Sir Moses Montefiore 'again sent medical supplies from Apothecaries Hall to the dispenser in Jerusalem', *Diaries* ii, p. 12.

65. See Frumkin, pp. 231—2.

66. The first mention of the threat of excommunication to any patient using the missionary hospital is in Ayerst, p. 395 (1844).

67. In all, five letters were published in the *J.C.*:
    1. Eight Sephardi dignitaries, Rosh Hodesh Teveth 5609 (24 December 1848) (*J.C.*, 28 March 1849).
    2. 'A leading man in the congregation', same date (*J.C.*, 31 March 1849).
    3. Sephardim and Ashkenazim, 1 Teveth 5609 (25 December 1848) (*J.C.*, 6 April 1849).
    4. R. Shmuel of Dolhinovo (January 1849) (*J.C.*, 12 April 1849).
    5. 'Principal Men', Ashkenazim, same date (*J.C.*, 18 April 1849).
    Professor Salo Baron has published a German letter written in Jerusalem (which bears no date and no signature), addressed to Sir Moses Montefiore. He attributes the letter to Rabbi Moshe Sachs and suggests a date about 8 or 9 August 1849, during Sir Moses' third visit to the Holy Land. However, there is no internal evidence to support these dates, and the suggested identity of the writer of the letter is only an assumption. The contents suggest rather the time of writing to be nearer the dates of the *J.C.* letters, i.e. the end of 1848 or beginning of 1849. If indeed the letter writer was Rabbi Moshe Sachs, it was true to form, as he was always ready to get on any bandwagon. See Salo Baron, 'LeToldoth Yehudey Germania b'Erets Yisrael', published in *Minha leDavid* (Jerusalem, 1935), pp. 113—18.
    B. Z. Gat, accepting Prof. Baron's suggestions as to the identity of the letter writer and date, draws the conclusion that the 1849 initiative to urge Sir Moses Montefiore to take upon himself the hospital building project originated at the *Kolel H'OD*, the German Jewish community of Jerusalem, of which Sachs was a vocal member (B. Z. Gat, *Mosdoth haRephua ha Rishonim b'Erets Yisrael* (Jerusalem, 1953), p. 263). Prof. M. Eliav, *Ahavath Zion veAnshey H'OD* (Tel Aviv, 1971), p. 216, is somewhat more guarded as to the identity of the writer of the unsigned

German letter when he says 'K'nireh miPri Ito shel Sachs'.

Another letter from the Ashkenazi rabbis of Jerusalem, dated Jerusalem 15 Av 5609 (3 August 1849), pleading with Sir Moses to provide a hospital for Jerusalem is in S. Baron, 'Mi Toldoth haYishuv haYehudi bi Yerushalayim' in *Sepher Klausner* (Tel Aviv, 1937), pp. 302—12, especially pp. 306—10.

However, neither Prof. Baron nor Dr Gat had knowledge of the letters published in the *J.C.* which prove a very broadly based initiative of the Sephardi and Ashkenazi Yishuv in Jerusalem. The unsigned German letter, if it was written by Moshe Sachs, added at the most his views to the discussion.

68. *Diaries* ii, pp. 11—12. Sir Moses was accompanied on this journey by Colonel Gawler. No date of departure is stated, but Wolf, *Biography*, p. 168: 'early in May'; P. Goodman, *Montefiore*, p. 100: 'left London May 16th', but gives no source.

69. Wolf, p. 168 'The Christian conversionist societies availed themselves of the opportunity to push forward their propaganda, and, being well supplied with funds, were for a time exceptionally fortunate in making converts. This only added to the distress of the remaining faithful and in March they addressed a letter to Sir Moses Montefiore to come to their assistance . . .'. The letters quoted in the *J.C.* during March and April were written during December and January.

70. Wolf, p. 169.

71. b. Pressburg, 1810—d. Vienna, 1891. Spent years in Oxford, London and Cambridge.

72. *J.C.*, 20 April 1849, pp. 225—7. The translator is not identified, but is possibly M. H. Bresslau.

73. *Diaries* ii, pp. 24—5. The year 1851 can be deduced from the narrative, but is not stated. Dr Loewe comes back to this architect's drawing on p. 35; writing in 1854 he states that the plans 'were made about a year before'. What is important is that they were drawn subsequent to the 1849 visit, but before Sir Moses Montefiore had any plans for a further visit to the Holy Land, and long before he had any funds available for so large a project.

74. In fact it was the design of two English architects. Count Pizzamano was also involved in the Rothschild hospital.

75. *Diaries*, ii, p. 36.

76. *Diaries*, ii, p. 36.

77. They permitted the sale of land to the Russians outside the city walls and also to Finn, who owned the *Talbiyeh* and *Kerem Abraham*.

78. P.R.O., FO 75/1024 dated Jerusalem, 27 July 1854, identical, but for slight differences in text with FO 195/448 (No. 28).

79. Hyamson, *British Consulate in Jerusalem*, i, p. 288, No. 166. Hyamson in a note refers to a similar dispatch of the same date from Finn to Lord Clarendon but this was not published by him. See also Finn, *Stirring Times*, vol. ii, pp. 79—80; Arnold Blumberg, *A View from Jerusalem* (Cranbury, NJ, 1982), Finn's entry, 26 July 1854.

III 80. See Hayim Eliezer Hausdorf, *Selig Hausdorf* (Hebrew) (Jerusalem, 1906 and reprint, n.d., [Israel, 1979]), the biography of Rabbi Selig Hausdorf by his son, Hayim Eliezer Hausdorf which is based on what was related orally by father to son and includes some documents.

81. b. Paris, 1829—d. 1911. He was very active in Jewish public affairs in France.

82. No exact date is stated.
83. Count J. Pizzamano, of Venetian origin, Austrian Consul in Jerusalem, 1849–60; promoted Consul-General, 1857 (Blumberg, *A View from Jerusalem*, index, s.v.). See also M. Eliav, 'HaConsulia ha'Austrit be-Yerushalayim', *Cathedra* (18 Jan. 1981).
84. Embassies and consulates in the Levant had interpreters who also acted as intermediaries with the authorities and experts on the affairs of the native communities. The word 'dragoman' is from the same origin as *Meturgeman*. In the British diplomatic service, the post was later dignified with the title of oriental secretary (even exceptionally, counsellor), especially if held by British officials.
85. Betty de Rothschild was one of those Sir Moses Montefiore informed of his intention to use the Touro funds for the building of the hospital in Jerusalem.
86. *AZdJ* (July 1854). On his way to the Holy Land, Dr Albert Cohn travelled to Vienna. There he obtained an audience with Franz Joseph, who assured him of royal patronage for his mission. The Austrian Foreign Minister assured him of the support of the diplomatic staff in the Middle East. (Dr N. M. Gelber, 'Dr Albert Cohn and his visit to Jerusalem [in 1854]' *Jerusalem* (Hebrew) Vol. ii, pp. 175–95, with full documentation; although the statements that Cohn asked the French and Prussians for patronage seem unlikely to me, in view of the recent French involvement in the Damascus Affair and other interests of the Prussians.
87. Hausdorf, pp. 17 *et seq.*
88. The rent agreed was 6,000 grosso per annum. L. A. Frankl's version (*Nach Jerusalem*, part ii, p. 115) is that the building belonged to the Sephardim and served previously as a Talmud Torah school. It became surplus to requirements and was sold for 60,000 grosso. Both figures are correct. It was rented in 1854, but bought in 1856 by Baron Alphonse de Rothschild (Dr B. Neumann, p. 402–3).
89. Erlanger (b. Weissenburg, 1828–d. Paris, 1892); assisted Dr Cohn; later a founder of the Alliance Israélite Universelle, a member of the Consistoire, and active in the Societé des Études Juives.
90. It is accepted that it was a happy coincidence that Dr Bernhard Neumann happened to be in Jerusalem. The source seems to be Frankl, *Nach Jerusalem*, p. 115: 'eine eigenthümliche Verkettung von Lebensverhältnissen fügte es so glücklich, dass Herr Dr Bernhard Neumann, ein geborener Russe der auf den Hochschulen von Krakau und Wien gebildet ist, sich eben in Jerusalem befand, als Herr Albert Cohn . . .'. This is contradicted by Dr Neumann himself. He states twice in his book, *Die Heilige Stadt und deren Bewohner* (Hamburg 1877), in the Introduction, p. vii, and on p. 140, that in 1862 he left Jerusalem after having spent fifteen years there. Thus he arrived in Jerusalem in 1847. The first eight years he served as 'Arzt der dortigen [i.e. Jerusalem] israelitische Gemeinden . . .'.
91. *Diaries* ii, p. 36.
92. L. A. Frankl, p. 117.
93. *J.C.*, 5 January 1855, p. 20. The appeal had raised nearly £20,000 since May.
94. Hausdorf, ibid. (freely translated).
95. Hyamson, i, No. 166, p. 228–9, dispatch from Finn, Jerusalem, 27 July 1854.
96. Correct title, 'Consistoire Centrale Israelite de France'.
97. A phrase that suggests that there were others who were not friends of Cohn.

98. Finn rather naïvely lists here the omission of the missionary medical institution.
99. i.e. the *Bikur Holim*, founded in 1844–5 by Sir Moses Montefiore.
100. *Diaries*, ii, p. 37 (no exact date). See Lucien Wolf, *Notes on the Diplomatic History of the Jewish Question*, pp. 18–19; Dr N. M. Gelber, 'Dr Albert Cohn u'Bikuro b'Yerushalayim', *Jerusalem* (Hebrew) vol. ii (Jerusalem, 5707) pp. 175 *et seq*. For the French side of the story, see Isidore Loeb, *Biographie d'Albert Cohn* (Paris 1875), pp. 48–9.
101. *J.C.*, 8 September 1854, p. 29.
102. In the report of his success in Constantinople which Cohn released to the press, he made the point that as 'he pronounced the blessing customary with Jews on beholding a crowned head, tears were seen in the Sultan's eyes' (*J.C.*, 8 September 1854). The same was also reported, on the authority of Cohn, in the *AZdJ* and probably in other papers too. Schreiner, the Dragoman of the Austrian Embassy in Constantinople, who was present at Cohn's audience with the Sultan, sent a long report on it to his superiors in Vienna (21 August 1854). He reported that his impression was that good results may be expected, '. . . wenn ich auch Dr Cohn's Behauptung dahin gestellt lassen will, dass der Sultan uber sein in hebräischer Sprache ausgesprochenes Gebet bis zu Thränen gerührt gewesen sei'. See Dr N. M. Gelber, 'Dr Albert Cohn u'Bikuro b'Yerushalayim', *Jerusalem*, vol. ii, Pt 3/4, (1949), pp. 193–4.
103. *J.C.*, 3 November 1854, pp. 29–30. The *J.C.* printed there two letters of Dr Cohn copied from the *Univers Israélite* of Paris, one dated Jerusalem, 27 July 1854, laudatory of his own work for the hospital, the other, Constantinople, 17 August 1854, addressed to the Chief Rabbi of France, recounting his success with the Sultan, with the text of the decree giving equal rights to all subjects of the Ottoman Empire. The *J.C.* published further letters on 17 and 24 November and extracts of Cohn's petition to Franz Joseph I.
104. i.e. Dr Albert Cohn.
105. A reprographic reprint (Israel [1979]) has been used. A copy of this rare pamphlet was discovered by G. Kressel in the National Library, Jerusalem; see his article, *Davar*, 18 Sept. 1963. cf. also Shoshana Halevi, *The First Hebrew Books Printed in Jerusalem in the Second Half of the Nineteenth Century* (Hebrew) (Jerusalem, 1975), no. 51.
106. The underlined words are in the Hebrew text in capital letters where *the house of Jacob* in the Hebrew text is printed in ordinary letters. 'House of Jacob' is an allusion to James de Rothschild whose Hebrew name was Jacob. This is rather typical of Albert Cohn.
107. *J.C.*, 29 December 1854 and 5 January 1855.
108. *Nach Jerusalem*, ii, p. 117. 'There is such a thing as jealousy of generosity'. That Paris was jealous of Sir Moses Montefiore's achievements was pointed out by Finn in his dispatch of 24 July 1855 to Lord Stratford de Redcliffe (Hyamson, i, p. 234). They were still smarting under the disappointment of Sir Moses Montefiore's success in Damascus.
109. i.e. Albert Cohn.
110. i.e. The Jews of Jerusalem.
111. *J.C.*, 29 December 1854.
112. *J.C.*, 6 January 1855.
113. i.e. Jerusalem.
114. Hyamson, i, doc. no. 6, p. 5. William Young, Consul in Jerusalem, to

Viscount Palmerston, Jerusalem, 25 May 1839, 'I found the religious prejudice so strong against being numbered at all ... at present I am only able to give your Lordship the aggregate numbers, which I think may be considered as pretty accurate, but certainly rather under than over stated ...'. The number of Jews in Jerusalem he gives as 5,500 souls. See discussion of population statistics, B. Z. Gat, *HaYishuv haYehudi b'Erets Yisrael*, pp. 12—16.

115. *AZdJ*, 4 September 1854 in footnote 'fur eine Bevölkerung von 8,000 Juden sind freilich 18 betten noch wenig!'.

116. *AZdJ*, 11 September 1854, p. 463, leading article, *Zur jüdisch-orientalischen Frage*, dated 1 September 1854.

117. The figure of 50,000 francs was mentioned as all that had come from Rothschild funds, whereas Cohn claimed to have spent 40,000 francs of his own as well as the above.

IV 118. *Diaries*, ii, p. 37.

119. *Diaries*, ii, p. 37.

120. *J.C.*, 19 January 1855, p. 37.

121. As so often Dr Loewe omits dates and he does not state when the first report was published. However, in *An appeal on behalf of the suffering Jews of the Holy Land*, Second report (London 1856), the report is signed and dated by Chief Rabbi Adler and Sir Moses Montefiore, London 14 February 5616 (1856). In the introductory paragraph it states that in February 1855 the same trustees 'had the honour to publish their first report'. I have not been able to locate a copy of it. It was printed in full in the *J.C.*, 2 March 1855 and the quotation in the *Diaries* is to be found there verbatim. It was also reprinted in full in *The Occident* of New York.

122. *Diaries*, ii, pp. 37—8.

123. Published in the *Asmonean* and reprinted from there in *J.C.*, 8 April 1855. Another letter also printed in the *J.C.*, addressed to A. Hart, Chairman of Palestine Fund Meeting, dated 5 February 1855 expresses thanks for the receipt of £60. 1s. 4d. Sir Moses also informed Hart of his intention to travel to Palestine after Passover.

124. *Diaries*, ii, p. 38.

125. Sir Moses Montefiore paid a short visit to Paris before he embarked on his journey to the Holy Land. He saw there Lord Cowley, in connection with the Damascus inscription (*Diaries*, ii, p. 39). There is no mention of Sir Moses having made contact with the Rothschilds in Paris.

126. *Diaries*, ii, p. 39. The words are Dr Loewe's but the facts are supposedly taken from Sir Moses' own diary.

127. In the first Report of the Palestine Appeal a sum of $288.98 received from New York is equated in the accounts with £66 1s 4d. This suggests a rate of exchange of £1 = $4.82. On that basis the £8,025 received represents approximately $38,600, which leaves as at that date approximately another $11,400 of the legacy in the hands of the executors in New Orleans.

128. That is to say, the available sources are silent on these points.

129. Guedalla, p. 6. Kursheedt is mentioned there as the trustee of £12,000 of the Touro legacy. See also *Diaries*, ii, pp. 39 *et seq.*

130. Author's italics.

131. As reported in the *AZdJ*, 20 November 1854. It is no coincidence that *The Occident* (New York, October 1854), p. 376, carried the report: 'we are informed that after mature deliberation, it has been decided that the bequest of the late Judah Touro for the benefit of the Palestine Jews shall be devoted to the foundation of a hospital and synagogue in Jerusalem.'

It was also stated on good authority that this would not retard the movement for furthering agricultural work in the Holy Land.

132. *J.C.*, 15 January 1855.

133. Written in Jerusalem, 24 July 1855. Sir Moses Montefiore was then already in Jerusalem.

134. 'Some Rothschild money'. The disdain in Sir Moses Montefiore's words is obvious. Finn refers to this in his earlier dispatch (Hyamson No. 166), quoted extensively above.

135. It is amusing to note the Anglo-phobia of the Pressburg-born Frenchman, Dr A. Cohn.

136. This does not take account of the large amount of the Appeal Fund which was also at Sir Moses Montefiore's disposal.

V 137. Guedalla, pp. 5, 6. See also, *Diaries*, ii, 39.

138. Joseph Sebag, later Sebag-Montefiore, (1822–1903), succeeded to Sir Moses' estate; son of Solomon Sebag and brother of Jemima Guedalla.

139. Benjamin Cohen (1789–1867) married in 1819 Justina (1800–73), sister of Sir Moses Montefiore. She was Jemima Guedalla's aunt.

140. This is the Guedalla diary version which was written at the time, whereas Dr Loewe reconstructed the events at a much later date and, in doing so, got some details wrong. Dr Loewe presumably came from his home in Broadstairs.

141. Guedalla, pp. 9, 10. See also Marcus N. Adler, *The Adler Family* (London, 1909), pp. 16, 17, where he gives a delightful description of his grandmother. She had been visited regularly by the Rothschilds and 'among those she captivated was Sir Moses Montefiore,' *J.C.*, 1 June 1855, taken from *Hannoverische Zeitung*, 24 May 1855. *J.C.* also reflected on Sir Moses Montefiore's visit to Mrs Adler.

142. *AZdJ*, 4 June 1855.

143. Guedalla, p. 10.

144. Guedalla, pp. 10–12. Haim Guedalla sent to the *J.C.* a short notice of the visit to the Synagogue and old burial ground at Prague, *J.C.*, 1 June 1855, p. 187. Also a lengthy report on Sir Moses Montefiore's stay in Prague, taken from the *Tagesbothe aus Böhmen* (Prague, 24 May 1855), was printed in translation in the same issue of the *J.C.*

145. Guedalla, p. 12; *Diaries*, ii, p. 40; *Wiener Mittheilungen*, 10 September 1855, adds that Sir Moses Montefiore also left in Kollin a considerable sum of money and sent from Vienna a gold Kiddush cup to Rabbi Frank. Dr Daniel Frank was Rabbi of Kollin 1839–1860; see Dr Richard Feder, 'The Jews in Kollin' (Czech), in *Die Juden und Judengemeinden Böhmens*, etc., ed. Hugo Gold (Brünn 1934), p. 291.

146. Guedalla, pp. 13–15, *Diaries*, ii, p. 40.

147. Guedalla, p. 16, who relates that Rothschild offered Sir Moses and Lady Montefiore his box in the Burg Theater which they did not accept, but Mr and Mrs Guedalla accepted the offer.

148. *Diaries*, ii, p. 41.

149. *Kochbe Jitzhak*, vol. xxi (Wien, 1856), pp. 58–61.

150. Now Ljubljana in Yugoslavia, capital of Slovenia.

151. Guedalla, p. 16.

152. Guedalla, p. 16; *Diaries*, ii, p. 41. Both extol the beauty of the place. The guide pointed out the stalactite they called 'Synagogue'. Dr Loewe assumes this was an *ad hoc* naming in honour of Sir Moses.

153. *J.C.*, 27 July 1855, quoted *in extenso* a column and a half report on the Trieste stay from the *Educatore Israelite*, 12 July 1855. See also *Diaries*, ii, p. 41 and Guedalla pp. 19–20.

154. The Chief Rabbi was R. Sabbato Grazido Treves, see Lelio della Torre, *Wiener Mittheilungen* (1855), p. 179. Rabbi Treves was then 78.

155. *J.C.*, ibid. A copy of this is in British Library 4033, aa. 51 (9). See also, on Sir Moses' visit to Trieste, *AZdJ*, 30 July 1855.

156. Letter dated Trieste, 8 June 1855, written in French and printed in English translation, *J.C.*, 12 September 1855.

157. Rachel Morpurgo (b. Trieste, 1790, daughter of Baruch Luzzatto, cousin of S. D. Luzzatto. Married to Jacob Morpurgo; d. Trieste, 1871). Her poems and literary letters were collected and edited by Castiglioni, *Ugav Rahel* (Krakau, 1890).

158. *Kochbe Jitzhak*, vol. xxi (Wien, 1856), p. 77.

159. Guedalla, p. 20.

160. Hazan, Dayan in Jerusalem, Rabbi of Rome, and Corfu (1852–5), later met Sir Moses in Alexandria, where he was then Chief Rabbi (*Diaries*, II, p. 71).

161. Guedalla, pp. 21–2.

VI 162. b. 1785 (?)–d. Paris, 1873. Ennobled by King Victor Emanuel. He was founder of the Central Consistoire of Turkish Jews, and took a great interest in the education of the Jewish children, cf. *Jüdisches Lexicon*, vol. i (Berlin, 1926), col. 1266; M. D. Gaon, *Yehudey haMizrah b'Erets Yisrael* vol. ii (Jerusalem, 1938), pp. 596 and 746. On his earlier visit to Constantinople in 1840 Sir Moses Montefiore stayed in the Camondo home (*Diaries*, i, pp. 260 *et seq.*). This is recalled by H. Ezra Ben Veniste, *Haye Moshe* (Jerusalem, 1886), pp. 32 *et seq.*, who was about Bar Mitzvah age at the time. He describes a most interesting discussion between Sir Moses and the Chief Rabbi.

163. Guedalla, pp. 27–37; *Diaries*, ii, pp. 40–45.

164. *J.C.*, 6 July 1855. The intention was to stay a fortnight in Constantinople.

165. *Diaries*, ii, p. 41.

166. Sir Stratford Canning, Viscount Stratford de Redcliffe (1786–1880); Ambassador in Constantinople 1825–9; 1831–2; 1842–8 (Hyamson, i, p. xiv).

167. See Blumberg, p. 305, n. 9.

168. Blumberg, p. 275, n. 24.

169. Lord Clarendon's draft dispatch of 2 July 1855.

170. *Diaries*, ii, p. 38, 25 March 1855. See below, marginal note by Lord Clarendon to draft of 7 April 1855.

171. PRO, FO 78/1062.

172. Drafts are instructions to secretaries to copy for signature by the Foreign Secretary, and make ready for onward dispatch.

173. The note is in Lord Clarendon's hand, but I could not trace the document referred to in the Public Record Office.

174. Etienne Pisani, engaged as Dragoman in 1852, was one of three members of the same family who filled that office in the British Embassy in Constantinople; another Pisani was acting in that capacity in 1840 when Sir Moses Montefiore visited Constantinople in connection with the Damascus affair, and was of great help to him. (*Diaries*, i, p. 271.)

175. *Diaries*, ii, p. 41, notes on 17 June, date of arrival, that Sir Moses Montefiore was 'most anxious to hear from Mr Pisani what arrangements had been made by the Turkish Minister regarding his audience with the

Sultan'. It is difficult to see how definite arrangements could have been made before Sir Moses' arrival in Constantinople. Is it possible that it is another inaccuracy of date? It is more likely that arrangements for the audience were made between the 17th and the 25th.

176. For Fuad Pasha, see Blumberg, p. 305, n. 9. He was Foreign Minister.

177. The endorsement is illegible beyond these words. Lord Ponsonby, a clerk at the Foreign Office, was currently Private Secretary to the Secretary of State.

178. *Diaries*, ii, p. 42.

179. *Diaries*, i, pp. 268 *et seq.*

180. *Diaries*, ii, p. 43. These are verbatim quotations from Sir Moses Montefiore's diaries and not Dr Loewe's edited version.

181. On Sir Moses Montefiore's earlier visit to Constantinople in 1840, he also received a Turkish decoration, *Diaries*, i, p. 277.

182. Guedalla, p. 34; *Diaries*, ii, p. 44.

183. Sir Moses Montefiore uses the plural *Firmans*, but I am not sure whether he meant two copies of the same *Firman*, as was the protocol: one copy for the Ambassador for onward dispatch to the Consul (in this case Constantinople Embassy to Consulate in Jerusalem), and one copy for the petitioner, in this case Sir Moses Montefiore. Alternatively, the plural may indicate two separate *Firmans*, in which case the second is the one permitting the rebuilding of the Hurva Synagogue which Sir Moses was to convey to Jerusalem.

184. This diary entry was jotted already on 28 June, *Diaries*, ii, p. 42. Sir Moses Montefiore repeated his sincere acknowledgements for the help received from Lord Stratford de Redcliffe in *An Appeal on Behalf of the Suffering Jews in the Holy Land*, Second Report (London, [February 1856]), p. 4, first published in *J.C.*, 22 February 1856, also reprinted in *The Occident* (New York, April 1856).

185. Guedalla, pp. 35—6.

186. Guedalla, pp. 37—40.

187. Guedalla, p. 38.

188. i.e. by the cholera epidemic.

189. See Guedalla, p. 38, on the methods of enforcing the quarantine regulations.

190. *Diaries*, ii, p. 45.

191. Guedalla, pp. 39—40.

192. 'Dragoman' (normally a title of an official at a foreign embassy or consulate), here indicates guide and translator.

193. Guedalla, pp. 41—2.

194. See A. L. Tibawi, *British Interest in Palestine 1800—1901* (O.U.P., Oxford, 1961), pp. 142—7, about As'ad Ya'cub Khayat and his family ramifications, and their connections with the British Consular Service in Beirut.

195. Sedan chairs, slung between two donkeys.

196. Guedalla, pp. 41—3.

197. Guedalla, p. 44; also, on p. 42, the twelve mounted guards led by Saladin; cf. *Stirring Times*, p. 325: '. . . by the escort of horsemen, who had been sent out by the Turkish authorities . . .'. *Diaries*, ii, p. 45, speaks of 'A guard of honour . . . drawn up by order of the Pasha . . .', that is on the approaches to Jerusalem. There is a cryptic entry in Blumberg, p. 197: 'July 18 . . . the Bin Bashi sent to the Chief Rabbi enquiring if he should place a guard of honour of Nizem infantry at the gate on the arrival of

Sir Moses. They referred him to the Consul, who decidedly refused to allow it, but recommended a detachment of half a dozen Beshi Bezuk.' It seems the Turkish authorities preferred to honour Sir Moses; Finn was more concerned to make sure of his safety, as he suggested six soldiers. However, there were twelve soldiers to guard them from Jaffa to Jerusalem, and a guard of honour to meet them at the approaches to Jerusalem. (Prof. Blumberg, p. 212, n. 54, has another explanation.)

198. Guedalla, p. 44; *Diaries*, ii, p. 45; *Stirring Times*, p. 325.
199. *Stirring Times*, p. 325.
200. Hyamson, i, p. 233, no. 174: Dispatch, Jerusalem, 24 July 1855. *Diaries*, ii, p. 45. It is interesting to note Sir Moses had hardly arrived in Constantinople when Moses Sachs wrote in a letter to the *Jewish Chronicle* (dated Jerusalem, June 5615) that 'there is a remarkable excitement just now in Jerusalem. In every street people ask each other what is the news? When will Sir Moses arrive?' (*J.C.*, 13 July 1855).
201. This is the correct date, as stated by Mrs Guedalla (p. 44). Hers is a day-to-day diary written at the time the events were taking place. This is borne out by Finn's dispatch (Hyamson, i, no. 174, p. 233: Finn to Lord Stratford de Redcliffe, Jerusalem, 24 July 1855). '. . . Sir Moses and Lady Montefiore arrived here on the 20th inst. . . .'. Also Blumberg, p. 197, 'July 20. Sir Moses Montefiore and party arrived.' When Dr Loewe (*Diaries*, ii, p. 45) wrote, 'On July 18th we arrived in Jerusalem', this is incorrect; and his chapter about his stay in Jerusalem is very much in need of correction of dates and clarification of events.
202. Guedalla, p. 44.
203. *Diaries*, ii, p. 45.
204. *Stirring Times*, ii, p. 325.
205. Guedalla, p. 44.
206. MS BZA.
207. Hyamson, i, p. 238, No. 175.
208. PRO FO/78/195/455; cf. also *Stirring Times*, ii, p. 326.
209. It must be stressed that, against common belief, the *Firman* to rebuild the Hurvah Synagogue was not issued at Sir Moses' request. Sir Moses never claimed it to have been. That it was issued was mainly thanks to the intercession in Constantinople of Lord Napier (later Lord Napier and Ettrick), then Secretary of the British Embassy. Sir Moses may have used his good relations with the Porte to expedite matters. It was his good fortune to have been the bearer of the document to Jerusalem.
210. That is the way his name is spelt in the Diaries. He was Governor of Jerusalem Feb. 1855–7. An enlightened man of liberal political views, he was helpful to Sir Moses. See Mrs Finn, *Reminiscences*, p. 128; Blumberg, s.v. Index, and in particular p. 207–8, n. 13.
211. Blumberg, p. 197.
212. Guedalla, p. 45. Jewish visitors were not received that day.
213. He was the Governor of Jerusalem in 1839, and later played an important role.
214. Blumberg, p. 197.
215. *Stirring Times*, p. 326; *Diaries*, ii, pp. 45–6.
216. *Stirring Times*, p. 326; *Diaries*, p. 46.
217. *Stirring Times*, p. 327.
218. Guedalla, p. 46; *Diaries*, ii, p. 47. While all rushed to have a glass of water, Sir Moses and Lady Montefiore 'proceeded, but slowly, to prepare for the breaking of the long fast' (*Stirring Times*, p. 327).

VIII   219. *Diaries*, ii, p. 46.
220. Dated February 1856, first published in *J.C.*, 22 February 1856.
221. *Diaries*, ii, p. 48.
222. *Diaries*, pp. 49–51.
223. London, 1862, pp. 311–315. Miss Rogers was the sister of Edward Thomas Rogers, the British Vice-Consul in Haifa.
224. 7 April 1855; cf. *Stirring Times*, ii, pp. 238–57; *Reminiscences*, pp. 130–1; Blumberg, p. 191, n. 37 on p. 210.
225. Finn, ii, p. 331. J. H. Tavijov's Hebrew translation of Montefiore's *Diaries*, *Sifrey haZichronoth l'Sir Moshe Montefiore* part ii (Warsaw, 1899), p. 86, left Loewe's entry completely untranslated. He obviously did not understand the allusion. It must be stated here that Tavijov's work, although quoted by scholars as an authoritative source, is completely unreliable and has no value for reference.
226. Guedalla, p. 45.
227. Misprint for Kiamil, Governor of Jerusalem, appointed 14 February 1855, Blumberg, p. 187; *Stirring Times*, ii, p. 217 gives 15 February as the date; Mrs Finn, *Reminiscences*, p. 128.
228. Here follows a description of what they saw. The other participants who left descriptions of the visit are James Finn, *Stirring Times*, ii, chap. 28, in particular pp. 323–39; Mrs Finn, *Reminiscences*, pp. 137–41; a further very interesting description was published in the *Wiener Mittheilungen*, vol. i no. 41 (Wien, 8 October 1855), pp. 161–2; *Ein Besuch in der Moschee Omar's*. Schreiben einer englischen Touristen aus Jerusalem, 26 July 1855. It is taken over from the M.f.d.L.d.A. [= *Monatschrift fur die Literatur des Abendlandes?*]. The identity of the writer can be gathered from the contents to be Mary Eliza Rogers. It is an interesting piece of descriptive reportage, penned on the day of the visit. Miss Rogers mentioned her visit together with Sir Moses and Lady Montefiore to the *M'kom HaMikdash* in her book, p. 58.
229. Blumberg, p. 197 and n. 58, pp. 212–213. Blumberg is mistaken when he says the Montefiore Diaries are silent on this event.
230. David de Sola Pool, *Some Relations of Gershom Kursheedt and Sir Moses Montefiore*, Publications of A.J.H. Soc. No. 37, p. 215. Kursheedt's letter is dated Alexandria, 3 September 1855.
231. Wien, 3 September 1855, p. 144.
232. *Reminiscences*, p. 139.
233. *Stirring Times*, ii, p. 237.
234. The Jerusalem Consulate had both Arab and Jewish interpreters, who bore the title of dragoman.
235. Blumberg, index s.v. Prof. Blumberg was at a loss in deciphering this name in Finn's handwriting, hence there are about half-a-dozen variant readings. Meyuhas was one of the inhabitants of Mishkenoth Sha'ananim in 1861 and as such signed a letter dated 4 Nisan 5621 (Hebrew University MS Var. 21). cf. Abraham Ben-Jacob, *Yerushalayim bein ha Homoth* (Jerusalem, 1977), p. 25.
236. M. Reischer, *Sha'arey Yerushalayim*, first edn. (Warsaw, 1868), p. 29. The facts he relates contradict in essentials what we know from Finn and others. The book was written during the winter months of 1868 in Lemberg to while his time away and entirely from memory. See approbation of Rabbi J. S. Nathanson, Chief Rabbi of Lemberg.
237. The Montefiores' first visit to the Holy Land.

238. *Stirring Times*, ii, p. 334. Finn insinuates that the religious fanatics (p. 333), the zealots, were only the front men for the Rabbis. This insinuation is unsubstantiated.

239. It is surprising that Finn's manuscript diary which goes into great detail makes no mention of a Herem. Dr B. Z. Gat, *HaYishuv haYehudi b'Erets Yisrael b'shnoth 5600–5641* (Jerusalem, 1963), p. 78, n. 59, refers to the *Stirring Times* quotation regarding the *Herem*. He expresses reservations with regard to Finn's words and suggests they need verification.

240. They arrived back in London on 20 September 1855. *J.C.*, 28 September 1855.

241. About them, Blumberg index s.v. In particular p. 121, n. 59.

242. *J.C.*, 30 November 1855.

IX 243. According to the First Report of the Appeal (February 1855), between May and September 1854 £3,250 was sent (*J.C.*, February 1855); by the time the Second Report appeared in February 1856, £6,364 was accounted for under the heading 'Money Relief'.

244. Quoted from *The Occident*, April 1855, p. 30, which reprinted the report in full. The *J.C.*, February 1855, seems to have had the full text before the separate booklet was published. I could not locate a copy of the Report issued as a booklet.

245. Sir Moses Montefiore on his earlier visits distributed large sums of money, much of it his own, and moneys entrusted to him to dispense at his own discretion. However, there was strong criticism of this as indiscriminate giving. The recipients were not always the most needy; the most insistent always received more than their fair share, whereas the humble and infirm were often left out. L. A. Frankl, *Nach Jerusalem*, ii, pp. 25–7, printed a dialogue between the author and 'M.S.', the son-in-law of Zadoc Levi, one of the richest Jews in Jerusalem, who certainly did not live in poverty. He admitted cynically '. . . if the foreigners are fools to send money should I be a fool and not accept it?' The fool who gave was, by implication, Sir Moses Montefiore, and the cynic who accepted was Moses Sachs.

246. *Diaries*, ii, p. 51.

247. Guedalla, pp. 52–4.

248. The dragoman brought by Sir Moses from Beirut.

249. This may well be to what Moses Sachs was referring (in his letter of 20 August 1855 to the editor of the *J.C.*,) writing about Dr Loewe: 'He is obliged to speak to every individual himself, in order to report to Sir Moses Montefiore. The patience, prudence and command over his temper, displayed during these tedious interviews excite general admiration.' (*J.C.*, 12 October 1855).

250. Blumberg, p. 198; n. 6, p. 123 (although it is necessary to refer to Mrs Guedalla's diary to understand this entry).

251. 3 September 1855.

252. i.e. Sunday the 5th, the day of the demonstration; 'The Rabbi' is not identified.

253. *Menschenfreund* is used in the original.

254. Letteris, the editor of the *Wiener Mittheilungen*, while he did not express any disapproval of the contents of the report, found it difficult to comprehend the attitude of the Jerusalemites. He stated that he left out the worst of the denigrating expressions of the letter '. . . der sonst achtbare Correspondent sich gegen Herrn Montefiore und Dr Loewe mit eine Leidenschaftlichkeit bedient welche eine allgemeine Unzufriedenheit mit dem Gebahren

dieser "Reformer" den Ausdruck zu geben scheinen. Und warum all dieser Lärm? Weil der Held von Damaskus . . . eine bleibende . . . Verbesserung . . . vorzieht.' The writer is obviously one of those Jerusalemites who were against Sir Moses and siding with Albert Cohn. Was it Hausdorf?

255. This story is told by the missionary Crawford and quoted from missionary sources by the *J.C.*, 14 December 1855. Crawford claimed that a Persian Jew turned up at his house telling him that he solicited Sir Moses Montefiore for alms; Crawford added: 'perhaps a bit insultingly'. At that a dragoman gave instructions to kawasses to have him removed. They in turn assaulted him brutally and in consequence he was laid up for some days. The Jew asked Crawford to complain to the British Consul, but he declined to do so, as he thought it would be of no use.

256. Guedalla, p. 54.

257. Both were non-Jewish daily papers in Vienna. As both papers printed the same report on the same day it suggests a concerted effort to denigrate Sir Moses Montefiore.

258. A well-known member of a Sephardi Jewish family, active in the *Türkische Gemeinde* (Turkish Congregation) in Vienna.

259. That is correct, but the popular enthusiasm soon waned when it was realized that this time the alms were to be channelled via the *Halukah*, that is through the Rabbinate.

260. 10 September 1855, vol. xvi, no. 37, n. on pp. 473—4.

261. L. A. Frankl was also of the same opinion '. . . und kein bahres Geld mehr verschleudern mochte, thaten sie ihm in den Bann, und nicht desswegen weil er die Omar Moschee . . . betreten hat'. *Nach Jerusalem*, ii. p. 212.

262. The letter quoted in the footnote in *AZdJ* (10 September 1855), pp. 473—4.

263. *AZdJ* (10 September 1855), p. 474. 'Nun, dass der *Cherem* nicht laut verkündigt worden ist, das die Glaubensgenossen in ihrem grossen Elende die spendende Hand nicht zurück stossen werden, wozu ja eine Nidduy-Erklärung notig ware — das glauben — das glauben wir dem Altonaischen Herrn Nassi de-Erez Israel leicht.'

264. Usually in cooperation with the *Pekidim v'Amarklim* of Amsterdam.

265. E. Dukes, *Iwah Lemoshav* (Krakau, 1903), Hebrew section, pp. 114—20 (Letter of appointment as *Nasi*, pp. 119—20). Rabbi Ettlinger discussed the subject of *Kedushat M'kom ha'Mikdash bi'Zeman hazeh* (Sanctity of the Temple Area in Contemporary Times) in *Shomer Zion haNe'eman*, the journal he edited, Altona 7 Heshvan 5616 (19 October 1855), also in no. 217, 4 Shevat 5616. Though the topicality of the discussion and publication is not indicated, it is obvious. Both these contributions were reprinted in Rabbi Ettlinger's Responsa, *Binyan Zion* (pt. 1), Responsa nos. 2 and 3. Cf. also Prof M. Eliav, *Ahavath Zion ve'anshey H'OD* (Tel Aviv, 1970), pp. 61—3 and 78—82.

266. b. Jerusalem, 1895—d. New York, 1980; one of the greatest experts on the history of Jerusalem of that period. His *Yehudim Mefurssamim she'nichnessu l'Mkom ha'Mikdash* was printed in *Bitzaron* (New York, 1968), pp. 88, *et seq.*, and reprinted in *Hatzofeh* (Tel Aviv, 12 Tishri 1968).

267. As quoted by Malachi from *HaZvi*, vol. i, no. 2, 12 Heshvan 1884.

268. Rabbi Samuel Weingarten in *Sinai*, vol. lxii (Jerusalem, 1967), p. 94, quoting from *Malkhi baKodesh*, part i (St Louis, 1919), p. 43.

269. b. Safed, 1857—d. Hoboken, NJ, 1935.

270. 1867 is a mistake. It should be 1855 on his fourth visit. This has already
been corrected by Malachi, *Sinai*, vol. lxiii (Jerusalem 1968), p. 285, in
his article *Ha'im Hecherimu eth Montefiore biYerushalayim?* It is strange
that Malachi, in an earlier article, *HaHerem b'Dorot haAcharonim*, reprinted in his *Perakim b'Toldoth haYishuv haYashan*, ed. Galia Yardeni
(Tel Aviv, 1971), p. 282, suggests that on two occasions the Herem was
pronounced against Sir Moses Montefiore, in 1855 and again in 1866.

271. 'Rabbi' in the sense of 'Haus Rabbiner' (i.e. domestic chaplain).

272. Two statements by Malachi also bear signs of originating in the folklore
of Jerusalem: that Dr Loewe never entered the *M'kom haMikdash*, which
is a mistake; and that Sir Moses Montefiore was carried in a sedan chair,
which may be true; and that thus *ipso facto* he did not transgress, which is,
of course, a misunderstanding of the *Halachah*.

273. This story is also printed by R. Yehuda Noah Brawer in *Sh'ar Dalthey
haLevanon* (Jerusalem, 1928) my original source. However, Weingarten
quotes Hirschensohn *Malkhi baKodesh*, part vi (New York), p. 265, who
claimed that the whole of Brawer's booklet was a plagiarism taken from
his work.

274. It should be stressed that Hirschensohn's book was published in 1919, that
is sixty-four years after the event.

275. *Sinai* (1968), vol. ii, pp. 282—5. The interview is reported in *HaZefira*,
vol. xii (3 Sivan 1867).

276. Jacob Goldman (b. Jerusalem, 1856—d. Tel Aviv, 1981) On him, see S.
Kressel, *Lexicon leSifruth ha'Ivrith*, etc., Vol. ii, (Merhavia, 1965),
cols. 418—419.

277. b. 1816—d., Jerusalem, 1909. He was a trusted friend and associate of Sir Moses Montefiore in his work for the Holy Land for some six
decades.

278. b. Tiberias (?)—d. Jerusalem, 5621. He was Chief Rabbi of Tiberias and,
after the death of Haham Bashi Itzhac Covo on 17 August 1854 (in
Alexandria), he succeeded to the post in Jerusalem.

279. b. Russia—d. Jerusalem, 5623; son-in-law of R. Yisroel [Poruch] Sklova,
Head of the Community of Perushim.

280. Rabbi Abraham ben David of Posquières (known as Rabad, i.e. Rabbi
Abraham Ben David), c. 1125—1198. Talmudic authority in Provence.
Born in Narbonne, died at Posquières, near Nimes, famous for its Yeshivah
he established there. In his marginal notes to Maimonides' *Mishneh Torah*,
he often expresses views different from those of Maimonides. See *En-
cylocpaedia Judaica*, ii, 136—40.

281. *Shulchan Aruch*, Orach Hayim, chap. 563, *Magen Avraham*, note 2.

282. Whether *Kudsha leShatho* is a commitment for *Kedusha laAthid* in
respect of *Issur Kareth*.

283. *AZdJ* (22 October 1855), p. 555.

284. This is absolutely correct. During this visit he set up at his father's wish,
a *Yesheeba* (talmudical college), which brought him in constant contact
with the Sephardi Hahamim. See Mrs. Guedalla's diary; cf. also Dr
Mordechai Rozen, 'Igroth Haim Guedalla le Rabbi Jacob Shaul Elyashar',
Vatikin (1975), pp. 163—86. It is now possible to give the exact date
when the *Yesheeba* was established: Rosh Hodesh Elul 5615, 15 Aug
1855.

X 285. First Report of the Appeal, February 1855 (quoted from *The Occident*
(New York, April 1855), p. 31): 'Another institution, the Lying-in-Charity,

established in Jerusalem, and in three other cities some years since by Lady Montefiore under the name of *Bekuur Cholim* . . .' (probably about 1840).
286. The amounts given to these are detailed in the Reports.
287. A. M. Luncz, 'Mosheh vi Yerushalayim', *Jerusalem*, vol. ii (Jerusalem, 1842), quoted from G. Kressel (ed.): *Nethivoth Zion viYerushalayim*, Selected Essays of A. M. Luncz (Jerusalem, 1970), p. 285. However, if M. Sach's words can be taken at face value, Luncz's statement does not accord with the facts. Sachs complained in a letter to the editor, dated Jerusalem, Ellul 5615, that there were no Talmud Torah schools in Jerusalem (*J.C.*, 29 September 1855).
288. Guedalla, p. 51.
289. Guedalla, p. 52.
290. MS BZA.
291. Blumberg, p. 198. According to L. A. Frankl, *Nach Jerusalem*, ii, p. 111, the rent for three years was 18,000 piastres [£50 per annum]. For repairs and refurbishing 8,000 piastres were spent [£67].
292. *Diaries*, ii, pp. 48–9.
293. *Diaries*, ii, p. 48.
294. Mrs Guedalla gives no figures. Dr Loewe's were not maintained, as will be seen.
295. MS BZA.
296. Finn's private diary noted on 23 August: 'Sir Moses is so infirm as to be obliged to use a sedan carried by four men and when walking very short distances has a man on each side.'
297. The first *Issur* [prohibition of the Rabbinate] seems to be the one issued in 1856 against the *Simon Edler von Lämelsch'en Lehr und Wohlthatigkeits Anstallt*. A full German translation was printed by L. A. Frankl in *Nach Jerusalem*, ii, pp. 153–5. It was originally printed in Hebrew as a leaflet, but is not listed in Shoshana Halevi, *The First Hebrew Books Printed in Jerusalem in the Second Half of the Nineteenth Century 1841–1890* (Hebrew)(Jerusalem, 1975). The Hebrew text was printed by R. A. J. Schlesinger, *Ma'assey Avoth* (Jerusalem, 1900), pp. 45–7.
298. *J.C.*, 30 November 1855.
299. It does not necessarily mean that Nicolayson was telling the absolute truth. However, hardly a year later the Sephardi Rabbinate signed a letter praising L. A. Frankl's school, which does not suggest that much coercion was needed to get their co-operation (*Nach Jerusalem*, ii, pp. 493–4). Dr Simon Fränkel and Dr B. Neumann also signed that letter. They were Ashkenazim but to all intents and purposes outsiders.
300. *Stirring Times*, ii, p. 434.
301. e.g. *Stirring Times*, ii, p. 433, the 'Rabbinists': there is an unpleasant undertone whenever he uses this epithet.
302. Miss Rogers (*Diaries*, ii, 50–1), inspected on her visit to the Montefiore girls' school two Ashkenazi classrooms which had between them fifty-five Ashkenazi girls. This was however one year later, in 1856; and by then the school was more acceptable than when it was established.
303. Guedalla, p. 54.
304. Cf. e.g. *Kol Bo* (Fürth, 1782), the last two folios of the volume.
305. 20 August 1855, the day before the party left Jerusalem for Hebron. Guedalla, p. 60; Blumberg, p. 200. The writer did not lose much time.
306. Nor can it be that one paper 'lifted' it from the other, a common occurrence in journalism in those days.

307. See below.

308. Guedalla, p. 58.

309. I am not sure that these two events took place after the inauguration ceremony of the Girls' School. The reasons are, first, why should 'H' break off his narrative of the matters connected with the opening of the school and insert the proceedings of the foundation stone laying; and second, how are the two pacifying attempts related? If the people were satisfied with Rabbi Bordaki's assurances, why should Dr Loewe have shown them the Hebrew by-laws? But if these things happened on the 9th, Dr Loewe would reasonably have gone out of his way to show the Hebrew text to all who were prepared to see it, as a preventive precaution. He wanted to anticipate and avert any possible trouble at the inaugural ceremony.

310. Guedalla, p. 56.

311. b. near Vilna, 1822—d. Jerusalem, 1885.

312. *Gey Hizayon* (Jerusalem, 1855); see Shoshana Halevi, No. 53. The poem was translated into English, probably by M. H. Bresslau, *The Valley of Vision*, *J.C.*, 23 Nov. 1855, pp. 386—7. An earlier cycle of poems in honour of Sir Moses Montefiore was published by Saphir under the name *Kether Shem Tov Kenaph Renanim* (Jerusalem, 1849). Cf. A. Schischa; 'Matay nidphasa Mahbarto shel Rabbi Jacob Saphir Kenaph Renanim? *Hadarom* (NY, 1968), pp. 226—231, see also Shoshanah Halevi, No. 15.

313. M. Sachs, *J.C.*, 3 April 1857. She was in Jerusalem in 1856—7. A long extract from her journal was printed in the *J.C.*, 13 November 1857. Her Jerusalem diary which appeared originally in Italian was recently translated into Hebrew by Profs. Daniel Karpi and Moshe Rinot, *Yoman Morah Yehudit miTrieste liYerushalayim 5617—5625* (Tel Aviv, 1982) Neither her teaching at the Montefiore School nor the very interesting details of her connection with Sir Moses and Lady Montefiore contained in her journal as printed in the *J.C.* are incorporated in her diary or the Hebrew translation. She met Sir Moses Montefiore again in 1875 (*Diaries*, ii, 272).

314. *Nach Jerusalem*, ii, p. 111. Not that Dr Albert Cohn's school fared better at the hands of L. A. Frankl (*Nach Jerusalem*, ii, p. 110). One has to bear in mind that Frankl was in Jerusalem to found a school in competition with the existing schools.

315. *Nach Jerusalem*, ii, pp. 7, 13.

XI 316. Hyamson, i, p. 233—5, Finn to Lord Stratford de Redcliffe, 24 July 1855.

317. MS BZA has it 'for building a hospital *outside* the city walls'. There is no significance in the omission of 'inside'.

318. Blumberg, p. 197; cf. also Hyamson, No. 234, Finn to Stratford de Redcliffe, 24 July 1855.

319. MS BZA, 25 July 1855.

320. Moses di Abraham Finzi, British Agent in Acre, of Italian Jewish origin, whose father and family emigrated to Safed. Finzi was asked, without the permission of Finn, to come to Jerusalem and stay there as long as Sir Moses wished him to stay. Finn was rather annoyed by that and dispatched him back to his post as quickly as he could (Blumberg, pp. 198—200). Finzi was approved as British Agent in Acre, 18 May 1837 (Hyamson, i, p. ix, n. 1 and index s.v.). For his report on the Jews in Safed in 1837 see Lady Montefiore, *Notes from a Private Journal* (London, 1844), pp. 377—80; see also *Diaries*, i, pp. 189—92, ii, 15—16.

321. R. Arye [ben Jerachmiel Markus]; cf *Toldoth Hahmey Yerushalayim* Pt. 3 (Jerusalem, 1929), pp. 263–4; for his address to Sir Moses in 1839, see *Notes from a Private Journal*, pp. 399–405. Wrongly identified by Blumberg as R. Arjeh Zvi Hirsch (index, p. 333, col. 2).

322. MS BZA.

323. Guedalla, p. 49.

324. Guedalla, p. 51.

325. [Lady Montefiore] *Notes from a Private Journal of a Visit to Egypt and Palestine* (London, 1844), pp. 273–95; cf. also Blumberg, index s.v. Ahmad Aga Inzdar [Tuzdar] (Blumberg misread Tuzdar for Inzdar, which looks rather similar in Finn's handwriting).

326. Guedalla, p. 54.

327. Italics in the original.

328. *Diaries*, ii, p. 51. This paragraph is taken verbatim from *An Appeal on Behalf of the Suffering Jews in the Holy Land*, Second Report (London, [February] 1856), p. 7. The only addition is 'in the most beautiful and salubrious locality'.

329. *Stirring Times*, i, p. 335.

330. Finn does not mention the purchase of the land either in his Official diary (Blumberg) or his private diary (MS BZA).

331. Dr Ruth Kark, 'He'aroth l'Parashat Batey Touro', *Cathedra*, vol. xviii (Jan. 1981), pp. 158–67, published a modern Hebrew translation of that document together with an apparently contemporary English translation of 1855. She also refers to another English translation dated 1886 (p. 161) which was at her disposal. She dates the purchase in the document, 9 August 1855. [Mordechai Rozin], *Mishkenot Sha'ananim* (Jerusalem, 1974). 1st edn. not seen by me, reprinted 2nd edn. (Jerusalem, [1982]), p. 12 reproduction and on page 13: 'The document confirming the purchase was signed on August 12th, 1855'. It should be noted that Finn was out of town on 9 August. He returned to Jerusalem on the 11th, Saturday. Did he, a devout Christian, sign an official document on 12 August, a Sunday — a non-legal date at that time? The exact dates need further investigation. (Mrs Shoshana Halevi, 'Ha'aroth l'Yetzias min ha'Homoth' printed in *Perakim b'Toldoth haYishuv haYehudi biYerushalayim* (Jerusalem, 1973), p. 148, gives the date of the purchase as 12 August 1855.)

332. MS BZA.

333. Blumberg, p. 199, 14 August.

334. *Stirring Times*, i, p. 335.

335. See Kark, *Cathedra*, Jan. 1981.

336. *Diaries*, ii, p. 52. It was to be very helpful, when the hospital project was changed to alms houses. It still needed clarification and regularizing, so as to carry on with building the alms houses. cf. *Diaries*, chap. xiii.

337. Dr Joseph Meisl, the official historian of the 'Sir Moses Testimonial Fund' *Eleh Toldoth Keren Mazkereth haSar Moshe Montefiore* (Jerusalem, 1939), p. 16, n. 3: 'as a matter of fact [the land] was bought with the legacy of Judah Touro'; Dr Alad'ar Fürst, *Yerushalayim Hehadash* (Jerusalem, 1946), p. 16; Kark, p. 164, n. 31.

338. Kark, ibid. and *Diaries*, ii, p. 52. It could have given Sir Joseph Sebag-Montefiore the reason to believe it was his by inheritance from his uncle Sir Moses Montefiore; and gave rise to much misunderstanding (Meisl, pp. 26–7, 70–1).

339. 'An Appeal', Second Report (London, [February], 1856). This is repeated in the Third Report, published in 1862.
340. As appears in contract. The rate was £1 to 120 piastres. See *Jewish Chronicle*, 27 June 1854.
341. Hyamson, i, p. 238, no. 176: Finn to Stratford de Redcliffe, Jerusalem, 30 August 1856. Finn, *Stirring Times*, ii, p. 335 changed 'hospital' into 'alms houses'. He wrote the book in 1870 by which time the hospital was long forgotten.
342. *Nach Jerusalem*, ii, pp. 116—7.
343. *Jewish Chronicle*, 6 November 1857.
344. *Jewish Chronicle*, 28 September 1855, letter dated Jerusalem, August 5615.
345. Guedalla, pp. 56—7.
346. *Jewish Chronicle*, Nov. 1856, the letter dated Jerusalem, 16 October 1856. It is interesting to note that by the early 1920s, 466 dwellings were erected on the land, apart from the synagogues and the communal buildings (J. Meisl, p. 92).
347. *Diaries*, ii, p. 53.
348. *Stirring Times*, ii, p. 336.
349. Guedalla, p. 58.
350. R. Jacob Saphir, *Gey Hizayon* (Hebrew) (Jerusalem, 1855), translated *J.C.*, 23 Nov. 1855 as 'The Valley of Vision'.
351. N. Laski, *The Laws and Charities of the Spanish and Portuguese Jews' Congregation of London* (London, 1952), pp. 127—8. The Elders of the Spanish and Portuguese Congregation accepted on 28 Tebeth 5616 [6 Jan. 1856] the trust of £3,000 Consolidated 3 per cent Annuities. This was converted in 1872 into the 'Trust of the late Judah Guedalla' and administered by the Elders. The bulk of the interest was an entitlement to the 'students in the Yeshiba founded by the donor in Jerusalem subtitled Beth Guedalla'; the money was transferred twice a year, in Adar and Ellul, 'according to the agreement made with the Rabbanim'.
352. Misprint for Abualafia.
353. Dr M. Wallenstein, 'Ktav yad Gaster no. 975: Tazkir shel Kotel haSepharadim biYerushalayim', in *Zion*, vol. xliii, pt 1—2 (1978), pp. 75—96. I am indebted to Dr Arye Morgenstern, Jerusalem, who drew my attention to the article and to that mentioned in the next footnote, and sent me off-prints of both.
354. This note reads, as copied by Dr Israel Bartal in his article, 'Birurim b'Shuley Tazkir Kolel haSepharadim biYerushalayim mi Shnath' (5616): 'An account of the income and expenditure of the Portuguese congregation in Jerusalem *given* to Sir Moses Montefiore Bart. during his stay in the Holy City in [*sic*] the 18th of Menachem Ab AN [?M] 5616.' Dr Bartal refers the reader to his paper in *Shalem* (Hebrew) vol. ii (Jerusalem. 1976), pp. 237, 246, 267, where he takes issue with Dr Loewe's 'use' of the papers gathered by Sir Moses on his travels and also with those that were sent to Sir Moses in England. Dr Bartal attributes, if I understand him correctly, ulterior motives to Dr Loewe's annotations which are to be found on the back of letters and papers addressed to Sir Moses. There seems to be a slight misunderstanding of the purpose of these notes. They were summaries penned by Dr Loewe to save Sir Moses from having to read the letters, nor could Sir Moses read the cursive Hebrew script of the letters.

XII

355. Among them H. H. Abualafia.
356. MS SMM 1855 (H. U. MS Var. 21).
357. Guedalla, p. 59.
358. 'H' in *Wiener Mittheilungen*, 12 Nov. 1855.
359. Second Report, p. 8. *Diaries*, ii, p. 53 gives a shortened version of the Report. By the time Loewe wrote the *Diaries* the Hospital was a long forgotten failure.
360. *Diaries*, ii, p. 53.
361. Saphir, *Gey Hizayon*, n. 15 reads (in Bresslau's translation): 'The large hewn stone was let down, containing a hollow ... with the contract of the purchase of the ground ... that the acquisition was effected by means of ... bequest of the late Juda Touro was deposited ... which document Rabbi Gershom Kursheedt ... seal of the late Judah Touro'.
362. Hühner, pp. 30–52 and 102–3. He suggests it was Catherine; see also on p. 137, para. 56 of Touro's Will. Dr Bertram W. Korn, *The Early Jews of New Orleans* (Waltham, 1969), pp. 76–7, dismisses the local New Orleans tradition, that Touro was engaged to one of his cousins, as a myth. It was, he suggests, invented to lend some colour to an otherwise monotonous life. This is suggested in spite of the text of the will.
XIII 363. Guedalla, p. 59.
364. Sir Moses Montefiore, MS 1855 (H. U. MS Var. 21).
365. Sir Moses noted as an aside that, while the Ashkenazim distributed the 'Halukah', i.e. the charity moneys sent for distribution to the Holy Land, only among the poor and needy, the Sephardim shared it out among all their members, to the deserving and to those who did not need it. Sir Moses did not like this arrangement.
366. Second Report (1856), pp. 9–10; *Diaries*, ii, p. 56. Dr I. Bartal, p. 100, suggests Sir Moses took no notice of the difficulties of the Sephardim contained in the petition, but the evidence of the Second Report and *Diaries* (ii, p. 56) is that he did, and reported to the Committee what he had gathered in personal interviews. This is confirmed by the MS Diary in H.U. MS Var. 21.
367. *Diaries*, ii, p. 56.
368. Guedalla, p. 59.
369. Wyatt Angelus Papworth de Sandau (1824–94), well-known architect of the later nineteenth century, was assistant surveyor to the Alliance Assurance Company under Thomas Allason. On Allason's death in 1852 he became sole surveyor. Allason's work for the Alliance (of which Montefiore was a founder) introduced him to clients such as the Montefiores, Rothschilds and Ricardos.
370. L. A. Frankl, *Nach Jerusalem*, ii, p. 117.
371. Presumably Eliyahu Pinhas Navon, father of Joseph Navon Bey (d., Jerusalem, 1896). See E. M. D. Gaon, *Yehudey haMizrah b'Eretz Yisrael*, ii (Jerusalem, 1938), p. 448. He was an active public worker in Jerusalem.
372. Son of Rabbi Shlomo Pach Rosenthal, one of the founders of the Ashkenazi community in Jerusalem. Rabbi Isaac Rosenthal was active in communal life (Frumkin/Rivlin, *Toldoth Hahmey Yerushalayim*, s.v. index).
373. Hebrew letter to Navon signed by Sir Moses Montefiore and Chief Rabbi N. M. Adler, London, Rosh Hodesh Shevat, 5616 (8 Jan 1856). While the letter is addressed to Navon, the contents concern both. cf. A. Ben-Jacob, *Jerusalem* (Heb. Quarterly), vol. iii (Jerusalem, Tishri 5610), pt. 1–2, pp. 60 and 65–6.

374. Dr L. Loewe's Hebrew letter to Rosenthal, 22 Tammuz 5619, written without the knowledge of Sir Moses. cf. P. Grayevski, *Sepher ha Yishuv* (Jerusalem, 1939), p. 6; also letters from Navon and Rosenthal to Sir Moses, 1857–9, MS AS.

375. Jewish building labourers were paid 4 piastres a day or 24 per week (Sir Moses Montefiore, MS Diary for 1855), which at a rate of 120 piastres to £1, was the equivalent of £0.20 per week.

376. R. Jacob Saphir, *Gey Hizayon* (Jerusalem 1855). The relevant passage was translated in the *J.C.*, (23 Nov. 1855). G. M. Luncz, *Moshe v'Yerushalayim*, in *Nethivoth Zion v'Yerushalayim*, ed. G. Kressel (Jerusalem, 1970), p. 284. This essay was originally published in 1885. (Saphir was the source for Luncz.)

377. Guedalla, p. 60, Blumberg, p. 200; MS BZA.

378. *Stirring Times*, ii, p. 333; *Diaries*, ii, p. 54; neither of these give the date when Sir Moses applied to Kiamil. Loewe states that on the next day they went to Hebron, which we know was 21 August. On the health hazard caused by lack of sanitation, see A. Schischa, 'Mikhtav Toda Shel Rabaney ha'Ashkenazim l'Consul Finn, 5621', *Ha'Ohel* (Hebrew) (1972) part 1.

379. Sir Moses MS Diary 1855 (H.U. MS Var. 21); Loewe and Blumberg, sv. index; *Stirring Times*, ii, pp. 336 *et seq.*

380. Sir Moses MS 1855 (H.U. MS Var. 21).

381. Second Report, p. 6; which is quoted almost verbatim in *Diaries*, ii, p. 56; for a description of the land in 1856, see L. A. Frankl, *Nach Jerusalem*, i, p. 7.

382. Sir Moses Montefiore MS 1855 (H.U. MS. Var. 21). Rabbi Judah Levy was the first Rabbi of Jaffa and apparently owned the land; a native of Ragusa, he was presumably a Turkish citizen.

383. *Diaries*, ii, p. 56.

384. Z. Vilnay, *Ariel* (Hebrew), Vol. A'yin-Kuf (Tel-Aviv, 1979), c. 6129–32.

385. Guedalla, p. 63; for the arrival in Jaffa, see Guedalla, p. 41.

ACKNOWLEDGEMENTS

I thank Dr V D Lipman for his help in locating documents and ancillary reference works in the Public Record Office; Mrs B. Z. Abrahams for her kindness in allowing me to use copies of the MS Diaries of James Finn; Dr A. Morgenstern, Jerusalem, for details culled from Sir Moses Montefiore's 1855 Diary in the National Library, Jerusalem; Mr Maxwell Whiteman, Jenkinstown, Pa, USA, for permission to reproduce the plan of the Hospital; Mr Ezra Kahn in his capacity as Librarian of Jews' College, London, and for the loan of Dr Neumann's book from his personal library.

PART IV

The Myth Emerges

1
The Testimonials and the Legend

MARILYN LEHRER WITH PETER SALINGER

A vivid demonstration of how Sir Moses Montefiore became a legend
in his own lifetime is provided by the form and wording of the
hundreds of testimonials and letters sent to him from communities
and individuals all over the world. A collection of them was held at
the Judith Lady Montefiore College in Ramsgate, although the
greater part must have been destroyed along with other manuscripts,
diaries and letters after Montefiore's death.[1] Others were scattered;
they are probably in different archives and have yet to be located.
About four hundred are held at the Mocatta Library, University
College London, and a catalogue of these is now in progress. So far,
two hundred have been studied in detail, provisionally catalogued in
a series numbered M.1–M.200. Most of the extracts quoted here
have been translated from the Hebrew, and we have endeavoured
to keep the flow of the original rather than giving a strictly literal
translation.

The testimonials illustrate Montefiore's life during a time when
minorities of many countries were fighting for equal rights, and they
show the extent to which he had a foot in both the Jewish and
non-Jewish worlds. For example, in 1846 he is spoken of by the
Manchester Hebrew Congregation as a man who unites

all the virtues of genuine patriotism with the ancient religious virtues of the
Hebrew nation (M.200).

This is an accurate reflection of his activity in Jewish communal
life, which was paralleled by his activity in the non-Jewish world.
At the core of his reputation was the perception that he had successfully combined the practices of an observant Jew with his secular
activities; and that the honours he received were bestowed on him as
a Jew, at a time when Jews were in general debarred from high
position.

Interwoven into the fabric of Montefiore's Jewish and civic life
was his love of the Holy Land, which he visited no fewer than seven
times. In 1831, to commemorate the visit by his wife and himself
to 'the City of Jerusalem in the Holy Land of their forefathers', he
successfully petitioned for the addition of the word 'Jerusalem' in

Hebrew characters to the banner of his coat of arms, granted in 1819, and when he was granted supporters to his arms in 1841, each supporter's banner was similarly inscribed. That he took every opportunity to give practical assistance to the Jewish population of the four Holy Cities (Jerusalem, Hebron, Tiberias and Safed), encouraging them to take up agriculture and become self-supporting, is reflected in many of the testimonials from the Holy Land. For example, the earliest testimonial in our survey, dated 1839, written by a group of Jews in Jerusalem, shows very clearly that Montefiore had already become to the Jews of the Holy Land someone to whom they could turn for practical help. A short extract from the Hebrew runs:

The man Moses is great among Jews, a chief of chiefs, a prince of princes; his praise is in the congregation of the pious: he is a king, helper and shield (M.69).

In 1840 came the Damascus Affair, which gained Montefiore an instant reputation throughout the Jewish world as a saviour who had achieved the 'honourable liberation' of the falsely-imprisoned Jews and received a *firman* (edict) from the Sultan of Turkey (the overlord of Syria) guaranteeing protection in the future to his Jewish subjects.

Twelve testimonials date from this time, nearly all of them poems from individual writers, which show the extent to which his achievement had fired popular imagination and inspired a heightened form of literary expression. Six came from Italy, all written in Hebrew in sonnet form, each entitled *Shir Zahav* (Song of Gold);[2] three came from Germany (also in Hebrew, which is a point worth mentioning, as nearly all the other testimonials from Germany were written in German), with the remainder coming from Austria and England.

With the Damascus Affair and its successful outcome, one is already able to picture the beginnings of the legend. In his subsequent journeys, Montefiore's aims were almost always crowned with at least the appearance of success, and on each occasion his reputation as a figure larger than life was reinforced. The fact that he survived to such a great age must also have played its part, and it is therefore no surprise that the testimonials increasingly show him as a man with more than human qualities — in fact, a legend, in his own lifetime. This underlying attitude towards him must have been the reason why he was treated with such graciousness and consideration by very powerful rulers. In 1863/4 Montefiore travelled to Morocco on his mission to release the Jews imprisoned there. His success in doing so, and in gaining a *dahir* from the Sultan, promising the Jews and other minorities equal rights before the law, is clear proof of the power of his reputation. The Sultan received him with great courtesy and ceremony and, as Montefiore reported to the Board of Deputies of British Jews on his return:

The Sultan expressed his pleasure in seeing me at his Court; he said my name was well known to him as well as my desire to improve the condition of my brethren . . . .[3]

There was a similar occurrence in 1872 when he travelled to Russia to present a special address to Tsar Alexander II on the bicentenary of the birth of Peter the Great. He was then eighty-eight years of age, and in order to spare him the difficulties and inconveniences of further travel, the Tsar of all the Russias came specially to St Petersburg from the military manoeuvres that he was attending to accept these greetings from him.

Besides testimonials written on the occasion of specific events such as the Damascus Affair, Montefiore received entreaties from communities asking him to intercede with their local governors, as well as requests for financial assistance. Other testimonials refer to special services and prayers said in his name, while still others mention the diverse ways in which he was honoured in their communities. The testimonials culminate in the great numbers that were sent to him on his ninety-ninth and hundredth birthdays, which were days of rejoicing not only among the communities of Anglo-Jewry, but also among Jewish communities all over the world.

The testimonials discussed here were sent to Montefiore at several different points in his life — after the Damascus Affair, on his visit to Russia in 1846, after his mission to Morocco in 1864, on his journeys to the Holy Land, and in celebration of his ninety-ninth and hundredth birthdays. They came from all over the world — from the countries of Europe as far east as Hungary, Poland and Russia, the small communities of the east and west coasts of America to which the great influx of immigrants was yet to come, South Africa and far-off New Zealand, and the Holy Land.

The testimonials are in a number of languages. Of the 200 under consideration, seventy-eight are in English, eighty-three in Hebrew and eighteen in German. Other languages include Italian, Hungarian, Russian, Yiddish and Swedish. Thirteen are in more than one language, generally Hebrew, together with the language of the country of origin. Those in English come from all over the English-speaking world. Those written in Hebrew come not only from the Holy Land, but also from many communities and individual writers in the

Diaspora, clear examples of the fact that Hebrew had remained a literary *lingua franca* throughout the centuries. Very few from Germany are in Hebrew. There is no reason to suppose that the authors could not write Hebrew; more probably, they preferred to use their native language, giving in some cases a Hebrew translation.

No trouble was spared to make all the testimonials as beautiful as possible. Some are of parchment or vellum, and a few are in the form of elaborate scrolls with satin ribbons and wooden rollers. Drawings, decorative borders and different coloured inks are all used. Where the testimonials are in English, scripts of varying types, sizes and colours are employed, giving a highly elaborate effect; the Gothic script is most commonly used in those from England. Montefiore's name is often written in a decorative manner, or picked out in special colours. Testimonials from the Holy Land have an added dimension of decoration, which is the use of Hebrew phrases and quotations to form arches, crowns and borders.

It is a common convention in Hebrew writing to give the Hebrew year by employing the technique of *Gematriah* (namely, using appropriate quotations, the numerical value of whose letters in Hebrew add up to the required number). This opportunity of paying a graceful compliment to Montefiore, in addition to the actual words of the testimonial, was very frequently used. Examples are *Roni Ve-simchi* (Exult and Rejoice) for the year 5624/1864 (M.145 and M.195), after the journey to Morocco, and *Vihi Shemo Mevorach* (May his name be blessed) for the year 5645/1884 (M.152 and M.184). Acrostics are also used; a typical example is *Meah Shanim Ha-yom* (A Hundred Years Today) (M.27), where the initial letters make up the name *Mòshe* (the Hebrew form of 'Moses'). More elaborate is an acrostic of Montefiore's full name in Hebrew, as in a poem from Revd Moses Mielziner, a professor at Hebrew Union College, Cincinnati, Ohio (M.87).

A few testimonials are printed, but most are written by hand. Of those in Hebrew, a number are in ordinary square script, but there are many in the finest script such as is used in a *Sefer Torah* (Scroll of the Law). As the scripts vary so do the styles, ranging from the somewhat stilted to beautiful free-flowing Hebrew, full of echoes of biblical phrases. For example, occurring several times is a quotation from the Book of Esther describing how after the fall of their enemy (Haman) the Jews had light and joy, gladness and honour (Esther 8:16). Solomon Mendilowitz, writing from Hebron, refers to the successful outcome of the Damascus Affair when he quotes from the previous verse, substituting the name 'Damascus' for the original Shushan: 'And the city of Damascus shouted and was glad' (M.142). Where script and words are equally beautiful, the result is outstanding. This is particularly the case with testimonials from centres of Jewish learning such as Odessa and Vilna.

The testimonials sent from communities are usually signed (in cursive script) by the communal leaders – the local rabbi, the *dayan* (lit., 'judge', a member of the Rabbinical court), the wardens and treasurer, and by scholars and other leading members of the community. These signatures are fascinating from a historical point of view, as they provide a record of the community at the time.

From east and west, these testimonials were sent to Montefiore in distant England, but they were not written to a figure who was remote and unreal. Because Montefiore did not believe in negotiating from a distance, but in personal intervention, he travelled wherever his fellow-Jews were in need of help, so that he became known directly in much of the Jewish world. Since his journeys covered such distances, and took him through many different countries on the way, he had the opportunity, which he almost invariably used, of visiting the communities of the towns through which he passed. Dr Louis Loewe, has described in detail[4] the enthusiastic reception that Montefiore and his party received wherever they went. Both his beloved wife Judith, who encouraged him in all his undertakings and accompanied him on all his journeys until she died in 1862, and Dr Loewe left a strong impression, and they are frequently mentioned in the testimonials with praise and affection.

The testimonials allude to the length and physical discomforts of the journeys. These were genuine enough; for example, there were periods of enforced quarantine on journeys to the Levant because of outbreaks of plague. There were dangers, too, such as storms at sea and the risk of attack by pirates. Two testimonials written in 1864 after Montefiore's mission to Morocco, one from a group of Jews in Hebron and Jerusalem, and another from the Brighton Hebrew Congregation, highlighted this aspect of the journey:

And what man would consider such a journey, at a time of old age and grey hair, to a desert and arid land, a fearful and terrifying wilderness! (M.145)

You left the quiet of home and your own fireside at an inclement season of the year accompanied by a small band of earnest men to do battle against ancient prejudices, not for the love of glory but to remove those oppressive burdens under which our brethren have so long suffered (M.156).

The first quotation refers to Montefiore's age when he undertook many of these journeys. That a man in his seventies or eighties leaves the comfort and safety of his home, and takes great risks in order to relieve the plight of his oppressed fellow-Jews in distant lands, naturally gives rise to testimonials of glowing and eulogistic praise. Time and again he is compared to the biblical Moses, and several testimonials are headed *Tehilah Le-Moshe* (Praise to Moses), which, in the context, is clearly a play on the title of Psalm 90, *Tefilah Le-Moshe* (A Prayer of Moses). The quotation: 'From Moses to Moses there has not arisen one such as Moses' appears a number of times, and with the biblical Moses, Maimonides and Mendelssohn, Montefiore takes his place as another great bearer of that name. These references appear in testimonials from many different countries, clear indication that such a view of him was widespread.

In these testimonials not only is the gratitude felt towards Montefiore by Jews all over the world made manifest, but also the deep affection that he inspired. This is most strongly expressed at the time of his hundredth birthday. Communities as far apart as New York, Budapest and Praga, near Warsaw, wrote to tell him of special services held in his honour on that day and special prayers that were recited. Particularly touching are the words written from the community of Kerch in the Crimea:

And it shall be, when you read today the great number of letters that come from all ends of the earth, pray remember also this little congregation that from afar bows down before your glorious majesty (M.4).

This phrase 'your glorious majesty' is used in Jewish liturgy to refer to God, and in these testimonials there are many instances where praise is expressed to Montefiore in phrases that echo the psalms or that are taken straight out of the synagogue service. Typical of such references is the praise expressed by the Chief Rabbi and the community of Ferrara, Italy:

Generation to generation shall praise thy works, for as thy name is so is thy praise. The earth is full of thy righteous acts . . . arise, let us bow down and worship before our lord (M.9).

In a testimonial already mentioned (M.87), Professor Mielziner wrote in similar vein: 'The words of thy servant who bows down from afar towards your glory (M.87)'.[5] Such hyperbole, reaching virtually the point of blasphemy, is not uncommon in the testimonials, and it is indicative of the extremely strong feelings that Montefiore evidently inspired in his fellow-Jews all over the world. Time and again the names of Damascus, Morocco, Russia and

Jerusalem recur, showing that his achievements have been remembered with gratitude; and as they are mentioned in greetings to him on his hundredth birthday, many years after the event, they obviously had become part of the legend that had grown up around him.

An extension of the gratitude and affection felt towards Montefiore was the wish that his name should be perpetuated among future generations. After Montefiore's first journey to Russia in 1846, a most interesting testimonial was sent to him from Jonas Gourland, Magister of the Imperial University of St Petersburg, recording in detail a visit made to the synagogue in the military barracks on a Friday evening, a two-mile walk each way. Gourland gives the wording of the tablet put up in the synagogue to commemorate the event, part of which runs as follows:

When Sir Moses Montefiore came from the City of London, the place of his greatness, he showed his himility and came to pray together with us, few in number, he and his noble wife Judith ... and his learned and perfect companion Eliezer Halevi (Dr Loewe) (M.126).

This testimonial, which was printed and sold in quantity, contains the request that everyone who buys a copy should frame it and put in on the wall 'as an everlasting memorial, so that when children not yet born grow up, they will tell their own children'.

Another most vivid example of this is a testimonial sent by one Abraham Morgenstern to Montefiore and his wife after their visit to Vilna in that same year, 1846 (M.194). He wrote that his new-born granddaughter had been given the name Judith, and went on to say that a wish had been expressed in the community that all baby boys born to their members should bear the name Moses, and all baby girls the name Judith; in this way the names of Montefiore and his wife would be perpetuated and the children would have examples to emulate.

But there were other and more permanent ways in which Montefiore's name could be honoured. Twenty-three of these testimonials are, in fact, certificates or, as they are often called, diplomas, in which he was made an honorary member of communal societies. Nearly all of these came from countries in Central and Eastern Europe, half of them from Hungary, and a quarter from Germany. The great number of these communal societies reflects the highly-developed structure of Jewish communities in these countries. They ranged from the *Chevrat Gemilut Chassadim* (Interest-free Loan Society) and the *Chevrah Kadishah* (Burial Society) to the *Talmud Torah* and *Beth Hamidrash* (School and House of Study). The community of Seyene, near Suwalki in Poland, sent a certificate making Montefiore an honorary member of all their societies (M.182); there were seven in all, and this in a relatively small community. Many of the certificates bear the special stamp of the society, and a number of them are extremely elaborate, with pictures illustrating their particular activities.

Some communities, such as Gorodyszyz, near Minsk, in Russia (M.27), decided to honour Montefiore in an even more permanent way by establishing schools and calling them by his name; in Miskolc, Hungary, every member of the community gave a donation towards the cost of founding such a school (M.193). Most of the certificates were sent to Montefiore on his hundredth birthday, as a positive way of showing him as much honour as was in the power of these communities to give.

Of the testimonials under discussion, nearly a quarter, forty-four in all, come from Great Britain, mainly from Jewish communities throughout the country. There are also a number from communal organizations such as the Board of Deputies of British Jews, the Anglo-Jewish Association, and the United Synagogue and Jews College, with all of which Montefiore was closely associated.

Nine testimonials were sent to him from non-Jewish organizations, half of them from Masonic Lodges — he had been a member of that ancient order for many years. Worthy of mention is an address that came from the Worshipful Company of Merchant Taylors of the Fraternity of St John the Baptist (M.132), to which in 1838 Montefiore had given money for a medal to be awarded for excellence in Classics and Hebrew at Merchant Taylors School. To honour him on his hundredth birthday, a decision was taken by the Company to invest £100 and to use the interest for a Montefiore Prize, to be given to the winner of the medal. But the most outstanding perhaps, is a testimonial from the Borough of Margate dated 1864, expressing gratitude to Montefiore for what he had achieved for the welfare of Christians in Morocco, as well as for the Jews (M.123). The testimonial speaks of

the generous efforts which, on many occasions, regardless of distance or personal inconvenience, you have made on behalf of your oppressed co-religionists ... We rejoice in the great triumph of the principles of civil and religious liberty in the protection and security attained at your instance for both Christians and Jews from the violence of a fanatical and barbarous people, and you have, Sir Moses, by your benevolent advocacy of the sacred rights of Man, merited the warm sympathy and approbation of all civilised nations.

Nine of the testimonials date from 1846, when Montefiore made his first journey to Russia. The travelling time was only a month, for contrary to his usual practice he did not stop to visit Jewish communities in the towns through which he passed. He did, however, receive a number of testimonials in the course of his journey, praising his achievements and wishing him success; poems from the community leaders of Riga in Latvia (M.169) and Kalvariya in Lithuania (M.188) are in the collection. In St Petersburg, after his audience with Tsar Nicholas I and talks with different ministers, he visited some of the synagogues in the city. One such visit has already been described in the testimonial sent by Jonas Gourland.

On his way homeward, Montefiore travelled by way of Vilna, Kovno and Warsaw. A testimonial from Kishinev in Bessarabia, sent to him on his hundredth birthday nearly forty years later, vividly recalls how he appeared at Vilna (M.192); it describes in detail the emotion that he showed when the time came for him to leave, and the tears that rolled down his cheeks. This corroborates his words at the time:

I leave you, but my heart will ever remain with you. When my brethren suffer, I feel it painfully; when they have reason to weep, my eyes shed tears.[6]

The recollection of this emotion, so long after the event, is one more strand in the legend that had built up around him.

Ten testimonials were sent to Montefiore from the Holy Land, ranging in date from 1839 to 1885. After the first of his visits, Montefiore became to the Jews living there someone to whom they could turn for practical help. In 1848 and 1849 he received heartfelt pleas for assistance from different groups of Jews in Jerusalem. Because of their extreme poverty, they felt themselves at the mercy of the missionaries who had gone out to the Holy Land. One group wrote to Montefiore how they feared for their ability to hold on to their faith against these outside influences, and begged him to build a hospital in Jerusalem, because the only one in existence which could treat those suffering from the diseases and infections that were rampant in the city was a mission hospital (M.79). In fact, Montefiore had in 1843 sent out a fully-qualified physician to help them.[7] Another group wrote to beg Montefiore to establish a *Talmud Torah* (Jewish school) for their children, to help them against the same influences (M.141).

During the same period, groups of Jews from Safed and Tiberias, who had come originally from Russia and Russian Poland, wrote asking for financial assistance both for themselves and for their fellow-Jews still living in those communities (M.111 and M.191). Incidentally, these early testimonials from the Holy Land are of great sociological interest, giving as they do full details of every member of the community — his name, age, place of origin and length of residence in the Holy Land, together with the names and ages of his wife and children.

It is not surprising that the Jews of the four Holy Cities felt that Montefiore was their benefactor. He personally gave very large amounts of charity to institutions and individuals while he was there, and also acted as agent for the North American Relief Society of Indigent Jews of Jerusalem, taking the funds with him and distributing them at his discretion.

A number of testimonials were sent by *Chovevei Zion* (Lovers of Zion), members of a Zionist movement that preceded political Zionism and was strong in Russia and Poland. Typical of these is one from Slonim, near Grodno in Lithuania, in which there is a fervent prayer for the rebuilding of Zion, and grateful thanks expressed to Montefiore for all that he had done in the Holy Land:

You have set your eyes and heart always to comfort the desolation of Zion and to be gracious to the dust of Jerusalem ... to revive the waste places of the land and to give a light to the people of Israel in its holy land ... to teach how to develop its earth and to plough its furrows, so that the Children of Israel should eat their bread in plenty and should not bear the reproach of famine among the nations (M.170).

This passage shows very clearly that the early Zionists in the Diaspora were fully aware of the practical assistance that Montefiore had given to the Jews of the Holy Land in his efforts to encourage them to till the land and grow their own food.

It was not only to the Jews in the Holy Land that Montefiore appeared as a benefactor and a source of hope. Soon after his visit to Russia in 1846, the community of Suwalki in Poland, then under the rule of the Russian Empire, wrote to him (M.143), begging him to intercede with their local governor to lighten their tax burden and allow them to live within the small town and not at the prescribed distance of ten miles. The testimonial describes their dire economic plight, giving a graphic picture of the situation of Jews in many of the countries of Eastern Europe: because they were forbidden to buy land, or live in or near to villages, they were forced to go to the cities to find work, which was extremely difficult to obtain. Here is a clear example of Jews who had never met Montefiore but had only heard of his achievements, who yet had faith that he could help them in their distress. We do not know if he was able to help in this particular case, but he certainly took all such entreaties very seriously.

In the same year he received a similar request from the community of Rossiena, near Kovno in Russia, also asking for help; no details are given, but the writers beg Montefiore to come and visit them and help them in their distress (M.25).

It was not only from communities that Montefiore received pleas for help. Ignaz Kirz, a poor Jew who had left Hungary to live in Vienna with his wife and five children, found it impossible to make a living. He wrote to Montefiore twice (M.166–7), appealing to him as a last hope, and asking for an annual sum of 200 gulden (£20.00); obviously Montefiore in no way seemed remote and unapproachable to him.

To the oppressed and downtrodden Jews in the countries of Eastern Europe and Russia, where there was endemic anti-semitism, Montefiore represented a source of hope, a man who had power to move mountains and who was yet eminently approachable. It must have seemed miraculous that a practising Jew should command such influence. Yet although his journeys were always paved with credentials from the British Foreign Office and with letters of introduction to local officials and dignitaries in the countries through which he passed, the testimonials clearly demonstrate that Jews abroad saw him as a personage in his own right, and not as an emissary of Great Britain.

There are comparatively few testimonials to Montefiore from countries of Western Europe. Besides those from Germany, Italy, and Great Britain already mentioned, there are three from Holland and one from Sweden. Almost all of these were written after his journeys to Damascus and Morocco, or in celebration of his hundredth birthday.

It must be mentioned here that not one testimonial in this selection was written after Sir Moses' journey to Romania, and very few refer to it. The communal leadership in Bucharest, from which official testimonials would have emanated, was violently opposed to his intercession on behalf of the Jewish proletariat.[8]

It is somewhat surprising that in the United States of America, to which Montefiore never travelled, so many organizations and communities, as well as individuals, wished to pay him honour. Twenty-six of the testimonials came from America, from New York in the East to San Francisco and Los Angeles in the West. They include testimonials from a number of lodges of the *International Order of B'nai Brith* (Sons of the Covenant), the philanthropic organization founded in New York in 1843. Several lodges took the name of Montefiore, including two in San Francisco; indeed, the second

Sefer Torah of the Emanu-El Congregation in that city was donated by Montefiore in 1851.[9]

In New York in 1879, the Young Men's Hebrew Association of Harlem named their social and cultural hall the Montifiore [*sic*] Hall (M.15), and on his hundredth birthday the organizers of the Hebrew Orphan Asylum Society, Brooklyn, wrote that he had been elected to honorary membership and that a Montefiore Wing was being built (M.51). Communities in the South and Mid-West were no less aware of his achievements. In the Congregation Temple of Israel in Wilmington, North Carolina, a special thanksgiving service was held on his hundredth birthday, and a subscription raised for a Sunday School prize to be awarded annually to the best pupil (M.37). The following week, at the Hebrew Union College of Cincinnati, Ohio, (the Reform seminary) the Sir Moses Montefiore Chair of Sacred Literature was officially dedicated; the money for the endowment of this Chair was raised through the Montefiore Testimonial Fund of the United States, which had been set up the previous year (M.100). But not every honour given to Montefiore was paid for by public subscription. Leaders of a community in St Louis, Missouri, wrote at the same time that their synagogue now bore the name 'Moses Montefiore Benei Amoonah Congregation', and requested financial assistance in establishing a permanent building (M.90). Nor was it only Jews in America that knew and honoured Montefiore's name; warm congratulations were sent to him on his hundredth birthday by The Irish Benevolent Union in Wheeling, West Virginia (M.99).

Such different and varied testimonials combine to indicate that, although Montefiore had never visited America, and in spite of the great distance that separated it from Europe, his reputation existed and flourished in the New World.

It is evident from the testimonials that Montefiore was seen as a saviour of his people, able to intervene successfully on their behalf whenever and wherever the need arose.

Perhaps this is best expressed pictorially in a testimonial sent to him on his hundredth birthday by a group of early Zionists in Odessa (M.5). Under a beautiful and mellifluous Hebrew text is a wash painting by Isaak Pasternak (later to become famous under his Russian name, Leonid), in which Montefiore, under a banner marked '100', is supporting a fettered Jew. In the distance is Jerusalem, and the hands of an angel or, anthropomorphically, the hands of God, are held above him in blessing.

This was how Montefiore was seen by his fellow Jews — as a

saviour of the oppressed and lover of Zion, with God's blessing on all his achievements. This was the legend that grew up around him in his lifetime, of which these testimonials provide ample evidence.

ACKNOWLEDGEMENTS

We are most grateful to Professor Raphael Loewe for his guidance and encouragement and to Professor Chimen Abramsky for his help in deciphering signatures.

BIBLIOGRAPHY

Loewe, L., ed., *Diaries of Sir Moses and Lady Montefiore* (London, 1890; new edition 1983)
Goodman, Paul, *Moses Montefiore* (Philadelphia, 1925)
Lipman, V. D., ed., *Sir Moses Montefiore: A Symposium* (Oxford and London, 1982)

NOTES

1.   (a) R. D. Barnett in *Sir Moses Montefiore: A Symposium*, pp. 3—4
    (b) Paul Goodman, *Moses Montefiore*. Bibliography of Montefioriana pp. 231—50. This indicates that a large number of items which cannot be identified with those in the Mocatta collection were on exhibition after Sir Moses' death and after many of his private papers had been destroyed.
2.   The numerical value of the letters in the word *Zahav* add up to fourteen, the number of lines in a sonnet.
3.   *Diaries*, ii, p. 155.
4.   *Diaries, passim.*
5.   Revd Moses Mielziner (1828—1903), reform rabbi and writer, was professor of Talmud and rabbinical literature at I. M. Wise's Hebrew Union College, Cincinnati.
6.   *Diaries*, i, p. 348.
7.   *Diaries*, i, p. 312.
8.   *Diaries,* ii, pp. 205—6.
9.   Fred Rosenbaum, *Architects of Reform* (Western Jewish History Center, Berkeley, 1980), p. 5.

2

The Times Leading Article:
23 October 1883

Tomorrow Sir Moses Montefiore enters upon his hundredth year, and the occasion will be celebrated in a fitting manner by the Jewish community all over the world. The people for whom he has done so much will do him honour. Not only from London and from Ramsgate, near which he lives, but from Russia, Poland, Germany, Italy, and, above all, from Palestine, are representations to be made to him, expressing the gratitude felt towards him by the Jews of every degree, and even by his Christian fellow-countrymen for the great services that he has rendered them. It is inevitable, as we have said in the opening of the detailed article in which we have reviewed his life, that the first thought of anyone who sees or speaks with Sir Moses Montefiore should be the thought of his immense age. Even now, though human life seems to be really lengthening, centenarians are rare enough to make themselves interesting — we extend the term, perhaps hardly legitimately, to Sir Moses Montefiore, who is ninety-nine — but when a man in a prominent position lives to that age, the thought of what he has seen and done, of the changes through which the world has passed during his time, becomes over-powering. Sir Moses has seen the great work of his life crowned with success in very many countries, and this thought, no doubt, is that on which he and his Jewish friends will dwell with the greatest satisfaction tomorrow. But outside observers will reflect, with almost greater interest, on the men that he has seen in this long life of his, on the epochs through which he has passed, and on the contrasts which the world of today presents to the world in which Sir Moses spent his youth.

Born in 1784, he may possibly remember the taking of the Bastille, and he will certainly recollect the execution of Louis XVI, and the fall of Robespierre. He can probably recall the sensation caused by each of Nelson's victories and will remember with accuracy the feelings awakened in England by the events of the Peninsular War. When the news of Waterloo came to his brother-in-law, Mr Nathan Mayer Rothschild, Montefiore, who was with him in business, probably shared with him the advantages to be gained from the exclusive information. He was past forty when Catholic Emancipation and the Reform Bill were carried and had arrived at full middle age when

Queen Victoria ascended the throne. Yet it is since that date that he has done the greater part of the work by which he is known throughout the world — the work of practically helping his suffering brethren wherever they were to be found. His journeys to Palestine began in 1827, and they only ended in 1875, when he was past ninety years of age. He visited the Sultan in 1840, the Czar in 1846, and Cardinal Antonelli, to try to rescue the boy Mortara, in 1859. No journey has been too long or too difficult and no work too tedious for him, if help could be gained for those who sorely needed it. Nor has his help been confined to those of his own race or religion. We tell this morning some curious stories of the aid that he has given to persons who had no claim upon him, except the claim of distress; and we quote the letter which he wrote to this journal in 1860 and which had so much effect in stimulating public sympathy for the unfortunate Christians of the Lebanon. The clerical and other speakers in the meeting at Ramsgate yesterday had good reason to speak of his universal benevolence.

The Montefiores are, as their name implies, Italian Jews, though there is a difficulty in deciding when and whence they settled about the little town on the eastern slopes of the Apennines which bears that name. In different countries the Jews have had different modes of choosing surnames; in England they are mostly called by Old Testament names, possibly somewhat altered — Levi, Lewis, Abrahams, Moss; in Germany and in some other countries they take the names of towns and call themselves Erlanger, Breslauer, Oppenheim. A fortunate chance gave to the ancestors of the venerable philanthropist the name of the little town near the Adriatic; but they are first heard of as settled at Leghorn, where the Jews number no less than 7,000 at the present time. The grandfather of Sir Moses, Moses Vita Montefiore settled in England 130 years ago, as a merchant trading with Italy. One of his many sons married Rachel Mocatta, one of the family of Spanish Jews whose name is still so well known in London; and the first child of this marriage was Moses, born at Leghorn in 1784, on the 24th of October, corresponding in that year to the 8th of the Hebrew month Cheshvan, which falls somewhat later in the present year. It is well known that the Jewish trading community is headed by a kind of close aristocracy of great financiers, who are closely connected with one another by marriage; and of this aristocracy, if such it may be called, the Montefiores are leading members. Sir Moses is half Montefiore and half Mocatta; he married Miss Judith Cohen, whose sister married the founder of the English house of Rothschild. These four names are, with one or two more, co-extensive with the inner circle of English Jews. Many of those who bear one or other the names have gone much more deeply into finance than Sir Moses, and have consequently left themselves neither the heart nor the time to do the good that he has done. He left the Stock Exchange early, and entered into other and less exciting kinds of business. He helped to found the Alliance Insurance office, the Imperial Continental Gas Association, and the Provincial Bank of Ireland. But though he did not cease his connexion with business, he was never absorbed in it. We have already said that his passionate devotion to his race led him to visit Palestine in 1827, and we give in another column, from Mrs Montefiore's diary, an account of the difficulties through which they had to pass – difficulties more like those which would now attend a journey to Bokhara or Yunnan than those which we associate with a trip to Jerusalem. But what distinguishes the work of Sir Moses Montefiore from that of any other philanthropist is the success with which he has pleaded the cause of the Jews in the quarters to which, under ordinary circumstances, their cry could not have reached. In 1840 he extracted from the Sultan a firman, which has been of real service, many times over, in the cause of the Jews of the Turkish Empire. He got something more than civil speeches from the Emperor Nicholas, and in 1872, in a second visit to Russia, he was deeply gratified to notice the improvement in the lot of his Russian brethren. He penetrated even to Morocco in 1863, and in 1867 to Bucharest, where the Jews are, perhaps, more hated than in any other city in Europe. Neither danger, nor distance, nor discouragement has ever prevented him going on his errands of charity.

Sir Moses Montefiore has seen many changes in European society, but none greater than that which has passed, since the beginning of this century over the condition of the Jews. In Russia and the backward regions of Eastern Europe they are still, indeed, miserably poor, and are as liable as ever to outbreaks of hatred on the part of the Christian peasantry and of those who wish to turn that hatred to account. Civilized Germany even is inclined to 'boycott' them; but the very fact is a proof that they have in the last half-century prospered so very much more than their rivals that the jealous hostility of the latter must from time to time break out. The difference is that what is now abnormal and exceptional was expressed by law fifty years ago. Jewish disabilities, not extending merely to the right of sitting in Parliament but to half the rights of citizenship, existed even in England, which boasts of being in the forefront of enlightenment, until Sir Moses Montefiore had himself had ample time to experience them.

Now not only have the Jews got rid of all their disabilities but their power in Europe is very great and far-reaching. Much of the

Continental Press is in their hands. They control the Bourses. National financial operations are regarded by them as to a great extent their own affair. Their well-known qualities of patience, insight, and mutual fidelity, and their habit of thinking nothing beneath the notice of a man of business, have given them success. What the future of the race may be no man would rashly prophesy; but if their progress is as rapid as it has been during Sir Moses Montefiore's lifetime, they will in the next century, be an important fact indeed.

THE TIMES LEADING ARTICLE: 24 OCTOBER 1884

Sir Moses Montefiore completes his hundredth year today, according to the Gregorian Calendar. He himself reckons his years by the Hebrew Almanack and will keep his birthday on the 8th of Heshvan, which coincides with Monday. The Chief Rabbi has fixed Sunday for the religious celebration; and the Ramsgate friends and neighbours of Sir Moses will hold festivities in his honour on Tuesday. But whatever the exact day of celebration, the occasion is felt almost as a national event. Centenaries have become common of late; many think, much too common. A centenary like the present stands apart from the rest and is not likely to have enough rivals to produce satiety. Public opinion is apt to be tardy in recognition of noble careers. Centennial celebrations fit its temper not the less that the subject of admiration is tolerably sure to have been by the time long safely in his grave. A festival of this sort with its hero for its living centre is in the nature of things, very exceptional. No magic hedges the especial date of a hundred years of life. If men can survive to ninety, there is no necessary bar to their attainment of a hundred, unless that the contingencies of death increase generally with the number of years. That is the true and sole impediment to centenarianism. It operates quietly and implacably, and medicine assails it in vain. Sanitary science has sensibly invigorated the tenacity of life at its other stages. Upon extreme old age, though it is not absolutely powerless, its influence is limited and very slow to extend. A generation excusably makes much of longevity such as Sir Moses Montefiore's, apart from higher considerations, because it is rare and strange. It is proof positive, after a fashion seldom exemplified, of the presence in the human constitution of a precious vital force not often displayed. Sir Moses Montefiore impersonates for mankind the ability to enjoy in the highest degree a gift which few actually possess, and all, in happy circumstances, would be glad to possess. Old age, when the conditions which harmonize with it are realized, is an end to be desired and valued. Honour and kindness wait upon old age because it is old age. The community takes pride in its patriarchs.

For the aged themselves there is an abundance of compensations for the loss of strength. The most unselfish cannot avoid a grateful pride that he has drawn a rich number in the lottery of life. He has the pleasures of memory. One like Sir Moses has the pleasures of hope. Mortal calamities, should they happen, visit the aged more lightly. They fall with the softness of snow-flakes, and are swept into the stored pile of historical reminiscences. Bodily pains usually are more endurable. To live is a satisfaction. The mere consciousness of existence, which youth perceives little and middle age not at all, affects healthy old age with a delighted thrill. The old see life both from within and without. They have been doers, and they are spectators. From either side it is permissible for them to believe that they have the best of the game.

Any old man to whom fortune has been moderately good, who has preserved his physical and mental energies according to the measure of old age, is to be congratulated on his accumulation of years. Had Sir Moses Montefiore been altogether obscure, his kindred and neighbours would have been moved to celebrate so extraordinary an occurrence as a hundredth birthday. Every emotion of popular sympathy is intensified by the knowledge of the career which thus culminates.

Sir Moses Montefiore's life marks an epoch in the existence of the country in which he is a citizen, and of the race he belongs to. When he began to participate in affairs the position he has reached and the affection with which he is regarded, would have been a vision too wild to imagine. Jews were still little more than connived at in England. Every act of theirs was suspected. Their number was small, and those who occupied a respectable rank in business might have been counted on the fingers. The improvement Sir Moses Montefiore, in his progress from youth to manhood, and from manhood to old age, has witnessed in the social and political state of his brethren is less marvellous than the revolution of thought in the English nation which rendered it possible. Since he entered life, the whole surface of English existence has been changed. The relations of classes have been utterly altered. The forces of industry have shifted their course.

To any educated man it would be inconceivable now that another should be refused his share in national privileges because he was a Jew. In several lands Sir Moses Montefiore has observed during his lifetime as entire an overthrow of the old persecuting disqualifications of his race as in Great Britain. Jews have the rights of citizenship in France, the United States, Belgium, Holland, and Italy, as freely accorded to them as here. Where they are stigmatized and harassed, the form and motives of their maltreatment have varied their character essentially. They are no longer despised so much as they are feared. Jew-baiting is the contemptible revenge of a jealous population upon its recognized superiors in intelligence. Fifty years ago none of the Governments which allow their Jewish subjects to be troubled by stolid Christian competitors would have held themselves bound to disguise the fact. At present the States which do not protect against outrages know them to be a shame and reproach. Sir Moses Montefiore has not only watched the gradual emancipation of his people from the bonds which dishonoured the gaolers as much as it; [*sic*] he has himself been foremost in the work of liberation. At a period when successful businessmen settle down to the occupation of becoming millionaires, he and his equally magnanimous wife, declared themselves contented. Had he gone on, he might now have been a lord of finance. He might have been moving the money market with a nod. All the qualities of skill, coolness, patience, sagacity and laboriousness, which rule the City were his. His acknowledged probity was itself an inestimable stock-in-trade which trebled the weight of his capital. He turned his back on the gambling table of commerce at the moment when the stakes were highest and all the chances were in his favour. He is neither a Stoic nor an Epicurean. He has never disdained, and he has never overesteemed the advantages of wealth and the enjoyments it can purchase. Simply he wished to apply his life to its best account. He felt he could get the most out of it by resting satisfied with the riches he had acquired, and by devoting them and the maturity of his vigour to the service of his race. Henceforward, if centenarianism is ever again questioned, it will be sufficient to point to Sir Moses Montefiore. In the same way, for the last sixty years, when the compatibility of Judaism with every endowment of an admirable citizen has been doubted, it has always been sufficient to name him. He has been the victorious defender of persecuted Jews because he was the perfect English gentleman. In his own person he has solved once for all the problem of the competence of the most faithful of Jews to be not the less a complete Englishman. Many others of his people have trod since in his footsteps. In the days when he was young the lesson had not been learnt either by Jews or by Englishmen; and the path was not always clear. He is entitled to the glory of a discoverer. His proficiency in the combination had the effect of a prodigy; and the Jewish cause gained through the amazement of strangers at the phenomenon. Both as Jew and as Englishman he demanded abatement of his kinsmen's grievances of Emperors, Sultans, Pashas, and Parliaments. None could dispute the union in him of the double claim. Redress which would have been denied scornfully to the Jew was often granted as of right to the Englishman.

Englishmen without distinction of creeds contemplate Sir Moses Montefiore's career with as much pleasure as his co-religionists. The English are a mixed race; and Englishmen believe they are greatly indebted to the mixture. Sir Moses Montefiore has helped to infuse a fresh element relieved from the alien strain which would have neutralized its utility. Englishmen have learnt also from him many ennobling lessons of charity. His hand has constantly been open for deeds of compassion. Christians and Jews have profited alike by his munificence. His gifts have been bestowed with a shrewd discrimination. His aim has been to raise as well as succour. Jewish communities, wherever they may be, would be wise to study no less than Christians the principles upon which his almsgiving has proceeded. He was aware of the danger of pauperizing the recipients of bounty. The encouragement he has extended to agriculture in Palestine indicates his comprehension of the direction Jewish subventions should follow. But the personal teaching of his own conduct is a larger contribution even than his princely beneficence to the promotion of the Hebrew cause. Jews are still persecuted in other countries. They will continue to be, until they can be persuaded, as in England, and like Sir Moses Montefiore, to reconcile their race and their nationality. Though by no means primarily through their own fault, they have contracted a habit in many lands of labelling themselves, and branding their race, with customs and pursuits unlike those of their neighbours. They have not thrown themselves into the general current of national life. Sometimes they appear as if they courted envy and odium. The will is needed in themselves as much as legislation to break down the inner wall of partition which isolates them within the States of which they are subjects. Sir Moses Montefiore has shown them the way. Champions of his people, on whom his mantle of leadership falls, it is to be hoped, keep, most prominently of all his admirable virtues, before the eyes of his fellow believers his representative characteristic — the determination to show, by his life, that fervent Judaism and patriotic citizenship are absolutely consistent with one another.

Index

Compiled by Walter M. Schwab

Note: The many individual references in the text to Sir Moses and/or Judith Lady Montefiore have not generally been indexed separately. However, references have been included where they relate to special aspects of their activities or character.

The Montefiore Family Tree

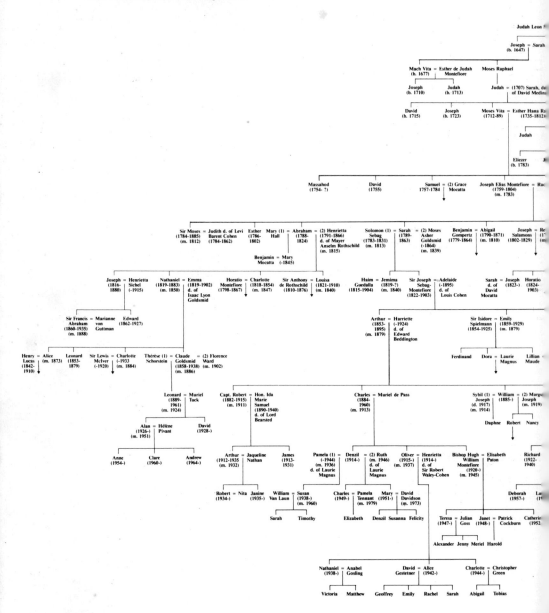

Adapted from the Family Tree given in the Jewish Encyclopedia 1904; C. B...